Now Available

Demonstrations of *Auditory Scene Analysis: The Perceptual Organization of Sound*

By Albert S. Bregman and Pierre A. Ahad

Audio CD

There are a few demonstrations of perceptual organization of sound on other CDs, but nowhere is there a CD that is completely dedicated to this goal.

This compact disk contains forty-one audio illustrations of the principles underlying the human perceptual organization of sound that were first described in Albert Bregman's book, *Auditory Scene Analysis* (MIT Press 1990). The CD can be played on any home CD player; for the most part the audio demonstrations can be listened to over loudspeakers, but a few are inherently stereo and require headphones. While referring readers to the relevant pages in the book, the CD can be used on its own. Each demonstration is described in the companion 78-page booklet, along with a diagram, an explanation, technical details, and suggested readings. There is also a 58-item bibliography.

The CD can also provide a set of perceptual phenomena that any computational model of auditory scene analysis should be able to explain. As such, it can serve as a test bed for theory.

Albert S. Bregman is Professor, Department of Psychology, McGill University.

See other side for Order Form

Order Form for

Audio CD

Demonstrations of *Auditory Scene Analysis: The Perceptual Organization of Sound*

By Albert S. Bregman and Pierre A. Ahad

Please send ____ copies of Bregman and Ayad, Demonstrations of *Auditory Scene Analysis* Audio CD

$ 25.00 per CD ISBN 0-262-52221-7 BREIP

$ _____ Total for CD(s)

$ 3.50 Postage for North American addresses

$ _____ Postage for addresses outside North America: $3.50 each book surface; $8.50 each CD air

$ _____ Canadian customers add 7% GST (MIT Press remits GST to Revenue Canada. Your CDs will be shipped from inside Canada, and you will not be assessed Canada Post's border fee.)

$ _____ Total due

❒ Payment Enclosed Charge to my: ❒ Master Card ❒ VISA ❒ AmEx

❒ Purchase Order Attached Card No.__________________ exp. date______

Signature______________________________

Send to:

Name____

Address____

____

Zip/Postal Code____________Country__________________

Phone____________________Fax______________________

Make checks payable to and send order to:

The MIT Press 55 Hayward Street Cambridge, MA 02142-1399 USA

To order by phone, call (617)625-8569 or 1(800)356-0343

Auditory Scene Analysis

Auditory Scene Analysis

The Perceptual Organization of Sound

Albert S. Bregman

A Bradford Book
The MIT Press
Cambridge, Massachusetts
London, England

Fourth printing, 2001

Second MIT Press paperback edition, 1999

This book was set in Bembo
by Asco Trade Typesetting Ltd. in Hong Kong
from computer disks provided by the author,
and was printed and bound in the United States of America.

Library of Congress Cataloging-in-Publication Data

Bregman, Albert S.
Auditory scene analysis: the perceptual organization of sound/
Albert S. Bregman.

p. cm.
"A Bradford book."
Includes bibliographical references.
ISBN 0-262-02297-4 (HB), 0-262-52195-4 (PB)
1. Auditory perception. I. Title.
[DNLM: 1. Auditory Perception. WV 272 B833a]
QP465.B74 1990
152.1'5—dc20
DNLM/DLC
for Library of Congress 89-14595
CIP

To Abigail

Contents

Preface

In the late 1960s, when I began to do research on the perceptual organization of sound, I naively thought that surely the questions that I was puzzling about had been studied to death. I could vaguely recollect the term tonal fusion and was sure that some hoary psychologist had figured it out. Gradually, as my own research progressed, I discovered that there had been a trickle of studies, but somehow the impetus was weak. Audition had not attracted the attention that vision had. Nonetheless, I started to explore a phenomenon that I called auditory stream segregation (later dubbed streaming by Ulric Neisser).

It was fortunate that I had never been trained in auditory perception and had only the most primitive idea about the structure of sound. I was free to pursue the phenomena as they unfolded without feeling the need to make them conform to existing psychophysical or neurological concepts. The fact that I was willing to strike off in a direction I knew nothing about can be blamed on one of my teachers in graduate school at Yale—Neil Miller. Miller advocated this strategy: If a phenomenon is strong enough to get in the way of something that you are trying to study, then perhaps it is worth studying in itself. He called it "making a silk purse out of the sow's ear." Auditory stream segregation got in the way of a study that I was trying to do on auditory learning and I decided to follow Miller's advice. I thought of it as a detour at the time, but the detour has occupied about 20 years.

Gradually, a body of research has accumulated, both in my laboratory and elsewhere, and I have developed a way of looking at it. For years I had vaguely thought of writing a book, but it was John Macnamara, a colleague at McGill, who convinced me to actually do it. He arranged for me to talk to his publishers, Harry and Betty Stanton, but I really did not think I would have the time to write the book. Fortunately, I was awarded a two-year research fellowship by the Killam Foundation to do so, and the publishing arrangement was soon concluded with The MIT Press. I was able to finish the writing on a sabbatical given by McGill University and spent at the Center for Computer Research in Music and Acoustics at Stanford.

Before I plunge into the main argument of this book, I want to take this opportunity to acknowledge the people and organizations who have made it possible.

The ideas and findings that I am going to talk about are the product of the cumulative work of many individuals. I have reworked these ideas and made up a slightly different story about them that makes sense to me, but it is clear that an entire research community has labored to gain an understanding of these problems for a good many years.

I want to particularly acknowledge the stimulation that I have received from the research work and theoretical writing of Christopher J. Darwin, Diana Deutsch, W. Jay Dowling, Stephen Handel, Hermann von Helmholtz, Ira J. Hirsh, Mari R. Jones, Bela Julesz, George A. Miller, Brian C. J. Moore, Otto Ortmann, Irvin Rock, Richard M. Warren, Leo van Noorden, and Giovanni Vicario.

The work in my own laboratory has been advanced by the contributions of many students, assistants, and associates. It would be impossible to mention all of them, but I would like to mention the following with particular appreciation: Pierre Abdel Ahad, Jack Abramson, André Achim, Gary Bernstein, Jock Campbell, Valter Ciocca, Gary Dannenbring, Peter Doehring, Magda Chalikia, Lynn Halpern, Robert Levitan, Christine Liao, Stephen McAdams, Michael Mills, Steven Pinker, Brian Roberts, Wendy Rogers, Alexander Rudnicky, Howard Steiger, Jack Torobin, Yves Tougas, Tony Wolff, and James Wright.

I want to thank John Chowning for inviting me to the Center for Computer Research in Music and Acoustics to spend the summer of 1982 and a sabbatical year in 1986 and 1987. These pleasant and productive periods gave me a chance to become familiar with what the computer music community, especially John Pierce, Max Mathews, and John Chowning, had discovered about the perception of musical sound.

I have also benefited from valuable discussions with other colleagues. These include Pierre Divenyi, Bernard Mont-Reynaud, Earl Schubert, William Schottstaedt, and Mitchell Weintraub. In addition, Alan Belkin, Valter Ciocca, Michael Cohen, Doug Kieslar, John Pierce, Martin Tenenbaum, and Meg Withgott were kind enough to read parts of the manuscript and give me their comments.

Not the least of my obligations are to the organizations whose financial support have made my research possible: the Natural Sciences and Engineering Research Council of Canada, the Defense

Research Board of Canada, the Faculty of Graduate Studies and Research of McGill University, and the Ministry of Education of Quebec (FCAC program). I am particularly indebted to the Killam Foundation for its two-year fellowship. I should also mention the Department of Psychology of McGill University, which has been a congenial place to work.

Finally, it is impossible to express the debt that I owe to my wife, Abigail Elizabeth Sibley. She has put up with me for many years and, although a historian by trade, has entered into my professional milieu with gusto, earning the affection and respect of my colleagues.

This book is a compromise. I was uncertain as to whether to write for the specialist or not. The nonspecialist might need a chapter on the physical nature of sound and might not be interested in the details of experiments. In the end, I decided to write two books in one. The first and last chapters can be read alone to get a general idea of the topic of auditory scene analysis. The first one lays out the problem, gives a few examples of it, and sets it in a theoretical context. The final chapter presents a brief summary of what we do and do not know about the subject.

The remaining chapters are addressed to the person who wishes to find out more about how the research is done and to what extent the evidence supports the conclusions. I have given more detail on research that is less accessible, either because it is unpublished or because it is published in the form of theses.

One way in which the scope of this volume has been limited is by omitting an originally planned chapter on the nature of sound. I have tried to assist the novice in the field of audition by explaining each concept in an intuitive way when I use it. As an additional help I have included, at the end of the book, an alphabetical glossary of terms that appear in the chapters.

Auditory Scene Analysis

Chapter 1

The Auditory Scene

Historical Difference between Auditory and Visual Perception

If you were to pick up a general textbook on perception written before 1965 and leaf through it, you would not find any great concern with the perceptual or ecological questions about audition. By a perceptual question I mean one that asks how our auditory systems could build a picture of the world around us through their sensitivity to sound, whereas by an ecological one I am referring to one that asks how our environment tends to create and shape the sound around us. (The two kinds of questions are related. Only by being aware of how the sound is created and shaped in the world can we know how to use it to derive the properties of the sound-producing events around us.)

Instead, you would find discussions of such basic auditory qualities as loudness and pitch. For each of these, the textbook might discuss the psychophysical question: which physical property of the sound gives rise to the perceptual quality that we experience? It might also consider the question of how the physiology of the ear and nervous system could respond to those properties of sound. The most perceptual of the topics that you might encounter would be concerned with how the sense of hearing can tell the listener where sounds are coming from. Under this heading, some consideration would be given to the role of audition in telling us about the world around us. For the most part, instead of arising from everyday life, the motivation of much of the research on audition seems to have its origins in the medical study of deafness, where the major concerns are the sensitivity of the auditory system to weak sounds, the growth in perceived intensity with increases in the energy of the signal, and the effects of exposure to noise.

The situation would be quite different in the treatment of vision. It is true that you would see a treatment of psychophysics and physiology, and indeed there would be some consideration of such deficits as colorblindness, but this would not be the whole story. You would also find discussions of higher-level principles of organization, such as those responsible for the constancies. There would, for example, be a description of size constancy, the fact that we tend to see the size of an object as unchanged when it is at a different distance, despite the fact that the image that it projects on our retinas shrinks as it moves further away. Apparently some complex analysis by the brain takes into account clues other than retinal size in arriving at the perceived size of an object.

Why should there be such a difference? A proponent of the "great man" theory of history might argue that it was because the fathers of Gestalt psychology, who opened up the whole question of perceptual organization, had focused on vision and never quite got around to audition.

However, it is more likely that there is a deeper reason. We came to know about the puzzles of visual perception through the arts of drawing and painting. The desire for accurate portrayal led to an understanding of the cues for distance and certain facts about projective geometry. This was accompanied by the development of the physical analysis of projected images, and eventually the invention of the camera. Early on, the psychologist was faced with the discrepancy between what was on the photograph or canvas and what the person saw.

The earlier development of sophisticated thinking in the field of visual perception may also have been due to the fact that it was much easier to create a visual display with exactly specified properties than it was to shape sound in equally exact ways. If so, the present-day development of the computer analysis and synthesis of sound ought to greatly accelerate the study of auditory perception.

Of course there is another possibility that explains the slighting of audition in the textbook: Perhaps audition is really a much simpler sense and there are no important perceptual phenomena like the visual constancies to be discovered.

This is a notion that can be rejected. We can show that such complex phenomena as constancies exist in hearing, too. One example is timbre constancy. A friend's voice has the same perceived timbre in a quiet room as at a cocktail party. Yet at the party, the set of frequency components arising from that voice is mixed at the listener's ear with frequency components from other sources. The total spectrum of energy that reaches the ear may be quite different in different environments. To recognize the unique timbre of the voice we have to isolate the frequency components that are responsible for it from others that are present at the same time. A wrong choice of frequency components would change the perceived timbre of the voice. The fact that we can usually recognize the timbre implies that we regularly choose the right components in different contexts. Just as in the case of the visual constancies, timbre constancy will have to be explained in terms of a complicated analysis by the brain, and not merely in terms of a simple registration of the input by the brain.

There are some practical reasons for trying to understand this constancy. There are engineers currently trying to design computers that can understand what a person is saying. However, in a noisy environment the speaker's voice comes mixed with other sounds. To a naive computer, each different sound that the voice comes mixed with makes it sound as if different words were being spoken or as if they were spoken by a different person. The machine cannot correct for the particular listening conditions as a human can. If the study of human audition were able to lay bare the principles that govern the human skill, there is some hope that a computer could be designed to mimic it.

The Problem of Scene Analysis

It is not entirely true that textbooks ignore complex perceptual phenomena in audition. However, they are often presented as an array of baffling illusions.[1] They seem more like disconnected fragments than a foundation for a theory of auditory perception. My purpose in this book is to try to see them as oblique glimpses of a general auditory process of organization that has evolved, in our auditory systems, to solve a problem that I will refer to as "auditory scene analysis."

Let me clarify what I mean by auditory scene analysis. The best way to begin is to ask ourselves what perception is for. Since Aristotle, many philosophers and psychologists have believed that perception is the process of using the information provided by our senses to form mental representations of the world around us. In using the word representations, we are implying the existence of a two-part system: one part forms the representations and another uses them to do such things as calculate appropriate plans and actions. The job of perception, then, is to take the sensory input and to derive a useful representation of reality from it.

An important part of building a representation is to decide which parts of the sensory stimulation are telling us about the same environmental object or event. Unless we put the right combination of sensory evidence together, we will not be able to recognize what is going on. A simple example is shown in the top line of figure 1.1. The pattern of letters is meaningful, but the meaning cannot be extracted because the letters are actually a mixture from two sentences, and

AI CSAITT STIOTOS

A I C S A I T T S T I O T O S

Figure 1.1
Top line: a string of letters that makes no sense because it is a mixture of two messages. Bottom line: the component messages are segregated by visual factors. (From Bregman 1981b.)

the two cannot be separated. However, if, as in the lower line of the figure, we give the eyes some assistance, the meaning becomes apparent.

This business of separating evidence has been faced in the design of computer systems for recognizing the objects in natural scenes or in drawings. Figure 1.2 shows a line drawing of some blocks.[2] We can imagine that the picture has been translated into a pattern in the memory of the computer by some process that need not concern us. We might think that once it was entered, all that we would have to do to enable the computer to decide which objects were present in the scene would be to supply it with a description of the shape of each possible one. But the problem is not as easy as all that. Before the machine could make any decision, it would have to be able to tell which parts of the picture represented parts of the same object. To our human eyes it appears that the regions labeled A and B are parts of a single block. This is not immediately obvious to a computer. In simple line drawings there is a rule that states that any white area totally surrounded by lines must depict a single surface. This rule implies that in figure 1.2 the whole of region A is part of a single surface. The reason for grouping region A with B is much more complex. The question of how it can be done can be set aside for the moment. The point of the example is that unless regions A and B are indeed considered part of a single object, the description that the computer will be able to construct will not be correct and the elongated shape formed out of A, B, and other regions will not be seen. It seems as though a preliminary step along the road to recognition would be to program the computer to do the equivalent of taking a set of crayons and coloring in, with the same color, all those regions that were parts of the same block. Then some subsequent recognition process could simply try to form a description of a single shape from each set in which the regions were the same color. This allocation of regions to objects is what is known to researchers in machine vision as the scene analysis problem.

There are similar problems in hearing. Take the case of a baby being spoken to by her mother. The baby starts to imitate her

Figure 1.2
A line drawing of blocks for visual scene analysis. (After Guzman 1969.)

mother's voice. However, she does not insert into the imitation the squeaks of her cradle that have been occurring at the same time. Why not? A physical record of what she has heard would include them. Somehow she has been able to reject the squeak as not being part of the perceptual "object" formed by her mother's voice. In doing so, the infant has solved a scene analysis problem in audition.

It is important to emphasize again that the way that sensory inputs are grouped by our nervous systems determines the patterns that we perceive. In the case of the drawings of blocks, if areas E, F, and H were grouped as parts of the same object, we would see the L-shaped object shown at the right. The shape of the object formed by this grouping of areas is an emergent property, since it is not a property of any of the parts taken individually, but emerges only as a result of the grouping of the areas. Normally, in perception, emergent properties are accurate portrayals of the properties of the objects in our environment. However, if scene analysis processes fail, the emergent perceived shapes will not correspond to any environmental shapes. They will be entirely chimerical.

The difficulties that are involved in the scene analysis processes in audition often escape our notice. This example can make them more obvious. Imagine that you are on the edge of a lake and a friend challenges you to play a game. The game is this: Your friend digs two narrow channels up from the side of the lake. Each is a few feet long and a few inches wide and they are spaced a few feet apart. Halfway up each one, your friend stretches a handkerchief and fastens it to the sides of the channel. As waves reach the side of the lake they travel up the channels and cause the two handkerchiefs to go into motion. You are allowed to look only at the handkerchiefs and from their motions to answer a series of questions: How many boats are there on the lake and where are they? Which is the most powerful one? Which one is closer? Is the wind blowing? Has any large object been dropped suddenly into the lake?

Solving this problem seems impossible, but it is a strict analogy to the problem faced by our auditory systems. The lake represents the lake of air that surrounds us. The two channels are our two ear canals, and the handkerchiefs are our ear drums. The only information that the auditory system has available to it, or ever will have, is the vibrations of these two ear drums. Yet it seems to be able to answer questions very like the ones that were asked by the side of the lake: How many people are talking? Which one is louder, or closer? Is there a machine humming in the background? We are not surprised when our sense of hearing succeeds in answering these questions any more than we are when our eye, looking at the handkerchiefs, fails.

The difficulty in the examples of the lake, the infant, the sequence of letters, and the block drawings is that the evidence arising from each distinct physical cause in the environment is compounded with the effects of the other ones when it reaches the sense organ. If correct perceptual representations of the world are to be formed, the evidence must be partitioned appropriately.

In vision, you can describe the problem of scene analysis in terms of the correct grouping of regions. Most people know that the retina of the eye acts something like a sensitive photographic film and that it records, in the form of neural impulses, the "image" that has been written onto it by the light. This image has regions. Therefore, it is possible to imagine some process that groups them. But what about the sense of hearing? What are the basic parts that must be grouped to make a sound?

Rather than considering this question in terms of a direct discussion of the auditory system, it will be simpler to introduce the topic by looking at a spectrogram, a widely used description of sound. Figure 1.3 shows one for the spoken word "shoe". The picture is rather like a sheet of music. Time proceeds from left to right, and the vertical dimension represents the physical dimension of frequency, which corresponds to our impression of the highness of the sound. The sound of a voice is complex. At any moment of time, the spectrogram shows more than one frequency. It does so because any complex sound can actually be viewed as a set of simultaneous frequency components. A steady pure tone, which is much simpler than a voice, would simply be shown as a horizontal line because at any moment it would have only one frequency.

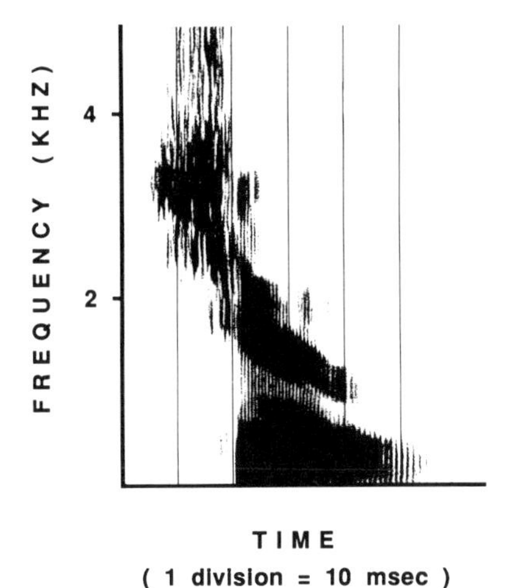

Figure 1.3
Spectrogram of the word "shoe" spoken in isolation.

Once we see that the sound can be made into a picture, we are tempted to believe that such a picture could be used by a computer to recognize speech sounds. Different classes of speech sounds, stop consonants such as "b" and fricatives such as "s" for example, have characteristically different appearances on the spectrogram. We ought to be able to equip the computer with a set of tests with which to examine such a picture and to determine whether the shape representing a particular speech sound is present in the image. This makes the problem sound much like the one faced by vision in recognizing the blocks in figure 1.2.

If a computer could solve the recognition problem by the use of a spectrogram, it would be very exciting news for researchers in human audition, because there is some reason to believe that the human auditory system provides the brain with a pattern of neural excitation that is very much like a spectrogram. Without going into too much detail, we can sketch this process as follows. As sound enters the ear, it eventually reaches a part called the inner ear where it affects an organ called the basilar membrane, a long coiled ribbon. Different frequency components in the incoming sound will cause different parts of this organ to vibrate most vigorously. It reacts most strongly to the lowest audible frequencies at one end, to the highest at the other, with an orderly progression from low to high in between. A different group of neurons connects with each location along the basilar membrane and is responsible for recording the vibration at that

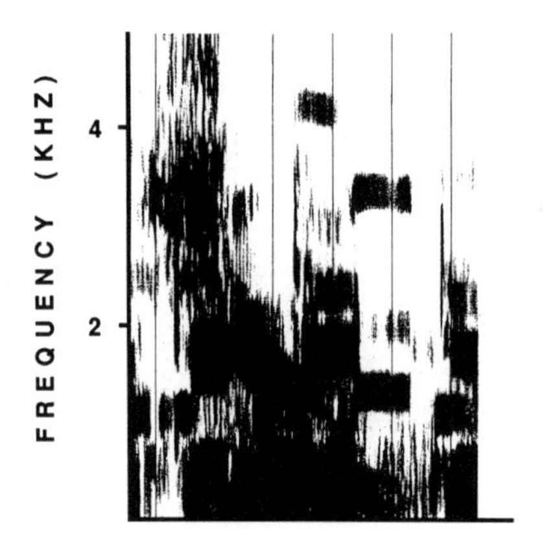

Figure 1.4
A spectrogram of a mixture of sounds (containing the word "shoe").

location (primarily). As the sound changes over time, different combinations of neural groups are activated. If we imagined the basilar membrane oriented vertically so that the neural groups responsive to the highest frequencies were at the top, and also imagined that each group was attached to a pen, with the pen active whenever a neural group was, the pens would write out a picture of the sound that looked like a spectrogram. So the brain has all the information that is visible in the spectrogram, and providing that it could store a record of this information for some brief period of time, it would have a neural spectrogram.

The account that I have just given hides a deep problem. The spectrographic record of most situations would not have the pristine purity of figure 1.3, which represents speech recorded in an absolutely quiet background. The real world is a great deal messier. A typical acoustic result is shown in figure 1.4. Here all the sounds are being mixed together in the listener's ear in exactly the same way that the waves of the lake, in our earlier example, were mixed in each of the channels that ran off it. The spectrogram for a mixture of sounds looks somewhat like a picture created by making a spectrogram of each of the individual sounds on a separate piece of transparent plastic, and then overlaying the individual spectrograms to create a composite. The spectrogram of the word shoe is actually one of the component spectrograms of the mixture.

Although the theorist has the privilege of building the composite up from the pictures of its components, the auditory system, or any machine trying to imitate it, would be presented only with the spectrogram of the mixture and would have to try to infer the set of pictures that was overlaid to produce it.

The recognizer would have to solve the following problems: How many sources have created the mixture? Is a particular discontinuity in the picture a change in one sound or an interruption by a second one? Should two dark regions, one above the other in the picture (in other words, occurring at the same time), be grouped as a single sound with a complex timbre or separated to represent two simultaneous sounds with simpler timbres? We can see that if we look at a spectrogram representing a slice of real life, we would see a complex pattern of streaks, any pair of which could have been caused by the same acoustic event or by different ones. A single streak could have been the summation of one, two, or even more parts of different sounds. Furthermore, the frequency components from one source could be interlaced with those of another one; just because one horizontal streak happens to be immediately above another, it does not mean that they both arose from the same sonic event.

We can see that just as in the visual problem of recognizing a picture of blocks, there is a serious need for regions to be grouped appropriately. Again, it would be convenient to be able to hand the spectrogram over to a machine that did the equivalent of taking a set of crayons and coloring in, with the same color, all the regions on the spectrogram that came from the same source. This "coloring problem" or "auditory scene analysis problem" is what the rest of this volume is about.

Objects Compared to Streams

It is also about the concept of "auditory streams." An auditory stream is our perceptual grouping of the parts of the neural spectrogram that go together. To see the reasons for bringing in this concept, it is necessary to consider the relations between the physical world and our mental representations of it. As we saw before, the goal of scene analysis is the recovery of separate descriptions of each separate thing in the environment. What are these things? In vision, we are focused on objects. Light is reflected off objects, bounces back and forth between them, and eventually some of it reaches our eyes. Our visual sense uses this light to form separate descriptions of the individual objects. These descriptions include the object's shape, size, distance, coloring, and so on.

Then what sort of information is conveyed by sound? Sound is created when things of various types happen. The wind blows, an animal scurries through a clearing, the fire burns, a person calls. Acoustic information, therefore, tells us about physical "happenings." Many happenings go on at the same time in the world, each one a distinct event. If we are to react to them as distinct, there has to be a level of mental description in which there are separate representations of the individual ones.

I refer to the perceptual unit that represents a single happening as an auditory stream. Why not just call it a sound? There are two reasons why the word stream is better. First of all a physical happening (and correspondingly its mental representation) can incorporate more than one sound, just as a visual object can have more than one region. A series of footsteps, for instance, can form a single experienced event, despite the fact that each footstep is a separate sound. A soprano singing with a piano accompaniment is also heard as a coherent happening, despite being composed of distinct sounds (notes). Furthermore, the singer and piano together form a perceptual entity—the "performance"—that is distinct from other sounds that are occurring. Therefore, our mental representations of acoustic events can be multifold in a way that the mere word "sound" does not suggest. By coining a new word, "stream", we are free to load it up with whatever theoretical properties seem appropriate.

A second reason for preferring the word "stream" is that the word "sound" refers indifferently to the physical sound in the world and to our mental experience of it. It is useful to reserve the word "stream" for a perceptual representation, and the phrase "acoustic event" or the word "sound" for the physical cause.

I view a stream as a computational stage on the way to the full description of an auditory event. The stream serves the purpose of clustering related qualities. By doing so, it acts as a center for our description of an acoustic event. By way of analogy, consider how we talk about visible things. In our verbal descriptions of what we see, we say that an *object* is red, or that it is moving fast, that it is near, or that it is dangerous. In other words, the notion of an object, understood whenever the word "it" occurs in the previous sentence, serves as a center around which our verbal descriptions are clustered. This is not just a convenience of language. The perceptual representation of an object serves the same purpose as the "it" in the sentence. We can observe this when we dream. When, for some reason, the ideas of angry and dog and green are pulled out from our memories, they tend to coalesce into a single entity and we experience an angry green dog and not merely anger, greenness, and dogness taken separately. Although the combination of these qualities has never occurred in our experience, and therefore the individual qualities must have been dredged up from separate experiences, those qualities can be experienced visually only as properties of an *object*. It is this "belonging to an object" that holds them together.

The stream plays the same role in auditory mental experience as the object does in visual. When we want to talk about auditory units (the auditory counterparts of visual objects), we generally employ the word "sound". We say that a sound is high pitched or low, that it is rising or falling, that it is rough or smooth, and so on. Again I am convinced that this is not simply a trick of language, but an essential aspect of both our conceptual and our perceptual representations of the world. Properties have to belong to something. This becomes particularly important when there is more than one "something" in our experience. Suppose there are two acoustic sources of sound, one high and near and the other low and far. It is only because of the fact that nearness and highness are grouped as properties of one stream and farness and lowness as properties of the other that we can experience the uniqueness of the two individual sounds rather than a mush of four properties.

A critic of this argument might reply that the world itself groups the "high" with the "near" and the "low" with the "far". It is not necessary for us to do it. However, it is not sufficient that these clusters of properties be distinct in the physical happenings around us. They must also be assigned by our brains to distinct mental entities. In auditory experience, these entities are the things that I am calling streams. As with our visual experience of objects, our auditory streams are ways of putting the sensory information together. This going together has obvious implications for action. For example, if we assign the properties "far" and "lion roar" to one auditory stream and the properties "near" and "crackling fire" to another one, we might be inclined to behave differently than if the distance assignments had been reversed.

When people familiar with the English language read the phrase "The gray wagon was on the black road", they know immediately that it is the wagon that is gray, not the road. They know it because they can *parse* the sentence, using their knowledge of English syntax to determine the correct "belongingness" relations between the concepts. Similarly, when listeners create a mental representation of the auditory input, they too must employ rules about what goes with what. In some sense, they can be said to be parsing this input too.

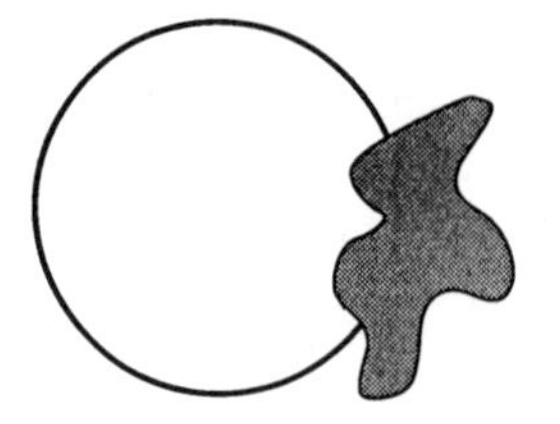
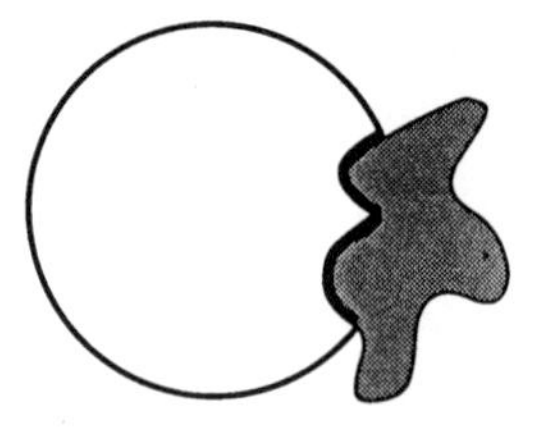

Figure 1.5
An example of "belongingness." The dark portion of the line seems to belong to the irregular form.

The Principle of Exclusive Allocation
Any system that attempts to build descriptions of a natural world scene must assign the perceptual qualities that it creates to one organization or another. The quality "loud" is assigned to the organization that represents the roar of the lion. The quality "far" is assigned as the distance of that same event. The Gestalt psychologists made this point by introducing the principle of belongingness. In describing the visual organization of drawings like the one in figure 1.5, they pointed out that the lines at which the drawn irregular figure overlaps the circle (shown as a dark line in part B of the figure) are generally seen as part of the irregular figure and not of the circle. That is, they *belong* to the irregular form. With an effort, we can see them as part of a circle; then they belong to the circle. In any mental representation of a drawing, a perceived line always belongs to some figure of which it forms a part. The belongingness may shift, for example, when we try to see the figure in a different way, but regardless of how we see it, it is always a property *of* something.

There is a second principle that I want to introduce here because it has a connection with the principle of belongingness. This is the principle of "exclusive allocation." It can be seen in an ambiguous visual figure such as the vase-faces illusion of the Gestalt psychologists. An example is shown in figure 1.6. We can interpret the figure as an outline of either a vase or two faces. The "exclusive allocation of evidence" describes how these interpretations affect the edge that separates the vase from a face. When we see the vase, that edge is allocated to the vase and defines its shape. When we see the face, the same edge is now allocated to the face. It is never allocated to both vase and face at the same time, but exclusively to one of them.

The exclusive allocation principle says that a sensory element should not be used in more than one description at a time. If the line is assigned to the vase, that assignment "uses up" the line so that its

Figure 1.6
An ambiguous drawing in which either a vase at the center or two faces at the sides can be seen.

shape cannot contribute to the shape of another figure at the same time. We shall eventually see in chapter 7 that there are certain limits to this idea, but it holds true often enough that it is worth pointing it out as a separate principle. It is not identical to the principle of belongingness. The latter merely states that the line has to be seen as a property of a figure, but does not prevent it from being allocated to more than one at a time.

There is a certain ecological validity of the principle of exclusive allocation in vision. The term "ecological validity" means that it tends to give the right answers about how the visual image has probably originated in the external world. In the case of edges separating objects, there is a very low likelihood (except in jigsaw puzzles) that the touching edges of two objects will have the same shape exactly. Therefore the shape of the contour that separates our view of two objects probably tells us about the shape of only one of them—the nearer one. The decision as to which object the contour belongs to is determined by a number of cues that help the viewer to judge which object is closer.

Dividing evidence between distinct perceptual entities (visual objects or auditory streams) is useful because there really are distinct physical objects and events in the world that we humans inhabit. Therefore the evidence that is obtained by our senses really ought to be untangled and assigned to one or another of them.

Our initial example came from vision, but the arguments in audition are similar. For example, it is very unlikely that a sound will

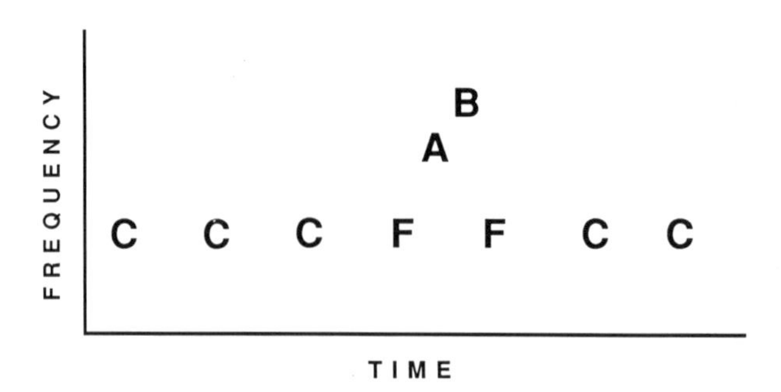

Figure 1.7
A tone sequence of the type used by Bregman and Rudnicky (1975).

terminate at exactly the moment that another begins. Therefore when the spectral composition of the incoming sensory data changes suddenly, the auditory system can conclude that only one sound in a mixture has gone on or off. We will see in chapter 3 that this conclusion can give rise to a search in the second sound for a continuation of the first one.

The strategy completes itself in the following way. Let us give the name A to the segment of sound that occurs prior to the change, and call the second part B. If spectral components are found in B that match the spectrum of A, they are considered to be the continuing parts of A. Accordingly, they can be subtracted out of B. This allows us a picture of the second sound free from the influence of the first. In chapter 3, this is called the "old-plus-new heuristic," and it is shown to be one of our most powerful tools in solving the scene analysis problem in audition. Here I want to point out that it is an example of the principle of exclusive allocation in which the allocation of the continuing spectral components to the first sound interferes with their being allocated to the second.

Another case of exclusive allocation is shown in an experiment by Bregman and Rudnicky, using the pattern of pure tones shown in figure 1.7.[3] In this figure the horizontal dimension represents time and the vertical one shows the frequency of the tones. The listener's task was to decide on the order of two target tones, A and B, embedded in the sequence. Were they in the order high-low or low-high? When A and B were presented alone, as an isolated pair of tones, this decision was very easy. However, when the two tones labeled F (for "flankers") were added to the pattern, the order of A and B became very hard to hear. Apparently when they were absorbed as the middle elements of a larger pattern, FABF, the orders AB and BA lost their uniqueness.

This experiment was about the perceptual allocation of the F tones. As long as they were allocated to the same auditory stream as A and B, the order of A and B was hard to hear. However, Bregman and Rudnicky reasoned that if some principle of grouping were able to assign the F tones to a different perceptual stream, the order of A and B might become audible again. With this in mind, they introduced yet another group of tones, labeled C (for "captors") in figure 1.7. They varied the frequency of these C tones. When they were very low, much lower than the frequency of the F tones, the F tones grouped with the AB tones and the order of A and B was unclear to the listeners. However, when the C tones were brought up close to the frequency of the F tones, they captured them into a stream, CCCFFCC. One reason for this capturing is that tones tend to group perceptually with those that are nearest to them in frequency; a second is that the F tones were spaced so that they fell into a regular rhythmic pattern with the C tones. When the capturing occurred, the order of AB was heard more clearly because they were now in their own auditory stream that was separate from the CCCFFCC stream. The belongingness of the F tones had been altered, and the perceived auditory forms were changed.

Scene analysis, as I have described it, involves putting evidence together into a structure. Demonstrations of the perceptual systems acting in this way are seen in certain kinds of illusions where it appears that the correct features of the sensory input have been detected but have not been put together correctly. Two examples will make this clearer.

The first is in vision. Treisman and Schmidt carried out an experiment in which a row of symbols was flashed briefly in a tachistoscope.[4] There were three colored letters flanked by two black digits. The viewers were asked to first report what the digits were and then to report on the letters. Their reports of the digits were generally correct, but the properties of the letters were often scrambled. A subject might report a red O and a green X, when actually a green O and a red X had been presented. These combinations of features often seemed to the viewers to be their actual experiences rather than merely guesses based on partially registered features of the display. The experimenters argued that this showed that the human mind cannot consciously experience disembodied features and must assign them to perceived objects. That is, the mind obeys the principle of belongingness.

The second example comes from audition. In 1974, Diana Deutsch reported an interesting illusion that could be created when tones were sent to both ears of a listener over headphones. The listener was presented with a continuously repeating alternation of two events. Event A was a low tone presented to the left ear, accompanied by a high tone presented to the right ear. Event B was just the reverse: a low tone to the right ear together with a high tone to the left. The high and low tones were pure sine wave tones spaced exactly an octave apart. Because events A and B alternated, each ear was presented with a sequence of high and low tones. Another way to express it is that while both the high and low tones tones bounced back and forth between the ears, the high and low were always in opposite ears.

However the experience of many listeners did not resemble this description. Instead they heard a single sound bouncing back and forth between the ears. Furthermore, the perceived tone alternated between sounding high pitched and sounding low as it bounced from side to side. The only way this illusion could be explained was to argue that the listeners were assuming the existence of a single tone, deriving two different descriptions of it from two different types of perceptual analyses, and then putting the two descriptions together incorrectly. Apparently they derived the fact that the tone was changing in frequency by monitoring the changes in a single ear (usually the right). However, they derived the *position* of the assumed single sound by tracking the position of the higher tone. Therefore, they might report hearing a low tone on the left at the point in time at which, in actuality, a high tone had been presented on the left. Here we see an example of pitch and location assigned in the wrong combination to the representation of a sound. Therefore, this can be classified as a misassignment illusion just as Treisman and Schmidt's visual illusion was.

The question of why this illusion occurs can be set aside for the moment. What is important is that the illusion suggests that an assignment process is taking place, and this supports the idea that perception is a process of building descriptions. Only by being built could they be built incorrectly.

These illusions show that there are some similarities in how visual and auditory experiences are organized. A thoughtful discussion of the similarities and differences between vision and audition can be found in a paper by Bela Julesz and Ira Hirsh.[5] There is no shortage of parallels in audition to visual processes of organization. This chapter cannot afford the space to mention many examples, but it can at least discuss two of them, the streaming phenomenon and the continuity illusion.

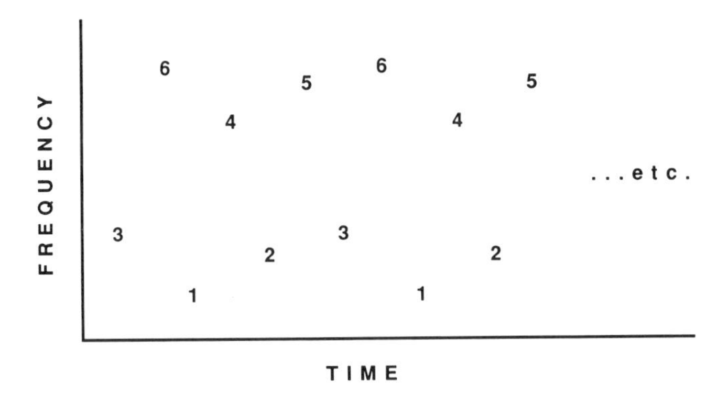

Figure 1.8
A repeating cycle of six tones, of the type used by Bregman and Campbell (1971).

Two Comparisons of Scene Analysis in Vision and Audition

Auditory Streaming and Apparent Motion

One auditory phenomenon with a direct parallel in vision is the auditory streaming effect. This is the phenomenon that originally got me interested in auditory organization. The effect occurred when listeners were presented with an endlessly repeating loop of tape on which were recorded a sequence of six different tones, three high ones and three low ones. The high ones were at least one and a half octaves above the low ones. High and low tones alternated. If tones are given numbers according to their pitches with 1 as the lowest and 6 as the highest the tones were arranged in the sequence 142536. The six tones, shown in figure 1.8, formed a repeating loop that was cycled over and over.

When the cycle of tones was presented very slowly the listeners heard the sequence of high and low tones in the order in which they occurred on the tape. However, as it was made faster, a strange perceptual effect became stronger and stronger and was extremely compelling when there was only one-tenth of a second between the onsets of consecutive tones. When the effect occurred, the listeners did not actually hear the tones in the correct order, 142536. Instead, they heard two streams of tones, one containing a repeating cycle of the three low pitched tones, 1–2–3– (where dashes indicate silences) and the other containing the three high ones (–4–5–6). The single sequence of tones seemed to have broken up perceptually into two parallel sequences, as if two different instruments were playing different, but interwoven parts. Furthermore it was impossible for the listeners to focus their attention on both streams at the same time.

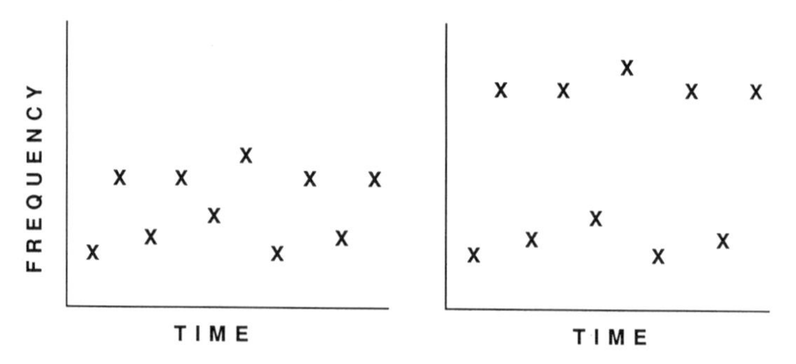

Figure 1.9
Stream segregation is stronger when the frequency separation between high and low tones is greater, as shown on the right.

When they focused on one of the streams, the other was heard as a vague background. As a consequence, while the listeners could easily judge the order of the high tones taken alone, or of the low ones taken alone, they could not put this information together to report the order of the six tones in the loop. Many listeners actually reported that the high tones all preceded the low ones, or vice versa, although this was never the case.

Other research has shown that the phenomenon of stream segregation obeys some fairly simple laws. If there are two sets of tones, one of them high in frequency and the other low, and the order of the two sets is shuffled together in the sequence (not necessarily a strict alternation of high and low), the degree of perceptual segregation of the high tones from the low ones will depend on the frequency separation of the two sets. Therefore if the two conditions shown in figure 1.9 are compared, the one on the right will show greater perceptual segregation into two streams. An interesting point is that visually, looking at figure 1.9, the perception of two distinct groups is also stronger on the right.

There is another important fact about stream segregation: the faster the sequence is presented, the greater is the perceptual segregation of high and low tones. Again there is a visual analogy, as shown in figure 1.10. We see the pattern in the right panel, in which there is a contraction of time (the same as an increase in speed), as more tightly grouped into two groups than the left panel is.

Gestalt Grouping Explanation

In the visual analogies, the grouping is predictable from the Gestalt psychologists' proximity principle, which states roughly that the

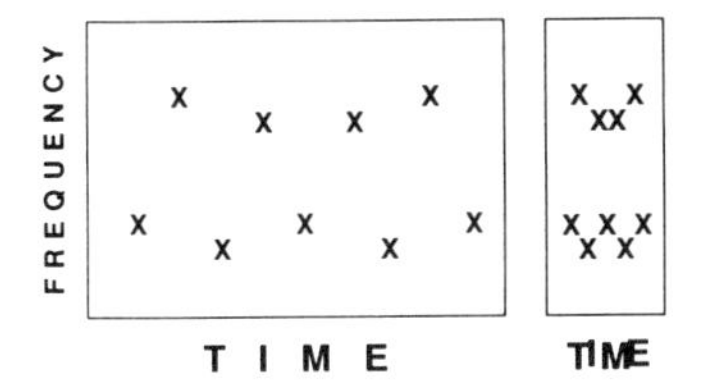

Figure 1.10
Stream-segregation is higher at higher speeds, as shown on the right.

closer the visual elements in a set are to one another, the more strongly we tend to group them perceptually. The Gestalt psychologists thought of this grouping as if the perceptual elements—for example, the tones in figure 1.9—were attracting one another like miniature planets in space with the result that they tended to form clusters in our experience. If the analogy to audition is a valid one, this suggests that the spatial dimension of distance in vision has two analogies in audition. One is separation in time, and the other is separation in frequency. Both, according to this analogy, are distances, and Gestalt principles that involve distance should be valid for them.

The Gestalt principles of grouping were evolved by a group of German psychologists in the early part of this century to explain why elements in visual experience seemed highly connected to one another despite the fact that the incoming light rays, pressure energy, sound waves, and so on stimulated discrete sensory receptors such as the ones found in the retina of the eye. The word Gestalt means "pattern" and the theory described how the brain created mental patterns by forming connections between the elements of sensory input. We cannot go into much detail here about this subtle and philosophically sophisticated theory. However, we can examine a few of the observations that they made about the grouping of sensory elements. They are illustrated in the present discussion by means of the set of diagrams shown in figure 1.11.

Distinct visible elements will be grouped to form coherent perceptual organizations if they fulfill certain conditions. The first is similarity. In the first part of the figure, the black and white blobs can be seen as different subgroups because of the similarity of color within each group and the contrast between groups. Similarly, in audition we find that sounds of similar timbres will group together so that the successive sounds of the oboe will segregate from those of the harp, even when they are playing in the same register.

The second part of the figure shows grouping by a second factor, proximity, where the black blobs seem to fall into two separate clus-

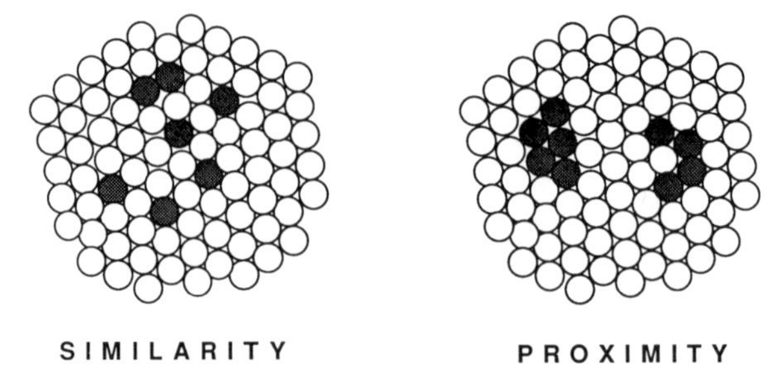

Figure 1.11
Illustration of the effects of the Gestalt principles of similarity and proximity on visual grouping.

ters because the members of one cluster are closer to other members of the same one than they are to the elements that form the other one. It would appear then that the example of stream segregation would follow directly from the Gestalt law of grouping by proximity. The high tones are closer to one another (in frequency) than they are to the low ones. As the high and low groups are moved further away from one another in frequency, the within-group attractions will become much stronger than the between-group attractions. Speeding the sequence up simply has the effect of moving things closer together on the time dimension. This attenuates the differences in time separations and therefore reduces the contribution of separations along the time dimension to the overall separation of the elements. In doing so, it exaggerates the effects of differences in the frequency dimension, since the latter become the dominant contributors to the total distance.

In both parts of figure 1.11, it is not just that the members of the same group go with one another well. The important thing is that they go with one another *better* than they go with members of the other group. The Gestalt theorists argued that there was always competition between the "forces of attraction" of elements for one another and that the perceptual organization that came out of this conflict would be a consequence of the distribution of forces across the whole perceptual "field," and not of the properties of individual parts taken in isolation.

The Gestalt psychologists' view was that the tendency to form perceptual organizations was innate and occurred automatically whenever we perceived anything. It was impossible, they claimed, to perceive sensory elements without their forming an organized

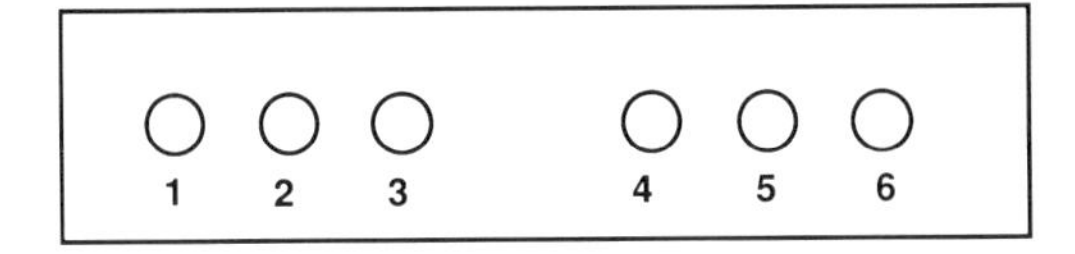

Figure 1.12
A visual display used to demonstrate visual motion segregation. Two groups of three lamps are arranged in a horizontal row.

whole. They argued that this organizing tendency was an automatic tendency of brain tissue.

Auditory Streaming versus Apparent Motion
We have been examining the phenomenon of auditory stream segregation as an example of how phenomena of auditory organization can exhibit the same complexities as are found in vision. This has led us to see interesting parallels in the principles that govern auditory stream segregation and visual grouping. But we have not yet discussed the most striking parallel, that between auditory stream segregation and the phenomenon of apparent motion in vision. Apparent motion is the perceptual effect that used to be very popular on the billboards of theatres, where the switching on and off of a series of electric light bulbs in sequence gave the experience of movement. In the laboratory it is usually created in a much simpler form. Two electric lamps, often seen as small white dots in an otherwise black room, are alternately switched on, each for a brief instant, so that a movement is seen that dances back and forth between the lights, always moving from the light that has just been flashed to the light that is currently being flashed. If the lamps are close together, it may seem that the light itself is moving back and forth. At greater distances the experience is just an impression of movement.

In 1915, Körte formulated a number of laws relating the duration, brightness, and spatial separation of the lamps to the strength of the impression of movement. Körte's third law stated that within certain ranges, if you want to increase the spatial separation between the lamps and still have a strong impression of motion, you had to slow down the alternation of flashes. It was almost as if the movement would not be able to keep up with the alternation of flashes if they were far separated in space unless the flashes were slowed down to compensate for their separation.

A more elaborate form of the apparent motion effect strongly resembles the streaming effect.[6] Instead of two lamps, there are six, arranged in a horizontal row as shown in figure 1.12. They are arranged so that there is a wider gap between the left triplet of lights and the right triplet than there is between the lights within each triplet. If we label the lamps with the digits 1 to 6 from left to right, the order in which the lights are to be flashed can be expressed as the sequence 142536, repeated endlessly with no pause between repetitions. In this sequence there is an alternation between left-triplet and right-triplet flashes. At very low speeds, there is no apparent motion at all. The lights appear simply to go on and off in sequence. At a somewhat higher speed, the true sequence (142536) is seen as a form of irregular left-and-right motion between members of the two triplets. Then, as the speed is increased, the motion appears to split into two separate streams, one involving the leftmost three lamps and the other the rightmost three. The leftmost path of motion is 1–2–3 and the rightmost one is –4–5–6 (the dashes indicating the time periods in which the lights from the other stream are active). This segregation is exactly parallel to what happens in the auditory streaming effect. However, it is also directly explainable through Körte's third law.

This law simply states that as the speed increases, the distance between flashes must shrink if good motion is to be seen. Therefore, if we assume that potential motions between successive and nonsuccessive flashes are competing with one another for dominance, and that we finally see the one that is most dominant, the results of our example follow directly. As we speed up the sequence there is an increased tendency for shorter movements to be favored by Körte's law so that the longer between-triplet motions are suppressed in favor of the stronger within-triplet motions.

I have set up the two examples, the streaming of tones and the splitting of apparent motion, in a parallel way so that the analogy can be directly seen. Horizontal position in space is made to correspond to the frequency of the tones, with time playing the role of the second dimension in both cases.

The success of Körte's law in explaining the visual case suggests that there is a parallel law in audition, with melodic motion taking the place of spatial motion.[7] This law would state that if you want to maintain the sense of melodic motion as the frequency separation between high and low tones increases, you must slow the sequence down. As with visual apparent motion it is as if the psychological mechanism responsible for the integration of auditory sequences could not keep up with rapid changes.

Scene-Analysis Explanation

However, Körte's law is not an accident of the construction of the human brain. In both visual motion and melodic motion, the laws of grouping help to solve the scene analysis problem as the sensory input unfolds over time. In both domains, Körte's law is likely to group information appropriately. In vision it tends to group glimpses of a moving object with other glimpses of the same object rather than with those of different objects. This is important in a world where many objects can be moving at the same time and where parts of their trajectories can be hidden by closer objects such as trees. The law assumes that if a hidden object is moving a longer distance it takes it longer to get there. Hence the proportionality of distance and time that we find in the law.

The proportionality of frequency displacement and time that we observe in the streaming effect also has a value in scene analysis. What should the auditory system do if it hears a particular sound, A1, and then either a silence or an interruption by a loud sound of a different quality, and then a subsequent sound, A2, that resembles A1? Should it group A1 and A2 as coming from the same source? The auditory system assumes that the pitch of a sound tends to change continuously and therefore that the longer it has been since the sound was heard, the greater the change ought to have been. This has the effect that longer frequency jumps are tolerable only at longer time delays.

The experience of motion that we have when a succession of discrete events occurs is not a mere laboratory curiosity. When visual apparent motion is understood as a glimpse of a scene analysis process in action, new facts about it can be discovered. For example, it has been found that when the apparent movement seems to occur in depth, in a movement slanting away from the observer, the visual system allows more time for the object to move through the third dimension than it would have if it had appeared to be moving only in the horizontal plane.[8] This happens despite the fact that although a slanting-away motion would traverse more three-dimensional space, it produces the same displacement of an object's image as a horizontal motion does on the retina of an observer. Therefore Körte's law applies to real distance in the world and not to retinal distance, and therefore can best be understood as a sophisticated part of scene analysis.

Another example of a discovery that was guided by the assumption that the rules of apparent motion exist to group glimpses of real scenes was made by Michael Mills and myself.[9] We worked with an animation sequence in which a shape disappeared from one part of a drawing and appeared in another. This change was seen as motion only if the shape was seen as representing the outline of a "figure" both before and after the disappearance. If the observer was induced to see it as "ground" (the shape of an empty space between forms) before it disappeared, and as "figure" (the shape of an actual figure) when it reappeared, the displacement was not seen as motion but as an appearance from nowhere of the figure.

Neither is the auditory streaming effect simply a laboratory curiosity. It is an oblique glimpse of a scene-analysis process doing the best it can in a situation in which the clues to the structure of the scene are very impoverished.

In general, all the Gestalt principles of grouping can be interpreted as rules for scene analysis. We can see this, for example, in the case of the principle of grouping by similarity. Consider the block-recognition problem shown earlier in figure 1.2 where the problem was to determine which areas of the drawing represented parts of the same block. Because this drawing is not very representative of the problem of scene analysis as we face it in everyday life, let us imagine it transformed into a real scene. In the natural world visible surfaces have brightness, color, and texture. It would be a good rule of thumb to prefer to group surfaces that were similar in appearance to one another on these dimensions. This would not always work, but if this principle were given a vote, along with a set of other rules of thumb, it is clear that it would contribute in a positive way to getting the right answer.

In the case of sound, the considerations are the same. If in a mixture of sounds we are able to detect moments of sound that strongly resemble one another, they should be grouped together as probably coming from the same happening. Furthermore, the closer in time two sounds that resemble each other occur, the more likely it is that they have originated with the same event. Both of these statements follow from the idea that events in the world tend to have some persistence. They do not change instantly or haphazardly. It seems likely that the auditory system, evolving as it has in such a world, has developed principles for "betting" on which parts of a sequence of sensory inputs have arisen from the same source. Such betting principles could take advantage of properties of sounds that had a reasonably high probability of indicating that the sounds had a common origin. Viewed from this perspective, the Gestalt principles are seen to be principles of scene analysis that will generally contribute to a correct decomposition of the mixture of effects that reaches our senses. I am not claiming that the auditory system "tries" to achieve this result, only that the processes have been selected by evolution because they did achieve them.

The argument that I have made does not imply that Gestalt theory is wrong. For the Gestaltists, the phenomena of perceptual grouping arose from the fact that there were forces of attraction and segregation that operated in a perceptual field. This may indeed be the mechanism by which the grouping occurs. I am simply arguing that even if this is the form of the computation, the particular grouping force given to each property of the sensory input and the way in which the grouping forces are allowed to interact have been determined (through evolution) to be ones that will tend to contribute to the successful solution of the scene analysis problem.

Closure and Belongingness

Our senses of vision and audition, living in the same world, often face similar problems. So we should not be surprised if we often find them using similar approaches to overcome those problems. We have seen how the two systems sometimes deal with fragmented views of a sequence of events by connecting them in plausible ways. Another strong similarity between the sense modalities can be seen in the phenomenon of "perceived continuity." This is a phenomenon that is sometimes said to be an example of "perceptual closure."

The tendency to close certain "strong" perceptual forms such as circles was observed by the Gestalt psychologists. An example might be the drawing shown on the left side of figure 1.5 in which we are likely to see a circle partly obscured by an irregular form. The circle, though its outer edge is incomplete in the picture, is not seen as incomplete but as continuing on behind the other form. In other words, the circle has closed perceptually.

It is commonly said that the Gestalt principle of closure is concerned with completing forms with gaps in them. But if it did that, we would not be able to see any forms with gaps in them, which would be ridiculous. The principle is really one for completing *evidence* with gaps in it.

The Gestalt psychologists argued that closure would occur in an interrupted form if the contour was "strong" or "good" at the point of interruption. This would be true when the contours of the form continued smoothly on both sides of the interruption so that a smooth continuation could be perceived. Presumably laws of similarity would also hold so that if the regions on two sides of an interruption were the same brightness, for instance, they would be more likely to be seen as a single one continuing behind the interruption.

Like the perceptual grouping of discrete events, closure can also be seen as a scene-analysis principle. This can be illustrated with figure 1.13 which shows a number of fragments that are really parts of a familiar object or objects. The fragments were obtained by taking the

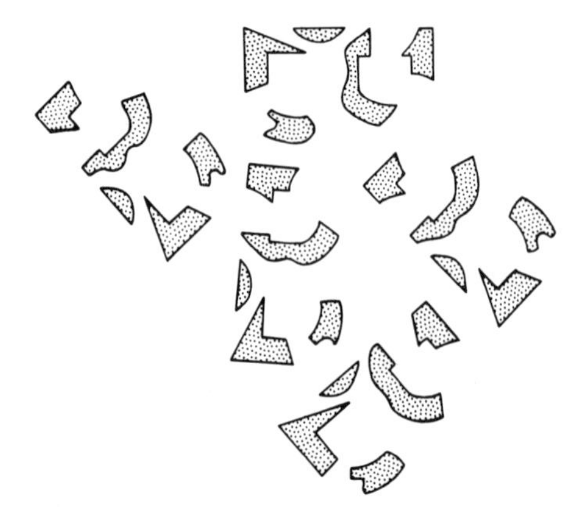

Figure 1.13
Fragments do not organize themselves strongly when there is no information for occlusion. (From Bregman 1981b.)

familiar display and laying an irregularly shaped mask over it. Then the parts that were underneath the mask were eliminated, leaving visible only those parts that had not been covered by it.

Why do the fragments not close up perceptually in this figure? A plausible Gestalt answer might be that the forces of closure are not strong enough. The contours of the fragments might not be similar enough or in good continuation with one another. However, it is easy to show that these are not the basic reasons for the lack of closure. The problem in this figure is that the visual system does not know where the evidence is incomplete. Look at what happens when the picture is shown with the mask present as in figure 1.14. The visual system quickly joins the fragments without the observer having to think about it. The Gestalt principle of closure has suddenly come alive in the presence of the mask.

What information could the mask be providing? It tells the eye two things. It explains which contours have been produced by the shape of the fragments themselves as contrasted with those that have been produced by the shape of the mask that is covering them. It also provides information about occlusion (which spaces between fragments were created by the fact that the mask occluded our view of the underneath shape). These spaces should be ignored and treated as missing evidence, not as actual spaces. The continuity among the contours of the fragments of a particular B undoubtedly contributes to their grouping, but this continuity becomes effective only in the presence of occlusion information.

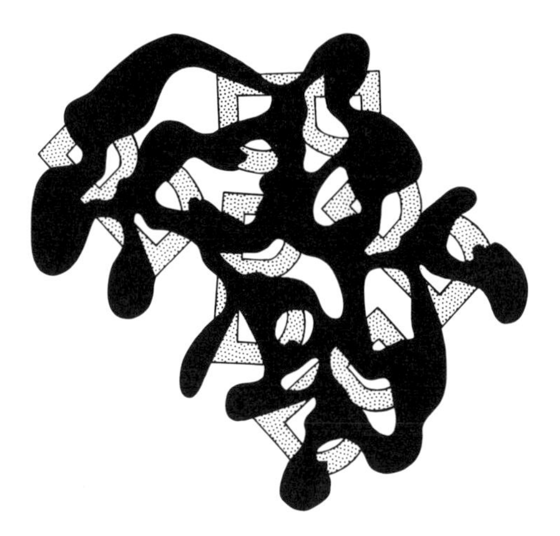

Figure 1.14
The same fragments shown earlier except that information for occlusion has been added, causing the fragments on the boundaries of the occluding form to be grouped. (From Bregman 1981b.)

The conclusion to be reached is this: the closure mechanism is really a way of dealing with missing evidence. But before our perceptual systems are willing to employ it, they first have to be shown that some evidence is missing. This explains how we can see figures with actual gaps in them; we have no reason to believe that the missing parts are merely being hidden. Figures 1.13 and 1.14 indicate that Gestalt principles are just oblique glimpses of a process of scene analysis that looks as much like an evidence-processing system as like the simple grouping-by-attraction system described by Gestalt psychology.

There is evidence that principles of grouping act in an equally subtle way in audition. There is a problem in hearing that is much like the problem of occlusion in seeing. This is the phenomenon of masking. Masking occurs when a loud sound covers up or drowns out a softer one. Despite the masking, if the softer sound is longer, and can be heard both before and after a brief burst of the louder one, it can be heard to continue behind the louder one just as B's were seen as continuing behind the occluding blob in figure 1.14, and as the circle seemed to continue behind the occluding form in the example of figure 1.5. What is more, even if the softer sound is *physically removed* during the brief loud sound, it is still heard as continuing through the interruption.

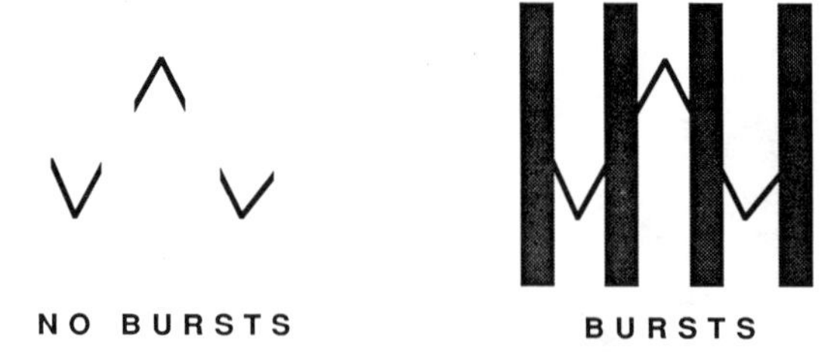

Figure 1.15
Tonal glides of the type used by Dannenbring (1976). Left: the stimulus with gaps. Right: the stimulus when the gaps are filled with noise.

This illusion has many names, but I will refer to it as the illusion of continuity. It occurs with a wide range of sounds. An example is shown in figure 1.15 where an alternately rising and falling pure-tone glide is periodically interrupted by a short loud burst of broad-band noise (like the noise between stations on a radio). When the glide is broken at certain places but no masking sound is present during the breaks, as in the left panel, the ear hears a series of rising and falling glides, but does not put them together as a single sound any more than the eye puts together the fragments of figure 1.13. However, if the masking noise is introduced in the gaps so as to exactly cover the silent spaces, as in the right panel, the ear hears the glide as one continuous rising and falling sound passing right through the interrupting noise. The integration of the continuous glide pattern resembles the mental synthesis of B's in figure 1.14. They are both effortless and automatic.

Again you could see the auditory effect as an example of the Gestalt principle of closure. However another way of looking at it may be more profitable. Richard Warren has interpreted it as resulting from an auditory mechanism that compensates for masking.[10] He has shown that the illusion can be obtained only when the interrupting noise would have masked the signal if it had really been there. The interrupting noise must be loud enough and have the right frequency components to do so. Putting that in the context of this chapter, we see that the illusion is another oblique glance of the auditory scene-analysis process in action.

We have seen how two types of explanation, one deriving from Gestalt psychology and the other derived from considerations of scene analysis, have been applicable to both the streaming and continuity effects. They differ in style. The Gestalt explanation sees the principles of grouping as phenomena in themselves, a self-sufficient

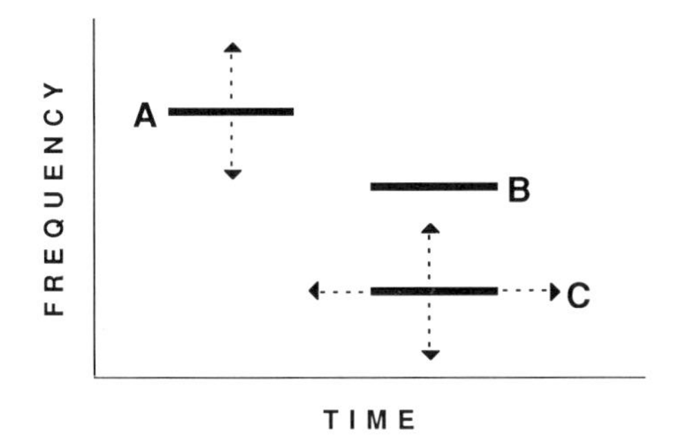

Figure 1.16
Stimulus used by Bregman and Pinker (1978). A, B, and C are pure tone components.

system whose business it is to organize things. The scene-analysis approach relates the process more to the environment, or, more particularly, to the problem that the environment poses to the perceiver as he or she (or it) tries to build descriptions of environmental situations.

Sequential versus Spectral Organization

Perceptual Decomposition of Complex Sounds
We have looked at two laboratory phenomena in audition that show the activity of the scene-analysis process: the streaming effect and the illusory continuation of one sound behind another. There is a third phenomenon that deserves to be mentioned in this introductory chapter. It is introduced here not to demonstrate a parallel between vision and audition, but to show another dimension of the grouping problem. This is the perceptual decomposition of simultaneous sounds. It can be illustrated through an experiment by Bregman and Pinker.[11]

The sounds used in this experiment are shown in figure 1.16. They consist of a repeating cycle formed by a pure tone A alternating with a complex tone that has two pure-tone components, B and C. This is inherently an ambiguous event. For example, it could be created by giving an audio oscillator to each of two people. The oscillator given to one of them puts out the pure tone A, while the one given to the other puts out the complex tone BC. The two persons are asked to play their oscillators in rapid alternation. If this were the way the sound had been created, the correct perceptual analysis would be to hear a pure tone alternating with a rich-sounding complex tone. This, however, is only one possibility for the origin of the sound. The second is that we have given out oscillators, as before, to two persons. This time, however, both of the oscillators can put out only pure tones. One person is told to sound his instrument twice on each cycle to make the tones A and B, whereas the other is told to play his tone only once on each cycle to make the tone C. He is told to synchronize his C tone with the B tone of his partner. If our auditory systems were to correctly represent the true causes of the sound in this second case, we should hear two streams: one consisting of the repetitions of tones A and B, accompanied by a second that contains only the repetitions of tone C. In this way of hearing the sequence, there should be no rich tone BC because the richness is an accidental by-product of the mixture of two signals. If the auditory system is built to hear the properties of meaningful events rather than of the accidental by-products of mixtures, it should discard the latter.

The experiment showed that it was possible to hear the sequence in either way, depending on two factors. The first was the frequency proximity of tones A and B. The closer they were to one another in frequency, the greater the likelihood of hearing A and B as forming a single stream separate from C. Apparently the auditory system uses the proximity of a succession of frequencies, much as it does in the case of the streaming phenomenon, as evidence that they are from a common source. The second factor was the synchrony of tones B and C. If their onsets and offsets were synchronized, they tended to be fused and heard as a single complex sound BC, which was heard as alternating with A. Furthermore, the effects of the BC synchrony were competitive with the effects of the AB frequency proximity. It was as if A and C were competing to see which one would get to group with B. If the synchrony of C with B was reduced, B would be more likely to group with A, unless, of course, the AB connection was made weaker by moving A further away in frequency from B.

Horizontal and Vertical Processes of Organization

There is a distinction that ought to be made now because it follows directly from the Bregman-Pinker experiment and because it is responsible for the structure of the later chapters. This is the distinction between the processes of sequential and spectral integration.

The process of putting A and B together into a stream can be referred to as sequential integration. This is the kind of integration that forms the melodic component of music. It is the process that connects events that have arisen at different times from the same source. It uses the changes in the spectrum and the speed of such changes as major clues to the correct grouping. The sequential process is what is involved in the streaming effect that was discussed earlier.

The fusing of B with C into a single sound is what will be referred to as simultaneous integration or, in special contexts, as spectral integration, a term borrowed from James Cutting.[12] It is this process that takes acoustic inputs that occur at the same time, but at different places in the spectrum or in space, and treats them as properties of a single sound. It is responsible for the fact that we can interpret a single spectrum of sound as arising from the mixture of two or more sound sources, with the timbre of each one being computed from just those spectral components that have been allocated to that source. This happens, for example, when we hear two singers, one singing "ee" and the other "ah", on different pitches. Despite the fact that all we have is a single spectrum, with the harmonics from the two voices intermixed, we can clearly hear the two vowels. Since a vowel sound is a sort of timbre, this example shows that we can extract two timbres at the same time from a single signal.

If we turn back to the mixed spectrogram shown in figure 1.4, we see that in order to put together the streaks of darkness belonging to the same acoustic source, the same two kinds of grouping are necessary: (1) putting together events that follow one another in time (sequential grouping) and (2) integrating components that occur at the same time in different parts of the spectrum (simultaneous grouping). Musicians speak of a horizontal and a vertical dimension in written music. By horizontal, they refer to the groupings across the page that are seen as melody. By vertical, they refer to the simultaneous events that form chords and harmony. These are the same two dimensions as the ones called sequential and simultaneous.

It is useful to distinguish these two aspects of organization because they are controlled by different acoustic factors. Of course they interact, too, but that can be described separately. Therefore, chapter 2 discusses the sequential aspect of organization and chapter 3 deals with the fusion of simultaneous auditory components into a single sound.

Types of Explanation of These Phenomena

In the following chapters, I will attempt to show how the auditory system goes about trying to solve the scene-analysis problem. The presentation will include a number of approaches. First, it will try to show what acoustic information the auditory system uses to solve this problem. An example of this would be the fact that the synchronous onset of two frequency components is taken as evidence that they are parts of the same sound. Second, it will show the perceptual effects that the grouping process has. For instance, if the two components are not allocated to the same stream, then properties that involve their combination, such as the timbre of the mixture, will tend not to be perceived. Third, it will point to a few general properties of the perceptual system that does these things, such as the fact that the groupings are competitive; for example, two components that, in the absence of any other components, might have been placed into the same stream can be captured into separate streams by other components with which they fit better.

This volume can be thought of as an attempt to build up a functional description of how the auditory system solves certain types of problems. It is possible to arrive at an appreciation of the problems of audition by taking the attitude of a researcher in artificial intelligence faced with the problem of trying to replicate human auditory functioning. Such a person, required to duplicate a skill such as segregating individual sound sources from mixtures, would first analyze the information available to the listener. What clues are available in the acoustic signal itself that could indicate which components arose from the same source? How can the environment alter the clues in ways that make them subject to error? What would be the best way to combine these clues if some of them are subject to error?

Whereas the following chapters maintain this attitude, they also deal with a large body of empirical data and try to keep the speculation within the bounds of what is supportable by that evidence. There are certain things that they do not do. They do not attempt to offer physiological explanations or proposals about explicit computational mechanisms. Their approach can best be viewed as an attempt to lay some constraints on theories of these two types.

Although the story is informal, it is interesting to take a moment to see how it is related to more developed theoretical positions. I will consider its relation to concepts drawn from computer modeling, syntactic theory, Gestalt psychology, and physiological explanation.

The computer modeling approach has contributed an important idea that will be used in the coming chapters. This is the notion of a heuristic. The idea was evolved in the process of designing computer programs to solve difficult problems for which no mathematical solution was known. The approach taken by the designers was to employ heuristics, which are defined as procedures that are not guaranteed to solve the problem, but are likely to lead to a good solution. An example would be the use of heuristic tests by computer chess programs to determine whether a proposed move would lead to a good position (e.g., to test whether the move would result in the computer controlling the center of the board or whether the move would lead to an exchange of pieces that favored the computer). Each move is evaluated by a number of such heuristics. No one of them can guarantee success, but if there are a large number, each with some basis in the structure of the game of chess, a move that satisfies most of them will probably be a good one. Furthermore, if each of the heuristic evaluation processes has a chance to vote for or against the move, the program will be less likely to be tricked than it would be if it based its move on only one or two criteria, no matter how good they were.

I believe that the perceptual systems work in similar ways. Having evolved in a world of mixtures, humans have developed heuristic mechanisms capable of decomposing them. Because the conditions under which decomposition must be done are extremely variable, no single method is guaranteed to succeed. Therefore a number of heuristic criteria must be used to decide how to group the acoustic evidence. These criteria are allowed to combine their effects in a process very much like voting. No one factor will necessarily vote correctly, but if there are many of them, competing with or reinforcing one another, the right description of the input should generally emerge. If they all vote in the same way, the resulting percept is stable and unambiguous. When they are faced with artificial signals, set up in the laboratory, in which one heuristic is made to vote for integration and another for segregation, the resulting experiences can be unstable and ambiguous.

My use of the word "heuristic" does not imply a computer-like procedure that involves a long sequence of steps, extended over time. We have to bear in mind that the decisions of the auditory system are carried out in very short periods of time. I use the word heuristic in its functional sense only, as a process that contributes to the solution of a problem.

Whereas the perceptual phenomena that we examined earlier are the province of psychologists, the problem of how people build mental descriptions is a topic that has been looked at by linguists too. As a result, they have provided us with a metaphor for understanding auditory scene analysis. This metaphor, "deep structure," derives from the study of the syntactic structure of sentences.

One of the basic problems in syntax is how to describe the rules that allow the speaker to impose a meaning on a sentence by adding, subtracting, or rearranging elements in the sentence. For example, in English one of these rules imposes the form of a question on a sentence by placing the auxiliary verb at the beginning of the sentence.

Thus, the active sentence "He has gone there" is expressed in a question as "Has he gone there?" The difficulty that occurs when a language loads a sentence with meanings is that when a large number of form-shaping rules are piled on top of one another, it becomes difficult to untangle them and to appreciate the contribution of each of them to the final product. Somehow all speakers of English come to be able to do this, but the learning takes some time. In the 1960s, Noam Chomsky introduced the notion of the "deep structure" of a sentence, a description of a sentence that separately and explicitly described all the underlying syntactic forms and displayed their interrelationships. When a theorist, or a listener, starts with a given sentence and builds a description of its syntax, this is called "parsing" the sentence. It was argued by psychologists who were inspired by Chomsky's approach that in the course of understanding a sentence, the hearer parses a sentence and builds a deep structure for it.

We can talk about perception in a very similar way. Just as a spoken sentence imposes an extraordinary decoding problem upon the listener, so does a nonlinguistic sensory input. Whenever we experience an event, the sensory impression is always the result of an elaborate composition of physical influences. If we look at a four-inch-square area of a table top, for example, the local properties of this area have been affected by many factors: the table's shininess, the variations in its surface color, the unevenness of its surface, the shadow of a nearby object, the color of the light source, the slant of the surface of the table relative to our eyes, and perhaps many more. These factors are all simultaneously *shaping* the sensory information; they are not simply inserted side by side. The shininess is not at one place in our visual image, the surface color at another, and so on. Neither can they be extracted from the sense data independently of one another.

The same thing happens in audition. If we look at any one-tenth-second slice of figure 1.4, the information shown in that slice represents a composition of influences. The spectrum may have been shaped by voices and by other simultaneous sounds. Somehow, if we are able to understand the events that have shaped it, we are succeeding, as in sentence comprehension, in developing a mental description that displays the simple causative factors and their interrelationships in an explicit way.

There is a provocative similarity among the three examples—the syntactical, the visual, and the auditory. In all three cases, the perceivers are faced with a complex *shaping* of the sensory input by the effects of various simple features, and they must recover those features from their effects. Transposing the linguist's vocabulary to the field of perception, one might say that the job of the perceiver is to parse the sensory input and arrive at its deep structure. In some sense the perceiver has to build up a description of the regularities in the world that have shaped the evidence of our senses. Such regularities would include the fact that there are solid objects with their own shapes and colors (in vision) and sounds with their own timbres and pitches (in audition).

Although the approach of this book is not physiological, it is important to see its relation to physiological explanation. We can take as an example the physiological explanations that have been offered for the streaming effect of figure 1.8. It has been proposed that the segregation into two streams occurs because a neural mechanism responsible for tracking changes in pitch has temporarily become less effective.[13] This interpretation is supported by the results of experiments that show that the segregation becomes stronger with longer repetitions of the cycle of tones. Presumably the detector for change has become habituated in the same manner as other feature detectors are thought to. This view of the stream segregation phenomenon sees it as a breakdown. This seems to be in serious conflict with the scene-analysis view presented earlier, in which stream segregation was seen as an accomplishment. So which is it to be, breakdown or accomplishment?

We do not know whether or not this physiological explanation is correct (the claim will be examined in chapter 3). But even if it is, its truth may not affect the scene analysis explanation of streaming. To demonstrate why, it is necessary to again appeal to an argument based on evolution. Every physiological mechanism that develops must stand the test of the winnowing process imposed by natural selection. However, the survival of an individual mechanism will often depend not just on what it does in isolation, but on the success of the larger functional system of which it forms a part.

Because of the indirect way in which the individual physiological mechanism contributes to the successful accomplishments displayed by the larger system, it is possible that what looks like a breakdown when seen at the single-mechanism level is actually contributing to an accomplishment at the system level. To take a homespun example, consider the case of a pitfall trap. When the top of the trap, covered with branches and leaves, "breaks down" and the animal falls through into the hole, we can see that the physical breakdown (of the trap cover) represents a functional success (of the entrapment). The breakdown and the achievement are at different levels of abstraction. By analogy, it would not be contradictory to assert that the streaming effect represented both the breakdown of a physiological mechanism and the accomplishment of scene analysis. This example illustrates how indirect the relation can be between function and physiology.

Scene-Analysis View Prevents Missing of Vision-Audition Differences

It was argued in the earlier discussion that Gestalt explanations had to be supplemented by ones based on scene analysis because the latter might lead us to new phenomena, such as the role of the occluding mask in perceptual closure. There is another difference between the two approaches. Because the Gestalt theorists saw the principles of organization as following from general properties of neural tissue they focused on similarities between the senses rather than on differences. The laws of grouping were stated in a general way, in terms of adjectives (such as "proximity" or "similarity") that could apply equally well to different sense modalities. This has had both useful and harmful effects. On the positive side it has promoted the discovery of the similar way in which perceptual organization works in different sense modalities. For example, the similarities between apparent movement and auditory streaming have become apparent. However, an exclusive focus on the common Gestalt principles, neglecting the unique scene-analysis problems that each sense must solve, is likely to neglect differences between them and cause us to miss some excellent opportunities to study special problems in audition that make themselves evident once we consider the dissimilarities between the senses. The way to get at them is to consider the differences in the way in which information about the properties of the world that we care about are carried in sound and in light. The fact that certain Gestalt principles actually are shared between the senses could be thought of as existing because they are appropriate methods for scene analysis in both domains.

As an example of the way that the scene-analysis approach can reveal important differences between the senses, let us go through the exercise of considering the roles of direct energy, reflected energy, and their mixture in the two senses.

Differences in the Ecology of Vision and Audition

There is a crucial difference in the way that humans use acoustic and light energy to obtain information about the world. This has to do with the dissimilarities in the ecology of light and sound. In audition humans, unlike their relatives the bats, make use primarily of the sound-emitting rather than the sound-reflecting properties of things. They use their eyes to determine the shape and size of a car on the road by the way in which its surfaces reflect the light of the sun, but use their ears to determine the intensity of the crash by receiving the energy that is emitted when this event occurs. The shape reflects energy; the crash creates it. For humans, sound serves to supplement vision by supplying information about the nature of events, defining the "energetics" of a situation.

There is another difference that is very much related to this one: sounds go around corners. Low-frequency sound bends around an obstruction while higher frequency sound bounces around it. This makes it possible for us to have a distant early warning system. The reader might be tempted to object that light too goes around corners. Although it does not bend around, in the way that low-frequency sound does, it often gets around by reflection; in effect, it bounces around the corner. But notice what a difference this bouncing makes in how we can use the light. Although the bounced-around light provides illumination that allows us to see the shapes of things on our own side of the corner, unless it has been bounced by means of mirrors it has lost the shape information that it picked up when it reflected off the objects on the opposite side. Sound is used differently. We use it to discover the time and frequency pattern of the source, not its spatial shape, and much of this information is retained even when it bends or bounces around the corner.

This way of using sound has the effect, however, of making acoustic events transparent; they do not occlude energy from what lies behind them. The auditory world is like the visual world would be if all objects were very, very transparent and glowed in sputters and starts by their own light, as well as reflecting the light of their neighbors. This would be a hard world for the visual system to deal with.

It is not true then that our auditory system is somehow more primitive simply because it does not deliver as detailed information about the shapes, sizes, and surface characteristics of objects. It simply has evolved a different function and lives in a different kind of world.

What of echoes? We never discuss echoes in light because its speed is so fast and the distances in a typical scene are so small that the echo arrives in synchrony with the original signal. Furthermore, in vision we are usually interested in the echoes, not the original signal, and certainly not in integrating the two into a single image. Light bounces around, reflecting off many objects in our environments, and eventually gets to our eyes with the imprint of the unoccluded objects still contained in it. Because the lens-and-retina system of the eye keeps this information in the same spatial order, it allows us access to the information about each form separately. Echoes are therefore very useful in specifying the shapes of objects in vision because the echoes that come off different surfaces do not get mixed together on the way to our eye.

The case is otherwise in audition. Because our ears lack the lenses that could capture the spatial layout of the echoes from different surfaces, we are usually interested in the source of sound rather than in the shapes of objects that have reflected or absorbed it. The individual spatial origins of the parts of a reflected wave front are barely preserved at all for our ears. Therefore, when the sound bounces off other objects and these echoes mix with the original signal, they obscure the original properties of the sound. Although echoes are delayed copies and, as such, contain all the original structure of the sound, the mixing of the original and the echo creates problems in using this redundant structural information effectively.

The two senses also make different uses of the absorption of energy by the environment. The fact that different objects absorb light in different ways gives them their characteristic colors and brightnesses, but this differential absorption is not as valuable in hearing because our ears cannot separate the reflections from small individual objects. We do hear the "hardness" or "softness" of the entire room that we are in. This corresponds to the color information carried in light, but the acoustic information is about very large objects, whereas the information in light can be about very small ones.

In summary, we can see that the differences in how we use light and sound create different opportunities and difficulties for the two perceptual systems and that they probably have evolved specialized methods for dealing with them. This realization will be useful in chapter 7 when we begin to search for reasons for apparent violations of the principle of exclusive allocation of sensory evidence.

Primitive versus Schema-Based Stream Segregation

It seems reasonable to believe that the process of auditory scene analysis must be governed by both innate and learned constraints. In the chapters that follow, the effects of the unlearned constraints will be called "primitive segregation" and those of the learned ones will be called "schema-based segregation."

One reason for wanting to think that there are unlearned influences on segregation is the fact that there are certain constant properties of the environment that would have to be dealt with by every human everywhere. Different humans may face different languages, musics, and birds and animals that have their own particular cries. A desert certainly sounds different from a tropical forest. But certain essential physical facts remain constant. When a harmonically structured sound changes over time, all the harmonics in it will tend to change together in frequency, in amplitude, and in direction, and to maintain a harmonic relationship. This is not true of just some particular environment but of broad classes of sounds in the world.

Such regularities can be used in reverse to infer the probable underlying structure of a mixture. When frequency components continue to maintain a harmonic relationship to one another despite changes in frequency, amplitude, and spatial origin, they will almost always have been caused by a coherent physical event. The later chapters show that the human auditory system makes use of such regularity in the sensory input. But is this innate? I think that it is. The internal organs of animals evolve to fit the requirements of certain constant factors in their environments. Why should their auditory systems not do likewise?

Roger Shepard has argued for a principle of "psychophysical complementarity," which states that the mental processes of animals have evolved to be complementary with the structure of the surrounding world.[14] For example, because the physical world allows an object to be rotated without changing its shape, the mind must have mechanisms for rotating its representations of objects without changing their shapes. The processes of auditory perception would fall under this principle of complementarity, the rules of auditory grouping being complementary with the redundancies that link the acoustic components that have arisen from the same source.

The Gestalt psychologists argued that the laws of perceptual organization were innate. They used two types of evidence to support their claim. One was the fact that the phenomenon of camouflage, which works by tricking the organizational processes into grouping parts of an object with parts of its surroundings, could be made to disguise even highly familiar shapes. Clearly, then, some general grouping rules were overriding learned knowledge about the shape of objects. The second was the fact that perceptual organization could be demonstrated with very young animals.

To the arguments offered by the Gestaltists can be added the following one: From an engineering point of view, it is generally easier to design a machine that can do some task directly than to design one that can *learn* to do it. We can design machines that can parse or generate fairly complex sentences, but there has been limited success in designing one that could learn grammatical rules from examples without any designed-in knowledge of the formal structure of those rules. By analogy, if you think of the physical world as having a "grammar" (the physical laws that are responsible for the sensory impressions that we receive), then each human must be equipped either with mechanisms capable of learning about many of these laws from examples or with a mechanism whose genetic program has been developed once and for all by the species as a result of billions of parallel experiments over the course of history, where the lives of the members of the species and its ancestors represent the successes and the lives of countless extinct families the failures. To me, evolution seems more plausible than learning as a mechanism for acquiring at least a general capability to segregate sounds. Additional learning-based mechanisms could then refine the ability of the perceiver in more specific environments.

The innate influences on segregation should not be seen as being in opposition to principles of learning. The two must collaborate, the innate influences acting to "bootstrap" the learning process. In language, meaning is carried by words. Therefore if a child is to come to respond appropriately to utterances, it is necessary that the string be responded to in terms of the individual words that compose it. This is sometimes called the segmentation problem. Until you look at a spectrogram of continuous speech occurring in natural utterances, the task seems easy. However, on seeing the spectrogram, it becomes clear that the spaces that we insert into writing to mark the boundaries of words simply do not occur in speech. Even if sentences were written without spaces, adults could take advantage of prior knowledge to find the word boundaries. Because they already know the sequences of letters that make meaningful words, they could detect each such sequence and place tentative word boundaries on either side of it. But when infants respond to speech they have no such prior learning to fall back on. They would be able to make use only of innate constraints. I suspect a main factor used by infants to segment their first words is acoustic discontinuity. The baby may hear a word as a unit only when it is presented in isolation, that is, with silence (or much softer sound) both before and after it. This would be the result of an innate principle of boundary formation. If it were presented differently, for example, as part of a constant phrase, then the phrase and not the word would be treated as the unit. The acoustic continuity within a sample of speech and the discontinuities at its onset and termination would be available, even at the earliest stage of language acquisition, to label it as a single whole when it was heard in isolation. Once perceived as a whole, however, its properties could be learned. Then, after a few words were learned, recognition mechanisms could begin to help the segmentation process. The infant would now be able to use the beginnings and ends of these familiar patterns to establish boundaries for other words that might lie between them. We can see in this example how an innate grouping rule could help a learning process to get started. (I am not suggesting that the establishing of acoustic boundaries at discontinuities is the only method that infants use to discover units, but I would be very surprised if it were not one of them.)

Another example of innate segregation that was given earlier concerned an infant trying to imitate an utterance by her mother. It was argued that the fact that the infant did not insert into her imitation the cradle's squeak that had occurred during her mother's speech displayed her capacity for auditory scene analysis. I am also proposing that this particular capacity is based on innately given constraints on organization.

There is much experimental evidence drawn from experiments on the vision of infants that supports the existence of innate constraints on perceptual organization. Corresponding experiments on auditory organization, however, are still in short supply.

One such study was carried out by Laurent Demany in Paris.[15] Young infants from $1\frac{1}{2}$ to $3\frac{1}{2}$ months of age were tested with sequences of tones. The method of habituation and dishabituation was used. This is a method that can be used with infants to discover whether they consider two types of auditory signals the same or different. At the beginning, a sound is played to the babies every time they look at a white spot on a screen in front of them. The sound acts as a reward and the babies repeatedly look at the white spot to get the interesting sound. After a number of repetitions of this "look and get rewarded" sequence, the novelty of the sound wears off and it loses its potency as a reward (the infants are said to have habituated to the sound). At this point the experimenter replaces the sound by a different one. If the newness of the sound restores its ability to act as a reward, we can conclude that the infants must consider it to be a different sound (in the language of the laboratory, they have become dishabituated), but if they continue ignoring it, they must consider it to be the same as the old one.

Using this method, Demany tried to discover whether infants would perceptually segregate high tones from low ones. The proof that they did so was indirect. The reasoning went as follows: Suppose that four tones, all with different pitches, are presented in a repeating cycle. Two are higher in pitch (H1 and H2) and two are lower (L1 and L2), and they are presented in the order H1,L1,H2,L2, ... If the high and low tones are segregated into different perceptual streams, the high stream will be heard as

H1–H2–H1–H2–H1–H2–. . .

and the low stream will be perceived as

L1–L2–L1–L2–L1–L2–. . .

(where the dashes represent brief within-stream silences). In each stream all that is heard is a pair of alternating tones.

Now consider what happens when the reverse order of tones is played, namely L2,H2,L1,H1, ... If the high tones segregate from the low ones, the high stream is heard as

H2–H1–H2–H1–H2–H1–. . .

and the low one as

L2–L1–L2–L1–L2–L1–. . . .

Again each stream is composed of two alternating tones. In fact, if the infant lost track of which one of the pair of tones started the sequence, the two streams would be considered to be exactly the same as they were with the original order of tones. Suppose, however, that the infant does not segregate the high from the low tones. In this case the forward and the backward orders of tones are quite different from one another and remain so even if the infant forgets which tone started the sequence.

To summarize, the segregated streams are quite similar for the forward and backward sequences whereas the unsegregated sequences are quite different. Using the habituation/dishabituation method, Demany tried to determine whether the infants considered the forward and backward sequences the same or different. The results showed that they were reacted to as being the same. This implied that stream segregation had occurred. In addition, Demany showed that this result was not due to the fact that the infants were incapable in general of distinguishing the order of tonal sequences. Pairs of sequences whose segregated substreams did not sound similar to an adult were not reacted to as being the same by infants. In general, the infant results paralleled those of adult perception and the older and younger infants did not differ in their reactions.

Undoubtedly more such research is required. After all, the infants were not newborns; they had had some weeks of exposure to the world of sound. But after this pioneering study, the burden of proof shifts to those who would argue that the basic patterns of auditory organization are learned. Unfortunately, working with very young infants is difficult and the amount of data collected per experiment is small.

The unlearned constraints on organization can clearly not be the only ones. We know that a trained musician, for example, can hear the component sounds in a mixture that is impenetrable to the rest of us. I have also noticed that when researchers in my laboratory prepare studies on perceptual organization, they must listen to their own stimuli repeatedly. Gradually their intuitions about how easy it is to hear the stimulus in a particular way come to be less and less like the performance of the untrained listeners who are to serve as the subjects of the experiment.

Undoubtedly there are learned rules that affect the perceptual organization of sound. I shall refer to the effects of these rules as "schema-based integration" (a schema is a mental representation of some regularity in our experience). Schema-based analysis probably involves the learned control of attention and is very powerful indeed. The learning is based on the encounter of individuals with certain lawful patterns of their environments, speech and music being but two examples. Since different environments contain different languages, musics, speakers, animals, and so on, the schema-based stream segregation skills of different individuals will come to have strong differences, although they may have certain things in common. In later chapters, I will give some examples of the effects of schema-governed scene analysis in the fields of music and language, and will discuss a theory of sequential integration of sound, proposed by Mari Riess Jones, that is best understood as describing the influence of schemas on stream segregation.

Verification of the Theory

The theory presented in this volume proposes that there is an auditory stream-forming process that is responsible for a number of phenomena such as the streaming effect and the illusion of continuity, as well as for the everyday problems of grouping components correctly to hear that a car is approaching as we cross a street, or "hearing out" a voice or an instrument from a musical performance. This is not the type of theory that is likely to be accepted or rejected on the basis of one crucial experiment. Crucial experiments are rare in psychology in general. This is because the behavior that we observe in any psychological experiment is always the result of a large number of causal factors and is therefore interpretable in more than one way. When listeners participate in an experiment on stream segregation, they do not merely perceive; they must remember, choose, judge, and so on. Each experimental result is always affected by factors outside the theory, such as memory, attention, learning, and strategies for choosing one's answer. The theory must therefore be combined with extra assumptions to explain any particular outcome. Therefore it cannot easily be proven or falsified.

Theories of the type I am proposing do not perform their service by predicting the exact numerical values in experimental data. Rather they serve the role of guiding us among the infinite set of experiments that could be done and relationships between variables that could be studied. The notion of stream segregation serves to link a number of causes with a number of effects. Chapter 2, for example, will show how stream segregation is affected by the speed of the sequence, the frequency separation of sounds, the pitch separation of sounds, the spatial location of the sounds, and many other factors. In turn, the perceptual organization into separate streams influences a number of measurable effects, such as the ability to decide on the order of events, the tendency to hear rhythmic patterns within each segregated stream, and the inability to judge the order of events that are in different streams. Without the simplifying idea of a stream-forming process, we would be left with a large number of empirical relations between individual causal influences and measurable behaviors.

A theory of this type is substantiated by converging operations. This means that the concepts of "perceptual stream" and "scene-analysis process" will gain in plausibility if a large number of different kinds of experimental tasks yield results that are consistent with these ideas. With this in mind, in the remainder of this volume I will try to set out the pieces of evidence that fit together into a mutually supporting whole.

Summary

I started this chapter with a general introduction to the problems that would be considered in more detail in later chapters. I began with the claim that audition, no less than vision, must solve very complex problems in the interpretation of the incoming sensory stimulation. A central problem faced by audition was in dealing with mixtures of sounds. The sensory components that arise from distinct environmental events have to be segregated into separate perceptual representations. These representations (which I called streams) provide centers of description that connect sensory features so that the right combinations can serve as the basis for recognizing the environmental events. This was illustrated with three auditory phenomena, the streaming effect, the decomposition of complex tones (the ABC experiment), and perceptual closure through occluding sounds.

The explanation that I offered had two sides. It discussed both perceptual representations and the properties of the acoustic input that were used heuristically to do the segregation. I argued that one had to take the ecology of the world of sound into account in looking for the methods that the auditory system might be using, and claimed that this could serve as a powerful supplement to the Gestalt theorist's strategy of looking for formal similarities in the activity of different senses. Finally I proposed that there were two kinds of constraints on the formation of perceptual representations, unlearned primitive ones and more sophisticated ones that existed in learned packages called schemas.

These theoretical ideas will be used in the remainder of the book to analyze the known evidence on auditory scene analysis. One chapter is devoted to looking at the problem of grouping auditory components sequentially. Another will look at the grouping of simultaneous sounds. There is a separate chapter that looks at the possible differences between primitive and schema-driven integration of sensory evidence. Eventually we look at the role of scene analysis in music and in speech. The reader will discover that there is actually an impressive body of data that can serve to constrain theorizing about auditory scene analysis.

The next chapters present a fairly detailed analysis of how auditory scene analysis is accomplished and analyze the supporting evidence. The reader who is interested only in the conclusions can turn to the final chapter for a summary of what we do and do not know at the present time.

Chapter 2

Sequential Integration

Auditory Stream Segregation

This chapter is about the process of sequential grouping of sounds. We will begin by looking closely at those factors that are responsible for the streaming phenomenon that was described in chapter 1. In this phenomenon the auditory system is grouping tones that are similar to one another in preference to grouping tones that follow one another immediately in time. This is an example of the sequential type of grouping. Both the elements being grouped and those being excluded follow one another in time rather than being simultaneous.

Before we begin, it is necessary to distinguish between two phenomena that have sometimes been called "streaming." The first is the general process of auditory scene analysis in which links are formed between parts of the sensory data. These links will affect what is included and excluded from our perceptual descriptions of distinct auditory events. This process will be referred to in this book as "auditory stream segregation." The second phenomenon is the laboratory effect created when, in a rapid repeating sequence of high and low tones, the high tone and low tones form separate streams. This will be referred to as the "streaming effect." Although the principles of stream segregation create the streaming effect, they do not just create odd phenomena in the laboratory. They are responsible for our normal perception of distinct sonic events.

In the mixed spectrogram shown in figure 1.4 of chapter 1, there are two interesting classes of regions: those in which the visible partials are primarily the result of one signal and others in which they are a hopelessly tangled mixture. If the auditory system were capable of taking the clear views of a single signal and grouping them sequentially with one another on the basis of similarity, it could get at least a partial picture of the individual signal, perhaps no worse than the picture of the B's obtained from the fragments of figure 1.13 of chapter 1. This application of sequential organization could help us deal with mixtures.

The process of sequential grouping could also exploit a related situation. If it could find a portion of the mixture that contained an unmixed signal, it could analyze the portion of the mixture that immediately followed it for components that resembled the unmixed ones, and extract them from the mixture. This second application of sequential grouping principles will not be discussed until chapter 3. Although it is also a sequential grouping process, it interacts with the processes that hold the simultaneous parts of a sound together and is therefore more naturally discussed together with them.

An Experiment with Artificial Words

I want to begin with a bit of personal history. My earliest encounter with auditory organization occurred by accident. A problem that J. R. Hayes and I had been discussing at the time was one presented in chapter 1: Is it possible for an infant to discover the boundaries of individual words in a continuous stream of speech? We speculated that perhaps the baby could learn to recognize repeating patterns of smaller speech sounds. If the sounds "B-A-B-Y" followed one another in that order often enough, perhaps the baby would associate them to make a unit. Remember that at the beginning the infant would have no already-learned units to serve as boundaries for any new ones that were sandwiched between them.

Preliminary to working with infants, I decided to do an experiment on myself to establish whether the idea had any plausibility. However, I tried to put myself into the same state of naivete as a baby by working with unfamiliar verbal material—backward speech. In backward speech, words become totally unfamiliar, and even some phonemes, such as "t", change drastically. I chose 10 English words of different lengths and wrote out a long sequence of these, arranging it so that each word followed every other one equally often. This was to make sure that only the within-word contiguities of sounds occurred with high frequencies, but that the frequency of transition between any particular word and the next one was not very high. I read this balanced sequence into a tape recorder in a monotone, making sure not to insert any pauses between the words. I then played the tape backward to myself repeatedly and hoped that I would eventually learn to hear it as built out of repeating units. Gradually, after about an hour of listening, I had discovered all but the shortest units.

But I began to wonder whether I had really done it by a pure process of association. Perhaps there were special features of speech that assisted grouping. A similar experiment without speech sounds had to be created. I recorded 26 continuous nonspeech sounds, such as water splashing into a sink, a doorbell, a dentist's drill, and so on, and created mock phonemes out of them. Because real phonemes are spoken at the rate of about 10 per second, I took an approximately one-tenth-second segment of each sound. Think of each one as a letter. I spliced the letters together to make artificial words of different lengths, and then made many recordings of each word. Then I made up a sequence of these "words" that was exactly like the sequence of the backward words I had used earlier and again set myself the task of listening to it and trying to discover the "word" units. This time I found it impossible. I could hear groupings that jumped out at me, but they happened too irregularly to be the "words" that I was looking for. Obviously there was something different in speech than in a sequence of arbitrary sounds. Real speech contained glides in frequency, alternations of consonant and vowel, and so on. In listening again to the sequence of random sounds, I noticed that the groupings that jumped out at me were ones in which the component sounds strongly resembled one another. This brought to mind the Gestalt principle of grouping by similarity. The problem with the sequence of arbitrary sounds now became clear. Accidental groupings of sounds in adjacent words had become unitized by similarity, and these chance units had bridged the boundaries between the arbitrary units that I had constructed randomly. Clearly, a perceptually based unit took precedence over one defined by a fixed sequence of arbitrary sounds.

The fascinating possibility occurred to me that acoustic similarities were playing a large role in how we heard sequences of sounds. However, it became obvious that unless the dimensions of similarity for these sounds could be specified, it would be impossible to do any real research on the subject. It seemed more profitable to simplify the sounds so as to be able to know how similar they were to one another. I decided to use pure sine tones of equal loudness. These differed from one another only in frequency.

Using a computer a long random sequence of tones was created in which fixed arbitrary tunes, 12 notes long, were embedded, but where other distractor tones occurred between the notes of the tune.[16] The tunes occurred only occasionally in the sequence of random tones. As these sequences were played, certain things became apparent. If the tunes were much higher in frequency than the distracting tones, they were easily detected. Even when the speed of the sequence was extremely high (over 20 tones per second) the tunes popped out when they were in a different frequency range. In fact, speeding up the sequence seemed to make them pop out even more strongly. It seemed that similarities in the frequencies of sine tones made them into coherent units and caused them to segregate from other less similar ones.

About a year later, I heard of an experiment done by Richard Warren and his colleagues.[17] They had spliced four sounds into a repeating loop and asked listeners to judge the order of the sounds. The listeners could easily do so when the four sounds were spoken digits but found it extremely difficult when the sounds were a hiss, a buzz, the phoneme "ee", and a whistle. For many subjects, the sequence had to be slowed down to over seven tenths of a second per sound before they could correctly judge the order. It occurred to me that Gestalt principles were again involved. It seemed likely that, at the faster rates, some of the sounds were grouping together and overriding the physical proximities (at least at the faster rates), as had happened in my artifical word experiment. So with the help of Jock Campbell I put together an analogue of Warren's experiment using sounds whose similarities could be known in advance: three high-pitched sine tones of different frequencies and three low-pitched ones.[18] The high and low tones were alternated, and the sequence was played to subjects at 100 msec per tone in a repeating cycle. In order to prevent the use of the onset and offset of the cycle as boundaries, the cycle was faded in, played for a while, then faded out. We found that many of the subjects, presented with alternating high and low tones, believed that the three high tones had been adjacent in the sequence and that the three low ones had formed another group. When we asked listeners to pick out a pattern that was embedded in the sequence, we found that if the pattern involved both high and low elements, it could not be picked out of the sequence. Listening to the stimulus, we had the experience of two independent streams of sound—one involving high tones and the other involving low tones. This "streaming" effect destroyed the true sequence of sounds.

I thought that I had discovered a new phenomenon, but I had not. Musicians had been using it since the Baroque period and psychologists had studied it more than once. The only thing that was new was the demonstration that the isolation of the streams could be so complete that you could not even tell the order of elements in the total sequence.

Previous Knowledge of the Streaming Phenomenon

We can look at the musical use of frequency-based segregation in chapter 5 after we have come to understand it a little better. There we will examine not only examples of musical use of stream segregation but also research on this topic by psychologists who were focused on its use in music. Right now we will focus on more general types of studies of the effect.

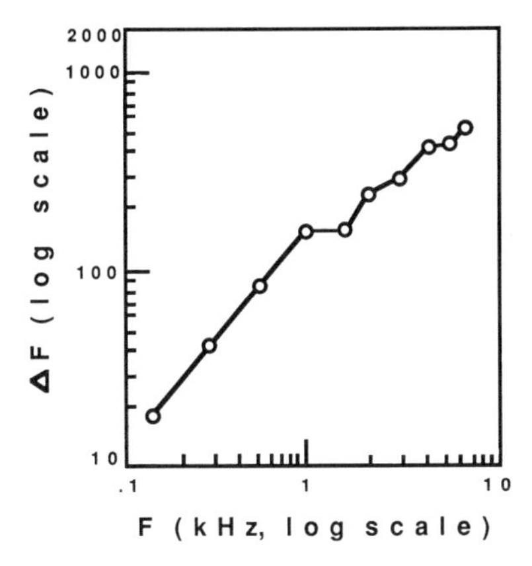

Figure 2.1
Size of trill threshold as a function of frequency. (From Miller and Heise 1950.)

Early Scientific Observation
In 1947, George Miller reported an incidental observation that he had made in an experiment concerned with the annoyance value of patterns of tones. He wrote that "listeners reported that the wide range of component frequencies tended to be perceived alternately, first as a complete pattern and then as two patterns, one of high and one of low pitch" and concluded that "this effect is very similar to figure-ground reversals in visual perception."[19] Three years later Miller and George Heise reported a more systematic experiment on this effect.[20] They presented listeners with a rapidly repeating alternation of two tones. The rate of alternation of the tones was fixed so that the onset-to-onset time of successive tones was 100 msec. The experience of the listener depended on the frequency separation of the tones. They reported: ". . . the pitch seems to move continuously up and down if the frequency difference is small. If the frequency difference is increased progressively, a point is reached at which the trill seems to break; then two unrelated and interrupted tones are heard. It is as if the listener's 'melodic tracking' could not follow a sudden change larger than a certain critical amount." They called this breaking point "the trill threshold." They measured the size of the trill threshold at a series of different frequencies. Figure 2.1 shows what they found. The *x* axis shows the frequency at which one of the tones was set by the experimenter. The *y* axis shows how far away from this tone in frequency the other tone had to be set by the subject to make the sequence split. The authors noted that the necessary frequency separation was approximately 15 percent of the frequency of the fixed

tone at the lower frequencies but became less at the higher ones. The possibility that this phenomenon could be explained by Gestalt principles of grouping did not escape the notice of these researchers: "If frequency and time in the tonal pattern are replaced by vertical and horizontal spatial coordinates (e.g., as in the sound spectrographs of visible speech), then the principles of visual organization discovered by the Gestalt psychologists are applicable to the auditory situation." (p. 638)

Since this research was published, a number of other authors have independently studied the streaming effect (in some cases not knowing that it had been studied earlier) and most have pointed out the relevance of Gestalt principles of grouping in explaining it.[21]

An example of this was a paper by Paolo Bozzi and Giovanni Vicario that reported a series of acoustic demonstrations created at the University of Trieste.[22] They distinguished two factors in the perceptual grouping of tonal elements, their temporal separation and their pitch separation. They showed that groups of tones that were closer in time to one another than they were to other tones would form perceptual units. The same happened when they were closer in pitch to one another than they were to other tones. Bozzi and Vicario emphasized the fact that the distances were to be thought of in relative terms. It is not merely the shortness of the distance between two tones that makes them group but their distance from one another *relative to* their distances from neighboring tones. They pointed out the analogy of these phenomena to the visual examples described by Wertheimer where grouping was thought of as being based on a field of spatial relations. They noted that there could be conflicts between these proximities: tones that were near to one another in pitch could be nonadjacent in time. In these cases pitch proximity might win. For example, a group of lower tones might group together to form a musical phrase that would essentially skip over a few high tones in their midst with the result that the high tones would be isolated from the lower phrase. Sometimes when tones occurred in both high and low ranges two lines of melody were formed. In other words, the two dimensions of time and pitch acted as if they were spatial separations in controlling the perceptual grouping.

Methodology for the Study of Stream Segregation

Before launching into a discussion of the nature of sequential organization in sound and the cues that are used by the auditory system to group sounds sequentially, I want to address two methodological issues. One is the question of what sorts of stimuli to use and the other is concerned with the question of what response measures to take from the listener.

Rationale for Recycled Sequences One of the more popular methods to study stream segregation has been to use a small number of sounds in a repeating sequence. Miller and Heise alternated only two tones, but others, for instance Bregman and Campbell, have used somewhat longer patterns. A repeating loop of a small number of sounds is not a pattern that is representative of sound patterns outside the laboratory. However, it has several advantages. First, it is a way of studying a temporal sequence of events that can be made very long (through repetition) while remaining the same in structure. It can retain the same types of relationships among its elements, and therefore be susceptible to a simple description, no matter how long the repetitions go on. This improves the chances that when we obtain an effect, we know what property of the stimulus has been responsible for it.

Second, it makes it possible to study the grouping process without the influence of starting and ending points. This is very important in the study of the effects of stream segregation on the perception of order of events, since it has been found that the first and last in a series of sounds can be used by listeners as reference points from which they can figure out the positions of the other tones. A loop of tones can be repeated over and over until the memory of the beginning point becomes less significant.

Third it has been found that the repetition pushes the segregation of the streams to above-normal levels. While this is not representative of natural signals, it is very convenient for the study of the factors that increase stream segregation because it acts as a sort of effect amplifier.

Finally, using a loop eliminates the use of certain slow cognitive strategies by the listener and increases the likelihood that basic processes of perceptual organization are being studied. For example, when a nonrepeating sequence is presented and then listeners are asked to make some judgments about it, they can use the silent period after the termination of the tones to review their briefly persisting sensory memories of the tone sequence and to figure out, in some problem-solving way, the answers to the questions of the experimenter. With a loop, however, a short rapid pattern occurs over and over, continually wiping out these memories and creating new ones, probably too fast to permit the use of slow cognitive processes that use memory to any great extent.

The method of repeating cycles has, however, one drawback: despite the continuous wiping out of briefly persisting sensory memories, some knowledge about the sequence gradually accumulates and it becomes predictable. Therefore, in all experiments in which repeating loops of sound are used, the observed effects that are observed may be influenced by this predictability as well as by the factors that are under study (this was pointed out by Jones, Kidd, and Wetzel).[23] As a consequence, while the repeating loop method has important advantages, any results obtained by this method should be verified using less predictable patterns.

How to Measure Streaming

The second question is concerned with how stream segregation should be measured. Is there a best way? I would like to argue that there is none. Stream segregation can have a large number of consequences for observable behavior. Any of them may be used to measure it. However, none of them is a pure measure. Each is influenced by other factors. For example, if you ask the listener to draw, on a picture of a sequence of sounds, the perceptual grouping of the sounds, the task is influenced not only by the grouping of the sounds but by the listener's ability to rapidly carry out the translation from what is heard to what is seen on the paper. Suppose it is found, using this method, that when the sequence is slowed down the grouping of tones becomes more reliable. Does this mean that the perceptual process is unreliable at higher speeds or merely that slowing down the sequence gives the listener a better chance to think and to plan his or her response? The result must be thought of as tentative until it is confirmed using another method. The amassing of support for a theory by different methodologies has been called the method of converging operations. I referred to it in the last chapter. It is an absolute requirement in a field such as experimental psychology where the observations in any individual experiment are always the result of the interaction of known factors with unknown ones.

We seem to be in a vicious circle, condemned to building our knowledge on quicksand, but things are not as bad as they seem. If we start by guessing which stimulus factors favor segregation and which perceptual tasks are affected by this segregation, we can start with this guess and see how well it explains things. When it fails we can guess about why, and gradually converge on a better description of the cause-effect relationships. As this bootstrapping process continues, we will also come to understand that the stimulus variations that we employed to manipulate stream segregation also had unwanted effects on other psychological processes and that our so-called response measures of stream segregation were also measuring other things as well. If it all makes sense at the end, we will have succeeded.

List of Measures That Have Been Used

Here is a partial list of the methods used to study the grouping of tones into separate streams. It is because they tend to give results that are consistent with one another that we believe that stream segregation effects are real. At this point I will list them but not cite the experiments in which they were used.

Method of Adjustment. The subject is asked to adjust a physical property of the sequence, such as the separation of high from low tones, until the sequence splits (or merges again). The average of the settings set for splitting and merging is taken as a threshold for stream segregation. This method is bedeviled by the problem of the "hysteresis" of perceptual organization, its tendency to remain the same even after the sensory input changes. Let us take an example. Suppose listeners hear the sequence as split into two streams. Even when they reduce the separation past the level that would normally yield the percept of a single integrated stream, the perceptual organization in terms of two streams will be held on to just the same. Once the sequence is heard as integrated and the listeners start to increase the frequency separation again, it may require a large separation to split the sequence. The threshold between the two percepts can be so unstable as a result of this hysteresis that the thresholds are very unreliable.

Method of Limits. In this approach, the properties of a repeating pattern are slowly changed. For example, the frequency separation of the higher and lower tones is increased. The subject signals when the perceptual organization shifts from a single stream to two separate streams (or the reverse). The average changeover point from one to two streams and from two to one is taken to be the stream segregation threshold. This method also suffers from hysteresis effects.

Proportion of Time Integrated and Segregated. The listeners are asked to hold one button down as long as the sequence sounds integrated and another during periods when it seems segregated. This is particularly suitable for experiments that expose the subject to the same signal for extended periods and where the tendency to split into substreams is not overwhelming. In such cases the organization will tend to shift back and forth between segregated and integrated organizations and the proportion of the total time that the sequence is split is a useful measure of the strength of segregation.

Rating Scale for Fixed Presentations. The subject is given a rating scale, running from (say) 1 to 5, with 1 indicating that the sequence is totally integrated or heard as a whole and 5 indicating that two wholly separate streams are heard. The subject hears a number of different conditions in a random order and assigns a numerical rating to each. This method has the advantage of being a direct report of the experience in which we are interested. However, since subjects are likely to adjust the use of the scale to the range of variation encountered in a particular experiment, the method makes it hard to compare the results of different experiments.

Pattern Recognition. If a target pattern lies wholly within a stream it is easy to recognize, but if its elements must be extracted from two different streams, the recognition becomes hard. At least two methods for studying the recognition of patterns have been employed. Both require the listener to judge whether or not a particular target pattern is in the stimulus sequence. The first one uses the listener's prior knowledge to provide the target. For example, the subject can be asked to listen for the presence of a familiar tune in the sequence. The second uses two steps: It first presents a short target pattern in isolation and then presents it as part of a longer test pattern. The listener is asked to detect the target pattern in the test pattern. The response of the subject may be to simply say whether or not the target is present in the test pattern, or to rate the clarity using a numerical scale. Like the method of direct rating of the degree of segregation, this method has a straightforward appeal because the essence of the scene analysis process is that it isolates patterns from one another. An important advantage of the second version of this method is that if the target is absent from the test series on half the trials, the score of the listener can be expressed as an accuracy score and this can be used to derive measures (such as thresholds or d') that are comparable from one experiment to another. The method is particularly convenient because it allows all the signals to be recorded ahead of time and does not require equipment that allows the subject to adjust the signal. Furthermore, it seems to give quite consistent results. It can also be used to assess which of several ways of hearing an ambiguous stimulus is stronger. The ambiguous sequence is used as the test pattern. Different target patterns are made up, each of which contains a sequence of tones that would be isolated if the listener were organizing the test sequence in a particular way. Then we can ask the listeners to give a scale rating of how clearly they can hear each target pattern.

Rhythm Changes. Since it appears that when streams split apart the perceptual rhythm is heard only within streams, listeners can be asked to report what rhythms they hear and how they change as stream-segregating factors, such as frequency separations, are increased. Because this is really a sort of pattern recognition task, the methods used to study the latter can be used with rhythm.

Drawing or Writing Down What You Hear. Some experiments, such as early ones by Heise and Miller, have failed to get listeners to do this reliably whereas others have been more successful. It probably depends on some particular skills of the listeners and how complex the drawing task is. If the listeners are musically trained, the task should be much easier, especially if musical notation is used. A variation on this task is to provide the listener with a set of cards, each representing one of the component sounds, and asking him or her to arrange them on the table to express the auditory experience. This method has been used quite successfully in Richard Warren's laboratory.

Judgment of the Order of Elements in a Repeating Sequence. This method can be used because the segregation of streams makes the overall order hard to judge. The order of elements seems to be one of those properties of sequences of sounds that is only readily judged when the elements to be ordered are within the same stream. The disadvantage of this method is that other factors than stream segregation may affect the perception of order.

Counting Tones. When a moderately long sequence of tones becomes split into two perceived streams, it is difficult to count all the tones. Some tend to get lost. However, since the ability to count a string of tones may be affected by other variables than stream segregation, and these, in turn, by the variables being used in the experiment, it is sometimes not clear what is being measured.

Stream segregation may be responsible for other effects as well, but the effects may not be clear enough for them to be used as measures of the effect.

Factors Influencing Stream Segregation

The next major section discusses the acoustic factors that influence the sequential grouping of sounds. The discussion of the perceptual effects of stream segregation is deferred to a later section. It is artificial to disconnect the two topics in this way. The only way we can study a cause of stream segregation is by knowing how to measure its effects. Our learning about the causes and effects of stream organization goes on in parallel. However, it is clearer to present the two topics separately; so that is how this chapter is organized.

The chapter is really on a narrower topic than sequential grouping. Most of the factors that influence the sequential grouping of sounds are those that affect their similarity. Also, since sequential grouping can be most easily observed in the case of stream segregation, most of the research concerns the formation of parallel streams of sound. Therefore much of what follows is a discussion of the effects of various kinds of acoustic similarities on stream segregation in rapid sequences of tones.

Frequency Separation and Rate

The first factors that were known to influence the streaming phenomenon were the frequency separation of the elements in the sequence and the speed of the sequence.

In the early 1970s, Leo van Noorden at the Institute for Perceptual Research in Eindhoven, Holland, carried out a series of experiments on these factors. His brilliant Ph.D. thesis used a number of techniques to thoroughly explore the perceptual grouping of tones.[24] In his first study he used rapid sequences of sine tones. The tones themselves were 40 msec long and the rate of the tones was varied in different sessions, onset-to-onset times varying between 60 and 150 msec. The sequence of tones consisted of a repeated alternation of F, a tone of fixed frequency, with V, a tone of variable frequency, in the pattern VFV–VFV–. . . (where the dash stands for a silent gap of the same length as a tone). When the entire sequence was heard as a single stream, it was heard as having tones of two different pitches, alternating in a galloping rhythm. However, when the frequency of the V tone was far from that of the F tone, and the V and F tones segregated into two streams, each stream sounded isochronous (its tones equally spaced in time). The F stream had the rhythm F–––F–––F––– . . . while the V stream had the rhythm V–V–V–V–. . . . In other words, the segregation left gaps in the component streams where the other tone (V or F) had been when there was a single united stream.

This experiment made clever use of the fact that when the streams segregated the rhythm seemed to change. This clearly audible change helped the listener to decide whether or not the segregation of streams had occurred.

The listeners' task was as follows: F was fixed at 1 kHz. As the two tones rapidly alternated, tone V was slowly moved downward from a frequency high above F until it reached a frequency far below F; then it turned around and moved slowly upward until it was far above F again. This sweeping of frequency up and down continued for 80 seconds. It was found that just asking the listeners to indicate whether the sequence was integrated or segregated was not sufficient. With intermediate differences in frequency between F and V they could hear it either way at will. When they made no special effort they heard it first one way and then the other. Therefore they were asked on some runs to try to hear all the tones as part of a single sequence and to signal whether they could or not. When these instructions were used, the point at which the frequency separation became too large to hear one coherent stream was called the "temporal coherence boundary" (TCB). Under a second set of instructions the listeners were asked to try to hear only one or the other of the streams and again to signal whether they could or could not. The point at which the two frequencies drew too close together for separate streams to be heard was called the "fission boundary" (FB). Figure 2.2 shows the two boundaries plotted as a function of tone rate. The tone rate is expressed as the onset-to-onset time and the frequency separation as the number of semitones separating tones F and V.

The exact numerical values in these results are not the main point of interest. They tend to vary from observer to observer and depend on the exact method used in the test. However, some important trends are visible that are valid across a wide range of experiments.

The first is that there is a broad region between the two boundaries, especially at slow rates (long tone-repetition times). For example, at the 150-msec tone-repetition time, if the listeners try to hear two streams, they can do so with frequency separations greater than about 4 semitones. But if they try to hear the sequence as a single stream they are able to do so below a frequency separation of about 13 semitones. These two facts taken together mean that at 150 msec, if the frequency separations are between 4 and 12 semitones, the listeners have their choice about whether to hear the sequence as one or as two streams. At higher rates (shorter tone repetition times), the range of ambiguity is smaller and the frequency separation tends to control the perception more effectively.

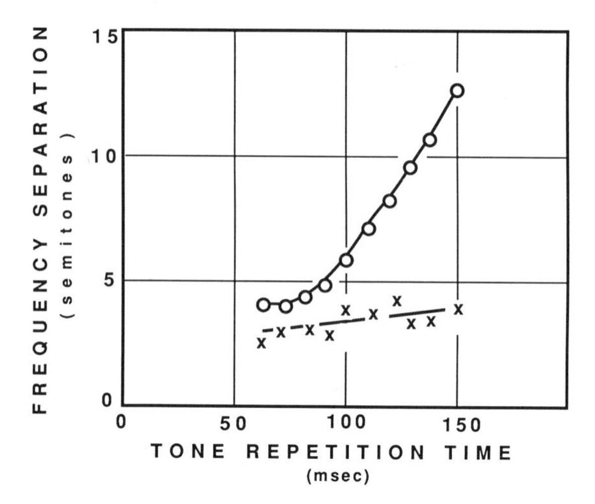

Figure 2.2
Temporal coherence boundary (o) and fission boundary (×) plotted as a function of the onset-to-onset time of adjacent tones. Higher times represent slower sequences. (From van Noorden 1975.)

It is extremely important to notice that only one of these boundaries, the one where the listener is trying to hold onto the experience of a single, integrated stream, is sensitive to the tone rate. It becomes increasingly harder to hear one coherent stream at high speeds. The task of trying to hear two streams (you can actually pay attention to only one at a time) is much easier. It is always possible to do this successfully unless the tones are less than a few semitones apart. This difference in the effects of speed on the two tasks, as reflected in the two boundaries, suggests that they are measuring different perceptual phenomena.

I will argue here, without supporting it yet, that the temporal coherence boundary indicates the point at which the auditory system is forced by automatic and primitive processes of organization to segregate the signal into two streams. The fission boundary, on the other hand, measures the limits of an attention-based process in creating a stream by a process of selection. This difference between automatic primitive processes and schema-controlled attentional processes in creating streams will be dealt with later in more detail under the heading of "schema-driven stream formation" in chapter 4.

Considering only the temporal coherence boundary, and hence, I would argue, only primitive segregation, figure 2.2 shows a rather simple tradeoff between frequency separation and tone rate. At slower rates, the listener can integrate the whole sequence even at fairly large frequency separations, but at high speeds, the separation must be less than 5 semitones. It is this kind of relationship that has prompted the hypothesis that the stream integration mechanism fails when it has to cross a large frequency gap in too short a period of time.

Van Noorden's study also showed another important fact. Segregation seems to be the same whether the variable tone is above or below the fixed tone in frequency when the results are plotted on a semitone scale. This seems to imply that the correct scale for the calculation of frequency separations for the purpose of assessing perceptual grouping is a logarithmic scale. However, this is confirmed only approximately by the "trill threshold" results of Miller and Heise (see figure 2.1, where the threshold seems to be a constant proportion of the frequency of the fixed tone only up to about 1,000 Hz). If frequency proximity were really based exactly on the logarithms of the frequencies involved, Miller and Heise's graph should show a constant slope all the way up.

Even though the logarithmic scale is not fully confirmed, the symmetry of van Noorden's results argues that a researcher need not be overly concerned about varying the frequency of a variable tone in both the higher and lower directions from a fixed tone when studying stream segregation.

The effects of frequency separation and speed were studied in a slightly different way in the author's laboratory at McGill.[25] The experiment studied the perceptual isolation of a tune that the subject was listening for from a set of distractor tones with which it was interleaved in time. It varied both the frequency separation of the distractor tones from the target tune and the loudness of the distractor tones. Two sequences of tones were created, called sequence I and II. These are shown in figure 2.3. Each sequence had one "primary tune" embedded in it, alternating with distractor tones. The tones forming primary tunes are marked in solid circles; the distractors are shown in open circles. The primary tune of sequence I was called tune A and that of sequence II was named tune B. They were both the same shape, having the following structure:

H–M–L– – –H–M–L– – –L–M–H– – –H–M–L– – –

The H, M, and L are high, medium, and low tones, respectively, and the hyphens represent the presence of other distractor tones. This is hardly a tune to be proud of, but our subjects found it fairly easy to learn and it was homogeneous in frequency range throughout.

Tune A was the frequency-isolated version. It was restricted to one part of the frequency range (1,389 to 1,841 Hz) and the distractors

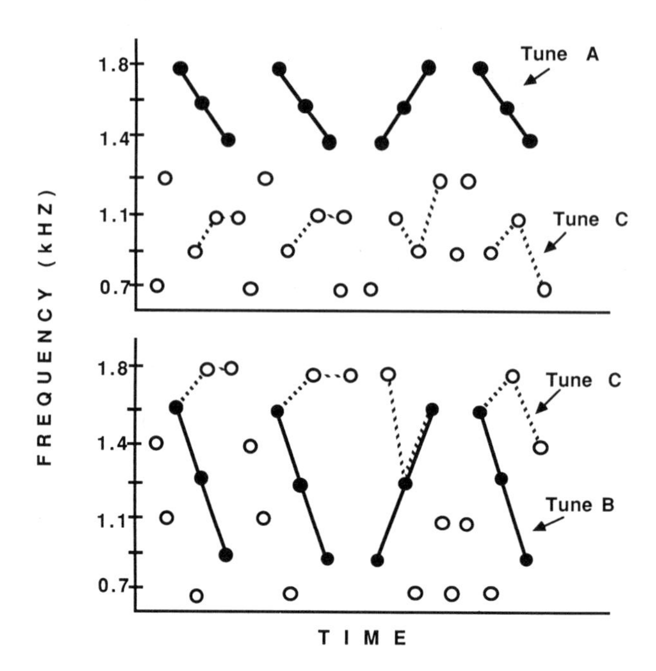

Figure 2.3
Sequences of tones used by Bregman (1971). Top: Sequence I. Bottom: Sequence II. Solid dots indicate the "primary" tunes, A and B. Dashed lines show tune C.

were restricted to a different one (794 to 1,207 Hz). Tune B, on the other hand, was a frequency-embedded tune. It was positioned in a wider frequency range (913 to 1,600 Hz) and the distractor tones were placed throughout this range and also bracketed the tune above and below. The set of tones used was equally spaced on a log-frequency scale. On this scale, the intervals between adjacent tones in tune B were exactly double those in tune A. Neither was a very good diatonic tune. The distractors in both tunes were placed at the same temporal positions. All the tones were sine tones.

It was expected that due to the frequency difference between primary tune tones and distractor tones, tune A would form a unitary subjective stream, segregated from the distractor tones. Tune B, on the other hand, should disappear under conditions that favored stream splitting, since its upper tones should split away from its lower tones, each joining up with the distractor tones of similar frequency to form new tunes. In order to avoid creating a situation in which the B tune would never be heard, we also "helped" the tunes in some conditions by attenuating the distractors.

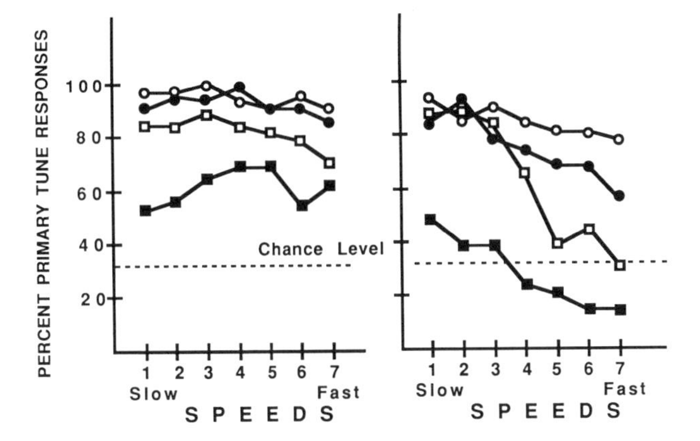

Figure 2.4
Reported hearing of embedded tunes at different sequence speeds. Left: speed conditions presented in ascending order. Right: speed conditions presented in descending order. Circles: narrow-range tune (A). Squares: wide-range tune (B). Open symbols: tune A or B is louder than distractors. (Unpublished data, Bregman, 1971.)

The factors that were varied in this study were (1) two tone sequences: I and II; (2) seven tone rates: 1.4, 2.7, 5.3, 6.7, 10.2, 14.3, and 20 tones per second; (3) attenuation of distractor tones relative to the tune: 0, 15, or 30 dB; and (4) order of presentation of conditions: from slow to fast rates for half the subjects, and from fast to slow for the other half. This variation of order was included to examine the effects of learning insofar as possible without a randomized presentation order.

The experiment began by training the subjects to distinguish tunes A and B from similar tone sequences that might emerge from grouping some of the tune's tones with distractor tones. Then they had to listen to unidentified examples of sequences I and II under different conditions, to say which tune they heard, and to rate how hard it was to hear it on a scale from 0 to 10.

Figure 2.4 shows the number of cases in which tune A was the strongest response in sequence I and tune B was strongest in sequence II. It combines the 15 dB and 30 dB conditions of distractor tone loudness since they gave very similar results. The slow-to-fast and fast-to-slow orders of testing are shown separately. The very large superiority of hearing A versus hearing B can be directly seen. There are more than three times as many cases of failing to identify tune B as of failing to identify tune A.

The open circles and squares show the cases of hearing the A and B tunes under conditions in which the distractors were attenuated by 15 to 30 dB. At slow speeds, this attenuation was sufficient to yield a high level of recognition of both tunes. However, at high speeds, as expected, the recognition of the B tune is very much worse than that of the A tune. Thus, there is a dominance of frequency-based streams over loudness-based streams at the highest, but not at the lowest, speeds.

It has been shown that increasing the speed of a sequence increases its tendency to split into substreams, and that this splitting affects the ability to track an auditory sequence even when this sequence is 30 dB louder than distractor tones. Hence frequency dominates over loudness as a grounds for segregation at high speeds. Unfortunately, we cannot make any general statements about the effects of particular speeds on streaming. It is true that in our data the frequency-based segregation seems to begin to dominate loudness-based segregation at above 5.3 tones per second; however, this value must certainly depend on the particular distribution of frequencies that were used. In this experiment, the tones were equally spaced on a logarithmic scale. Hence the distractors for Tune A were as close as one logarithmic step away from the tune. But suppose, instead, that we had used two highly separated bands of frequencies (300 to 500 Hz and 1,800 to 3,000 Hz) and had required subjects to follow a single tune across these two highly separated bands. The high and low tones would undoubtedly have segregated at lower speeds disrupting the perception of the tune.

This experiment demonstrated that the streaming phenomenon performed a scene-analysis function. The auditory system seemed to be calculating only those melodic relations that occurred between members of same perceived stream.

The effects of speed were studied using a different method by Anstis and Saida.[26] Their subjects listened to a continuous 30-sec sequence of tones that alternated between two frequency values at different rates. They indicated what they heard by pressing down one key if they heard a single stream jumping up and down in pitch and another key if they heard two separate streams at different pitches. The results showed that the probability of hearing a single coherent stream fell approximately in direct proportion to the logarithm of the number of frequency alternations per second. They also showed that at a fixed rate of four alternations (i.e., eight tones) per second, the probability of hearing a single stream in a continuous alternation of high and low tones fell linearly with the size of the frequency separa-

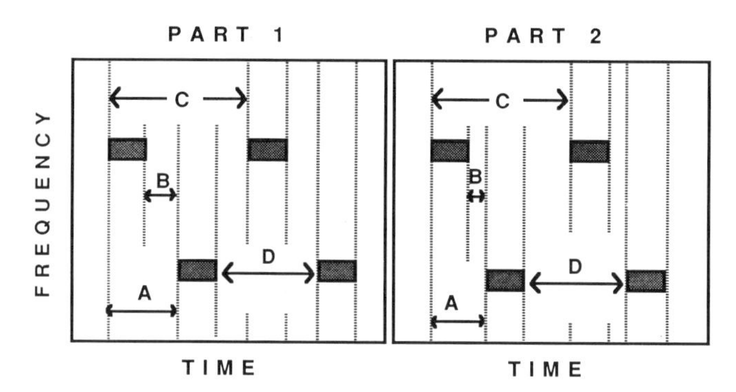

Figure 2.5
Time intervals in a streaming experiment. Higher tones are symmetrically spaced in time between lower tones in part 1 and asymmetrically in part 2. A: onset-to-onset interval between temporally adjacent tones. B: silent gap between temporally adjacent tones. C: onset-to-onset interval between tones in the same frequency range. D: offset-to-onset time between tones in the same frequency range.

tion between high and low tones expressed in semitones. This relation held in the range from 0 to 12 semitones. It agreed with the results of van Noorden in supporting the idea that frequency separation should be expressed on a logarithmic scale to obtain the simplest relation to segregation.[27]

What Property of Time Intervals Influences Streaming?

Many experiments have shown that the streaming phenomenon becomes stronger when the rate of alternation of the tones increases. However, it is not certain which of the time intervals involved is responsible for the effect. Consider figure 2.5, part 1, which shows a diagram of the time intervals involved in a streaming experiment. It illustrates a typical case in which the tones alternate between high- and low-frequency ranges and there are silences between them. The interval marked A shows the onset-to-onset time for adjacent tones; B is the *offset*-to-onset time for adjacent tones; C is the onset-to-onset time for tones in the same frequency region; and D is the *offset*-to-onset time for tones in the same region. Since most experiments do not vary these independently of one another, we do not know which of them is responsible for the effects of rate on streaming. However, the different theories that have been evolved to explain the illusion consider different intervals to be the effective ones. For example, the Gestalt view that it is the proximity of the tones in a time-by-frequency space that counts should find the lengths of the silences crucial, since these silences are what separate the tones and determine their temporal proximity. For Gestalt theorists, then, it would be intervals B and D that would be important. On the other hand, intervals A and C would be significant for any theory that proposed that the auditory system uses rhythm in determining what tones to group, since it is the onsets of tones that define the rhythm. (Mari Reiss Jones has proposed such a theory, in which the auditory system prefers to group tones that both have a regular rhythmic pattern in time and follow smooth frequency trajectories.[28])

Which intervals are important? Unfortunately, different studies have produced different answers. Van Noorden kept the onset-to-onset time constant and lengthened the tones; in other words he shortened intervals B and D.[29] He found that this increased stream segregation. His interpretation is that interval D was the important one. However, van Noorden's conclusions were based on the results of only a single subject—himself.

Dannenbring and Bregman, using a different method, got different results.[30] They fixed the length of interval B, the gap between adjacent tones, to a different duration on each trial. Different trials had different gap durations ranging from 0 to 100 msec. Their subjects controlled the tone length and, in this fashion, the repetition rate. They were asked to find the duration that produced an experience that was just at the threshold between one and two streams. The results were quite simple. On trials where the experimenter lengthened the gap, the subjects shortened the tone to compensate, and vice versa. They were essentially trying to hold interval A, the onset-to-onset interval, constant at about 200 msec. Since the experiment failed to independently vary intervals A and C (the across-stream versus the within-stream onset-to-onset intervals), either one might have been critical for stream segregation.[31]

In either case we are dealing with onset-to-onset times. This suggests that in at least some cases, the auditory system is focusing on the onset of events. This is very sensible of it. It is at the onsets of sounds that things are happening. It is the onset of the piano tone that tells you when the pianist's finger hit the key. The tone's duration tells you about the resonance characteristics of the piano but not about *when* anything has happened. Two percussionists, playing in time with one another, one on wood blocks and the other on a vibraphone, will synchronize their attacks, or tone onsets, and let the offsets fall where they may.

When the auditory system places a sequence of such short percussive sounds into the same stream, it is not treating them as parts of a single environmental event, but as a series of distinct short events that have all arisen from a common source. By measuring their onset-to-onset times, it is determining whether they are close enough in time to be grouped.

Not all sounds come from sudden transfers of energy. Sounds with slow attacks, such as the growth in loudness of the wind in the trees, also occur in nature. They tend to be continuous and to die out slowly. In these cases we are likely to be less concerned with the moment of onset of the sound and more with the mere fact that it is happening. The onset does not signal the occurrence of a discrete event whose point in time needs to be estimated. As far as grouping the sounds of these gradual events is concerned, since they are likely to be continuous, the grouping will not have to bridge silences at all. Rather it will have to bridge interruptions by louder sounds. In such cases, it will probably be the time between the last clear glimpse of the sound and the next one that is important (that is, something resembling offset-to-onset time).

Different experiments on the temporal separation of tones have given different results. Evidently more research is needed to determine exactly when the onsets of sounds are critical in perceptual grouping and when they are not.

We can ask a general question here: Is it the timing relations between the tones of the same frequency range that are important (intervals C and D) or those between frequency ranges (A and B)? There is one study that is relevant to this question. Van Noorden used a pattern of alternating high and low tones in which the tones in one frequency range were not exactly half-way (in time) between the tones of the other range, although the tones in each range, considered alone, maintained a regular spacing.[32] The perceptual effect on the listeners was that sometimes, instead of hearing two separate streams, each with its own regular rhythm, they would hear a grouping of the tones by pairs, these pairs being the consecutive pair of high and low tones that were closer together in time. This shows that neither of the intervals C or D alone is critical since neither of these intervals is affected by shifting one sequence as a whole forward in time relative to the other. However, this result in itself does not imply that these intervals are not taken into account in determining streaming. Part 2 of figure 2.5 shows that not only have intervals A and B changed as a result of van Noorden's manipulation, but the size of these intervals have also changed in relation to the sizes of the C and D intervals. If it is this relation that is important, then manipulating A and B was only an indirect way of manipulating this relation.

What Are the Elements?

How to Define Onsets The trouble with having a theory that relates stream segregation to onset-to-onset intervals is that in real life onsets may not be so well defined. Even in the punctate signals that we have in western music (and perhaps in most music), where each note has a definite beginning, the notion of onsets is not entirely cut and dried, because the rise times of the notes of different instruments are not the same. The piano tone reaches its maximum intensity almost immediately while the cello tone does not. Can we really talk, then, about when notes begin? It appears that we can. The perceived onset time of musical tones has been studied in an experiment in which people were asked to adjust the spacing of a series of tones until they were heard as equally spaced in time.[33] The sequence contained two tones, A and B, that were alternated, except that the B tones were not fixed at exactly halfway between the A tones and the listeners were allowed to alter this position. Furthermore, the two types of tones had different rise times. The results showed that the listeners adjusted the tones so that the intensity at the beginning of the tone reached a certain level at regular intervals. Therefore the more slowly rising tone had to be set to start a bit earlier than halfway between the more rapidly rising tones. The fact that a certain intensity of the tone defines its beginning is a useful fact because it is simple, but does this simplicity exist in cases in which the events are not as discrete as in a sequence of tones?

In listening to speech, listeners appear to judge its rhythm not according to the points in time at which the intensity itself changes but at the points at which the speaker initiates articulatory movements.[34] This suggests that the listeners are using some abstract knowledge about the relations between speech sounds and speech movements. Although this knowledge affects their judgments of rhythm, it is still possible that the onsets that control raw perceptual grouping are defined by acoustic variables alone.

When we speak about the rate of onsets of units of sound, we presuppose that we know what a perceptual unit is. Yet it is far from certain that we have anything better than our own intuitions to go on. Any physical definition that we can give at this time is sure to be wrong. Consider, for example, the word "cat" spoken in isolation. We know that words consist of sequences of phonemes, and that the word "cat" has three of them, "k", "a", and "t". But is it correct to say that the word consists of a sequence of three sounds, each of which functions as an auditory unit? We should remember that even the simple sound "k", when examined at a microscopic level, consists of three acoustically distinguishable parts, a brief silence when the closure occurs, a sharp burst of noise when the closure is released, and a longer "h" sound (aspiration) at the end. The "k" has no special claim to being a true acoustic unit. It is a phoneme, which is a linguistic unit, not an acoustic one. Might it be that the word "cat" is heard as a single acoustic unit when spoken in isolation, and then by a process of pattern analysis is understood as having been shaped by the three phonemes in question? Asking the question another way, is it true that larger units are always built up by first perceiving some smaller ones and then sticking them together?

There is very little real research on this question. However some related research has led to interesting speculations. Ira Hirsh and his colleagues carried out a series of experiments in the late 1950s on the question of how rapidly a sequence of sounds would have to be presented before people could no longer tell what order they were in.[35] This seemed to be an important question at the time because it appeared that speech could be understood even when the rates of the individual speech sounds (if you thought of each phoneme as a separate sound) were very high, perhaps up to 10 per second in normal speech and up to 15 or 20 per second in artificially speeded-up speech.

Using brief pairs of sounds such as click-hiss, Hirsh determined that a difference in onsets of about 20 msec was required before highly practiced subjects could tell which of the two had come first.[36] However, other experiments showed that these results did not reflect a simple spontaneous ability to name the order of events; the high level of practice was the relevant factor. Broadbent and Ladefoged reported that their subjects, in a very similar experiment, began by being unable to tell what order the pairs of sounds were in, even when the individual sounds lasted for 125 msec.[37] However, after much practice they could name the order even when the sounds were only 30 msec long. This in itself would not argue against the idea that in recognizing words we apprehend both the individual elements and their order. After all, we have enormous amounts of practice with the recognition of words. But the subjects told them something that does jeopardize this theory. They said that they were able to attain the high levels by noticing a qualitative difference between the sound of the pair taken as a whole when it appeared in the two orders. This implies that they were perceiving the sequence as a single event, not as a sequence of two sounds.

Basing his argument on observations of this type, Richard Warren has concluded, after reviewing a large number of experiments on the recognition of the order of rapid events, that there are two ways of accomplishing this task.[38] These are the direct "identification of components and their order," and, second, "holistic pattern recognition." The astounding success of subjects in experiments in which they are required to recognize the order of events in extremely rapid sequences (having onset-to-onset times as low as 2.5 msec) is achieved by first recognizing some quality of the sequence as a whole that changes when the order of elements changes, and then remembering that this quality is what is experienced when the components are in a certain order. Hirsh has reached essentially the same conclusion.[39] Both authors agree, then, that we deal with rapid sequences of speech sounds by recognizing units that are larger than the phoneme.

There is another problem with the notion that longer sounds are built up perceptually by concatenating our percepts of smaller units. Consider a long sound, such as a steady pure tone, that lasts for 10 seconds. Is our experience of it built up of smaller perceptual units? If so, where do the units start and stop? How could a theory of perceptual unification that talked about the grouping of units deal adequately with the obvious perceptual unity of this sound? To deal with this question we are forced to fall back on an idea of the Gestalt psychologists: A homogeneous perceptual input contains no units. Only when it is broken up by some sort of discontinuity does it organize itself into units. According to this way of thinking, the perceptual unit is itself formed by a process of perceptual organization. After being formed, units can be grouped by similarity and other factors to form higher-order organizations.

Still, there is a problem with units. When an acoustic event occurs that we know is physically composed of a series of distinct components, how can we predict whether the auditory system will treat these as distinct or will blend them to derive a holistic quality? What are the speeds and other physical parameters that determine which alternative will occur?

Only a bare beginning has been made on studying the formation of perceptual units in sound. Royer and Robin studied what they called "unitization" by presenting repeating patterns consisting of sequences of 1,200-Hz sine tones and silences to listeners at different speeds.[40] The patterns were not strict alternations of tones with silences but rather patterns such as

T–T– –T– – –T– –

where the T's are tones and the dashes are silences. At slow speeds the individual tones could be distinguished, but at higher speeds, the whole pattern was heard as a unitary repeating sound, "a repeating packet of sound bursts," in which the individual components lost their identities. The research suggested that the process that defines units uses dips in intensity to discover them, but can follow intensity changes only at a certain rate. When the dip is too fast it is missed and larger units are formed.

Two observations reported by van Noorden also link the formation of units to sudden rises in intensity.[41] The first (p. 36) concerns what is heard when a tone is subjected to rapid cyclical variation in amplitude (amplitude modulation or AM). If the AM is slow, the tone is simply heard as a single tone whose loudness alternately rises and falls. As the AM speeds up, a series of separate tone bursts is perceived, the bursts corresponding to the loud phase of the AM cycle and the interunit gaps to the attenuated phase. Instead of hearing one sound, a series is now heard. Presumably this happens because the rate of change of amplitude exceeds a critical value and a perceptual boundary is formed at each change in amplitude.

It is likely that it is really the rate of *rise* in intensity that controls the formation of units. A possible illustration of this fact is our perception of a rapid series of guitar tones. A plucked string sound has a very sudden attack but decays gradually so that rapidly played tones will overlap in time. Despite this, in a rapid series of plucked guitar notes, each one sounds like a discrete event. In our laboratory, we have synthesized these tones backwards so that the onset is slow and the decay rapid, maintaining the same overlap in time. When we listen to these, the discreteness of the individual sounds is less definite (and the pitches are less precise). Apparently, abrupt rises in intensity tell the auditory system that a new sound has joined the mixture and that it should begin the analysis of a new unit.

The second of van Noorden's observations (p. 47) concerned a pair of 40-msec tones presented in rapid succession. When the time between tones was short (less than 10 msec) and the frequency separation was small (for example, 4 semitones), they sounded like a single tone that was changing in pitch. When the time between them was increased, the two separate tone bursts were clearly heard, but the listener got a clear impression of a jump in pitch between them. At longer time intervals, the two tones sounded more independent. These observations, like those of Royer and Robin, seem to indicate that silent gaps of sufficient duration will cause sound to segregate into separate units, but even at the point where they just separate, there will still be strong perceptual relations between them (the jump sensation).[42] Therefore there appears to be a continuum between complete unification and complete independence.

Hierarchy of Time Scales with Properties Computed at Each Sequential units are formed by our auditory system for the same reason that parallel streams are: to create auditory entities that can serve as centers for description. If units are formed whenever a region of sound has uniform properties and boundaries are formed whenever properties change quickly, it follows automatically that units will tend to have relatively simple descriptions. A simple description is equivalent to an economical theory. So we can imagine that the finding of unmistakable units in an input represents good progress along the road to pattern recognition. A series of dissimilar units probably represents a series of distinct happenings in the world. The unit plays the same role in segregating events in time as the stream does in segregating them in frequency. In fact it is possible that the terms "unit formation" and "stream formation" simply pick out different aspects of a single process, the formation of auditory entities that represent distinct happenings in the world.

In talking about units we must remember that units can be perceived as embedded in larger ones. The spoke of a bicycle is a unit and so is the rim. However, spokes and rim together form a higher order unit, the wheel. The wheel in turn can be seen as part of a larger unit, the bicycle. I would like to emphasize that I am talking about actual seeing, not just conceptualization. The spoke is a unit because it is smooth and continuous in its properties. The wheel is a visual unit because it is bounded by a strong contour, the circle, and also because it rotates as a unit. The bicycle is seen as a unit because of the connectedness of its parts and because it moves as a unit. So all these levels exist in the sphere of perception.

The situation is similar in sound. In a bird song, there may be distinctly audible chirps; some rapid sequence of them can form a trill, and the trill itself may be embedded in the larger sequence that defines the song. Furthermore there may be different levels of description that apply to the different sized units. The chirps may be short and descending in pitch; the trill may be slowing down as it proceeds, and the song as a whole may contain exactly three buzzes and one trill, with certain time relations between them. There seems, in sound, to be a hierarchy of units spanning different scales of time.[43]

As units are formed, the auditory system computes properties that derive from just the energy that gets packaged in that unit. So, for example, suppose we had a long gliding tone that contained gradual changes in its properties. These would be heard as shifts in its quality, and probably would not be very noticeable. If, on the other hand, the glide were broken in three places, each of the glides packaged between these breaks would be experienced as having its own separate properties, such as starting pitch, slope of glide, or loudness. These properties would now belong to the individual short glides and could affect their grouping with other sounds in their neighborhoods.

Steiger and Bregman have shown that glides with similar slopes and in the same frequency region, for example, will group sequentially into streams.[44]

We must bear in mind, then, as we continue to discuss the various properties that govern the sequential grouping of sounds that we have to stop ourselves occasionally and ask, "properties of what?" Most laboratory research in audition works with materials such as tone bursts, noise bursts, and clicks, whose units are strongly predefined. It is convenient to have these ready-made units. The description of our research becomes simpler. However, not all of nature comes so neatly packaged, and we therefore can surmise that the packaging decisions made by our perceptual systems may have important consequences. When we hear an acoustic change, it can be dealt with as a transformation of the qualities of a single sound, as the ending of one sound and the beginning of a new one, or as the interruption and masking of a first sound by a second. Therefore, although we hope that the following discussion of the factors that control grouping may have general applicability, we have to remember that they have been investigated, for the most part, with sequences of discrete sounds.

Spatial Location

One would think that the most powerful principle of all for the perceptual decomposing of a complex mixture of sounds should be to group, as part of the same stream, all components of sound that come from the same position in space. It would be a good bet that sounds emanating from the same location have been created by the same sound source. We are familiar with the fact that we use our spatial hearing to help us to follow a particular conversation in a noisy room. If we block one ear and interfere with spatial localization, the task becomes much harder.

If the auditory system is to group sounds by their locations, it must have a method for representing locations on some sort of continuum. We know that space is physically a continuum and to move from any position in it to another, any object must pass through all the intermediate positions. It is this property of space, for example, that justifies the existence of perceptual rules that favor the grouping of visually perceived movements that lie on smooth trajectories. But it is not sufficient that space have this property. The perceptual representation of space must also have it. Roger Shepard has called this the "psychophysical complementarity" principle.[45] This sort of complementarity has been found in vision and in touch.[46] The auditory system, for instance, should behave as though there were a continuum of locations and that to get from one place to another, a sound must pass through intermediate places. Then, if two moments of sound were acoustically similar, but were too far apart in space to have arisen from the same source, and were not joined by a continuous movement from one location to the other, they would likely be treated as having come from different sources.

There is one piece of evidence that space is considered as a continuum by the auditory system, the results of an experiment by Gillian Rhodes.[47] Rhodes has suggested that the human auditory system maintains an analog representation of space in which the transformations that can occur in physical space are mirrored by operations in the representational system. One might suppose that the reason that vision and touch represent space in an analog fashion is that in both modalities, the representations of space at the surface receptors and in the primary sensory cortex take the form of a topographical map. It seems, however, that audition is different. In audition it is frequency for which the representation is laid out like a map in the peripheral levels of the system. At higher levels of the nervous system, though, there are spatial maps of sound. Evidence has been found that at the level of the superior colliculus of the nervous system the spatial origin of auditory inputs is coded topographically.[48]

Rhodes carried out an experiment whose results supported the idea that in order to shift our attention from one point to another in space, we must, in effect, shift it through all the intermediate positions. The listeners in her experiment were blindfolded in front of nine loudspeakers that were laid out in a semicircle in front of them. A short tone was played over one loudspeaker and the subject was required to call out as quickly as possible the label for the speaker from which it had come. Immediately afterward another tone was played from the same or a different loudspeaker, and so the experiment proceeded. The experimenters found that the time taken to respond to a tone was proportional to the spatial separation between it and the previous tone, as if the subjects had to swing their attention across the intervening space, each bit of that space taking a certain time to traverse. Rhodes interpreted this as evidence that auditory space acts like a continuum.

I would like to believe that her interpretation is correct. However, it is possible that the increase in time with more distant speakers was not occupied by the listeners swinging their auditory attention over, but by their trying to determine the label for the new speaker. Since the speakers were labeled by numbers, the listeners might have counted their way over from the last speaker (and hence the last number that they had used) to find the label for the subsequent sound.[49] The time taken for this counting process would be proportional to the displacement. The correct interpretation of this particular experiment is therefore unclear, but there is indirect evidence to support the theory behind it. If auditory space is a continuum, we might expect the same sorts of perceptual grouping of sounds as we find for visual elements. The fact that we do find such grouping, as we shall see below, argues that it is a continuum.

One might expect from an examination of the research on signal processing that grouping sounds by spatial origin is the only principle that is needed. Most engineering attempts to automatically reject extraneous sounds from a signal have used spatial location as the criterion for accepting the signal.[50] However, human beings are not so trusting of this "best" principle. While spatial location is used, it by no means overpowers other bases for grouping when in conflict with them. That is why humans can segregate different voices even when they hear them coming over a monophonic radio.

Stream Segregation Based on Spatial Location

There have been a number of laboratory studies on how spatial separation affects the sequential grouping of sounds. Many of these have involved the streaming phenomenon.

The first mention of streaming on the basis of differences in location that I am aware of was by Donald Norman, who observed that "the continuous up-and-down movement of the pitch in a trill does not occur when the alternate tones are presented to different ears."[51] He argued that "dichotic presentation of the two tones could never lead to perceptual continuity because the tones could never be attended to simultaneously" (p. 7).

The streaming of sequences of tones when they alternated between the ears was also observed by Leo van Noorden.[52] He also found that the temporal links between the tones in the two ears were weak (p. 61). Using himself as a subject, and using sequences in which all tones had the same frequency, he found that it was hard to judge whether the tones sent to one ear were exactly halfway in time between the tones that were sent to the other ear. This judgment was harder when the tones alternated between the ears than when all the tones were sent to both ears (diotic presentation) and became even more difficult when the tone rate increased. This relation of the effect to the rate of presentation was not found (or at least not very strongly) for the diotic presentation. The difficulty grew most strongly as the tone rate changed in the region between 160 and 120 msec per tone. (Incidentally, this is the region in which the effects of frequency separation also grow most strongly with increasing tone rate.) Van Noorden offered a physiological explanation for the streaming of dichotic tones: Successive tones had to stimulate overlapping populations of hair cells along the basilar membrane before they could be integrated into a single stream. This requirement would automatically rule out the integration of tones arriving in sequence at opposite ears since there would be no shared population of sensory receptors.

The hypotheses of Norman and van Noorden were not confirmed by later findings. When factors other than spatial separation were introduced so as to favor the integration of tones into the same stream, it was possible for a person to hear dichotically alternating tones as an integrated sequence and to not even realize that they were alternating between the headphones.

Diana Deutsch's "scale illusion" is an example of this.[53] In it, the principles of grouping by frequency proximity and by spatial location are put into conflict with one another, with frequency proximity winning out. The stimulus for this illusion is shown in figure 2.6, part 1. It is a musical scale, presented simultaneously in both its ascending and descending form. The pattern is played to listeners over headphones. The two ears receive different signals. When a note from the ascending scale is played to one ear, a note from the descending scale is sent to the other ear. The notes in part 1 are marked L or R according to which ear received them. Each tone in Deutsch's original version of the illusion was 250 msec in duration. If the listeners had heard the tones grouped by their ear of arrival, the listener would have heard the two irregular patterns shown in part 2 of the figure, one in the left ear and the other in the right. What most listeners actually perceived is shown in part 3. In one earphone, they experienced a sequence formed by the higher tones, and in the other they heard a sequence formed by the lower ones. Rather than grouping the tones by their ear of presentation, they grouped them by their frequency range.

The fact that Deutsch used a rate of presentation slower than we normally have to use in order to obtain strong stream segregation might lead a proponent of the attention-switching theory to propose this criticism: She failed to get a dissociation of the tones in the two ears because her sequence was too slow. The listeners had time to switch their attention back and forth; under these circumstances they were able to track the tonal sequence on the basis of frequency proximities. After writing this, I decided to test the validity of this criticism. I went to the laboratory and created versions of the scale illusion at rates of up to 20 tones per second. Although at higher rates it is harder to hear distinct tones and the sequence sounds more like a

Figure 2.6
Part 1: stimulus pattern for the scale illusion of Deutsch (1975). The letters show the ear of presentation. The tones of upper and lower staffs are presented at the same time. Part 2: tones grouped by ear of arrival (upper staff for left ear, lower staff for right). Part 3: tones grouped by frequency range.

ripple, at all rates the trajectories that I heard corresponded to a grouping by frequency proximity as shown in part 3 of figure 2.6.

The failure of spatial grouping to effectively compete with frequency proximity in Deutsch's scale illusion seems to have something to do with the fact that different tones are being presented simultaneously to the two ears. Tedd Judd argued that the illusion arose because the cues for spatial separation of the tones were weakened by the particular conditions of the illusion.[54] In addition he showed that "spatial stream segregation," as he called it, could be made to interfere with the ease of recognizing a tonal sequence. He asked subjects in an experiment to decide which of two patterns had been presented. The patterns were the ones shown in figure 2.7. The two channels were presented to different ears. The hyphens represent silences and the numbers 1 to 4 represent four tones that are fairly close in frequency to one another (restricted to an eight-semitone range).

```
Pattern A
  Channel 1          ... 1 - 4 - 1 - 4 - ...
  Channel 2          ... - 2 - 3 - 2 - 3 ...

Pattern B
  Channel 1          ... 1 - 4 - 1 - 4 - ...
  Channel 2          ... - 3 - 2 - 3 - 2 ...
```

Figure 2.7
Segregation by spatial location. Patterns presented by Judd (1977).

Observe that the channel 1 sequence is the same in both patterns. Furthermore, since the stimulus is a repetitive cycle, the channel 2 sequence is really the same in the two patterns, merely starting at a different point. Therefore the distinction between the two patterns does not reside in either channel taken alone but in the amalgamation of the two channels. The listeners experienced a certain difficulty in distinguishing the two patterns.

There was also a second condition in the experiment in which the silences were replaced by white noise with an amplitude equal to that of the tones. Surprisingly, many of the listeners reported that when the noises were present, it was easier to hear the pattern as an integrated whole. Those who reported this typically did much better in this condition than in the one with silences. This result supported the idea that a noise in the opposite ear acts to reduce the cue for location that is based on intensity differences in the two ears, and thereby reduces the degree of perceived spatial separation of the two channels and thus their segregation into separate streams.

Judd also showed that if a stimulus like the first half of Deutsch's scale illusion is altered so that the left- and right-ear notes are not presented at exactly the same time, but instead noises are presented to the contralateral ear, segregation of streams according to ear of arrival can be induced.

Picking up on Judd's demonstration, Deutsch went on to confirm that streaming by ear could be suppressed by a contralateral "drone."[55] She required her subjects to identify eight-tone melodic patterns in which the component tones switched between the ears. The onset-to-onset time in the tone sequence was 130 msec. As predicted by both Norman and van Noorden, the task was very difficult. But then, accompanying each tone, Deutsch introduced a drone (a tone with a fixed frequency) into the ear opposite to the one that was receiving the tone from the melody. This drone, like the noise in Judd's experiment, was intended to equalize the intensity of sound in the two ears and thereby reduce the cue for spatial location that depends on intensity differences in the two ears. At the same time she used tunes with very narrow frequency ranges that provided a strong frequency-proximity cue to integrate the melody. The drone was effective in reducing the apparent spatial separation of the tones of the melody. As a result, the melodies could be recognized more easily. This experiment argues that the difficulty with tones that alternate between two ears is not that they are coming into different "channels" in the head in some physiological sense. Rather, it implies that the difficulty arises because there is acoustic evidence to suggest that the tones have come from two different places and this causes the auditory system to assign the tones to separate streams.

The discovery of the scale illusion has provoked other analytic studies that have attempted to discover its underlying basis. For example, the illusion is not restricted to sounds presented over headphones. Butler found that it also occurred when the tones were presented over two spatially separated loudspeakers.[56] This is not surprising, given Judd's interpretation of the scale illusion, because the cues for localization of the sounds are even less strong in a normal room where not only the sound from the opposite loudspeaker but also the reverberation is weakening the cues for the spatial segregation of the two channels. Therefore the weakened spatial cues should lose out even more readily to the frequency-proximity cues.

Switching Signals between the Ears

Stream segregation by spatial location may also be involved in a number of experiments in which sounds, rather than being played to both ears at once as in the scale illusion, are rapidly alternated between the ears. Cherry and Taylor played speech to listeners through an apparatus that could shunt the sound back and forth between the left and right headphones so that alternate segments were played to each ear (none of the speech signal was physically absent; it was present at either one ear or the other).[57] This research came out of Broadbent's framework in which the individual ears were viewed as separate channels, each with its own individual memory that was capable of holding material until a limited capacity central processor (attention) could get around to dealing with the information that had arrived through that channel. It was thought that attention could not be paid to more than one channel at a time.[58] The listeners had to shadow the speech, that is, to say it back continuously as they listened to it. At slow rates, they were able to follow what was said, presumably by shifting their attention back and forth. But as the rate of alternation increased they had a harder and harder time until a worst level of performance was reached at about three alternations per second. At this rate it was thought that attention could no longer switch back and forth between the ear channels rapidly enough to thread the speech back together in the proper integrated sequence. As the rate of alternation was speeded up past this hardest rate, the intelligibility of the speech began to improve again because as the rate of alternation approached the rate of occurrence of phonemes in speech, even a single ear would have some (although not perfect) information about every speech sound and therefore the process of stitching the alternating information back together would no longer be necessary.

The notion of channel that was used to make sense of this result differs in some very important ways from the concept of stream that I have been using. A perceptual channel was understood as being like an input channel on a computer. The events that it contained were thought to be linked together by the fact that they had arrived through some common input device such as an ear. In contrast, the events in a stream are conceived of as having been linked together by the fact that the perceptual system has concluded that they must have come from a common source. It is reasonable, therefore, to say that the concept of channel is focused on the mechanical structure of the listener while the concept of stream is focused on the listener's apprehension of the structure of the external world. Auditory stream theory would argue that the listener is not built to listen to ears but to events, and it is among these events that attention must be switched. Therefore, according to stream theory, the results of Cherry and Taylor would have been due to the fact that the sounds entering the two ears had been segregated into two streams by their difference in apparent spatial location since one of them would have been localized at the left ear and the other at the right.

Some evidence that supports the explanation based on streams comes from the results of an experiment that was similar to the one done by Cherry and Taylor except that as each segment of speech occurred in one ear, it was accompanied by a noise burst in the opposite ear.[59] This noise burst would have had the effect of equalizing intensity at the two ears and therefore moving the perceived location of both the left-ear and right-ear speech segments to a more centered position. This would have reduced the strength of the streaming by location. The results of this experiment showed that the presence of the opposite-ear noise actually made the speech easier to follow. It is hard to see how the channel theory could explain this result. Simply adding a noise in the opposite ear cannot affect whether or not the ear is a channel in Broadbent's sense. If it can, then Broadbent's notion of channel corresponds to that of stream. In that case, the various Gestalt principles of organization would have to be taken into account in deciding whether or not a pattern of sounds did or did not enter through the same channel. This type of theory was not at all what Broadbent was proposing.

Another interesting laboratory effect that seems to be related to the perceptual segregation of sounds by location is the incorrect perception of the rate of dichotically alternating clicks. The effect, as studied by Axelrod, Guzy, and their associates, is created by presenting a rapid series of clicks, uniformly spaced in time, to listeners over headphones, with alternate clicks sent to right and left headphones (alternating presentation).[60] This form of presentation is contrasted with the situation in which all the clicks are sent to both headphones (binaural presentation). When the alternating presentation is used, the sequence appears to be slower. This perceptual effect can be demonstrated using a number of different types of response measures. If the listeners are asked which sequence is slower they say that the alternating one is. If they are asked to count the number of clicks, they estimate that there are fewer in the alternating sequence. If asked to adjust a binaural sequence to the same rate as the alternating sequence, they slow it down.

There is some controversy about whether the apparent slowing of the alternating sequence is fully accounted for by the explanation that the left and right ear clicks have segregated into separate streams. Huggins argued that it was.[61] When he asked his subjects to adjust a binaural sequence of clicks to a rate at which it sounded just as fast as an alternating sequence, he found that at slow rates (below eight tones per second) the subjects set the binaural sequence to the same rate as the total event rate in the alternating sequence. However at higher rates the subjects began to slow down the binaural sequence relative to the alternating sequence until at very high rates (more than 20 clicks per second) the subjects set the binaural rate to one-half the alternating rate. With these very fast rates they seemed to be matching the binaural sequence to the rate heard by just one of their ears.

These results are exactly what you would expect if the sequence of alternating clicks split into two streams as the rate went up. However, the streaming explanation has a clear-cut explanation only for those portions of the results in which the subjects matched the rate of the binaural sequence to the exact rate of the alternating sequence (single-stream perception) or to exactly half this rate (two-stream perception). Yet Huggins' results for click rates between 8 and 20 per second show that the subjects used some compromise settings that were slower than the total rate but not as slow as the single-ear rate. It is possible that these intermediate settings are only the result of taking averages between the one stream and two ear settings that occurred on different trials. After all, we know that perceptual organization tends to be unstable when the cues favoring segregation are not decisive. Therefore it is not unreasonable to assume that at intermediate rates on some trials the clicks formed an integrated stream and on others they segregated into two streams. However, Huggins' presentation of his data does not permit us to tell whether this was what happened at the intermediate speeds.

Gert ten Hoopen and his co-workers at the University of Leiden have argued that the streaming explanation is not a sufficient explanation for what happens under conditions in which listeners match the binaural rate to neither the total rate of the alternating clicks nor the rate at a single ear.[62] They have proposed that what happens instead is that there is a genuine perceptual slowing down of the rate of alternating clicks.

Despite the argument of the Leiden group that alternating sounds generate a real perceptual slowing of the sequence, they have shown that although the results favor their time distortion explanation under some circumstances, under others they are unquestionably a consequence of stream segregation.[63] Since my purpose in this section was to show that streaming *could* be based on rapid spatial alternation of sounds, rather than to show that the alternation could do nothing else, the finding of ten Hoopen and his colleagues that their perceptual distortion explanation will not cover all the cases and that streaming by ear must be postulated for at least some of them is a sufficient demonstration for my purposes.

We have now seen a number of cases in which the presentation of a sound to the opposite ear reduces illusions based on the alternation of sounds between the ears.[64] It seems reasonable to suggest that an explanation for all of these is that location-based stream segregation becomes weaker when an opposite-ear sound is present. The question of why segregation by location sometimes generates a distortion of time that is not generated when segregation is based on frequency is not yet understood.

Although some of the research that I have cited seems to show that stream segregation based on spatial location can occur, it seems to lose out when it is placed into conflict with other bases for grouping (as in Deutsch's scale illusion). This suggests that segregation by location alone is not very strong. Is this an oversight of nature? After all, one would think that the spatial location of two sounds should be an excellent indicator of whether they came from the same source or not. However, we might have to think again. We should remember that the sounds made by one event, say a musical instrument, can pass around another musical instrument that lies between it and the listener, so that both sounds may appear to be coming from the same place. Also, because of echoing, reverberation, and wrapping around obstructions, the spatial origins of a sound may be very unclear. Perhaps location information should not count too strongly unless it is supported by other bases for segregation. Maybe we should expect to find that location differences alone will not be powerful influences on grouping, but will have a powerful multiplying effect when they are consistent with other information such as frequency-based ones. There is some evidence for this type of interaction in the segregation of simultaneous speech sounds described under the topic of "duplex perception" in chapter 7.

Spectral Frequency and Fundamental Frequency

So far we have been talking about experiments in which the sounds were pure sine wave tones. In such tones, since the frequency composition is so simple (only one component per tone), no distinction can be made between three different properties of a tone: its fundamental frequency, its pitch, and its spectral balance. The case is different with complex tones. Let us take the three properties in turn. The fundamental frequency of a tone is the frequency of the repetition of the waveform. If the tone is composed of harmonics of a fundamental, this repetition rate will be at the frequency of the fundamental regardless of whether the fundamental is actually present. Next the pitch. In harmonic tones like this one, the perceived pitch of the tone is determined by the fundamental of the series, despite the fact that it is not present.[65] This phenomenon is sometimes called "the perception of the missing fundamental." (The perceived pitch of nonharmonic tones is controlled in more complex ways.) Finally, the spectral balance is the relative intensity of the higher and lower harmonics. This feature controls our perception of the brightness of the tone.

Tones can differ in one or more of these ways. Take as an example the four tones whose spectra are shown in figure 2.8. Tone A has a (missing) fundamental frequency of 128 Hz and has been passed through a filter that produces a spectral peak at 1,000 Hz. Notice that the tone is built out of many harmonics of 128 Hz but that the fundamental itself is not present. Tone B has the same (missing) fundamental frequency as Tone A but has a nominal spectral peak in a different position (2,161 Hz). Tone C has a different fundamental (277 Hz) but it has been passed through the same filter as A (yielding the

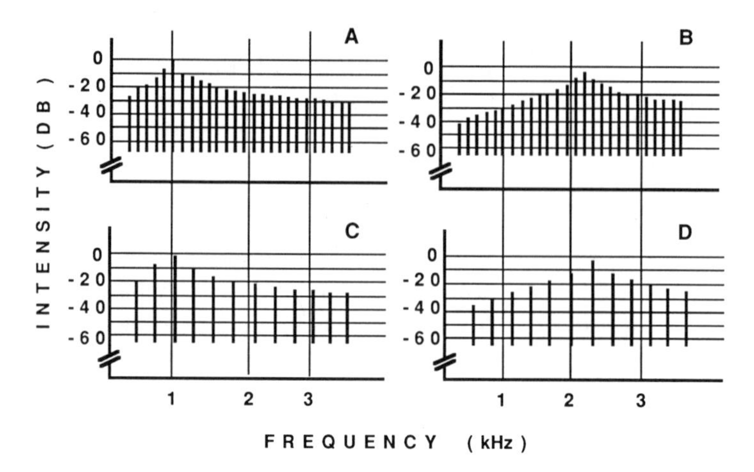

Figure 2.8
Four tones that differ in fundamental frequency and in spectral peak (formant) frequency. (From Bregman and Levitan 1983.)

same nominal spectral peak). Finally tone D differs from A in both its fundamental and its peak. Its fundamental matches C's and its spectral peak matches B's. What sort of stream segregation would occur if a repeating cycle of these four tones were played rapidly? One might imagine two different bases for grouping. If the pitch (more precisely, the fundamental frequency) is dominant, tones A and B should group to form one stream and tones C and D another. If, on the other hand, the spectral peak position is dominant, the groupings should be AC and BD.

The question of whether the pitch of a tone, as distinct from its spectral components, affected its grouping was addressed by van Noorden.[66] He carried out two experiments. In the first one he alternated a pure tone with a complex tone in the same way that Bregman and Pinker did (see figure 1.16 of chapter 1).[67] He had already shown an interesting phenomenon that occurred when a complex tone was rapidly alternated with a pure tone. If the complex tone contained a harmonic that was at the frequency of the pure tone, the pure tone would capture this harmonic into a sequential stream. He then decided to make a complex tone that was composed of a large number of harmonics, but where the first two harmonics were taken away. Despite the removal of these harmonics, the tone was left with the same pitch, the pitch of the now missing fundamental. In one experiment (p. 18), van Noorden wanted to see whether the perceived missing fundamental could be captured out of the complex tone. He

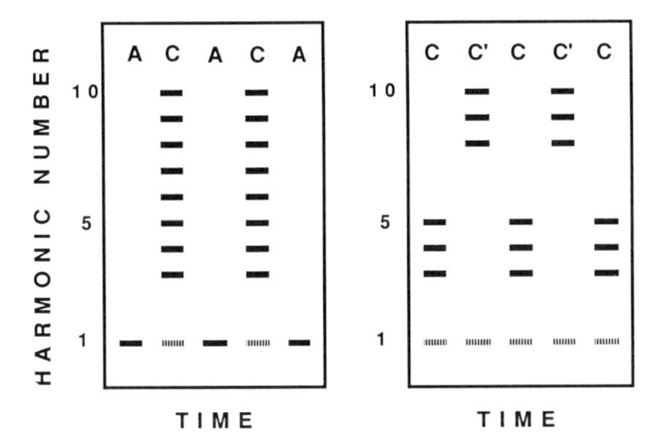

Figure 2.9
Left: alternation of a complex tone having a missing fundamental with a pure tone placed at the fundamental. The shaded dash represents the missing fundamental of the complex tone whose actual harmonics are shown above it. Right: alternation of tones that have the same missing fundamental but are formed of different harmonics. (From van Noorden 1975.)

placed the pure tone captor at the frequency of the missing fundamental. The two tones, the pure and the complex, had the same pitch, and they were alternated rapidly (see figure 2.9, left panel). However, the pure tone did not capture that ghostly missing fundamental pitch out of the complex tone. The two tones, the pure and the rich one, entered separate perceptual streams. The listener heard a stream of pure tones accompanied by a stream of rich tones. They had the same pitch but were nevertheless definitely in different streams.[68]

This result led van Noorden to speculate that perceived pitch itself played no role at all in sequential grouping. Otherwise the pure and rich tones should have entered the same stream. Normally when two tones have the same pitch they also have the same fundamental and their spectra overlap in the frequency domain. Perhaps it is this overlap and not their common pitch that is responsible for their grouping.

A second experiment led van Noorden to the same conclusion. He alternated two tones that had the same missing fundamental, 140 Hz. But the first tone was formed of the third, fourth, and fifth harmonics of 140 Hz while the second was formed of the eighth, ninth, and tenth harmonics (figure 2.9, right panel). If you listen to a pair of tones like these, they have the same pitch but quite different timbres, the one formed of the higher harmonics having a tinnier or brighter quality. When this pair of tones was alternated, again they formed two separate streams. It is likely that the spectral difference (or the timbre difference that resulted from it) was responsible for the segregation.

Van Noorden's experiments, however, did not give fundamental frequency a fair chance. The only way that fundamental frequency could have had an effect on segregation would have been by overpowering the grouping effects of spectral peaks. Because the spectral components of the alternating tones were in two different frequency ranges, each tone preferred to group with its own occurrence on the next cycle rather than with the other tone. If a real effect of fundamental frequency had existed, but if its strength was less that that of the frequency proximity of the components in controlling sequential integration, its effects would have been swamped in van Noorden's experiment.

Bregman and Levitan decided to study the role of fundamental frequency in sequential grouping in a different way.[69] They arrived at the hypothesis, by considering speech sounds, that both fundamental frequency and spectral peaks would affect grouping. They noticed that in speech, there are two distinct physical causes that control the spectrum of the signal. The tension across the vocal cords controls the fundamental frequency or pitch whereas the shape of the vocal tract (determined by the positions of the tongue, jaws, lips, etc.) controls the peaks in the spectrum (called formants). Therefore the two factors, fundamental frequency and spectral peaks, are independently controllable, to a reasonable degree, in the speech signal. If van Noorden had been right, only the formants and not the pitch would be able to help the auditory system to put together the components arising from a single voice despite interruptions by other voices. Yet one would expect that an effective scene-analyzing mechanism would make use of both aspects of the signal in determining whether one moment of sound is a continuation of an earlier one, since both arise from parts of the speech apparatus that cannot change instantly from one setting to another. For this reason, the changes in both the pitch and the formants are fairly often continuous. Therefore the closer that two parts of the same signal follow one another in time, the more strongly they are likely to resemble one another in both of these ways. Performing the same reasoning backward, if two nearby bits of signal resemble one another on either fundamental or formant frequency, one ought to judge that they are parts of the same signal.

Bregman and Levitan studied the stream segregation of a rapidly repeating four-tone pattern. They used groups of four complex tones such as those shown in figure 2.8, except that the fundamentals were present (though considerably attenuated). The similarity relations are shown schematically in figure 2.10. In such sequences of tones,

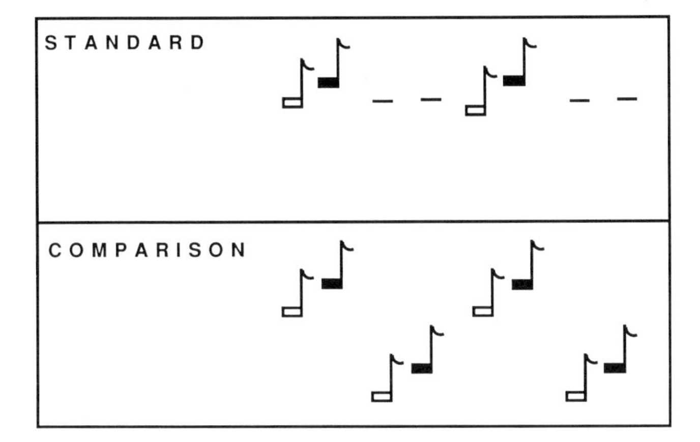

Figure 2.10
The similarity relations in the cycle of tones used by Bregman and Levitan (1983). Vertical position represents fundamental frequency and note darkness represents the frequency of the spectral peak.

streaming by fundamental is set into opposition with streaming by formant frequency. In the figure, the fundamental frequency is represented by the vertical position of the note and the frequency of the formant peak is shown by the note's darkness. If we look at the sequence labeled "comparison," we see that if the tones group by fundamental frequency, notes 1 and 2 will form one group and 3 and 4 another. However, if spectral peak position is the major factor controlling streaming, note 1 will group with 3 and 2 with 4. It was expected that even if one factor was stronger than the other, if the differences on the weak factor were made very large and the differences on the strong factor made small or nonexistent, the influence of the weak factor would be detectable.

The experimenters studied the perceptual grouping by seeing which subsets of tones were perceptually isolated. Before each presentation of a cycle of the four tones to listeners, they presented, as a "standard," a repeating cycle of four events. It consisted of a selection of only two adjacent tones from the forthcoming "comparison" cycle, the other tones being omitted. The two tones were followed by two silences that were the same length as the omitted tones so that the resulting two-tone-plus-silences cycle (the standard) had the same duration as the subsequent four-tone cycle (the comparison). The standard cycle was presented 20 times and then was followed, without a pause, by 20 cycles of the comparison cycle. Listeners were asked to indicate on a rating scale how clearly they could hear the standard pair continue when additional tones were added in. They were to direct their attention to both the quality and the rhythm of the two target tones within the group of four. The argument of the authors was that if the two tones grouped together to form a separate stream, they would remain audible as a distinct part of the signal; on the other hand, if each was captured into a different stream, grouping with some other tone, the two-tone pattern would tend to be very hard to hear as a distinct unit within the four-tone pattern and this difficulty would become greater and greater as the strength of these separate groupings increased.

The pattern of four tones in the comparison cycles was varied on different trials to independently manipulate the frequency separation of the spectral peaks and the fundamental frequencies. Each four-tone pattern was tested with two different two-tone standards, one testing how clearly the listeners could hear the groupings based on fundamental frequency differences and the other testing how easily they could hear those based on formant frequency differences. The sizes of frequency separations were the same for both factors when expressed in terms of a ratio measure (such as octaves).

The results of the experiment are shown in figure 2.11. This figure displays the results by showing which test was easier for the subjects and by how much. The row and column headings represent the separations (expressed in octaves) between the tones on the two factors that were studied in that condition. If any cell in the table contains an ellipse, this means that the listeners could hear the groupings based on fundamental frequency more easily; if, on the other hand, it has a cross, the grouping based on formant frequency was stronger. The height of the symbol indicates the degree of superiority. The results in the first column show what happened when only the fundamental frequency was varied and the formant frequencies of all four tones were the same. It shows that the grouping based on the fundamental frequency grew stronger as the separation grew larger. Similarly, the top row shows that when there was only one fundamental frequency, the grouping responded to the degree of formant frequency separation. The other cells of the matrix show what happened when both types of difference were varied at the same time.

Generally speaking, an increase of the difference between the tones on each factor increased the ease of the test based on that factor and interfered with the test based on the opposing factor. The figure shows that both factors were effective. The fact that more cells have crosses than have circles means that in this experiment, taken as a whole, the grouping based on formant frequency was stronger. The same thing is shown by the fact that along the diagonal from upper

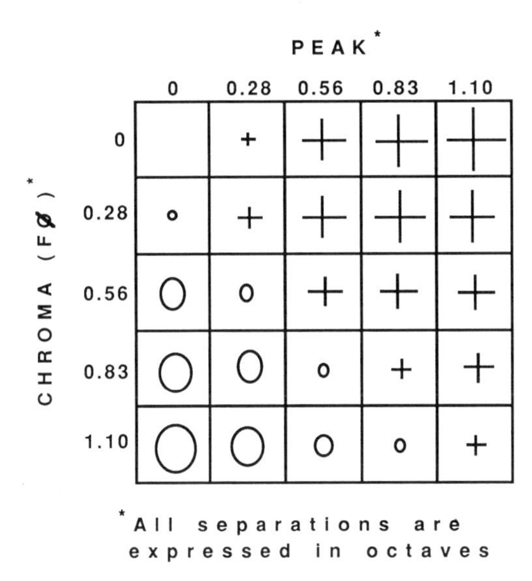

Figure 2.11
The dominance of spectral peak versus fundamental frequency in sequential grouping of tones. Symbols: O is fundamental frequency; + is formant frequency. (From Bregman and Levitan 1983.)

left to lower right, that is in conditions where the two separations were the same in terms of octaves (or ratios of frequencies), there are only crosses.

Therefore these results differed from van Noorden's. They showed that there is a real effect of fundamental frequency on sequential grouping and that the effect is independent of and additive with the effects of the shape of the spectrum. However, it could be argued on behalf of van Noorden that in the experiment of Bregman and Levitan the spectrum was really manipulated differently. There were two major differences. The first was that in van Noorden's experiment, when two tones were supposed to segregate from one another on the basis of fundamental frequency, the two different fundamentals were not actually present. Only some of the harmonics related to each of them were. Perhaps the fundamental of a series of harmonics can play a role only if it is actually present. Perhaps it defines the lower edge of the spectrum of the tone and it is through this role, rather than the role of fundamental, that it exerts its effects on grouping.

The second difference between the two experiments was that when van Noorden's tones were in different frequency regions, there was no spectral overlap between them. The experiment of Bregman and

Levitan, on the other hand, shaped the spectrum more gradually. Tones differing in frequency region did so only by having a peak in a different region; they still covered the same broad range of frequencies (roughly speaking). This difference between the experiments is not really germane to the question of whether or not differences in fundamental can affect grouping. It is important, however, in what it shows about grouping based on the frequency region of the harmonics. It shows that it is not necessary for harmonics to occupy totally nonoverlapping regions of the spectrum before differences in the spectral frequencies can affect grouping. It is sufficient that the spectra of two tones be shaped differently with peaks in different regions.

A second experiment was carried out by Bregman and Liao to further clarify some of these issues.[70] The basic design was the same as the experiment by Bregman and Levitan but the tones were constructed differently.[71] The first difference from Bregman and Levitan's tones was that all tones, no matter what their pitch or formant frequency, spanned exactly the same spectral range, sharing the same lowest and highest harmonics (500 and 4,000 Hz, respectively). This ruled out spectral "edges" as a basis for grouping. Second, the fundamental frequency was always missing as in van Noorden's experiment. Even with these controls, the experiment showed a clear effect of fundamental frequency in segregating tones. This result shows that the effectiveness of pitch in controlling grouping that was found in Bregman and Levitan's experiment was not due to the fact that the fundamentals themselves were present in that experiment.

The question of whether differences in fundamental frequency can cause the segregation of streams seems to have been settled in the affirmative by the experiment of Bregman and Liao. However, there is one discrepant piece of data that still remains unexplained. Van Noorden, like Bregman and Liao, also did an experiment that varied the fundamental frequencies in a rapid sequence of tones while keeping the frequency components of all the tones in a fixed band.[72] Yet in his case, using himself as a subject, he was able to hear perceptual coherence up to a separation of an octave. This discrepancy with the results of Bregman and Liao will have to be explained as arising either from differences in the way the spectra of the tones were designed or by the task that was required of the listeners.

One possibility is related to the strength of the pitch percept. Bregman and Liao used tones that had many harmonics and therefore very strongly defined pitches. The tones used by van Noorden had only a few harmonics. Such tones might be expected to have a weaker pitch. If a difference in perceived pitch was the means by which the difference in fundamental influenced stream segregation, the stronger pitches created by Bregman and Liao would have been more likely to find an effect. A second difference was that Bregman and Liao used a cycle containing four different tones and the cycle used by van Noorden had only two tones. Perhaps, having only two tones to deal with, van Noorden could anticipate the next tone more easily, and therefore hear the coherence that his hypothesis predicted.

Finally, Bregman and Liao used a task in which there was a competition between two factors and the listener's job was to isolate two tones from a four-tone sequence when the two tones were labeled by a similarity in pitch. It is possible that this task taps a different psychological process than the task of trying to hear a sequence as coherent. In particular, it may be sensitive to what I have earlier referred to as schema-based stream segregation, in which stream segregation is based on a learned criterion or on an expectancy. If this is so, the results of the experiments of Bregman and Levitan and Bregman and Liao concerning grouping by fundamental frequency may not reflect the process of primitive stream segregation at all.

There are other experiments that concern the effects of fundamental frequency on sequential grouping, such as the one by Darwin and Bethell-Fox.[73] However, because they deal with the grouping of speech sounds, discussion of them is put off until chapter 6 in which we deal with speech.

Van Noorden's finding about the importance of the frequency position of the spectral content in affecting the grouping of sounds receives support from an experiment in which there was no fundamental frequency at all. Dannenbring and Bregman used two sounds consisting of filtered noises.[74] They were rapidly alternated and listeners were asked to judge how segregated the sounds were. The noises were created from white noise that had been filtered so that the intensity dropped off by 48 dB per octave on both sides of a peak in the spectrum. It is important to study stream segregation in such sounds because they have no fundamental frequency and no harmonic structure, and give only a weak pitch sensation. Therefore any segregation between them must be due to the frequency location of the spectral content taken as a mass. When the two alternated sounds in this experiment had spectral peaks at 1,000 and 1,200 Hz, the listeners reported strong continuity between them, but when the peaks were at 1,000 and 3,000 Hz, they were heard as strongly segregated. The reported degree of segregation for these pairs of sounds was about as strong as the segregation for pairs of pure tones separated by the same amounts. Therefore stream segregation is not restricted to pure tones or harmonically structured complex tones.

It is important to point out that each of the filtered noise bursts used by Dannenbring and Bregman was heard as a single sound. There is some likelihood that if each of them had contained more than one spectral peak, for example, two peaks widely separated in frequency, each peak might have given rise to a separate experienced sound and the predictions about streaming would have had to take into account all four spectral peaks as if they were separate sounds.

Timbre

The Problem of the Definition of Timbre We have examined a number of acoustic factors that can influence the similarities between successive sounds. These have included fundamental frequency, spectral component frequency, the balance of the spectrum, and possibly individual peaks in the spectrum. One might be tempted to say that a number of these have their influence through their effects on the timbre of the sounds. For this reason, we should look at the concept of timbre.

The problem with timbre is that it is the name for an ill-defined wastebasket category. Here is the much quoted definition of timbre given by the American Standards Association: "that attribute of auditory sensation in terms of which a listener can judge that two sounds similarly presented and having the same loudness and pitch are dissimilar."[75] This is, of course, no definition at all. For example, it implies that there are some sounds for which we cannot decide whether they possess the quality of timbre or not. In order for the definition to apply, two sounds need to be able to be presented at the same pitch, but there are some sounds, such as the scraping of a shovel in a pile of gravel, that have no pitch at all. We obviously have a problem: Either we must assert that only sounds with pitch can have timbre, meaning that we cannot discuss the timbre of a tambourine or of the musical sounds of many African cultures, or there is something terribly wrong with the definition. Even if we accept the limitation of the definition to sounds that have pitch, many qualities are hidden in the words "similarly presented." We can judge the dissimilarity of a sound presented to the right ear from one presented to the left and yet any fool knows that this is not a difference in timbre, so we can conclude that they were not similarly presented. Does a tone pulsed twice per second differ in timbre from one pulsed three times per second? Probably not; therefore since they are dissimilar in some way, they must not have been "similarly presented". This argument implies that rate of presentation must be held constant. But if we accepted that conclusion, we could never discover the obvious truth that tones pulsed 20 times per second are different in timbre from those pulsed 40 times. I think the definition of timbre by the American Standards Association should be this: "We do not know how to define timbre, but it is not loudness and it is not pitch."

The exclusion of loudness and pitch from the category may be due to the fact that these perceived qualities are founded on fairly simple properties of sound and are easy to manipulate in musical instruments. Most often loudness is strengthened by applying more force whereas pitch is increased by shortening the length of the vibrating structure. The remaining qualities of sound, the ones we call timbre, are harder to describe and to manipulate, and the methods may vary from instrument to instrument. Furthermore, the variations that can be obtained by varying the manner of playing one instrument are not comparable with those available in another one. When we do find a characteristic of sound that can be obtained on different instruments, such as vibrato, the characteristic tends to be given a label and no longer falls into the nameless wastebasket of "timbre."

Another way of defining timbre is to link it to the differences between the sounds of different instruments. A drum has a different timbre than a tambourine or castanets. The names of the instruments can be used as labels for the timbres, as they are in the case of pipe organs where the stops, those mechanisms for activating different combinations of pipes so as to alter the timbre of the mixture, are labeled as "cello," "trumpet," and so on. If one merely wants a name that communicates the general impression given by a sound, this method of naming timbres by their usual sources is perfectly satisfactory. We can have not only a "cello" timbre but a "rattling" timbre, and so on. However, if we want to know what qualities of sounds will affect their fusion when played at the same time or their sequential grouping when played in succession, we will have to have more analytic concepts of timbre. For example, we shall look at Wessel's demonstration of the effects of spectral balance, or brightness, in affecting sequential grouping. Wessel refers to it as a demonstration that timbre can control grouping, and so it is. But this demonstration would not tell us anything about whether some other acoustic dimension that we also called timbre was capable of controlling grouping. The fact that we referred to variations along both of these dimensions as variations in timbre would not in itself allow us to unhesitatingly transpose facts that we had learned from one of them to the other.

What we need is a better vocabulary concerning timbre. But the vocabulary should not be selected arbitrarily. The dimensions that are wanted should ideally have two properties: (1) they should act in psychologically simple ways (that is, they should act in independent or perhaps additive ways in controlling scene analysis), and (2) they should, if possible, have straightforward physical definitions. What we need to do is to develop descriptive terms for timbre, find ways to measure them, and do careful studies of how they affect perceptual grouping.

Until such time as the dimensions of timbre are clarified perhaps it is better to drop the term timbre and talk simply in terms of those features of sounds that can affect sequential integration.

Nonanalytical Studies of Grouping by Timbre

There are a number of demonstrations that show the effects of timbre upon sequential integration of sounds but in which the acoustic dimension that is responsible for the effect cannot be further specified. One such case is an experiment by Smith, Hausfeld, Power, and Gorta in which the the different timbres resulted from the use of the "piano," "ocarina," "harpsichord," and "saxophone" settings of a commercial electronic music synthesizer.[76] The stimulus pattern that was used was the one that gives rise to Deutsch's scale illusion (see figure 2.6 and the accompanying description). Normally, in this setup, it is very hard to hear the irregular pitch sequence that arrives at each ear. However, when the ear distinction was reinforced by playing the tones arriving at the left ear using one synthesizer setting and those at the right ear using another setting, the listeners more frequently were able to report what was happening at each ear. Also when each of the two rising and falling scale sequences was played in a different timbre (the timbre bouncing back and forth between the ears), the listeners were able to hear the two sequences crossing one another, rather than being forced to hear them as bouncing apart. Therefore the timbre did play a role in determining what sequential stream was formed.

An early observation of the difficulty of naming the order of rapid sequences of unrelated sounds can be interpreted as resulting from the stream segregation of sound on the basis of timbre differences. Warren and his colleagues presented subjects with cycles of unrelated sounds such as a pure tone, a hiss, a vowel, and a buzz.[77] Untrained listeners could name the individual sounds but were unable to name their order, sometimes even when the sequence was slowed down to less than two sounds per second.[78] It seems that accurate judgments of order require sounds to be in the same stream and that sounds with grossly different timbres resist being assigned to the same stream.

An analytic study based on this assumption was undertaken by McNally and Handel.[79] They examined the streaming of 100-msec sounds of a number of different timbres, presented in a cycle at a rate

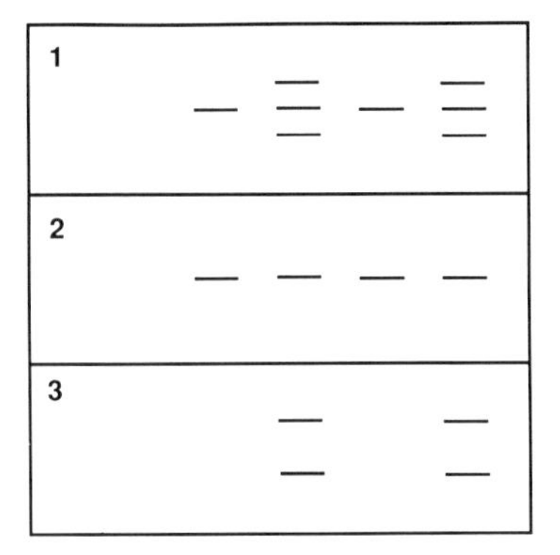

Figure 2.12
1: alternation of a pure with a complex tone. 2: stream formed by captor and one harmonic. 3: remaining harmonics of complex tone.

of five tones per second. The cycles consisted of different combinations of pure tones of different frequencies, clicks of different spectral compositions, white noise, and buzz (40-Hz sinusoid). Listeners were asked to indicate the order of the component sounds by arranging a sequence of cards in front of them, each with the name of one of the sounds printed on it. The reports of order were more likely to be correct when two sounds of the same type, for example, two tones, occurred next to each other in the presented cycle. This is explainable under the assumption that these two sounds, being similar in timbre, would enter the same perceptual stream, that their adjacency in their own stream would lead to their being reported as adjacent, and that this would correspond correctly to their adjacency in the presented sequence. Although this study demonstrated streaming based on similarities in timbre, it did not ask what the dimensions of timbre were, or the relative potency of different kinds of timbre differences. In this respect, it resembles much of the existing research on the grouping of timbres.

Simple and complex tones can be thought of as differing in timbre and they will segregate from one another as long as the pure tone does not group with a pure tone that is part of the complex tone. If you rapidly alternate a simple and a complex tone as in part 1 of figure 2.12, two perceptual results can occur. If the pure tone is close in frequency to one of the harmonics of the complex tone, it may capture that component into a sequential organization (part 2), leaving the remainder of the complex tone in a separate stream (part 3). This, of course, is not a case of grouping by timbre. However, if the pure tone is unable to capture a component of the complex tone,

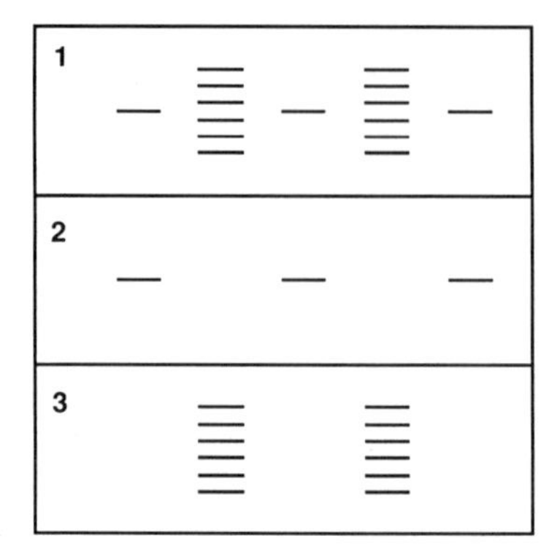

Figure 2.13
1: alternation of a pure with a complex tone. 2: stream including only the pure tone. 3: stream including only the complex tone.

either because it does not match one particular component in frequency or because the set of components is too dense, there is a different perceptual result, shown in figure 2.13.[80] The repetitions of the pure tone form one stream (part 2) and the repetitions of the complex tone form another (part 3). In this case, instead of decomposition of the complex tone, we experience an example of segregation based on timbre.

Steiger also made some informal observations concerning the grouping of complex patterns of gliding tones.[81] One observation was that steady-state tones seemed to segregate away from complex glides even when there was no gap between them. One of the sound patterns that Steiger listened to is shown in figure 2.14. Part 1 shows the acoustic pattern and parts 2 and 3 show the two perceptual streams into which it most often split. The steady tones shown in part 2 segregated from the gliding segments shown in part 3. The latter were heard as vaguely resembling a repeating sequence of speech sounds. We do not know what differences between the steady-state and the glide portions of the sequence caused them to split apart. It may have been the fact that a steady state is perceptually different from a glide or the fact that a complex sound with more than one harmonic tends to segregate from a pure tone.

Brightness and Timbre Wessel reported a demonstration that he had made to show how timbre could control stream segregation.[82] Actually what he manipulated was the "brightness" of the tones. Roughly speaking this is the balance of high and low partials in the spectrum.[83] It is very much like the frequency that is at the mean of

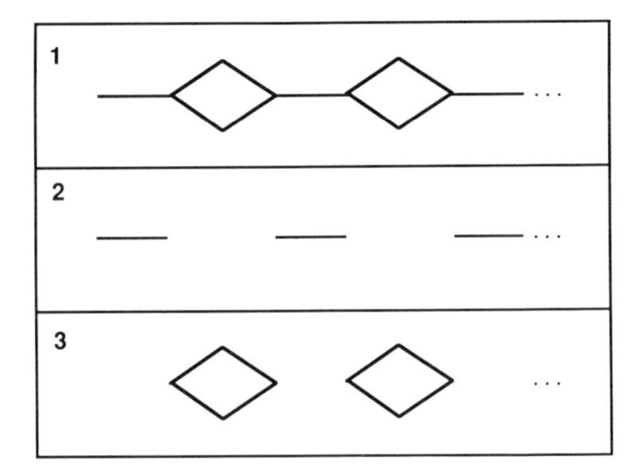

Figure 2.14
1: alternation of a glide pattern with a steady-state tone. 2: stream including only the pure tone. 3: stream including only the glide pattern.

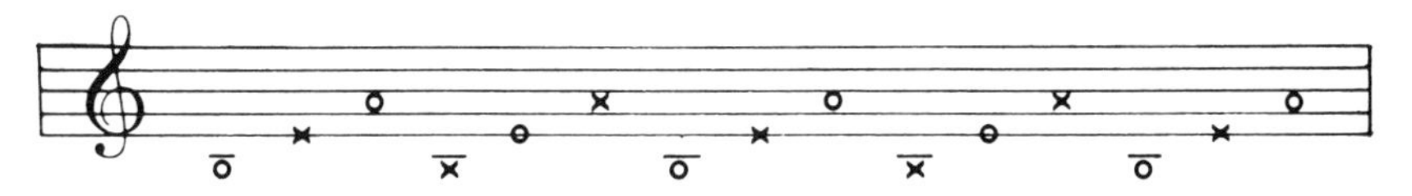

Figure 2.15
Demonstration of the effects of spectral "brightness" on stream segregation by Wessel (1979). The tones shown as ○ and × have different levels of brightness.

the distribution. If a tone has a higher brightness than a second one has, it has relatively more energy in the higher frequencies.[84] The tone pattern that he used is shown in figure 2.15. The pitch sequence is a repetition of an ascending three-note pattern. The brightness of the tones is shown by the × or ○ used to represent them. The tones labeled × always had one level of brightness and those labeled ○ had a second. When the two types of tones differed very little in brightness, the sequence of tones was heard as a repeatedly ascending triplet. However, when the × and ○ tones were quite different in brightness, the perceptual organization shifted. Now the ear followed the tones that had the same brightness and heard the sequence of descending triplets that is shown by the consecutive ×'s or ○'s in the figure. The demonstration shows that brightness itself can control sequential grouping, a fact that suggests that the spectral peak results of Bregman and Levitan and of Bregman and Liao could have been due to this factor.

The mention of brightness leads to the question of whether all sequential grouping by spectral peaks can be attributed to this factor. It appears that the answer is no. Brightness and spectral peak position are correlated only in the case of sounds that have only a single spectral peak. Speech sounds, most notably vowels, have a number of spectral peaks. As we shall see later, in the section on the grouping of speech sounds, it is possible to cause a vowel spectrum to be perceptually decomposed by capturing out the spectral region containing a single formant of the spectrum; this can be done by taking a sound that has a vowel spectrum and preceding it by a sound whose spectrum contains only the formant that is to be captured out, and then rapidly alternating the two sounds.

Two Kinds of Spectral Constancy

We have observed that similarities in the spectrum of a tone can affect sequential grouping. However, it is important to recognize that there are two different kinds of spectral similarity and that these have different physical causes. They are both based on the strength of different harmonics, but the cases differ in how these harmonics are strengthened. The spectrum of sounds is influenced in two ways. Let us take the human voice as an example. The original sound is caused by the vibration of the vocal cords. Not everybody's vocal cords are the same. Some vibrate in a different pattern than others, and the result is that two people could generate vocal cord spectra in which the tenth harmonic, for example, might have a different intensity relative to the first harmonic.

After being generated in the vocal cords, the sound passes up through the air chambers in the cavities of the throat, mouth, and nose where it resonates. Here the effects on the spectrum can also be different at different times as the speaker moves his mouth and jaw and allows air to flow through his nose or not. Because these resonance cavities in one speech sound (such as "ee") could be different in size and shape from those for another (say "ah"), the spectral regions enhanced by these resonances (the formants) will be at different frequencies.

Notice that I said "at different frequencies" in the case of "ee" and "ah" and mentioned "the tenth harmonic" in the case of the vocal cords. This was not an accident. In the case of the vocal cords, differences in flexibility might affect a particular numbered harmonic, such as the tenth, but the spectral region occupied by this tenth harmonic would change as the fundamental, or pitch, of the voiced changed. If the vocal cords were tightened so as to raise the fundamental by 40 percent, the frequency of the tenth harmonic would also be raised by 40 percent. However, its strength relative to the fundamental could remain much the same. Therefore the individuality of a particular pair of vocal cords would be marked by the strength of particular numbered harmonics, not particular frequency regions in the spectrum.

On the other hand, the individualities of the air-filled cavities in different speech sounds would cause formants to occur at particular places in the frequency spectrum, not at particular harmonics. If the fundamental rose, in the course of speaking, by 40 percent, the strength of the tenth harmonic would change as it entered a frequency region that was being enhanced by a resonance. For this reason, the frequency positions of the formants would remain constant but a different set of harmonics would populate them as the fundamental frequency changed. That is the way resonances work, not on particular harmonics but on frequency regions.

It is not only the human voice that can be talked about in terms of two factors that are responsible for shaping the spectrum. Most musical instruments can be described as having a source vibration and a resonance shaper. In the violin, for example, the string is the source vibration and the hollow violin body is the resonance shaper.

We can now ask this question: If we lost track of a particular voice in a jumble of sounds, what should we listen for, a sound with certain numbered harmonics stronger than others, or a sound with peaks in the same region of the spectrum? The answer is "Both, but for different reasons." In the first case we would be listening for a particular pair of vocal cords and in the second for a particular vocal tract resonance pattern.

Do we in fact use both methods when grouping sounds over time?

There is some evidence that we group sounds together when they have energy in the same part of the spectrum. Experiments by van Noorden, by Kinney, and by Levitan, Liao, and myself in our laboratory seem to confirm this idea, but as I pointed out before, all these experiments used sounds that had only a single formant, so that we cannot say that the grouping was by *spectral peak pattern.*[85] It could have been by brightness, for example. The research that addresses the problem of grouping by spectral pattern is primarily about the grouping of speech sounds and will be dealt with later in chapter 6.

However, it should be mentioned here that research has been done on how well people can discriminate one spectral pattern from another. This is relevant to the question of grouping because unless people can register the differences between different spectral patterns, we could hardly expect that they would group successive sounds on this basis. The research of David Green and his colleagues at Harvard University on the recognition of spectral "profiles" (the pattern of intensity of partials in the spectrum) has shown that people are quite good at doing this. Their subjects have been able to remember a simple spectral profile, compare it with a subsequently presented one, and tell whether one of the partials of the profile has been changed in intensity.[86]

Furthermore, we have long been aware that people discriminate vowels from one another on the basis of where the formants are in their spectra. So the fact that people recognize sounds as being different when their spectral peaks differ cannot be in question. We also know that we are generally able to "set" ourselves to listen for those sounds that we know how to distinguish from others. For this reason we would expect that at least schema-based streaming would be able to be done on the basis of formant patterns. What we *can* question, however, is whether automatic primitive stream segregation is capable of grouping sounds by their spectral patterns, or whether, instead, this simpler, more involuntary process analyzes only some cruder property of the sound with no computation of the formant pattern as such. This uncertainty leads us to be cautious in our claims.

There have been studies that looked at whether the ear groups sounds that are similar in their harmonic structure. By the latter, I mean the numbers of the particular harmonics that are present in the tone rather than the spectral region occupied by these harmonics. We should remember that it is hard to modify harmonic structure without at the same time altering other factors. Suppose, for example we create two sounds, different in harmonic structure. We make the first one out of the third, fourth, and fifth harmonics of one fundamental and the second one out of the seventh, eighth, and ninth harmonics of another fundamental. To find out whether these two sounds will segregate from one another on the basis of their harmonic numbers (3, 4, and 5 versus 7, 8, and 9) we have to make sure that other factors are held constant. We may, for example, hold the frequency region constant by making sure that the center harmonics of the two sounds are at the same frequency. But when we do this, we will have made the (missing) fundamental much lower for the tone consisting of the higher harmonics. Alternatively, if we try to hold the fundamental constant, we know that the sound composed of the higher numbered harmonics will occupy a higher spectral region and therefore have a greater brightness.

The only way to select the harmonics of two tones differently while holding both spectral balance and fundamental frequency constant is by making sure that the distribution of harmonics in both tones covers the spectrum in a similar manner. For instance, we could use the same fundamental for both tones, and could make sure that the lowest harmonic chosen and the highest harmonic chosen was the same for the two tones. Between these two limits we could choose every harmonic for one of the tones and every second, or possibly every third, harmonic for the other tone. Both tones would then have spectra that evenly covered the range from low to high, but one spectrum would be denser than the other. Of course we would have to boost the intensity of the tone with fewer harmonics to make it as loud as the denser one. Some musical instruments differ in this way. The clarinet has only odd-numbered harmonics while the violin has all harmonics.

I have tried to do an experiment of this type informally. I created two tones, A and B, both based on harmonics of 200 Hz. Tone A consisted only of odd harmonics, beginning with the first and ending with the fifteenth. Tone B consisted of every harmonic, also starting with the first and ending with the fifteenth. The intensities of the harmonics of both tones decreased with harmonic number (falling 6 dB per octave). I rapidly alternated these tones in a galloping rhythm, ABA–ABA–. . . , as van Noorden had done, and listened for whether they segregated.[87] At high enough speeds they did clearly segregate. The segregation seemed to be based on a qualitative difference between the two sounds: the tone with all harmonics seemed smooth and the one with odd harmonics had a buzzy quality.

There were two experiments done in 1977 in my laboratory at McGill, one by Stephen McAdams and the other by Lynn Halpern, when they were both undergraduates, that manipulated the harmonic structure of tones and influenced how strongly they segregated.[88] McAdams used a rapid cycle of four tones, two high and two low, and found that he was able to increase their segregation by adding the third harmonic either to the low tones or to the high ones. However, it is quite likely that the increased segregation was due to a change in the brightness of the tones resulting from the added harmonic. This interpretation is strengthened by the fact that the segregation was helped more when the harmonic was added to the higher tones than it was when the harmonic was added to the lower ones. Since brightness depends on the relative intensity of higher harmonics in the spectrum of any sound, higher pure tones are already brighter than lower ones. Therefore, adding a harmonic to the higher tones (that is, the already brighter ones) would create a greater separation in brightness between the two sets of tones than adding it to the lower ones.

The experiment by Halpern involved stimulus patterns built out of simultaneous tonal glides.[89] The patterns are shown in figure 3.9 in chapter 3. Each stimulus consisted of one or more gliding sinusoidal tones that ascended in frequency and one or more that descended. The set of glides that moved in the same direction also maintained fixed harmonic relations to one another as they rose or fell. In the figure, the numerals that are adjacent to a set of parallel glides indicate the harmonic numbers of the corresponding glides relative to a missing fundamental. The dotted lines show where the fundamental would have been had it been presented. Each stimulus was of 1-second duration.

In listening to a pattern of this sort, the set of ascending glides (when more than one ascends) fuses together to form a single rich glide as does the descending set. Two sounds can be distinguished at any given time, a rising one and a falling one. However, what happens at the crossing point differs in the different conditions. For example, in condition A, in which there is a single rising and a single falling glide, if you begin by tracking the falling glide to the crossover point, rather than following it through the intersection you find yourself listening to the second half of the rising glide. The net effect is that you hear a glide that falls until it reaches the midpoint and then "bounces" up again. If you start by listening to the rising glide, you hear it rise to the midpoint and then fall again. There seems to be a bias in favor of connecting segments of glides that stay in the same frequency region. However, this is not true in condition C where the listener can hear the rising sound continue to rise right through the crossing point, and the falling one continue to fall past the crossing point. In this case the auditory system has connected up the two glide segments (preceding and following the crossover point) that glide in the same direction, and has based this grouping on the similarity in harmonic structure.

The number at the bottom of each box in the figure is proportional to the preference for hearing the bouncing percept over the crossing percept. It appears that crossing was best (the numbers lowest) when the timbre of the rising glide set was most different from that of the falling set. Note, for example, that in both conditions A and D the ascending and descending sets have the same number of glides in the same harmonic relations and therefore the continuation at the crossover point is inherently ambiguous. However, in condition F, while both the ascending and descending sets contain the same number of glides, and these cross in frequency, the tendency to hear bouncing is much lower. Instead one hears two glides, different in timbre, crossing each other at the midpoint. In this stimulus, the difference in timbre is due to the different spacing of the partials in the two glides, or, putting it another way, to the difference in the harmonic numbers of the partials present in the two glides. Here, then, is an example of a type of timbre that is based on the presence of a particular pattern of harmonics and of a sequential grouping that is based on similarities among timbres generated in this way.

The crossing of streams was also the subject of an experiment by Tougas and Bregman.[90] However, the stimuli in their experiments were ascending and descending sequences of 100-msec pure tones. An ascending and a descending sequence crossed each other at a middle frequency. The pattern is shown in part 1 of figure 4.2 of chapter 4. The listeners tended to not be able to follow one sequence right through the crossover point, but instead, as in the Halpern experiment described earlier, they heard a bouncing pattern. Making the short tones into short glides (part 2), all aligned on a common trajectory, made no difference in the perceptual organization. The listeners tended always to group the portions of the two sequences that were in the same frequency region. Only one change in the stimulus made a difference: if harmonics 2 to 4 were added so as to enrich the tones of either the ascending or the descending sequence (but not to both), the listeners were easily able to follow either the rich or the pure sequence through the crossover point. It appeared that the streams were being formed on the basis of a timbre that was generated by a certain selection of harmonics (either 1 only, or 1 to 4). However, as in the earlier studies, the experiment was not analytical enough to know whether it was the choice of harmonics per se that was responsible for the segregation. It could have been many other things, such as the brightness of the spectrum or even the bandwidth of the tones.

We have evidence that grouping of successive sounds can take place either on the basis of a similar harmonic structure or a similar spectral shape, but we may want to know which is stronger. We can get some clue about this from considering how strongly each of these factors may be weighted when listeners judge the similarity of pairs of sounds. I have already argued that the fact that some particular acoustic difference between two sounds is audible does not imply that this difference will play a role in primitive stream segregation. All the same, in the absence of contrary evidence, it is reasonable to assume that it will. Plomp and Steenecken studied the perception of harmonic nonvowel sounds with different pitches.[91] They showed that pairs having the same spectral envelope (profile) were much more similar than pairs with constant amplitude relations between harmonics.[92]

Beyond the Study of Steady-State Tones

We should stop for a minute and consider the problem that we are faced with. We have been studying cases in which the sequential integration of sounds depends on their properties on a number of dimensions. However, the experimental cases of grouping are not important in their own right. Their significance lies in what they tell us about how the auditory system solves the scene analysis problem. It appears that one of the more important rules that it uses is to consider sounds to be part of the same stream if they resemble one another in certain ways. We have already looked at some of these ways. In asking the question as to whether timbre affects grouping, we are really asking whether there are any other acoustic similarities that we have not already mentioned that also promote grouping.

We have seen that similarities on a number of acoustic dimensions promote sequential grouping. What other properties of sound might do this? There are certainly a very large number of possible properties. Of course all sounds can be described as the behavior of a (possibly changing) set of partials over time. But different patterns of these may function differently in affecting perception and we do not know how many different *types* of patterns to distinguish in a theory of auditory perception. However, to constrain the problem a little we can ask this question: are there any properties at all that allow us to hear that two sounds are qualitatively different but do not affect the way that one sound will group with another? One might conclude from the research that I have already described that the answer to this question will be no. However, this implies that the qualities that have already been mentioned are the major properties of sounds. I agree that they are the major properties of the types of tones that have been studied in the laboratory, but not of the types of sounds in the world.

For one thing, despite the fact that the steady tone is the laboratory favorite because its acoustic description is simple, the steady tone is very rare in nature. It is even rarer than the straight line, which you can see on the horizon when looking out to sea on a calm day. The steady pitch is an idealization that probably was discovered when humans invented musical instruments. Its great attractiveness for us as a sound suggests it plays a central role in the perceptual system, perhaps as a physiologically based ideal, or reference point, against which natural sounds are measured. It is also possible that sustained pitches may play some other biologically significant role. Perhaps a clue to this role is the fact that sustained tones occur mainly in animal vocalizations. Yet even these animal sounds are not steady-state. They consist usually of glides either in pitch or in the filtering of the spectrum. So the steady pitch is an idealization of even these sounds.

The second laboratory favorite is the noise burst, either white or filtered in some fashion. Again it is a favorite because its description is simple. It is unlike the steady tone, which is an example of a spectrally coherent or stable sound. Other examples, only a little less coherent than the steady tone, are a singer singing a vowel sound, or an oboe playing a single note. Coherent sounds can be analyzed into sinusoidal components or partials, and the particular partials that are present remain unchanged for appreciable periods of time. Incoherent sounds, or noises, can be thought of as being composed of a constantly shifting set of partials. Their spectra are not constant and can only be described in a statistical way by probability distributions. Although the shapes of the spectral distributions of noises may be relatively constant on the global level, at the microscopic level they are continually changing. In nature they arise very often from turbulence in air. Examples outside the laboratory might include the sound of a steady wind blowing, or of the sound "s" in speech.

Could the coherence or spectral stability itself be a basis for the grouping of sounds? Only a very primitive beginning has been made in the study of this question. Gary Dannenbring and I alternated pure tones with noisy sounds.[93] Each of these noisy sounds consisted of a sample of white noise that had been filtered so as to have a sharp peak in its spectrum, the energy dropping by 48 dB per octave on both sides of the peak. We found that there was a substantial degree of segregation between a 1,000-Hz pure tone and a noise with a peak at 1,000 Hz. We remarked that "the segregation effects seen with these stimuli are the strongest that we have observed." Such pairings gave a stronger segregation than was obtained with similar frequency separations in noise-noise or tone-tone pairs. There was even more segregation when the tone was raised to 3,000 Hz. We found that we could explain our results by assuming that there were two types of acoustic differences at work and that our results were additive. The first was the frequency separation of the two sounds (considering the spectral peak position to be the frequency of the noise), and the second was the type of sound, noise versus tone. We really cannot tell from this experiment, however, whether the difference between the two types of sound that affected our segregation was really their degree of frequency stability. It could have been something else, such as their bandwidth; the pure tones had, of course, a very narrow bandwidth, whereas the bandwidth of the filtered noises was larger. Perhaps it would be better to alternate filtered noises with filtered complex tones because we could then shape the overall spectrum identically for the two types of sound, while retaining differences in frequency stability.

If it should turn out that there is a tendency for tones and noises to segregate from each other, we would be forced to explain why certain speech sounds remain coherent. For example, the word "see" has

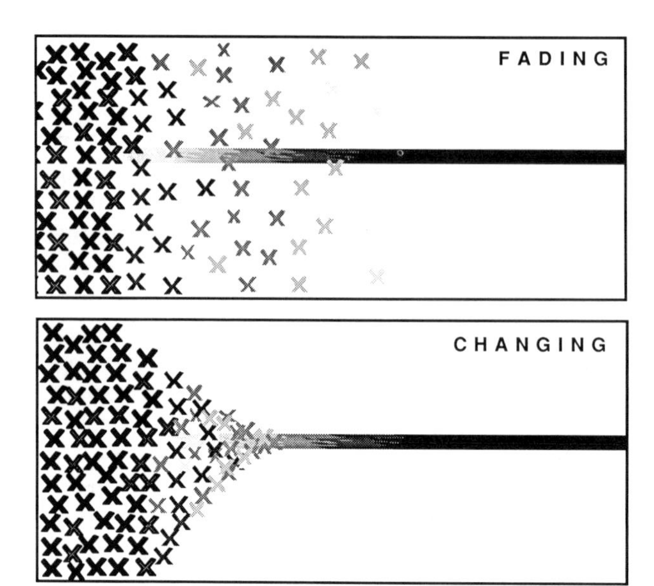

Figure 2.16
Transition of a noise to a tone by fading (top), and by filtering (bottom).

two parts: the "s" sound, which is a noise burst, and the "ee", which is an almost periodic sound (similar to a tone). How is it that they form a single syllable? Is it because they are speech sounds or is there some other reason? We return to this question in chapter 6.

The resistance of speech to segregation may have something to do with spectral continuity. The effects of such continuity should be investigated with simpler stimuli, sequences of nonspeech noises and tones. I suspect that it would not be sufficient to simply fade out a noise as you faded in a tone (shown in the top panel of figure 2.16) for the two to be grouped as a single sound. You would probably just hear one sound fade out and another one appear. Would you have to gradually turn the noise into a tone by some filtering process as in the lower panel of the figure, before the two were heard as coherent? Would the rate of change have to fall into the same range as the transition from noise to tone at the onset of the notes of natural instruments? Research on these questions is sorely needed.

What Remains to Be Studied

In pursuing the question about what properties might affect the sequential grouping of sounds, it is worth offering suggestions about what might be studied in the future. Even in the study of steady-state tones with stable frequency content, we have barely begun to study differences in the sounds of tones. An important difference between sounds is their roughness or buzziness. This can be affected by the choice of harmonics. For example, a sound might be built out of a set of adjacent harmonis, or only odd harmonics or even ones, or only every *n*th harmonic or only harmonics spaced an octave apart. The beats produced by the interference of harmonics contribute to perceived roughness. This can be shown by creating complex tones that contain only partials that are separated by more than the width of a critical band and therefore do not interact perceptually to produce beats. Such tones sound very smooth.[94] It would be important to know whether the dimension of roughness itself, independently of what caused it, was responsible for the segregation of tones.

Although we have neglected certain properties of steady sounds, an even greater oversight is that most of the acoustic properties studied so far pertain to tones that do not change very much over time. Perhaps the use of the word "change" needs some qualification. Sound itself is a change in the pressure of a medium such as air. How then can sounds be unchanging? By the word "unchanging" we refer to sounds that are repetitive in nature (harmonic sounds) or are built of components that are repetitive in nature (inharmonic complex tones), and in which the component repetition rates do not change. Furthermore, we are generally referring to sounds in which the repetition rate is high enough to be heard as a quality of the sound, rather than a repetitive pulsation in the loudness of the sound. In changing sounds, the frequency components change in frequency or amplitude over time.

We will exclude noise bursts from the category of changing sounds. Noises possess a funny sort of blend of the properties of changing and unchanging. A comparison of successive very brief time periods would show that the frequency composition was changing constantly in erratic ways. Yet with some sorts of noises (perhaps we could call them steady noises), a comparison of successive long time intervals would show that the statistical distribution of the strength of frequency components was remarkably stable, and, correspondingly, the noise is heard as having a constant quality over time. Just as steady tones are rare in nature, so are steady noises. Yet the simple describability of both types of sound has led to their use in the laboratory. We have seen how pure tones will segregate from noises having the same central frequency as the frequency of the pure tone. However, we were not sure whether the segregation arose from the difference between the internal coherence of the two types of sound or from some other property, such as bandwidth.

You would think that between the steady tone and the noise burst, we have covered the field. The steady tone has a constant and coherent spectrum and the noise does not. However, much of the sound in the world is neither periodic nor random. Think, for example, of the sound of a falling jar breaking on the floor, a car passing by, and snow crunching as it is walked on.

We have no knowledge of how to characterize these sounds or of how they are classified and organized by the auditory system. We can assign only metaphorical descriptions to their changes. We can say that the sound becomes rougher over time, or less squeaky, and so on. But we know of no metric of similarity, and no obvious physical dimensions to account for these metaphors. An important beginning has been made in the study of these changing sounds by Warren and Verbrugge under the rubric of "ecological acoustics."[95] They have investigated the acoustic patterns created by glass jars either breaking or bouncing when dropped and have shown that these two classes of changes can be recognized by their temporal patterns. However, they have not addressed the question of how different classes of sounds are segregated from one another when mixed.

Another important beginning has been made on the problem of how we ought to classify changing sounds (mainly different types of onsets) by musicians who have been trying to understand what we mean by timbre, but these efforts, often employing the methods of multidimensional scaling, have been applied to only a very limited range of sounds and depend on a subjective judgment of similarity that may or may not be correlated with how these sounds will segregate from one another.[96] Yet segregate they must. In natural situations we encounter a mixture of these changing sounds with one another and with sounds of the sustained periodic and noisy types. The mixture must be taken apart and the correct acoustic components grouped together.

It is interesting to examine whether or not the temporal changes in a sound can influence the way in which it groups with other sounds. A simple laboratory model of a changing sound is a pure-tone glide, the kind of sound you get by twisting the dial of a tunable oscillator. The sequential grouping and spectral fusion of such sounds have been studied by Steiger and Bregman.[97] The sound pattern used in their experiment is shown in figure 2.17. The pattern resembled the one used by Bregman and Pinker which was shown earlier in figure 1.16 of chapter 1. The pattern again involves three elements, two simultaneous ones, Y and Z, preceded by an isolated element, X, that is supposed to capture Y into a sequential stream. However, where the

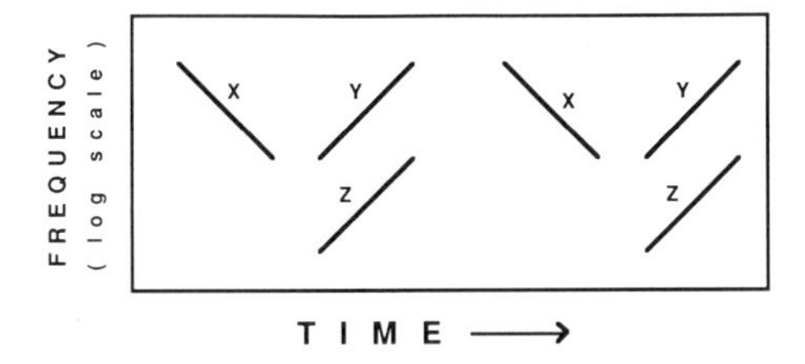

Figure 2.17
Stimuli used by Steiger and Bregman (1981). Repeated alternations between a pure-tone captor glide X and a pair of synchronous glides Y and Z.

Bregman-Pinker experiment used steady tones as elements, the Steiger-Bregman elements were short glides, 230 msec per glide in a slower condition and 130 msec per glide in a faster condition. The glides Y and Z were set an octave apart and each of them glided for one-half an octave. Since they moved in parallel on log-frequency coordinates, they maintained an exact octave separation throughout the glide. Furthermore they started and stopped at the same time. For these reasons they tended to fuse perceptually into a complex tone YZ. The basic question asked in this experiment was whether X, a preceding single glide, could capture Y, one of the parallel glides, so that it no longer would be fused with its parallel partner. Of particular interest was the relation between the slopes of glides X and Y.

The subjects were instructed to call the stimulus fused when it sounded like a rhythmically regular alternation of a pure glide (X) and a rich one (YZ). They were to call it decomposed when it appeared to contain two streams, one with a rhythm twice as rapid as the other, all sounds having a fairly pure quality. In the latter case the subjects would be hearing the repetitions of the sequence XY as one stream and the repetitions of Z as the second. Across a group of conditions, the slope of glide X was varied from being the same as Y's to exactly the opposite of Y's (going up if Y went down or vice versa, as shown in the figure). The results showed that the more similar the slope of glides X and Y, the more strongly Y was pulled by X into a sequential stream.

The effect of similarity of slope shows that the auditory system registers the slope of a glide and uses it as a descriptive feature for that sound, a feature that influences the grouping of successive sounds. Does this make sense in nature? Is it likely that a series of related acoustic events will have the same slope? One might argue just the opposite. Since changes in the pitch of sounds are related to either changes in the rigidity of vibrating objects (e.g., vocal cords) or to

Figure 2.18
The glide pattern of part 1 segregates into the two patterns of parts 2 and 3.

changes in the velocity of the driving force (e.g., wind whistling through telephone wires) and since both sorts of changes would appear to be operating within fixed physical limits, a rising sound might be expected to be more likely to turn around and come down again in pitch than to repeat the same pitch trajectory again. Why does the auditory system seem to look for repetition? It could be that this anticipation of repetition is a specific consequence of our evolution in a world of animal sounds. In a forest it is the animal sounds, such as the gliding whistles of the cardinal, that are repetitive. The hearing of a gliding sound with little difference in slope or center frequency from the previous sound is likely to be the next in a series making up an animal call.

There is evidence that the measurement of the slope of a glide is carried out by prewired mechanisms in the auditory system. Both physiological observations and indirect psychophysical findings point to the fact that specialized cortical cells in mammals register the rate of a frequency modulation (the slope of a glide).[98]

The experiment by Steiger and Bregman also showed that glides tend to group according to the principle of frequency proximity.[99] When glide X in figure 2.17 was set to the same slope as glide Y, then it captured Y best when its frequency midpoint was also the same as Y's. As its frequency midpoint was moved away from Y's (either higher or lower), its capturing effect became less and less. Therefore the frequency proximity basis for grouping applies to glides as well as to steady-state tones. Another example of such grouping is shown in figure 2.18 where the complex glide pattern shown in part 1 segregates into two subpatterns on the basis of frequency proximity, as shown in parts 2 (the upper part of the total pattern) and 3 (the lower part).[100]

A question that arises when using glides is "Where does a glide start and end?" Is a long glide really a long glide or just two short glides laid end to end? This may sound like a silly question. However, in informal observations that were made when preparing the stimuli for the experiment that we have been discussing, Steiger also noticed

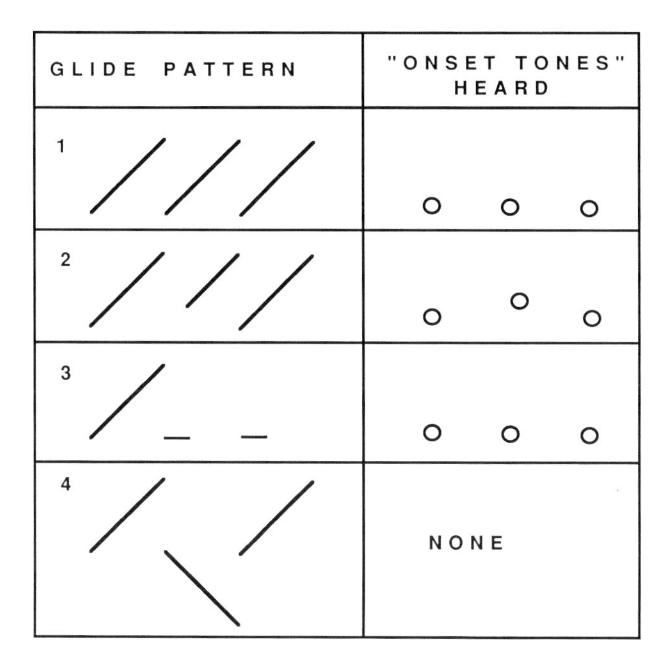

Figure 2.19
Perceived "onset" tones in a sequence of glides. (From Steiger 1980.)

that a long continuous glide could sometimes be broken apart by the stream-forming process. A series of examples of the types of glides that Steiger examined is shown in figure 2.19. When listening to a rapid sequence of glides that start at or near the same frequency, Steiger noticed that in addition to the sequence of glides, he heard a series of onset tones that corresponded in pitch to the beginnings of the glides. In figure 2.19, the drawings on the left show the glide pattern that was played, and those on the right the pattern of onset tones that was heard. The glides could be short or long, spanning from one to three octaves, without any change in the effect, and the onsets could be up to a quarter octave apart. In part 1 of the figure, the glides start and stop at the same frequencies and yield an experience of a series of onset tones at the same pitch. In part 2, the glides start at different frequencies and, correspondingly, there is a series of onset tones of different pitches. In part 3, glides are alternated with short tone bursts and again the onset tone of the glide is heard. Part 4 shows an interesting variation. Here all the glides started at the same pitch but they alternated in orientation. In this stimulus, *no* onset tones were heard. This fact suggested the following possibility to Steiger:

> Maybe when the second tone onset occurs while memory for the first tone onset is still strong, and both onsets correspond in frequency, the repeated excitation in a similar region is interpreted as representing the repetitions of a unique stimulus (one separate from the rest of the glide). The initial portions of glides in [part 1], [part 2], and [part 3] . . . therefore segregate from the rest of the glide pattern. In [part 4] the second glide onset is unlike that of the first glide. Since successive excitations are therefore not similar, perhaps there is less tendency for the second onset to be captured by the first. (p. 5)

Steiger also noticed that offset tones could also be heard in the stimuli of parts 1 and 2 but the offset tones sounded smoother than the onset tones.

> Instead of being percussive, they sound like they have a smooth onset and an abrupt offset. (This is presumably due to the fact that, while offsets of tones also capture each other, there is no abrupt onset to give "offset tones" definition. In the case of "onset tones," there is such an onset, and this may explain why "onset tones" have much better definition.)

Steiger's observations show that a long acoustic glide does not always give rise to an indivisible perceptual glide. In fact, one should be sensitive to why one calls it a single glide to begin with. Apparently one does so because there are no inhomogeneities on the glide that lead one to segregate it into parts. In other words, the reasons for considering it to be a unit are perceptual. Our perceptual systems tend to break an array of sensory input into separate units only at points of discontinuity of properties. If there were a sudden dip in intensity or a sudden discontinuity in the middle of a long glide, we would tend to hear this as a sequence of two shorter glides. However, Steiger's observations show that discontinuity within a glide is not the only perceptual reason for breaking it into parts. Another reason seems to be that part of the glide (preferably its beginning or end) corresponds to something that has occurred a moment earlier, and that this justifies factoring that segment out of the larger unit in which it is embedded.

A final observation of Steiger's is relevant to the question of whether a glide can be thought of as just a sequence of short pure tones increasing in frequency with no breaks. If a sequence of pure tones rising in frequency is played as in part 1 of figure 2.20, it does not sound like a glide. Perhaps the pulsating sound that we hear in the sequence arises from the fact that in each frequency region we hear

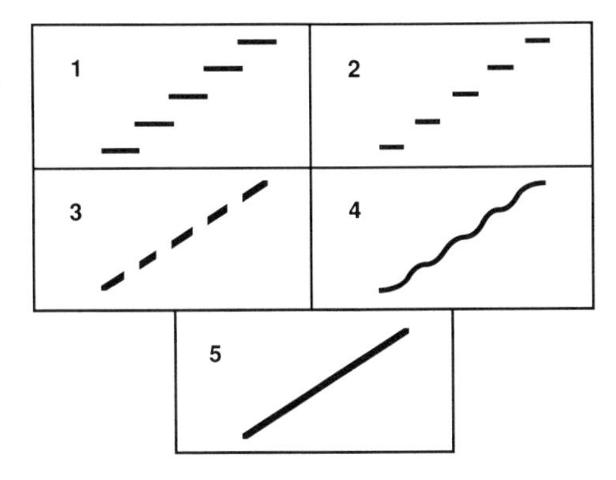

Figure 2.20
Perception of an interrupted ascending pattern of sound. (From Steiger 1980.)

sudden onsets and offsets of tones which are not present in the continuous glide shown in part 5. Although it is impossible to get rid of these acoustic onsets and offsets it is possible to mask them. Steiger created two stimuli for comparison, the ones shown in parts 2 and 3 of the figure. The one in part 2 consists of a sequence of 50-msec steady pure-tone segments, rising in frequency, with 10-msec silences between the segments. The stimulus of part 3 had the same timing, but the segments were 50-msec pure-tone glides. Both of these patterns have a rough pulsating sound because of the discontinuities that result from the silences. The next step was to introduce loud noise bursts to just fill the gaps between segments. The result was striking. In both stimuli, the noise bursts were perceptually grouped into a separate stream from the tonal segments. However, the sound of the tonal portion was quite different in the two cases. The stimulus derived from part 2 had a sound that is represented in part 4, a ragged upward series. However, the stimulus derived from part 3 sounded like the long ascending glide shown in part 5. With the discontinuities masked, part 3 stimulus became a continuous glide but the part 2 stimulus did not. Therefore even 50-msec disconnected portions of a glide still have glide properties, even though the glide property may not be clearly audible. They are not equivalent to steady-state tones. This proves that the measurements made by the auditory system on the slope of a glide can be completed in 50 msec.

Another extremely important property of changing tones, either pure or complex, is their temporal envelope, that is, how their intensity changes over time. The most important part of this is what musicians call the "attack"—how the sound begins. One of the important features that listeners use to discriminate the sounds of different musical instruments is the rise time of the tone, also referred to as its onset or attack.[101] The sounds of plucked instruments such as the guitar begin with a sudden rise in intensity (as the pluck is released) followed by a slow decay. On the other hand, the notes of bowed musical instruments such as the violin rise more gradually in intensity as energy is slowly transferred from the bow to the resonant air chamber inside the violin body. The suddenness of onset of energy is such a good cue to the distinction between plucked and bowed instruments that even a pure tone sounds either plucked or bowed depending on whether its onset is sudden or gradual.[102] Although a difference in the suddenness of the attack of two sounds gives rise to a clear perceptual difference between them, it is not clear whether differences in attack can lead to the perceptual segregation of rapid attack from slow attack tones in a rapid sequence. At least two researchers have reported that the rise time of tones did not affect their sequential integration.[103]

I have made informal observations in my own laboratory on whether differences in rise times of tones affect their segregation. A difficulty arises if we study this with pure tones. A sudden onset has the acoustic effect of splashing energy across the spectrum. If there is a rapid series of pure tones with sudden onsets, it appears that the auditory system will segregate the spectral "splashes" that arise from the sudden onsets into a stream of their own. You hear a series of tones accompanied by a series of clicks that seem not to belong to them. This effect can be reduced by using complex tones that are rich in harmonics. Then the spectral splashes at the onsets are not so different from the spectra of the tones themselves and they are less likely to segregate from them.

In 1986, I made a galloping pattern similar to the one used by van Noorden.[104] It had the form LHL–LHL–LHL–. . . , where H and L refer to high (600 Hz) and low (400 Hz) tones, respectively. The tones were each 80 msec long and presented at a rate of 110 msec per tone. The silences separating LHL groups were also 110 msec long. The frequency separation between H and L tones was chosen so as to lead, at the rate that was used, to an ambiguous degree of segregation between high and low streams. Then I tried to see whether adding a difference in onset time to the difference in frequency would promote a greater degree of segregation between H and L tones. What I did was to synthesize all the low tones with a slow onset (30 msec), a 20-msec steady-state part and a 30-msec exponential decay. The high tones had a sudden onset (1 msec), a 49-msec steady state, and a 30-msec decay. I tried to balance them for subjective loudness. It seemed to me that the difference in onset suddenness did make it more likely that the high and low tones would segregate from each other, but the effect was not strong. The particular manner in which I listened to the tones, either trying to hear the high (or the low) tones as a separate stream or else trying to hold them together in the galloping rhythm, made a much greater difference than the onset differences, and I could not tell whether or not the small effect that I detected was merely the result of a listening bias. I concluded that if onset differences of the size that I had studied did facilitate segregation, the effect was small compared to that caused by other differences such as changes in frequency or in spectral peak position.

In pure tones there is only a single frequency component whose intensity evolves over time. In complex tones, such as those that are created by musical instruments, there are many spectral components and the intensity of all of them may not evolve in the same way. For example, in a guitar, the initial pluck gives rise to a very complex spectrum. As the tone dies off in intensity, the intensities of the higher harmonics tend to die off faster, so that toward the end of the note the fundamental is about all there is left; the brightness of the note seems to be concentrated at its onset. On the other hand, in the trumpet note, the midrange harmonics grow more slowly in intensity than the lower ones, so that the note appears to grow brighter over time. In instrumental notes, and presumably in other naturally produced sounds, it seems to be the case that the more intense parts of the sound also contain a greater intensity of higher harmonics. This will be at the onset of the note in struck or plucked instruments where the energy is injected in a single shot, and may occur later in the note for bowed or blown instruments that are fed by a sustained stream of energy.

We may ask whether the differences in the temporal evolution of the harmonics, as found in different instruments, affect the perceptual segregation of musical tones of different instruments when they occur in a series. We know from ordinary listening that the differences in timbre of instruments favor the segregation of melodic lines in music, and Robert Erickson has composed a piece called LOOPS as an experiment on the effects of timbre on sequential grouping.[105] Unfortunately, the sounds of the natural instruments differ from one another in so many ways that it is hard to say what acoustic factors will integrate sequences. More analytic experiments are required.

A sound can change in intensity over time in a periodic way. This in known as amplitude modulation (AM). If the repetitions are fast, we refer to the changes as tremolo or warble. Although sounds can easily be distinguished by their degree and speed of warble (depth and frequency of AM), I do not know of any observations on whether these factors aid in the grouping of sequential sounds. However, as we shall see in chapter 3, the synchrony of the warble in *simultaneous* sounds does influence whether they fuse perceptually.

Similarly, the frequency of sounds can change over time. This is called frequency modulation (FM). Rapid repeated changes, especially small ones, give rise to musical vibrato. The situation with vibrato is much as it is with warble—known effects on the fusion of simultaneous sounds but unknown effects on sequential grouping.

When we think of amplitude or frequency modulation, we tend to envision a regularly repeating change. However, many natural sounds are not like that. Think of the sound of a piece of metal being dragged across different surfaces. The amplitude changes rapidly over time in an irregular pattern. However, it is not entirely irregular. We can tell a lot about the roughness of the surface by listening to the sound. The best way to describe it is to say that the sound is granular, reflecting the granularity of the surface over which it is being dragged.

The analogy to such sounds in vision is surface texture. Steven Zucker at McGill University has a theory of two types of primitive visual organization.[106] The first, Type A, is not directly relevant here. It pertains to the organization of shapes. It is responsible for the detection of edges, and groups them to find the shapes of objects. It is very accurate at measuring the positions of lines and their alignment along common trajectories. The second process, Type B organization, is the process that I want to describe here. It is less accurate at detecting lines, but more robust in determining whether different patches of the surface show the same sort of general statistics of line orientation. This process, for example, is responsible for detecting the general way that a person's hair is lying. It does not detect the position of each strand of hair but generally can tell from the fact that continuities are detected along a certain axis of flow that the hair has been combed so as to lie in a certain direction. Another example is seeing the water sprayed by a shower as moving in a certain direction. The individual globules of water may not really be tracked, but the viewer gets the general sense of the motion.

Zucker's Type B perceptual organization has been described by other researchers as "texture" and it has been found that that if adjacent portions of an image have similar textures they will group, and conversely if the texture suddenly changes, a discontinuity will be seen on the surface. By texture is meant the quality that is given by the tiny irregularities of a surface which, though irregular, may show a certain consistency of patterning. As an example, when a heap of fish netting is piled on a surface of concrete, although the surfaces of both are irregular, they are irregular in different ways and, because of this, we will see a discontinuity at the boundary even when the netting and the concrete have the same average brightness and color and when the netting casts no shadows at its boundary. This grouping has been the subject of much research. Both Bela Julesz and James Pomerantz have written excellent reviews of the work done by themselves and others.[107]

Many pieces in contemporary music create sound masses analogous to the spraying shower or the flowing hair in vision. Though individual lines are not perceived, the granularity is, and the granularity of one piece can be quite unlike that of another. Similarly, we can distinguish between the sound of a hand winnowing dry rice and the squeak and crunch of a footstep in low-temperature snow. Here we have differences of two types, at gross and fine time scales. The footstep, taken as a whole, has a different temporal course of loudness and frequency than the finger. The footstep has two distinct temporal phases, the transfer of weight to the foot and the rolling of the body over the pivot of the foot, and these can be heard. The winnowing of the rice may have its own phases, including a final one in which the fingers come away from the rice, dripping occasional bits of rice back onto the pile. These properties at the gross scale reflect the difference in the two types of action. However, there are differences in how grains of rice react to displacement as opposed to how crystals of snow react, and these differences are reflected in the shorter-term properties of the sound, the "whooshing" of the rice versus the "crunching" of the snow (we really have no good words to describe these sounds). These sorts of sound occur widely in nature. They are much more common than those laboratory favorites, sustained tones and spectrally stable noise. They must be tracked over time and separated out of mixtures. How do we do it?

Before we will be able to find out we will have to have a quantitative language to describe such sounds. First of all, I suppose, we should test the adequacy of the languages that we now have. The most manageable description would be one in terms of a succession of short-time spectra, that is, a spectrogram. You could simply try to describe the main spectral peaks in the short-time spectrum of each sound and then ask whether two sounds would group together sequentially if the initial part of the second one resembled the last part of the earlier one in its spectral composition.

However, I suspect that the ears are better than the spectrogram at registering differences in granularity (between a rough and a smooth sound, for example). I believe that a promising direction toward the analysis of complex sounds has been shown in an experiment by William Warren and Robert Verbrugge.[108] In this experiment, the authors tried to synthesize the sound of a glass being shattered upon impact on a floor using a mixture of repetitions of simpler sounds. They chose as elementary components first the initial bursting sound, and second, the subsequent complex pattern of bouncing fragments. It was this second aspect that they synthesized from simpler sounds. First they recorded on a computer one bounce from each of four different fragments of glass and treated these as what I will call "acoustic grains." Then they used the computer to create for each grain a sequence of repetitions that could occur if that piece of glass were repeatedly bouncing (the repetitions speeding up over time). Each fragment was given a different bouncing rate and then the sounds of the four fragments were mixed to produce the complex result, which turned out to be a good representation of the "bouncing fragments" part of the sound of a shattering glass.

Let us imagine how we could use this approach to describe what I have called granular sounds. The use of acoustic grains serves to factor the problem of description into two parts, the description of some characteristic grain of sound and a description of how this grain is repeated in the sound. Warren and Verbrugge bypassed the first problem, the description of the grain. They simply recorded a simple impact and used it as a grain. They did, however, describe (and create) the time-varying pattern of impacts.

Probably Warren and Verbrugge produced only a caricature of a glass shattering, because there were only four different kinds of "tinkle" in their synthesis, whereas in reality the impacts of many different tiny pieces of glass would be slightly different in quality. This implies that the description of a complex granular sound would not only need to specify some pattern of replications of a grain over time, but a range of variations in properties that the grain could undergo (for example, in pitch and intensity). Conceivably, in the general case of granular synthesis, both the times of occurrence of the grain and the range of its properties might be described by statistical distributions.

Returning to the problem of hearing roughness in natural sounds, we could make sense of roughness through the concept of acoustic grains. Such factors as the density of grains in the sound, the length of each grain, and the intensity envelope within each grain might represent dimensions of roughness.

This concept of a grain has already been the subject of acoustical analysis. Gabor objected to Helmholtz's idea that subjective hearing could best be represented by Fourier analysis: "Fourier analysis is a timeless description in terms of exactly periodic waves of infinite duration. On the other hand, it is our most elementary experience that sound has a time pattern as well as a frequency pattern. . . . A mathematical description is wanted which *ab ovo* takes account of this duality."[109]

Gabor proposed that a granular or quantum representation would be able to describe any sound, and Bastiaans went on to verify this conjecture mathematically.[110] However, the acoustic grains that I have proposed are not exactly the same as Gabor's. His grains are all identical, except for their frequencies. They have identical (short) durations, sinusoidal waveforms, and Gaussian (bell-shaped) amplitude envelopes. I see no reason, from the perspective of possible neural analyzers in the human auditory system, to restrict the grains to all be the same, either in terms of their frequency or their time characteristics.

My notion of an acoustic grain is more like Bela Julesz's concept of "texton" and it is interesting to speculate on whether auditory textures might have analogous properties to visual ones. Julesz's texton, the unit of texture, is conceived to be an elementary local property of the visual field, such as a small elongated blob with a particular color, angular orientation, or length.[111] The visual system is conceived of as containing a preattentive subsystem that carries out a parallel, instantaneous analysis of the visual field and registers the density of textons of different types in different parts of the field. Regions of the field that, according to the texton analysis, have homogeneous texture (textons with similar properties) within themselves, but are different from the texture of other regions, will segregate into visually distinct regions.

Analogously, one might speculate that grain analyzers in audition describe the texture of sounds as having acoustic grains of some particular range of properties and that scene analysis might segregate regions of sound for which the descriptions were different enough.[112] This segregation might be expected to occur along the two dimensions of a spectrogram. Along the time dimension, the process might segregate different sequential events, leading to the perception to event boundaries. In the frequency dimension, different frequency bands with the same granular properties might be grouped together to create the spectral profile of a single source of sound. The theory could be verified by means of listening tests carried out on the sounds created by computers using a granular synthesis technique of the type used by Curtis Roads to compose computer music. Roads' approach has two useful features. It allows the spectral and temporal properties to vary across grains, and it makes use of the concept of an "event," which is the larger unit in which the grains are embedded. The global description of an event specifies the temporal change in the grains within it with respect to their density, their frequencies, and their harmonic content and bandwidth (they are not necessarily pure sinusoids). In Roads' system, "Sound spectra can vary from a single isolated pitch (formed by a chain of grains at a given frequency) to groupings of simultaneous frequencies, glissandi, and clouds of granular particles over the entire audio spectrum."[113]

The granular approach to the perception of changing sounds must remain speculative, of course, until some serious perceptual research based on these concepts is carried out. Even so, we might take some intuitions about the properties of sounds and see how they could be translated into a description in terms of acoustic grains. For example, let us take the difference between the sounds of two percussion instruments, the rattle and the tambourine. Intuitively, the rattle has a less ringing quality than the tambourine. Furthermore the tambourine sound has two components, the drum sound contributed by the drum head and the sound of the jingles. Let us focus our attention on the latter sound. It can have an irregular pattern of components like the sound of the rattle, so both can be thought of as consisting of a random pattern of grains. However, there are some differences. In the tambourine, the initial impact is likely to excite a large number of jingles at the same time, whereas at the onset of each beat of the rattle, the synchronization of pellet impacts is less precise. Therefore the degree of synchronization of grains at onset is a global property that distinguishes the two sounds. Another distinction is based on the sound of a single grain. The grains of the tambourine are generated by metal jingles and therefore have a sustained vibration that lasts longer that the brief impacts of the grains of a rattle.

But are granular sounds common enough in nature that we might imagine that the human auditory system has evolved specific ways of dealing with them? Here is a smattering of cases that come to mind: dead leaves rattling in the wind, a person walking in snow, a door creaking, a person snoring, dragging a metal object across a concrete surface, the act of riffling through the pages of a book, and water splashing at a waterfall. Most of these would have granular properties that change over the course of the event, such as the change in the temporal density of grains from beginning to end of the global event, so that a time-varying granular description, such as the type used by Roads, would be required. One might expect that the time variation of granular properties would be in itself an important feature for recognizing a particular sound. The research of Warren and Verbrugge that I mentioned earlier seems to show this to be true.

I think it is evident, even from this short discussion, how a granular analysis might provide a perceptually relevant description of the sounds of events that can be considered iterations of multiple small events. This is a rich field for study and one that is still unmined.

But can differences in granularity affect the sequential organizing of auditory evidence? Let us think of the differences that visual texture and auditory granularity might play in scene analysis in the two sense modalities. The analogy to a visual object is an auditory stream, and the analogy to the visual features that define objects are the acoustic factors that help define streams. In vision, brightness differences create strong edges between surfaces and are one of the most important features by which the boundaries are discovered. Differences in surface texture play a smaller, though definite, role in helping us to detect boundaries.

Similarly in the auditory sense the texture or granularity of sounds is probably not the main factor that tells the listener that a new sound is appearing. The new sound is probably more reliably signaled by a sudden rise in amplitude within some set of frequency bands. This is because, unlike in vision, auditory objects are transparent and add their energies to the auditory input. In vision when a new object moves into view and is seen against a background, if the object and background have the same brightness, there will be no brightness change, and no brightness will be lost if the foreground object is removed. Furthermore, when it is present, there will be no brightness change at the object's edge. In such a case the chromatic color or the texture of the object, if different from that of the background, may help us to see it. In audition, on the other hand, a new event will always add its energy to the input. If it is taken away, the input energy in some frequency bands must drop. There is less need to depend on other changes. Therefore we may not rely on granularity to create sequential boundaries.

A difference in granularity may also be a hard cue to use in the creation of temporal boundaries. The auditory system might need a temporally extended sample in order to assess the statistical properties of each granularity. Therefore the use of granularity statistics to create a sharp boundary may not be practical.

Sequential organization, however, is not only the creation of boundaries, but the grouping of sounds over time. This process might not have to be as temporally precise as the forming of boundaries. There is some evidence that the auditory perception process lags real time by some amount anyway. This can be seen, for example, in the continuity illusion, in which a portion of a sound is cut out and replaced by a loud burst of noise and in which we seem to hear the sound continuing through the noise.[114] Apparently the decision as to whether to hear the sound as continuing through the noise depends on whether the properties of the sound that comes out of the noise match those of the one that went in.[115] Therefore the details of our perception of the period of noise are not made until later. The grouping of sounds over time might be done slowly enough that there would be time to sample the statistics of the later event in time to make the decision.

Timbre Space or Single Properties? Metameric Timbre

We have discussed the perceptual grouping that was based on a number of acoustic dimensions that we would describe in commonsense terms as affecting timbre. Earlier, I introduced a word of caution, arguing that the notion of timbre was poorly defined and that for the moment it was wiser to simply describe the acoustic dimension that was responsible for the segregation of sounds rather than calling it a segregation by timbre. Unfortunately, we have seen that there are a very large number of ways to describe how one sound may differ from another. This being the case, we are surely going to ask whether there is no simpler set of dimensions that describes timbre. The phenomenon of timbre can be seen as similar to the phenomenon of color in vision. Physically, every color can be viewed as a mixture of a set of components of light, each with its own frequency and intensity. Given that there are a large number of visually distinguishable frequencies, there are an incredibly large number of combinations of frequencies that might occur. Nevertheless, all the colors that we can see can be described in just three dimensions. Two of these dimensions generate the familiar color circle, with the colors red, orange, yellow, green, blue, violet, purple, and red again running around the circumference, and colors becoming less saturated and grayer as they move from the edge toward the center. The circle can be considered as having a red-green dimension at right angles to a blue-yellow dimension. The third dimension is the light-dark dimension that stands at right angles to the circle, and on which, for example, the color blue runs from an inky black, through midnight blue, through royal blue and powder blue, to white. Since there are many more combinations of physical light frequencies than there are dimensions of color, different combinations of spectral components can yield perceptually identical colors. These are known as metameric colors.[116]

The search for a reduced number of dimensions of timbre boils down, then, to answering the following question: "Are there metameric timbres?" In other words, can you select two entirely different combinations of acoustic properties and still be left with the same timbre? If so, what are the simple dimensions of timbre that are analogous to the long, medium, and short wavelength components into which light is analyzed by the eye?

Multidimensional Timbre Space There have been attempts to find a small number of dimensions on which differences in timbre can be represented. The method most often used is called multidimensional scaling, which starts with judgments of the degree of similarity between sounds presented in pairs and tries to infer the dimensions on which the judgments were made.[117] Each study that has used this approach, however, has imposed limitations on the set of sounds that was included and this has restricted the generality of the conclusions.

Plomp and his colleagues have studied the differences in the timbre of different musical instruments using the method of multidimensional scaling.[118] The instruments were violin, viola, cello, oboe, clarinet, bassoon, trumpet, French horn, and trombone. Artificially steadied tones were created by using only a single period from the waveform of each instrument and repeating it over and over to create a longer tone. It was found that the sizes of the judged differences could be accounted for by assuming that the listeners were hearing three dimensions of variation in the sound.

Then a second sort of analysis was done. The sounds of the instruments were subjected to a physical analysis in which each was represented by the output of 15 one-third-octave bandpass filters when each of the sounds was fed into this set of filters. Then, since the variations in the energy levels in these 15 spectral bands across different instruments were not all independent of one another, the correlations in the outputs were subjected to principal-components analysis. It showed that the spectra could be considered to be varying from one instrument to another in four independent dimensions, each dimension affecting the set of 15 filters in a different way. It was possible to "rotate" three dimensions from the physical analysis to quite closely match the three dimensions derived from the analysis of perceived differences.

What this means is that the listeners were making use of the correlations in the spectral differences between the instruments. It does not necessarily mean that the characteristic physical ways that this particular set of sounds differed among themselves, as discovered by the physical analysis and used by listeners in their difference judgments, represent features of timbre that are central in the perception of timbre in general, that is, for a wider variety of sounds. For example, if the researchers had added the sound of a rattle, the dimension of noise versus tone would probably have emerged as a new component, and if they had allowed the different sorts of onsets and vibrato to appear in the sounds, or had included a sine wave oscillator as one of the sounds, other dimensions of variation would have been found. Does this mean that if they had done these things the multidimensional scaling procedure would have found the original dimensions *plus* several new ones? Not at all. When you ask subjects to judge differences that are present in a particular set of stimuli, they tend to fasten on the two to four most salient ones. Therefore multidimensional scaling tends to come out with this number of dimensions whatever the stimuli. However, these will shift depending on the set of stimuli that is used. This can be summarized by saying that what you get out of the analysis depends on what you put in. What is particularly worrisome in the just cited research is that the researchers did not interpret the mathematically derived dimensions into meaningful properties that could be used to describe new sounds without having to enter them into the same principal components analysis with the old ones.

Another attempt to try to find a reduced number of dimensions for describing a large number of sounds was carried out by von Bismarck, who asked listeners to describe the timbre of 35 selected sounds by the use of a semantic differential scale.[119] This involved asking them to assign a number from 1 to 7 for each sound with respect to each of 30 dimensions defined by adjective pairs such as "hard-soft," "dead-lively," and "dim-brilliant." The sounds were either complex tones with varying number of harmonics or noise bursts. They were filtered to produce a number of spectral shapes, including (for the harmonic spectra) the profiles of vowels. The method of principle-components analysis was used to show that the similarity patterns in the use of the 30 scales could be explained by assuming that there were four perceptual dimensions on which the subjects were judging and that the various adjectives were tapping these dimensions in different combinations. The most reliable of these dimensions seemed to be one that was best represented by the adjective pair "sharp-dull" and seemed to relate to the center of gravity of the spectrum (high versus low harmonics). This dimension of sharpness is the same as the one discussed earlier as brightness. The second important dimension was best represented by the adjective pair "compact-scattered" and related to whether the sounds were tones (compact) or noises (scattered). We have previously seen that both the brightness dimension and the tone-noise distinction are strong bases for the stream segregation of sequences of sounds. Again, we must note that the method that was used is highly sensitive to the experimenter's choice of sounds, and had he included pure tones or tones with octave harmonics only, other dimensions such as purity or smoothness might have dominated the judgments.

Multidimensional scaling was also used by Grey to study the perceptual similarities in sounds derived from musical instruments.[120] He took 16 recorded instrumental sounds derived from 12 different instrument types and used computer-based signal processing to simplify the sounds and equate them for loudness, pitch, and perceived duration. The listeners rated the dissimilarity between pairs of these sounds and these ratings were scaled.[121] It was found that three dimensions gave an adequate account of these difference judgments. The first dimension seemed to pertain to what proportion of the energy was contained in the lower versus the higher harmonics. It is perhaps best thought of as brightness or sharpness. The second dimension described the synchrony of onset of the attacks and decays of the higher harmonics and the corresponding degree of spectral fluctuation throughout the signal (static versus dynamic sound). The third dimension seemed to relate to the presence of high frequency, possibly inharmonic, energy at the onset of the tone (grating versus clean attack). We see that when differences in onsets are allowed to enter into the set of stimuli, they overpower all but the brightness factor in the spectral distribution. Perhaps this is a tribute to the importance of brightness as a dimension of timbre. It is the one dimension that tends to be found across a variety of studies.

None of these attempts to find a reduced number of dimensions to account for differences in perceived timbre has been able to show that the dimensions identified as the important ones are completely adequate, even within the restricted range of stimuli used, to account for differences in the qualities of the sounds. Even sounds that are the same on the most important dimensions can be heard as different if their spectra are different. They are not fully equivalent in the same way that two metameric mixtures of light can be with respect to judgments of color. Perhaps, then, a way to approach the problem of whether it will ever be possible to reduce timbre differences to a small number of dimensions would be to try to find some examples of metameric sounds, sounds which, though spectrally quite different, are perceptually indistinguishable.

Perhaps we might be satisfied with a more modest result. We might find that there is a small number of dimensions on which any sound can be situated for purposes of predicting grouping. Although two tones might not be metameric in the sense that it is impossible to tell their timbres apart, they might be metameric in the sense that they group as strongly with each other as they do with exact copies of themselves, and also group with other tones in identical ways.

Amplitude Differences A very obvious candidate for a factor that might influence sequential grouping is loudness, and there have been a few studies that asked how differences in loudness would affect the grouping of sounds. Van Noorden presented a series of tones that were the same in frequency but alternated between soft (S) and loud (L).[122] The onset-to-onset time was 100 msec (40-msec tone and 60-msec silence). When the intensity difference was less than 3 dB the tones S and L were heard as having different loudnesses but as being part of a single coherent stream. When the L's intensity was between 3 and 40 dB louder than S's, the listener's attention could be directed to either the soft or the loud tones. Using sequences of different rates, van Noorden had his subjects reduce the intensity difference between S and L to the point at which they could just still hear separate streams. In the range of speeds from about 2.5 to 10 tones per second, the threshold was about 3 to 4 dB and showed a negligible effect of speed in this range. At slower and higher speeds the required difference was higher.

Notice that van Noorden measured the minimum loudness difference under conditions where the listeners were *trying* to hear separate streams. I have argued earlier that this task is not a measure of the automatic process of stream segregation that is governed by principles of grouping, but of the limits of the psychological mechanism of selective attention. Recall that when van Noorden had measured the segregation of a sequence of tones on the basis of rapid alternation between low and high *frequencies*, as shown in figure 2.2, he had found that the frequency difference needed for segregation when the listener was *trying* to segregate the streams was very low (about three semitones) and was unaffected by speed over a wide range. He found the same thing with loudness differences. However, although he appeared to believe that loudness differences created the same sorts of phenomena as frequency differences, he did not report the effects that loudness differences had when the listener was trying to hold the loud and soft tones together. The obvious reason is that in a rapid sequence, the softer tones tend to disappear unless you pay special attention to them. If they are heard at all, they tend to be heard as a faint echo of the louder tones or as a constant hum in the background. This is quite unlike the situation that exists for frequency differences. Frequency-based segregation is symmetrical. Later, in chapter 4, I will argue that this symmetry is one of the important distinguishing properties of the automatic process of primitive segregation.

For the moment let us consider this question of symmetry in the context of loudness-based streaming. In the extreme, when the softer stream gets infinitely soft, one would not want to give the name "streaming by loudness" to the resulting ability to hear the loud tones as a separate stream. Even in less extreme cases, we know that soft sounds interfere less with the ability of loud tones to be heard. Therefore, the ability to hear the soft tones as a stream is a much more convincing demonstration of stream segregation than the ability to hear the loud ones.

In addition, if we want to demonstrate loudness-based segregation, we should ask the subject to try to hear an integrated sequence despite the segregating tendencies of the loudness alternation. It would have to be found that it was harder to *integrate* a sequence with large loudness differences. One indication of this difficulty might be the inability to detect a pattern that crossed loudness ranges. There could be slight frequency differences between the elements of the pattern (enough to give them distinct identities but not enough to cause segregation by frequency proximity). Suppose that L1, L2, and L3 were loud tones and S1, S2, and S3 were soft ones, and the repeating sequence L1,S1,L2,L3,S2,S3, . . . , was presented. And suppose that the subject's task was to decide whether the subsequence L1,S1 (presented in isolation first, as a standard) occurred in either that order or in the reverse order in the longer sequence. If streaming is affected by loudness differences, the task should be harder than making a similar judgment on the pattern S2,S3, whose elements had the same loudness.

Even if this result were found, there would be a problem in interpreting it. It could simply be due to the fact that the loud tones were having forward and backward masking effects on the soft ones. You would have to rule out masking effects as the explanation, and it is not obvious to me how this could be done. What the difficulty about masking means in practical terms is that in natural environments it is unlikely that the auditory system could make much use of the fact that the constituent sounds of a sequence were all soft in order to segregate them from loud tones with which they were closely intertwined.

In summary, I do not think that loudness differences can be used to segregate signals in the same powerful way as frequency or timbre differences can. Loudness differences, however, are not irrelevant. I think sudden loudness *changes* do introduce boundaries into signals, but these boundaries are heard as being beginnings or endings of the louder event not the softer one (this idea will be dealt with at greater length in chapter 3 in the discussion of the continuity illusion).

Cumulative Effects of Repetitions

As we have seen, when you rapidly play either a short cycle repeating endlessly or a long nonrepeating pattern composed of tones from two frequency ranges, the high and low tones segregate from each other. However, the segregation does not occur right away. The first few tones seem to form a coherent sequence.

This effect was apparently noticed by van Noorden.[123] In his instructions to listeners in one of his experiments, in which they were asked to adjust the tempo of a sequence until the sequence just held together as a single stream, he cautioned them that "there are some sequences which sound all right at first but suddenly lose their coherence; this is a sign that the tempo is too high" (p. 44).

The effect was studied more extensively in our laboratory at McGill.[124] The basic stimulus was a four-tone sequence with two different high-frequency tones (H1, H2) and one low one (L), arranged in the order H1, L, H2, L. As this four-tone sequence was played repeatedly without intervening silences, the segregation effect was found to be cumulative. If a 4-sec silence was introduced at any point, it seemed to reset the process so that the sequence tended not to segregate. In one experiment, there were four conditions. The sequence either had a silence after every 4 tones (one cycle of the basic 4-tone sequence), every 8 tones (2 cycles), every 16 tones (4 cycles), or had no silences (I). Therefore we were able to observe the effects of the number of tones packaged between silences on the degree of segregation. The strength of segregation induced by the length of the unbroken sequences was measured by titrating it against the speed of the sequence, which is another variable known to affect segregation. The subjects were asked to speed the sequence up until the point of splitting was obtained. Figure 2.21 shows what happened. The greater the length of the "tone package," the slower the speed threshold for stream segregation (since the y axis of the figure is tone onset-to-onset time, not speed, the line rises on the graph). This meant that the longer sequences had a greater tendency to form streams since they would segregate at slower speeds.

We also looked at the decay of streaming with different lengths of silence from 0 to 4 sec inserted between 4-tone packages of alternating high and low tones in a long repeating sequence. Again the subjects adjusted the speed of the sequence to obtain splitting. The streaming was indeed reduced by the presence and length of the embedded silences. With longer silences there was a need for higher speeds before streaming occurred.

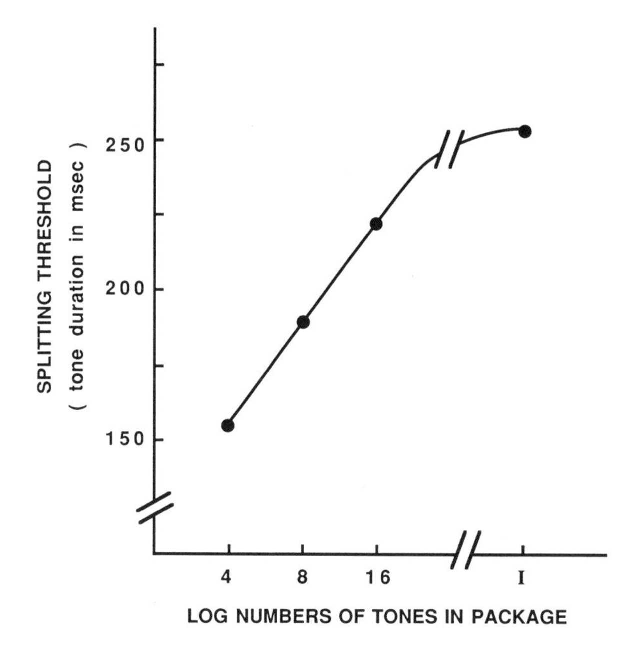

Figure 2.21
Cumulative effects in stream segregation.

The effect of repetition was studied using related methods by Anstis and Saida.[125] Their subjects listened to a continuous 30-sec sequence of tones that alternated between a higher and a lower frequency value. They described what they heard by pressing down one key if they heard one coherent stream jumping up and down in pitch and another key if they heard two streams. The results showed that the probability of hearing a single coherent stream was high at the beginning of each sequence but became progressively less likely over time. The experimenters then allowed the listeners to null out the increased tendency to hear streaming by slowing down the alternation. In a plot that showed both listening time and rate of alternation on logarithmic scales, the alternation rate used by the listener to maintain perceptual coherence fell linearly with listening time from 2 to 10 sec and then with a slower linear decrease from 10 to 60 sec.

These researchers also showed that the buildup of the streaming tendency with listening time is very specific to the frequencies involved. If the listeners are exposed for an extended period to one pair of alternating tones and then are shifted immediately over to a second pair as a test, there is no carryover of the buildup of the tendency to form streams unless the second pair is within one or two semitones of the first pair. They also showed that if the extended listening is done with a pair of tones presented to one ear, and the subsequent testing is done with the same pair presented to the other ear, there is no carryover. Therefore the buildup of the tendency to form streams is specific both with respect to frequency and to ear of presentation.

Explanations of the Cumulation Effect

Although Anstis and Saida obtained results similar to those of Bregman, the explanation that they offered was quite different and in examining this difference we have a good chance to contrast a functional with a physiological explanation. The physiological approach sees stream segregation as a breakdown while the functional approach sees it as an accomplishment.

The functional explanation sees the cumulative effect as the way that the auditory system deals with evidence in a complex world. When a series of sounds appears after a silence, the system begins with the simplest assumption, namely that the elements of the sequence have all arisen from the same external source. Only after there has been repeated activity in one or more restricted frequency regions does the system develop a bias toward restricting the streams to those regions. I have described the behavior of the system as follows:

> The biasing continues for more than 4 sec. Either a period of silence or of wide-band noise can gradually remove this bias. The recovery process probably also continues for more than 4 sec. Why should this sluggishness exist when other processes in the auditory system are carried out in milliseconds if not in microseconds? This relatively slow biasing and unbiasing of the streaming process is valuable because it acts as a conservative evidence-accumulating process. Streams are not split until evidence for substreams continues for a few seconds. Similarly, our auditory systems do not assume that a substream has ceased to exist simply because it has not been heard from for one or two seconds. This conservatism prevents the system from oscillating wildly among perceptions of various numbers of streams in a complex environment.[126]

The description so far seems to imply that a single brief sound in an isolated frequency region would either have to be heard as part of an ongoing stream or else not at all. Yet we know that this is not true. For example, if an electronic click sound is heard concurrently with a sentence, it appears unrelated to the speech sounds and the listener cannot tell exactly where it occurred in the sentence.[127] It is clearly heard in a separate stream. While repetition is important in the formation of streams, it seems not to be absolutely essential for the segregation of grossly dissimilar sounds. Although there is a bias for a single stream in the absence of any accumulation of evidence, very dissimilar sounds will still not be well integrated. This can be seen, for example, in the fact that when two tones are played in succession, the further apart they are in frequency, the harder it is to judge the length of the time interval that separates them.[128]

Although it is possible that repetition is not essential, it may play a role even when only one of the classes of sounds is repeated. In the experiments in which clicks occurred in sentences, while the click was not repeated, the verbal sounds were. A number of words in the sentence occurred before the click and the stream-forming process may have had a chance to lock on to the characteristics of the speech sounds prior to the occurrence of the click. It may be sufficient that one stream be formed on the basis of some coherent set of auditory properties in order for it to become biased toward rejecting sounds that have quite different properties. If this is true, an interesting question arises: If a single stream is gradually formed on the basis of some shared features of its sounds, and it is suddenly mixed with a set of different sounds, will all the nonfitting sounds tend initially to be considered to be part of a single added stream until the evidence accumulates that they, in turn, should be formed into more than one stream?

A physiological model to explain the growth of segregation with longer sequences was proposed by Anstis and Saida.[129] Like van Noorden, they proposed that the sequence of tones is heard as a coherent sequence when an adjacent pair of tones, say a high one and a low one, stimulate a pitch motion detector (an FM detector).[130] They argue that the auditory system uses the output from these detectors to create "fusional links" and that stream segregation may be a breakdown product: ". . . segregation is not itself an active process which positively isolates streams but refers merely to a lack of links, so that adaptation in our experiment broke down the fusional links between tones of different frequencies, leaving intact the simpler fusional links between tones of the same frequency."

There are two differences between the explanations offered by myself and by Anstis and Saida. The first concerns the level of description. I have already argued in chapter 1 that a breakdown at the physiological level can be the mechanism behind an accomplishment at the functional level. I shall not repeat that discussion here. The second is empirical in nature. For my explanation, the important thing about the repetition is that evidence has accumulated in the

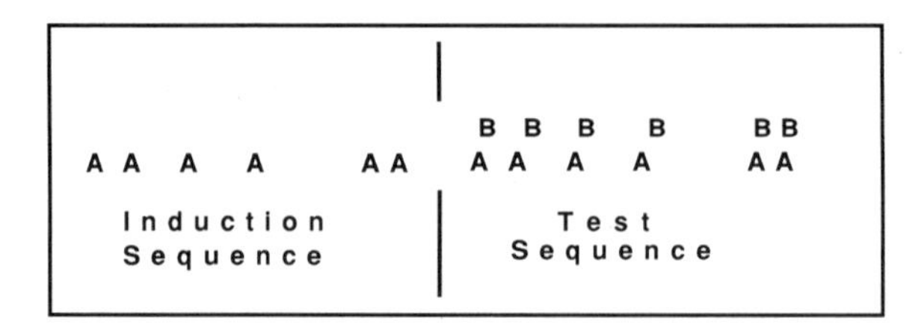

Figure 2.22
Test of habituation theory.

form of repeatedly presented tones in different frequency regions. It is not the jumping back and forth that is important but the distribution of tones in two distinct frequency regions. For Anstis and Saida, it is the jumping back and forth between frequency regions that is important. Therefore the two explanations would have different predictions in the following experiment:

Suppose that we are interested in the segregation of A from B in the sequence ABABAB. . . . Let us call this the test sequence. Prior to starting the test sequence, we could play an inducing sequence that contained a long string of occurrences of only tone A. This is shown in the left part of figure 2.22. Care would have to be taken not to make the A sequence isochronous either in the inducing or the test sequences so as to avoid the auditory system's tuning into this periodicity. Notice that the inducing sequence contains no AB or BA jumps to tire out the corresponding jump detectors.

In effect, this experiment has already been done by Bregman and Rudnicky.[131] In their experiment, the perception of the order of two target tones, A and B (2,200 and 2,400 Hz), was made more difficult by bracketing them between two distractor tones, both at a somewhat lower frequency, X (1,460 Hz), so that there was a four-tone sequence, XABX, that began and ended on the same frequency. The difficulty arose from the fact that the four tones formed a coherent perceptual unit of which the inner events, A and B, were not very prominent. Their prominence could be restored by capturing the two X tones into a separate stream. This was done by preceding and following the four-tone sequence by a series of captor tones at the X frequency. This led to the stimulus pattern shown in figure 1.7 of chapter 1. The added C tones formed a stream that captured the distractors that surrounded the AB pair and left the tones AB in a separate stream. In a later discussion of this experiment, I made the connection between this result and the idea of the cumulation of evidence as follows:

> Why, in the experiment just cited, was a captor stream required to strip the distractor tones off the target tones? Why did the distractors not strip themselves off to form a separate stream from the targets regardless of the presence of the captors? The answer is that in the four-tone pattern [XABX] . . . there was no cumulative build-up of a stream in the lower [X] frequency range; hence the distractors and targets formed one coherent stream. Adding the captors allowed evidence to build up for a stream in the 1,460-Hz frequency range and to therefore affect the streaming of the captors.[132]

There is one factor in the Bregman-Rudnicky experiment that prevents it from being an exact analog to the experiment that I have just proposed as a test of Anstis and Saida's explanation versus my own. Jones and her colleagues pointed out that the X's in the Bregman-Rudnicky experiment all occurred at the same regular temporal rhythm, and showed that this rhythmic regularity facilitated the capturing effect that was observed.[133] This criticism would not help the jump detector explanation since there were no frequency jumps in the inducing sequence of captors. However, the regularity of the X tones may have made it possible for an attention-based mechanism that exploits the regularities of sequences to have been responsible for the capture of the distractors. The attention-based mechanism is what I shall refer to in chapter 4 as schema-based stream segregation and this appears to be different from the primitive stream segregation that is the focus of the present chapter.[134]

Another fact that argues against a simple explanation of streaming in terms of the breakdown of frequency-jump detectors is the fact that a sequence of tones all having the same fundamental frequency but with two different timbres will also form two streams based on the two timbres. To bring this under the "breakdown of detectors" rubric, there would have to be timbre-jump detectors, presumably one detector for each pair of perceptibly different timbres. While this is a conceivable strategy for explaining things, it would be useful only if there were a fairly small number of types of detectors.

Continuity

It was recognized by the Gestalt psychologists that the continuity or smoothness of a change promoted the perceptual integration of the changing experience. For example, if a sheet of paper has a gradual change in brightness from left to right, the brightnesses will be integrated and seen as a brightness modulation of a single colored surface. If a line is drawn vertically down the page at the midpoint, the page

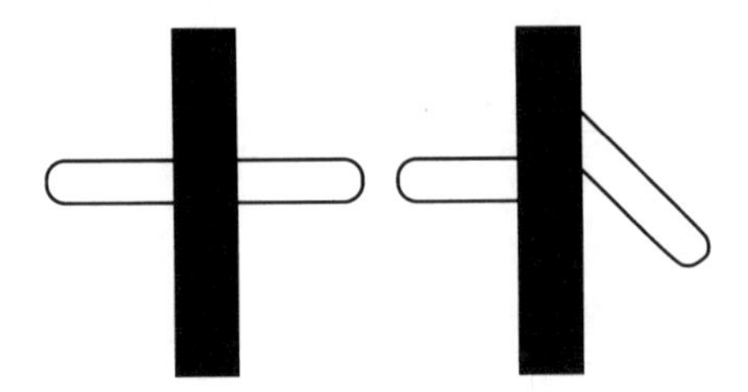

Figure 2.23
Role of continuity in visual grouping.

will break up into two distinct regions, a darker region on one side of the line and a lighter region on the other side. The line breaks up the continuity of the color change and prevents integration across the discontinuity. Smooth changes hold perceived regions together. Discontinuities cause them to break up. This applies also to visual contours. An outline contour that is smoother is more easily seen as a single boundary and more likely to be perceptually restored by closure when it is missing. Figure 2.23 shows an example of this. On the left the parts separated by the overlapping shape tend to be perceived as a single interrupted form because of what the Gestaltists called the "good continuation" of its lines. On the right the disconnected parts are not perceptually unified because they do not have such continuity.

Gary Dannenbring and I investigated the question of whether an analogous principle could be found in audition.[135] We asked whether a smooth frequency transition would serve to perceptually integrate a sequence of tones that might otherwise form two streams. We used, as stimuli, cycles of alternating high and low tones, manipulating the way the tones started and ended as shown in figure 2.24. The cycle consisted of two high tones at 2,000 Hz (H1) and 1,600 Hz (H2) and two low ones at 614 Hz (L1) and 400 Hz (L2). The figure shows the adjacent edges of a consecutive pair of tones in each of three conditions. The central third of the figure represents the 40-msec interval that separated the steady-state full-intensity part of one tone from the corresponding part of the next. During this interval there were three possible ways in which the sound could change. In the *discrete* (standard) condition the first tone faded out in 10 msec, there was a 20-msec gap, and then the next tone faded on in 10 msec. In the *ramped* condition, the first tone was joined to the next one by a frequency glide at full intensity. Finally, in the *semi-ramped* condition, the first tone began to glide toward the second one and at the same time to fade out. The offset glide "pointed" to the the frequency of next tone. The next tone had a corresponding onset glide that pointed back to the frequency of the previous one.

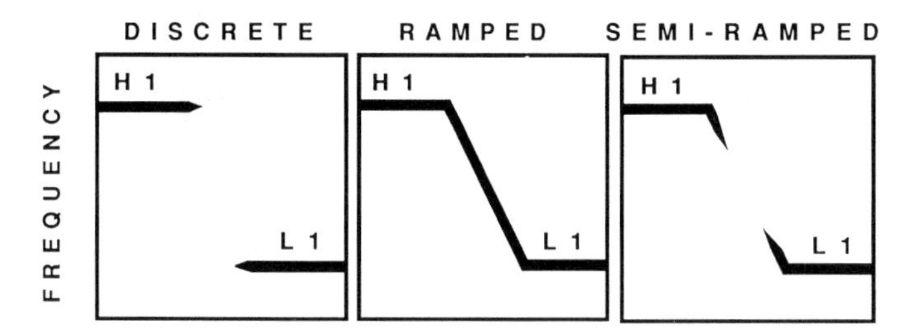

Figure 2.24
The adjacent edges of consecutive tones in the three continuity conditions used by Bregman and Dannenbring (1973).

The listeners heard two different sequences, a standard and a comparison, each consisting of a 5-second cycle of the four tones. They were asked to judge whether the tones were in the same order in the two sequences. The order was either H1,L1,H2,L2, . . . , or it was H1,L2,H2,L1, ... A full segregation of the high and low streams makes these two orders indistinguishable because the within-stream sequence (in either the high or the low stream) is simply an alternation of the two tones that fall in that range. Therefore the failure of listeners to accurately judge whether the two cycles were in the same order was taken as a measure of the degree of segregation of the high and low streams. The worst accuracy was obtained in the discrete condition; the streams segregated as they normally do. The best accuracy was found in the ramped condition, indicating that the frequency glides held the sequence together to some degree. The semi-ramped condition yielded an intermediate degree of accuracy. A further experiment using direct judgments of the number of streams showed that the ramped condition seemed more like a single stream, the discrete sequence more like two streams, with the semi-ramped condition in between.[136]

We argued in 1973, incorrectly I think, that our finding that the semi-ramped condition was more integrated than the discrete condition showed that even a mere pointing of one tone to the next could help to integrate the sequence. This meant, we claimed, that the auditory system probably was able to use these brief glides to predict the frequency region of the next tone. We pointed out the similarity of the sounds in this experiment to the formant transitions that are seen in speech spectrograms and speculated that it was these transitions that helped to keep the speech signal coherent. However, since this experiment was done, other evidence has thrown the notion of trajectory-following into question. The issue will be discussed more extensively in chapter 4. For the moment it is sufficient to mention that not only does the semi-ramped condition cause one tone to point to the next one, but it also brings the end of one tone closer in frequency to the beginning of the next one, as compared with the discrete condition. Therefore the integration could be due to frequency proximity rather than pointing.

In the ramped condition, there is a continuous set of frequency proximities throughout the glide. This is a rather strange way to talk, because there are no discrete tones at all in the ramped condition. Therefore how can their proximity be discussed? Obviously, we are discussing an analytical fiction obtained by considering each very short bit of sound as a separate unit. If we permit ourselves to consider such units, however, we can see that in the ramped condition there is never a jump in frequency between each unit and the next. This is what we mean by continuity.

We should not be surprised to find that the continuity of changes in audition are taken as an indication of a single environmental event. It is a good betting principle that if one moment of sound strongly resembles the previous one, the two are part of the same event. Indeed, the frequency-proximity principle itself is just a degenerate case of the continuity principle that we have to use in cases in which there is a temporal gap between successive sounds.

Trajectory-Based Integration

Among the factors that favor sequential grouping, many people would include the regularity of the sequence. Heise and Miller found that when they played a sequence of tones that followed a regularly ascending or descending frequency trajectory, if one of the tones deviated too much from the frequency that would place it on the trajectory, that tone seemed to pop out of the sequence.[137] Building on this finding, Jones has proposed a theory of sequential integration that is based on the predictability of the sequence.[138] For example, if a sequence follows a simple, regular pattern on frequency-by-time coordinates, it will be easy to integrate. There have been a number of research findings that are consistent with this hypothesis. However, I wish to explore the idea that it is not primitive stream segregation but a different process, schema-based stream segregation, that exploits the regularity in sequences of tones. By regularity, I include things such as isochrony (regular spacing in time), other simple repeating rhythms, and regular steps in frequency or in any other acoustic dimension. The argument is rather complicated and requires us to look at a number of experiments. Therefore it is given its own chapter (chapter 4).

Effects of Streaming

In this section I would like to discuss the perceptual consequences of preattentive segregation. In a way it is artificial to separate the discussion of the results of segregation from its causes because in an actual experiment you cannot study an acoustic factor that has been proposed as a cause of of segregation without having some way of measuring its effects. Therefore many of the effects of segregation will have been mentioned in an incidental way in the previous sections. I will attempt here to consider them in more detail. It is important to do so for three reasons.

The first is that, as I have already said, we often use some consequence of primitive segregation to measure the effects of a proposed cause. However, it is important to remember that each measurable behavior or judgment that we can use as an index of segregation is actually influenced by many factors, only one of which is segregation itself. Therefore we must evaluate the research findings that claim to measure segregation in the light of this fact.

The second point follows from the first. Given that each measure of primitive segregation is affected by many factors, then whenever we, as researchers, claim that some factor influences the forming of streams, we are obliged to show the effects of this cause on more than one measure of segregation. This is what is called the method of converging operations. It was discussed in the final section of chapter 1. If a number of tasks respond in a predictable way to a factor that is thought to influence segregation, this suggests that segregation has actually been influenced by that factor. This strategy is particularly useful in psychology where we understand, at best, only a small fraction of the human system and where it is impossible to freeze the activity of the rest of the system while we study one part. Even if we allow only one physical factor (such as the length of a tonal sequence) to vary across the conditions of an experiment, we have no way of knowing whether it affects only one psychological mechanism. Since really powerful scientific knowledge is about the nature of basic internal systems rather than about patterns of observable responses to observable stimuli, we must concern ourselves with the issue of converging operations. Otherwise we are forced into the kind of blind behaviorism that brought psychology to a standstill for much of this century.

The third reason for examining the various effects of segregation is that, taken as a whole, they give us a clearer idea of the role that streams play in the overall task of perception. In particular, they provide a picture of segregation as a scene-analysis process.

Focusing on the Stream as a Unit

The major effect of sequential integration and segregation is that when acoustic material is bound into a primitive stream, it is easy to pay attention to it and to follow it over time. Although we have a considerable degree of voluntary control over our attention, this control is not absolute and some things are easier to attend to than others. An integrated stream is the natural subject for an act of attention. It is obvious why this should be so. The perceptual stream-forming process has the job of grouping those acoustic features that are likely to have arisen from the same physical source. Since it is profitable to attend to real sources and to determine their qualities, locations, and so on, rather than to arbitrary sets of features, attention should be strongly biased toward listening to streams. This clearly cannot be the whole story because we are capable, with effort and with practice, of listening to individual features of sounds or to arbitrary collections. But the words "effort" and "practice" are revealing. It is only to streams that we can listen in a naive way.

This bias toward attending separately to different streams showed itself in a striking way in one of our earliest experiments on primitive segregation.[139] The subjects were presented with a repeating loop of tones that included three different high tones (A, B, and C) and three different low ones (1, 2, and 3). Say, for example, that the order was A,1,B,2,C,3. . . repeatedly. When listeners were asked to report the order of the tones, 59% of all judgments reported that the order of the tones was A,B,C,1,2,3 or 1,2,3,A,B,C. The listeners were apparently attending to the order within each frequency-based stream and then concatenating the two remembered perceptual results in their answers. This is strong evidence that the two streams were perceptually isolated from each other and could not be focused on at the same time.

Computation of Within-Stream Emergent Properties

Treating a stream as a unit involves calculating its properties from only that set of acoustic features that has been assigned to it. Sometimes, in the study of perception, we speak about emergent features. These are global features that arise at a higher level when information at a lower level is grouped. One often hears that "the whole is greater than the sum of its parts." I have always found this sentence mysterious. When you weigh a whole, it weighs no more than the sum of its parts. Actually what this cryptic sentence is pointing out is that a whole has properties and functions that its parts, taken individually, do not. If this were not true we would never manufacture anything by putting pieces together. For example, a bicycle is usable as a means of transportation although none of its individual parts is. Its "transporting" function is emergent from the particular way in which the parts are put together. But what does this have to do with perception? The answer is this: Because nature allows structures to behave in ways that are derived from the properties of parts but are unique to the larger structure, perception must calculate the properties of structures, taken as wholes, in order to provide us with valuable information about them.

Since we are concerned with the properties of the meaningful structures of our environments such as bicycles and people, and the meaningful events such as a car roaring by us or a child singing a song, it is these structures and events whose properties we should calculate with our senses. Perception should be concerned, then, with properties calculated on the basis of an appropriate grouping of information, rather than with properties calculated from isolated flashes of light or squeaks of sound. If this is true, researchers should be able to find strong evidence that the auditory system uses mainly within-stream information to calculate emergent properties. Without giving away the whole story now, we should find that properties such as melodic form and rhythm, the order of components, the swelling of intensity, or any other property that unfolds over time should be calculated within an individual stream.

The relative ease with which the auditory system combines information within and across streams was the subject of a study by Jock Campbell and myself.[140] We asked our subjects to listen first to a standard pattern—a repeating cycle containing three sine tones and three silences. Then they heard a comparison pattern; like the standard, it was a repeating loop, but the three silences of the standard were replaced by three additional tones so that the comparison sequence always contained six tones. Three of these were always high in frequency (A, B, and C) and three were low (1, 2, and 3). This comparison pattern always segregated into two streams, one containing the high tones and another containing the low ones. The listeners were asked to judge whether or not the three tones of the standard appeared in the same order and temporal spacing in the six-tone comparison cycle.

If the tones chosen for the standard all fell in the same stream in the comparison, the task was easy. However, if two of them fell into one stream and the third into the other, the task was virtually impossible. Apparently to judge the order of a group of tones requires the listener to be able to perceive them as a group. This appears to be impossible when its members alternate between different streams.

A more direct example of the way in which the forming of streams affects the patterns that can be perceived was shown in a set of experiments by Jay Dowling. I will describe them in more detail in chapter 5 but will present a brief summary now. Dowling interleaved the tones from one simple melody with those of a second one.[141] When the two sets of tones spanned the same frequency range, it was impossible for listeners to recognize the individual melodies. But when one of the melodies was transposed upward so that it occupied a nonoverlapping frequency range, it was possible to hear the two melodies as separate figures and to recognize them. Dowling's experiments illustrate the fact that a frequency separation that leads to the formation of two separate streams allows the auditory system to compute separate global properties, in this case distinct melodic shapes, within each stream.[142]

The fact that auditory shapes are computed within streams is also responsible for certain difficulties in recognizing sounds. Let me give an example from the experiment of Bregman and Rudnicky.[143] I have mentioned this experiment before (it was illustrated in figure 1.7 of chapter 1) but let me describe it again for a different reason. Suppose we play two tones, A and B, to a listener rapidly (65 msec per tone, including rise times and silences) and ask whether the pair ascends or descends in frequency. Given that the two tones are far enough apart in frequency to be discriminable, the task is easy. But we can create a very hard task from this pair of tones. We bracket the pair by two extra tones, say both at frequency F, where F is in the same general frequency range as A and B but a bit lower. It becomes almost impossible to discriminate FABF from FBAF. The reason seems to be that the two patterns both start and end with the same frequency, and that both have a top frequency B somewhere in the middle. The exact position of A, which is neither the highest nor the lowest, neither the first nor the last, seems not to be clearly appreciated. However, if more tones are added near the frequency of F, they capture the F tones into a separate stream. It now becomes possible for the listener to report the order of A and B. Why? Apparently whatever auditory interaction made the order of A and B less salient in the four-tone sequence operates only among tones that are in the same stream. The interaction appears to be one in which individual tones lose some of their original salience when they are incorporated into a larger unit. Many experiments have observed this loss of salience of certain sounds (usually those in the middle of the frequency range or of the temporal series) when they are embedded into a larger pattern.[144] This bears on the point that we made earlier about shapes being perceived within streams: When the flanking sounds are not part of the same stream, the embedding effects do not occur.

The reduction of salience for tones embedded in a larger group and the requirement that the embedding tones be in the same auditory stream as the embedded ones may be seen in a phenomenon that Pierre Divenyi and Ira Hirsh called sequential blanking.[145] In their experiment the listeners were asked to identify the order of three 20-msec tones that were immediately followed by an additional tone. The addition of the fourth tone made the order of the three-tone sequence harder to identify. This difficulty, however, was eliminated when the fourth tone was remote in frequency from the preceding three. In the original report, Divenyi and Hirsh viewed this as a sort of memory erasure effect. However, a later experiment that they did, in which they embedded a three-tone sequence in a longer one, made it clear that the effect was really due to the formation of auditory "figures."[146] In this later experiment they varied the frequency proximity of the target triplet to the other tones and found that the interference by the embedding tones on the identifiability of the target tones was very much reduced when the two sets of tones fell in different frequency ranges. It is as if the separation of frequency prevents the two sets of tones from being part of the same auditory figure and that only parts of the same figure suppress one another's individual identities.

This loss of salience within larger groups may be the basis for two effects reported in the research literature. The first has been called "backward recognition masking" by Dominic Massaro.[147] When a brief tone is followed rapidly by another one, it is hard to perceive the exact pitch of the first. The masking effect is greatest when the second tone follows the first immediately and it becomes smaller as the silent interval between the two increases. It seems to me that some or all of the masking may really be due to the perceptual grouping of the two tones. This interpretation is supported by the results of an experiment by Idson and Massaro.[148] In that experiment, the pattern to be recognized contained three tones, a low, medium, and high one (L, M, and H), covering a six-semitone range and appearing in any of six possible orders. A single masking tone (X) was always interleaved between the target tones—for example,

L,X,H,X,M,X.

Only when the masking tone X fell in the same frequency range as the targets did it make the task difficult and only in this frequency range did its time delay relative to the target make any difference. This suggests that when extra tones are incorporated into a stream, they change the shape of the forms that are perceived and make it difficult to extract an embedded form. In a different frequency range they will fall into a separate stream and not embed the target in this way.

Idson and Massaro were loath, however, to explain the simpler case of backward recognition masking of a single tone by a second one via the argument that a single pair of tones forms a new "Gestalt" in which the first one loses its identity. A troublesome fact prevented them from doing so: When only two tones are used, a target and a masker, the difference in frequencies between the target and the masker seems not to matter. It is possible, however, that frequency proximity has a relatively weak effect in this case because with only two tones present, the segregation is not very strong. This would be consistent with a view of stream formation in which the segregation "force" starts off slowly and becomes strong only gradually with a buildup of evidence that we are hearing two narrow-range signals rather than just one wide-range signal. Perhaps the two-tone experiment has missed a frequency-proximity effect because it is weak. A frequency effect has been found by another researcher.[149] Therefore current evidence still leads me to believe that the backward recognition masking effect and the sequential blanking effect may both be consequences (entirely or in part) of the within-stream process of forming auditory figures. This conclusion is supported by the finding that it is easier to mask the recognition of a tone by inserting a second tone after it than by inserting a noise.[150] A stream-segregation interpretation of this result is consistent with the finding by Dannenbring and Bregman that tones segregate strongly from noises in sequential presentation.[151]

There is one final study that I want to cite to show that the interaction of tones occurs primarily within streams. It was carried out by Woods, who reasoned as follows.[152] When we observe a strong destructive interaction between tones that are near to one another in frequency and a lesser interaction between tones that are distant in frequency, we cannot conclude that the differences are due to stream segregation because we already know that tones that are proximal in frequency ought to interact more strongly due to the nature of the resolving mechanism in the inner ear. Therefore we must manipulate stream segregation by some factor that does not relate to frequency differences. For this reason, Woods used the apparent spatial location of tones (controlled by their relative intensity in the listener's two ears) to cause them to segregate into different streams. When two streams were formed on the basis of spatial location, it was found that only tones that were in the same stream showed interactions based on frequency proximity.

Stream segregation can even affect the listener's ability to count the tones in a sequence. Dominic Massaro asked his subjects to count the tones in sequences in which the tones either alternated between two frequency ranges or did not.[153] The number of tones was less accurately counted if the sequences alternated between frequencies that differed by 14 semitones (which would have broken the sequence into two subjective streams at most of the tone rates utilized in this experiment). The accuracy of counting, however, did not further deteriorate if the frequencies alternated over still larger intervals (38 semitones). If the frequencies alternated over an interval of only two semitones, no deterioration of counting accuracy could be established, in comparison with the nonalternating condition. Massaro concluded that it was not the frequency alternations as such, but rather the sensation of streaming, that hampered counting performance. Apparently the stream segregation makes it hard to catch every event when trying to count all the sounds in the two streams.

Temporal Relations

One of the most important aspects of sounds is the temporal relation between them. This includes how far they are apart in time, any temporal patterns that they may generate, and their temporal order. In this section I want to show that when a sequence is segregated into separate streams, the listener loses the finer details of the temporal relation between sounds that are in different streams and focuses instead on the temporal relations that exist among the elements of the same stream. This focus follows from the nature of stream segregation as a scene analysis process. It is the individual streams that represent meaningful environmental events and it is the temporal properties of these events that are of interest to the listener.

Recognition of Order I began to suspect that stream segregation influenced the listener's ability to judge the order of events when I read a remarkable result reported by Richard Warren and his coworkers.[154] Unpracticed listeners had been asked to listen to a repeating cycle of four sounds, a hiss, a tone, a buzz, and the speech sound "ee". Each sound was 200 msec long. Although the listeners could detect each of the individual sounds in the cycle fairly easily, it was virtually impossible for them to report the order of the four sounds in the cycle. Warren and his colleagues were impressed with the difficulty of this task because earlier Ira Hirsh had shown that the order of pairs of unrelated sounds could be detected when their onsets occurred as little as 20 msec apart.[155]

Earlier, in listening to rapid sequences of short, steady-state, natural sounds, such as water splashing in a sink, a doorbell ringing, or a dentist's drill, I had noticed that often the perceptual groupings of similar sounds with one another would camouflage the real order of the sounds. It seemed to me that in the experiment of Warren et al., subsets of the sounds must be falling into different perceptual streams making it difficult for the listener to perceive the temporal relations between some of the items. This led me to the study of the perception of temporal order in cycles of pure tones. With pure tones we know more exactly the similarity of one sound to another since it depends on the frequencies of the tones.[156] An experiment that I described earlier was carried out with Jock Campbell. It showed that the reports of temporal order in a sequence of strictly alternating high (H) and low (L) tones (that is, HLHLHLHL . . .) was quite distorted.[157] More than half the subjects reported orders in which the tones were grouped by frequency (HHHLLL or LLLHHH).[158]

There are numerous examples in the research literature in which it is difficult to report the order of rapid sequences formed by different types of sounds.

For instance, Broadbent and Ladefoged had played pairs of unrelated sounds to listeners.[159] Each pair was selected from a set of three—hiss, buzz, or pip (short tone). The listeners first heard a sequence of two different pairs, call them A and B, and then one of the pairs again. They had to say whether it was pair A or B that had been played again. To do this task you obviously have to be able to discriminate pair A from pair B. If both pairs consisted of the same items with the order simply reversed they could not be discriminated from one another by unpracticed listeners even though the onset-to-onset time was fairly long (150 msec). With practice, listeners were able to learn a strategy for succeeding even with very fast pairs by listening for the *quality* of the pair rather than for the order of its component sounds.

In an unpublished report written 5 years later, Donald Norman, in describing the rapid alternation of tones from different frequency ranges, wrote that "the resulting impression that the tones are unrelated in time is very strong".[160] He reported an informal experiment. The stimulus was a 10-tone sequence formed from the repeated alternation of a higher and a lower tone, not far enough apart in frequency to form separate streams. Each tone lasted 100 msec, and 30-msec silent gaps separated them. In one of the silent gaps there was a 30-msec probe tone. The listeners had to judge whether the probe tone occurred after a low tone or after a high one, in other words whether they had heard "L,probe,H" or "H,probe,L." When the probe tone was far away in frequency from the other tones, the subjects could not do it. The difficulty did not occur when only the probe and one other tone were present. It seemed to require the presence of a series of tones. (This is probably due to the fact that a strong stream will form only after several tones have occurred in a fixed range of frequencies.)

Giovanni Vicario in Italy also noticed that the order of unrelated sounds could be perceptually distorted. He reported the results of an experiment with a sequence of three sounds (A,X,B) where A and B were tones that were close together in frequency and X was either a tone from another frequency range or a noise.[161] There were frequent errors in the reported order with the two related tones often reported first. In the case in which Vicario had used three tones, the strength of the dislocation increased with an increasing frequency separation between tone X and the other two.

McNally and Handel studied the effects of similarity relations between the sounds in cycles. Did they affect the listeners' ability to report the order of the sounds?[162] The experiment used repeating cycles of four sounds selected from an inventory that included different kinds of clicks and buzzes, tones of different frequencies, and white noise bursts. Their innovation was to control similarities between subgroups of sounds in the cycles. Their basic finding was that when similar items were temporally adjacent in the cycle, the order was more accurately reported.

When the cycle consisted of two frequencies of tone and two types of click, the reports of order were only better than chance when items of the same class had been placed adjacent in the sequence by the experimenters. For such sequences there was a strong tendency for the listeners to describe the items from the same class as being adjacent in the sequence whether or not they were. This was very analogous to the finding of Bregman and Campbell. Another important point is that the similarities seemed to be relative rather than absolute. The experimenters wrote, for example, "it should be noted that [when each tone was widely separated in frequency from all the others] the tones, although far beyond the frequency separation limit for temporal coherence when trilled separately . . . stream together when opposed to a buzz and white noise, thereby demonstrating that stream segregation is a function of all the elements in a pattern."

Why Effects of Streaming on Order Perception Are Not Always Clear

Not every experiment that has asked listeners to report the order of rapid sequences of tones has observed difficulties that could be attributed to stream segregation. Some seemed to show that the factors that are known to affect stream segregation did not affect order discrimination. For example, neither Nickerson and Freeman nor Warren and Byrnes found a decrease in accuracy in sequences of four tones when the frequency separation between the tones increased.[163]

Other studies showed that some of the difficulties in reporting the order of unrelated tones could be attributed to factors other than stream segregation. For example, it is much easier to report the order of four unrelated sounds in a cycle when, instead of calling out their order verbally, listeners were allowed to give their answer by arranging, on a table top, a set of cards bearing the names of the four sounds.[164] Other studies showed that the performance of listeners could be greatly improved by giving them extensive training,[165] or by using response measures that did not put a strain on their memories.[166]

Richard Warren has argued that such results suggest that stream segregation may be a rather restricted phenomenon: "While there can be little doubt that splitting into parallel auditory streams occurs in Baroque compositions having 'compound melodic lines,' it appears to be rather difficult to obtain analogous splitting with non-melodic recycled tonal sequences."[167]

I would like to offer a different interpretation of these facts by stating three points: first, it is always true that the more different the items in a cycle are from one another in frequency content, the more they tend to segregate from one another. Second, when stream segregation occurs, it always makes across-stream order judgments harder than within-stream judgments. Third, and this is the important point, the experiments that have failed to obtain effects of streaming on order perception either did not produce streaming, or, if they did, the listeners were able to make the required order discriminations without the necessity of making across-stream judgments. In the light of this third point, let us look at some of the experiments to see whether they invalidate the claims for stream segregation.

One of the experiments that failed to find any effects of frequency separation (and therefore, presumably of stream segregation) on order judgments was done by Nickerson and Freeman.[168] This is a case in which, because of the method that was used, the subjects did not need to employ across-stream judgments to get the right answers. The experiment presented the subjects with four-tone cycles. The listeners were required to memorize a number to identify each of six possible orders of the four tones. They later used this number to identify which of the orders they had heard. The results showed that performance on this task *actually improved* with an increasing frequency separation of the tones. However, a close look at the cycles that were used reveals that all but a single pair of these could be distinguished from one another on the basis of within-stream frequency-and-rhythm patterns. The remaining two orders, which could not be distinguished by their within-stream patterns were the only ones that were hard for the subjects to discriminate. Even these last two orders could have been discriminated from one another on the basis of within-stream information, providing that the subjects could have known with what note the first cycle had started, and since the cycles were not faded in slowly, the listener could have determined the starting note of the sequence. In any case, it was these two orders that were the hardest to discriminate. Nickerson and Freeman were aware of the within-stream solution strategy and discussed it extensively, showing how their results could be entirely explained by it. Therefore this experiment is not a counterexample to my earlier claims.

If an order-discrimination task is being used to study stream segregation, rather than to study order-detection itself, it is necessary to use tasks that are sensitive to stream segregation. Order detection is not sensitive to streaming whenever the ordering task can be solved in any manner other than by experiencing the entire sequence as a coherent perceptual organization. We must avoid using a task in which whatever fragments are left in the same stream after segregation occurs are sufficient to make the identification. Such cases occur when there is a small set of alternative patterns known to the listener in advance or when the test involves a forced choice between only two alternatives.

In the Bregman-Campbell experiment, there were only two six-tone comparison sequences offered to listeners for each three-tone standard sequence. However, the researchers made sure that the two alternatives would sound identical if the listeners could pay attention only to one stream at a time. They did this by requiring the subjects to discriminate two sequences that would contain the same within-stream orders only if they segregated. This is how it was done: Remember that the stimulus is a repeating cycle, and when it segregates it becomes two repeating cycles (a high one and a low one). Consider figure 2.25. If we can consider that cycles have no beginning or ending points, one of the ways that the high-frequency cycle can be interlaced with the low one to make the total cycle is shown in case 1. However, if the starting point in the high cycle is changed, the sequences are as shown in case 2. The difference between the two cases can be seen clearly in the total sequences where, for example,

Case 1:

High sequence: A — B — C — A — B — C — A ....etc.
Low sequence: — X — Y — Z — X — Y — Z — X ....etc.

Total Sequence No. 1: A X B Y C Z A X B Y C Z A X ....etc.

Case 2:

High sequence: B — C — A — B — C — A — B ....etc.
Low sequence: — X — Y — Z — X — Y — Z — X ....etc.

Total Sequence No. 2: B X C Y A Z B X C Y A Z B X ....etc.

Figure 2.25
Stimuli for studying the effects of streaming on the discrimination of order.

the sequence A,X appears in the first case but not in the second. Yet *viewed as closed cycles* the high and low sequences are the same in the two cases. Therefore when the streams segregate, as long as the listeners cannot remember where the cycles began on their first iteration, they should not be able to discriminate the first case from the second. The precaution of making the stimuli in this way is essential in experiments in which a same/different judgment is being used to determine whether the listener has detected across-stream order relations.

Another argument against attributing the difficulty of rapid sequences to stream segregation has been to attribute it to something else—the reporting process itself. Before we consider this argument in detail, we should ask ourselves what is involved in an experiment in which the order of events in a sequence must be discerned.

Ulric Neisser proposed mental representations that people might use to remember a sequence of sounds and how people might learn to use them better with training.[169] He described a type of mental representation that he called a "string." These were composed of successive parts, each of which was in correspondence with one of the elements in the acoustic sequence. When the time for making the report arrived, listeners could use this string to generate, one by one, the series of verbal labels for the elements or to decide how to place response cards on the table. It is to such strings that we refer when we say that we can remember the order of events in a sequence.

Neisser also proposed a less articulated type of representation, called an "analog." This was a representation that encoded some of the sequence's properties but that was not subdivided into parts that explicitly represented the individual parts of the sequence. Even though an analog did not explicitly store the sequence of events, it could be used to accomplish some kinds of order discrimination. For example, some experiments play two sequences to listeners and ask them to report whether the two sequences are the same or different.[170] We find that listeners have some sensitivity to the order of sounds at speeds that are much faster that the ones at which they are able to report the actual order. If the listeners can store analogs for the two sequences, they can compare them and see whether or not they are different. This may be what happened in an experiment by Broadbent and Ladefoged.[171] Listeners had a hard time discriminating "hiss-buzz" from "buzz-hiss" at fast presentation rates. The experimenters themselves learned to do it with practice, but did so by noting a qualitative difference between the two orders, rather than a change in perceived order. In Neisser's terms, this qualitative difference was a difference in the mental analogs of the two pairs; the performance was not based on a string representation. The experimenters learned to attach the names "hiss-buzz" and "buzz-hiss" to these two analogs. An essentially similar argument has been made by Warren.[172]

Presumably it is due to the use of these analogs that listeners can learn to discriminate the onset asynchrony of two sounds at durations as low as 20 msec[173] or to discriminate the order of two clicks of unequal intensity (Huffman sequences), or of other sounds at asynchronies of as low as 2 msec.[174]

Even some tasks that seem to require a naming of the elements of a sequence in the right order might be accomplished through the use of analogs. For example, if you play the various permutations of a four element one-shot sequence such as "low-tone, high-tone, hiss, scratch" on enough different trials to subjects and tell them which order they have heard, they can learn to use cues from the analogs to give the correct answer (as long as the experiment does not use too many different orderings). Neisser gives an account of the reasoning process by which he himself was able to do this.[175] "The low tone was certainly first . . . there was a hiss-high transition . . . the scratch certainly wasn't *before* the hiss . . . so it must have been low, high, hiss, scratch."

Neisser and Hirst argue that "the overt response string may really be a complex post hoc construction based on minimal cues available in an analog form."[176] The idea that listeners have two different methods for dealing with tasks that involve the order of stimuli has been proposed by others as well. Warren and Byrnes made essentially the same distinction as Neisser, but instead of calling them strings and analogs, used the terms Type I and Type II judgments.[177] Warren later referred to them as the "identification of components and their order" and "holistic pattern recognition."[178] Perhaps these last are the clearest terms.

In an experiment in which untrained listeners must report on the order of a fast sequence of unrelated sounds, they are unable to create strings at such a high speed and because they are untrained, they do not yet know how to decode the analog memory that they do have into a sequence of names. Therefore they fail at the task. This evidently happened in the experiment by Warren, Farmer, Obusek, and Warren on cycles of unrelated sounds. Yet in that same experiment, the subjects succeeded when the elements of the cycle were words or musical notes. Other research has shown that sequences composed of verbal elements such as spoken digits or vowels are easier, the ease increasing with the naturalness of the presentation of the item.[179] How could listeners form strings for words or musical notes at high rates?

Neisser argues that maybe they could not: "maybe subjects form unsegmented analogs while listening to such sequences, and subsequently *expand* them into a listing."[180] Subjects may not be able to form single coherent analogs for incoherent sequences of unrelated sounds, but can form coherent ones for words and musical sequences. For speech sounds, this probably occurs because the verbal elements are likely to be acoustically similar (for example, in fundamental frequency) and hence not likely to segregate from one another, and if spoken in a natural sequence, to contain acoustic transitions that hold the sequence together.[181] For musical sequences, the successive tones are likely to be close together in frequency and to therefore be grouped into a coherent stream, allowing within-stream relations, such as musical contour, to be calculated and to become part of the analog. The problem in the ordering of unrelated elements or of tones that are far apart in frequency is that it becomes impossible to code the sequence as a series of relations (e.g., pitch changes). Instead the coding must be of an arbitrary sequence of mental symbols, apparently a more cognitive form of coding that must be done fairly slowly.

Another reason why sequences of meaningful words or familiar syllables may be easier is that they are more easily encoded into strings by the listener. The name by which the item is reported is the same or similar to the sound of the item; therefore no arbitrary translation between sound and name is required. Furthermore the listener is experienced at recognizing verbal items.

We have already seen that the ability to name the order of sequences of unrelated sounds can improve with training. Does this mean that somehow a person can be trained to penetrate, so to speak, through the psychological boundaries within which auditory streams are contained? In some cases, at least, I think that the effects of training on the order-discrimination task can be explained by learning to discriminate the set of alternative sequences by using their holistic qualities rather than by perceiving their components. However, the fact that the experiments on training can be interpreted in this way does not allow us to rule out the possibility that it is possible to learn to overcome the perceptual segregation that occurs in rapid sequences of sounds.

The experiment of Neisser and Hirst might be an example of such learning.[182] There were 24 different possible orders of stimuli and the listeners would have had a hard time remembering separate qualitative features for all of them, even in the 3 or 4 days of practice in which most of the learning occurred. If actual across-stream order information was used by the listeners in this experiment, it was not a spontaneous capability, and therefore falls in the category of the schema-based stream segregation that will be discussed in chapter 4.

In effect, what we have been saying so far is that there are many factors, specific to the identification of order, that do not arise due to stream segregation. Furthermore there is a known limitation of stream segregation itself that must be taken into account when trying to see how it affects the perception of temporal order.

I have frequently noticed in the laboratory that it is easy to recognize the order of the first few and the last few sounds of a long streaming sequence. This observation has also been made in a number of experiments.[183] The ease of ordering the first few sounds is explainable by the fact that stream segregation grows with the number of repetitions.[184] It would follow from this that the first few tones are not yet very strongly segregated. But what of the effect at the end of the sequence? The sequence ought to be most strongly segregated at this point. The ease of detecting order at this point shows that there is more to the detection of order than the effects of stream segregation.

One possibility is that there exists, concurrent with the existence of a stream-based representation of the sequence, another one that preserves a record of the unsegregated sequence and that this memory can be accessed at the end of a sequence (and perhaps at the beginning). It is conceivable that this is the representation that has been called echoic memory.[185] On the other hand, Divenyi and Hirsh have interpreted these "end" effects as resulting from the listener's ability to more easily perceptually isolate these tones from the others because they occupy salient positions in the sequence.[186] To support their interpretation, they point to analogous effects in vision in which a visual target is more easily detected when it is located near the edges rather than at the center of a visual display. In conformity with their explanation, they suggest that it should be possible to perceptually isolate a short sequence that is embedded in the middle of a longer sequence of tones by placing short silences before and after the embedded sequence.

Whatever the explanation of end effects, they do not lend themselves to an explanation in terms of stream segregation. Therefore any test of the effects of streaming itself on the perception of order must eliminate these phenomena. If a short repetitive cycle is used, as in most of the existing research, the effect at the beginning can be minimized by fading the sequence in slowly, gradually raising its intensity from zero to maximum over the course of from 1 to 5 seconds.[187] The effect at the end can be avoided in two ways. One is simply to fade the sequence out slowly. Another is to require the listener to make the required judgment while the cycle is still repeating. Nobody knows why fading the sequence on and off slowly will reduce end effects, but it seems to do so. This might be a fruitful line of investigation and might clarify two questions that are of theoretical interest: (1) What forms of perceptual, or perhaps neural, representation of the sequence are responsible for end effects? (2) What is the perceptual usefulness of the mechanism that produces these effects?

It goes without saying that end effects will be a contaminating factor when the experiment uses short, nonrepeating, sequences (sometimes called one-shot sequences).[188] The effects of stream segregation on the perception of order will be greatly lessened and other effects may dominate. End effects will also be present in experiments in which the listeners are allowed to listen first to one then another cycle of tones.[189] If the signal presentation device is under the control of the listener, so that either cycle can be turned on at will, the listener can create end effects in the process of switching back and forth, creating a new end and beginning each time the switch is made. In the process, the contribution of stream segregation may be held at a rather low level and other perceptual factors may be responsible for any observed differences in difficulty among the various conditions of the experiment.

Despite the various reasons proposed as explanations of the difficulty in reporting the order in rapid sequences, none can explain why it is so much harder to report the order of tones that are in different streams than those that are in the same stream when the two sorts of judgments are made on the identical sequence of sounds. Recall that in the experiment by Bregman and Campbell the within-stream judgment was pretty easy while the across-stream judgment was impossible. No appeal to general difficulties of reporting can explain this difference without recourse to the idea of stream segregation. This illustrates how important it is to have an a priori idea of which sounds will fall into the same substream so as to be able to compare within-stream order judgments to across-stream judgments on the same sequences.

The reader has the right to be wondering, by this time, what all this discussion (of two types of order discrimination and of the fact that different tasks assess these capabilities differently) has to do with the original question—does stream segregation make the perception of across-stream temporal relations difficult. The discussion is intended to show that there are many factors that affect the outcome of an experiment that purports to be measuring the perception of order relations. Not all such experiments tap the same mental mechanisms. Therefore we must be clear as to what it is that the stream segregation mechanism is supposed to affect. Only in this way will we know what kinds of judgments should be made harder by factors that are known to affect stream segregation.

I think that the notion of a stream is equivalent to the notion of a coherent analog. Therefore, using Neisser's language, my claims can be stated as follows: (1) analogs are designed so as to represent sources in the world; (2) parts of the presented material can be excluded from an analog by stream organizing processes; (3) it is analogs, not strings, that are directly affected by stream segregation; when material is presented slowly enough for string formation to occur, primitive stream segregation processes either do not operate at all or are quite weak; (4) with training, listeners can learn to re-extract string descriptions of a stimulus from a retained analog.

Difficulties in the formation of string descriptions may not always arise from the insufficiency of the analog representations of the stimulus. For example, when a subject is asked to report the order of the elements of a recycling sequence, he or she may not have enough time to perform the procedure of converting the analog into a string description. Providing cards for the listeners to arrange to describe the heard sequence allows them to keep track of where they are in the procedure and may change the nature of the conversion task entirely. Warren supports this idea: "Card ordering permitted listeners to break the task into parts by listening for one sound, and then trying to identify the sound immediately preceding or following" (p. 126).[190]

Listening for one sound is an essential part of the above procedure. Yet, from the work of van Noorden, we know that extracting a single sound from a sequence is limited by the "fission boundary" not the "coherence boundary" and therefore is almost unaffected by speed or by the frequency separation between tones.[191] Trying to identify the next sound is an attention-dependent process, and according to the theory that this book is proposing, falls in the province of schema-governed stream segregation, and, as such, is a skill-based process that is affected by learning and by the predictability of the sequence. We can see that the card ordering task is affected by stream segregation only to the extent that the listeners are *unable* to take advantage of the special strategies permitted by the presence of the cards that allow them to defeat the effects of streaming.

Donald Norman and Daniel Bobrow defined two sorts of limitations on the performance of judgments or other responses in experiments on human information processing.[192] They argued that performance can be data limited or resource limited. If you imagine the subject trying to perform a response based upon an internal representation of a stimulus, the performance could be limited by the inadequacy of the stimulus representation (data limited) or of the resources, such as attention or memory, that can be brought to bear on the task. In these terms, what I am saying is that stream segregation affects the nature of one sort of data available to the listener (organized streams), but that performance in a judgment task can also be affected by the resource limitations imposed by the experiment. It is only when the primary limitation comes from the nature of the data itself (the streams) that an experiment will be sensitive to stream segregation. In addition, when one shows that an experimental task is primarily resource limited, it does not rule out the possibility that it is also data limited.

It is therefore necessary to know the strategies that the subjects will employ before we can unambiguously interpret an experiment on streaming. In practice, knowing all the influences on an experiment is not usually possible. As an alternative we must fall back on a method of converging operations in which we do not try to argue that the proof of the existence of some proposed underlying factor such as stream segregation comes from a single crucial experiment. Instead, we try to show that the proposed factor shows its effects in a variety of tasks, each of which requires a different set of other mental resources, skills, or activities. If we are successful, this gives us confidence in the theory. Our confidence will be even stronger if we can explain why certain experiments failed to find any effects. Often such after-the-fact explanations seem suspect. Only if they appeal to well known facts about human psychology or are supported by further analytical experiments can we feel comfortable with them.

This section has attempted to show an effect of stream segregation on the perception of temporal order. The reader will have to judge whether there are enough experiments showing a difficulty in using across-stream temporal relations, and a sufficiently persuasive discounting of the experiments that failed to find this difficulty, to conclude that it truly arises from the stream-forming process. The remainder of this chapter is an attempt to validate the notion of auditory streams and their effects on perception through the use of convergent operations.

Other Measures of Temporal Relations

Considering that the order-reporting task makes such strong use of a specialized form of representation (the string), why has it been so popular an experimental paradigm? Apparently it was taken at first to be an experimental analog of the problem that the brain faces in distinguishing the word "ghost" from "goats".[193] Obviously the brain does not need to form a "string" (or reportable sequence) to distinguish the two words, but can do it on the basis of any sequential or transitional information that distinguishes the two words. Order reporting is an unnatural task and is not normally what we do when we make use of the order of events in natural situations. I believe that the research community has come to a consensus on this point.[194] Therefore, to see whether stream segregation has an important effect on how we use temporal information in more natural cases, we should look for tasks in which the temporal information is utilized rather than reported.

There are a number of tasks in which this is done. One of these focuses the listener's attention on the perception of temporal patterns such as rhythms. A second asks listeners to judge how overlapped in time the sounds from different streams appear to be. A third looks at how accurately a listener can judge the length of a silent gap when it occurs between two sounds that are very qualitatively different, since such sounds might be expected to have a tendency to segregate from each other. A fourth looks at the perceived changes in the speed of a sequence when it segregates into separate streams.

Generation of Within-Stream Rhythms To my mind, one of the most convincing demonstrations that stream segregation strengthens the perception of within-stream temporal relations at the expense of

PART 1: HLH-HLH-HLH-HLH-... etc.

PART 2:

High stream: H-H-H-H-H-H-H-H...

Low stream: -L--- L---L---L-...

Figure 2.26
Part 1: van Noorden's stimulus with a "galloping" rhythm. Part 2: perceptual segregation causes the galloping rhythm to disappear.

between-stream relations is what happens to rhythm. When we listen to a repeating cycle of tones that is gradually speeded up until it segregates into substreams, we are struck by the fact that when it segregates the rhythmic experience seems to change. Instead of hearing a repeating rhythm that is defined by the relative onset times of all the sounds in the sequence, we begin to hear a pair of rhythmic patterns, each defined by the tones in a single stream. If the two rhythms that emerge when the sequence splits are quite different from the original rhythm, it becomes easy for the listener to tell when the segregation has occurred. This effect further strengthens the picture of stream segregation as a scene-analysis process. If the individual streams are the mind's description of the meaningful sonic objects in the environment, then only the rhythmic pattern computed within that stream tells about the pattern of activity of a meaningful object. The between-stream rhythms are likely to be merely chance combinations of within-stream patterns.

In discussing the fact that rhythms are computed within streams, we should try to be more general and to talk about temporal patterns rather than rhythms. A rhythm is only one type of temporal pattern, which is given the name rhythm when it is repetitive. Obviously we can hear temporal patterns, such as those of speech, that are not repetitive.

The appearance of new rhythms when streams split into segregated substreams makes certain experimental tasks easier. This fact was exploited by Leo van Noorden.[195] In some of his conditions, the total sequence was constructed of the alternation of a high tone (H) and a low one (L), and silence (hyphen) as shown in part 1 of figure 2.26. This pattern contained a silence after every three tones so that it generated a triplet or galloping rhythm. The high tone was gradually made higher until the sequence split into two streams. At that point the streams appeared to have the two rhythms shown in part 2 of the figure. Now neither stream contained a triplet rhythm; therefore that global rhythm disappeared from perception. Instead the listener heard two new rhythms, a faster isochronous rhythm of high tones and a slower isochronous rhythm of low ones. This change was clear enough that it assisted the listener in deciding whether the sequence was integrated or segregated.

The emergence of new rhythms when segregation occurs is powerful enough to be used as an experimental measure of stream segregation. This measure has the virtue that it does not require the recognition of the order or the identity of the individual sounds in the sequence, nor is it evident to the listeners what the experimenters are looking for. Therefore it is not susceptible to some of the criticisms of other measures of segregation.[196]

Van Noorden did an experiment that showed how the perception of the rhythmic pattern generated by alternating pairs of sounds becomes less precise when the two sounds are organized into different streams.[197] First the listeners heard an alternation of two tones of different frequencies in which the tones of the higher frequency (A) were situated exactly halfway in time between the tones of the lower frequency (B). When the tones were close together in frequency this arrangement of tones led the listener to hear an alternating rhythm A,B,A,B, ... When they were far apart in frequency, they heard a two-stream percept with an isochronous sequence of tones in each stream.

As well as manipulating frequency separation, van Noorden also varied the temporal position of the higher-frequency tones. During a trial they drifted either forward or backward in time, moving further away from the exact halfway position between the low-frequency tones. This caused the rhythm to change to one in which the nearest pair of tones grouped into a sort of rhythmic unit, producing either a pattern sounding like AB–AB–AB . . . or like BA–BA–BA . . . , depending on the direction of the displacement. The listeners were required to press a button as soon as they could detect this change in rhythm. At a slow rate (400-msec onset-to-onset time), at which there was no compulsory stream segregation, the listener could always hear this rhythm change from a simple alternating one to an iambic or trochaic pattern and this happened even with large differences in frequency. However, at intermediate rates, such as 158 msec onset-to-onset, the experience depended on the frequency difference between the high and low tones. With small frequency differences, where stream segregation did not occur and the sequence remained temporally coherent, the change in rhythm was perceptible with even small off-centerings of the tones. When larger frequency differences were employed at this rate, it took a large off-centering to be detectable. Finally, at high speeds, such as 100 msec per tone, and with large frequency separations, it took very large off-centerings to be detectable.

Another way to describe van Noorden's results is to observe what happens to the temporal threshold (the amount of off-centering) required to detect the change in rhythm at different rates. We want to express the threshold as a fraction of the tone onset-to-onset time at that rate (let us call this the relative threshold). The relative threshold is used rather than the absolute amount of off-centering to compensate for the fact that it takes a proportionately larger shift in a large time interval to affect a noticeable change in its duration.

Van Noorden's results showed a strong interaction between the effects of frequency separation and speed, as might be expected from the known interaction of frequency separation and speed on stream segregation. At very slow speeds, say 400 msec per tone (onset-to-onset time), the relative threshold was quite small (about 5 percent), and was not affected by frequency separation. Presumably this was due to the fact that at low speeds, there is little stream segregation regardless of frequency separation. However, at high speeds, where stream segregation depends very strongly on frequency separation, the off-centering threshold for tones with a 25-semitone frequency separation was about 10 times greater than for tones with a one- or two-semitone separation. This showed that the rhythmic relation between high and low tones was very hard to hear when the tones were in different streams.

The emergence of separate rhythms with increased stream segregation can be used in music to assist the listener in the perception of polyrhythms. A polyrhythm is produced when two different simpler rhythms are played at the same time, for example, when one sound divides each measure into three beats and another divides it into four (this is called "three by four"). Unfortunately, the polyrhythm is often not heard as such but as the more complex cross-rhythm that arises from the combination. But when the component rhythms are carried by two notes of different frequencies, it makes it clearer to the listener that the rhythm being presented is actually a polyrhythm generated by two different rhythms being played at the same time. A good indication that stream segregation is involved in this separation is the fact that the perceptual isolation of the two component rhythms can be strengthened in two ways: by increasing the frequency separation of the two tones and by increasing the speed of the sequence.[198]

Perception of Overlap An odd feature of hearing two segregated streams is that often the elements of the high and low streams seem to overlap in time even when they do not. Suppose you are presented with a repeating cycle formed of an isochronous alternation of high and low tones that forms two streams. Each of the two streams is also isochronous. At first the rate of the two streams seems the same, but after you listen for a while, you are not sure at all. It seems that one of the cycles could actually be faster than the other. You are not sure whether the sounds of the two streams alternate in time, occur at the same time, or are partly overlapped. There has been one controlled study of this effect using an experimental setup in which the listener was required to judge the degree of overlap of two sounds that were rapidly alternating, and also to directly rate the amount of stream segregation.[199] The two sounds were either a pair of tones of different frequencies, a pair of noise bursts filtered at different frequencies, or a tone and a filtered noise burst. In the actual physical sequences there was no temporal overlap of the two sounds. In fact, in some conditions there was a 50-msec silence between them. Nonetheless, the listeners reported substantial amounts of temporal overlap. Some of this perceived overlap came from the continuity illusion, but when the effects of that phenomenon were accounted for, it was found that the remainder of the perceived overlap could be predicted by the degree of stream segregation which, in turn, depended on two factors: (1) the separations of the frequencies of the tones or of the center frequencies of the noise bands, and (2) the speed of the sequence.

Effects on Gap Discrimination The dissociation between the temporal positions of the events in different streams can also be seen in another way. If one is asked to judge the lengths of silences embedded in a stream, the judgment is much harder when the two sounds bracketing the gap fall into separate streams.

This is not something that could be explained though other auditory phenomena such as masking. The effects of the frequency separation of the tones that bracket the gap are the opposite of what you would expect from masking: increasing the frequency separation between two tones decreases the masking effect of one upon the other and makes each of them easier to hear clearly. Nevertheless, it makes it harder to judge the duration of the silent gap between them. Really this is not a contradiction. A decrease in masking means that the tones are dissociated from one another perceptually. This is also what it means to say that it is hard perceive the relations between them (such as the duration of the gap).

An early study of perceived gap duration was done by Jo Ann Kinney.[200] She asked her subjects to judge the temporal gap between sounds that had different frequency separations. Each tone was composed of two adjacent harmonics. To define the gap between tones, she used either a pair of tones or a pair embedded in a longer sequence, and varied the shape of the sequence (e.g., ascending sequence, up-and-down "pyramid," frequency alternation). The listeners were required to discriminate one pattern containing a 50-msec gap from another one in which the gap was shorter. Their judgments were more accurate when the frequency separation was lower. This result appeared regardless of the type of sequence.

A related experiment was done by Fitzgibbons, Pollatsek, and Thomas.[201] Their listeners heard sequences of four sine tones, two high ones (2,093 and 2,394 Hz) and two low ones (440 and 494 Hz). There was a silent gap in one of the intertone intervals. On each trial, the subjects heard two repetitions of one of the sequences, and their task was to determine whether the twice-presented sequence had a gap in some location. They were highly accurate in determining the location of a gap that occurred within either of the frequency groups (high or low), but were extremely poor at detecting a gap between the two frequency groups. The authors invoked the idea of stream segregation to explain their results.

Leo van Noorden made an interesting set of observations on his experiences in listening to a sequence of two 40-msec tones with a variable length silence between them:

> With small [frequency separations] and [short] tone repetition times, the two tone bursts fuse to a single tone burst whose pitch varies with time. When the tone repetition time is increased [longer time gap] the two tone bursts are heard quite separate, but one gets the clear impression of a jump in pitch between them. When [the time interval] is made even longer the impression of a jump in pitch is gradually lost and the two tones appear to be more independent. The jump in pitch is, as it were, postponed until the arrival of the second tone burst; until then, the first tone burst 'stays in your mind'. When the [frequency separation] is larger, a clear transition between 'simultaneity' and a jump in pitch is heard as [the time interval] is varied. The 'simultaneity' at short [time intervals] is characterized not so much by the fact that that the two tones are heard to coincide as by the fact that the observer has no impression of movement: the direction of the jump in pitch cannot be distinguished.[202]

Van Noorden also noted that this loss of a feeling of transition or jump from one tone to the next, which he took as a loss of coherence, depended on the frequency separation. If the latter was small the transition could be heard even with short gaps, while if it was large the transition was lost with short gaps. These results parallel the effects of stream segregation with longer sequences of tones.

Van Noorden also measured how the frequency difference between two tones affected the listener's ability to judge the time gap between them. The listener was presented with two pairs of tones and asked whether the same time interval existed between members of the two pairs. As the frequency separation grew, the detection of the change in the time interval got harder. He also devised a method for comparing the listener's ability to detect changes in the time gap between a high tone (H) and a low tone (L) in two cases: cyclic presentations of the sequence HLH, for example

HLH–HLH–HLH–HLH–HLH–. . .

and spaced repetitions of the sequence HLH, for example

HLH——HLH——HLH–. . . .

He found that the continuous sequence made the judgment harder and made it much more dependent on the frequency separation of the high and low tones (pp. 63–64). This is consistent with the idea that stream segregation, which cumulates over repetitions and decays with silences, was responsible for the effect.

A number of other studies have also found that the judging of the length of a gap between two tones gets increasingly harder as the frequency separation between the tones marking the beginning and end of the gap increases.[203]

Despite the resemblance of the effects in gap discrimination and stream segregation, only one study has made a direct comparison between the two. It was done by Neff, Jesteadt, and Brown.[204] They compared direct judgments of stream segregation to measures of gap discrimination. Although both measures showed an effect of frequency separation in the expected direction, there were certain differences between the behavior of the two. Because of these differences they argue that "gap discrimination may not be related to [stream segregation] in any direct way" (p. 499). It may be presumed that they attribute the difficulty in gap discrimination it to the separation in neural channels stimulated by two signals when they differ a lot in frequency.

The effect of frequency separation on stream segregation judgments showed a much greater variability from subject to subject than did the effect on gap discrimination. This in itself is not a very strong argument that the gap discrimination effects do not derive from stream segregation. I am not convinced that the relative strength of two measures can reveal which phenomenon is primary. To take a fanciful example, suppose we were to compare two ways of measuring a person's gender (and suppose we had an omniscient knowledge of the true situation for each person). In one case we ask a person to check off one of two boxes labeled "male" and "female" on a questionnaire. Suppose this turns out to be 100 percent reliable and valid. Suppose we use as a second method a chromosome analysis and, because of technical problems, this is only 88 percent accurate. Would we be right to conclude that the chromosome difference was only a secondary consequence of the tendency to answer "male" or "female" on a questionnaire? The reason that this sounds ludicrous is that we have a fairly advanced scientific understanding of gender and this makes our use of evidence about relative reliabilities look very naive indeed. The point of this example is that we cannot infer causality or the lack of it from the relative reliability of two effects. The less reliable effect may merely appear that way because it is measured by a method that is more subject to error, where by error I mean the influence of irrelevant factors on the measurement situation. Gap discrimination may just be a very sensitive measure of stream segregation.

What we have to do, instead, is to explore the whole causal nexus surrounding the two phenomena. For example, does gap discrimination get worse whenever any factor that is supposed to increase stream segregation is introduced? Neff and her colleagues varied a factor of this type in their experiment. They embedded a gap discrimination in a longer sequence of tones and varied the rate of the sequence. Sequences had 4, 8, or 16 tones in a fixed time interval; this meant that the presentation rates varied from 50 to 200 msec per tone. Speeding up the sequence increased stream segregation but did not affect gap discrimination. However, in their experiment, no matter how long (i.e., fast) the sequence was, the gap discrimination was always embedded in one of the three final intertone intervals (i.e., near the end of the sequence). As observed earlier, stream segregation is weak at the beginning and ends of sequences, and may be contributing little to the gap discrimination in these positions. This may explain why the speed and length of the sequence did not affect the gap discrimination. Just the same, the presence of a strong gap discrimination effect, unaffected by variables that affect streaming, does seem to support the authors' case that the frequency effect on gap discrimination, or at least part of this effect, may have nothing to do with streaming.

We need further studies to find out. Some of these could be done with complex tones in which the spectra overlap completely and therefore stimulate the same neural channels. For example, we have to know whether increasing the timbre difference between two complex tones of the same fundamental frequency (perhaps by manipulating their brightness) would make gap discrimination worse. Brightness could be manipulated while ensuring that the spectra of the two tones occupied the same frequency regions (though not with the same intensities). Another manipulation would be to vary the difference between the fundamental frequencies of the two tones while keeping them under identical spectral envelopes, as Bregman and Liao did.[205] We also need to know whether across-stream gap discrimination is much worse in the middle of a long sequence than at its ends. By gathering evidence on the connection of gap discrimination to factors such as these, we may be able to sort out the causal links.

Effects on Apparent Rate There is another effect on time perception that seems to be due to the segregation of perceptual streams. It has already been mentioned in an earlier section on factors that affect stream segregation. This is the perceptual change that occurs when two tones are alternated rapidly and repeatedly between the ears or between two different frequency ranges. Under these conditions, the apparent tone rate drops. When a sequence of tones splits into two streams, the rate that is heard is the rate of each separate stream, but when it holds together as a single stream, the perceived rate is the rate of the full set of components. I refer the reader to the earlier section for a fuller discussion. At this point it simply should be mentioned as another effect on temporal perception that may be due to stream segregation.

Conclusions about the Effects on Temporal Relations This section has reviewed a number of experimental and observational findings that show how stream segregation makes a difference in how the listener forms auditory representations of the acoustic signal. It is likely that the difficulty in some of the tasks may be strongly affected by factors that are related only remotely, if at all, to stream segregation. I am thinking of the difficulty in tasks such as reporting the order of sound in a rapid sequence or judging the length of a silent gap between tones of two different frequencies. Despite this qualification, I believe that the weight of the evidence from experiments in which the use of temporal relations *is* affected by the formation of substreams is massive enough for us to conclude that the effect is real.

Because of the variety of measures of the effects of streaming on the use of temporal information, it is tempting to ask what the best measure might be. To answer this we must recollect for a moment what the assumed purpose of stream segregation is. I have argued that its function is to isolate the pattern of sound emanating from one physical source from the patterns emanating from others so that accidental patterns that result from mixtures of sound will not be analyzed as a pattern. The temporal properties by which we recognize events tend to be located within the patterns that are generated by the events themselves rather than in the patterns formed by the accidental co-occurrence with other events. Therefore it is in the perception of the temporal properties of patterns that the effects of stream segregation should be most visible.

The role of stream segregation in isolating the temporal patterns is perhaps most directly seen in the case of polyrhythms. When the frequencies of all the pulses are the same, the listener hears only the complex cross-rhythm even though it is more complicated than the simple component rhythms. The restricted range of frequencies causes the scene-analysis process to conclude that it is all one pattern. Yet when the frequencies of the two components are widely separated, the stream-forming process dictates that only the component rhythms should be heard.

Another clear example is Dowling's demonstration in which a sequence of tones was created by alternating the notes of two different melodies.[206] When the alternate notes (the ones from each melody) were in the same frequency range, the sequence of all the tones formed a new melodic pattern that was unrecognizable. Only when the frequency ranges occupied by the two melodies were separated were the individual melodies audible.

Complete Loss of Across-Stream Information? It is clear that when substreams of sounds are formed, there is a substantial loss of information about the temporal relations between items of different streams. However, it seems that the loss may not be total. For example, when listeners judge whether two orders of a cycle are the same or different they can often do better than chance. Although sometimes these results can be attributed to the fact that stream segregation actually did not occur, this may not be the only factor involved.[207]

There has been another experimental demonstration in which stream segregation does not totally segregate the elements in different streams. Some, but not all, listeners can ignore the segregation into streams when judging the overall tempo of a sequence.[208]

Finally there is a more common example in which the isolation of streams is not complete. In music, two lines of melody can often remain distinct in the sense that you can choose to pay attention to either one or the other. However, the experience is not like the one that you have when you hear two different players practicing different pieces in the same room. When a single piece is involved, although you are aware of the two different lines, you also experience how the two fit together to create the whole piece.

There is only one explanation of this example that comes to mind. For some reason, the mental representation of the piece of music is unitary, although it is experienced as having two parts. This is not an unusual case in human perception. In vision, we can experience the human body as having parts and at the same time as having a unity. Clearly there must be perceptually available information that tells the listener both about wholes and about parts. When an event or object is experienced as being a whole but having parts, we say that it is hierarchically structured. So far I have not considered this aspect of segregation and integration, but I will do so in a later section. For the moment I will continue to deal with the issues of segregation and integration in sounds that are not hierarchically structured.

Competition among Alternative Organizations

Belongingness In the next section, we discuss the effects of the competition among the various factors that favor the organization into streams. Let us begin by looking again at an observation that we discussed in chapter 1. Whenever a total sequence of sounds is experienced as the intermingling of two streams that are more basic, the scene-analysis system seems to be working to place any single sound either in one stream or another, but not in both at the same time. This is what we referred to earlier as the rule of exclusive allocation. An example is seen in the experiment of Bregman and Rudnicky.[209] It will be useful to refer to figure 1.7 of chapter 1 in the present discussion. A rapid four-tone pattern (F,A,B,F) was played to listeners, who were asked to judge whether the pattern formed by tones A and B ascended or descended. This was extremely difficult because the two tones, A and B, were embedded in a larger perceptual organization F,A,B,F, in which the individual pitches of A and B were partly lost as individuals, contributing instead to the formation of the up-and-down shape of a larger pattern. The two patterns F,A,B,F and F,B,A,F had the same general shape. It was also difficult because A and B were embedded in the middle of the pattern. However, when a sequence of captor tones (C) was brought close to the frequency of the F tones, they captured them into a lower stream that was at least partially segregated from A and B. The order of A and B became easier to judge.

This example seems to be governed by the rule of exclusive allocation. The F tones seem not to be able to contribute both to the F,A,B,F up-and-down pattern and the pattern formed by the C and F tones at the same time. It is interesting to note that it is also visually impossible in figure 1.7 to see the two F's as part of the FABF pattern and the horizontal line of C's and F's at the same time. With inspection and effort we can flip the organization from one form to the other, but we feel that we cannot see both at once. It is as if the two organizations compete for the belongingness of the F's.

The idea of competition implies the idea of exclusive allocation. If a sound could be in more than one stream at a time, the notion of competition would be meaningless. What does it mean to compete for something if the two competitors can have it at the same time? Therefore whenever we observe a competition between streams for a sound, we are observing the principle of exclusive allocation in action. The belongingness of an element can shift from moment to moment, but at any one time it tends to be definite.

Experimental Data on Competition A study by van Noorden showed how frequency proximities can compete with one another. He found that a single pair of tones presented once ("one-shot" presentation) tended to remain coherent over much wider frequency separations than they would when cycled in a long sequence.[210] This may have been due to the fact that stream segregation takes time. However, another factor also seems to be playing a role in one-shot sequences: When only two tones are presented, there is no competition for the grouping of the high or the low one. The only sounds available for the two tones to group with are each other. This interpretation is supported by the results with one-shot sequences that consisted of three tones. With "angular" sequences, those in which one pitch interval (the first or second one) ascends and the other descends, perceptual coherence was lost more readily than in "linear" ones (where they both ascend or descend). Although the linear sequences remained as coherent, or even more coherent, than two-tone sequences, the angular ones were much less so. Van Noorden argued that "it follows from the results that the presence of a third tone prevents the perception of temporal coherence when the third tone is close to the first in frequency." He offered an explanation in terms of the

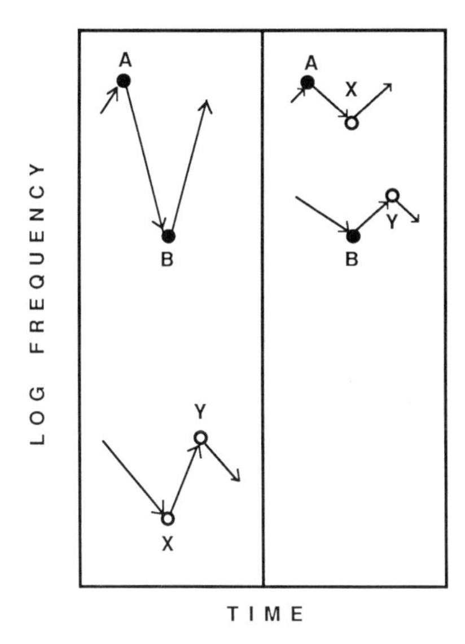

Figure 2.27
Competition of frequency proximities in sequential grouping. Left: A and B enter the same stream. Right: A and B are captured into separate streams. (From Bregman 1978b.)

competition of stronger signals from jump detectors that detect small frequency transitions and weaker signals from detectors for large frequency transitions. Stripped of its physiological trappings, this theory says that frequency proximities are calculated among different pairs of tones and that there is a competition among frequency (and time) proximities in determining the grouping of tones.

At McGill, we have looked more directly at the competition between alternative frequency-based groupings.[211] The listeners heard a cycle of four tones, A,B,X,Y, in which two of the tones, A and B, were always the same but the frequencies of X and Y varied. If only the frequency separation of A and B mattered in determining whether A and B would be heard in the same stream, then their fate should have been the same in all the conditions. However, this did not happen. Figure 2.27 shows two of the conditions in the experiment. In the first, tones X and Y (the open circles) were much lower in frequency than tones A and B (the closed ones). In this case, A and B grouped to form one stream and X and Y formed their own. In the second, shown on the right, X was close to A in frequency and Y was close to B. In this case, A and B were absorbed into different streams, A with X and B with Y. This result can be explained by the notion that all streams are formed by competition among frequency and temporal proximities. Auditory events that are located on the dimensions of frequency and time will group in just the same way as their pictures do when they are drawn as in figure 2.27, with frequency represented by the vertical axis and time by the horizontal. In the first case, shown on the left of the diagram, A and B are closer to one another than to the other tones, so they form a stream. In the case shown on the right, A and X are closest, so they group with one another. It appears the relative separations are important, not just absolute separations.

The competition of grouping was also found in an experiment by McNally and Handel. They contrasted this finding with expectations derived from van Noorden's temporal coherence boundary, remarking that "It should be noted that the tones, although far beyond the frequency separation limit for temporal coherence when trilled separately (van Noorden 1975) stream together when opposed to a buzz and white noise, thereby demonstrating that stream segregation is a function of all the elements in a pattern."[212]

A result reported by Idson and Massaro can also be interpreted as deriving from competition of frequency proximities.[213] The experiment, which we discussed earlier in this chapter, studied the accuracy of discrimination of the pitches of one or more tones when they were followed by an interfering tone. Often, in such cases, following a short tone by a longer one makes it very hard to judge the frequency of the first one with any accuracy. This is called recognition masking by Massaro. In the case of a single tone followed by a second one (the usual recognition masking paradigm), the frequency separation of the tones does not influence the masking.[214]

However, an experiment using a three-tone pattern (ABC) that had all of its tones in the same frequency range showed a different result. When a constant interference tone (X) was placed after each of its tones (that is A,X,B,X,C,X), the ability to discriminate the frequencies of tones A, B, and C depended on how far tone X was away from them in frequency. When it was far away, as in figure 2.28, it was easier to discriminate their frequencies. It is easy to use a stream segregation explanation for these results, with streams based on frequency proximities developing in the high- and low-frequency ranges. But why was the effect of frequency proximity not found in the case of two tones (the standard recognition-masking paradigm)? It is possible that the explanation is this: Frequency proximity may produce streams only when there is a competition of proximities that acts to reject distant frequencies through a tighter coupling of close ones. Unless tones of neighboring frequencies are present to form a best

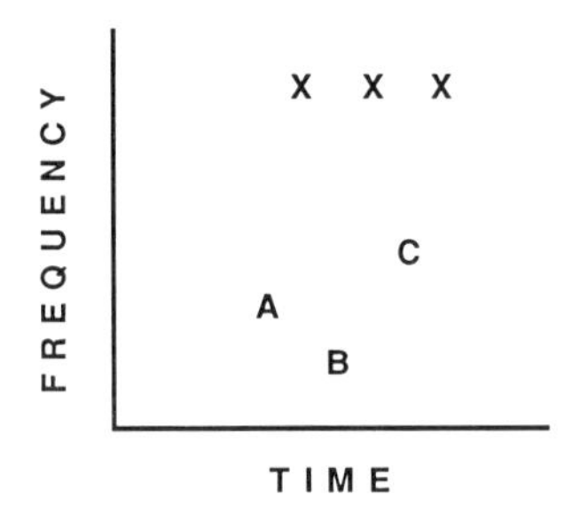

Figure 2.28
Stimuli of Idson and Massaro (1976).

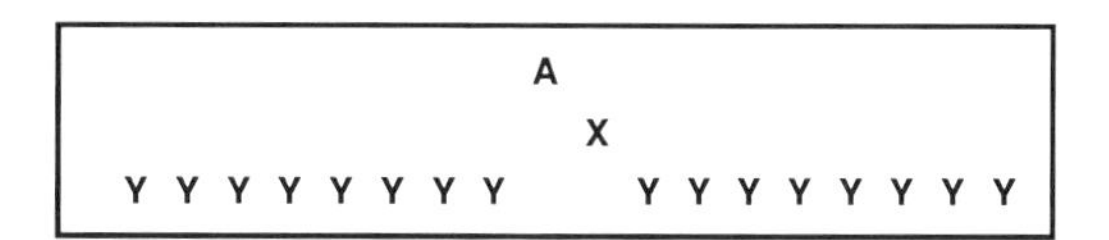

Figure 2.29
Stimulus to demonstrate release from masking.

stream, more distant ones may bind together almost as well as nearby ones. When this binding occurs, the tones become part of a larger Gestalt in which the distinctiveness of its members is lost. This might be what happens in the two-tone sequence.

To reiterate, it is the competitions among frequency proximities that determine grouping and not merely pairwise frequency proximities. Massaro's recognition masking may occur because the target and masker tones have become part of the same stream, which is formed of frequency-separated tones that are nonetheless permitted to group because there are no better tones in their temporal vicinity for each of them to group with. If this is true, the simpler stimulus pattern shown in figure 2.29, which employs a target tone A, a masker tone X, and a set of captor tones (Y Y Y . . .), should also release a target tone A from the effects of the masker. This release from masking should work best when X is distant in frequency from A and close in frequency to the Y's. The reader will notice that this stimulus pattern is very similar to the one employed by Bregman and Rudnicky.[215] The difference is that the latter authors looked for the listener's ability to make order judgments among two elements (A and B), whereas in the present case we would look at how well the listener could discriminate the frequency of a single tone (A). If frequency-proximity effects were found between X and Y tones in this case, it would strengthen the idea that recognition masking is the consequence of the perceptual grouping of tones A and X, which can be prevented if either tone has something better to group with.

The previous examples might have led the reader to expect that the only competition that ever takes place among grouping tendencies occurs along the dimension of frequency. This is not true. It takes place whenever there are multiple ways in which sounds can be grouped. Sometimes the competition is between different criteria for grouping. Such criteria can include all of those that were mentioned earlier in this chapter. They include, for example, similarities in frequency region, in spectral characteristics, in spatial location, and in fundamental frequency. Not very many experiments have put a number of these in conflict with one another. Bregman and Levitan and Bregman and Liao played a repeating cycle of complex tones for their listeners and varied the fundamental frequency and the spectral shaping of the tones.[216] They found that similarities on both dimensions affected the stream segregation of tones and that the effects seemed independent of one another. This means that, in effect, they competed with one another to control the grouping.

Another experiment that clearly demonstrated the effects of competition was the one carried out by Smith, Hausfeld, Power, and Gorta that I described in our earlier discussion of the role of timbre in streaming.[217] It showed that the perceptual grouping was affected by the competition between the grouping tendencies deriving from a number of different factors. These included the continuous trajectory of pitch change as well as similarities in pitch, timbre, and spatial origin. My examination of their data suggests that frequency proximity was the strongest cue, followed by timbre (depending on the instrument), followed by spatial origin, with trajectory the weakest.

Validity of Competition Why is such competition useful for the listener? In most natural situations, sounds that arise from the same source will resemble one another in a variety of ways. The auditory system seems to be designed according to the assumption that the more ways in which sounds resemble one another, the more likely they are to be from the same source. Therefore it computes the similarities among the sounds that it hears and sets up tendencies (one could think of them as votes) favoring each possible grouping. Then it lets the groupings with the highest numbers of votes be formed. It is probably also true that not all these groupings are equally strong. If a stream is formed on the basis of some factor that is very weak (for instance, timbre differences that are not really very different) or if the grouping is the result of a narrowly resolved conflict between opposing factors, we will find weak groupings. The idea behind using the word "weak" is that it is possible that all streams may not have equally strong effects on pattern-recognition processes. A weak one may not enforce the same barriers to attention that a strong one does. It may be easier, for example, to recognize a pattern that is formed of elements from more than one weak stream.

An interesting metaphor for this process is the crystallizing of coalitions at a political convention. People are competed for on the basis of different types of claims until they make commitments to coalesce with certain other delegates. As a coalition gets more members it finds it easier to attract even more of them, and so it goes. In auditory streaming we find both the competition on the basis of many types of similarities, and also the growth of the power of a stream over time. This suggests that, just as the Gestalt psychologists maintained, certain descriptions of grouping have a universal validity.

Limitation of the Principle of Exclusive Allocation Exclusive allocation seems to always hold true when the sounds do not overlap in time, but it may not always be true when sounds are overlapping. Even though Bregman and Pinker found that a complex timbre generated by a mixture of two tones would be suppressed perceptually when the tones were allocated to different streams, the suppression was not complete.[218] There is also a counterexample to the rule of exclusive allocation in the field of speech perception. When two formants are presented at different locations or at different fundamental frequencies, even though the two formants will be heard as distinct streams, a vowel sound, created by combining information across the two simultaneous streams, will also be heard.

The violations of the rule of exclusive allocation will be pursued further in our discussions of fusion and of duplex perception, but for the moment it is sufficient to offer a hint about the explanation that will emerge. In principle, since the information arising from simultaneous sounds gets mixed together in our ears, any evidence for energy in a certain spectral region could actually represent some summation of energy from two or more sources. Therefore the allocation of some of it to more than one source is not always a bad idea. We will want to understand when it will be done and to what degree.

Summary of Effects of Streaming To summarize, the effects of stream segregation on perception seem to be that the auditory system seems to be biased toward computing pattern properties within streams. These pattern properties are what we sometimes refer to as Gestalten or emergent properties. They are based on the relations among the elements of a pattern. In a piece of music, its melody and rhythm are examples. We should not be surprised, therefore, to discover that research on rhythm and melody shows strong effects of stream organization. However, even in simpler experiments, where a listener hears a short pattern of sounds and then is required to recognize the same pattern embedded in a longer one, the target pattern can be easy to recognize if the added sounds in the longer sequence are such that the stream segregation process puts the to-be-recognized pattern into its own stream and the added sounds into a different one.

On the other hand, if elements of the target pattern become parts of different streams, the pattern is almost impossible to recognize. The pattern also becomes difficult to recognize even when stream segregation allows the target pattern to remain together in one stream. This happens when extra sounds also become part of the target's stream, particularly when the added sounds bracket the target pattern so that it becomes part of a larger one and loses its own identity. This may be the explanation of the phenomenon known as "sequential blanking" or "recognition masking."

There are some secondary effects of stream segregation as well. One of these is that the temporal relationships between the elements in different streams are hard to judge. An example of this can be observed when a repeating cycle of tones segregates into two streams on the basis of frequency differences. The listener often has the impression that the two resulting streams are cycling at different speeds, or that the elements of the different streams are overlapped in time. These difficulties may occur because the temporal relationships are not being perceived directly but are being inferred from mental representations of holistic patterns that are formed within streams. Because of this indirect way in which listeners (especially trained ones) can extract information, stream segregation may not always cause disruption in order-discrimination tasks.

There is a phenomenon that is in dispute. This is the effect of frequency separation on the accuracy of judging the length of a temporal gap between a pair of tones. This may be due to stream segregation or to some more fundamental effect of frequency separation.

Taken as a group, the effects reviewed in this chapter are what would be expected if the auditory perception system were focused on within-stream relationships.

Stream Segregation and Vision

Similarities with Vision

The reader will have remarked many times on the fact that in the diagrams in this book the visual grouping that occurs is analogous to the grouping that occurs in the illustrated sounds. This analogy between visual and auditory grouping has been noticed by a host of writers.[219] The diagrams show frequency as vertical distance and time as horizontal distance. The Gestalt laws of grouping by proximity seem to hold as validly for sounds as for visual objects. Perhaps this is one of the reasons for the popularity among speech scientists of showing speech in a spectrographic (frequency by time) representation that is like most of the diagrams of sound in this book.

There is no well-defined way to convert the auditory dimensions to visual ones and still obtain analogous perceptual groupings. Given that I have decided that one horizontal unit on the drawing will represent 1 second of time, the correct amount of grouping will not occur unless I make the correct intuitive judgment about how many vertical units should be equal to one octave in frequency. While this choice seems rather arbitrary, it does show that there exists some mapping for frequency and time into the two dimensions of space that permits some of the auditory grouping processes to be seen visually.

Musical notation also benefits from this analogy. Because of its choice of the two spatial dimensions to represent pitch and time, the visual groupings that emerge often correspond to the auditory groupings that are heard. The analogy is not exact in musical notation and this will be discussed in a later section on perceptual organization in music.

There is another sort of analogy between vision and audition. This is the one between perceived pitch (or frequency) change in sound and perceived spatial movement in vision. Suppose we took a diagram that showed pitch changes over time and relabeled the y axis so that it referred to spatial position in the up-down direction. If we did so, a curve drawn on this diagram would represent a simple form of motion: an object that moves only up or down in the vertical dimension over time. The spatial movement of this object would correspond to an auditory "motion" in frequency. Is there any usefulness to such an analogy? Well, musicians use words such as "pitch motion" or "melodic motion" to describe a change in pitch, and a number of writers have proposed that following a melody is like following an object's motions in space.[220]

This makes us wonder whether there are any analogies between principles of auditory grouping and those that govern the grouping of movements of seen objects. Most of the research on auditory grouping has been done with sequences of discrete sounds, such as tones, and so it has seemed natural to look for an analogy between auditory sequences composed of discrete changes in *frequency* over time and visual sequences that are composed of discrete changes in *position* over time. Fortunately there is a long history of research on how we see such sequences of positions. Sometimes we simply see them as one or more objects that appear at a series of different locations over time, but when the displacements are at the right speed we see a sort of motion that is called "apparent" or "stroboscopic" movement. This is the type of movement that used to be so popular on theatre billboards, where the impression of movement was conveyed by illuminating a sequence of light bulbs at the right time intervals.

The analogy with auditory grouping is fairly straightforward: When we see a series of spatial displacements as motions, this is analogous to hearing a series of tones as a coherent auditory stream.[221] To make the analogy even more exact, let us imagine a visual display in which there are two light bulbs in an otherwise dark room. One is placed about 1 meter directly above the other. The higher one is called H and the lower one L. The lights are to be lit in alternation: H,L,H,L, ... The corresponding auditory situation consists of a pair of tones, a high one (H) and a low one (L). They, too, occur in alternation: H,L,H,L, ... As the speed of alternation of the sequence is increased, the phenomena are quite similar in the two cases. At a very slow speed in the visual case we see the successively illuminated lights but do not have any experience of either of them having moved. In the auditory case, at slow speeds we hear simply a succession of tones with no grouping into streams. At an intermediate speed, in the visual case, we see a light jumping back and forth between two locations. With the tones at an intermediate speed we get an impression of melodic jumps back and forth between the high and low tones; the tones are now part of a single stream.[222]

At a high speed the effect in the visual case is that we no longer see a single light moving up and down in the visual field, but instead we see the two lights, each remaining in one position, flickering.[223] This is analogous to what happens at the high speed with the alternating tones. What we hear is two streams of sound, a high tone repeating and a low one also repeating. The fact that each light flickers continuously and that the flickering of one light appears to have nothing in particular to do with the flickering in the other is analogous to the unrelated repetitions of the two tones when stream segregation occurs. Bregman and Achim have called the visual case "visual stream segregation" and have argued that what is happening is that two streams of visual motion are being segregated from each other.[224] It is hard to think of a single stationary flickering light as a stream of motion, but it is, in effect, a degenerate form of motion. But, by analogy, it could be argued that an unchanging, repeating tone is a degenerate form of auditory pattern.

To see more clearly what it means to say that at high speeds you have a breakdown of the total motion into two streams of motion, we have to look at a more complicated pattern, both in the visual and auditory cases. Instead of having only two events, let us have four. In the visual case, this means four lights arranged in a vertical column, two grouped together higher up and two grouped together lower down. In the auditory case, we have four different pitches, two high ones and two low ones. Let us label the events, going from highest to lowest, as H1, H2, L1, and L2. These labels will be used for both the lamp positions and the tone pitches. Now let us present the sequence H1,L1,H2,L2 repetitively. Let us look, in particular, at the effects at medium and high speeds. At a medium speed, the effect in the visual case is that we see an oscillatory motion up and down between the high and low sets of lights. The effect in the auditory case is that we hear a melody that jumps up and down between the high and low tones in an analogous way.

When the sequence is speeded up we already know what happens in the auditory case. The sequence breaks into two streams, one consisting of an alternation between the two high tones (H1,H2,H1,H2, . . .) and the other of an alternation between the two low ones (L1,L2,L1,L2, . . .). The result in the visual case is analogous. We see two streams of motion, one between the two upper light positions and the other between the two lower ones.[225] This is what Bregman and Achim meant by visual stream segregation.

Figure 2.30
Crossing trajectories of tones.

There is yet one more similarity between auditory streaming and apparent motion and it has to do with the crossing of "motions." Suppose we have a sequence of tones that alternates between a rising and a falling trajectory, crossing in the center as shown in figure 2.30. In this diagram, the numbers represent the order in which the tones are sounded and the horizontal and vertical dimensions, as always, represent time and frequency. With such an arrangement, the perceived streams never follow the individual linear trajectories so as to cross the midpoint. Instead the tones group by frequency range. For instance, one of the streams will be 1, 3, 5, 7, 8, 10, 12. However, if the tones that constitute the falling trajectory are given a different timbre than those that constitute the rising one, two crossing streams can be heard, segregated by timbre.[226]

There is an analogous phenomenon in vision. Suppose four lights are laid out in space as shown in figure 2.31, two high positions, A1 and A2, and two low ones, just below them, B1 and B2. Suppose that at time 1, the two on the left are briefly illuminated and at time 2 the two on the right are. Two of the logically possible apparent motions that can be seen are as follows: (1) a light moves from A1 to A2, while another one moves from B1 to B2; (2) a light moves from A1 to B2, while a second one moves from B1 to A2, the two motions crossing en route. In actual experiments only the first percept occurs. The trajectories prefer not to cross. However, the crossing percept can be easily obtained if we arrange it so that the observer sees the lights A1 and B2 at one distance and the other two lights at a different distance.[227] This difference in perceived depth can be arranged by manipulating the disparity between the images in the two eyes. In this example the preference for grouping of the pairs that have the least retinal separation (the analogy to grouping by frequency proximity) is overcome by introducing a difference on a third dimension (depth). Therefore, depth in this case takes the place of timbre in the auditory example, allowing trajectories to cross on a pair of dimen-

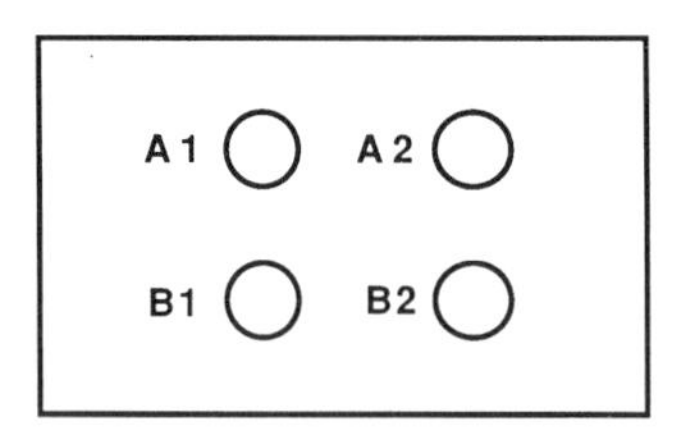

Figure 2.31
Lack of trajectory crossing in ambiguous apparent motion.

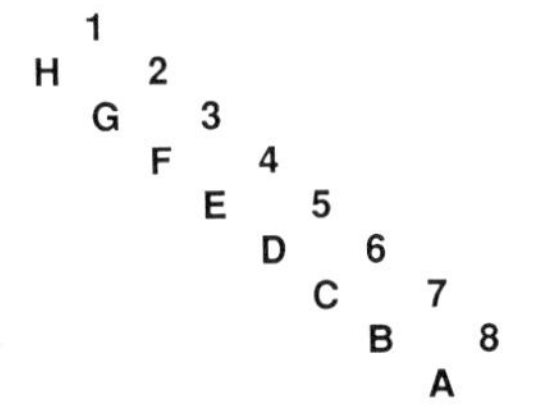

Figure 2.32
Trajectory following in visual apparent motion.

sions as long as there is a third dimension on which the crossing paths differ.

However, despite the analogy between apparent motion and auditory grouping that we see in this example, there are some differences. In visual motion the trajectory effect is much stronger. Let us examine an example of this trajectory effect. We begin by observing that in apparent motion there is a tendency for grouping to be based on spatial proximity. For example, if light A is flashed briefly at one moment and then lights B and C are flashed simultaneously at the next, motion will be seen between A and one of the other two depending on which is closer to A. This tendency for motion to favor shorter paths has been put into competition with a tendency to follow a continuous trajectory.[228] There were two rows of lights, lights 1 to 8 and A to H as shown in figure 2.32.

The lights in a row were flashed in succession (1, 2, 3, . . . and A, B, C, . . .). The two rows were synchronized so that 1 flashed together with A, 2 with B, 3 with C, and so on. This caused two streams of apparent motion, one running down the sequence labeled by numbers and one running up the sequence labeled by letters. You can see that the flash of light 4 was followed immediately by those of lights 5 and E, so that there was a competition at this point between where the descending stream should go next. It could either continue descending through 6, 7, and 8, or else move over to E and run up through F, G, and H. The experiment showed that this choice of direction was not just controlled by which distance was shorter (4 to 5 versus 4 to E), but that the choice was biased in favor of continuing along the same downward trajectory. Similarly, the upward movement seen in the lights labeled by letters was also biased in favor of continuing rather than reversing and running down again. This biasing by trajectory contrasts with the observation that auditory streams will not cross even when hearing them cross would permit us to follow a simple trajectory.

Early in this century Körte noticed a number of regularities in the perception of stroboscopic motion.[229] Among them was his third law that said that for the best apparent motion to be produced there had to be a sort of proportionality between the interflash time interval and the spatial separation of the lights that were illuminated. If the spatial separation was increased, the rate of alternation of the flashes had to be slowed down to obtain a good motion percept. The analogy with auditory stream segregation is clear if we take frequency separation as analogous to spatial separation in vision. As the frequency separation is increased, the alternation of high and low tones must be slowed down to maintain the experience of a single coherent stream. (The coherent stream is the analog of a good motion percept). It appears that Körte's third law also explains the preference for two streams over one stream when the speeds are too high or the separations (visual or auditory) too large. Under these conditions the optimum proportionality for the single single-stream "motion" percept is violated, but a two-stream percept restores the proportionality by reducing the amount of change per unit of time.

The analogy between auditory stream segregation and the breakdown of apparent motion at high speeds has led to the hypothesis that the physiological basis is similar in the two cases. The explanation of the visual case has been the existence of jump detectors.[230] Both van Noorden and Anstis and Saida have proposed that the basis of auditory stream segregation is the tiring out of pitch motion detectors.[231] I will put off a lengthier consideration of this hypothesis until a later section on theoretical explanations of stream segregation. For the moment it is sufficient to point out that the analogy between visual motion and pitch motion has given rise to a common physiological explanation.

The analogy even covers what happens when the auditory or pitch motion is made either continuous or partly continuous. Bregman and Dannenbring found that when there was a rapid alternation between tones that were in a higher and a lower frequency range, the tones broke apart perceptually into a higher and a lower stream.[232] However, they found that the breaking into substreams could be reduced when instead of the tones being discrete there was a frequency glide joining the higher and lower tones. Analogously, Anstis, Giaschi, and Cogan found that prolonged inspection of visual motion between a pair of illuminated spots led to the breakdown in the perception of a coherent stream of motion so that the two spots each appeared stationary and flickering in place (we have interpreted this as analogous to stream segregation).[233] However, they also found that prolonged inspection of sinusoidal real motion never degenerated into flicker but always looked like motion, although the motion had a decreased vividness. Although this experiment did not show it, we know that even continuous motion can exhibit "streaming": if you wave a pencil back and forth in front of your face fast enough you will have the experience of seeing more than one pencil, the dominant perceptual organizations being the pencil in each of the two end positions of the motion where it moves most slowly.

The two experiments show that in both sense modalities, continuous change maintains a single coherent stream better than discrete stepwise change does. This has been interpreted as due to the fact that continuous change stimulates motion detectors better than discrete changes do.[234]

It is important to remember that continuity in frequency change is merely an extreme case of frequency proximity. Looking at it the other way around, the frequency proximity that causes the streaming of discrete sounds is simply a degenerate case of continuity in frequency. By analogy, stroboscopic movement in vision is just a degenerate case of continuous real movement. If the analogy between pitch streams and visual movement is a good one, then we should be able to find an effect in vision that is analogous to what Bregman and Dannenbring found with a semi-ramped condition.[235] In this condition, the successive tones were not joined by complete frequency glides but by glides that had their center portions missing; the end of a high tone, for example, would begin to glide downward to the next low tone, pointing to it in some sense, and the onset of the low tone would actually be a brief glide coming from the direction of the previous high tone. They found that the effects of the partial glides, while weaker than the full glides in holding the successive tones together, still had some beneficial effect.

By analogy, semicontinuous motion should be clearer than stroboscopic discrete motion. Semicontinuous motion could be set up by using a pendulum swinging back and forth between two locations and using a screen to block out the middle part of the movement from view. In fact this setup has not been thought of as a special case of apparent movement but as a different effect with its own name, "the visual tunnel."[236] In this phenomenon, two objects are in motion. One goes behind a screen where its motion stops. The other object begins its movement behind the screen and emerges from behind the screen in a direction that continues the trajectory of the first object. The viewer will often experience a continuous motion despite the missing information about what is happening behind the screen. We can see that the visual tunnel effect falls between the cases of true continuous motion and the typical laboratory demonstration of apparent motion. Apparent motion is simply the case in which the screen is so wide that it covers every part of an oscillatory motion except the endpoints that are just visible as they poke out past the ends of the screen. Furthermore the screen is not usually explicitly shown to the viewer in the apparent motion paradigm.[237]

Earlier, I made the argument that auditory stream segregation served a useful function in dealing with the environment. I presented it as one of a set of heuristics that grouped sounds that had the same source in the environment together. I think the same argument can be made for the organization of perceived visual movements. In a sense, I am trying to answer a view that holds that the parallel phenomena hold because the auditory and visual systems just happen to be built in analogous ways or built out of the same stuff. I do not think that it "just happens to" at all. The same kinds of problems exist in the grouping of discrete glimpses of motion as in the grouping of discrete moments of sound. The stroboscopic motion experiment has been viewed as essentially a laboratory abstraction and as having little to do with real world situations. We can see that this is not true when we realize that the experimental situation with a light appearing in only the end positions of the motion is just the same as a continuous motion, part of which is blocked from sight by a screen. The stroboscopic case is just the limit when the screen gets so large that only the endpoints of the motion are visible. In the natural environment, there are screens all over the place. Objects in motion tend to disappear behind things that obstruct our view of them and then appear again on the other side, possibly disappearing again, and so on. Imagine tracking a fleeing animal in a forest and obtaining glimpses of the motion between the trees. To make matters worse, there can be more than one fleeing animal and it is important to track the movement of just one of them at a time. Therefore it is necessary to correctly group the motion fragments into continuous motions of single objects and to segregate the motions of different objects. That is why the laws of apparent motion exist. For example, if an animal in motion disappears from view for a longer time, it is likely to reappear further away from the last place than if it had disappeared for only a short time. This must be the reason for Körte's third law concerning the rough proportionality between time and the amount of displacement.

Why should Körte's law be useful in audition? Why should a sound have to be more similar if it occurs again after a very short time and less similar if it occurs again only after a longer time? If we think of a sequence of disconnected sounds as being produced by some activity that stops and starts, perhaps there is no usefulness to such a law. But if we think of a continuously changing activity that we are able to hear only intermittently because of masking by other sounds, then the law makes sense. The activity is likely to have changed more the longer we have been unable to hear it. This suggests that many of the perceptual rules that apply to tone patterns were not evolved to integrate such intermittent sounds but to integrate continuous sounds that were audible only intermittently.

Therefore there are similar ecological reasons for the existence of stream segregation in the two sense domains.

Interactions with Vision

Perhaps a more profound reason for the similarity of principles of organization in the visual and auditory modalities is that the two seem to interact to specify the nature of an event in the environment of the perceiver. This is not too surprising since the two senses live in the same world and it is often the case that an event that is of interest can be heard as well as seen. Both senses must participate in making decisions of "how many," of "where," and of "what."

It appears as though, either at birth or shortly afterward, the human brain is already prepared to respond to correlations in the temporal patterns of vision and audition. Young infants are already extremely sensitive to such correlations. If you present an infant with two simultaneous visual recordings of different women speaking and at the same time present the audio recording of the speech of one of them from a speaker located halfway between the two images, the infants prefer to look at the face that belongs with (and therefore is synchronized with) the voice they are hearing.[238] Furthermore, the time that an infant will spend looking at a videotape of a woman reciting nursery rhymes is significantly reduced if a 400-msec lag is introduced between the picture and the sound.[239]

The value of having a brain that is already prepared to coordinate the two sense modalities has been stated clearly by O'Leary.[240]

> The coordination of the two systems would constitute a marked advantage for a neonate entering an unfamiliar world. Many objects emit sounds which change over time in a manner covariant with their (visually perceivable) motion: faces move as people talk; the sound of a box or toy covaries with its motion as it is dragged along the ground; the sound of leaves rustling in the wind covaries with the swaying of the tree's branches.

Not only are people sensitive to correlations between temporal patterns in audition and vision but they use each sense to correct the scene-analysis decisions of the other one, as we can see in the following example. Subjects in an experiment were presented with a simultaneous auditory and visual display.[241] The auditory display was a typical stream segregation arrangement, with a loop of three high and three low tones, alternating between high and low tones. The visual display was a visual stream segregation setup using six dots, three high (in space) and three low, also alternating between high and low. First, in a pretest, the experimenters assessed separately for each sense modality the speed at which the sequence would split into substreams for each of four separations in "height" (frequency or spatial location). In the main experiment, they presented the visual and auditory displays in synchrony. Each tone was associated with a dot that had the corresponding "height" and was presented in synchrony with it. On each trial of the experiment, one of the two dimensions (visual height, for example) was designated as the target dimension. It was the streaming on this dimension that was to be influenced by what happened on the other dimension (in this case, frequency height), which was called the inducing dimension. Based on the information gleaned from the pretest, the experimenters were able to choose separation values for the visual and auditory stimuli so that the streaming on the target dimension would be ambiguous and the streaming on the inducing dimension clear (definitely one stream on some trials and two streams on others). The goal was to see whether the ambiguous streaming would be influenced in favor of one versus two streams by what was happening in synchrony on the other dimension. The experimenters reported consistent but small effects. Visual streaming was affected by only about 5 percent and auditory by 8 percent. In this experiment, of course, the subjects had a clear presentation of both the visual and auditory stimuli. Often, in real life, some of the auditory or visual information would be missing or unclear; therefore larger induction effects might be expected.

Sometimes the interaction of the two senses can create interference. If you create an artificial laboratory setup in which the senses give flatly contradictory information, the decisions of the individual sense are interfered with. Suppose a visual apparent motion oscillates back and forth between a left and a right position, and in synchrony with the visual events, a sound is presented through headphones to either the corresponding ear or the opposite ear; in this case, the sound will affect the apparent movement. When the sound is presented to the opposite ear, there is an inhibition of apparent movement.[242] Even if the sound is presented to the ear corresponding to the light, if the speed is too slow for the sound to give the sensation of moving back and forth between the ears, the corresponding visual motion can be inhibited even though it would have been experienced at that combination of speed and horizontal separation if the sound had not been there.[243]

Other research that has synchronized light flashes with sound pulses has shown that the apparent location of events in one modality can be affected by our localization of the events in the other one. This has been named the ventriloquism effect after the ability of stage ventriloquists to make an audience believe that the speech of the dummy is actually emanating from the dummy's mouth. Common belief has it that ventriloquists can actually throw their voices, but we skeptical psychologists prefer to see it as a perceptual illusion in which the ventriloquists' words, rather than being correlated with their own facial movements, are correlated, instead, with the movements of the dummy's face. In a laboratory version of this effect, subjects were asked to point to locations of *both* visual and auditory signals, sequences of light flashes and sound pulses that occurred simultaneously in discrepant positions. Effects in both directions were found, but the effects on auditory localization were much greater.[244]

Not only does the correlation of events registered by the two senses tell us how many events have occurred and where, but also what the events were. An example is lip reading. We are aware that the hearing impaired use this method of recognizing speech extensively. We are less aware, however, of how much the normal listener also employs it. It is much easier, for example, to follow the speech of a particular talker at a crowded party when you can see the person's face.[245]

We unconsciously combine visual and auditory information. An amazing proof of this was given in an experiment by McGurk and MacDonald.[246] The subjects saw a videotape of the face of a person pronouncing a consonant-vowel syllable (for instance "ga-ga") but the sound track had been altered. Although it was in synchrony with the picture, some of the phonemes were altered (for example "ba-ba"). The result was that the subjects heard sounds that were a blend of what they received by eye and by ear (in the present example, "da-da"). The illusory "da-da" in our example, when actually spoken, has some of the acoustic qualities of the actually presented "ba-ba", but is pronounced with the lips open, like the visually presented "ga-ga". As an indication of how unconscious the integration is, the listeners did not experience the final percept as a conclusion derived from conflicting evidence but as the actual sound that they heard. I was present at a demonstration of this illusion by McGurk and was astounded to discover that with my eyes closed I heard the sound that was actually presented but that with my eyes open I truly heard the illusory blend. Apparently conscious knowledge of what is happening cannot prevent the illusion.

The correction of one sense by another has great utility. The senses operate in different ways and are good at different things. Sound misses some aspects of events because of reflections. The reason for this is that the reflections of sound mix with the original waves in the ear of the listener in such a way as to obscure some of the properties of the original source. Although reflection of light also occurs, the eye, with its lens and two-dimensional retina, can distinguish original from reflected light by the direction from which it is coming with greater precision than the ear can and can also keep the two more distinct by registering them at different places on the retina. The ear, however, has certain advantages over the eye. Sound can bend around large obstructions whereas light cannot. The best strategy then is to combine the information from the two. The human nervous system even goes one step beyond this. It not only combines the information but goes back and corrects the low-level description that is specific to each sense organ. This seems a little odd. If all that needs to be done is to combine the information from the two senses, the perceiver might simply take some combination of evidence and store the resulting decisions in some sense-independent description of the environment. It would not be necessary to go back and correct the auditory and visual descriptions themselves. But apparently the human nervous system takes the latter approach. Why should it? Perhaps the answer is that the sensory record of an event, say the auditory one, is used again by the auditory system in combination with other auditory records to compute new auditory relations. By going back and correcting the raw auditory record and not just the abstract conceptual one, the brain may guarantee that subsequent within-sense computations will be correct.

Theoretical Explanations of Stream Segregation

Scene Analysis and Other Forms of Explanation

Naturally the existence of the sequential grouping of sounds and the stream segregation that it gives rise to has led to a certain amount of theorizing. The theories fall into two categories, physiological and functional. The former tries to explain the effects by appealing to pitch motion detectors or other brain mechanisms. The explanations of the second type try to describe laws of auditory perception itself without reference to physiological structures in the brain.

Physiological Hypotheses
Some of the physiological explanations have concerned fairly peripheral mechanisms of the auditory system. An early hypothesis, offered by van Noorden, was that "overlapping groups of hair cells have to be excited if temporal coherence is to be heard" (p. 21).[247] Two facts made him believe this. The first was that frequency separation, which we know to be effective in perceptually segregating sound, corresponds to a spatial separation of stimulation on the basilar membrane of the inner ear. The second fact was that when he was listening to tones that alternated between the two ears he could never hear them as a single stream. Obviously the tones in different ears could not be stimulating overlapping groups of hair cells, since each ear had its own separate hair cells. The overlap hypothesis was, however, damaged by subsequent findings. We know now that you can integrate sounds that alternate between the ears as long as the energy at the ear that is being stimulated is balanced by some energy (a noise burst or a drone) at the opposite ear.[248] So if you rapidly alternate a series of tones between the ears but accompany each tone by a sound at the other ear, the listener will, contrary to van Noorden's observation, be able to hear the melodic pattern carried by the alternating tones despite the fact that alternate tones are stimulating different hair cells. The overlap theory also has the defect of not accounting for the effects of speed and its interaction with frequency separation in controlling segregation. Nor does it deal with such subtleties as the effects of context that are described further on.

Van Noorden, himself, found two reasons to criticize this theory. First, he noted that listeners can direct their attention so as to select a subsequence of tones on the basis of their loudness. Since tones of different loudness still mostly stimulate the same hair cells he concluded that "contiguity at the level of the hair cells is not a sufficient condition for observation of temporal coherence" (p. 29). He also took note of the tendency for pure and complex tones of the same fundamental frequency to segregate with one another despite the fact that their stimulation of the hair cells coincides at the fundamental. We should also recall that the results of Bregman and Liao show that complex tones can segregate from one another even when they have a complete overlap on the basilar membrane providing they have their peaks of spectral energy at different frequencies.[249]

The theory that segregation arose if nonoverlapping cells were stimulated was an attempt to deal with the effects of frequency separation on perceptual integration. The next theory that I shall discuss attempted to explain two effects: (1) the interaction of frequency separation with speed of presentation and (2) the fact that frequency-based streaming increases with prolonged listening. The theory was proposed independently by van Noorden and by Anstis and Saida.[250] I have already commented on the theory of Anstis and Saida in an earlier section on the cumulative effects of listening upon stream segregation. Both theories proposed that a change in frequency is registered in some physiological structure whose job it was to detect changes in frequency. Noticing the similarity between stream integration and apparent motion, these authors speculated that the phenomena in both sensory domains were the result of the activity of "change detectors." Both theories also proposed that when a stream splits into substreams, as a result of a high event rate or a large frequency separation, the splitting occurred because these frequency-jump detectors could not follow such a large jump at that speed. The theorists also cited the physiological findings on the existence of cells in the cortex that are sensitive to frequency changes, and both explained the increase in streaming that happens with prolonged listening as resulting from a reduction in the sensitivity of these detectors as a consequence of repeated stimulation.[251]

At the moment there are pieces of data that these theories (more accurately, this theory, since the theories are identical) cannot handle. It is possible that the theory could be expanded to accommodate them, but at the moment it has not been. The first is this: The question of whether two tones in a sequence will or will not be perceived as part of the same stream does not depend only on the particular proximity, in frequency or in time, of the two tones that we are talking about, but on competitive tendencies for grouping with other tones. At the very least, the theory would have to be expanded to state that transitions in frequency are being detected for all pairs of tones that occur within some range of one another and not just for transitions between adjacent tones. The closer the two tones are to each other in both frequency and time, the stronger the signal from the detector that is responding to that pair. The grouping that finally results depends on which detector puts out the strongest signal. Hints about expanding the theory in this direction are present in both of the works that I cited but are not worked out explicitly in either one.

Another difficulty is that while Anstis and Saida proposed that the adaptation of the detectors was frequency-specific and presented evidence in support of this, the frequency specificity of the jump-detector adaptation failed to show itself in an experiment by van Noorden that I describe in some detail in chapter 4.[252] Instead of having tones alternate between two frequency regions as a way of creating incoherent sequences, he generated a semirandom sequence

A B A B A B A B A B ... etc.
C C C C C

Figure 2.33
Alternation of pure and complex tone as in Bregman and Pinker 1978.

in which the frequency of each tone deviated from that of the previous one (randomly upward or downward) by a certain number of semitones. On each run of the experiment, the average absolute deviation in semitones from one tone to the next was set at a particular value and each actual deviation was allowed to vary by at most one semitone from this average. The listeners adjusted the speed of the sequence to the fastest rate at which a single coherent stream could still be heard with no tones detaching themselves into a separate stream. The usual increase of segregation resulted from increases of the intertone frequency jump. What is more important is that the results were about the same for these random walk sequences as for a condition in which the sequence stayed in particular frequency regions longer. This latter condition resulted from requirements for a strict alternation of direction of jump and a small variability in the amount of jump. The sequence tended to hop up and down in a given frequency range for a longer period of time. According to the theory, the detectors should have become more tired out in this latter type of sequence but there was no evidence for more segregation with these sequences.

Another fact that is left out of this theory is that a separation in space or a difference in timbre of the tones acts in much the same way as a frequency difference and therefore the theory would have to expand itself to incorporate timbre change detectors and spatial change detectors as well. The need for explaining timbre-based segregation is the more complex requirement since there may be many dimensions of timbre that affect perceptual grouping, requiring each aspect of timbre to be detected by a different detector (if we were to have grouping that was based on each of these dimensions).

The theory, in its present form, is also unable to account for sequential capturing. My earlier discussion of the theory of Anstis and Saida pointed out the difficulty in explaining the results of the experiment of Bregman and Rudnicky on the capturing by one stream of tones that would otherwise belong to another stream.[253] The same difficulty occurs in a different form in the experiment of Bregman and Pinker.[254]

The stimulus pattern is shown in figure 1.16 of chapter 1 and is reproduced schematically in figure 2.33. It rapidly alternates a pure tone A with a complex tone that has frequency components B and C. The experiment showed that one of the pure tone components (say B) could be captured by the preceding pure tone into a sequential stream, A,B,A,B. . . . This capturing can dissociate it from the complex tone BC of which it is a part. The strength of the capturing grows weaker as the capturing tone, A, is moved further and further away in frequency from B. The capturing by proximity resembles the proximity effects in stream segregation and furthermore the repeating sequence A,B,A,B . . . has the perceptual properties of an auditory stream. However, the detector theory cannot deal with this phenomenon. The detectors might conceivably detect the frequency transition between A and C, become tired out, and not link them sequentially, but this does not in itself explain why tone B gets factored out of the BC complex.

Perhaps the theory could be extended to accommodate this example. It is interesting to carry out an exercise along these lines. Let us make a number of suppositions. The first is that that the detectors treat *no change* as a form of change. The second is that the strength of the signal that is output from a change detector (or perhaps from an array of such detectors) is proportional to the degree of frequency change, with a minimum output when there is no change. Suppose also that all transitions within a certain temporal range are detected unless the onsets of the two tones are simultaneous (in which case the relation between them cannot properly be thought of as a transition at all). In order to accommodate the facts about the effects of speed, we will have to introduce detectors of *temporal* separation as well. Finally, we will suppose that the frequency and time proximities that are detected in this way will compete to form streams. In this formulation, tones will be grouped with those neighbors that provide the lowest jump-detector output and that have the lowest temporal separation, the two factors of frequency separation and time separation being combined in some mutually supportive way. Either large frequency transitions or long temporal separations (or both) would contribute to the barrier against grouping, and the groups would be formed accordingly.

Notice that the effects of speed fall out automatically from this model. If we speed things up, then we decrease the time between tones without affecting their frequency separation, and the temporal distance between nonadjacent tones does not inhibit their grouping as much as their frequency separation does. Therefore nonadjacent tones will group as long as they close together in frequency.

The effects of continuous listening in increasing stream segregation would be explained as follows. Repeated listening modifies the output of the array of frequency transition detectors such that it starts to behave as if the frequency differences were larger than they really are. This would have the effect of increasing the contribution of frequency separation relative to temporal separation in the decision of whether to group a particular sequence of tones.

Applying this theory to the example of capturing a tone out of a mixture of tones, all we have to say is that the AB separation is detected and since it is a small separation, it contributes to the integration of A with B. A will not group with C because the frequency separation is greater. We may have to talk about the tendency for B to group with C, but that is best left for the chapter on spectral integration.

As the astute reader will already have noticed, the theory really works because it is simply a neural version of the Gestalt rule of grouping by proximity where frequency separation and temporal separation both contribute to the perceptual grouping of tones in the same way as the two dimensions of visual distance in a picture contribute to the grouping of visual elements.

Even the theory as expanded in this way faces a difficulty. This is that the buildup of the stream segregating tendency can occur with no frequency transitions at all. Some unpublished experiments that I carried out at McGill with the assistance of Tina Dornbusch were based on the stimulus pattern used by Bregman and Rudnicky.[255] That pattern used a series of tones at a single frequency to capture some later tones. The unpublished study simply varied the number of tones in the capturing series from one to four and found that the longer the series the better the capturing. Researchers in Darwin's laboratory have found similar effects of number of tones in a capturing series when trying to capture a tone from within a vowel spectrum.[256] The increased capturing could not be due to changes taking place in frequency-jump detectors with repeated activation because there were no frequency jumps in the capturing series. Instead, the results suggest that the narrowing of the criteria for inclusion in a stream that takes place with increased listening is not caused by rapid jumps back and forth between two different pitches (or between two different sets of tones differing in any other way) but to the buildup of an "expectation" for tones with certain properties that occurs when you repeatedly hear tones with two distinct sets of properties and no tones that have properties in between. We learn that the distribution of tones in our multidimensional acoustic space is not uniform and that certain areas in this space are heavily populated. This learning may encourage the formation of streams in these regions.

Functional Explanation

We have seen what the flavor of physiological explanations for stream segregation would be. Let us now look at explanations of a different sort—functional explanations. These try to view the perceiver as a functioning system and to determine rules that govern the system. Often, use is made of metaphors that employ ideas from current technology. We will see an example of this in the idea that the tones that become members of a stream can be viewed as having passed successfully through a filter that has rejected the tones that are not in the stream. Functional explanations come in two flavors, those that talk about the parts of the process as if they were mechanisms and those that talk about the purposes of the parts. Let us take these in turn.

Mechanistic Forms of Explanation

Mechanistic explanations of two sorts have been offered. One tries to explain stream segregation by processes that operate on a purely local level. By this I mean processes that look only at the relation between an adjacent pair of sounds. In contrast to these, there are theories that use the properties of an entire sequence of tones to decide what sort of grouping will occur. We can refer to these as theories that use global rules rather than purely local ones.

Local Rules

One of the theories that employs local rules was offered by van Noorden.[257] He was thinking of the type of experiment in which there is a rapid sequence of tones of different frequencies; at slow speeds the sequence remains coherent, and the sequence splits into two streams when it is speeded up. He thought of the process that accepts a sequence of tones into a coherent stream as a sort of filter that passes the next tone through it if the filter is tuned to a frequency that is near the frequency of that tone. It would obviously have to be a self-adjusting filter that would sense the frequency of the incoming tone and then shift its tuned frequency in the direction of that tone. One of the properties that van Noorden proposed for the filter was that it could not shift its tuned frequency very quickly, but had only a limited velocity of change. At a slow speed, this would be no problem and the filter would be able to keep up with the jumps in frequency, passing all the incoming tones into the same stream even if they were widely separated in frequency. However, as the sequence was speeded up, the relatively sluggish filter would not be able to keep up with the rapid changes in frequency and the elements of the sequence would no longer all be passed and treated as parts of a coherent stream.

Norman has referred to the process that must switch from one frequency to another as "attention" and has reminded us that we can attend to only a limited number of things at once.[258] He has proposed, in particular, that attention can focus only on a limited range of frequencies at any one time and that when the incoming tones fall outside this range, the attentional process begins to have difficulties.

Both the theories of van Noorden and Norman explain the loss of coherence of a sequence in terms of the relation between the present frequency to which a tunable process is set (a filter in one case and attention in the other) and the frequency of the next incoming tone. This is the only relation that counts, and that is why I have classified these theories as ones that use local rules. The difficulty with such theories is that they cannot take context into account. We have seen that frequency proximities compete when streams are being formed and there is no way for this to happen in either of these two theories. Neither is there any provision for the cumulative effects of listening, although one could imagine saying that the filter (or attention) gets gradually tired of re-tuning itself. This would serve much the same theoretical purpose as Anstis and Saida saying that frequency-transition detectors become habituated or put out a weaker signal with repeated use.[259]

A theory that is related to the two we have just discussed was offered by Idson and Massaro.[260] These authors use an information-processing framework in which the nervous system is described as performing computations on the sensory input. Their argument about why tones in different frequency ranges are treated independently of one another is that the processing system may be limited as to the frequency range over which exact pitch intervals (such as those that define a melody) can be computed. As in the previous two theories, the segregation occurs because an integrative process breaks down (in this case, a calculator of pitch relations). Like the other two, it has trouble with the striking fact that in stream segregation not only does the single-stream integration break down but that, in addition, two new integrations (streams), each with its own coherent structure, are formed.

It is not clear how the breakdown of an integrator (a filter, or attention, or a relation calculator) can leave us with two nicely packaged streams.

The strategy taken by these theories has been to attribute the loss of coherence of the sequence to the fact that not all the tones can be dealt with by some integrative process, and that "being able to be dealt with" is what defines a stream. In that case, there is never more than one stream.

If we get the impression that there are two, the argument might continue, it is just that when we shift our attention (or "filter," or "computer of relations") into a new frequency region it creates a stream in that region and we feel that the stream was there all along. This feeling, though, is wrong. Only one stream at a time is created by this process. In fact, calling it a stream is misleading. A stream is merely what happens to be dealt with by this process. There can never be more than one at a time.

Handling this set of theories as a group requires us to determine whether more than one stream can exist at a time. This is a difficult problem. Nobody denies the fact that attention has a very limited scope. We cannot pay attention to everything at once. When we listen to a sequence of tones that has split into substreams, we have the impression that there are two streams but that we are unable to pay attention to both of them at the same time. A straightforward incorporation of this fact into a theory would be to say that the streams are formed by some other process, not the one we call attention, but that attention can select one of these already formed streams for further processing. But how could such a theory be verified? We can report on some experience only when we are paying attention to it. Does a tree falling in the forest make a sound if there is nobody to hear it? Does an auditory stream exist when we are paying no attention to it? We can leave the first question to philosophers, but unfortunately the second one is our responsibility. Can one ever discover whether a stream exists when we are not paying attention to it?

The argument made by Bregman and Rudnicky is that a stream can be said to exist if it has an effect on the contents of consciousness even though the stream itself is not being consciously attended to.[261] An attempt was made by these authors to show that an unattended stream could capture members from a stream that the listener was attending to. We have discussed this experiment before and diagrammed it in figure 1.7 of chapter 1. The central part of the sequence was a four-tone pattern, FABF. The listeners were asked to judge whether tones A and B formed an ascending or a descending pair. It was a hard task, and to do it the listeners had to pay close attention to tones A and B. There was no difficulty in hearing A and B in the same stream. The problem was that the F tones were also in the same stream. The four tones together formed a pattern and the subpattern involving B and C was hard to extract. However, when a series of capturing tones, labeled C in figure 1.7, preceded and followed the F tones, they captured the latter into a stream with them. This seemed to remove them from the same stream as A and B, and for this reason the order of A and B was easier to report.

Bregman and Rudnicky argued that this result showed that two streams existed at the same time. The first stream was the one containing A and B. Since the report was to be about A and B and the listeners were trying hard to hear them and were able to detect their order, they must have been the object of attention. This would put them into the same auditory stream in anybody's theory. The authors also argued that the sequence of C's was a second stream that was in existence at the same time. How do we know that the C's really were a stream and not just a sequence of unattended tones? In what ways were they acting like a stream? First of all, they were able to capture the F tones out of the stream that contained A and B. We know that the F tones would have been in the same stream as A and B if the C tones had not been present. Capturing new tones is a property that we have already postulated that streams have. Therefore the C sequence is acting like a stream. Second, the closer the C tones were in frequency to the X tones, the better they captured them. This is an example of the frequency proximity effect that is always seen in stream segregation. Third, from unpublished research in our laboratory at McGill, it appears that the more C tones there are preceding the F tones, the better they capture them. This is an example of the buildup in the strength of a stream with the passage of time that was described by Bregman.[262] These are the reasons for considering the C tones to actually be a second stream.

There is one final question. How do we know that the C stream was in existence at exactly the same time as the AB stream? The answer involves recalling first that the subjects were able to detect the order of A and B. Therefore the AB stream was in existence at that moment. Furthermore they were able to do so because the F's were being captured by the C stream at that same moment. Therefore it seems that the two streams were active at exactly the same time.

The utility of grouping tones even though they may not be in awareness may be that this makes it easier to reject them as a group. We could call this method the "wrap up all your garbage in the same bundle" heuristic.

The existence of simultaneous streams is a challenge to any theory that sees the sounds that have been left out of the currently attended stream as existing in a wholly unorganized state. This includes all theories in which only a single grouping process is active at any moment. The theories of Norman, van Noorden, and of Idson and Massaro are of this type. In fact, any theory that uses only local relations to determine streaming will fall into this category; however, the use of global relations will not necessarily prevent a theory from falling into the class of one-stream theories.

Clearly something very special is happening to auditory material when we are paying attention to it, but it seems that even when we are not doing so, it is being organized. It is this sort of reasoning that has led me in the past to propose that there is at least a primitive structuring of streams that occurs without the involvement of attention.[263] I would like to call it "primitive stream segregation." In so naming it, I mean to contrast it with schema-based stream segregation, a process that involves attention and is affected by different factors than the primitive process, which I see as simpler and innately determined.

My current view is that that the detailed conscious perception of a sequential auditory structure (a stream) is the result of a description-forming process that is at a higher level than primitive grouping. But the organization and packaging of the sensory evidence to facilitate the construction of such a percept is done in parallel for more than one cluster of evidence at the preattentive level.

Global Rules

This brings us to another major group of theories that uses global rules to determine sequential integration. That is, the grouping of a pair of sounds with one another does not depend solely on the relation between that pair but on their relations to a larger group of sounds.

The theory of Mari Riess Jones is one of those that uses global rules to determine grouping.[264] It sees auditory integration as the activity of an attentional process that integrates incoming material with an already attended-to sequence if the new material can be caught by the attentional process. The ability of the attentional process to catch new material depends on the pattern properties of the already caught material. Let me explain what I mean when I say that new material is caught. Jones's theory uses a spatial analogy when describing a sequence of sounds. Sound is seen as laid out in a multidimensional space in which time is one dimension (say laid out from left to right) and frequency is another, as in a spectrogram. However, there are more dimensions as well, one for each property of sound that is significant for the auditory system. The process of attending to successive sounds is analogous to moving through this space, always from left to right along the time dimension, but dodging back and forth along the other dimensions to catch as many sounds in the sequence as possible. If they are caught they become part of the integrated sequence. Otherwise they do not. In this respect it resembles the theories of van Noorden and of Norman.

The atttentional process in Jones's theory is seen as one that attempts to predict the multidimensional position of the next sound in the sequence from the positions of the preceding ones. Furthermore, it is restricted to using certain kinds of rules for doing so. The rules are global in nature, in the sense that they are designed to fit the pattern properties of the sequence that has been received up to the current moment in time. The factor that determines the acceptance of the next tone is therefore not based only on the local relation between that sound and the one before it. In addition, the theory argues that a sequence that obeys rules of a certain type will be easier to perceive and learn, and among rules of this type simpler ones will make a sequence easier to attend to.[265]

In Jones's theory, the rules that have been picked up by the listener tell the process of attention where to move next in the multidimensional acoustic space in order to capture the next sound. There is also a limit on the speed at which attention can shift to the predicted position of the next sound. This velocity constraint is similar to the one proposed by van Noorden and serves the same theoretical purpose.[266] It explains why more rapid sequences are more likely to split apart perceptually. In this regard, Jones talks of an optimum rate of movement of the attention along the dimensions of the space (for example, along the pitch dimension). Finally, to soften the effect of the previous constraints in governing what can or cannot be attended to, she introduces the idea of a "serial integration region" a region in the time-by-pitch space that surrounds the optimum rate of movement and within which the attention will be able to catch sequences of sounds even if their separation does not maintain the optimum proportionality between pitch change and time change.

The problem with this theory is that it is in some sense too rule-bound and therefore not general enough. Because it bases the activity of the integrative process on a rule-based description of the stimulus, it fails to explain how we can perceive and group random sequences. For example, let us suppose that we hear a random sequence of tones, consisting of only two frequencies, A and B, with one of the two frequencies chosen randomly as the next tone. In addition suppose that the time between two successive tones can take only two values, T1 or T2, chosen at random. Although Jones' rules could not describe the sequence at all, the sequence would be integrated or segregated depending on the frequency separation between tones A and B and the overall rate of the sequence. It is not clear what happens in Jones' theory, or any other rule-governed one, when there is no rule to be found. Another problem is that though the theory claims to deal with

PART 1:

XXX XXX XXX XXX XXX

PART 2:

XXX   XXX   XXX   XXX   XXX

PART 3:

XXX XXX XXX XXX XXX

Figure 2.34
Grouping by (relative) temporal proximity.

perceptual integration, it has mostly been verified through studies of memory. These issues will be discussed again in chapter 4.

There is another way of letting global relations determine perceptual organization—the way chosen by the Gestalt psychologists. Rather than talking about a rule-based description that unites the sequence into a whole, they talked about forces of integration. Like Jones, they saw the necessity of having the grouping of perceptual elements based on something other than the local relations between parts; but rather than basing this grouping on some mathematical regularity in the sequence of events, they based it on the competition between "forces of attraction" between the elements.

In chapter 1, I introduced the Gestalt psychology explanation of the streaming effect. It was based on the proximities between the tones in the pitch-time space. In the present section I would like to list some of the main elements of Gestalt psychology and to apply them to the phenomena of perceptual organization that we have been discussing.

1. *Proximity*. Parts of a sensory input will organize themselves into groups based on proximity. If temporal separation is viewed as a sort of proximity, then sounds that are near to one another in time will group with one another. In part 1 of figure 2.34, all the tones have the same frequency but differ in their temporal spacing; the sound will be heard as a series of triplets. It is not the absolute proximity that counts, but the relative proximities (there are certain limits to this statement when distances get too large or small). For this reason the sequence in part 2 would be more strongly organized in terms of triplets than the previous one. Although the spaces between the nearest tones are the same, the gaps separating the triplet groups are longer. The same enhancement of grouping can be achieved by reducing the within-triplet spacing, as in part 3.

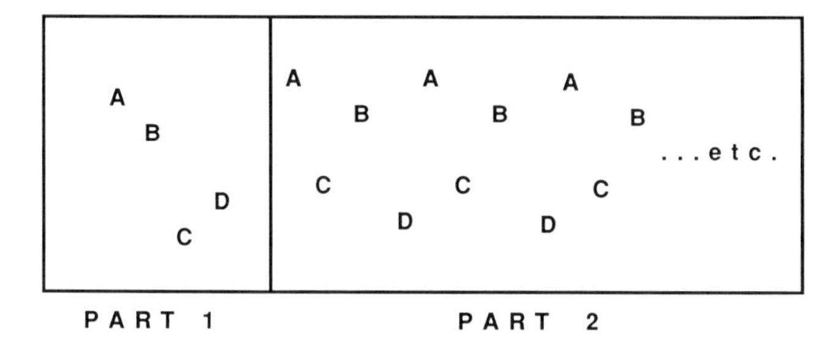

Figure 2.35
Grouping by (relative) frequency proximity.

Sounds that are near one another in frequency should also show a tendency to group with one another as in part 1 of figure 2.35. Although A, B, C, and D are equally spaced in time, the clustering of A with B and C with D in frequency will cause them to be heard as two groups. Very often, the two bases for grouping by proximity (by time or by frequency) will be in conflict as is the case in the streaming effect, diagrammed in part 2 of the figure. Although A is closest to C in time, it is closest to B in frequency. (Actually A is closest to the frequency of the next occurrence of itself in the sequence, but this occurrence is too far away in time to compete effectively.) The effect of increasing the frequency separation between the high and low groups would be to increase the perceptual coherence of each of the groups. This is a well documented effect. Reducing the within-group frequency separations would be expected to accomplish the same result, but this effect is not well documented. I once tried to demonstrate it in an experiment and failed.[267]

The effects of increasing the speed can be thought of as reducing the separations of the sounds on the time dimension while keeping their frequency separations as they were before. The effects of doing this are seen in figure 2.36. Even visually, the A's (and also the B's) seem more tightly clustered in the case shown on the right. The reason is evident when we think in terms of separations rather than proximities. By compressing time differences, we reduce the contribution that time makes to the total frequency-time separation; therefore the separation of the tones will mainly be affected by frequency. It is easiest to see this at the limit of compression where (given the freedom allowed to theorists) we eliminate time entirely. In such a case there would be only two simultaneous tones whose separation would be entirely one of frequency.

2. *Similarity*. It is hard to know where proximity leaves off and simi-

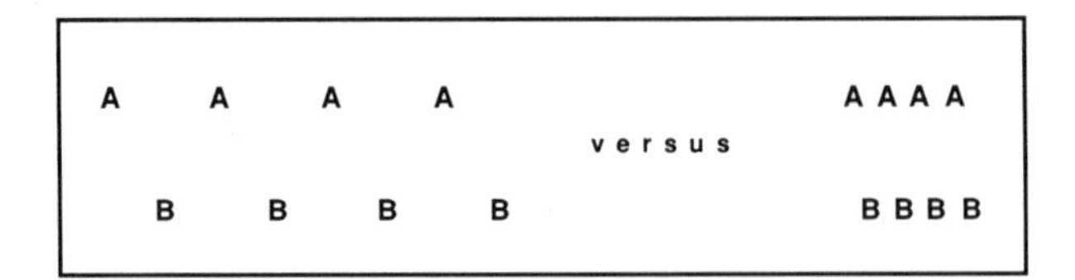

Figure 2.36
Effects of speed on overall frequency-time proximity.

larity begins. Proximity really refers to spatial proximity and when we say that two frequencies are near each other we are really employing a spatial analogy. We could just as easily have said that they were *similar* to one another. However, it really does not matter since the effects of the two are the same. Things that are either more similar to one another than to their neighbors, or nearer to one another, will tend to be grouped together perceptually. Perhaps we might reserve the use of the word similarity for cases in which we were unable to physically describe the dimension of similarity, but when we could describe the physical basis of the dimension, we might say that the sounds were near on that dimension. If we followed this rule we would talk about the perceptual grouping of a sequence of notes formed by different instruments as being based on the similarities of their timbres rather than on their proximities.

3. *Good Continuation and Completion.* When the Gestalt psychologists looked at visual patterns, such as line drawings, they discovered that they did not all have the same resistance to disruption. One test of such resistance is the tendency of a line in a drawing to be seen as complete when part of it is hidden behind a screen. If the visible parts have certain continuities with one another, the line will seem to complete itself and be seen as a single contour; otherwise the disconnected line segments may seem unrelated. When we say that the line seems complete, we do not mean that the viewers of it will be deluded into thinking that the whole line is visible. Rather they will see the missing part as covered rather than as missing and may not even remember later that a part of it was covered. Two examples, one in which there is good completion and one where the completion is poor, were given in figure 2.23. The goodness of the continuity seemed to depend on whether the two disconnected segments fell into a regular, smooth trajectory when connected. In the case of auditory research there is some evidence that sequential grouping is better when the frequency changes that precede an interruption by noise or by silence are consistent with the changes that follow the interruption.

4. *Organization.* The Gestalt theorists believed that all perceptual entities were organized. One mark of this fact is the tendency of a picture that we are looking at to organize itself into figure and ground. When we see a line in a drawing, we generally see it as an edge that represents the occlusion of a more distant object by a nearer one. The shape of the edge is seen as the boundary edge of the nearer object. In some ambiguous drawings, such as the ambiguous vase-faces drawing of figure 1.6 of chapter 1, the line can be seen as either the boundary edge of object A or of object B. When object A is seen, the area that would have been seen as object B is seen as unstructured space falling behind object A. The experience seems to oscillate back and forth, with one interpretation of the image dominating for a number of seconds and then the other taking over. The point that the Gestalt psychologists liked to make was that the experience was *always* organized, even if there was no completely dominant organization. It was as if human nature abhorred a vacuum of organization and always imposed the one that was momentarily favored by the forces of organization.

The experience in listening to the streaming effect is quite similar to the visual example. As one listens, first one stream seems like an organized experience while the other seems to coexist vaguely in the background; then the other one moves to the foreground for awhile. This "foregrounding" of auditory experiences is not restricted to the streaming effect but exists whenever we select one of a set of concurrent sounds to listen to. Auditory organization can also show the same kind of ambiguity as we see in the vase-faces figure. In the streaming effect, when the sequence is played with an intermediate speed and frequency separation, the sequence can often be heard as either a single stream or as two, first one then the other organization taking charge. I think what this shows is that the auditory system, like the visual one, is weighing evidence for alternative organizations but is always maintaining one of them as the active one at any given moment. It, too, avoids unorganized experiences. The fact that it gradually tends to move to a two-stream organization over time does not obscure the essential point: at no time is the experience ever free of either one organization or the other.

5. *Context.* The Gestaltists emphasized that the way in which we experienced the properties of the component parts of visual scenes depended on the role that the part was playing in the currently dominant perceptual organization. The properties were always experienced in relation to the organization of the whole. As an example, figure 2.37 shows how we experience the motion of a tiny light mounted on the rim of a rolling wheel. If it is seen in a normally

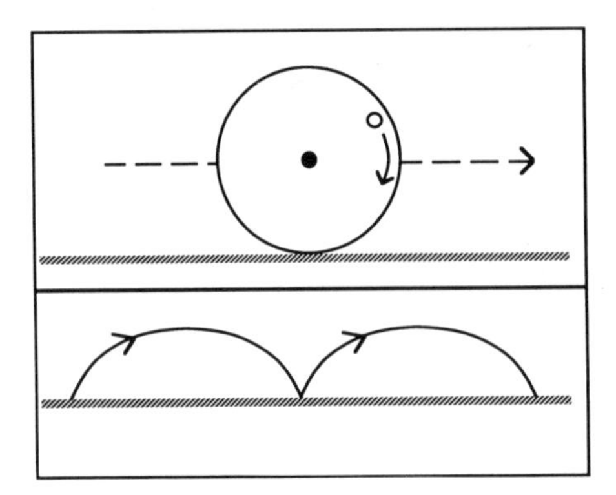

Figure 2.37
The role of context in determining the perceived motion of a small light attached to the edge of a wheel. Top: room illuminated. Bottom: room darkened.

illuminated room in which the light, the wheel, and the floor are visible, the light appears to be rotating around the hub of the wheel as the wheel, in turn, moves sideways across the floor (as shown in the top panel). However, when the normal illumination is extinguished so that only the tiny light can be seen in an otherwise black room, it is now seen as moving in a cycloidal trajectory, because it is no longer seen in relation to the wheel but only in relation to the floor of the room (this is illustrated in the bottom panel).

In auditory organization there is a similar dependency of perceived properties on the nature of the larger organization. In the Bregman-Rudnicky experiment, for example, the A and B tones were perceived in relation to the flanking distractor tones when the latter were bound into the same organization as they were.[268] However, when the distractor tones were peeled away into a different organization, the A and B tones were perceived only in relation to each other and under these circumstances their order was easier to judge.

6. *Belongingness.* One of the manifestations of this dependency of perceived properties on context was the idea of belongingness that is discussed more extensively elsewhere in this volume. In previous discussions and in chapter 1, I have tended to interpret it in its strongest form.[269] I have seen it as forcing the exclusive allocation of properties. It is sufficient to point out here that the principle does not always work in this form, and I refer the reader to my discussion of duplex perception in chapter 7. Just the same, there is a weaker sense in which it always does hold true—if a property of an experience is perceived, it is always experienced as a property "of" something in that experience. Although, as we shall see, the same piece of sensory

input can contribute evidence to specify more than one property of a sound, the properties, once formed, never float around unattached. They are always properties *of* something. If theorists believe that the individual properties of sensory experiences are detected by specialized neural detectors, there is all the more reason for them to see the need for organizational processes to put them all together into coherent mental descriptions.

7. *The Perceptual Field.* The Gestalt psychologists used a metaphor drawn from physics to describe the organizational process. They said that it resembled the action of competing forces of attraction in a "field." Think of the bodies of our solar system exerting simultaneous forces of attraction on one another and setting up regular orbits, or the mutual forces governing the molecules of a bubble and tending toward a symmetrical organization, and you will have a reasonable picture of what they had in mind. In perceptual grouping, the proximities and alignments of the components of the sensory field were seen as setting up simultaneously acting forces that cooperated and competed with one another to yield the final groupings. The Gestaltists imagined that in vision, things such as the boundaries of figures or the clustering of perceptual groups came into existence in this way. For them, the idea of simultaneously acting forces explained a number of things. For example, there could be such things as strong stable organizations that were hard to disrupt that would occur when a number of forces all favored the same organization. On the other hand there could be weak and shifting organizations when the forces operated in different directions. I have usually referred to them as factors favoring grouping rather than forces, because I did not want to prejudge the exact nature of the process. However, I have offered essentially the same account of how these factors compete and collaborate in auditory grouping.

Certain geometric figures were called strong forms by the Gestaltists. An example is a circle. We can immediately see why this is so by drawing a circle (it has to be a very good one) and then trying to camouflage it by adding lines to the picture anywhere we wish. The task is virtually impossible. The picture always ends up containing a visible circle. According to a Gestalt view, this occurs because the parts of the contour of the circle will group better with one another than they will with anything else. By analogy we should expect to find strong forms in audition. To my mind, the strongest form is a steady tone. Its parts will be grouped with one another by frequency proximity, timbre similarity, and temporal continuity; we cannot imagine anything that could group with a segment of that tone better than the remainder of the tone does. You would think that this should also be true of continuous glides in pitch, but it is not. We can often derail the listener who is trying to follow one glide by intersecting it with another one. For instance, if we are trying to follow a glide that is falling in pitch and it is intersected by a rising one, our attention is usually forced onto the rising one so that we follow it up again in pitch.[270]

8. *Innateness and Automaticity*. The Gestalt psychologists recognized the role of learning and volition in the organizing of experience. After all a viewer can, with effort, search for and find camouflaged objects in the various hidden-figures puzzles, such as the ones studied by Gottschaldt.[271] However, the thing that makes these puzzles hard is the automatic organization that forces some of the parts of the sought-after figure to group with extraneous lines against the will of the viewer. The Gestalt psychologists believed that certain principles of organization were both automatic and innate. They supported this belief with demonstrations of organized perception in newborn animals. I have already mentioned the research of Laurent Demany in Paris that demonstrated auditory stream segregation in infants.[272] This is just what the Gestalt psychologists would have expected.

As we can see, there are a goodly number of ways in which the facts of auditory perception can be seen in relation to the organizational phenomena that were described so carefully in vision by the Gestalt psychologists. Many of these auditory analogs have been described by psychologists and music theorists.[273]

I have already pointed out, in chapter 1, that the Gestalt principles of grouping can be seen as ones that ensure that scene analysis will take place correctly. Parts of a visual field that are similar to one another, close together, whose contours follow a smooth trajectory are likely to be the visible parts of the same physical object. Similarly in audition, sounds that are close together in time and similar in pitch and other acoustic properties are likely to have arisen from the same acoustic source. In some cases the source is not a single individual, but there is some other important reason to group the components. Examples are a flock of birds in a tree, several people walking together on gravel, or a group of children yelling to one another.[274] Although the grouping of these sounds does not isolate the behavior of a single individual it does isolate a coherent social phenomenon.

However, the contribution of Gestalt theory is not limited to this. Their central point was that perception at all levels is organized, and that the organization at each level is adjusted by the brain to be consistent with those at more global levels as well as at more microscopic levels. The case of the appearance of the wheel with the light on its rim that we looked at earlier is a good example of the consistency requirement that flows down from higher levels. So far I have shown no cases of this in auditory perception, but it is an issue that I will discuss in the chapter on schema-based stream segregation.

Recent work in computer vision has emphasized the importance of the grouping processes that were described by Gestalt psychology. Witkin and Tenenbaum have argued that the purpose of these processes is to find regions of scenes that have some sort of coherence or regularity within them.[275] These, they say, are very likely to correspond to parts of meaningful objects. The grouping, therefore, can simplify the discovery of the identity of the meaningful objects in the scene. For this reason, these authors have proposed that grouping on the basis of similarities and continuities be built into computer programs for visual recognition. I am very much impressed by their arguments.

Although there is a tendency to want to see the perceptual organizational process as highly integrated and consistent, a tendency that was strong in the Gestalt psychologists and can be seen today in the "perceptual intelligence" approach espoused by Rock and by Bregman, care must be taken not to go too far in this direction.[276] It seems that some of the organizational processes are fairly local in their application. Global rules cannot explain, for example, why the tip of a long tonal glide (its first little bit) can break off perceptually from the rest of the glide in the manner observed by Steiger (see the subsection on changing sounds in the section in this chapter on timbre).[277] After all, the tip fits in very consistently to the description of the glide taken as a whole. However, grouping the tip with the rest of the glide can sometimes be in conflict with grouping it with the tips of glides that have preceded it. The conflict seems to be entirely between local, low-level processes of grouping that operate with little consideration of the larger perceptual description that is being formed for the sequence.

Hierarchies in Auditory Organization So far in this volume I have presented the problem of scene analysis as though every portion of the incoming sensory evidence could be allocated to simple and distinct perceptual organizations. If that were true, then if a piece of pink surface were seen as a part of one of a person's fingers, it would not be able to be seen as part of another finger. So far so good; everything is as it should be. However, the fingers of a hand are not wholly unrelated to one another. They are seen as parts of a larger organization—the hand. The accurate recognition of a hand is dependent on the correct grouping of the regions of light that arise from the various fingers (despite interruptions by the outlines of other objects, and differences in lighting of the different fingers) in just the same way that the accurate recognition of one of those fingers is dependent on the correct grouping of the sensory evidence arising from the parts of that finger. It looks as though the scene-analysis problem repeats itself on the way up from fingers to hands to limb to body and that there can be, in our visual experience as in the outside world that gives rise to it, a hierarchy of organizations of different sizes, the smaller ones being parts of the larger ones.

The same fact is true of audition. In audition, I have called the perceptual organizations streams, and in the preceding sections of this volume have implied that when we package incoming auditory information into separate streams, we prevent it from interacting with the information in other streams. But is it really true that auditory streams are wholly distinct from one another in this way? Consider the perceptual streams that arise when you hear a musical composition, for example, one for two instruments. If my earlier arguments were strictly true, there would be only two possible organizations of the sounds. In one of these, they would be heard as a single stream that contained the emergent pattern that is formed by all the sounds taken together. This would be unsatisfactory because we would not be able to distinguish the contributions of the two instruments as we do when we follow a melody being carried by one of them. In the other organization, each instrument would be heard as a separate stream and any pattern formed by the two taken together would be discarded by the auditory system as an accident. This would be equally unsatisfactory. The pattern created by the two instruments in concert is as much the subject of perceptual analysis and "description" as the pattern created by each of them. If the mental representations of the instruments were completely distinct, there would be no point in having them play together. Furthermore, we intuitively know, even without reference to a musical appreciation of the ensemble, that even though the two instruments are heard distinctly, still, as a group they are heard as distinct from the coughing of a neighbor. It makes sense, therefore, to think of the auditory perceptual organization of the duet as having a hierarchical structure just as the visual one representing a hand does.

This argument implies that there are levels of perceptual belongingness intermediate between "the same thing" and "unrelated things." Yet it is imaginable that only the raw organization into basic streams, such as the one that represents a single instrument, is the job of the perceptual system and that the job of putting these streams into a hierarchical structure belongs to some more conceptual faculty of mind. While it is hard to pry open the mind to see which is true, we can at least ask whether the two kinds of decisions, the isolation of the basic streams and the grouping of them into hierarchies, is based on the same type of information. It is conceivable that the decision about basic streams uses only low-level acoustic information, whereas the one about the hierarchical grouping uses the listener's learned knowledge about musical styles. Although this is conceivable, it seems unlikely. There are many low-level acoustic properties that relate the sound that arises from the members of an ensemble and that are not present with two wholly unrelated sounds. One is the fact that (at least in traditional folk and art music throughout the world) they form parts of a coherent rhythmic structure. This means that at the very least, there will be a fairly large number of synchronies between onsets of sounds of the different instruments. Furthermore, in many forms of music, sounds that happen at the same time are usually harmonious, meaning that they have certain types of acoustic relations among them. As we shall see in chapter 3, the existence of synchrony and harmonicity between sounds tends to bind them into the same perceptual stream.

There may also be other properties that serve to promote hierarchical grouping just as they promote the grouping of sounds into basic streams, such as parallel frequency changes in different basic streams and common spatial location. We are left with the possibility that the grouping of the sounds of an ensemble is just a weaker form of integration by exactly the same set of factors that holds together the sounds of a single instrument.

The kind of hierarchy that we have just considered is one in which the things that form the parts of a higher level grouping are the different instruments that are playing at the same time. There is another kind of hierarchy that exists in both music and other types of sound. This kind of hierarchy exists due to the fact that even within a single basic stream, such as a single voice or instrument, there are embedded units. In a sequence not every pair of sounds goes together in the same way. In music there are short phrases whose elements belong with one another more than they belong with elements that are not part of the same phrase. It is more accurate to say that the individual sounds go together to form a group, and that it is the group, rather than the individual sounds within it, that belongs with the adjacent groups of sound. The hierarchy can have more than two sizes of units. A sequence of short phrases can, in turn, be grouped into a longer phrase, and so on.

This kind of grouping at higher and higher levels in music is surely not all part of the same system that is responsible for the phenomena of auditory stream segregation that we have been examining in this chapter. The higher levels of grouping span much larger time intervals than are involved in primitive auditory stream segregation. They undoubtedly depend on learned musical concepts.[278]

Relation to Other Psychological Mechanisms: Attention When we think of the segregation of clusters of auditory evidence as being formed by a mechanism, it is natural to ask how this mechanism is related to other ones that psychologists have talked about. In particular, we might want to see how attention is involved in this segregation.

It is undoubtedly true that a person can try to listen for a particular sound, for instance, when trying to follow a single talker in a crowded room, and that this process of selective attention is assisted when the voice of the target talker has some acoustic properties that distinguish it from the other voices with which it is mixed. The acoustic differences that make this task easier strongly resemble those that I have described earlier as those that increase stream segregation. They include such differences as those of pitch and spatial position. This seems to be an argument for thinking that stream segregation is just a form of attention. After all, if the factors that influence two phenomena are the same, it seems reasonable to think that the two are related.

Just the same, there is disagreement among theorists concerning the relation between auditory stream formation and attention. Both Norman and Jones, for example, have interpreted stream segregation as a failure on the part of an attentional mechanism to follow all the tones in a sequence.[279] Norman assumed that this was because the attentional mechanism cannot shift rapidly enough from one critical band to another, whereas Jones has interpreted it as the inability of the attentional mechanism to move rapidly enough in a multidimensional auditory space to catch tones that violate good-sequence rules.[280]

I, on the other hand, have viewed the phenomenon of stream segregation as being largely the result of the grouping performed by a pre-attentive mechanism. I have done so partly on the basis of the Bregman-Rudnicky experiment that showed that a sequence of tones to which the listener was not paying attention could capture tones from the field of attention.[281] This capturing is, in my opinion, the mark of an organized perceptual structure. It provides evidence that a second stream can exist even though attention is not being paid to it.

There is another interesting observation that seems to show that more than one auditory grouping can exist at the same time. Richard Warren and his colleagues have created conditions in which a listener heard either two or three streams of speech by having the streams come from different places in space.[282] In each stream there was a voice repeating the word "tress" over and over again at about half-second intervals. It was the same recording in all streams, but the onset times were staggered; for example, when two streams were employed, the onsets of the repetitions in the second stream were exactly halfway between the onsets of the repetitions in the first. The researchers were looking at the phenomenon of verbal transformation in which a repeated word undergoes illusory perceptual changes, presumably due to some sort of neural adaptation. The word "tress", for example, might change eventually to "stress", then to "distress", then to "Esther", and even to such apparently different words as "commence". The researchers were interested in whether the changes occurred simultaneously or independently in the different streams. The results showed that the changes were independent. This suggested to them that there were functionally separate sets of verbal analyzers associated with the different streams. These observations may bear on the question of whether streams (or at least "proto-streams") are structured preattentively or not. If you think of attention as a mechanism that focuses on some sensory material and relegates the rest to background, you would imagine that the material in the foreground might be the subject of pattern analysis, in this case analysis of verbal patterns. It seems likely that the listeners were switching their attention back and forth between bodies of sense data that had already been primitively organized. Remember that the words in the different streams were identical. So when a person shifted attention to another stream, more repetitions of the same physical signal would be encountered. If a single "stream of consciousness" were involved, you would imagine that the word detection system would continue on from the state that it was in when focused on the previous repetition. Instead, it seemed that there were structured and partially analyzed streams present at two or three spatial locations and that the illusory changes that took place followed their own separate course in each stream. This finding supports the idea that there can be preattentive structuring of more than one cluster of sensory evidence at a time. The independence of changes in all three streams in the three-stream condition suggests that the two streams that were not attended to at any given moment nonetheless maintained their distinctness from each other.

Confirmation that two bodies of perceptually integrated material can exist at the same time also comes from an experiment on conditioning. The subjects participated in an experiment in which they were presented with two different sequences of words, one sequence in the left ear and one in the right. They were asked to shadow (that is, to continuously repeat with as little delay as possible) the material that was being sent to one of their ears. In such a task, the subjects can usually not report afterward what words have been presented to their nonattended ear. But in one experiment, the subjects were conditioned by the pairing of electric shocks with certain selected words that were received in the nonattended sequence.[283] Afterward, the subjects were given a shadowing test in which there were no shocks but where their galvanic skin response (GSR, a measure of autonomic arousal used in lie detector tests) was measured. The subjects showed a GSR response to the words that had been paired with shock as well as to words that were similar in meaning or in sound to those words. This showed that despite the fact that these words had not been the focus of attention, the sounds out of which they were made had been perceptually organized into units that were separate from all concurrent sounds and the units had even been reacted to in terms of meaning.

There are also masking experiments that suggest that both of a pair of concurrent sounds are analyzed as separate entities. The experiments show that when a to-be-reported signal was masked by a tone, the listeners did better when the frequency of the masking tone was known in advance. This improvement of segregation when the masking signal was familiar suggests that the listeners were able to process both sounds at least to a certain level: they attempted to hear the target sound and at the same time directed some process of inhibition toward the unwanted sound.

If primitive organization and auditory selective attention are different, why do they make use of the same acoustic features? If I may be excused an analogy at this point, I would like to propose that this may be due to convergent evolution. In biological evolution we often see similarities of form developing in species that are very far separated on the evolutionary tree. This convergence occurs when the two species have evolved into the same ecological niche, where they have had to solve similar problems in order to survive. By analogy, the mental processes that form coherent clusters of sensory evidence and those that select them for more detailed processing live in the same acoustic world. In this common world it is a good bet that all the members in a sequence of similar sounds come from the same acoustic source and conversely that when members of the sequence come from a different spatial origin this suggests that they have come from different acoustic sources. Stream formation has the job of grouping sounds that have arisen from the same source and attention must select distinct sources for further analysis. It should not, then, be surprising that they both make use of those properties of sound that are ecologically useful in labeling distinct sources.

Despite these arguments, however, I do not think that the issue of whether segregation is preattentive or not will be able to be resolved until there is some agreement in the research community about what the properties of attention are and how to distinguish experimentally between attention and a process that is preattentive.

Teleological Approach

Earlier in this section on theoretical approaches, the distinction was offered between two kinds of functional explanation. One of these explains auditory organization through the nature of the mechanism that does it. We have just finished considering theories of this sort. The other type of functional explanation explains auditory organization by showing how it solves practical problems for the listener. Since Aristotle, this form of explanation has been called "teleological," a word that refers to the purposes or goals toward which natural processes move. For a long time, it was in disfavor because it was often applied inappropriately. For example, in Aristotle's time the falling of a stone was seen as guided by the goal of getting to its natural place—the ground. Not only was teleological explanation unhelpful in the explanation of falling stones (due to the fact that stones do not really have their own purposes) but it also gave the illusion of explaining things, and diverted people from developing more suitable explanations. Unfortunately, the whole teleological approach got blackened by the fallout from such inappropriate attempts and when it was later applied as an explanatory framework for the behavior of human beings, who clearly do have purposes of their own, it was ruled out of science by well-meaning philosophers who were, like old generals, treating the next war as if it were an exact repetition of the last one. I have given the justification for the teleological approach in chapter 1 and it is that approach that I will continue to pursue. It should be obvious by now that the scene-analysis approach is teleology in a new guise.

To proceed with a scene-analysis approach to the sequential organization of sound is not merely to offer the explanation that we sequentially group sounds that have arisen from the same source because it solves an important problem for us. If this were all there was to it, the criticism that it was an empty explanation would be perfectly correct. Instead we can push the idea of "solving a problem" further by asking what it takes to solve the problem. What clues would be helpful in deciding whether or not two components of sound have arisen from the same source? By seeing it as solving a problem, we can generate hypotheses about what forms of information are used by the auditory system to solve it. Furthermore, we no longer see perceptual organization as an isolated idiosyncrasy of the auditory system but as contributing to the success of the plans and actions of the perceiver. This can lead us to ask questions about the role of the process of perception itself and what its properties would have to be in order to fulfill this role. This, in turn, could lead us to ask how perceptual organization could contribute to the general perceptual process in useful ways.

The major contribution of the "what for" approach to phenomena of auditory organization is to help us to see these phenomena as part of a system and to guide us in studying the properties of this system. This has a relation to explaining the process of audition as the product of a physiological system. The two modes of explanation are complementary. Physiology is there to support a function, and the analysis of the physiology can be assisted by asking "what is the physiology there to do?" The individual physiological mechanisms must have evolved a complementary set of systems to create a consistent higher level system of functions.

The "what for" question can clarify the relations between the level of physiology and the level of function. There has been some discussion as to whether stream segregation, and especially its increase with repeated listening, is a breakdown or an accomplishment. At the physiological or mechanistic level, the strongest current contenders are models that see it as a reduction in something, either in the sensitivity of frequency-transition detectors or of the ability of some filter-like process to follow rapid transitions. In chapter 1 we came to the conclusion that it is possible for a system to achieve a useful outcome for itself as a whole by allowing some local process to break down. Therefore what appears as a breakdown at the level of physiology is an accomplishment at the level of function. Physiology, in itself, cannot tell us about function.

Formal versus Informal Theorizing There is one last point to make about theorizing. It is clear that the ultimate goal of any theory is to operate according to formal logical rules, to describe the essential patterns of a domain in mathematical form, and to make testable predictions of a quantitative nature. The finest examples of this are in the field of physics. In the hope that psychology, or at least some parts of it, can some day be as strong as physics, many psychologists have taken the direction of developing formal quantitative models of particular psychological phenomena. The reader will notice that there is no such attempt in this volume and may be troubled by its absence.

My feeling on this issue is that there is no point in trying to develop formal models before we have at least a reasonable idea of what kind of beast we are dealing with. Otherwise the formal theories are almost certain to be useless and, what is worse, may divert useful energy from more valuable endeavors. It is just as bad to develop formalisms on the wrong problems as to apply teleological explanation to the wrong ones. Choosing the right approach at the right stage in the study of a problem is an art, not a science, and only historical hindsight can tell us when it has been done appropriately. In rereading this chapter what strikes me is the absence of answers to so many questions of a very basic and factual type, such as "What sorts of natural sounds will group with one another?" I think the first order of business is empirical research, in which useful questions are suggested by an orientation that sees the perceptual systems as solving practical problems.

Chapter 3

Integration of Simultaneous Auditory Components

The task of segregating sounds that had arisen from different sources was described in chapter 1 through the example of the spectrogram of a mixture of sounds (see figure 1.4). It was apparent that there are two kinds of grouping to be done. First, a process of sequential grouping was needed to put some of the spectral components that followed one another in time into the same perceptual stream, where they could be used to calculate the sequential properties of a source of sound in the environment (such as its melody or rhythm). This process was the subject of chapter 2.

A second process was needed to partition the set of concurrent components into distinct subsets, and to place them into different streams where they could be used to calculate the spectral properties of distinct sources of sound (such as timbre or pitch). It is this process that will be the subject of the present chapter.

The question of how to study the process of simultaneous grouping and segregation is not obvious. However, in the summer of 1975, Alex Rudnicky and I began work on a set of auditory demonstrations that were related to the question of whether two tones could be overlapped in time and still separate into two perceptual components, as opposed to becoming a simple complex tone. The first demonstration made use of a repeating cycle of two discrete tones, A and B, each of the same fixed duration and a fixed rate of repetition. The two tones were at different frequencies, but overlapped in time as shown in figure 3.1. The percentage of the length of the tone that overlapped the other tone was varied. We found that if we used tones whose duration was, for example, 250 msec per tone, and that were only 25 percent or 50 percent overlapped (i.e., relatively asynchronous in onset) the tones would segregate clearly into separate streams. When the temporal overlap reached 88 percent (almost synchronous onsets) the tones fused into one percept. When the two tones fused the resultant tone sounded complex, but when they segregated each sounded pure. Segregation was clearer when the frequency separation was

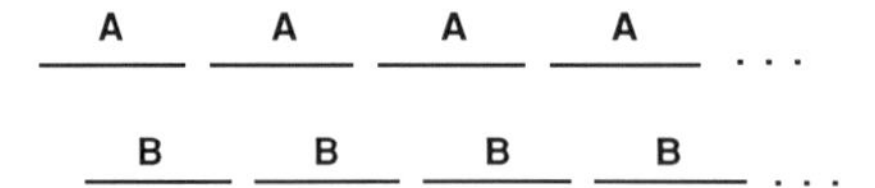

Figure 3.1
Repeating cycle of overlapping tones.

greater; this suggested to us that some sort of stream segregation phenomenon was involved.

This demonstration used tones with silences between them. We decided to see whether two simultaneous and continuous tones of different frequencies could be induced to segregate or fuse depending on brief amplitude changes that were synchronous or asynchronous for the two frequencies. We introduced brief amplitude drops (8 per second) in the two, otherwise continuous, tones, causing a warbling sound in each tone. This is illustrated in figure 3.2, with the two dashed lines representing the tones and the V's representing the dips in loudness. (In the example the dips are not synchronous.) We could not cause the tones to totally segregate on the basis of asynchronous warbling. When the warbles were at different rates for the two frequencies, the two different rates could be heard, but the tones were not really perceptually segregated; the quality of each one was affected by the presence of the other.

So far, we had seen that when each component switched completely on and off, with a sizable off period, stream separation was high under asynchronous conditions; however, where the amplitude merely dropped off briefly, asynchrony did not produce complete separation. We then decided to confine our attention to an intermediate condition, which used 224-msec tones with 32-msec silences between repetitions. When the tones had asynchronous onsets in this condition, we were able to perceptually pick out the top or bottom stream. An analogy to our earlier studies of stream segregation was noted: *The relatively pure-sounding tones of the streams emerged only after several cycles, a period of time that apparently was required for the buildup of the stream criteria.*

We next made a series of observations employing two tones, a high and a low, repeating at different rates, e.g., 5 tones per second for the high tone and 4 tones per second for the low tone. Thus, once per second the high and low tones would have synchronous onsets; otherwise they were out of synchrony. The perceptual experience consisted of two streams, but with some interesting effects. Every time the onset synchrony occurred, a rich tone was heard in the lower

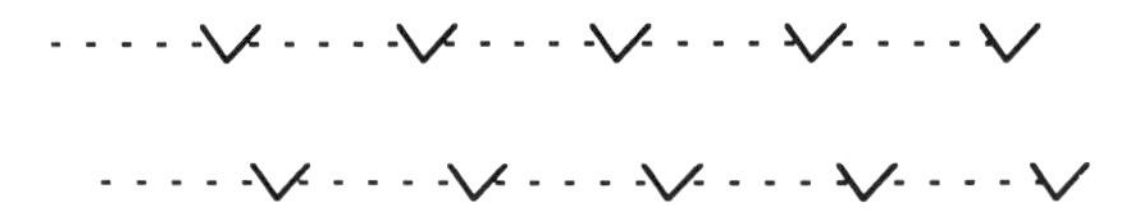

Figure 3.2
Partial segregation with brief amplitude drops (represented by V's).

stream and the corresponding tone in the upper stream was weak or missing. The lower tone was heard to be louder as well. The lower tone percept thus seemed to capture the energy of the synchronous higher tone. This reminded us of the exclusive allocation principle in perception which states that a piece of perceptual evidence has to be allocated to one perceptual entity or another, but not to more than one at a time. Here a certain amount of the energy was being subtracted from the upper tone and added to the lower one.

We then went on to listen to cycles that contained repetitions of three tones of different frequencies that might or might not overlap in time. In this example, it was possible to hear three streams. Asynchronous onsets of three tones did produce segregation, but not as strongly as with only two tones. Nonetheless we made an interesting observation. One of the patterns in this series included a temporal point at which a tone in all three streams had a simultaneous onset. At this point a strong "vertical" fusion took place. This fusion was different from the one we had encountered in the two-stream situation in that now the fusion was so compelling that it rendered the new fused unit quite perceptually independent of the single-tone streams, and did not simply color the timbre of the tone in the lowest stream.

We should note that since only about one-eighth of each stream was composed of silence, most of the time all three frequencies were present simultaneously. Hence all combination tones, beat phenomena, dissonance, and so on, were occurring most of the time. Yet when the streams segregated they sounded pure, all those acoustic combination effects being ignored by the ear. Apparently when the contributing tones were assigned to separate perceptual objects (streams) the awareness of these interactions was suppressed. We might ask, if this is the case, why the ear ever hears these interaction phenomena if it is capable of rejecting them. The answer may depend upon the fact that in some cases, such as when the combination effects are caused by the interaction of acoustic components that all belong to the same real-world sound, these phenomena are as characteristic of that source of sound as the pure-tone components are and therefore should be incorporated into the description.

But how can our auditory systems tell the difference between acoustic phenomena that are an intrinsic part of a sound and those that arise from the accidental co-occurrence of two unrelated sounds? It must obviously fall back on some of the same techniques that it uses to decide whether pure-tone components belong to the same sound. These cues may act to bind the interaction effects into one or another stream. Take, for example, a case in which two complex tones, each composed of a simple harmonic series and therefore heard as having no internal dissonance, are sounded at the same moment. In this case the combination phenomena have a synchronous onset with the pure-tone components, and therefore are also captured into the stream, adding to its timbre or perceptual complexity. On the other hand, if one of these tones occurs for a short time by itself and then is joined by a second tone, the interaction properties will not appear until the second tone is sounded and therefore the onset of the interaction phenomena starts in synchrony with the second tone but not the first. Under these circumstances, the richness or dissonance would be expected to be assigned to the second tone but not the first. However, if the second tone lasted longer than the first, so that it appeared at the end without any interaction components, the auditory system would have evidence that it, too, was pure and might not assign the interaction properties to it either.

The most important observations of Rudnicky and myself could be summarized by saying that the onset synchrony of elements in two streams increased the perceived intensity of the element in the lower stream and decreased the intensity of the one in the upper stream, and that this effect decreased with an increase of frequency separation between the two simultaneous tones.

Although the experimenters were trained listeners and could describe the phenomena reliably to one another, the requirement of replicating the observations with naive subjects required us to reduce the task to one involving simple comparisons or descriptions. For this reason, the experiment by Bregman and Pinker was undertaken.[284]

A Miniature Scene-Analysis Problem

This experiment has already been described in chapter 1 and illustrated in figure 1.16. It involved the sequential capturing of one component from within a two-component tone. It used a cycle in which a pure tone A was followed by a pair of more-or-less simultaneous pure tones B and C. The latter pair could be viewed as forming a complex tone BC. The timing was as follows: 117 msec of silence, A for 117 msec, 47 msec of silence, and then BC, with each of tones B and C lasting for 117 msec. This pattern was repeated cyclically. In figure 1.16, tone A is just a little higher in frequency than B and tone C comes on a bit earlier than B; however, not all the conditions were like this.

The cycle could be heard in more than one way depending on the frequencies and timing of the three-pure tone components. One way was as an alternation of a pure tone A and a rich tone BC, the repetitions of each of these belonging to a stream of its own. Another way was to hear the pure tones A and B in one stream (AB AB AB . . .) and the isolated pure tone C in another (C C C . . .). There were, of course, some ambiguous cases in which the listener experienced some mixture of these two percepts. The way the listener heard the sounds depended on two factors that were manipulated in the experiment: (1) the frequency separation between tones A and B, tone A varying in frequency from a semitone above B to 1.7 octaves above, and (2) the asynchrony of onset of B and C, tone C either coming on synchronously with B or else leading it or lagging it by 29 or 58 msec (25 or 50 percent of the length of one tone).

In one experiment the listeners were asked to judge the richness of the timbre of tone C. "Timbre" was defined for them as "the quality that distinguishes, for example, the sounds of different musical instruments producing notes of the same pitch." They were asked to judge this richness in relation to two standard tones that were presented before each judgment was made. The "pure" standard tone contained only tone C, but the "rich" one contained both B and C. In the rich standard tone, the richness of the BC complex was heard because there was no capturing tone to break it up. In effect the subjects were being asked how much the C tone sounded like it did when embedded in a BC complex, versus sounding like it did when played in isolation. It was assumed that if B fused with C this would make C sound richer.

When tone C was less synchronous in onset (and therefore in offset) with tone B, the former was heard as more pure. We interpreted this as meaning that C fused less with B when the two were not synchronous. However, a critic might have offered a simpler explanation. Perhaps when C was not synchronous with B, the listener could hear C alone for a brief moment and this was sufficient to reduce the richness ratings that were given to it. However, there was also a more remarkable result that could not be explained in this way: when A was closer in frequency to B, tone C sounded purer. We explained this by arguing that when A was close to B in frequency, it captured B into a sequential stream (AB AB . . .). This tended to remove B from its perceptual association with C, and this, in turn, released C to be heard as a pure tone.

In a separate experiment, the listeners were asked to make a different judgment: whether A and B were heard in the same stream. Of course, in order to be able to do this the listeners had to be trained on what it meant to hear one stream as opposed to two. Their training consisted of a tonal sequence that contained a rapid alternation of a higher and a lower tone. At first the tones were near one another in frequency and sounded like a single coherent sequence, but gradually they moved apart in frequency until they split perceptually into two streams.

The main experiment yielded two results. The first was that when the frequencies of A and B were more different, the two tones sounded less like they were in the same stream. We interpreted this as showing that the capturing of B depended on the frequency proximity between A and B. However, as in the previous experiment, a simpler explanation might have been sufficient. Since the listeners were trained to call a stream "single" when its members were close together in frequency, they might have simply used this criterion, rather than the actual stream segregation, to make their judgments. Fortunately, just as in the previous experiment, there was a second result that called for an explanation in terms of perceptual grouping: the synchrony of B and C affected the perception of A. In conditions in which B and C were less synchronous in onset and offset, A and B were more strongly judged as being in the same stream. Our explanation for this result was that when B and C were asynchronous, they tended not to fuse as well into a single sound. This released B so that it could more easily be captured by A into a sequential AB stream.

The results of these experiments seem to be describable in terms of the competition between two types of organization. One is a sequential process that groups A and B into the same stream, with the strength of their grouping depending on how similar they are. The second is one that fuses B and C into the same simultaneous grouping and does so with a strength that depends on how synchronous they are. The effect of the competition is such that it takes less strength to capture a component into a sequential organization if it is less strongly bound into a simultaneous organization (and conversely).

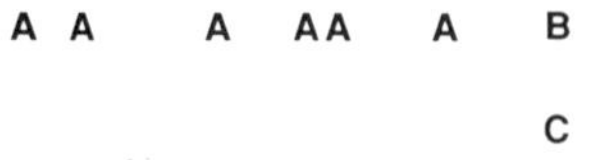

A A A AA A B

C

Figure 3.3
Effect of a sequence of captors.

My interpretation of the Bregman-Pinker experiment using the ABC pattern depends on the assumption that it is the same sequential grouping process at work in their experiment as in the experiments on sequential streaming that were described in chapter 2. If this assumption is true then several predictions can be made for experiments using the ABC pattern.

1. Increasing the rate of the sequence (or perhaps decreasing the distance between the offset of A and the onset of B) should strengthen the AB grouping. The former effect has been observed by van Noorden.[285]
2. Because sequential grouping builds up with repetition of components in a given frequency region, increasing the length of time that one listens to the cycle should increase the AB grouping.
3. For the same reason as given in the previous prediction, if a single occurrence of Bregman and Pinker's ABC pattern were preceded by a long string of A's as shown in figure 3.3, then as this string was made longer, the AB grouping should become stronger (and the BC grouping thereby weakened). (In the figure the timing of the captors is irregular to avoid effects of rhythmic regularity.)
4. The next prediction applies to the pattern shown in figure 3.4. If a three-component sound (call it XYZ) were repeatedly alternated with a simpler tone, XY, where two of the partials in XYZ appear in XY, XYZ should be divided perceptually into two pieces, XY and Z. (This might be more likely if the two parts of XY were more integrated, e.g., by starting synchronously.)

Although these predictions are in agreement with informal observations that I have made, as far as I am aware there has been no formal experimentation that confirms them (except where noted).

Before we leave our discussion of the ABC experiment, we should consider a possible criticism. How could we answer a critic who

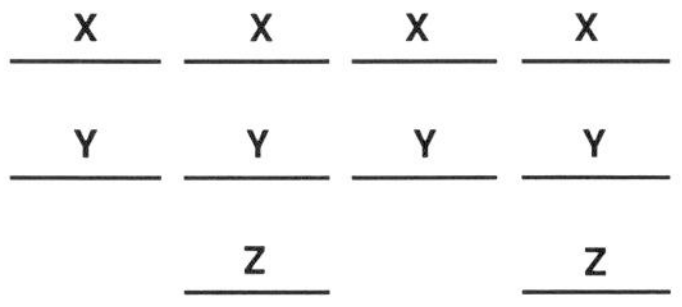

X X X X
Y Y Y Y
Z Z

Figure 3.4
Decomposition of a three-component tone through capturing.

claimed that when we heard tone A repeating again as part of B, it was just a figment of our imaginations, a memory of A that was somehow being activated again by the BC mixture? Helmholtz raised the question and answered it in 1859.[286] He was discussing the fact that he could help himself hear a harmonic of a complex piano tone by preceding it with a tone whose fundamental was at the frequency of the desired harmonic. He pointed out that when the prior tone was very close but not identical in frequency to the desired harmonic, he could hear that the prior tone and the harmonic were not the same. Furthermore, if the complex tone did not contain a component that was close to the priming tone in frequency, no harmonic would be heard. A result similar to the latter was reported by van Noorden when he alternated a pure and a complex tone rapidly.[287] We can see that a frequency identical to the captor's is heard in the complex tone only when it is really there.

Another demonstration that it could not be just a ringing in the ears comes from a repetition of the ABC experiment using as A, B, and C, tones that glide from one frequency to another rather than tones that remain steady at one frequency. Howard Steiger and I carried out this experiment.[288] The stimulus was shown earlier in figure 2.17 of chapter 2. A pure tone glide X alternated with a complex glide whose components were Y and Z. Glides Y and Z moved in parallel on a log frequency scale. X acted as a captor that, under certain conditions, could capture Y into a sequential stream so that Y no longer fused with Z. This capturing was strongest when Y was an exact copy of X. Then the listener heard X occurring again in the mixture. Clearly, since Y was a complex event, hearing it could not be explained as "hearing a ringing in ones ears." If by a ringing, we mean a replaying of the memory of X, that memory must be complex enough to encode a glide.

Even if we are not just replaying our memory of X but actually pulling Y out of the mixture YZ, we know that the memory of X that is influencing this decomposition must involve the glide property. We know this because the most effective captor of a glide is another identical glide. A steady-frequency tone, matching either Y's mean log frequency or the frequency of its beginning or end points, is not as effective. If the only part of the memory of X that counted was some single fact about its frequency, a steady-frequency X should serve just as well. The effectiveness of the capturing, however, even depended on the match in the direction of gliding of X and Y. If X was ascending and Y was descending, both centered on the same frequency, the capturing of Y was weaker than if both were ascending or descending. We can conclude that there is a fairly complex memory for X that is employed to look for near matches to X at subsequent moments of time.

It is important at this point to recall the significance of the ABC experiment as a model of the scene analysis process that we have been discussing. In ordinary listening we have to group acoustic components both sequentially and simultaneously in order to allocate them appropriately to streams that represent individual sources of sound. The ABC experiment provides a glimpse of this process working on a very simplified problem. Because of the simplification, we cannot say that the factors that controlled grouping were representative of those that work in real life. However, we have learned that the factors of frequency proximity and synchrony are among those that are usable and have also learned about the competition between the two types of grouping.

Factors Influencing Integration of Simultaneous Components

The discussion of the process of the integration of simultaneously present acoustic components divides naturally into two questions. The first of these asks what the acoustic clues are that tell the auditory system which components have come from the same physical event. The second question asks about the perceptual consequences of having grouped spectral components; what features of our perceptual experience depend on this grouping? The first question is the topic of the following sections.

How do we know which acoustic components have arisen simultaneously from the same physical event? The answer that I would like to propose is this: If a group of components have arisen from the same physical event, they will have relationships between them that are unlikely to have occurred by chance. The relationships that I am thinking of are of an entirely physical nature and concern properties such as timing, frequency, and the differential effects on our two ears. They are the consequence of the physical laws that govern the sounds and their effects on our ears. We can view the scene-analysis system as trying to take advantage of these physical relationships in order to put the components together appropriately. In effect, they are trying to run the laws of acoustics backwards to reconstruct the original sounds. It is unlikely, however, that the grouping principles directly resemble the physical laws that have created the sounds. Rather, the principles have evolved to take advantage of relationships that the laws create. This section, then, will discuss those relationships that are likely to exist between simultaneous components that have arisen from the same physical event, but are unlikely to exist between those that have arisen from unrelated events.

The "Old-Plus-New" Heuristic

The results of the Bregman-Pinker experiment suggest that the auditory system uses a rule that we might label "the old-plus-new heuristic." It could be stated as follows: "If you can plausibly interpret any part of a current group of acoustic components as a continuation of a sound that just occurred, do so and remove it from the mixture. Then take the difference between the current sound and the previous sound as the new group to be analyzed." I use the word heuristic in the same sense as it is used in the field of artificial intelligence, as a procedure that tends to give the right answers, or at least improve the quality of the answers, but is not guaranteed to do so in all cases.

As we find with many principles of audition, when we think we are the first to notice something we discover that Helmholtz, the great nineteenth-century German physicist, was ahead of us. So it is for the old-plus-new principle. Helmholtz was a strong supporter of the idea, proposed by the physicist G. S. Ohm, that the auditory system registers the individual spectral components of a sound. Realizing the implications of this idea, Helmholtz knew that in the case of acoustic mixtures, there would be a problem in deciding which components had arisen from the same source. Here is an excerpt from a passage that describes a person listening to a group of musical instruments. It describes the old-plus-new heuristic clearly.

> Now there are many circumstances which assist us first in separating the musical tones arising from different sources, and secondly, in keeping together the partial tones of each separate source. Thus when one musical tone is heard for some time before being joined by the second, and when the second continues after the first has ceased, the separation in sound is facilitated by the succession of time. We have already heard the first musical tone by itself, and hence know immediately what we have to deduct from the compound effect for the effect of this first tone. Even when several parts proceed in the same rhythm in polyphonic music, the mode in which the tones of different instruments and voices commence, the nature of their increase in force, the certainty with which they are held, and the manner in which they die off, are generally slightly different for each. . . . When, then such instruments are sounded together there are generally

> points of time when one or the other is predominant, and it is consequently easily distinguished by the ear.

In the same passage Helmholtz describes other factors that promote appropriate separation of sounds. They will all turn out to be important in the discussion that follows.

> But besides all this, in good part music, especial care is taken to facilitate the separation of the parts by the ear. In polyphonic music proper, where each part has its own distinct melody, a principle means of clearly separating the progression of each part has always consisted in making them proceed in different rhythms and on different divisions of the bars; or where this could not be done . . . as in four-part chorales, it is an old rule, contrived for this purpose, to let three parts, if possible, move by single degrees of the scale, and let the fourth leap over several.

Helmholtz also goes on to point out that the factors that distinguish the partials of different sounds that have been mixed together will not segregate the partials of a single sound.

> All these helps fail in the resolution of musical tones into their constituent partials. When a compound tone commences to sound, all its partial tones commence with the same comparative strength; when it swells, all of them generally swell uniformly; when it ceases, all cease simultaneously. Hence no opportunity is generally given for hearing them separately and independently.[289]

Helmholtz, however, gives the reader a special method for hearing out the third harmonic of a *c* played on the piano:

> In commencing to observe upper partial tones, it is advisable just before producing the musical tone itself which you wish to analyze, to sound the tone you wish to distinguish in it, very gently, and if possible in the same quality of tone as the compound itself. . . . First gently strike on a piano the note *g′* [the *g* in the octave above the *c* that is to be analyzed] . . . and after letting the [piano key] rise so as to damp the string, strike the note *c*, of which *g′* is the third partial, with great force, and keep your attention directed to the pitch of the *g′* which you had just heard, and you will hear it again in the compound tone of *c*.[290]

He showed how by the use of a similar method a listener could hear individual partials in different sorts of instruments and even in the human voice. Notice how closely Helmholtz's method resembles the method used by Bregman and Pinker. Helmholtz was not proposing a full-blown theory of perception and would probably have been amazed at our giving a name such as the old-plus-new heuristic to what seemed like a commonsense method for directing the listener's attention to the appropriate part of the spectrum. In his view, no doubt, he was simply using his knowledge of the physical structure of sound and his experience in the laboratory to indicate how these perceptual problems could be solved.

One of the modern experiments that has examined how a partial can be heard out from a complex tone was carried out by Leo van Noorden in the early 1970s.[291] He showed that if we listen to a rapid alternation of a pure tone A and a complex tone C that contains A as one of its components, and if A is presented at the right intensity on every cycle of the AC pattern, we will hear A occurring twice on each cycle (we will discuss the intensity issue later). That is, A will appear to repeat with twice the tempo of C. This experiment demonstrates only one-half of the old-plus-new heuristic. The component of C that matches the frequency of A is indeed being extracted from C as a separate sound; we know this because we can hear it. But because this component is such a small part of the harmonic structure of C (only 1 partial out of 10) we are not able to hear whether the remainder has a different quality after the extraction of this component.

Another fact about the old-plus-new heuristic is also visible in van Noorden's results. The capturing of the embedded harmonic improves with a shorter interval between the pure tone and the complex tone. It became stronger as the rate of alternation was sped up from 91 msec to 63 msec onset-to-onset time (for tones of a fixed duration of 40 msec). This dependence on temporal proximity operates in the same way here as in the streaming illusion that occurs with rapid alternations of high and low tones where the grouping of tones in the same frequency region gets stronger as the time delay between them is reduced. This suggests that the sequential integration is carried out by the same process in both cases.

The old-plus-new heuristic might be restated as follows: "Look for a continuation of what went before and then pay attention to what has been added to it." We must remember that the new thing that gets added might conceivably contain components at some of the same frequencies as the earlier sound. If the auditory system took away all the frequencies that matched those it had heard earlier it might take away too much. The later arriving tone might be left with no energy at the shared frequencies. Amazingly, the partitioning process seems to take away just enough and no more.

This was demonstrated in an experiment by Richard Warren and his colleagues.[292] The stimuli were noise bursts that were filtered to be one octave wide. Two bursts of noise of the same spectral content were alternated. The only difference between them was that one was more intense than the other. Under these conditions, the listener heard the less intense one as continuing through the more intense one. That is, the less intense one appeared to be present all the time, with the more intense one joining it at regular intervals. One strange effect occurred when the intensity difference between the two alternating sounds was less than 3 dB, for example, when an 80-dB sound alternated with one at 82 dB. The "added" sound (the one heard when the 82-dB burst came on) seemed less loud than the "constant" one (at 80 dB). This can be explained by remembering that because of the nature of the decibel scale, the decibel values of two sounds cannot simply be added together when the sounds are added. In the case of noise bursts, when two bursts of equal intensity are added together they make a sound that is just 3 dB louder than each of the originals. The auditory system was apparently mindful of this fact. Because of the similarity of spectral content, it thought that the more intense noise was a continuation of the less intense noise with an additional noise added to it. Then it had to calculate how intense the "added" noise must have been to augment the total intensity by 2 dB. It concluded that the added noise could not have been as intense as the constant noise since the increase was less than 3 dB. This explanation is supported by the results from another condition in which the stronger of the two alternating noises was exactly 3 dB more intense than the weaker one. In this case, the auditory system heard a constant noise joined periodically by another that was equal to it in intensity. The arithmetic of the auditory system seemed to be fairly precise.

I have used words such as "thinking" and "concluding" metaphorically to describe what the auditory system does under these circumstances. It is a metaphor because the process being carried out by the auditory system differs from ordinary thought in that we are not conscious of any inference process going on. Helmholtz called it unconscious inference and we can do so too, as long as we realize that the metaphor that we are using is based only on the results of the process and not on its detailed inner nature, which may or may not work like a thinking process. It is best, perhaps, to think of it as a process that has evolved in our nervous systems to deal with problems in the accurate use of sensory information. To do so, its information-processing rules must respect certain physical laws that govern how our senses receive the information. In audition, this means respecting the laws of mixture of sound.

To respect a law does not necessarily mean having that law explicitly encoded in the neural circuitry that processes the information. It simply means that the process should deal effectively (by whatever means) with a world that is structured by these physical laws. To do so may sometimes requires the neural process to have distinct parts that mirror distinct physical laws or the relations imposed by those laws on the information that reaches our senses. This would allow the neural system to somehow model the interaction of a number of physical laws as they shape the evidence that strikes our sense organs. I have dealt with the issue of the composition of physical effects on sense data in my earlier writing.[293] The issue of the complementarity of perceptual processes to physical laws has also been dealt with by Roger Shepard.[294]

Before drawing conclusions about what the experiment on alternating bursts of noise means, we have to remember that the system, although not really faced with a mixture of sounds, was acting as if it were. The spectral similarity of the two bursts of noise pointed to the conclusion that the first burst continued through the second. After this conclusion was reached, the auditory system showed that is was able to deal with the physics of mixtures by extracting from a mixture just the amount of energy that might have been contributed by a continuing sound and by using the residual energy to build a description of an added sound.

This experiment on alternating noise bursts seems to indicate that the auditory system makes just the right computation about the components of mixtures. However, a second experiment points to a limitation of the ability of the auditory system to do so. Van Noorden found this limitation when he alternated a pure tone, A, with a complex tone, B, to get A to capture one of B's harmonics into a sequential stream. In his experiment, the best capturing did not occur when the intensity of A was the same as that of the harmonic it was capturing. The best intensity for A depended on the degree to which the target harmonic was masked by the other harmonics of B.[295]

The factor of masking showed itself in the following ways: The higher the harmonic he was trying to capture, the lower he had to set the intensity of A. We know that the higher components of a mixture are masked by the lower ones more than the lower ones are by the higher. It seems, then, that the intensity of A was required to match the "sensory strength" of the target as it existed after masking, not its physical intensity. This conclusion is supported by the finding, in the same experiment, that if van Noorden removed some of the other harmonics from the mixture, reducing the masking of the target harmonic, he had to make the capturing tone louder.

How does this finding relate to the observation that the auditory system knows what happens to sounds in a mixture? It seems that it does not know enough about masking to match the original physical levels of A and the target harmonic. If A had really continued into the mixture, we would expect it to remain at the same intensity, and therefore the auditory system should find the best match between a target and a captor of the same physical intensity. However, it did not. I have tried out a number of explanations for the masking findings that employ the assumption that the nervous system knows about masking and tries to cancel its effects, but they all fail to explain the results of this experiment.

These results, then, show less ability on the part of the auditory system to arrive at the true facts about a mixture than did the earlier experiment on the alternation of louder and softer noise bursts. But there is a difference in what was being asked in these two experiments. In the case of the alternation of noise bursts, the question was not whether A (the the less intense burst) would be factored out of burst B; it was how much of B would be left behind. That was not the question being asked in van Noorden's experiment. In it, there was a competition between factors that favored taking the harmonic out (sequential similarity) and those that favored leaving it in (harmonicity and simultaneous onset). The experiment tried to find the best way to capture the component. So the two experiments are not exactly comparable. Perhaps the apparent knowledge that the auditory system has of the laws of physical mixture and of masking depends on the task and on the stimuli. This may be because the design of the auditory system has been optimized for several factors, not only the ability to deal with mixtures.

Spectral Relations

So far we have seen one way in which the auditory system deals with the problem of grouping the simultaneously received sensory components into sets that represent different sound sources. The old-plus-new heuristic looks at the sequence of events to find continuing ones that are hidden in a mixture. Other methods for deciding on the grouping of components do so without looking at earlier events. They group simultaneous components at different frequency regions by a consideration of certain relations between them. The next family of methods to be discussed is concerned with spectral properties that relate the different simultaneous components.

Properties of the Harmonics
All other things being equal, it appears likely that the further apart in frequency two simultaneous components are, the less likely they are to fuse. I recall once, when listening to an air conditioner, hearing two distinct noisy sounds, a low one and a high one. This prompted me to wonder whether I was hearing two sounds because there was a concentration of energy in two parts of the spectrum with a gap in between. It seemed to me that the auditory system might find some utility in segregating disconnected regions of the spectrum if it were true in some probabilistic way that the spectra that the human cares about tend to be smoothly continuous rather than bunched into isolated spectral bands. Since then I have collected a number of experimental observations, demonstrations, and theoretical speculations that bear on this issue.

The first has to do with the perceptual isolation of harmonics in a complex tone. When we listen to a complex tone in a nonanalytic way it seems that the first two partials are well integrated perceptually with one another and with all the rest of the harmonics. But are they really? We know that the harmonic series hangs together to generate the percept of a single tone, but are all the harmonics equally strongly bound into the fused mass? It has often been reported that it is easier for a listener to hear out the fundamental and the lowest partials of a complex tone.[296] A possible explanation for this finding depends on one of the properties of the peripheral auditory system.[297] Harmonics in sounds are linearly spaced in frequency whereas the mapping of frequency onto place on the basilar membrane is logarithmic. In log-frequency units the lower harmonics are spaced further apart from one another than the higher harmonics are. The way to tell whether this spacing is important is through experiments in which the harmonic in question is captured by a preceding pure tone of the same frequency into a sequential stream. Van Noorden used a stimulus in which a rich tone with 10 harmonics was alternated with a pure tone and supplied three pieces of evidence on this question. The first is that the lower harmonics were easier to capture out of the complex than the higher ones were. This was explained by saying that their representations on the basilar membrane are further apart. Second, it was easier to capture the components from a spectrum that contained only the odd harmonics than from a spectrum that contained consecutive ones. Again the explanation is that in the odd-harmonic spectrum the harmonics are twice as far apart as in the consecutive-harmonic spectrum. Third, a harmonic was easier to capture out of the complex tone when neighboring harmonics were removed. We can conclude that the greater the frequency separation between a harmonic and its

		Cond. 1	Cond. 2
———	tone 1	523	538
—————	tone 2	440	440
———	tone 3	370	360

Figure 3.5
A tone passing through a "field" of other partials. Left: diagram of the stimulus pattern. Right: the frequency for each of them in two conditions. (After Vicario 1982.)

nearest frequency neighbors, the easier it was to capture it out of the complex tone.[298]

There is another effect, reported by Giovanni Vicario, that is consistent with van Noorden's findings.[299] It was obtained using the pattern of tones shown at the left in figure 3.5. A pure tone (tone 2) was sounded alone briefly and was then joined by another set of partials (tones 1 and 3); the accompanying partials were then shut off and the tone continued briefly by itself. In some cases, tone 2 could be heard as passing right through the rich tone generated by the field of partials and in others it did not pass through but seemed to be replaced by the rich tone and then to reappear afterward. Vicario found that the perceptibility of tone 2 was not reduced by increasing the number of tones that it had to pass through. He added four more, two higher than tone 1 (622 and 740 Hz) and two lower than tone 3 (311 and 262 Hz). The lack of any effect suggested that it was only the local proximity of tones 1 and 3 to tone 2 that made tone 2 hard to hear. The result is suggestive rather than conclusive. It may be that the immediate neighbors of tone 2 had some special harmonic relations to it as well as being closer to it in frequency. However, the suggestion that nearest neighbors exert the strongest effects in absorbing a tone into a complex is consistent with van Noorden's observations.

The basilar-membrane explanation for these frequency proximity effects has nothing to do with the utility of these effects for scene analysis. If the nervous system cannot resolve simultaneous tones that are close in frequency it will not be able to put them into separate streams no matter how desirable this might be. Yet I do not believe that an inability to resolve the separate harmonics can be the entire explanation for the greater tendency of the auditory system to fuse partials that are nearer in frequency. I grant that it could apply to tones that were very close in frequency, let us say within a critical band of each other (on the order of three or four semitones). However, it cannot apply to a tendency observed in some other experiments. These experiments used patterns like the one used by Bregman and Pinker and shown in figure 1.16 of chapter 1. The only difference was that each of the two simultaneous tones, B and C, was an amplitude modulated tone. The experiments on the perceptual fusion of such sounds will be discussed in more detail later. For the moment, I want to focus on one finding. Even when the partials are as much as 14 semitones apart, they tend to fuse more strongly than partials that are separated by 16 semitones.[300] With such large frequency separations between pairs, there is no question of whether the nervous system is capable of resolving them as separate sounds. The preference for fusing sounds that are nearer in frequency must have some other basis and may well be "designed in" for scene-analysis purposes rather than being a by-product of a failure to resolve parts of the spectrum.

When Pinker and I found that a partial could be captured out of a mixture we were using a mixture of two partials separated by about an octave (see figure 1.16).[301] Although an octave may seem large, these partials were no more separated than the first two harmonics of a harmonic series, f and 2f, are. Yet, in informal experiments, I have found that the second harmonic of a complex tone that contains many harmonics is harder to capture than the higher partial in the two-partial complex. Plomp has also observed that the ability of listeners to identify a partial in a two-partial complex tone was very much better than in a tone containing more partials. The frequency separation between adjacent partials that permitted perceptual isolation of the partial was as much as three times smaller in the case of the two-partial tone.[302]

What of the observation that higher harmonics are harder to capture out of a complex tone than the lower ones? Can this effect be explained by the greater crowding of the representations of higher partials on the basilar membrane? An experiment done by Gary Dannenbring and myself bears on this question.[303] It employed a complex tone whose three partials were logarithmically spaced in frequency and hence equally spaced on the basilar membrane. The stimulus pattern consisted of the rapid alternation of a pure tone with this complex tone. In different conditions, the pure tone was set to the frequency of one of the harmonics of the complex tone and therefore acted as a captor that tended to capture its target harmonic out of the stream and into a sequential stream that included both the captor and the target. The three components of the complex tone were spaced by octaves, at f, 2f, and 4f. Even with this logarithmic spacing, the higher the harmonic, the harder it was to capture.

Therefore an explanation in terms of basilar-membrane spacing was not adequate.

However, there is another high-low asymmetry in the auditory system that may be used to explain this result. This is the well known "upward spread of masking." It is found, using a variety of methods, that lower tones mask higher tones better than higher ones mask lower.[304] This could explain why the higher partials are hard to extract from the complex tone. Remember that the ease of extracting them is judged either by just listening for them or else listening for them in the sequential stream into which they are pulled out by a captor tone. In both cases, since they are less audible, they may appear harder to capture. Two experimental results seem to support this explanation. The first is the observation that if you want to capture a harmonic out of a complex by alternating the complex with a captor tone, you get the best results when you make the captor softer when trying to capture a higher harmonic.[305] This seems counterintuitive; you would think that a louder captor would be better. However, we must remember the manner in which the experiment is usually carried out (for example, by van Noorden). The listener hears the rapid alternation of a pure tone with a complex tone and listens for a double beating of the pure tone, that is, for the pure tone appearing twice as often as the complex tone. This double beating means that the target harmonic is being heard as a sound separate from the complex tone, so that there are two pure tones (captor and target harmonic) for every repetition of the complex tone. Now suppose that due to upward spread of masking the target partial is registered very weakly by the auditory system. Then even if it were pulled out of the complex by the captor the pure-tone stream would contain a strong tone (the captor) alternating with a weak tone (the target) and the listener might be affected by the contrast between a strong and a weak tone and be led to believe that the weak tone was just not there. On the other hand if the physical intensity of the captor were lowered so as to achieve an equality of perceived intensity between the captor and the target the listener would judge that both were present in the pure tone stream. This masking-based explanation of the difficulty of hearing out the higher harmonics is also supported by the following finding: If you raise the intensity of the target harmonic it is easier to pull out of the complex, and this effect is more pronounced for the higher partials.[306] This would be expected if the perception of the higher partials were especially hurt by masking and if raising the intensity helped to overcome the masking.

Dannenbring and I found that the intensity pattern in which higher harmonics were hardest to capture was one in which a higher harmonic was weaker than a lower one. Despite the ready physiological explanations that come to mind to explain this fact, we should not neglect its implications for scene analysis. Most natural pitch-like sounds, such as the vowels of the human voice or most instrumental tones, have a long-term spectrum in which the higher partials are weaker than the lower ones. Sometimes this pattern is temporarily violated when strong resonances are imposed on the spectrum, as happens when the human speech apparatus forms the resonances that define one particular vowel, but if we average over many specific examples, the spectrum does have the property of a falling intensity with a rising frequency (at least in the range above 300 Hz).[307] If the auditory system prefers to accept as parts of the same sound, partials that fall off in intensity with increasing frequency, this will give a statistical boost to the grouping process and increase the likelihood of fusing partials that have arisen from the same acoustic event. The fact that this may be the result of a capacity limitation at the physiological level may be another example of the point that I made earlier—a functional accomplishment may be subserved by a physiological breakdown. Indeed, this point encourages us to ask the question "Why is the auditory system arranged so that lower partials mask higher ones? Does this arrangement serve some purpose?"

It also appears that the smoothness of the spectrum is important and that harmonics that are raised in intensity will segregate more readily from the others.[308] This can be understood in terms of the masking of one tone by another. A louder component is less likely to be masked and more likely to mask the others that accompany it. It is hard to find a direct explanation, in scene-analysis terms, for the segregation of more intense components from weaker ones that accompany them. Are they less likely to be parts of the same sound? Perhaps this basis for segregation is a by-product of the evolved design of the system and not specifically evolved to serve a function of its own.

Harmonic Relations (Harmonicity) in Complex Tones

There is a particular relation that can hold among a simultaneously present set of partials. They can all be harmonics of the same fundamental. There is a good deal of evidence to suggest that if they are, they will tend to be assigned to the same stream; that is, they will be fused and heard as a single sound. Let us call this the "harmonicity" principle.

There are a number of facts that point in this direction. One is the simple observation that a set of harmonics arising from a single fundamental is not heard as a large number of individual partials but as a single sound. This has been noticed over and over again.[309] While this placing of related partials into a single package serves to group components that have come from the same source there is a more definite purpose as well—to calculate the pitch of the fundamental. Most objects, when they are set into vibration, move not just with a single vibration frequency but with a large number of frequencies. In many cases, including the human voice and all instruments with clear pitches, the frequencies of vibration are all multiples of the lowest frequency (the fundamental). In such cases, the different frequencies are called harmonics. If the lowest frequency is called f, the harmonics have the frequencies f, 2f, 3f, 4f, ... Our auditory system seems to have evolved a method of finding out what the fundamental is, even if only some of the higher harmonics are present, with the result that the pitch we hear is the pitch of that fundamental. Even if we filter out the fundamental frequencies of the successive notes in a melody, as for example when we play it over the telephone or any equivalent low-fidelity reproduction equipment, we still hear the melody with its pitches unchanged despite a change in the fullness of the sound. How can we be hearing the pitch of the fundamental even though the fundamental has been filtered out? This question has been referred to as the mystery of the missing fundamental. How can the auditory system hear a sound that is not there? Apparently it is capable of making use of the regular spacing between the existing harmonics to determine the pitch of the missing fundamental.

It is important to the auditory system to group the harmonics together into the same analysis. This will seem to be a strange statement to those hearing scientists who are used to thinking of the typical laboratory setup in which only a single set of harmonics is played to the listener at any one time. In this case the issue of grouping seems meaningless and it seems sufficient to say that the listener just finds a fundamental that accounts for all the components that are heard. But the situation changes as soon as two complex tones are played at the same time. If the two fundamental frequencies are unrelated, an analysis that tries to find a single fundamental for all the partials that are present will fail. Yet we know through listening to music that we can hear two or more pitches at the same time. There has to be a way to base the computation of each component pitch on only a subset of the partials. Assuming that this is somehow done, what we hear in the presence of a mixture of two harmonic series (as when two musical tones are played at the same time) is not a large set of partials but two unitary sounds with distinct pitches.

Models of the Pitch-Analysis Process

Because of the intimate connection that probably exists between the computation of pitch in the auditory system and the perceptual grouping (fusion) of simultaneous partials, it is necessary to discuss theories of pitch perception. I cannot describe all the theories that have been proposed to describe how the auditory system calculates the fundamental from a set of harmonics. They are discussed in many textbooks.[310] I want, however, to discuss some of the issues in pitch perception.

There are two phenomena that current theories of pitch have tried to explain. The first is how we can hear the pitch of the fundamental even when it is filtered out of the spectrum. The second is how we derive a pitch for a spectrum whose components are not exactly harmonically related. I have already described how one can physically create a spectrum in which the fundamental is missing. Let me now describe how an inharmonic spectrum gives rise nonetheless to a pitch.

Due to the genius of modern sound-producing equipment, it is possible to present a listener with a tone formed of partials that are inharmonic. That is, they do not fall into a neat harmonic series. Nonetheless, they often give rise to a pitch that is not simply the pitch of one of the partials that is present. Apparently this happens because our mechanism for deriving a pitch from a set of partials goes to work on this inharmonic array of partials and comes up with an answer which is simply the best it can do with this weird input. It should be noted, however, that the pitch sensation derived from an inharmonic set of partials is never as strong and clear as the one derived from an equal number of harmonic partials.[311] Furthermore, the sound that one of these sets gives rise to is not as perceptually unified as the one that a harmonic series provides. Much research has been carried out on the perception of the pitch of inharmonic partials.

One way to derive inharmonic partials is to start with a set of harmonic ones and then shift their frequencies up or down by adding or subtracting the same constant to each. For instance, let us take some of the harmonics related to a fundamental of 100 Hz, for example 300, 400, and 500 Hz. These are all multiples of 100 Hz and they will yield a pitch related to 100 Hz. Now let us add 7 Hz to each frequency so that they are 307, 407, and 507 Hz. Notice that they are no longer multiples of any fundamental frequency (except 1 Hz, which is too low to be heard as a pitch). Despite the inharmonicity of the shifted group of partials we will still hear a pitch. The pitch will be just a bit higher than the 100-Hz pitch that we heard before we added the 7 Hz.[312] At the same time we may hear the pitches of the separate partials. Apparently in this case inharmonic tones are accepted into a pitch analysis, at least partly. While they may not lose their individual identities entirely, they contribute to a global estimate of pitch. This pitch experience is, however, weaker than the one that occurs with a harmonic series. It appears, therefore, that the admitting of partials into a pitch computation is not all or none. They can be weakly included as in the present example.

Theories of Pitch Analysis Different theories of auditory pitch analysis have addressed two problems: How we can hear the pitch of the missing fundamental in a harmonic series, and how we can hear a pitch in shifted sets of partials. The theories tend to differ on two dimensions: (1) whether they see pitch analysis as based primarily on "place" information or on "periodicity" information, and (2) what method is used to derive the pitch from the type of information that is used.

Some theories use the fact that different places on the basilar membrane of the inner ear respond maximally to different pitches. Therefore, if the auditory system knows what places on the basilar membrane are responding, and with what amplitude, it can infer a lot about the spectrum of the stimulating sound. This is the "place" information. Other theories use the fact that the part of the basilar membrane that responds best to a given frequency component also tends to vibrate at the frequency of that component. Therefore there is information in the vibration rates (or periodicity) at each position along the basilar membrane, and the auditory system could use it to infer the spectrum of the stimulating sound. This is the "periodicity" information. A neural recording of this periodicity is provided by the fact that each small region of the basilar membrane has its own nerve supply that primarily registers the frequency to which that portion of the basilar membrane is tuned. If the local region of the basilar membrane with its associated nerve supply is thought of as a channel, we can see that the output of this channel behaves like a band-pass filter. The filter, however, does not completely exclude nearby frequencies, especially those that are lower than the tuned frequency. Therefore the neural record of each frequency in the incoming signal is perturbed by the existence of other frequencies.

So far we have described how the theories differ in their description of how the spectrum of the incoming signal is estimated by the auditory system. They also differ in how they think that the estimates are used to derive a pitch. The methods appearing in different theories all try to derive the fundamental frequency of the incoming spectrum, but they go about it in different ways and therefore are fooled in different ways when an inharmonic spectrum is encountered. The most direct way of using the spectrum is by a calculation of the fundamental to which the received partials are all related harmonically. One of the theories assumes that there can be some error in the original estimation of the frequencies of the partials and that the system overcomes this problem by doing a "best fit" calculation on the set of estimated frequencies.[313] Models of this type have been referred to as pattern-recognition models because they require the auditory system to recognize the incoming pattern of partials as a set of harmonics that is appropriate for some particular fundamental.[314] That is how they solve the problem of the missing fundamental, the first phenomenon that was a challenge for modern-day theories of pitch. They explain the second phenomenon, the pitch of an inharmonic spectrum, by assuming that the auditory system still treats the partials as if they had arisen from a common source and tries to find the fundamental of which they are harmonics. Because the partials are really not harmonically related, the fundamental that is found will not fit very well, but the system will put out the pitch of this tone as its best guess.

The second method for deriving the fundamental does not directly use the information about the frequencies of the detected partials, but uses information about the beats between them. To understand this theory it is important to remember that equal steps along the basilar membrane do not represent equal steps in frequency but equal steps in log frequency. Octaves (doublings in frequency), for example, are equal steps apart. Therefore the harmonics, because they are equally spaced in frequency rather than log frequency, will stimulate a set of tuned basilar-membrane locations that are crowded closer and closer together as the harmonic number goes up.

The neural outputs of an individual basilar membrane location is not entirely driven by the single frequency to which that location is tuned, but by adjacent frequencies as well. For a harmonic series, this would happen more for higher harmonics because they are more crowded on the basilar membrane. Therefore, if you could look at the neural output of the basilar membrane, in its lower channels you could see firing rates corresponding to individual harmonics; in higher channels you would mainly see firing rates caused by the interaction of two or more harmonics. Any physical system (such as a band-pass filter) faced with unresolvable combinations of frequencies will register beats (periodic fluctuations in the amplitude envelope) whose rate will correspond to the differences in frequencies between pairs of harmonics. Recall that in a harmonic series the harmonics of a fundamental frequency, f, are f, 2f, 3f, 4f, ... Notice that their frequencies go up in increments of f. That is, they are spaced from their nearest neighbors by f, the frequency of the fundamental, and from their nonnearest neighbors by multiples of f. When a set of harmonics is not resolvable, the beat rate will be dominated by f and have multiples of f as well. This means that the interference pattern between adjacent harmonics will be repeated at a regular period. Conveniently, this period is the period of the fundamental. This will hold independently in every spectral band in which there are unresolvable harmonics. In these frequency regions, in the higher parts of the spectrum, while the neural mechanism is not fast enough to follow the repetitions of the waveforms of the individual harmonics it is fast enough to follow these beats. Therefore, there can be an independent estimate of f in a number of spectral bands in the higher parts of the spectrum. In the lower parts, where the auditory critical band is narrower and the harmonics are fully resolvable, the harmonics themselves are of a low enough frequency that their individual periods can be registered by a neural mechanism. It is, in principle, possible for a neural mechanism to use both the beat rate in the upper part of the spectrum and the rate of the separable harmonics in the lower part.

According to the proponents of "temporal" theories, it is totally unnecessary to compute the fundamental from the pattern of frequencies of the incoming fundamentals. The interference pattern in each basilar membrane channel does it for us. That is the explanation of how we hear the missing fundamental. The explanation of the pitch of inharmonic complexes is derived in the same way. Let us suppose that we have taken a group of three harmonics, 500, 600, and 700 Hz, that would normally be sufficient to specify a missing fundamental of 100 Hz and shift them all up by 15 Hz so that the frequencies are now 515, 615, and 715 Hz. In contrast to the case of harmonically related partials, the interference patterns for these shifted partials will not be exactly periodic and therefore the process whose job it is to detect the periodicity in the interaction of harmonics will find a pitch that is partly related to the 100-Hz separation between them, but which is a bit higher due to the nonexact repetition of the interference pattern.

Listening to Inharmonic Partials

As I have already pointed out, sounds that are composed of inharmonic partials give a weak sense of pitch and do not fuse very well.

For example, an inharmonic set of partials can be derived by simply mathematically stretching the separations between the partials of a harmonic series. Consider the ratio of 2. In a harmonic series, this is the separation between the frequencies of the first and second harmonics, or the second and fourth, or the third and the sixth, and so on.

By stretching all the frequency separations between the partials (on a log scale) so that the frequency ratio that relates these particular pairs of harmonics is now 2.2 instead of 2, a new set of frequencies can be derived for all the partials so that they are no longer harmonically related. The partials are now only 10 percent further apart than they were before (for octave relations) but they now no longer are heard as a single coherent sound. Instead, the lower partials are often heard as individual tones and the higher ones remain undistinguished from one another as a buzzing tonal mass. The sense of pitch is very indistinct. The judged fusion seems to continuously get worse when we either gradually stretch the spacing of the partials from what it is in a harmonic series to 7 percent further apart or shrink their spacing gradually to 7 percent closer together (for octave relations).[315] John Pierce, who has a lot of experience in listening to such sounds, has also noticed that when two stretched series of partials are sounded at the same time, you do not hear only two distinct sounds as you do when listening to two harmonic sounds.[316]

Clearly two things happen with the harmonic partials that do not with the inharmonic ones: the set of partials is heard as a single coherent tone, and that tone has a clear pitch. Therefore we see differences both in perceptual unification and in pitch extraction. A natural question comes to mind: is it the same process that extracts pitch and that unifies the partials into a single sound? Although we do not know the answer, we can remark that both accomplishments require the auditory system to group acoustic components. There have been recent attempts to extend the theory of how the human auditory system does pitch extraction so that it can explain how it is possible to hear more than one pitch at a time. Briefly, the older single-pitch theory supposed that the auditory system had some way of examining the neural impulses coming out of the inner ear and calculating the fundamental frequency that would best explain this neural output. The newer approach extends the method so that it finds the two best fitting fundamentals.[317] Undoubtedly, the approach will be further generalized to find the number of pitches that the human ear can hear, a number greater than two in many listening circumstances. Any theory of this type would group the separate sets of harmonics in the course of finding the separate fundamentals.

We have looked at the case in which all the partials are inharmonically related to one another. What happens if we start with a tone that is built from a harmonic series and then mistune just one partial from the rest of the partials? It has been reported that this partial becomes easier to hear out from the complex tone.[318]

Here is a description of what it sounds like when a harmonic partial is gradually mistuned:

> When a low harmonic component is mistuned by a small amount, less than 1%, the pitch of the complex as a whole shifts a little, but the tone still sounds like a harmonic complex, and the mistuned partial is not heard as a separate tone. When the mistuning is increased to 1%–1.5%, the pitch of the complex shifts further, and the complex can now just be distinguished from a truly harmonic complex. However, the mistuned partial is usually not heard as a separate tone. If the mistuning is increased to 1.5%–3%, the pitch of the complex shifts still further, but the mistuned partial is now just heard as standing out from the complex. If the mistuning is increased to 6%, the pitch shift of the complex generally declines, and the mistuned partial is heard even more clearly as standing out from the complex.[319]

Basically what happens is that at first the mistuning of the tone changes the pitch of the complex tone. This is consistent with the idea that some pitch-determining mechanism is trying to estimate the fundamental of the set of partials and the mistuning of one of them throws its calculations off. With greater mistuning the partial is somehow excluded from the pitch computation and the pitch returns to what it would have been if the partial had not been present. This intimate connection between the calculation of pitch and the decision about which tones go together suggests the existence of a single system whose job it is to carry out both tasks and that uses the harmonicity of the set of partials to make its decisions.

Logically, either group of theories, those that depend on recognizing a pattern of partials indicative of a certain fundamental or those that depend on the interference pattern within frequency-specific neural channels, could explain how the pitch system could exclude some partials from a global pitch analysis. A system using the pattern-recognition approach might be able to look for the set of harmonics related to every possible fundamental (within a certain range of possibilities) at the same time. For convenience we can imagine the system as possessing a set of harmonic-series templates, each one specific to a particular fundamental, which it applies to the pattern of active frequency channels. For example, the template for the 100-Hz fundamental would look for activity at 100, 200, 300, ... If a sufficient number of these were showing activity, it would register a global pitch at 100 Hz. Providing it could tell which partials had contributed to the decision, it might remove the partial pitches of these components from perception, leaving only the partial pitches of the badly fitting partials that had not activated the template. The method can be thought of as a "harmonic sieve," which allows through its holes only those tones related to the template and stops ones that are too far away from the frequencies of the acceptable harmonics.[320]

If, on the other hand, our auditory system estimates the fundamental from the repetition rate of within-channel interference patterns, it would have to "sift out" nonharmonics in a different way. It could look for neural channels whose periodicities were related (or almost so) and accept only those similar channels into the same pitch analysis. The remainder would be excluded.[321] There is some reason to believe that it would have to do this even if it were not interested in partitioning the spectrum to assist later pattern recognition. If it allowed badly fitting channels into the pitch estimation process, then, when it was estimating the pitch of a human voice, for example, it could come up with an estimate that was really a mixture of the effects of two different voices and hence not the pitch of anything at all.

We see then that any theory of pitch computation that can compute the pitch of a sound and not get confused by other co-occurring sounds would be, in effect, doing a scene analysis based on the harmonicity principle. That is why I said earlier that pitch estimation and sound separation were so intimately linked.

We should recall again at this point what the examples and theories mean for scene analysis. When a mixture of sounds is encountered, it may be useful to analyze the mixture for the existence of one or more good harmonic series. This strategy is useful since in the most important sound to us, the human voice, the partials come very close to forming a harmonic series. If we are able to detect a harmonic series, we can determine its fundamental frequency, assign a pitch to it, and then remove all the harmonics related to this pitch from the set of partials still being considered. Then the remainder can be taken alone and subjected to further analysis to discover other groups of partials that go together.

One consequence of the exclusion of a partial from a fusion group is that it should become freer to enter into sequential streams with earlier sounds that resemble it. We saw an example of this in the experiment of Bregman and Pinker where the upper tone, B, of a two-tone complex, BC, was freer to group with a preceding pure tone when the conditions were less favorable to the fusion of B and C (see figure 1.16). We should find, then, that inharmonic partials will more readily be captured away from their simultaneous companions and into sequential streams. This property would make it more likely that a sound that was suddenly joined by another that was unrelated

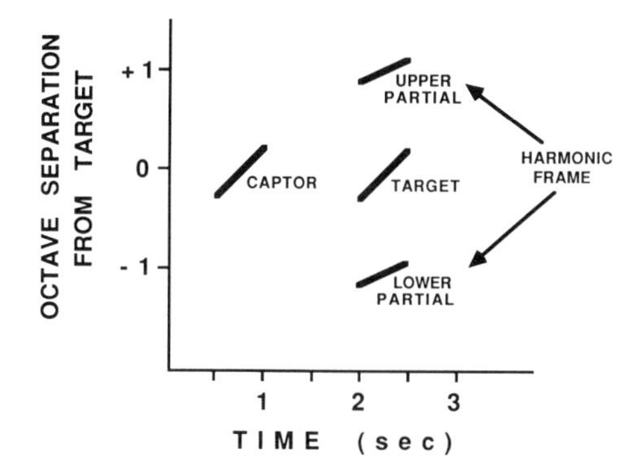

Figure 3.6
Capturing the central glide in a three-component glide. (After Bregman and Doehring 1984.)

to it would be more easily grouped with its own earlier part than with its accidental companion.

There is evidence both for and against this prediction. In one of Bregman and Pinker's experiments, they varied the relation between B and C so that they either formed ratios of 3:2, 2:1, or 3:1 or else were mistuned by a semitone from each of these simple ratios. They found no evidence that the harmonicity played a role in the ability of A to capture B into a sequential organization. Similarly, Plomp found it possible to "hear out" unrelated tones as easily as harmonic tones from a tonal complex.[322]

On the other hand, harmonicity did play a role in another experiment that was very much like the preceding one except that the component tones were all sinusoids gliding in a straight line on log-frequency-by-time coordinates as in figure 3.6.[323] A pure tone glide alternated repeatedly with a complex of three simultaneous glides and had the same frequency and slope as the middle of the three simultaneous glides so that in some conditions it captured the middle one into a sequential stream. Now in one set of conditions, the three simultaneous glides were all parallel on the log scale (unlike the case shown in figure 3.6 where the "target" glide does not move in parallel with the glides of the "harmonic frame"). In the parallel conditions, the glides remained in the same frequency ratio to one another throughout their gliding paths. In some of these conditions, the three glides were spaced by octaves, forming the ratios 4:2:1 throughout (the octave relation is a very powerful one for fusing tones). In other conditions, the two outer glides, the highest and the lowest, remained in the two-octave (4:1) relation as before, but the middle glide was mistuned from the octave relation by a quarter octave so that now the ratios between the glides were 4:1.68:1. Under these conditions, where the middle glide was mistuned from the other two, it was much easier to capture it into a sequential stream.

The discrepancy between the results of the two experiments cannot be attributed to the use of glides in the second because in that experiment there was a condition in which the slopes of the glides was 0 octaves per second (in other words, they were constant-frequency tones). This condition showed the same effects of harmonicity as the other ones. The only important difference was that the glide experiment used three simultaneous components instead of two. I think this was the crucial difference. In the inharmonic condition the outer two glides defined a harmonic frame into which the middle tone did not fit. Apparently it is not sufficient to have only a single tone define a potential harmonic series into which the other does, or does not, fit. I suspect that in the Bregman-Pinker experiment there was no real manipulation of harmonicity because there were too few partials to define it. If I am right, we should find that increasing the number of partials that maintain a harmonic relation to one another should increase the isolation of a partial that is mistuned from this group. To my knowledge, there has been no definitive study of this sort.

One of the surprising things about inharmonic complexes is that they have pitches. Somehow whatever process normally computes the pitch of harmonic complexes is activated sufficiently to generate a pitch. However, when we listen to an inharmonic complex we are often most aware of the pitches of certain individual partials that are not fusing with the others. We need a vocabulary for talking about different kinds of pitches. I would propose that we assign the name "partial" pitch to the pitch of an individual partial and the name "global pitch" to the pitch that is computed on the basis of a set of partials. The first thing to notice when we listen to an inharmonic complex is that the global pitch is weak. Partial pitches are more strongly heard. In harmonic complexes, this is rarely the case. How can this be explained?

First of all, we know that the auditory system can compute more than one pitch at a time, otherwise we would not be able to hear the individual pitches in a musical chord. The fact that we hear both the pitches of partials as well as a global pitch in inharmonic complexes is simply another example of the fact that more than one pitch can be calculated at once. Furthermore, it seems plausible that the frequencies of the partials that we are hearing as partial pitches are contributing to the computation of the global pitch as well. Why, then, are the partial pitches heard with such difficulty in complexes that contain only harmonic partials? The harmonics can be heard out by most people only if a pure tone, at the same frequency as the harmonic that they want to hear, precedes the complex tone.

Two explanations come to mind. The first is that we can hear out only the nonintegrated partials, those partials that are not being integrated to yield a global pitch. This would explain why we do not hear the partial pitches in harmonic tones: none of the partials is being rejected from the pitch analysis. This makes sense of the findings that I discussed earlier about the experience of a listener when a single partial in a harmonic series is gradually mistuned. Before it is rejected from the global analysis, the global pitch changes since the latter is now incorporating discrepant information. However, after the partial is rejected two things happen. The global pitch returns to what it was before and the partial pitch of the mistuned partial is heard. The implication of this explanation is that no matter how you remove a partial or a set of them from a global pitch analysis, whether by mistuning or by sequential capturing, the global pitch will be altered. As far as I know, this prediction has never been tested.

There is a second possible explanation for the absence of partial pitches in a harmonic complex. They may be actively inhibited by the nervous system. It would work this way: first, there would be a detection process for the existence of a harmonic series. This process would "know" the frequencies of the partials that were harmonically related to every fundamental. If a sufficient number of harmonically related partials were present at the same time, the detector would signal the existence of a global pitch appropriate to the inferred fundamental. At the same time, it would remove the individual harmonically related partials from the pitch analysis. Once a global pitch had been formed, the auditory system would try to inhibit the independent partial pitches of just those harmonics that were multiples of the perceived fundamental, in order to favor the perception of the global pitch.

The same theory would explain why we can easily hear both a weak global pitch and other partial pitches in an inharmonic complex. The existence of the global pitch would occur because some subset of the inharmonic partials managed to weakly satisfy the requirements of the detection process (which might not be precisely tuned so that it could tolerate some error). However, since even that subset of partials would not provide very strong evidence for a harmonic series, the global pitch would be registered only weakly. Furthermore we might expect the attempt by the global process to fail in its attempt to inhibit the partial pitches. This failure might occur because the pitch process knew only the set of *harmonic* partials associated with each computed global pitch. Even when it was fooled into registering a global pitch by an inharmonic complex, it would try to inhibit the partial pitches for the set of *harmonics* that normally trigger it. Since the partials that actually stimulated it would not be the ones that it knew how to inhibit, its inhibition would miss them and their partial pitches would be heard.

This theory has a nonintuitive prediction to make: If we started with an inharmonic complex and mixed it with a pure tone whose frequency we could adjust by means of a knob, and began to adjust the tone up and down in frequency, we would be able to hear the partial pitch of this pure tone. (We might, of course, need some assistance in hearing the partial. This could be provided by alternating an isolated copy of the pure tone with the mixture.) However, certain frequencies of this pure tone would be predicted to be harder to hear as partial pitches in the mixture. These would be at the frequencies that were harmonically related to the weak global pitch that was being heard at that moment, and therefore being actively inhibited by the pitch detector. Again, as far as I know, there are no experimental data to support or refute this prediction.

However, we do have some information that pertains to one presupposition of the theory. We need to be able to assume that the auditory system has the ability to direct inhibition very precisely to just that set of partials that is related to a particular fundamental. This assumption is supported by an observation reported to me by Quentin Summerfield. It is based on the earlier observation that if a person is exposed to a harmonic spectrum that has a shape to it (that is, where certain frequency regions are enhanced) and then is switched to a flat spectrum (where all frequency regions are equally intense), the flat spectrum will be heard as having a shape that is the complement of the one that was listened to first. You can use this effect to make a person hear a flat spectrum as if it were a vowel. First you present an inducing spectrum that has the complement shape to that of the desired vowel, intense at frequencies where that vowel is weak and weak at frequencies where the vowel is intense. A subsequently presented flat spectrum will sound like the vowel.[324] This is interpreted as resulting from a briefly persisting inhibition of those frequencies at which the inducing spectrum was intense.

The relevance of this phenomenon to our previous question becomes visible when we look at a fact discovered by Summerfield and his co-workers in the course of studying this way of inducing a vowel percept.[325] In the previous case the fundamental of the spectrum of the inducing stimulus and the vowel were identical, but now they arranged it so that the fundamental frequencies of the inducing stimulus spectrum and the subsequent flat spectrum were different (that is, the spectra had different frequency components as well as different spectral shapes). In this case the induction of the vowel percept did not occur. This shows that the inhibition process is accurate enough to target only the partials that were present in the first tone.

We are left with two possible explanations of why we can easily hear partial pitches in an inharmonic complex and not in a harmonic complex. Either the heard pitches are available because they were never integrated into the computation of the global pitch or because despite being integrated they have not been properly inhibited by the global process. Whatever the mechanism, we can see a good scene-analyzing reason for their being perceptually available when they are not harmonically related to the dominant global pitch. The harmonicity heuristic has decided that they are not part of the sound that generated the global pitch and therefore should be available to be heard in their own right or as part of some other sound or sequence of sounds.

Fusion and Segregation of Simultaneous Complexes

We have seen that if we hear a simultaneous set of partials in which some partials do not fit into a harmonic series, they are not fused with the ones that do. But what about more complicated cases in which we hear a group of instruments playing at the same time or a group of singing voices? Musicians believe that a simultaneous set of tones will blend better if they are in a harmonious or consonant relation to one another. This is different from the cases that were described previously. The earlier discussion concerned the rejection of components that were not part of a single harmonic series. In the present case, there are a number of tones present, each with its own harmonic series.

To simplify the discussion, let us consider only two notes of different pitches played together. In each note, the partials relate to a common fundamental, but this fundamental is different for the two notes. This being the case, our earlier discussion would lead us to think that the two sets of partials would be allocated to two pitch analyses. This is true; in such a mixture we will usually hear two pitches. However, our discussion led us to believe that as long as there were two different pitches, the tones would always be perceived as equally distinct from one another. This goes against the beliefs of musicians who generally hold the opinion that some pitches blend better than others.

It seems that two tones blend better when more of their harmonics coincide. We can start with the example of two tones, spaced by an octave, where the higher tone will (by definition) have a fundamental that is double the frequency of the lower one. Take a concrete case in which the fundamentals are at 100 and 200 Hz. The harmonics of the 100 Hz tone will be at 100, 200, 300, 400, 500, 600, 700, 800, . . . , whereas the harmonics of the higher one will be at 200, 400, 800, ... With these fundamentals, every harmonic of the high tone coincides in frequency with a frequency of the low one, and half the frequencies of the lower one appear in the higher one. This is the highest overlap that the harmonics of two different pitches can have. The only way tones can have more than 50 percent of their components in common is if both are at the same pitch.[326] It is probably not a coincidence that the perceptual fusion of tones is highest if they both have the same pitch and next highest if they are an octave apart.[327]

The blending of tones to create an experience of a single richer tone is clearly exemplified in the design of the pipe organ. This use of harmonic relations will be described in chapter 5 in a discussion of the role of scene analysis in music.

Another example of the principle that tones with simpler harmonic relations blend better was provided by a demonstration created by Giovanni Vicario.[328] First a pattern was demonstrated in which a 440-Hz complex tone was accompanied by two other complex tones for part of the time that it was on. This was shown earlier in figure 3.5. Tone 2 was 2.5 seconds long and it was accompanied by the other tones for its middle 1.5 sec. In a first condition, the fundamentals of these tones were spaced by a minor third, which is approximately the ratio 6:5. Such a spacing made the harmonics of the adjacent pairs of tones fall into a moderately simple harmonic relation with one another but the extreme tones (tones 1 and 3) fall into a more irregular relation. In this case, tone 2 seemed to partially disappear at that point in time at which the other tones were switched on. In the second condition tones 1 and 3 fell into the ratio 3:2, which put their harmonics into a fairly simple relation with one another; however, the middle tone was mistuned to both of the others. In this case it sounded more independent of the others and did not tend to disappear when the other two came on. This effect can be thought of in the following way: Because the part of tone 2 that co-occurred with tones 1 and 3 was rejected from an otherwise good harmonic grouping, it was more easily grouped with its own parts that extended outside the three-tone complex and was therefore heard as a continuous long tone.

Perhaps the reason for the fusion of related tones can be most easily understood by thinking not in terms of fusion but its opposite, segregation. We then see that two individual pitches are more prominent when the two fundamentals have few frequencies at which their harmonics coincide. If the pitch calculation system tends to eliminate a harmonic from further consideration after it has used it in the calculation of a global pitch, shared harmonics might not serve to define two different pitches very well. An absence of coincidence would allow the pitch calculation system a clearer, more independent look at the harmonics of each fundamental, and hence would allow it to clearly see that there were two.[329]

An indication that the auditory system prefers to have independent evidence that two pitches exist comes from an experiment in which listeners were required to separate the global pitches generated by two simultaneous sets of harmonics, each related to a different (missing) fundamental. The task involved recognizing the musical harmonic interval between pairs of tones.[330] Recognition was particularly hard when the harmonics were close enough to beat with one another; it was not so bad when they exactly coincided because at least the beating was eliminated. It was easiest when the harmonics occupied completely nonoverlapping regions of the frequency spectrum. Besides showing that the auditory system is least confused when the evidence is spectrally clear and separate, this finding suggests that the computations that calculate the pitch of a complex tone operate independently in local regions of the frequency spectrum.

The question of how the auditory system separates simultaneous speech sounds has attracted a lot of attention in recent years. This topic will be dealt with more thoroughly in chapter 6. For the moment we might simply point out that many theories of voice separation, both those that have been devised to explain human performance data and those that have been used to program computers to separate concurrent speech signals, start by trying to find the set of frequency components present in a mixture and then attempt to divide the total set into subsets that are harmonics of different fundamentals. There have been demonstrations with synthesized speech sounds that show that the auditory system tends to fuse two sets of partials that are in different portions of the spectrum, even sets presented to different ears, when each set is formed of consecutive harmonics and the two sets of harmonics are related to the same fundamental frequency. When the two sets are related to different fundamentals, they are heard as two separate sounds. There is some controversy about whether this segregation affects the listener's recognition of what is being said, but I believe that it has been clearly shown to do so in certain cases.

In the preceding section, I have presented evidence that the pitch estimation system acts to group harmonically related partials. We might conclude that this grouping is then used to derive other properties of the now segregated partials. This description implies a one-way transaction, the pitch system influencing the grouping system and not vice versa. However, this appears not to be true. There is evidence that the pitch that is calculated can depend on cues other than harmonicity, cues that we think of as operating outside the pitch system. These will be discussed more fully later when we get to those particular cues. To give a brief preview, however, we will see that when coherent frequency modulation is applied to a set of partials, it increases the likelihood of the calculation of a global pitch based on that set, whether the set is harmonic or not. This suggests that other factors that can affect the grouping of simultaneous components of a sound can affect the computation of global qualities of the subsets of sounds that are derived from this grouping. In chapter 5 we will see that even such basic properties of sound as the *dissonance* of a group of musical tones, which was thought to be based on a raw acoustic phenomenon, can be strongly reduced if the tones that are acoustically dissonant with one another are caused to be perceptually segregated from one another. We will be able to add dissonance to the list of basic qualities that are affected by the segregation (or fusion) of simultaneous auditory components.

This section has reviewed the role of spectral relations in the decomposition of mixtures of sounds. Many observations have suggested that one of the heuristics for simultaneous grouping of spectral components is whether or not they fit into the same harmonic series. The auditory system can detect more than one harmonic series at a time, each related to a different fundamental, and construct a number of pitches. This pitch generation seems to go along with a merging of the identities of the individual components into larger masses, each mass with its own global properties, of which pitch is only one. It is consistent with our earlier discussion to call each such mass a stream; by doing so we point out that such global organizations have a time dimension to them as well as a spectral structure.

To summarize our discussion thus far, it appears that many factors in complex spectra affect the ability of the auditory system to parse them and uncover the individual acoustic sources that gave rise to them. These include the density of the spectra (how closely partials are spaced), the relative intensities of the partials, the match in the perceived intensity of the partials to the intensities of earlier sounds, as well as the harmonic relations between the partials.

Common Fate (AM and FM)

The factors that have just been discussed—the harmonicity principle, for example—make use of properties of a sound that remain steady for at least a short time. The principles that we will examine next concern changes in the sound over time. Changes can provide us with a powerful rule for deciding whether parts of a spectrum belong together. The rule is this: If different parts of the spectrum change in the same way at the same time, they probably belong to the same environmental sound.

By way of introduction, I would like to describe a principle of grouping put forward by the Gestalt psychologists, the principle of "common fate." Let us imagine that we had a photograph taken of the sky. It shows a large number of birds in flight. Because they are all facing the same direction and seem to be at the same distance from the camera, we think that they are a single flock. Later we are shown a motion picture taken of that same scene. On looking at this view, we see that there were two distinct flocks rather than only one. This conclusion becomes evident when we look at the paths of motion. One group of birds seems to be moving in a set of parallel paths describing a curve in the sky. Another group is also moving in a set of parallel paths but this path is different from that of the first group. The common motion within each subgroup binds that group together perceptually and, at the same time, segregates it from the other group. The common motion within each group is an example of the Gestalt principle of common fate.

The segregating effects of common fate need not be restricted to motion. Suppose we were faced with an array of identical disks, each at a different randomly chosen level of illumination. A still photograph of the disks might cause us to group clusters of them on the basis of similarities in brightness. Because of the random brightnesses, this grouping would not yield clusters with simple shapes. However, a motion picture of that same array might reveal that the disks on the right half of the display were undergoing parallel changes (possibly only a slight flickering) in brightness, and this would cause us to see them as a group. The synchronous change would not necessarily cause the disks on the right to be more similar in brightness to one another than to those on the left. At any given moment, a still photograph would always find a haphazard array of brightnesses. The change itself is the important thing.

The common fate heuristic in vision groups any subset of elements of a scene whose changes are proportional and synchronous and it segregates them from other elements of the scene that are changing in a different way. We can see that this is a good way to do things. It is very unlikely that unrelated elements in a scene subset will undergo parallel changes by accident.

The principle of common fate also has an application in audition. Suppose it was found that two frequency components were changing synchronously by proportional amounts. This would seem to be very unlikely by chance. It is much more reasonable to assume that the two are parts of the same sound, that is, that they have arisen from the same physical disturbance in the environment. It is likely in our world that those frequency components that arise from a single acoustic source will go on and off at more or less the same time, will glide up and down in frequency together, will swell and decline in intensity together, and so on.

There are two types of synchronous changes that have been studied, changes in frequency (called frequency modulation or FM) and changes in amplitude (called amplitude modulation or AM). One would expect both of these to be useful in the listener's task of parsing the set of simultaneous components into streams.

FM: Parallel Changes in the Frequency of Partials

The first type of correlated change that we will examine is frequency modulation. An everyday example of this is in the human voice. As we tighten our vocal cords, the pitch of the voice rises. Physically, the fundamental frequency rises and all the harmonics rise in a proportional way as they must.[331] As the fundamental doubles in frequency, say from 100 to 200 Hz, the fifth harmonic must also double, from 500 to 1,000 Hz, since it always remains in the fixed proportion 5:1 to the fundamental. In fact all the harmonics must double in frequency to maintain their fixed ratio relation to the fundamental. Therefore all the harmonics must change by the same proportion. This is the same as saying that they must change by an equal amount in log frequency. If we look at a set of harmonics of a 100-Hz fundamental as it rises in frequency, the harmonics rise together on a log frequency scale as in figure 3.7. The first thing we notice is that their motion is parallel on the logarithmic scale. Second, they appear more and more crowded together as we increase the harmonic number. This latter fact arises from the relation between the harmonic series and the logarithmic scale. The successive harmonics in a tone are not spaced from one another in equal logarithmic steps. Instead they are spaced by a fixed number of cycles in frequency, and this fixed difference appears smaller and smaller as you move up a logarithmic scale. However, the choice of a logarithmic scale is not arbitrary: The mapping of frequency onto the basilar membrane also is logarithmic. Therefore, we can take figure 3.7 as a picture of how the peaks of activity on the basilar membrane will change over time.

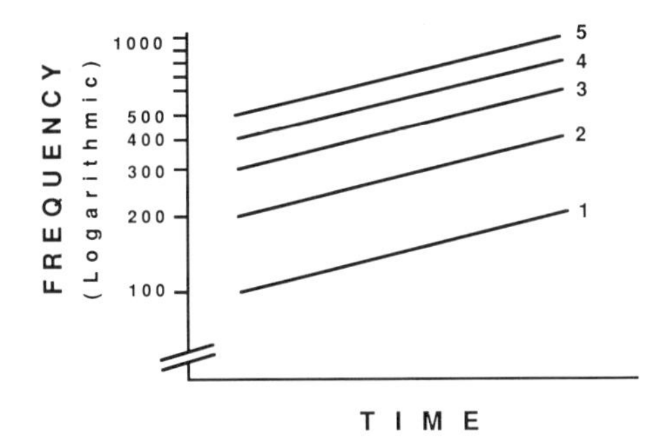

Figure 3.7
The spacing and the parallel motion of harmonics on a log frequency scale.

We would expect that since nature causes harmonics to move in parallel, our auditory systems take advantage of this regularity. In a mixture of sounds, any partials that change in frequency in an exactly synchronous way and whose temporal paths are parallel on a log-frequency scale are probably partials that have been derived from a single acoustic source. Therefore the spectral grouping process should unite them for subsequent global processes to work on. There is some evidence that the auditory system works this way.

We do not know what the physiological mechanism for this is. The fact that as harmonics move up and down in parallel they maintain a constant separation on the basilar membrane implies that there is a simple change on the receiving organ as well as in the external world. However, we do not know whether the auditory system exploits this anatomical simplicity. Before looking at the evidence for a grouping principle based on parallel FM, we must bear in mind the close relation between such a principle and the one based on harmonicity that we have already discussed. If we see the auditory system grouping harmonics that move in parallel frequency paths together, how do we know whether they have been grouped because they were *moving* together? Perhaps it was just that they always retained a harmonic relation to one another. Perhaps the fact that they were moving had no significance. Before we could attribute the grouping to the movement itself, we would have to see it adding some extra strength to the tendency for harmonics to group or else showing some ability to cause inharmonic partials to be perceptually fused. Much of the research that has been done on the perceptual grouping of modulated harmonics does not distinguish between the retention of harmonicity over time and the effects of the common motion.

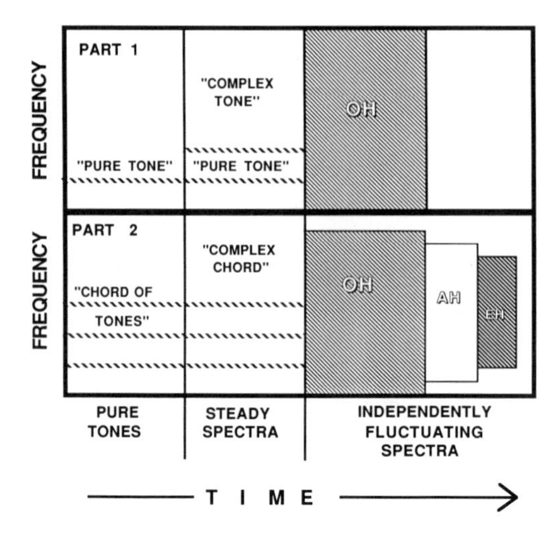

Figure 3.8
A demonstration of the power of coherent frequency fluctuation to integrate the harmonics of singing voices. Part 1: progression from a pure tone to a complex tone to the perception of a singing voice. Part 2: progression from a chord of pure tones to three singing voices. (After Chowning 1980.)

Micromodulation

In 1979, John Chowning of the Stanford University Center for Computer Research in Music and Acoustics reported some results that he had obtained when trying to synthesize a human singing voice. It appeared that the sound would not fuse and become a unitary percept unless a small amount of frequency fluctuation was added to the fundamental, and hence to all its harmonics.[332]

Basing his work on the assumption that it was the parallel frequency fluctuation that caused the harmonics to fuse, he created a fascinating demonstration that is illustrated in figure 3.8. In part 1 of the figure, we see first a pure tone at 400 Hz. It is then joined by harmonics that would be present in a vowel, in the intensities that would be present in that vowel, but with no frequency fluctuations. What the listener will hear at this point is a continuation of the 400-Hz tone, but now joined by a second tone that is harmonically complex, like an organ tone. The combination is not yet heard as a voice. In the final period all the harmonics have a coherent frequency fluctuation imposed on them; now the fusion of the set of harmonics is much better, and the sound is heard as a voice singing a vowel (for example, "oh") at a pitch of 400 Hz.

In part 2, the same game is played with a mixture of three singing voices, one singing an "oh" with a fundamental of 400, one singing an "ah" at 500, and the third an "eh" at 600 Hz. The demonstration begins with three pure tones, the fundamentals of the three voices, at 400, 500, and 600 Hz. This is heard as a chord containing three pitches. Then the full set of harmonics for all three vowels is added, but without frequency fluctuations. This is not heard as a mixture of voices but as a complex sound in which the quality of a chord is present but the three pitches are not clear. Finally, in the third section, the three sets of harmonics are differentiated from one another by their patterns of fluctuation. We then hear three vocal sounds being sung at three pitches (300, 400, and 500 Hz).

Let me explain how the three sets of harmonics were caused to segregate from one another and yield three voices. It is possible to impose a frequency fluctuation on a fundamental and all its harmonics so that they all move together in parallel on log frequency coordinates. Chowning chose a pattern of frequency variation that was like the vibrato of a singer. It had a repeating up and down sinusoidal variation but some irregularity was also added to the pitch change so that it did not sound mechanical. Each of the three sets of harmonics had a different pattern of fluctuation in frequency, the differences being in the rates of vibrato (4.5, 5.0, and 5.5 Hz) as well as in the patterns of irregularity. As a result, the harmonics of the same synthesized voice moved in synchrony and in parallel, retaining their harmonic relations to one another over time. However, the partials from one voice had a constantly changing relation to the partials of each of the other voices. The size of the frequency fluctuation that Chowning imposed on the frequencies was about plus or minus 5 percent (or 10 percent total excursion), a typical figure for a vibrato in a singing voice.

Small fluctuations in frequency occur naturally in the human voice and in musical instruments. The fluctuations are often not very large, ranging from less than 1 percent for a clarinet tone to about 1 percent for a voice trying to hold a steady pitch, with larger excursions of as much as 20 percent for the vibrato of a singer. Even the smaller amounts of frequency fluctuation can have potent effects on the perceptual grouping of the component harmonics. Small frequency modulations of this type have been called "micromodulation" by Jean-Claude Risset, a French composer of computer music.

Micromodulation has been the object of intense study in a Ph.D. thesis by Stephen McAdams.[333] One of the important questions addressed by this thesis was whether it was necessary to have parallel motion on log frequency coordinates before fusion was induced. What about another type of parallel modulation in which the frequency components move up and down together but instead of maintaining their frequency *ratios* as they move, maintain their frequency *differences* instead? In the latter type of modulation, if you started with three harmonics, of 100, 200, and 300 Hz, and shifted the 100-Hz component up by 37 Hz, all the harmonics would go up by 37 Hz, yielding frequencies of 137, 237, and 337 Hz. Notice that these new partials would no longer be harmonically related. This kind of change is called constant-difference (CD) modulation. It is contrasted with the more normal case where all the partials are *multiplied* by a constant amount and thus maintain their ratio relations to one another; this is called constant-ratio (CR) modulation.

McAdams started with 16 harmonics of a 220-Hz fundamental, and imposed a frequency fluctuation of about 6 per second on them all.[334] In different conditions, he imposed different degrees of fluctuations, ranging from less than 1 percent (the variation of pitch that occurs in a clarinet) to just over 3 percent (a relatively small vibrato in a singing voice). The listeners were presented with two sounds, one containing constant-ratio modulation and the other containing constant-difference modulation. They were asked to judge which one seemed to have more "sources" in it. Their overwhelming choice was that the constant-difference modulation gave the impression of more sources, their choice of the CD tone increasing from about 60 percent with the small fluctuations to 90 percent or more when the large fluctuations were used. Evidently the constant-difference modulation, instead of helping the tone to fuse, actually caused its partials to segregate from one another. For example, the fundamental frequency was clearly heard as a separate sound. The reason for the breakup should be obvious. This sort of modulation destroys the harmonic relations among the partials. Evidently the benefit of concurrent modulation of this type, if it exists at all, is outweighed by the harm caused by reducing the harmonicity of the sound.

This is another example of where the Gestalt principles are best understood within a scene-analysis framework. There is no reason to reject CD modulation as an example of the Gestalt principle of common fate. After all, it consists of synchronous and similar changes. However, CD modulation is unnatural. There is no such regularity in nature and therefore we have no reason to expect our auditory system to be able to exploit it for purposes of scene analysis.

McAdams also ran a series of experiments comparing stimuli that either had incoherent or coherent micromodulation. There were a number of experiments, but they all had the same form. A complex sound containing many partials was played. There were two basic conditions: In the first, called coherent modulation, the same jitter pattern was applied to all the partials so that they changed in synchrony and in parallel on log frequency coordinates. In the second condition, incoherent modulation, the total set of partials was divided into two subsets by the experimenter. One jitter pattern was applied to one of these subsets of partials and a second, independent, jitter pattern was applied to the second subset. The frequency fluctuation of each subset of partials was coherent internally but was not coherent with the fluctuation of the other subset. In various experiments, he tried out frequency fluctuations as low as .01 percent and as high as 5 percent. The question was whether the ear would organize the two subsets into separate sounds.

In one experiment, for example, a single partial was given one pattern of fluctuation and all the rest received a second pattern. In different conditions within this experiment, the selected partial ranged from the first to the sixteenth. McAdams reported that in a pretest that used a 3–5 percent frequency fluctuation, the pitch of the selected partial could be heard as a separate pitch for any selected partial up to the sixteenth.[335] In the experiment proper (using much smaller fluctuations), once the size of the fluctuations reached 0.5 percent, the subjects virtually always chose the incoherently modulated sound as having more sources in it than the coherently modulated sound. The "more sources" judgment is a tricky one, however. McAdams reported that this judgment was based on different experiences depending on which partial was involved. In the case of the lower ones, the listener heard the partial standing out as a separate pitch. But with higher harmonics, the listener heard a kind of choral effect, the effect that you hear when you listen to a choir, in which you cannot distinguish individual voices but you know from some incoherence in the sound that more than one voice is involved.

These results supported the same conclusion as a pretest that McAdams reported in his thesis.[336] It was possible for trained listeners in a laboratory situation to hear out partial pitches for any of the first five to seven individual harmonics of a complex tone if the tone was sustained and unmodulated. However, when all the harmonics were modulated coherently, the listeners could no longer do this. The only pitch that they heard was the global pitch of the fundamental. Apparently in this case, as well, the coherent modulation increased the fusion of the harmonics.

McAdams also reported another pretest that showed how important coherent modulation is in encouraging the auditory system to compute the global pitch of a sound in preference to the partial pitches of its frequency components. He mixed three signals together and asked some musically trained listeners to tell him how many pitches they heard. Each of the three was a synthesized harmonic sound with the spectrum of a vowel. When two or three of the sounds were steady (not modulated), the listeners reported sometimes hearing four to six pitches. However, when each was given its own pattern of frequency fluctuation, the listeners reported that the three global pitches belonging to the three vowel spectra were clearer and less equivocal. He argued that these results were in agreement with findings reported by other researchers that the global pitches of sounds that have little or no energy at the fundamental are stronger when the partials are modulated coherently than when there is no modulation.[337]

It appears that even the global pitch associated with inharmonic complexes gets stronger with micromodulation. Once, when I was at IRCAM (Institut de Recherche et Coordination Acoustique/Musique), the world-renowned center for computer music in Paris, McAdams played me a demonstration in which micromodulation was applied to a mixture of three inharmonic sounds. Each sound was made by stretching the harmonic series in the way that I described earlier. When these were played without modulation, I could hear a weak sense of global pitch but certainly not three separate ones; I also heard a number of partial pitches. When modulation began (a separate pattern for each set of partials), I heard the three global pitches get stronger. The only difference between what is heard with a mixture of inharmonic spectra and a mixture of harmonic spectra is that in the case of the harmonic spectra the partial pitches often completely disappear whereas in the case of the inharmonic spectra many of these partials remain audible.

McAdams has reported an interesting musical effect that was created for a composition by Roger Reynolds at IRCAM.[338] The sound of an oboe was analyzed and then resynthesized with the even and odd subsets of harmonics sent to two different loudspeakers on different sides of the room. When the sound began, the two subsets were given exactly the same pattern of frequency fluctuation and this served to hold them together as a single sound heard somewhere between the loudspeakers. However, as the sound continued, the frequency fluctuations of the two subsets gradually became independent, with a separate pattern of fluctuation for each loudspeaker. This caused the listener to segregate the two subsets and hear two sounds, one coming from each speaker. The effect was that of "a soprano-like sound an octave higher (the even harmonics) and one of a hollow, almost clarinet-like sound at the original pitch (the odd harmonics)."[339] Why the two different pitches? Because of any tone that contains the even harmonics of a tone at frequency f (2f, 4f, 6f, . . .) can just as easily be viewed as containing all the harmonics of a tone at frequency 2f, a tone an octave higher.

This demonstration does two things. It displays the power of modulation to overcome even the classical clues to spatial location and it also makes us wonder about the order in which the qualities of a sound are computed in the auditory system. The demonstration suggests that frequency modulation affects perceptual grouping and then grouping determines perceived pitch and perceived location. In short, grouping determines location. Yet we know from other cases that cues for location can determine grouping: It is easier to follow one voice despite the presence of another if the two are at different locations. Which way does it go then? Does grouping determine location or does location determine grouping? We see this sort of pattern again and again in this book. My resolution of the contradiction is to imagine a highly interactive scene-analysis process in which all the major forms of evidence enter into the analysis. The function of this analysis is to converge on the interpretation of the scene that best satisfies the evidence.

Glides

We have seen that small fluctuations in pitch can serve to segregate subsets of partials that have different patterns of fluctuation. We would expect similar results in cases in which subsets of partials underwent longer (and slower) glides in parallel on log frequency coordinates. Only a few experiments on the fusion and decomposition of gliding partials are available.

One experiment of this type was done by Lynn Halpern and myself in 1977.[340] We asked people to listen to sounds that were made up of partials that were gliding in straight lines on a log frequency scale. Examples are shown in figure 3.9. There were always two subsets, each of which included one or more partials. One subset glided up and the other glided down in frequency. The glides were 1 second in duration. Within each subset, the partials maintained a fixed harmonic relation to one another throughout the glide. These ratios are marked on the figure. For example in part E the ascending glides maintain the fixed relation 3:4:5 throughout; that is, they could be considered to be the third, fourth, and fifth harmonics of a low tone. Similarly, in part E, the descending glides are in the ratios 10:11:12. Rather than hearing a confused mass of sound, the listeners heard two distinct sounds, one gliding up in pitch and the other gliding down. The two sounds were distinct enough that the listeners could make

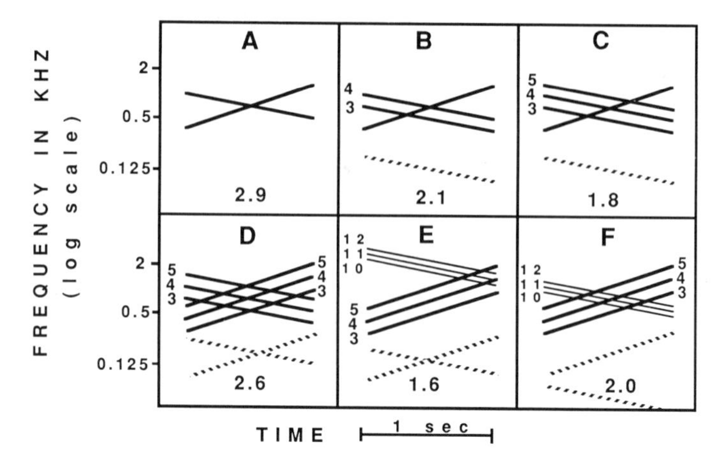

Figure 3.9
Patterns of crossing parallel glides. (From Halpern 1977.)

reliable judgments about whether the two sounds crossed in the middle or bounced apart. When they consisted of only single partials (part A), they tended to be heard as drawing together for the first half second and then bouncing apart. If we look at the figure, we can see that in the case of two pure-tone glides, the pattern is somewhat ambiguous to the eye. Nothing tells it whether the glides actually cross or meet at the middle and then bounce apart. If the eye has any preference at all, it prefers to see the lines cross. The situation is quite different for the ear. Rather than following a glide through its intersection the ear prefers to hear it stay in the same frequency range.

This preference applies whenever the two subsets of partials have the same internal frequency ratios. For example, in part D the partials in both the ascending and descending subsets maintain the ratio 3:4:5 to one another throughout their glides. Again the listener prefers to hear them approach and then bounce apart. The numbers at the bottom of each panel represent the preference (on an arbitrary scale) for hearing the tones bounce apart as measured in two replications of the experiment. Scores above 2.5 indicate that bouncing was more audible and scores below 2.5 mean that crossing was. The patterns shown in parts A and D show the strongest preference for bouncing. However, in some of the other conditions, where the within-subset ratios differ for the two subsets, the preferred organization is to hear the two sounds cross in the middle. In these cases the listener hears two tones with different qualities and uses the quality of the tone that is being focused on as a way of following it through the crossover point. What all this means is that if there is a difference in quality between the rising and falling subsets, the glides will be heard to cross. For example, the descending set in part F sounds like the yowling of a cat while the ascending set sounds more melodious. But notice what this description implies. If the difference in quality between the subsets is to affect the preference for hearing crossing or bouncing, the quality has to be derived from within each subset. The auditory system has to have grouped together only the partials that were gliding in parallel in order to have come up with this separate assessment of quality. Parallel modulation, then, appears to encourage the fusion of partials.

Unfortunately, there is some uncertainty about the cause of this segregation. It is possible that it was due to the parallel frequency change (frequency modulation) of the glides. This would make it an example of the Gestalt principle of common fate. However, there is another equally good explanation: It was not the parallel frequency change itself that was responsible for the segregation but the mere fact that the partials, by moving in parallel, maintained their harmonic relations to one another. Since we know from our earlier discussion that harmonically related partials will fuse, we might argue that there is nothing new here. The subsets would have segregated just as well had they not been gliding, as long as the two subsets did not bear a harmonic relation to one another. As with the case of micromodulation, it must be shown either that gliding harmonic tones fuse together even better than steady ones do or that gliding can fuse even nonharmonic tones.

A more analytic experiment was done sometime later at McGill by Peter Doehring and myself.[341] I have described it earlier in this chapter when discussing the effects of harmonicity upon fusion. The stimulus pattern was shown in figure 3.6. A pure-tone glide repeatedly alternated with a set of three simultaneous equal-duration glides, one of which, the target, was always the same as the captor in all respects. Therefore, it could be captured into a sequential stream by the captor and heard as a separate tone in the mixture. The two glides that were presented simultaneously with the captor tone were referred to as the frame. The two glides of the frame were always the same as one another in slope (on a time by log frequency scale) and were always two octaves apart throughout their excursions. This good harmonic relation (ratio of 4:1) tended to encourage their fusion.

The slope of the target relative to the frame was varied in the experiment. As the slope difference increased, the glide became easier to capture. This suggests that a parallel change in frequency caused the target to fuse with the frame. However, the results suggested otherwise. The conditions that showed this effect were all ones in which the target was positioned exactly between the glides of the frame and maintained a one octave separation from both of them. However, in other conditions the target was kept parallel to them but shifted up or down by a quarter octave from the perfect octave separation. In these conditions the target was no easier to capture when parallel to the frame than if it had an altogether different slope. The common slope alone was not enough. It seemed that a good harmonic relation had to be maintained.

Was it simply that there was no effect of the modulation and all that was important was maintaining good harmonic relations? This hypothesis fails to explain one fact about the data. The effects of the parallelness of the target to the frame were not all or nothing. A difference in slope of .5 octave per second had a less segregating effect than a difference of 1 octave per second. Yet in both cases, the deviation of slopes would effectively destroy any harmonic relations. Maybe some auditory analysis actually looks at the slopes after all. The question is still open.

It is hard to know what to conclude from this single study. McAdams maintains that parallel micromodulation will cause even inharmonic partials to fuse at least a little better than they would without modulation. In such a case there is no harmonicity to be maintained by the parallel modulation. Two explanations come to mind to explain the contradiction between this claim and the parallel-glides experiment. The first possibility is that although slow continued parallel modulation cannot fuse inharmonic partials, micromodulation can. This would make micromodulation and slower modulation different sorts of beasts. The other explanation relates to the fact that in the parallel glides experiment that Doehring and I did, the frame defined a strong harmonic framework that could have made the mistuned glide stand out very clearly. It may be that this provoked an active rejection of the nonfitting component and made it unlikely that even parallel modulation could cause it to fuse with the other glides. If all the partials were badly related to one another, as in the inharmonic stimuli that McAdams used, this positive rejection process might not occur since no strong harmonic framework would exist and therefore nothing could stand out as being mistuned from it. This hypothesis again brings up the need that I mentioned earlier for experiments to find out whether the strength with which a set of partials establishes a harmonic framework can affect the capacity of the ear to reject tones that do not fit.

AM: Common Amplitude Change at Different Spectral Locations

Onset-Offset Asynchrony

Earlier I presented an experiment that I did with Steven Pinker in which the tendency of two pure tones to fuse depended on the synchrony of their onsets.[342] There are really two ways of explaining this result. One is by the "old-plus-new" heuristic that was the subject of our earlier discussion. Briefly, this principle says "if part of a present sound can be interpreted as being a continuation of an earlier sound, then it should be." An explanation of the experimental finding by this principle would say that when two sounds come on asynchronously, one of them is first heard without the other and we can get a better fix on its properties so as to extract it from the mixture. Is this the whole explanation of the effects of the synchrony or asynchrony of the onset of partials? I think not. Although this factor surely plays a role, I believe that the synchronies themselves also play a role. This idea is attractive when you consider that in the normal acoustic world, it is exceedingly improbable that unrelated sounds will just happen to go on or off at exactly the same time. Therefore synchrony is an excellent indication that acoustic components must have arisen out of the same sonic event.

The first piece of evidence that suggests that there is an independent effect of synchrony comes from an experiment that looked at offset synchronies as well as synchronies at the onset.[343] It looked at the tendency for a group of three simultaneous pure tones (actually the harmonics f, 2f, and 4f) to fuse and resist the capturing effect of a preceding pure tone. The onsets and offsets of the three harmonics could be varied independently of one another. The experiment found that a harmonic that extended past the other two, either by coming on sooner or going off later, was easier to capture out of the mixture.

The old-plus-new heuristic was able to explain how we can segregate a partial that comes on ahead of the others. But what about the case where a later offset of a partial helps us to segregate it from the others. We also get to hear it alone in this case, but only after the mixture has gone by. Can a piece of knowledge acquired later help us to decompose a mixture that happened earlier? Or more generally, are there retroactive effects in auditory perception? There is ample evidence that there are. I am not referring to the higher-order examples in speech understanding in which, for example, the interpretation of the word "check" in the sentence "A check is not a checkmate" depends on the later word "checkmate". Such examples seem a bit more sophisticated than the simple hearing of two sounds rather than one. However, there is evidence for retrospective effects in even simple perceptual phenomena. For example when we perceive a sound as continuing through a very noisy masker even when it is not there, this illusion depends, in part, on the sound appearing again at the moment the noise ceases.[344] This means that something heard during the noise depends on what is presented to us after the noise has ceased. We think that we heard it at the time that it happened, but we must have revised our memory of it at a later time.

Here is a puzzle: When a component comes on a little before the rest of the spectrum of which it is a part, or ends shortly after it, do we use that information to really hear that component out of the mixture or is this "hearing out" just an illusion? We might just be basing our judgment of the tone on the part that sticks out and might be getting no information whatever about the part that is inside the mixture. There is some evidence from masking experiments done by Rasch that this description is true.[345] It will be discussed later when we look at masking studies. However, there is an observation that can easily be made by anybody with several audio oscillators that will demonstrate the segregative effects of onsets and offset that do not extend the target tone outside the mixture. If we tune the oscillators to a harmonic series, we will hear a fairly thick, single sound. However, if we take the oscillator that is playing the third harmonic and turn it on and off repeatedly while the remainder stays constant, we will hear the third harmonic as a separate pulsing tone. The independent temporal changes in that harmonic will isolate it. If all the harmonics had been pulsed together, we would simply have heard the global sound pulsing.

This effect was studied carefully by Michael Kubovy.[346] He created a monaural complex of nonharmonically related partials (whose frequencies were selected from a diatonic scale) with frequency separations ranging from two to six semitones between successive partials, and played it with equal intensity for each partial. This sounded like a complex chord. However, the sound could be changed by selecting one of the partials as a target every 300 msec or so and briefly lowering its intensity and then restoring it to its original level. When this was done, the pitch of that partial became prominent. By selecting a different partial every 300 msec, he could create the experience of a tune. The emphasis that the selected partial received was not just due to the fact that it had received a boost in amplitude at a moment when the other partials had not. In a variation of the experiment, every 300 msec or so a selected partial was attenuated by 12 dB for 77 msec, then restored to its original level by increasing it by 12 dB. At the same time as the target was incremented, all the other partials were also incremented by 12 dB and remained briefly at this higher level.

Despite the fact that all the partials rose in intensity at exactly the same moment, it was the pitch of the target partial that became prominent. If successively higher partials were chosen in turn to be the target partial, the listener could hear an ascending series of pitches. It was not the rise in intensity that distinguished the target partial from the others in this case, but the order in which the rise and fall in intensity took place, the order being down-up for the target and up-down for the others. The auditory system seems therefore to have a great sensitivity to differences in the amplitude *pattern* for different partials and can use these differences to segregate them.

Another experiment done in Kubovy's laboratory showed that if one partial in a steady complex tone was suddenly thrown out of phase from the others its pitch became audible.[347] The stimulus was a tone whose fundamental was 200 Hz. It contained all harmonics from 3 to 14. They were aligned in sine phase; that is, at the instants (200 times per second) when the absent fundamental would have been passing through 0 phase angle, all the harmonics that were present were passing through 0. At certain moments in time, all the harmonics except one were instantly reset to zero phase and, at the same instant, the remaining harmonic was reset to some other phase angle. The difference in treatment made the pitch of this particular harmonic audible. A succession of interruptions of this type occurred, each choosing a different harmonic to be the odd man out. The harmonics selected for emphasis in this way formed an ascending scale on some trials and a descending scale on others, and the listeners were required to decide whether the scale ascended or descended. Their sensitivity to the phase change depended on how far out of phase the selected harmonics were thrown. When they were 20° out, the listeners were getting about three-quarters correct, and at 40° they were almost always correct.

This result seems to imply that the ear can instantaneously compare the phase of all the components and find subsets that are incongruent, but the authors of this experiment pointed out a mechanism, known to exist in the peripheral auditory system, that could change a phase difference into an amplitude difference.[348] Therefore the more central auditory system may actually be detecting the same sort of change as when the amplitude of a partial is shifted suddenly with respect to that of other partials.

So far it sounds as if different patterns of amplitude change can segregate different partials of a complex sound. But what about the reverse: Can a synchronous change in amplitude cause sounds that would otherwise not fuse to do so? Elisabeth Cohen studied our perception of a tone that was formed of "stretched partials."[349] The frequencies of the partials of such a tone are derived from the frequencies of the harmonics of a normal tone as follows: Plot the frequencies of the harmonics on a log scale and then stretch the separations out uniformly and read off the new frequencies from the log scale. The new frequencies are no longer harmonically related. If the stretch factor is large enough, the tone will be less perceptually coherent than normal tones and we will tend to hear some of the partials as separate pitches. However, there is a method that we can use to encourage the listener to fuse these partials into a coherent tone. That is to play all the partials with a synchronous onset and an exponential decay. This percussive amplitude envelope is similar to those found in plucked instruments such as the guitar or harpsichord or in struck instruments such as the piano or gong. The exactly synchronized onset seems to tell the auditory system to fuse sounds that it would not fuse without this cue.

The role of synchrony and asynchrony of onset in the partitioning of mixtures of sounds faces us with a puzzle. In the tones of many musical instruments some of the partials rise and fall in amplitude at different times than others. For example, one study found that in a D4 (D in the fourth octave) played by a trumpet, the fifth, sixth and seventh harmonics reached their maximum amplitudes about 20 msec later than the first three harmonics did.[350] Why do we not hear the delayed harmonics as defining a separate sound? There may be a number of reasons.[351] First, the the asynchrony is small, usually less than 20 msec for most instruments. Second, there is often a noisy onset of the tone, which serves to mask the asynchrony of the onsets. In addition, the rise times of the various partials may not form two distinct clusters, and therefore distinct onsets may not be detected; if there is simply a mush of partials coming on at different times, the onset of any one of them may not be distinct enough from the others to cause the partial to be treated as a separate sound. In other cases, the later-rising partials may increase too gradually in intensity to be detected as a separate tone. Finally, since we know that fusion competes with sequential streaming, there may not be an ongoing stream at the frequency of the delayed partial to capture it, and it may remain in the stream of its own instrument. On the other hand, even if there is a capturing stream (perhaps a partial from some other instrument in a complex orchestral piece) the listener may simply group the asynchronous partial with the spectrum of the other instrument without noticing that it is gone from the spectrum of its own instrument. In short, under conditions of isolation the decomposition is not likely to happen, and in a mixture it is not likely to be noticed.

There is further confirmation of the role of asynchrony in segregating components of sounds. This evidence comes from experiments on masking. It is harder to mask a target if it comes on when the masker is already present.[352] However, we will discuss this evidence later when we consider the findings of masking experiments and how they relate to questions about the simultaneous organization of sound.

The partitioning of spectra by means of synchronous amplitude changes is consistent with our understanding of neurology. A neural model for the grouping of parts of the auditory spectrum has been proposed by Malsberg and Schneider.[353] The synchronous activation of neurons that are responding to different parts of the spectrum causes them to remain in synchronized oscillation for a short period of time. By this means the spectrum is broken into regions that these authors call segments. Neurons are synchronized within each segment and desynchronized between segments. Later recognition processes can get an unobstructed view of one of the segments by oscillating in synchrony with it.

Common Periodicity (AM) at Different Spectral Locations

As we saw earlier, there is good reason to believe that the basilar membrane of the cochlea decomposes the spectrum of the incoming sound into what we can think of as a neural spectrogram. If we look at a spectrogram of a complex sound, speech being a good example, we find that there are different temporal patterns going on in different temporal regions. As Schubert and Nixon put it,

> . . . in our immediate classification of the sounds of continuous speech . . . in the recognition of fine temporal nuance in musical performance, and particularly in our ability to separate simultaneously present broad-band sound sources, such as the instruments of an ensemble or competing talkers, there is convincing evidence that the system must either include an analyzer for direct coding of the original broad-band waveform or must routinely coordinate internally derived temporal patterns from different spectral locations in the cochlea.[354]

The question that we are examining is whether something about the temporal patterns themselves, as they occur in different spectral regions, allows the listener to put them together.

Even earlier, in 1957, Donald Broadbent and Peter Ladefoged had showed a clear understanding of this issue.[355] They, too, put it in terms of activity on the basilar membrane. How, they asked, could we understand speech when other simultaneous speech was present?

The regions on the basilar membrane that responded to the spectral bands containing energy from the two sounds would be intermixed. To segregate them, they argued, "the neural messages from sense organs [in those regions of the basilar membrane that are] stimulated by different formants of the same voice must resemble one another in some respect; and differ from the messages leaving sense organs stimulated by irrelevant sounds." They proposed that the distinguishing mark might be that the neural output of every region of the basilar membrane that was stimulated by the same sound would have a matching periodicity, since all these outputs would pulse at the fundamental frequency of the signal. We will discuss the research that was stimulated by these ideas later in a section on speech perception. For the moment it is sufficient to note that their thinking implied that common amplitude modulation in different spectral regions (and hence a common rate of neural periodicity) could bind regions of the spectrum together into a single perceived sound.

It was pointed out by others that

> Many real-life auditory stimuli have intensity peaks and valleys as a function of time in which intensity trajectories are highly correlated across frequency. This is true of speech, of interfering noise such as 'cafeteria' noise, and of many other kinds of environmental stimuli. We suggest that for such stimuli the auditory system uses across-frequency analysis of temporal modulation patterns to help register and differentiate between acoustical sources.[356]

In other words, when we are listening to a signal from a single source, the intensity changes at different places in the received spectrum tend to be correlated and the auditory system should be able to make use of this fact.

The analysis of correlations in firing rate at different parts of the basilar membrane may be an incidental by-product of the temporal mechanism, that I described earlier, for finding the fundamental frequency of a complex tone by analyzing the pattern of timing in the neural impulses activated by the sound.

Here is an example of how such a mechanism might work in detecting a correlation in the temporal fine structure at different frequency regions. When we utter a vowel sound, the acoustic result is a set of harmonics spaced from one another by F0 (the fundamental frequency). The resulting neural output from the the basilar membrane depends on the filtering activity of that organ. The output has been modeled by Richard Lyon, who displays the results in what he calls a cochleagram.[357] The latter is meant to represent the nervous

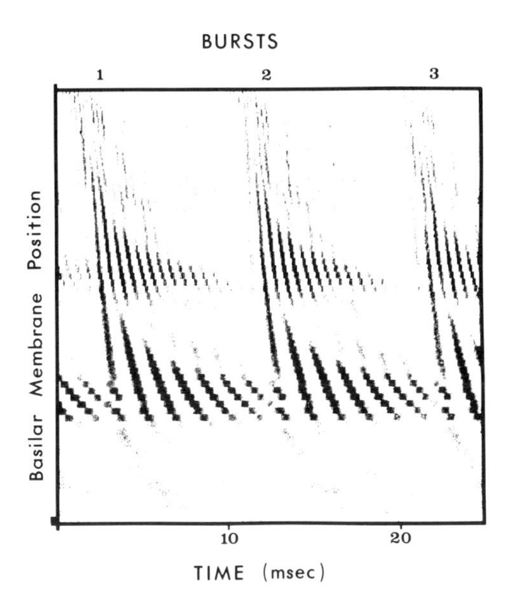

Figure 3.10
A cochleagram of a brief speech utterance, produced by Richard Lyon's computational model of cochlear output; see Lyon 1982.

system's version of the acoustician's spectrogram. An example of a cochleagram is displayed in figure 3.10. Its *x* axis represents time and its *y* axis, frequency. Darkness represents the strength of neural output at each time and frequency. We can see large temporal fluctuations in darkness (labeled bursts 1, 2, and 3) that represent beats in each frequency channel. The finer vertical striations (curving off to the right in the lower frequencies) represent the neural following of the individual frequencies. Recall that the beat rate is dominated by the fundamental. The lower fine striations are at simple multiples of the fundamental. All this regularity is extremely convenient. It means that if the auditory system groups those neural outputs from the basilar membrane where related periodicities are detected, it will probably be grouping the harmonics of a single voice, since it is extremely unlikely that two voices will be at the same fundamental frequency at the same time. If two or more voices are actually at the same fundamental frequency at the same time, as when a number of voices are singing in unison, we know that we experience great difficulty separating the individual voices from each other. To use the beats that occur at different regions of the spectrum, the auditory system would have to have a mechanism that grouped those regions of the spectrum that were exhibiting the same amplitude modulation at the same time, and would have to be sensitive to modulations that were at the rate that corresponds to the fundamental of the human voice (roughly, from 80 to 300 Hz). We shall see below that there is evidence for the existence of such a mechanism.

The alert reader will have come up with an objection by this time. I have proposed that the auditory system could decide which regions of the spectrum of a voice have come from the same source by examining the beat rate of local regions of the spectrum. The objection is that we already know of a grouping mechanism that could do the same job without any concern for the beats. This is the mechanism that groups harmonically related partials. It simply has to decide that sets of partials in different frequency regions are harmonically related to the same fundamental (a task it has to do anyway to calculate the pitch). Why should we postulate another redundant mechanism? In the interests of parsimony we should not, for it seems that whatever cases of grouping the beat-detection mechanism might explain could easily be explained by the harmonicity mechanism.

This argument is plausible except for two facts. The first is that the human sensory systems—because they are capable of processing many features in parallel—are probably not as concerned with parsimony as theorists are. They may, indeed, have evolved redundant mechanisms because no single mechanism (or subset of mechanisms) is 100 percent reliable. The second is the fact that we can imagine situations (such as when the sound is not harmonic) in which the beat detection mechanism might solve problems that the harmonicity mechanism might not. An example is the regular pulsing of the spectrum of a motorboat, where the pulsing appears in all spectral regions but the sound is not strongly harmonic. Another occurs in the human voice in the sound "z", which is a mixture of a noisy sound with a voiced sound. In the "z", the higher-frequency noise component, made by the front of the tongue, is actually being powered by the glottal vibration, which is periodic. This imparts the periodicity of the fundamental to the noise. So although the noise component is not harmonic, and could not be grouped with the voiced component by a harmonicity analyzer, it contains the same periodicity of amplitude fluctuation as the voiced component. Therefore a mechanism that tended to group different spectral regions by similarity of amplitude modulation could put together the sound components of the "z" as easily as it put together the parts of the motorboat sound. To summarize, we can say that the harmonic analyzer cannot deal with noisy sound, but an analyzer for beats or local periodicities could deal with both inharmonic and harmonic sounds with equal facility.[358]

Before looking at the evidence for whether similar periodicities at different spectral locations could be used to group portions of the spectrum for the purposes of subsequent pattern recognition, we should ask whether there is any evidence to suggest that the auditory system has the capacity to compare, or to combine, the periodicity information in different parts of the spectrum. One piece of evidence that it can do so comes from a study of pitch perception.

We must first recall that the pitch of the fundamental of a set of harmonics is often perceived when the fundamental itself is not present. The most convincing explanation of this is one which sees the auditory system as registering the firing rate of neurons in each separate frequency region. After this is done, the system compares all the firing rates and calculates a fundamental rate of which the rest are all multiples.[359] The theory that firing-rate evidence is accumulated is supported by the finding that the pitch seems to be detected better when more harmonics are present.[360] There is independent evidence that periodicities that are too low to hear as pitches, but are heard as beats, can also be combined across the spectrum to yield the perception of a beat rate of which all of the detected ones are multiples.[361] Although this accumulation of information about periodicities in the spectrum in different frequency regions is concerned with the detection of a fundamental firing rate, this apparent ability makes it more plausible that the auditory system could use a common periodicity for a second purpose: to group those regions that were related to one another. The only added capability that would be needed to achieve the latter result would be the ability to detect more than one fundamental at a time and then to put the spectral regions that were related to different fundamentals into their own separate groups.

The detection of different periodicities may be responsible for some part of the segregation of ordinary tones of different pitches. Magda Halikia, in a Ph.D. thesis done at McGill, studied the perceptual segregation of two complex tones that were mixed and presented binaurally over headphones.[362] Each tone was composed of up to 32 different harmonics (different numbers in different experiments). It lasted for 1 second including gradual onsets and offsets of 200 msec. The two tones were either at the same pitch or were separated by different numbers of semitones. The fundamentals of the two were always placed symmetrically above and below 140 Hz on a log frequency scale. The listeners were asked to write down how many sounds they heard, one or two. When the two had the same frequency, they said (of course) that they heard only one tone (because mixing two identical tones simply gives the same tone at a higher intensity). But as the fundamentals of the tones were moved apart in frequency, each increase in separation brought a greater tendency to judge that there were two. Interestingly enough, the greatest increase in segregation came with the change between no difference and a difference of 0.5 semitone, where the mean number of tones reported by the group of listeners changed from 1 to over 1.8. That is most of the time, at 0.5 semitone separation, the listeners heard two tones. This separation was equal to about 4 Hz. The sensitivity to the difference in fundamental frequency might actually have been more acute, but 0.5 semitone was the smallest separation used.

Halikia wanted to know whether the auditory system had to be able to resolve the frequency of the individual harmonics in order to segregate the two tones. Therefore she included conditions in which she gradually simplified the tones by removing their lower harmonics. But even when the two fundamentals were defined only by harmonics above 2,600 Hz (that is, above the eighteenth harmonic) the listeners almost always judged that there were two tones when their (missing) fundamentals had only a .5 semitone separation. This is puzzling because it is generally agreed that the adjacent harmonics in the region of the eighteenth harmonic of a 140-Hz tone could not be distinguished by any mechanism that looked for different sites of maximum stimulation on the basilar membrane. Furthermore it is generally believed that the perception of pitch cannot be stimulated by such high harmonics.[363] Nevertheless, these upper harmonics were sufficient to evoke a judgment of twoness when they were multiples of two different fundamentals. It is likely that the physiological mechanism responsible for the segregation was one that detected two different periodicities in the spectrum. Unfortunately, Halikia did not report the subjective experiences of her subjects. It is possible that they did not actually hear two tones when there were only very small pitch separations and very high harmonics. In such signals, small separations would give rise to prominent audible beats at a large number of multiples of the difference between the fundamental frequencies. It might have been the presence of the beats, rather than a clear perception of two tones, that prompted the listeners to judge that more than one tone was present.

Amplitude Modulation of Subsets of Partials We have been examining examples that suggest that the detection of matching periodicities at different sites along the basilar membrane could help to partition the spectrum. We have seen how these similar firing patterns could occur because of a common fundamental. Yet the grouping of spectral regions by shared periodicity may not be restricted to this one case. In his book *Introduction to the Psychology of Hearing*, Brian Moore describes a demonstration that shows how common changes in a set of frequency regions can cause those regions to group with one another perceptually and to segregate from others that are not changing in the same pattern:

> For example, if we present a steady complex sound containing many components with randomly distributed frequencies, a single noise-like sound will be heard, with a certain timbre. A subgroup of components in the complex can now be made to stand out perceptually from the rest by making them vary in a coherent way in either frequency, amplitude, or both. This group will be perceived as a prominent "figure" against a steady background, and both the figure and the background will have a timbre different from that of the original unvarying sound.[364]

A series of experiments have been done in my laboratory at McGill to study the integration of different spectral regions that showed the same amplitude modulation. These experiments followed the pattern of the Bregman-Pinker experiment in which a simple sound, A, is alternated with a mixture of two simple sounds, B and C, in such a way that A can capture B into a sequential stream (AB AB AB . . .). The new twist in the experiments was that A, B, and C were all pure tones that were amplitude modulated with a raised cosine wave (a sinusoidal pattern that starts at zero and oscillates between zero and one) at a frequency of about 100 Hz. That is, the amplitude of each tone rose and fell in a sinusoidal pattern about 100 times per second. The purpose of the experiments was to show that if tones B and C were both modulated at the same frequency, they would show a stronger tendency to fuse, so that B would not be free to group with A into a sequential stream.

When a sine wave is modulated with a sinusoidal pattern there are two equivalent ways of describing the result. These are shown in figure 3.11. Suppose, for example that tone B is a 1,500-Hz sine tone modulated at 100 Hz. We can describe it as I just did: as a 1,500-Hz sine tone rising and falling in intensity 100 times per second. This is shown in the upper half of box 1 of the figure. However, if we look at its long-term spectrum we will discover that there are three frequency components in it, not one. Not only is there a component at 1,500 Hz, but ones at 1,400 and 1,600 Hz as well, each having half the amplitude of the 1,500-Hz tone. This spectral result of the amplitude modulation (AM) is shown in box 2. The two additional frequencies introduced by AM are called "sidebands" and the modulated tone is called the "carrier" (these names originated with their functions in AM radio transmission). The sidebands lie above and below the

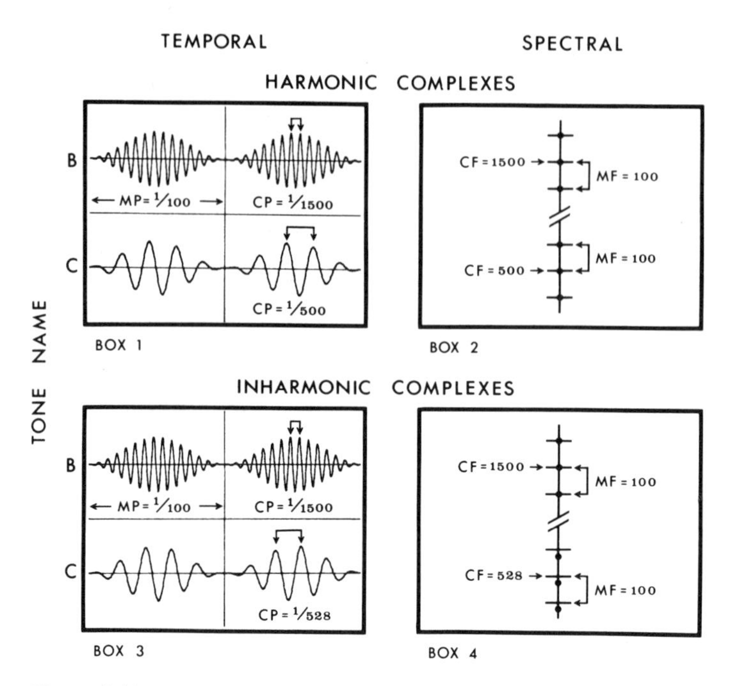

Figure 3.11
Stimuli used by Bregman, Abramson, Doehring, and Darwin (1985). Each of boxes 1 to 4 shows a representation of tones B and C. Boxes on the right, showing frequency components as the horizontal lines crossing the vertical scale, are spectral representations of the waveforms shown in the corresponding boxes on the left. MP, modulation period; CP, carrier period; MF, modulation frequency; CF, carrier frequency.

carrier frequency, separated from it by the modulating frequency (MF). Since in this example, the modulating frequency is 100 Hz, the sidebands are 100 Hz above and below the 1,500-Hz carrier.

Suppose that tone C, the one that we wanted to fuse with B, was at 500 Hz and was also modulated at 100 Hz. This would create sidebands for C at 400 and 600 Hz. Again the three resulting partials would be spaced by 100 Hz, as we see in the figure. If we look at tones B and C together, we realize that the modulation has created a situation in which all the partials are actually harmonics of 100 Hz. If such modulation were actually found to cause B and C to fuse, we would not know whether it was because they rose and fell in amplitude together, as shown in box 1, or because they simply fell into the same harmonic series, as shown in box 2. We already know that the harmonicity relation will promote fusion, so we would not know whether there was also an effect of the amplitude modulation itself.

The fact that the three components were all harmonics of a 100-Hz fundamental occurred because the carriers that I chose for this example, 1,500 and 500 Hz, were harmonics (exact multiples) of 100 Hz. Had I chosen a modulating frequency of 105 Hz, the three components that came from the 1,500-Hz carrier, 1,500, 1,605, and 1,395, would not be harmonics of any audible frequency. (Of course they are all multiples of 5 Hz, but this frequency is too low for the auditory system to hear as a missing fundamental pitch. Therefore it treats the partials as an inharmonic set.) Selecting the right modulating frequency enables an experimenter to choose whether the resulting components will or will not be related to a common audible fundamental. This means that it is possible to arrange it so that the modulation of two carriers by the same modulator does not automatically place them into the same harmonic series. There is also another way to ensure that the partials of C do not fit into the same harmonic series as those of B. We can choose a carrier frequency for C, (an example might be 528 Hz) that is not a harmonic of the 100-Hz modulating frequency that is being applied to both B and C. This situation is shown in boxes 3 and 4 of the figure. The AM has the same periodicity (100 Hz), but the partials in C are no longer harmonics of a fundamental of 100 Hz.

There is another problem that we have to guard against as well. If we change the harmonic series of C by changing its modulating frequency (keeping its carrier at 1,500 Hz), we create an inharmonic set of partials. One might think that now that it was not harmonically related to any audible fundamental it would have no pitch at all. However, this is not true. Apparently the auditory system computes the best-fitting pitch. Raising the modulator raises the pitch, but by much less than the raise in the modulator. This pitch, although weaker than a pitch based on true harmonics, creates a difficulty for our experiment. Although we have done away with harmonicity we have not done away with pitch. It could be argued that if we cause two carriers to fuse by modulating them at the same frequency, they will end up with the same pitch, and this, not common amplitude fluctuation, will cause them to fuse. Fortunately there is a way around this problem, because it is possible to create sounds with the same pitch by using different combinations of carrier frequency and modulating frequency. Optionally, we can keep modulating frequency constant while varying the pitch.

All these factors were taken into account at once in an experiment done in our laboratory.[365] Three complex tones, A, B, and C, were presented in a cycle with tone A first, then a mixture of B and C.

Table 3.1
The eight stimulus conditions used by Bregman, Abramson, Doehring, and Darwin (1985).

	Pitch	
Periodicity	100	105
100	(1) Harmonics of 100 no shift HARMONIC (400, 500, 600)	(2) Harmonics of 100 shifted up (+28 Hz) INHARMONIC (428, 528, 628)
105	(3) Harmonics of 105 shifted down (−28 Hz) INHARMONIC (392, 497, 602)	(4) Harmonics of 105 no shift HARMONIC (420, 525, 630)
	Pitch	
Periodicity	100	95
100	(5) Harmonics of 100 no shift HARMONIC (400, 500, 600)	(6) Harmonics of 100 shifted down (−28 Hz) INHARMONIC (372, 472, 572)
95	(7) Harmonics of 95 shifted up (+24 Hz) INHARMONIC (404, 499, 594)	(8) Harmonics of 95 no shift HARMONIC (380, 475, 570)

Each cycle, including the silences between the tones, lasted for 750 msec. Tone A was always identical to tone B and tended to capture it out of the BC mixture. Both A and B were always generated by a 1,500-Hz carrier modulated at 100 Hz (by a raised cosine). Therefore they were always harmonic and had a pitch related to a 100-Hz fundamental. The experiment consisted of varying the structure of tone C and seeing how this affected its ability to fuse with B and to prevent the latter from being captured out of the mixture. Table 3.1 shows the eight versions of tone C that were used. In each cell of the table, the number of the condition (from 1 to 8) is shown in parentheses. Each version of C was created by modulating a tone in the region of 500 Hz by a sinusoidal modulator (raised cosine) of about 100 Hz. The headings on the left show the exact frequency of the modulation. This is referred to as the periodicity of the resultant complex.

Let us focus on the pitch and periodicity of tone B, which was always the same. It had a periodicity of 100 bursts per second and a pitch related to a 100-Hz tone. Furthermore it was a harmonic tone; that is, it was formed of harmonics of 100 Hz. The side headings of the table show the periodicity of the C tones. All the tones shown in the first and third rows of the table (conditions 1, 2, 5, and 6) had the same periodicity, their modulating frequency being 100 Hz. The remaining C tones had a periodicity of 105 Hz. The headings across the top show the pitch of the tones. This pitch was determined by listening to the inharmonic tones and matching them to either a 100- or 105-Hz harmonic tone (in the upper half of the table). The lower half of the table is like the upper half, but instead of some of the periodicities being at 105 Hz, they are at 95 Hz.

Some of the complexes (three-component tones) are marked as harmonic complexes and others as inharmonic in the table. We can think of the inharmonic complexes as having been made by shifting the frequencies of the three partials of a harmonic complex up or down by 28 Hz. This was found, by trial and error, to change their apparent pitch by about 5 Hz and shift it to the desired value. However, it did not change their periodicity (burst rate) because this is related to the frequency separation of the three components and we have not changed this. The actual values of the three partials (carrier and sidebands) are shown in each cell.

The results are shown in figure 3.12. In it we see the results of two slightly different experiments (the solid and dotted lines) but the results are very similar. The bottom *x* axis is labeled as frequency separation. This factor is important because some of the conditions brought the harmonics of C closer to those of B and this caused B and C to fuse more strongly. The *y* axis represents the degree to which the C tone segregated from the B tone. We can see first that all the lines slope upward to the right. This means that moving the partials of C further from those of B increased the segregation of B from C. The different slopes of the solid and dotted lines simply show that this frequency-separation effect was stronger in one experiment than in the other.

The top *x* axis has a different labeling. It shows what the pitch of C was and whether it matched that of B. If the pitch match made a difference, the conditions under the "100" label should be stronger than the ones under either the "105" or "95" labels, since tone B had a pitch of "100." There was no sign of any effect of pitch match. Finally the two lower lines in the graph represent cases in which the periodicity of B and C was matched and the two upper lines relate to the conditions in which periodicity was unmatched. Obviously we would not see such a separation on the graph unless the mismatch in periodicity tended to segregate B from C. The difference in segregation between tone B and C in the conditions in which their periodicities were mismatched (3, 4, 7, and 8), as compared to those in which

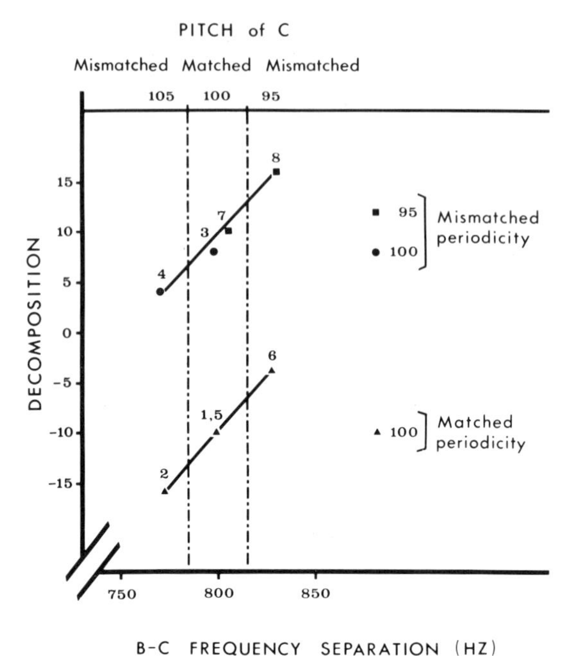

Figure 3.12
Results from experiment 1 of Bregman, Abramson, Doehring, and Darwin (1985).

their periodicities were matched (1, 2, 5, and 6), was the strongest difference found in this experiment. Furthermore, the results from the inharmonic conditions (2, 3, 6, and 7) did not deviate in any way from this overall pattern. We are able to conclude that periodicity itself has an effect on segregation independently of the effects of harmonicity, pitch, and the frequency separation of C from B.

A word of warning: The differences look very large on the graph, but that is only because a very sensitive method was used. Just listening naively to the stimuli, it does not sound as though the match in periodicity between B and C has a very strong effect on perceptual segregation. Probably the smallness of this effect was due to the use of such a narrow range of periodicities (100 Hz versus 105 or 95 Hz). But this had to be done to manipulate the pitches of the inharmonic C complexes appropriately.

Another reason for the small effect of AM may have been the fact that it was sinusoidal. Earlier, we saw that the natural-life relevance of grouping of spectral regions by their amplitude modulation was the fact that if we pass human speech sounds through a series of band-pass filters, as we believe that the auditory system must do, we discover that the amplitude in each channel is modulated by the fundamental frequency of the voice. But unlike the case in the experiment of Bregman et al., this is not a sinusoidal modulation. The effect of the modulation, in each pitch period of the voice, is to cause a sudden rise in the intensity of the carrier signal followed by a gradual dying out. Perhaps the auditory system can use this natural form of modulation more easily than the sinusoidal modulation used in this experiment. However, the experiment used the sinusoidal form because its effect on the spectrum of the resulting complex tone is simple and its effect on the pitch of the complex is fairly well known. Modulating with a fast-rise, slow-decay waveform would spread the spectrum of the complex tone out more, so that the neural effects of modulation of different carriers would be more overlapped on the basilar membrane. We were hoping to examine the perceptual integration of signals that were neurally separated to begin with.

There is, perhaps, a way of using the more natural modulation without spreading its effects across a large number of neural channels. This would be to study the effects of AM on the integration of neural channels in patients who are fitted with multichannel electrical stimulators implanted in their cochleas. To the extent that the electrical signal sent to different locations in the cochlea actually stimulated only a restricted local region, it might be possible to study the effects of different patterns of modulation on the integration of the neural information coming from different parts of the cochlea.

A related experiment was done, again using an alternation between a single tone, A, and a mixture of two other tones, B and C.[366] Once more A, B, and C were pure tones that were amplitude modulated. As before, A and B were always identical and remained unchanged throughout the experiment. Only the structure of C was varied. Two things were varied: the match between the modulation frequencies applied to tones B and C and whether the partials of B and C did or did not fall into the same harmonic series. The listener's task was to rate the clarity of hearing tone A repeating again in the BC mixture that followed it. Tone B was always a 3,000-Hz carrier amplitude that was amplitude-modulated at 125 Hz.

Figure 3.13 shows the results for three different conditions, using different carrier frequencies for tone C: 2,000 Hz, 2,050 Hz, and 1,951 Hz. The different modulation frequencies that were applied to the carrier are shown on the *x* axis. The *y* axis shows the fusion between B and C, the lower the value the stronger the fusion. The results are quite clear in showing that the closer the modulation frequency of

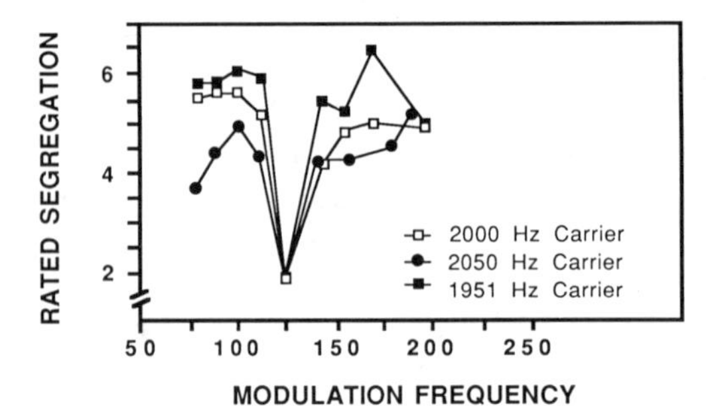

Figure 3.13
Segregation of tone B with changes in the AM match between tones B and C. (From Bregman and Levitan 1983.)

tone C approached the 125-Hz modulation frequency of tone B, the more strongly B and C fused.

There is a second aspect worth noting in the figure—the effects of harmonicity. Since the modulation frequency of tone B was always 125 Hz and its carrier frequency was 3,000 Hz (a multiple of 125 Hz), all partials of B were harmonics of 125 Hz. This was not always true for C. Recall that three different carrier frequencies were used for tone C in different conditions. One of these carriers, 2,000 Hz, had some unique properties. When it was modulated at exactly 125 Hz, it, too, gave rise to three harmonics of 125 Hz. Furthermore, when it was modulated at any of the other modulation frequencies that were used, it always gave rise to a trio of harmonics of that modulation frequency. (It was evenly divisible by all the modulation frequencies.) The other two carriers did not have this property. When modulated at any of the modulation frequencies, they gave rise, instead, to an inharmonic trio of partials.

However, the harmonicity of C made little difference. The figure shows that for all three carriers, when they were modulated at the 125-Hz frequency that matched tone B, fusion of B and C occurred regardless of harmonicity. Perhaps there is a slight tendency for the harmonic condition (2,000-Hz carrier) to fuse better, but you have to squint to see it. As in the previous experiment, the effect of a match in amplitude modulation did not depend on harmonicity.

There is another point to mention. When the C carriers were modulated at a frequency different than 125 Hz, it did not matter whether this caused C to be harmonic (within itself) or not. The curve for the 2,000-Hz carrier is not higher than the others at the AM frequencies that did not match B's. Therefore although there may be a hint of a tendency for the harmonicity of B with C to fuse them, there is no

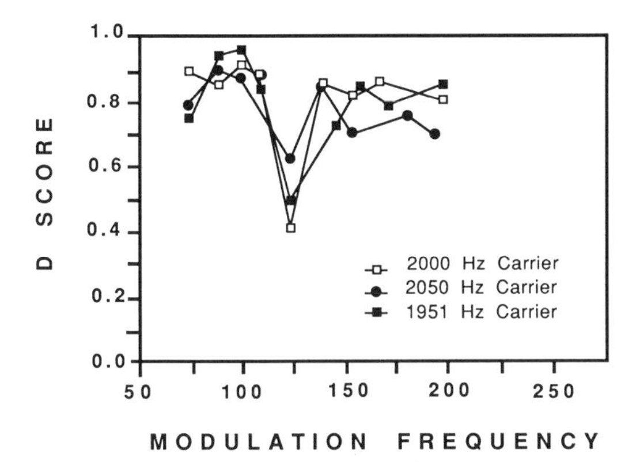

Figure 3.14
Results of accuracy judgments in an experiment on fusion by AM. (From Bregman and Levitan 1983.)

evidence that their segregation is increased when C belongs to a different harmonic series (as opposed to belonging to no harmonic series at all).

The experiment that we have just discussed depended on a subjective judgment by the listener—how clearly tone A could be heard repeating again in the BC mixture (recall that tones A and B were identical). We might wonder about the validity of accepting a listener's rating of a subjective experience. This concern motivated a second experiment done with exactly the same stimuli but with a different task.[367] On some trials, tone B was present as before but on others it was deleted. The listeners had to guess whether it was there or not and were scored according to whether they were right or wrong. The reasoning behind the experiment was this: If B and C truly tended to be more segregated in some conditions than in others, the listener's judgments of the presence or absence of B should be more accurate in these segregated conditions. As in the previous experiment, the carrier frequency for tone B was fixed at 3,000 Hz and its modulation frequency at 125 Hz. Two ranges of carrier frequency were used for tone C in different conditions. In some, the carrier was in the vicinity of 2,000 Hz as before; in others, it was in the vicinity of 1,600 Hz. Sometimes the trio of partials in C was harmonically related (carriers at 2,000 Hz and 1,600 Hz) and sometimes not.

The results, shown in figure 3.14, displayed certain similarities to the ones found with the clarity-judgment task, but also some differences. First the similarities. We see that when C had the same modulation frequency as B, the presence or absence of B was harder to detect (low scores). The difference from the previous results is that this effect of AM was much stronger when C was formed from carriers of 2,000 Hz and 1,600 Hz. These were the carriers that generated harmonics of 125 Hz (the fundamental of tone B) when modulated at 125 Hz (the modulation rate of tone B). That is, they matched B in terms of both periodicity and harmonic series. Therefore the fact that B and C were composed of harmonics of the same fundamental made B particularly hard to detect.

Harmonicity had a much stronger effect in this experiment, where the task was merely to detect B's presence, than in the previous one, where it was to rate how clearly B could be heard. What this could mean is that when harmonicity is violated, the presence of an inharmonic B causes a dissonance to arise that colors the mixture so that it can be discriminated from the case in which there is no B present; this is an additional effect that is not the same as really being able to hear B in the mixture. Although I believe that there is enough evidence from other experiments that harmonicity and inharmonicity promote fusion and segregation, respectively, we have to be sure that in any particular case, the apparent effect is not the result of the listener's being able to accomplish the experimental task without actually being able to hear the target as a separate sound. The experiment that I just described can be called an accuracy task, and such tasks are often thought to be more objective than rating tasks, where the listeners rate how clearly they can hear the target. However, they may purchase this objectivity at the expense of measuring something quite different from the perceptual effect that the experimenter is interested in.

So far we have looked at the role of the match in periodicity of amplitude pulsing at different spectral locations. Even a 5-Hz discrepancy in these rates of pulsing can reduce the tendency of these regions to fuse in perception. This requires the auditory system to have a fine level of sensitivity. However there is another experiment that shows that the system has an even finer sensitivity. It can distinguish between two pulsation patterns of the same frequency but of different phase.[368] The experiment resembles those we have just been discussing. Each of tones A, B, and C, was created by sinusoidally modulating a carrier frequency, and again tone A alternated with a mixture of B and C. However, tones A and B were not identical. Tone B was always either higher or lower than A in frequency and the listener had to report whether the high or the low version of B was heard. In all cases, B and C were modulated at the same frequency. Furthermore, B and C were both harmonics of the 100-Hz modulating frequency and therefore their partials were all harmonics of this frequency. All this should cause them to fuse together strongly. What was varied was the phase of the amplitude modulation applied to B and C. In one condition it was in phase; the amplitudes of both A and B rose and fell in synchrony 100 times per second. In the other condition, again the amplitudes of A and B rose and fell 100 times per second, but 180° out of phase (when A rose B fell and vice versa). The results showed that there was a greater fusion between tones B and C in the in-phase condition. The listener was less able to decide whether B was higher or lower than A. This sort of result suggests that the auditory grouping mechanism may not be looking at the frequency of modulation itself, but merely at whether increases of intensity (for example) are happening synchronously at different spectral locations.

Although phase information (or, perhaps, synchrony of changes in amplitude) may affect the grouping of spectral information for some purposes, it does not seem to affect all forms of spectral grouping. For example, there is evidence that the grouping of information from different frequency regions or bands *for the purpose of deriving a pitch* does not require a phase match of the intensity variations in different frequency regions. We know that a periodic waveform (say at 200 Hz) composed of harmonics with random phases and amplitudes will give a pitch that is appropriate for the repetition rate of the waveform and that this pitch will remain even when the fundamental and the next few harmonics are removed.[369] This means that the pitch is not derived by finding points in time where the pulses in all frequency regions are in the same phase. There would be no such points (because of the random phase). Instead one would have to be able to compute the actual repetition rate of the neural activity within each frequency region, and somehow compare this computed rate in different frequency regions rather than comparing the raw pulsations themselves.

How can we reconcile the following two facts: (1) that pitch computation (really a computation of the repetition frequency of the waveform) seems to be a within-region computation that does not care about the relative phases in different frequency regions, and (2) that the grouping of regions in the experiment that we just examined does depend on phase? One possibility relates to the size of the effect. Grouping may care about phase, but not very much. If separate computations of within-band periodicity are compatible across bands, grouping may be favored even when the phases are out of line. However the alignment of phases might improve it. To investigate this possibility we would have to compare the strength of the pitch percept when the phases in different frequency bands were either aligned or random. A second possibility is that the grouping of pitch information across frequency regions does not follow the same rules as the use of periodicities to group the regions for the extraction of other properties. It is too early to decide between these alternatives.

Perhaps the following experiment could tell us how important the synchrony of pulses in different regions was, independently of local pitch estimates. Suppose we used a series of short bursts of a sinusoid, where the carrier had a fixed frequency but where the bursts were scheduled to occur at random intervals varying, for example, between 2 and 20 msec, with a mean burst rate of 100 per second. We could have this occur with carriers of two different frequencies, with either the same schedule of bursts governing the two burst trains or else two independent schedules with the same overall statistical properties. In this case, if the synchronies themselves were important, the two frequency bands should fuse much better when they were both activated with the same schedule for the bursts. One would expect stronger differences between the synchronized and unsynchronized conditions than were obtained with the experiment on out-of-phase AM that I described earlier. In that experiment, the bursts in one frequency region always had a fixed delay relative to the bursts in the other (one-half of the modulation period). The regularity of this relation may have reduced the segregating effects of the asynchrony of the bursts. The auditory system may treat an irregular asynchrony as offering better evidence for the existence of separate sources than a fixed and repeating asynchrony does. A mere displacement of the pulses in one spectral region relative to those in another is not really very good evidence that two separate sounds are occurring. A fixed-delay asynchrony will occur, for example, between the amplitude changes in the low frequencies of a sound and the high frequencies of its echo (which may be mixed with the original sound). A statistical independence in the changes is a much better clue that there are two sounds than is a mere asynchrony of the changes.

Simultaneous amplitude changes help us to appropriately fuse or segregate sound that comes not only from different parts of the spectrum but also from different places in space. If you present different tones to the two ears, for example, 750 and 800 Hz, they will not fuse. But if you add an in-phase amplitude modulation of 8 Hz to both, they will.[370] An interesting side effect is that the single sound image seems to be localized on the side of the ear receiving the higher frequency. (This localization toward the ear receiving the higher tone also occurs in Diana Deutsch's octave illusion.[371])

We might ask ourselves whether a tendency to fuse the information from different directions when their pulsation is synchronized has any value in a real-world listening situation. The clue to its utility might be the fact that when we are standing close to a wall or other reflective surface, a significant amount of energy may be reaching one of our ears by a path that distorts the information about its true spatial origin. Furthermore, because the wall may be absorptive, the energy coming off it may have a different spectrum than the direct energy does. If the amplitude pulses are slow enough that their phase misalignment (resulting from the fact that they have traveled by different paths) is not large in comparison with the period of the pulsation, their approximate synchrony may provide information that the different spectra received at the two ears are really parts of the same source spectrum. It might be that the 8-Hz modulation demonstration gives us a glimpse of a mechanism evolved to exploit this sort of cue.

I have left out some studies that show strong effects of correlated AM in different frequency bands in uniting the information from those bands. They are concerned with masking, and I want to discuss all the masking experiments together later in this chapter.

We have seen that even though two sources of acoustic energy (for example, two instruments) are sounding at the same time and their partials are mixing at our ears, their momentary changes in intensity may tell us that there are two groups of partials.

We have examined the auditory system's use of correlated changes in amplitude in different spectral bands as evidence that the bands were created by the same physical source. We have only looked, so far, at rapid fluctuations in intensity. However, we must also consider slow changes. These might occur, for example, because of the spatial movement of either the source of sound or the listener. The partials of an approaching source will all become more intense together at our ear relative to the partials from sources that are not approaching. The same thing will happen when we ourselves are moving toward some sound sources and away from others or even when we turn our heads.

The issue of *changes* in intensity is unfortunately complicated by the issue of momentary *differences* in the intensity. If one physical source (a set of partials, A) swells and becomes considerably louder than another simultaneously active source (B), the spectral shape of the mixture will undoubtedly be very close to that of the spectrum of the louder sound, A, taken alone. The memory for that spectrum, created at moments when A is much louder, may make it possible to isolate A's spectrum from the mixture of A and B at a later moment when A is not emphasized by loudness.

When sources are changing in loudness relative to one another, therefore, we do not know whether to explain our ability to subdivide a mixture by appealing to a mechanism capable of using the correlations of the changes in loudness or one capable of exploiting momentary differences in loudness. We could imagine mechanisms that worked in either way. For example, a mechanism that looked for correlated intensity changes would first measure the intensity change over some brief time period for each resolvable part of the spectrum and then look for regions of the spectrum that showed the same changes. We have already discussed how useful such a mechanism might be in segregating a human voice from other periodic sounds.

However, a mechanism that used its memory for earlier events would also be useful, particularly in isolating a part of the spectrum in a very dense mixture. In such a mixture, especially where the components of two or more sounds were overlapped in frequency, the overlap might prevent the listener from obtaining separate assessments of the local properties of the different regions of the spectrum (such properties as frequency or amplitude changes or direction of arrival) so as to correlate them with properties found elsewhere in the spectrum. In such a case, getting clear "peeks" at the individual spectra would become particularly useful. Fortunately, sounds are rarely steady. The human voice, for example, changes constantly in frequency composition and in amplitude. If two voices are mixed together, there will be moments when one is relatively quiet and we will get a good peek at such properties as the spatial location and the shape of the spectrum of the other one. Even those moments when the components of one spectral region in one of the voices cease may allow us to get a peek at the components of the other voice in that region. To take advantage of these moments, the auditory system would have to be able to keep a record of them and then compare them with, and possibly group them with, later-arriving parts of the mixture.

Although it is hard to imagine exactly how this could be done by the auditory system, we already know that something very much like it would have to be done in order to carry out the old-plus-new heuristic that we discussed earlier. Recall that this heuristic examines a mixture of components to see whether it contains components that were present alone just before the mixture occurred. In order to carry this out, the auditory system would need a record of the components that were present at that earlier moment. In the experiments of the type done by Pinker and myself, memory for a single simple sound would be adequate. However, in real-life environments, the system could never know when a new source would become active and add its spectrum to the mixture. Therefore, its record of the components that were candidates for extraction from a later complex spectrum would have to be continuously changing and represent the entire recent spectrum.

I think there is every reason to assume that it is the same sequential grouping process that forms the sequential streams discussed earlier that records the peeks we are discussing now. If we make this assumption, it can suggest properties that a peek-using process might have. For example, we know that when we rapidly alternate two tones of quite different frequencies, the stream segregation that occurs can group a sound not just with the previous sound but with an earlier one. Therefore we suspect that the peek-using process has the ability to keep a record not only of the most recent sound but of earlier ones as well. How this could be done is a mystery, but our attempt to unify a variety of grouping phenomena strongly suggests that it must happen. Perhaps the record that is kept is more like a spectrogram (a time varying "picture") than like "the most recent spectrum," and the process that uses it can match up "subpictures" that are separated in time but resemble one another.

The strong likelihood that a listener has the capacity of recording time-varying spectra and following them into subsequent mixtures creates a problem for us as theoreticians: When we want to assert that the auditory system has decomposed a mixture by making use of correlated amplitude *changes*, we must try to rule out the use of simple momentary amplitude *differences*, which can give the system a peek at one of the component spectra. At the present time there has been, as far as I know, no systematic investigation of these issues.

Comparison of AM and FM Effects

We have seen how the grouping of regions of the spectrum can be affected by two sorts of correlations between changes in those regions. These are correlation between variations in frequency (FM) and in amplitude (AM). I have described AM and FM as different sorts of changes in the signal, but the auditory system may not always detect them in a different way. Let me describe a case in which the auditory system may be treating FM as just another form of AM. First let us set look at the cochlear transformation of the incoming signal and then see how it might be responding to AM and FM. The cochlea may be viewed as an array of band-pass filters, each of which is centered on a different frequency and has a neural output that shows a maximum when the input frequency is at the tuned frequency, a sharply falling off of response to frequencies above the tuned frequency, and a more gentle decline of response to frequencies below it. This is shown schematically in figure 3.15. The asymmetrical shape

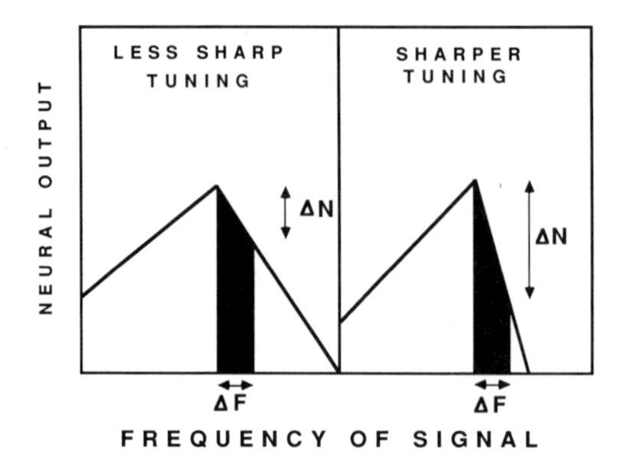

Figure 3.15
The magnitude of neural output of a local frequency region of the cochlea to inputs of different frequencies.

of the filter transfer function that is shown here summarizes the finding of a large number of neurological and psychophysical studies. Although the asymmetry is more or less agreed upon, the sharpness of the tuning is not. What is important in the figure is that the filter seems more sharply tuned on the high-frequency side, showing large changes in neural output (labeled *N* in the figure) for small changes of the frequency of the input (labeled *F*). Because of this sharp tuning, frequency changes are converted to changes in neural output.

Let us consider what happens in response to modulation in the frequency of a partial. The effects of two different assumptions about the sharpness of the filtering are shown. Suppose that the modulation moves a partial from the tuned frequency of a filter to a frequency somewhat higher. The intensity of neural response from that filter will drop substantially. When the frequency comes down again, the intensity of response will rise. As we see by comparing the two halves of the figure, the change in output activity for a fixed change in frequency depends on the sharpness of the tuning.

Now let us imagine that the partial that we are considering undergoes a changes in amplitude rather than frequency; again the neural output intensity will rise and fall in step with the modulation. We can see, then, that both FM and AM can cause the filter outputs to modulate in intensity.

It is therefore theoretically possible that the perceptual grouping of different spectral regions that are changing in a correlated way may be based on this modulation of the bursts of neural output both for AM and FM. This does not mean that listeners cannot tell the difference between frequency changes and amplitude changes. Clearly they can. However it could still be the case that the grouping process treats them as equivalent.

Pierre Abdel Ahad and I carried out an experiment to try to throw some light on this question.[372] It compared how well different types of modulation promoted the grouping of frequency regions. The type of stimulus pattern resembled that of Bregman and Pinker, as shown in figure 1.16 of chapter 1. It was a repeating cycle composed of a tone A, alternating with a mixture of two tones, B and C. Tones A and B were identical and the listener's task was to try to hear tone A repeating in the BC mixture. As in many of our experiments, A, B, and C were not pure tones but complex ones. The characteristics of tone C were varied in different conditions to see how this affected the listener's ability to segregate B from it. Each of tones A, B, and C consisted of one or more sinusoidal components. The components within a tone were all modulated in the same way. Tone C was either modulated in phase with B or in exactly opposite phase and it was the difference between these two conditions (in phase versus out of phase) that was the focus of interest. The rate of modulation was 6 Hz, which is slow, but at a rate that is not unlike the vibrato of the human voice.

So far I have not said anything about the type of modulation that was used. There were, in fact, three types, but only the first two are relevant to the present discussion. The first was amplitude modulation (AM). This was sinusoidal in form with a frequency of 6 Hz. Amplitude modulation can be described by its depth. That is, the modulation need not change the signal from full amplitude to inaudible. In this experiment, the difference between the most and least intense phase of the signal was either 4, 8, or 16 dB. We wanted to see how different depths of AM applied to tones B and C would affect their fusion when the modulations were either in phase or out of phase.

The second type was frequency modulation (FM). Frequency modulation can be described by its excursion factor, that is, by how far the frequency of the carrier is varied around its central frequency. It is convenient to express this as a percentage of the frequency being modulated, because if we want to preserve the harmonic relations among the components being modulated, we must modulate them all by the same fixed percentage of their frequencies. In this experiment we used excursion factors of 2, 4, and 8 percent. Again these were applied to tones A and B either in phase or out of phase.

We wanted to find some level of AM that gave the same effects on the segregation and fusion of tones B and C. From this, using the ideas shown in figure 3.15, we could estimate what the slope of the cochlear filter must be if AM and FM were actually both detected by their effects on the changes in the amount of neural output from individual filters. If this estimate gave a plausible value for the slope, it would support the idea of a common mechanism for AM and FM effects.

In order to accommodate a third condition (whose description is omitted here) we made each of the tones A, B, and C out of three partials, a carrier accompanied by two sidebands that were separated from the carrier by 100 Hz and had half its amplitude. The carrier frequencies for tones B and C were always 3,600 and 2,400 Hz respectively, and tones A and B were always identical.

The 6-Hz modulation had different effects in the AM and FM conditions. In the AM condition, the intensity of the three partials (e.g., those in A) simply rose and fell as a group six times per second. In the FM condition, the frequency of each component of the three-component tone rose and fell by the same excursion factor six times per second, maintaining the same harmonic relations to one another throughout.

The task of the listener was to reduce the intensity of tone C (which started off very intense) until A and B could be heard together in their own stream. The results are shown in figure 3.16. The loudness of C that could be tolerated while still hearing a separate sequence of tones A and B is shown as a function of the amount of modulation for the two forms of modulation. Higher levels of the curves represent increased degrees of segregation of tones B and C. For both forms of modulation, the segregation is greater when the modulation of B and C is out of phase than when it is in phase. Since the results are in decibels, they may be directly compared across conditions.

Comparing the FM and AM conditions, and interpolating a little, we see that an 8 percent excursion produced by FM is worth about the same as perhaps a 10-dB change introduced by AM. Using the reasoning represented in figure 3.15, we can calculate that the results of AM and FM could be the result of their effects on the intensity of the gross bursts of neural output if the falloff of the cochlear filters had a slope of at least 90 dB per octave. This is a simplification based on the assumption that the falloff is symmetrical in the low-frequency and high-frequency direction. We know that this is not true and that the falloff in the low-frequency direction is slower. Since we know that the falloffs observed on the high-frequency side of the tuning

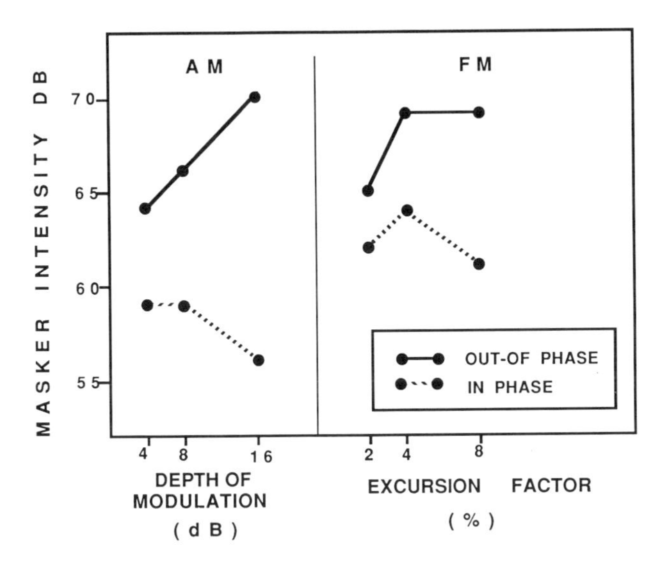

Figure 3.16
Results of a comparison of the effects of AM and FM on perceptual fusion. Left panel: AM results. Right panel: FM results. (From Bregman and Abdel Ahad 1985.)

curves of primary auditory neurons can be in the range of 200–500 dB per octave, there is more than enough sharpness in the tuning of the local regions of the auditory system to account for the grouping effects of FM on spectral fusion purely in terms of its effects on the *amplitude* of neural pulsations.[373]

A second experiment was done comparing the effects of these two forms of modulation. It was identical to the previous one except for the fact that tones A, B, and C had much denser spectra, 12 partials each. The results were much the same with these denser spectra as with those of the previous experiment.

These results suggest that it is possible that the same neural mechanism may be responsible for the effects of AM and FM on the perceptual grouping of frequency bands. They do not rule out the possibility that an entirely different mechanism underlies the two effects, but they show that a common mechanism is not implausible given the relative sizes of the two effects. If the FM effects had been much larger than could be explained by amplitude changes in basilar membrane filters, we would have had to postulate that FM was detected in a different way.

Correlation of Auditory with Visual Changes
We do not just live in a world of sound. Many of the events that make sound also have visible effects. Furthermore the effects on the sound and the light will often correspond in time. This correspondence is another example of the Gestalt concept of common fate. As I hit the keys of the keyboard upon which I am writing this chapter, there is an audible click at a certain phase of the motion. A person listening and watching should be able to utilize this temporal correspondence to determine which sounds, in a collection of intermingled sounds, are coming from the typing. If the position of the motion in the visual field is more clearly defined than the spatial origin of the sound, we could draw the inference that the sound was coming from a corresponding location in auditory space. We might then be able to direct our auditory attention to that location. Conversely, if the auditory location were clearer, the correspondence would tell us where to direct our visual attention. In other words, the correspondence, in time and in space, of auditory and visual changes should allow auditory and visual computations to help each other.

There have been a number of studies on how visual and auditory information is blended to allow the perceiver to know where in space an event is taking place, or what the identity of that event is.

One sort of study concerns the "ventriloquism" effect in which a sound appears to come from the spatial location in which a correlated visual event is occurring. This has been the subject of a great deal of study.[374] Another coupling between audition and vision that has been experimentally studied is the tendency of infants to prefer to look at objects whose motions are correlated with changes in a sound that they are hearing, or who show in other ways that they are treating the auditory and visual information as coming from the same object.[375] As I mentioned earlier, there is also evidence that the tendency to integrate a rapid sequence of auditory events into the same stream depends on whether a sequence of visual events, synchronous with the auditory ones, is seen as integrated into a single stream of motion.[376] Despite all this research, there have been no studies of whether the correlation of a subset of sounds with a sequence of visual events can assist the listener in extracting that subset from the auditory mixture.

There is perhaps one exception to this lack of research. There have been studies showing that if we see a speaker's face in a noisy environment, we can more easily understand what is being said.[377] However, there is reason to believe that in the case of speech perception the visual events are not just telling us that the acoustic components correlated with it are coming from the same source. Instead, the visual modality is actually supplying information about what the person is saying. We know how to recognize words both auditorily and visually. When we hear a word and see it spoken at the same time, we combine the evidence from the two sources. Experiments have been done in which the information sent visually (in a video image) and auditorily (in a synchronized sound track) was discordant.[378] For example, "ba-ba" might be presented auditorily and the word "ga-ga" visually. The actually perceived sound would be one that is as consistent as possible with both sources of information. In this example, we would hear "da-da", since it agrees with the visual "ga-ga" in being spoken with the lips open and with the auditory "ba-ba" in being a voiced stop consonant that is articulated at the front of the mouth. The integration is not a conscious one. Knowing what is happening does not prevent the illusion.

However, this form of unconscious integration must surely depend on our knowledge of the language and therefore does not fall into the category of scene-analysis processes that we have referred to as primitive ones. These latter exploit regularities that occur in a wide class of listening situations, not just in speech. It is possible that the primitive, general process of integrating simultaneous sounds and visual events is involved even in the auditory-visual integration of speech. However, it is hard to prove that it is since the highly trained skill of listening to speech is functioning at the same time and perhaps obscuring the effects of the primitive process. This difficulty is particularly evident in interpreting the duplex perception of speech, discussed in chapter 7.

Although there is no formal research on the role of auditory-visual temporal correspondences in primitive scene analysis there are some informal examples that suggest that they may be used. If you want to help a person to hear something in a mixture—for example, in an orchestral piece—a strategy that is often used is to synchronize the gestures of your hand with the loudness swells or rhythmic accents in the target sound. Here you correlate the property of intensity in your hand and the sound. In common language, you beat out the notes. Another strategy is to correlate the vertical position of your hand with the pitch of the notes as you beat them out. There seems to be a natural association between the following pairs of properties that change at the same time in vision and audition: (1) changes of intensity of motion (speed and amplitude) in vision with changes in amplitude of sound, and (2) change of vertical position in space with change of pitch.

Summary of Effects of Common Fate

We have seen that the Gestalt concept of common fate has provided us with a way of talking about the auditory system's use of a number of different types of clues that could tell it whether to treat co-occurring auditory events as having arisen from the same signal. A number of clues have been mentioned. These have included corresponding changes in frequency in different parts of the spectrum. These could be the large slow changes that occur when the voice is gliding in pitch or the very tiny fast ones when there are rapid fluctuations in the voice. These correlated changes lead to diverse effects. One is an improvement of the quality of the pitch sensation derived from a subset of partials. Another is the isolation of the timbre of the set of correlated partials. Single partials that change in ways that are uncorrelated with the others are heard as pure tones and a group of partials changing together define a single sound with its own perceptual qualities. Unfortunately we cannot tell from the existing research whether all these effects can be explained by the fact that the parallel changes in log frequency that have been used in most of these studies had their effect simply by maintaining good harmonic relations within subsets of partials.

Correlated amplitude changes are also important. These changes include the synchrony or lack of synchrony of onsets and offsets, and of changes in amplitude (and possibly in phase). The detection of these amplitude changes can act in support of other detected changes, as when the beats between harmonics that are detected in auditory "filters" occur at the same rate as the fundamental and give support to evidence that might be found from a more direct assessment of the spacing of the harmonics on the basilar membrane. On the other hand they can oppose other clues, as when a rapid onset followed by exponential decay can lead the listener to fuse a set of inharmonic partials that would otherwise not have fused.

Finally, there is some suggestion that correlations between some spectral activity in audition and some visual activity will help to isolate acoustic components from a mixture.

All these clues can be described by the same principle: If there is a correspondence between a change in an auditory component and in something else (either another auditory component or a nonauditory event) this is probably not an accident and the auditory component should be assigned to the same perceived event as the other change with which it is correlated.

Spatial Correspondence

We will now shift our attention to one of the strongest scene-analysis principles. This is the one that says that acoustic components that can be localized as coming from the same position in space should be assigned to the same stream. We know that the cue of spatial location is a very important one in allowing a listener to follow the words of one speaker in a noisy environment.[379] If we cover one of our ears in such a situation our ability to select the desired voice gets much worse.

It is evident that the frequency components arising from the voices of different speakers will be interleaved in frequency, and that the early spectral analysis done by the auditory system will not in itself be sufficient to segregate them. To compute a separate identity for each naturally occurring sound in the mixture, the auditory system has to be able to group the overall set of resolved frequency components or frequency regions into the subsets that represent the individual sounds. Could this grouping be done according to the spatial origin of the components?

There is a difficulty involved. At the stage in processing that grouping must be done, the system is still working with frequency components, not whole sounds. Therefore, in order to know how to group these components, it has to be able to assign a spatial origin to each one separately. Only then could it know which ones came from the same location. What evidence is there that the auditory system can compute location on a frequency-by-frequency basis?

We saw in an earlier chapter that the principle of grouping sounds that come from a common spatial origin was used to create separate perceptual streams for sounds that were rapidly alternating between the ears. However, we are now dealing with events that happen at the same time, not in succession. We know intuitively that we can hear two sounds at the same time and know that they are coming from different spatial locations. But what more do we know about this impressive capability?

Kubovy has presented an argument that does not assign a central importance to spatial location in audition.[380] He has argued that while it may be true that space is an "indispensable attribute" in vision, it is frequency that plays that role in audition. An indispensable attribute is a feature of the sensory input that permits the perception of the twoness of two simultaneous signals that are identical except for that feature. In vision, two otherwise identical objects that are either separated in time or in space can be seen as two things. Therefore space and time are both indispensable attributes in vision.

In audition, Kubovy argues, the indispensable attributes are time and frequency. Frequency is considered indispensable since two simultaneous sounds differing only in frequency can be heard at the same time. The role of time (in the range of the longer time intervals that do not give rise to the perception of frequency) is the same as in vision. But space, according to Kubovy, is not an indispensable attribute in audition. He argues that two sounds that differ only in their spatial origin will be fused in perception and heard as emanating from some intermediate location. (We shall see shortly that this is not always the case.) Similarly loudness is not an indispensable attribute of audition, since two otherwise identical and simultaneous sounds of different intensities coming from the same position in space will simply sum at the ear and be heard as one.

Since frequency and time are Kubovy's indispensable attributes of hearing and we have already seen that they appear to be the ones involved in stream segregation, it would be tempting to guess that only his indispensable attributes are used in the segregation of simultaneous sounds. Unfortunately for this hypothesis, this volume contains counterexamples that suggest that spatial separation plays an important role. It is true that a spatial difference alone cannot cause segregation of two simultaneous tones that go on and off at precisely the same time. However, as soon as the situation becomes more complex, two simultaneous frequency components differing only in place of origin can be heard as parts of two separate sounds at different spatial locations rather that uniting to form a sound heard between those locations.[381] In addition, when a spatial difference is added to some other difference (say in frequency or in a match to a prior event in one ear), it greatly increases the amount of segregation.

Evidence That Ear Comparisons Must Be Frequency Specific

Let us return to the question of whether the spatial origins of different frequency components can be assessed independently. There is some indirect evidence from physiology. If a cat is operated upon and parts of its primary auditory cortex are lesioned, it may no longer be able to tell where a sound is coming from in space when tested with a short burst of a certain frequency; at the same time its spatial localization for other frequencies may be intact and normal.[382] Larger lesions may wipe out the ability to localize most frequencies but may not affect the ability to localize the frequencies that are handled by the part of the cortex that is still intact. Furthermore the deficit will occur only in the half of the auditory field on the opposite side to the lesion. The cortical locations that will produce deficits at different frequencies are arranged in regular strips along the cortical surface. The results cannot be attributed to simple deafness to those frequencies resulting from by the operation. Frequency-specific deficits have also been reported in humans with brain damage. These results support the idea that the auditory system is capable of frequency-specific localizations.

There is also evidence gathered in psychoacoustic experiments that show that two pure tones of different frequencies at different locations can be heard simultaneously. When one is presented to each ear over headphones, they will not fuse to generate a single image unless the tones are very close in frequency. For example, when the frequency of one tone is 250 Hz, the other one must be less than 6.6 Hz (3 percent) away from it before fusion occurs. In the range from 250 to 4,000 Hz, the maximum mistuning that is tolerated is never greater than about 7 percent.[383] Therefore this fusion is quite finely tuned.

This experiment measures fusion, but not its opposite—independent localization. There will have to be extensive research on separate judgments of locations for simultaneous pure tones before we can know exactly how finely tuned the auditory system is for making separate frequency-specific localizations. The research will be hard to do because the mere simultaneity of the tones will tend to fuse them. We may need special indirect methods for the study of such localizations.

Such an indirect method was used in a fascinating experiment done by Kubovy and Howard that showed not only that closely spaced parts of the spectrum can be localized separately from one another but that the separate location information is remembered for some time.[384] They played to listeners a chord of six pure tones ranging from 392 Hz to 659 Hz. These tones spanned a range of less than an octave, and corresponded to the musical pitches G, A, B, C, D, and E. All the tones were sent to both ears over headphones, but the two ears received slightly different temporal information about each tone. It is possible, in the laboratory, to specify a location for a tone along the left-right dimension by delaying the phase of the sound a bit in one ear relative to the other. This simulates what happens in real life: the sound takes a little longer to get to the ear that is further from the source. Taking advantage of this cue for location, Kubovy and Howard introduced a different delay in phase for each tone, thus specifying a different horizontal location for each one. Even when this was done, the overall sound was confused, because no single frequency stood out of the mixture. Then, after a brief pause, the chord was played again, but the specified location of one of the tones was changed while the others were held constant. Now the tone with the changed location popped out of the mixture and its pitch was heard faintly, separate from the confused mass. The change was made during the silence between the two presentations so that each of the presentations, if heard alone, sounded like a blurred mass. It was only when the listeners heard one presentation shortly after the other that they heard a tone pop out. The researchers argued that in order to know which tone's location had changed on the second presentation, the auditory system must have had separate records of the previous locations of all the tones. It would have had to preserve these records until after the silence and then compare them to the new ones that came after the silence. Over how long a silence could these records be preserved? For most of the people in the experiment, the silence had to be less than 1.5 seconds. However, one unusual listener could detect the changed tone with 100 percent accuracy even across the longest silence that was tested, 9.7 seconds. Therefore not only did this experiment demonstrate the existence of a computation of location that is separate for each frequency, but also a separate memory for each.

At this point I would like to cite not a scientific study but a sound pattern that was created at IRCAM, the computer music center in Paris, for use in a piece of music.[385] It was created by synthesizing the even and odd harmonics of an oboe tone on separate channels and sending the channels to two different loudspeakers, to the left and right of the listener. A small amount of frequency fluctuation (FM micromodulation) was imposed on the harmonics. At the beginning of the sound, the fluctuations of all the harmonics were synchronized and identical, and the listener heard a single oboe centered between the speakers. Then the fluctuations of the harmonics in the left speaker were gradually made independent of those on the right, but within each speaker the harmonics fluctuated in synchrony. As the two channels became independent, the sound seemed to split into two separate sounds, one based on the even and the other on the odd harmonics, coming from separate speakers. We can understand why the two sounds would be heard as one when the fluctuations were correlated. But in the case of the two uncorrelated channels, how could the listeners know which harmonics to hear in each speaker unless they were able to assign independent locations to the individual harmonics and then group those that came from the same location and had a common micromodulation? The different qualities of the two perceived sounds furnished evidence that the segregation had actually caused the listeners to group the same-channel harmonics together. The sound coming from the speaker containing the odd harmonics had the characteristic, hollow, clarinet-like quality associated with a sound composed of only odd harmonics. Furthermore, the sound composed of the even harmonics sounded, as it should, an octave higher. The amazing thing is that the even and odd harmonics are closely interwoven in frequency and that not only the two pitches but the two qualities were correctly assigned to separate locations.

A reader might object that there is nothing unusual about hearing the sound that comes from a speaker as actually coming from it, or in hearing two sounds coming from the places that they are actually coming from. However, the initial fusion of the two sets of partials shows that this accomplishment is not inevitable, and makes us more sensitive to the magnitude of the accomplishment. We must remember that the auditory system does not have access to the two subsets of partials as whole signals. It first takes the sounds apart into their frequency components. If it is to put together all those that came from the same place, it must first figure out which place each of them came from. When the micromodulation in the two channels was correlated this acted to promote fusion; that is, it operated to contradict the directional cues, causing the partials to blend even though they did not all come from the same place.

This is a good example of how different cues will compete to control the fusion of the components. The usefulness of this particular competition in natural situations is that sometimes we may hear a sound in which a single signal has been bounced off different reflectors on two sides of us before it reaches our ears. In such a case, the reflectors may each absorb different frequency bands in different amounts, causing the input to one of our ears to have quite different acoustic parameters than the input to the other. A simple interaural intensity comparison (for example) might find different points of origin for different frequency components. If, however, the different inputs shared a common frequency-modulation pattern, this common-fate cue might cause the components to be fused, thereby overcoming the distorting effects of the environment.

There is another phenomenon that shows the effects of the ear's ability to make a separate estimate of point of spatial origin for different frequency regions. This time the segregation protects the weaker sound from being masked by the louder. The phenomenon is called the "binaural masking level difference" (BMLD) effect. I will discuss it later in a section that collects together different masking effects that are related to scene analysis.

Here is yet another demonstration of the ear's ability to separate different spectral components on the basis of their points of origin in space. Let us start with a broad-band noise that is created by a single white noise generator and choose a narrow band of its spectrum, lying below 1,000 Hz.[386] Then, for the frequency components in this part of the spectrum only, we delay the phase of the copy of the signal going to one ear relative to the copy going to the other. For the rest of the spectrum we send identical copies to both ears with no time difference. This acoustic stimulus causes the listener to hear a pitch that is like the pitch of a narrow band of noise at the ear that gets the earlier version of the narrow-band signal. This pitch stands out faintly against the rest of the broad-band noise, which is heard as centered. The segregation does not depend on the sound actually starting in one ear first, but on the ongoing disparity in phase between the two ears. As long as the phase leads continuously at one ear, the signal is heard at that ear. The isolated pitch cannot be heard by either ear taken alone but depends on the cross-ear comparison. In other words, the band of noise in which the components are out of phase at the two ears, as they would be if an environmental sound were on one side of the listener, is assigned a location different from the other spectral components. This segregates the frequency bands and the pitch of the narrower band is heard. The ears are acting as if there were two different sounds in the environment.

An important sort of fusion takes place when the echo of a sound is fused with the original so that we hear only a single sound. This interpretation is valid since only one sonic event has actually occurred. If the fusion is a sort of scene-analysis phenomenon, we would expect it to be affected by the spatial origins of the two sounds. For example, if the original sound came from straight ahead, the strength of fusion should depend on where the echo came from. If it also came from straight ahead (echoing off a wall behind the source), it should show a greater tendency to fuse with the original than if it came from the side (bouncing off one of the side walls). This is exactly what has been observed.[387]

As a brief interruption of our discussion of spatial effects on fusion, we might consider other plausible expectations about echoes. It is reasonable to expect that any of the factors that influence the segregation of two sounds would affect the segregation of an echo from an original. For instance, if the room resonances were to color the echo, giving it spectral characteristics different than the original, we would expect that the two would segregate more readily. The research on the role of onset asynchrony in segregation (as well as common sense) would tell us to also expect the amount of asynchrony to be important.

Thinking of the suppression of perceived echo as a scene-analysis problem leads us to note the following: A sound that is varying in frequency or intensity will be accompanied by an echo that is undergoing an identical series of changes, but with a certain delay. This common fate, even though slightly out of phase, may promote the fusion of the sounds. However, this common fate could be detected only if the ear's "covariation detector" could detect covariations even if they were displaced in time. The question of whether the auditory system can do this deserves experimental study.

The evidence that we have reviewed points to a capacity to segregate different components of a total acoustic input into streams that come from different locations. The perceptual result that we have mentioned thus far has been an ability to separate the subsets that come from different locations. But how about the ability to perceptually integrate such subsets? The following experiments suggest that, under some circumstances, we cannot put them back together even when an experimenter asks us to do so.

David Green and his associates at Harvard University explored an auditory capacity that Green called "profile analysis." Listeners can learn to discriminate two different spectrum shapes independently of their loudness. For example, if two sounds are played with different overall loudnesses and listeners are asked whether they have the same spectral shape, they can correctly judge them as different even if the difference involves a modest increase in the intensity of one spectral component (at 949 Hz) *relative to the others.* That is, boosting the intensity of the 949-Hz component in the spectrum makes it sound different and this difference is not just a loudness difference but a difference in some globally computed quality. Now let us suppose that we separate the 949-Hz component from the others and send it to the opposite ear. Can the listener now integrate the spectrum across the two ears so as to evaluate the *shape* of the overall spectrum without regard to any change in overall loudness? Experimental results have suggested that the listeners could not integrate the left and right ear sounds into a single qualitative analysis.[388] They simply heard the left and right ear signals as two individual sounds. Sometimes the segregation by spatial location is quite compelling.

The tendency to segregate sounds that come from different spatial locations can help us hear them more clearly. In San Antonio, Texas, there is a type of grackle that likes to congregate with its fellows in the same large tree, shrieking loudly. Although one of these birds is not unpleasant to listen to, a large number of them calling at slightly different times and pitches creates an unholy cacophony. Once when I was listening to this sound, I thought of covering one ear to see what the effect would be. Despite the lowering of loudness, the sense of dissonance and roughness rose. Uncovering the ear, I realized that

I was now aware of more individual components, even though the intermingling was such that the individual sounds poked their head, as it were, out of the mixture for only brief instants, giving the sound a sort of glittering quality. When one ear was covered these highlights were not as evident and the whole sound seemed more smeared and dissonant.

This effect seems to show that even the partial segregation of a multiplicity of sounds through spatial segregation prevents the auditory system from computing certain dissonances between them. As we shall see later, when we examine the case of musical dissonance, there seems to be evidence that if we can prevent the individual notes of a potentially dissonant chord from fusing by capturing these notes into separate auditory streams, the combination will not sound dissonant. Dissonance seems to be strongest when all the components are part of a single undifferentiated stream. Perhaps this lack of differentiation was what occurred when I covered one ear in the presence of the grackles.

Not all the evidence for the role of spatial differences in enhancing the segregation of signals is as impressionistic as this. In the 1950s there were a number of studies that showed that if a person were asked to repeat one of two mixed verbal messages, it helped a great deal if the two voices were presented over different headphones.[389] To cite another example, Robert Efron and his associates at the Veterans Administration Medical Center in Martinez, California, in the course of studying the effects of brain damage, presented a mixture of five sustained natural environmental sounds, such as violin, saw, cat meow, ping-pong, and human voice, to normal control listeners. They found that these were better identified when the sounds were made to seem to come from different locations (inside the head of the listener) by separately adjusting the loudness balance for each sound in the left and right headphones.[390]

Computer Programs That Use Spatial Correspondence The idea of using the direction of origin to segregate sounds has occurred to engineers designing computer systems to segregate simultaneous voices. Apparently if the number of microphones is larger than the number of voices and the location of each voice is known in advance, it is possible for a machine to filter out all but the desired voice. However, it is harder do this with just two microphones, analogous to the two human ears. In this case one cannot, according to theory, eliminate the offending voices, but it is possible to attenuate them.[391] One attempt required the target voice to originate at the center of a rectangle formed by four microphones.[392] If a different voice had been designated as the target, the microphones would have had to be rearranged so that the new target voice was at the center of the rectangle. A computer program operating on the input from these four microphones processed the signal. It did not split the signal into separate frequency bands and assess their spatial origins separately as we believe people do. However, it had some success; when a recording of the processed signal was played to listeners, the unwanted speech was both attenuated and distorted. The distortion of the unwanted speech seemed to increase the intelligibility of the target speech. This method seems far inferior to the capabilities of persons who work with only two ears that do not have to surround the target signal, and who, if they can segregate two voices sufficiently, do not have to change position to switch their attention from one to the other.

There has been another attempt to segregate voices using only two microphones that were implanted in the ears of a dummy head. It employed a mathematical method known as adaptive noise canceling.[393] The computer processing was able to separate one target voice from a single interfering one almost completely and from three other ones quite well. However, the system had to be supplied with information about the direction of the desired speaker (by having him speak alone) before it could do this processing, and the position of the target voice or the microphones could not change thereafter. Furthermore, these results were obtained with a silent and nonreverberant environment.

The unnatural limitations on the recording situation that must be imposed when employing the existing engineering approaches to this problem suggest that if machine-based attempts at voice segregation were based on the way in which people do it, they might be more flexible. An attempt to model how the human auditory system may be using spatial location in speech separation was begun by Richard Lyon, who created a computational model in which the delay of information in one ear relative to the other was assessed separately for 84 different frequency channels.[394] It was based on a model for binaural location estimation that was proposed by Jeffress in 1948.[395] The channels in Lyon's computer model were meant to correspond with the output of 84 small regions of equal size on the basilar membrane of the human cochlea, covering the range 50–10 KHz. A comparison between the ears gave a separate apparent direction for each frequency channel. The estimation procedure was repeated every .5 msec. In many of the channels, the apparent direction did not correspond to any real sound source but was due to a mixture of sound energy from more than one source. However, the individual directional estimate for each small "sound fragment" (extending over a narrow band of frequencies and short stretch of time) was dominated, more often than not, by the effects of a single source. Lyon had a restricted goal for this labeling, to use it to resynthesize the voice of one of two speakers, one to the left and one to the right of the listener. The way in which Lyon used these estimates after they were obtained reflected the limited goal that he had for it, but I see no reason why these estimates could not be combined with other sorts of information to decide how to connect Lyon's sound fragments over frequency and over time.

Interaction with Other Cues in Determining Grouping It seems that spatial origin, in itself, is such a good cue to whether or not spectral components come from the same sound, that we might need no other. Yet human auditory scene analysis does not put all its eggs into one computational basket. While spatial cues are good, they are not infallible. For example, they can become unusable in certain kinds of environments. One such case is a very reverberant environment. Another involves a situation in which the evidence for a particular sound is masked at one ear by a sound very close to that ear.

Even when the environment is more favorable, the mere fact that two auditory components have come from the same direction does not mean that they have originated from the same acoustic event. In vision, the surface of the nearer object occludes the sight of the further one, but this occlusion of evidence will not necessarily occur with sound. We have to remember that sound is transparent. Therefore two sounds that are coming at a listener from the same direction may mix their effects in the air. So when we hear two acoustic components coming from the very same place in space, we still cannot be sure that they came from the same acoustic event. Even a single frequency component arriving from one spatial direction could be the summation of corresponding frequency components arising from two different events. We do not know, in an ecological sense, how often the various cues are available or reliable in a random sampling of the environments in which humans find themselves. Very often, we suspect, the environment nullifies the usefulness of one cue or another.

For these reasons, the human auditory system does not give an overriding importance to the spatial cues for belongingness but weighs these cues against all the others. When the cues all agree, the outcome is a clear perceptual organization, but when they do not, we can have a number of outcomes.

When cues compete, the outcome may be determined by the extent to which the individual requirements of different cues are met. We can see how this works by looking at an experiment on the competi-

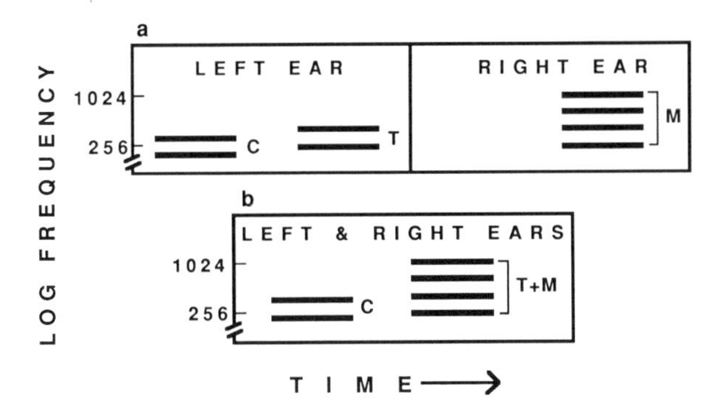

Figure 3.17
An example of a sequence of complex tones used as a captor (C), target (T), and masker (M) in an experiment by Steiger and Bregman (1982b). Presentations were either (a) dichotic or (b) binaural.

tion of cues done by Howard Steiger and myself.[396] The stimulus in this experiment consisted of a repeated cycle of two sounds, a captor tone, C, and a complex sound consisting of a mixture of two tones, T and M (see figure 3.17). The total length of one cycle was about 0.4 second. In the mixture (T + M), T was the target tone. The captor, C, was always very similar to T (same partials, each lowered by about 3 percent) and could pull T out to form a sequential stream, CT–CT–CT, and so on. M was the rest of the sound, which acted as a masker of T. Each of the sounds (C, T, and M) could consist of more than one partial.

As described so far, this stimulus offers the possibility of a competition between the sequential grouping of the captor and target (CT) and the spectral fusion of the target and the masker (T + M). However, there was also another type of competition: Sometimes the masker was in the ear opposite to the target and some partials in the masker could fuse with it to create a sound localized in the center of the listener's head. Therefore spatial cues sometimes entered into the competition. The listener's task was to adjust the intensity of the masker until a level was reached at which the target, T, was just audible.

The main purpose of the study was to find out which sort of fusion best opposed the sequential capturing effects of C. In other words, which masker, going on at the same time as T, best absorbed or masked it. The relations between the masker and the target were varied in three ways: harmonicity (relation to a common fundamental), number of corresponding harmonics, and same- or opposite-ear presentation. We found that when the opposite ear heard a masker that *matched all the target's harmonics exactly*, the fusion tended to be strong and to prevent T from being segregated from the mixture. Under these conditions of an exact match, binaural fusion was much more effective in preventing segregation than the best case of ordinary spectral fusion was. However, when the match in harmonics was not precise, either because the harmonics in the masker were tuned to a different fundamental or were not precisely the same harmonics as in the target, monaural spectral fusion was stronger than fusion across the ears. In other words, binaural fusion appeared to be very narrowly tuned and to happen on a harmonic-by-harmonic basis. This finding supports the results that have been obtained in a different type of experiment on the binaural fusion of harmonics. These latter studies asked whether the harmonics would fuse across the ears to generate a single pitch or remain separate and be heard as two pitches, one at each ear. The results suggested that the across-ear fusion of pitches occurred only when every individual partial in one ear was close enough in frequency to its counterpart in the other ear to fuse with it.[397]

What does all this tell us about the functioning of the auditory system in real life? It says that the system expects a very precise match in frequency (within about 4 percent at frequencies below 1,000 Hz) between the harmonics at the two ears if it is going to have this match overrule alternative clues to the belongingness of acoustic components. The requirements are less stringent for the fusing of partials within an ear than across ears. This makes perfect sense in natural environments. Correspondences across the two ears will arise when the two ears are both hearing the same sound. If the sounds in the two ears are merely *similar*, this is not sufficient evidence that they are different views of the same event. Nature never sends the same sounds to different ears with their frequencies lowered in one ear. It is able to do so for loudness, but not for pitch. Therefore the ear should require a reasonably precise match in the frequencies of the components before it decides that it is hearing only one sound.

The reasoning is different when it applies to different partials received at the same ear. When these come from the same acoustic event, they correspond to one another in a different way than those that arrive at opposite ears. At opposite ears, it is possible for us to receive two separate registrations of the very same partial. In a single ear, each partial is represented only once; so when we hear two distinct partials, they are never just two snapshots of the same one. They may, of course, have arisen from the same acoustic event, but the conditions under which they should be accepted as such are not as precisely defined as in the across-ear case. It may happen that two partials in the same ear are not exactly harmonically related, but what of this? Very often the partials in a natural sound may not be. So harmonicity is not a fixed requirement. The same pair of harmonics may have occurred together a bit earlier, but again this is not a prerequisite for accepting them as parts of the same sound. These ecological arguments may explain why within-ear fusion requires less exact relations between partials, but never ties partials too strongly together, and why across-ear fusion is so strong when its exact conditions are met.

The exactness of the requirements for across-ear fusion of speech sounds was demonstrated in experiments done by James Cutting, who sent a synthesized syllable "da" to both ears of a listener, but with slight inter-aural differences.[398] In one experiment, the two signals were identical except that one was delayed relative to the onset of the other. At delays of as little as 4 msec, the listeners began to segregate the signals at the two ears more often than they fused them. Remember that a syllable is a complex, time-varying signal; even though the "da" is synthesized on a constant fundamental frequency of 100 Hz (it sounds like a monotone), since the distribution of energy in the spectrum of the syllable is changing over time, as soon as one is displaced in time relative to the other, the spectra do not match exactly at the two ears. Cutting also did a version of the experiment in which the two "da" syllables were synthesized with different steady fundamental frequencies (pitches), but were otherwise identical. He found that with identical fundamentals there was 100 percent fusion of the two signals as one would expect, since the signals were then identical. However, with differences of as little as 2 Hz, which represents only one-third of a semitone at 100 Hz, the listeners almost always heard two sounds. In addition to being an illustration of the exactness of the requirement for spectral matches across the ears, this experiment may also be a demonstration of another point: although a spatial difference (having the sounds in two different ears) may not, in itself, segregate two signals, it may strongly assist other factors (such as a spectral mismatch) in doing so.

Contribution of Perceptual Grouping to Perceived Location So far, we have seen that conflicting cues can vote on the grouping of acoustic components and that the assessed spatial location gets a vote with the other cues. What is even more striking is that the other cues get a voice in deciding not only how many sounds are present but even where they are coming from in space. The auditory system seems to want to hear all the parts of one sound as coming from the same location, and so when other cues favor the fusion of components, discrepant localizations for these components may be ignored. It is as if the auditory system wanted to tell a nice, consistent story about the sound.

We saw this earlier in some of the illusions generated by a rapid alternation of tones between the ears. Take, for example, Diana Deutsch's octave illusion, where there might be a 400-Hz pure tone at one ear and an 800-Hz tone at the opposite ear, with the positions of the two tones switching repeatedly at a fixed rate.[399] Many listeners will hear an illusion in which there is only a single sound, which alternates between the ears, following the position of the high sound, but whose apparent pitch alternates between high and low. Apparently this is the way that some listeners resolve a conflict of cues where (1) the harmonic relations vote that there is only one sound, (2) the appearance of the same sound alternating between the ears votes that every successive sound is part of the same stream or possibly the same event, and (3) the independent localizations for the frequency components vote that there are two separate sounds. If we eliminate the good harmonic relation between the two sounds by making the relation different than an octave, the illusion disappears, and the listeners' ears produce a more accurate account of what is going on.

Although we are always much more struck by the interaction of cues when they produce an illusion, we should be aware of the importance of this interaction in everyday life. As I pointed out earlier, comparisons of our left and right ear inputs are not always good cues for how to group spectral components. They are also not always very reliable in telling us where those components are located in space. For example, in chapter 7, I describe a synthetic pattern of sound in which identical frequency components presented to the two ears do not fuse to form a single sound in the center. Instead the co-occurrence is interpreted as an accidental correspondence of a frequency component from two different sounds. It is conceivable that the momentary binaural correspondence causes a centered location to be computed, but that the larger context in which it occurs corrects the interpretation so that we never hear a centered sound.

Less dramatic examples of the same type of correction must occur a hundred times a day. As our ears pass close to reflective or absorptive surfaces, and as different sounds start and stop, the classical binaural cues to localization must momentarily give incorrect answers and their short-term decisions must surely have to be compared to the previously computed description of the environment so that wild fluctuations of our perceptual descriptions can be prevented by some conservative strategy for updating them. This would be a bad approach to take in a world in which each harmonic was on its own, not bound to acoustic events. In our world, however, harmonics and other products of our auditory system's analysis of acoustic events are treated as what they are: views of the same real-world events through different peepholes, where the glass in one or another peephole may momentarily be distorted or clouded.

We have seen, earlier in this chapter, that the apparent location of a sound in space can be corrected by the ventriloquism effect, the correlation of the behavior of the sound with that of a visual movement whose spatial location is different from the one that has been computed by the auditory system.[400] In this case, the typical perceptual result is the choice of an intermediate location for the sound. We think of this effect as an illusion, a view represented by the very name we give to it—ventriloquism. Yet it too is an example of the cleverness of our perceptual systems at resisting error by using the assumption of a coherent environment in which sounds should come from the places that are occupied by the events that made them. Once this assumption is built into our perceptual apparatus, it can correct errors in the estimates of the positions of events that it has obtained through sound by using estimates derived from vision.[401] Vision, of course, is not the ultimate criterion; so the final result takes both estimates into account. There is a problem, however, in the use of this procedure. When more than one event is occurring at the same time, which of the ones that have been located using vision should be treated as the same event as one that has been located using hearing? There are probably at least two criteria: one is that the two spatial estimates should not be too far apart, and the second is that the temporal patterns received by the two senses should show a weak synchrony. By "weak synchrony" I mean that not every event detected by one sense should necessarily be detectable by the other, but there should be a substantial number of correspondences. The cues might not be required to be absolutely synchronous but be allowed to be offset by some amount (perhaps up to 200 msec). When the perceptual systems decide that they are receiving information about the same event, they will merge information even when the auditory cues and visual ones are discrepant by as much as 30° (measured in terms of the visual angle).[402]

Interaction with Sequential Integration In an earlier section on sequential integration, I have reviewed a number of studies that show how sequential grouping by frequency can overcome spatial cues for the grouping of simultaneous sounds. I will now describe some experiments in which the sequential cues were deliberately manipulated so as to segregate a part of a mixture from the rest and this affected the perceived location of that segregated component.

The first one, done by Howard Steiger and myself, involved cues for vertical localization.[403] Calling high pitches "high" is not just an arbitrary metaphor. Higher pitched tones actually seem to be coming from higher in space.[404] It has been suggested that this effect is related to normal spectral cues for vertical location where, because of the filtering effect of the pinna of the outer ear, the incoming waveform is modified differently depending on its vertical angle of arrival.[405] Whatever its cause we have a phenomenon in which the monaural spectrum is linked to localization.

The purpose of our experiment was to build a signal out of two parts, a white noise burst and a pure tone. If the tone was high in frequency and was fused with the white noise, it would color the noise burst so that it sounded high and was localized higher in space, but if it was low in frequency it made the noise burst sound lower with a corresponding effect on its localization. The trick of the experiment was to see whether capturing the tone into a sequential stream with other tones would cause it to no longer contribute its highness to the noise with which it was mixed. First we did an experiment to verify that high- and low-frequency pure tones would be localized as high or low in space even if they were presented over headphones. We deceived our subjects by placing two dummy loudspeakers on the wall in front of them, one above the other, and asked them to judge the vertical positions that each of a sequence of two pure tones came from. They were told that they would be hearing the tones over headphones at the same time but to try to ignore the headphone signal and to try to focus on the signal coming from the loudspeaker. It was believable to the subjects that they could be hearing sound from the speakers even with their ears covered by headphones because the headphone speakers were encased in a foam plastic pad that let external sounds through. In actual fact, there was no signal from the loudspeakers. The results showed that in the sequence, the higher tone seemed to come from a higher position than the lower one.

This cleared the way for a second experiment in which tones and noises were played together. In this experiment, the noises came out of one or other of the pair of loudspeakers and the tones were presented over the headphones, synchronous with the noises. The loudspeakers were hidden from the listeners by a curtain, but four vertical positions were marked on the curtain. The listeners were asked to judge the vertical location from which the noise had come and to ignore, as far as possible, the tones that, they were told, were there

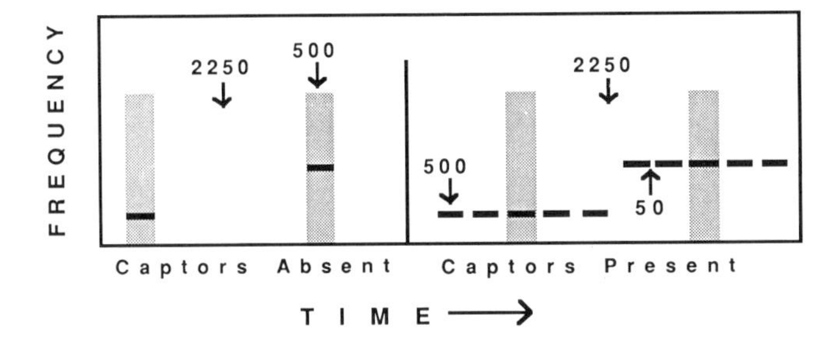

Figure 3.18
Stimuli used by Bregman and Steiger (1980). The vertical bars represent noise bursts and the dark horizontal bars are tones. The numbers represent the durations (in milliseconds) of the events or intervals.

only to distract them. A diagram of the stimuli is shown in figure 3.18. There were two conditions. In both of them, there was a sequence of two noise bursts synchronized with two pure tones of different frequencies. In one condition (captors present), each tone/noise burst was preceded and followed by two tones of the same frequency as the one that was present in the tone/noise mixture. These extra tones were intended to act as captors, capturing the tone into a separate stream from the noise. It was expected that under these conditions, the perceptual fusion of the tones and noises would be reduced and the tones would no longer determine the judged vertical positions of the noise bursts. The results supported this expectation: The direction of pitch change in the pair of tones affected the change in the judged position of the noise bursts only when the captors were absent and the tone and noise were allowed to fuse into a single stream. In a last condition, where there were no tones accompanying the noise bursts, the listener's judgments of their positions tended to be determined by the actual direction from which they had come.

This experiment showed how the fusion of simultaneous acoustic components can cause the spatial location information from them to be pooled into a single decision. Factors that cause the segregation of parts of this information, such as being captured into a simultaneous stream, can alter the perceived spatial properties of the auditory scene. Again we observe the effects of perceptual organization on the actual perceived location of sounds.

I have designed a simple demonstration to show that scene analysis can use sequential cues to influence localization in the left-right plane. It is created by playing the identical pure tone over channels A and B to stereo headphones. Then, using a volume control, channel B is repeatedly turned up and down between two limits—the intensity of channel A and silence. When the intensity is raised and lowered slowly, the location of the tone seems to move from the A side of the head to the center and back again. This is what we would expect from our understanding of binaural cues for location. However, when B is raised and lowered rapidly, two tones are heard, one staying on the A side of the head and the other pulsing on the B side. The effect is enhanced by using briefer rise times for B, by keeping B at its full intensity for shorter periods of time relative to its time at zero, and by alternating the two intensities more rapidly.

The similarity of these conditions with those required for good illustrations of the continuity illusion (of a tone through noise) suggests that we are dealing with the same sort of effect. Although I will deal more thoroughly with the continuity illusion later in this chapter, let me anticipate that discussion by a brief word here. The present demonstration resembles the continuity illusion in that in both cases the sensory evidence, received when a signal is present, is partitioned into two parts, one treated as a continuation of the signal that precedes it and the other heard as an added sound. Both are examples of sequential integration overcoming simultaneous integration. There are two new features of the present example: First, the integration being overcome is binaural rather than spectral integration, and second, not only is the sensory evidence partitioned into two streams, but each is assigned a separate location. This example shows again that scene analysis can affect where we hear sounds to be and not just how many there are or what their auditory properties are.

In the examples examined so far, when there is a discrepancy between different cues that are used to calculate the location of sounds, the auditory system seems to adopt a few sensible strategies. In some cases, it allows one cue to win. In others it takes some sort of average between them. When the discrepancy is very large, the system may decide that two things have happened and may hear two sounds at different locations. In natural environments this third strategy is normally correct, but sometimes in the laboratory it can give rise to illusions in which things are heard at one location with properties derived from other locations. Some examples of this are the studies by Diana Deutsch and her colleagues on the octave illusion, the scale illusion, and the effects of a contralateral drone. We have already discussed these phenomena in an earlier section on the effects of spatial cues in sequential integration.

Conflicting cues can be used in a fourth possible way so as to generate the illusion of "duplex perception." Duplex perception can occur when different parts of a synthesized speech sound are presented to different ears over headphones. A sound presented in one ear plays two roles at once. It can be heard as a sound in that ear and at the same time it alters the perceived identity of the sound that is heard in the other ear. Duplex perception has been thought to be such an unusual effect that it implies something special about the neural basis of speech perception. Although phenomena closely related to duplex perception can be observed with signals other than speech, I have decided not to discuss them now, but to do so in a section on exclusive allocation that follows the section on speech perception. This will allow me to address the apparent implications for the neurology of speech perception.

Interaction with Cues for Spectral Fusion The decision as to whether to merge information about spatial location from different spectral regions can depend on other sensory evidence that tells us that all these regions are registering the effects of a single sound. We have already discussed the demonstration made at IRCAM in which the even and odd harmonics of an oboe sound were sent to different loudspeakers. When the two sounds were encouraged to fuse, by giving them the same micromodulation, they were heard as coming from a single place, between the two speakers. When they were encouraged to segregate by being given different patterns of micromodulation, two separate localizations were made by the auditory system. This is another case in which scene analysis has controlled how classical cues to localization are allowed to operate.

A similar observation was made in an experiment by Donald Broadbent and Peter Ladefoged, in which two synthetic speech formants were presented to the same or different ears.[406] The formants could also be related to the same or to different fundamental frequencies. When the formants presented to different ears were related to the same fundamental, only one sound was heard and its location was more centered than in cases in which two formants with different fundamentals were presented. In the latter case two sounds with different positions were heard. The experimenters noted that the same factors that influenced the spectral fusion of sounds in one ear also controlled the fusion of sounds across ears. This supports the idea that all factors relevant to decisions about spectral parsing get to vote on it and when acoustic components are grouped into the same stream, for whatever reason, a single location is decided upon.

Conclusion: Classical versus Organizational Cues The most general conclusion that can be drawn from all these examples is that we must make some additions to the list of cues for spatial location that are typically given in textbooks on audition. Normally we would find three cues. For left-right position there would be intensity and delay, that is the increased intensity of the sound in the ear that is pointed more directly at the sound source and the relative delay of the sound in the ear that is further away. For the vertical and front-back distinctions, certain properties of the shape of the spectrum that are affected by the shapes of our ears would be mentioned. We might call these "classical cues," but a better name for them is "ear cues." They are based on the shapes of our ears and how they are placed on our heads.

However, there is an entire other family of cues that we might call "world structure cues" because they have nothing to do with the placement of our ears. It is a property of the world, and not of our ears, that events create changes both in the light and the sound, and it is this property that is responsible for the ability to correct the location estimates that we derive from vision by using ones derived from audition and vice versa. Another important fact about the world is that sounds tend to last for a while and not to change very rapidly in their qualities. This fact make it very unlikely that if the sounds in a sequence have great acoustic similarities and are very close together in time, they are wholly unrelated. They probably came from a common source and should be put into the same perceptual stream. This justifies the system's adjusting the estimate for the location of each part of the stream by taking into account the estimated locations for the moments of sound that occurred immediately before or after it in the same stream. I do not claim that the human auditory system is actually doing anything like the logical calculations that I have just described. It simply puts together whatever it is built to put together. My statements about "justification" have merely described the utility of putting things together in this way. Presumably the utility is the same whether we are discussing people, earthworms, or robots. However, they may not all be built to exploit this utility. People are.

Other Factors Affecting Fusion of Simultaneous Components

So far, when we have discussed the segregation of spectral regions, we have typically spoken the language of Fourier analysis, in which the spectrum is filled with sinusoidal components. Alternatively, we have thought of the spectrum as filled with noise. We must, however, also consider sounds that are more like textures, the "granular" sounds that we considered in chapter 2 in our discussion of the acoustic factors that led to sequential integration. We mentioned sounds such as the crunching of the boots of a walker in snow, or the sound of something being dragged, or the riffling of the pages of a book. Analogous visual examples might include the hair of one's head, where individual hairs are lost in an overall sweeping texture, or the appearance of a sheet of burlap.

In our earlier discussion, we found that since a certain amount of time was required to estimate the statistical description of the granularity, a difference in granularity would probably not be usable to create temporal boundaries, but might be usable for grouping separated sounds. Here we must do a similar analysis of the usefulness of differences in granularity for spectral integration. If we consider a spectrogram as a surface and if we looked at one that had a sufficiently high degree of resolution, these granular sounds might not look like individual spectral components (horizontal lines on the picture) or random noise (totally random dots) but might appear as different sorts of textures. If two spectral regions in this picture were filled with sufficiently different types of textures, the regions would visually segregate from one another.

There has been a considerable amount of research on the segregation of visual textures. One approach has been to describe textures as a distribution of grains on a surface where the grains have a limited number of shapes and the distribution has certain statistical characteristics.[407]

The question that we should address is whether different auditory textures in different frequency regions will tend to segregate from one another so that we hear two sounds with different qualities rather than only one. Unfortunately, no research has been done on this topic in audition. The critical step would be to devise some descriptive system for irregular sounds that could predict whether spectral regions filled with these sounds would segregate from one another. Then we would have to ask whether discontinuous parts of the spectrum (say in different frequency regions) would be integrated perceptually if they had the same description.

The problem gets more difficult if we ask whether differences in granularity could segregate two sounds when their spectra were overlapped. The granularity of the mixture will be the sum of the granularities of the two components and it might be very hard to recover the separate statistical properties with any degree of precision. Unfortunately we are left alone with our speculations on this matter. There is no evidence from the laboratory on the effects of granularity on spectral grouping.

We have now surveyed a large number of factors that affect how the auditory system carves up the immediately present spectrum and allocates parts of it to the perceptual representations of different events. I do not claim to have mentioned them all. For example, I have not mentioned the idea, put forward by Helmholtz in the passages that I quoted earlier, that different rhythmic patterns, present in different parts of the spectrum, indicate that there were different sounds embedded in it. Is this just an example of the use of synchronized onsets and offsets, factors that we have already examined, or does the periodic repetition of these synchronies make it easier to exploit them? There has been no research on this question.

All we can say is that there are a large number of factors that are useful in making this partitioning of the spectrum and are actually used by the human auditory system. We have seen that each cue has a partial validity in coming up with the right answer. For this reason I have called the auditory system's use of them "heuristic," a term in the theory of problem solving that means "tending to lead to good answers." What remains an open question is the exact method by which the auditory system combines the results of these heuristics to arrive at a decision that is usually right. There are researchers who are studying how computers could be made to recognize familiar acoustic patterns that might be present inside mixtures, and they would love to know the answer to this question. It might be very helpful if they, as specialists in system architecture, could suggest plausible ways that this might occur, so that students of perception could design experiments to determine which of these ways is used by the human perceiver.

Comparison between Fusion and Masking

This chapter has been describing how various factors promote the allocation of simultaneously present frequency components to the same stream. The evidence that I have used, in many cases, was that some components could be heard as perceptually separable sounds whereas others could not. This follows from the idea that when an acoustic component becomes absorbed into a stream that contains other simultaneous components, it gives up its perceptual identity in favor of contributing to the global features of the whole sound.

I now want to address the following question: What is the relation between perceptual fusion (absorption into a stream) and masking? I am prompted to ask this question for two reasons: the two phenomena are similar in their definitions (in both cases the listener loses the distinct qualities of one of the sounds), and the two phenomena seem to respond to the same variables in the same way. What then is the relation between perceptual fusion and masking?

The first thing to look at is the difference between their definitions. Helmholtz described our ability to hear a component in a mixture as analytic listening and referred to the tendency to hear the properties of the mixture itself as synthetic perception. He thought of the latter as a less refined form of consciousness:

> We then become aware that two different kinds or grades must be distinguished in our becoming conscious of a sensation. The lower grade of this consciousness is that where the influence of the sensation in question makes itself felt only in the conceptions we form of external things and processes, and assists in determining them. This can take place without our needing or indeed being able to ascertain to what particular part of our sensations we owe this or that relation of our perceptions. In this case we will say that the impression of the sensation in question is *perceived synthetically*. The second and higher grade is when we immediately distinguish the sensation in question as an existing part of the sum of the sensations excited in us. We will say then that the sensation is perceived analytically. The two cases must be carefully distinguished from one another.[408]

I propose to examine how studies of perceptual fusion and masking relate to Helmholtz's ideas, but first I want to say a few words about the notion of analytic listening as a skill. It is surely the case that our ability to hear out components from mixtures is a learned skill whose execution may be deliberate and involve attention. Helmholtz himself became very good at hearing out several of the lower harmonics in a complex tone. Yet despite the fact that individuals may vary in this ability, I think there is a general rule that cuts across all cases. Everybody will find some components easier to hear out of mixtures than other components. This will depend on physical relations between the components of the sound and how our primitive processes of scene analysis can make use of these relations. So despite the presence of practiced skills, I think we will always be able to find evidence for the more primitive processes that depend very directly on the physical structure of the sound.

One might think that the studies both of masking and of perceptual fusion and segregation are looking at the listener's ability to do analytic perception of the target. Yet the measurement of this ability in the two types of experiments is quite different. In a typical masking experiment there are two sounds presented at the same time, a masker and a target. The listeners are supposed to listen for the target. The masker is made louder and louder until the target can no longer be detected. So far this sounds very much like a task involving analytic perception, and therefore resembles many of the tasks that I have described as showing the effects of perceptual fusion. However, in practice, the masking experiment is done a little differently. The listeners are played a sound and must decide whether it consists of the masker alone or the masker accompanied by the target. Therefore they really do not have to detect the particular quality of the target sound in the mixture. All they have to do is to determine that the quality of the masker is different when a target is also present. The detection of this difference is not the same as hearing the target in the mixture, and does not imply that the target and mask are perceptually segregated. Masking studies, therefore, often measure the effects of the presence of the target on synthetic perception, because any global feature of the mixture can be used to make the discrimination.

When we say that the target has fused with the other sound, we are not implying that it will make no detectable contribution to the global qualities of the sound. On the contrary, the target might have fused with the masker but, in doing so, might have changed the quality of the masker. For these reasons, the typical masking experiment does not necessarily provide a measure of perceptual fusion. In a fusion experiment, on the other hand, the listeners are asked either whether they can or cannot hear the target in the mixture or, even better, to rate how clearly they can hear the target there. What we want to know is whether the target has retained its individual identity in the mixture. Ideally, they should also be told to ignore any qualities of the mixture that relate to *neither* the target nor the masker. (These would be emergent properties that arise from the combination of the two sounds.) There is an even better task to study the ability to perform analysis of the mixture. If a large set of recognizable and namable alternatives is used (such as words) the listener can be asked for the identity of the item. This task can clearly not be accomplished by basing one's judgment on some global property of the mixture. The study of the masking of speech, therefore, is not truly a study of masking but of perceptual fusion.

Despite the difference in the definition of fusion and masking, there are a number of results from experiments on masking that support the results on fusion. Variables that help to segregate one acoustic component from others seem to also prevent that component from being masked by the other ones. There are two possible explanations for this fact. The first possibility is that in many cases of masking, the listeners are actually trying to hear the target inside the mixture rather than just listening for a change in the global qualities of the mixture. By doing so, they are turning the task into one concerned with fusion.

The second alternative is that masking and fusion are different perceptual effects but that they both depend on the same underlying physiological phenomenon. For example, suppose a target is mixed with a masker and the intensity of the target is gradually turned down. At first (let us call it the first stage) the target may be perfectly audible. Then, in a second stage, the target might not be audible as a separate sound but might still color the quality of the masker. In a final the masker might be heard as identical to how it appears when there is no target buried in it. The factors that favor segregation might act so as to make the physiological registration of the target stand out in some way so that it affects both the first and second stages of this sequence, requiring a greater strength of the masker to cause perception to move from one stage to the next.

An example that lends some validity to this description comes from the study of harmonicity. In a complex tone that contains many harmonics, one of the harmonics is gradually mistuned. Before it is mistuned the the complex tone has a single pitch and sounds like a single tone. With a large amount of mistuning, say over 6 percent, the mistuned harmonic is perceptually dissociated from the complex tone (i.e., no longer fused) and has its own pitch. However, with a small amount of mistuning, say from 1 to 5 percent, the change is detectable not as the appearance of a separate tone but as an alteration of the pitch of the complex tone. In the latter case, if we asked whether the complex tone were masking the mistuned partial the answer would be no, because the complex tone that contained it would have a different pitch than one from which it had been removed.[409] This demonstration of the effects of violations of harmonicity on both masking and perceptual isolation may arise from its action on a common mechanism.

For whatever reason, results from the two types of experiments tend to agree; so let me proceed to review some results from masking experiments that show the influence of factors that I have already described as being used by the auditory system to partition the spectrum into separate streams.

The first experiment that I want to describe showed that the segregation that comes from having different patterns of micromodulation can also affect how strongly a loud sound masks a weaker one. In 1978, a Dutch researcher, R. A. Rasch, of the Institute for Perception (TNO) in Soesterberg, reported a study of this effect.[410] He played subjects a sequence of two chords. Each chord consisted of two harmonically rich tones. Each tone had 20 harmonics with successively higher harmonics attenuated more and more so that a harmonic an octave higher than another one would be 6 dB less intense. The lower tone was always the same in both chords but the higher tone was different, either higher or lower in the second chord. Each tone was 200 msec long. The listeners had to say whether the high tone moved up or down across the pair of chords. Typically the low tone was much louder than the high tone and acted to mask it.

Before describing the results, we should observe that despite the fact that the experiment is often described as a study of masking, according to our earlier definitions it is really about analytic listening or its opposite, perceptual fusion. This follows from the fact that the listeners had to make a decision about a quality of the target itself (its change in pitch) and not just a quality of the mixture.

In some conditions of the experiment, Rasch applied a simple frequency modulation (vibrato) of 4 percent to the high tone, the modulation being sinusoidal in form and repeating at 5 cycles per second. The low masking tone, however, was always steady in frequency. He found that the high tones were harder to mask when they underwent frequency modulation than when they were steady. If we were to set the low tone to a level loud enough to mask a steady high tone and then started to modulated the frequency of the high one, the low tone would no longer mask it and we would have to crank up the intensity of the low tone by about 17 dB (about a seven-fold increase in amplitude) to restore the masking effect. It is unfortunate that Rasch did not compare the effectiveness of the masking tone when it was modulated coherently with the target tone to the case in which it was modulated in an uncorrelated way. As the results stand now, I can think of two possible explanations for them: The first possibility is that the presence of two different forms of pitch modulation (sinusoidal for the target and nothing at all for the masker) improves the segregation of the two tones and thereby prevents the weaker from losing its identity in the mixture. This is what I would like to believe. However, there is a second logical possibility. Frequency modulation of a tone may improve the definition of its pitch, perhaps because the auditory system tends to habituate to steady tones, and this might make it harder to mask, even by a tone that was changing in parallel with it. Until experiments are done with frequency modulation of both masker and target, we will not be able to tell whether FM-based segregation is the cause of the release from masking that Rasch observed.

A second experiment was also done by Rasch as part of the same series. This one showed that asynchrony of onset prevented masking. In some conditions the target tone started a bit before the masker but the two ended at the same time. This made the target easier to hear. Each 10-msec increase in the time interval by which the target's onset preceded that of the masker made the target as much easier to hear as increasing its intensity by about 10 dB. The listeners were not aware that the onsets of the two notes were asynchronous; they knew only that they could hear the target better in these conditions.

Rasch was concerned about whether the listener was just basing this increased ability to hear the high tone on the few milliseconds of it that preceded the onset of the masker. To find out, he included a condition in which the target came on before the masker, but when the masker came on, instead of allowing the target to continue along with it, he allowed it to accompany the masker for only about 30 msec and then shut it off. If the listeners' detection of the high tone depended only on the part that preceded the onset of the masker, their ability to perceive the target should not have been affected by shutting it off in this way. And indeed it was not. This implied that they were not really segregating the spectrum of the target tone from the complex target-plus-masker spectrum but simply getting a glimpse of the target when it "stuck out" of the mixture. The listeners, however, thought that the high tones had lasted throughout the duration of the masker.

Before concluding that onsets or offsets that occur inside a mixture have no segregating effect, we should remember that in Rasch's study the masker tone was never *turned on* inside the mixture. That is, he never tested asynchronies where the target came on second. Michael Kubovy has shown that changing the intensity of a component tone inside a mixture of tones makes that tone stand out of the mixture.[411] Also Scheffers, in research that will be discussed in chapter 6, found that in mixtures of vowels, turning on the target vowel a few tenths of a second after the masking vowel had begun made the target much easier to hear than if the two started synchronously.[412]

Incidentally, a study of asynchronies by Dannenbring and myself gave a result that tends to support Rasch's conclusion that only the part of the target that sticks out of the mixture affects its perception.[413] We found that onset and offset asynchronies of a target harmonic relative to two accompanying harmonics made this harmonic easier to capture into a sequential stream, but this advantage seemed to be restricted to those cases in which the target tone stuck out of the mixture. Probably this was due to the fact that when the target went on or off when the rest of the mixture was on, the onset or offset was masked by the nearby onsets and offsets of the other tones as well as by their mere presence. Judging from Kubovy's results, if the onset of the target had occurred further inside the mixture, it probably would have escaped these masking effects and the target would have become audible.

There is one final point on the topic of onset synchrony that is of interest to musicians. Rasch pointed out that in polyphonic music the asynchronies of onset that occur because of the normal variability in human performance would be sufficient to isolate notes from one another despite the fact that they were nominally synchronous in onset. He verified this claim in a later experiment that directly studied how exactly musicians synchronized their playing in an ensemble.[414] He found that nominally synchronous onsets typically had a standard deviation of differences in onset time ranging from 30 to 50 msec.

One other observation shows that it is easier for a masking sound to mask a target when both come on at the same instant (by "easier" I mean that the masker does not have to be so close in frequency to the target to mask it). Masking is harder when the masker is present continuously and the target comes on periodically than when both the masker and the target are gated on at the same time.[415] This is consistent with our observation that onset synchrony tends to fuse two sounds into a larger spectral pattern.

Comodulation Release from Masking

There is a phenomenon that shows an effect on masking that is similar to the effects of common amplitude modulation that I described in an earlier section. In that section, we saw that two simultaneously presented tones tended to segregate from one another perceptually if they were amplitude modulated at different frequencies or if their amplitude modulation was out of phase. The related masking effect is called comodulation masking release. It was discovered by Joseph Hall, Mark Haggard, and Mariano Fernandes of the MRC Institute of Hearing Research in Nottingham, England.[416]

Let me describe it. The detection threshold was measured for a 400-msec, 1,000-Hz pure tone when it was masked by different types of noise. In one set of conditions, the masker was a band of random noise centered on the frequency of the target tone. In different conditions, the bandwidth of this noise was increased, while holding the spectrum level constant. What this means is that the bandwidth was increased by adding new energy in the sections of the spectrum on both sides of narrower band without altering the energy in that narrower band. As energy was added and the noise band became wider, the target became harder to detect. However, after a certain width was reached, the interference got no worse when the band was made even wider. The existence of an upper limit derives from the fact that only the energy in a spectral band adjacent in frequency to a given target is effective in masking it. This region is called the critical band. If you add energy outside it, it has no further effect on masking. So far, then, the results were entirely predictable.

There were, however, a set of conditions in which the masker was not a simple noise band but a noise that, after being generated, had been amplitude modulated in a random pattern.[417] Because of this way of generating the signal, the intensity fluctuation in the noise occurred in much the same pattern in all the frequency bands contained within the noise. As you increase the bandwidth of this type of modulated noise, you are adding energy that has the same pattern of amplitude fluctuation that is present in the narrower band. This is quite different than what is true in ordinary random noise, in which the intensity fluctuation is independent in each frequency band. There was a corresponding difference in what happened to masking when this type of noise was used as a masker and was varied in bandwidth. As with the unmodulated noise, the amount of masking rose as the noise band was made wider, up to the limit of the critical band. But as the bandwidth of the masker was made even wider, instead of remaining the same, the masking began to *fall* in effectiveness. In some paradoxical way, adding more energy to the masker was reducing its ability to mask.

The scene-analysis explanation of this result reduces to the statement that "it is easier to protect oneself from an enemy whose characteristics are known." The experimenters argued that because of the fact that the amplitude fluctuation was similar in different spectral regions, the auditory system was able to integrate the fluctuation knowledge from across the spectrum and use it to better cancel its effects out of the signal. It is possible to look at it a little differently, in a way that relates it to spectral grouping. The experimenters' explanation makes an assumption that we also have had to make in order to explain the segregation and fusion of amplitude-modulated tones, namely that the amplitude variation occurring in different parts could be separately detected and compared. Only in this way would amplitude fluctuation be useful in deciding which parts of the spectrum should be put together into the same stream. Following that same line of explanation in the present example, we would say that because the same amplitude fluctuation was detected in a number of frequency bands, those bands were linked together into a common stream. As more frequency bands were added, each containing a similar pattern of amplitude variation, the tendency to reject a band that did not have this pattern grew stronger and the target became more audible. This form of the argument shows explicitly the relation between the present effect and the general process of scene analysis.

Although this was discovered in the laboratory, the people who discovered it were aware of its importance in daily listening environments. I have quoted their argument earlier. I shall do so again:

> Many real-life auditory stimuli have intensity peaks and valleys as a function of time in which intensity trajectories [changes] are highly correlated across frequency. This is true of speech, of interfering noises such as "cafeteria" noise, and of many other kinds of environmental stimuli. We suggest that for such stimuli the auditory system uses across-frequency analysis of temporal modulation patterns to help register and differentiate between acoustic sources.[418]

This experiment is also relevant to the "peek" theory of the effects of amplitude modulation that I discussed earlier. According to that theory, the reason that it is easier to hear a target sound when it is present at the same time as another one that is being amplitude modulated in a different pattern may not be directly related to any strategy for parsing the spectrum. The auditory system may simply be getting a better peek at the target component at those instants of time at which the others have been reduced in intensity by the modulation. There is some experimental evidence to support this theory.[419] Still, the peek theory could not explain the present results. In particular, it cannot explain why the peeks should get more effective when the bandwidth of the masker increases.

An additional finding about the comodulation masking release phenomenon is that it does not work with frequency fluctuations.[420] If the target tone is masked by a signal that is varying in frequency in a random pattern, you cannot reduce the masking by adding a second signal that is varying in frequency in the same pattern and that lies outside the critical band of the target. This result may shed light on a question that was raised earlier in this chapter: Could the apparent integrative effects of parallel frequency modulation of subsets of partials be attributed entirely to other causes, leaving nothing over to be explained by "common fate in FM" principle? The comodulation data suggest that the answer could be yes.

There is another paradoxical masking effect in which adding more energy to the masker reduces the amount of masking. This one, too, is susceptible to a scene-analysis explanation. The effect occurs in forward masking in which a loud noise burst masker precedes a fainter pure-tone target. The masker is a band of noise centered at the same frequency as the target. If the bandwidth of this masker is increased, there is less forward masking. It has been argued that this occurs because a wide-band noise does not sound as much like the target as a narrow band of noise does. Therefore, a wider bandwidth of the masker will reduce forward masking because you can tell more easily where the noise ends and the signal begins.[421] Notice that this explanation has the flavor of a scene-analysis explanation. It is not really in the tradition that attributes masking to the swamping out of the target information by the masker energy within a critical band. In that tradition, nothing that happened outside the critical band could have an influence. The explanation that says that the additional energy makes the masker more distinctive is really talking about the fusion of the various spectral regions in the wide-band noise to create a larger perceptual entity that has global properties that are different from the properties of its parts. Furthermore, it no longer talks about the swamping of the target by the local energy of the masker, but about the degree to which the auditory system integrates or segregates the target and the masker. I would suspect that when the process of spectral integration fuses the spectral components of the noise into a single sound, it has two beneficial effects. As well as computing a global quality for the noise, it integrates the simultaneous "energy-going-off" information across the spectrum that signals the turning off of the masker; it may therefore be able to get a more precise fix on when the target turned off. This may aid it in calculating that there is one frequency band (the one occupied by the target) at which energy did not turn off at the same time and that therefore there is something different going on at that spectral location.

There is also evidence that when a target and a masker are perceived to be at two different spatial locations, masking is weaker. For example, when a listener is presented with a voice that is being masked by noise, the intelligibility of the speech signal depends on whether the speech and the noise are coming from the same spatial location. With increasing separations the speech becomes more intelligible.[422] Actually many of the studies have manipulated the interaural time delay rather than the actual position in space of the signals.[423] Masking drops off with increases in the spatial separation between target and masker.

This spatial release from masking can be seen in a phenomenon known as the binaural masking level difference (BMLD).[424] To illustrate it, we begin by presenting, over headphones, a mixture of a tone and a noise binaurally (i.e., with identical copies to the two ears). Then we increase the intensity of the noise until the tone is no longer audible. That is stage 1. In stage 2, we simply shift the phase of the tone in one ear, so that it is now out of phase by 180° across the ears while leaving the noise identical in the two ears. The tone will now become audible again. We will need to boost the intensity of the noise again in order to mask the tone. The difference between the intensities of noise needed in stages 1 and 2 to mask the tone is known as the binaural masking level difference.

Another example of the same phenomenon is also accomplished in two stages. In the first, we present a mixture of the tone and noise to a single ear and increase the intensity of the noise until it just masks the tone. In the second stage, we keep the first-ear signal as it was, but we now present a signal to the opposite ear. This signal contains only the noise, but as soon as we present it, the tone at the first ear becomes audible.

It is tempting to conclude that the results are due to the fact that phase relations between the two ears are a cue to spatial location. In all cases of the BMLD effect, one signal (target or masker) is in phase at the two ears and the other is out of phase. Therefore the two signals should appear to have different spatial locations. If the auditory system segregated them on this basis, this might make them less likely to fuse and would make the target more audible as a distinct sound. Indeed, in many examples of the effect, such as the second example that I gave, the sounds are heard as having different locations.

However, in cases where there is a reversal of phase between the signals in the two ears, as in the first example that I gave, the phase difference is greater than what would occur in natural listening situations and the localization of the phase-reversed sound is diffuse. Therefore it appears that a clear localization of the target and mask in different places is not required for obtaining the BMLD. The only thing that seems necessary is that the between-ear phase comparison should give a different result for the target and the masker. This requirement does not destroy an explanation based on scene analysis, only one based on a scene analysis that occurs after separate spatial locations are assigned to target and masker. We have seen that the auditory system can make use of any one of a number of acoustic relations to decide whether or not two parts of the spectrum should go together. Perhaps one of them is interaural phase relations. If two parts of the spectrum come from the same source, then they should be coming from the same spatial location and be subject to the same echoes; therefore, the delay between time of arrival in the two ears should be the same for both parts. Working this reasoning backward, if the auditory system receives two spectral regions with the same interaural phase difference, it should fuse them; however, when the two regions show different interaural phase differences, the regions should be segregated.

Perhaps this heuristic can work even in cases where the spatial location of one or the other sound is ambiguous. Even though location cannot be fully decided on when the phase is reversed in the two ears, it can still be decided that one part of the spectrum has a different interaural phase than another part. Therefore phase relations may be able to provide segregation of identity even when they cannot give definite locations. Earlier in this chapter, I said that separate assessments of spatial location had the power to segregate and group parts of the spectrum. However, what I took to be decisions about spatial location might have actually been something that is a simpler precursor of spatial localization, namely separate assessments of interaural phase relations.

I would not like to argue that it is the phase relations alone, and never the spatial estimates themselves, that are used to parse the spectrum. There are other cues to spatial location besides interaural phase relations. For example, there is the rule that a sound should not change its location too rapidly. There is evidence that these other cues can also affect the parsing of the spectrum.

To sum up the evidence from masking experiments: We see that masking and fusion seem to be affected by the same sorts of acoustic relations between a target component of a larger sound and the remainder of that sound. Generally speaking, these are relations that, in a natural listening environment, are useful for deciding whether different spectral components have arisen from the same acoustic event. Despite the differences in the measurement operations that define fusion and masking, the two may be affected by common underlying mechanisms.

Meaning of These Findings for Biology It is interesting to step back and look at the scene analysis heuristics from a biological perspective. We have looked at a number of relations between simultaneous components of a sound that are unlikely to have occurred by chance and therefore offer the auditory system an opportunity to exploit them for scene analysis. We have found that the auditory system seems to have evolved ways of taking advantage of them so as to make the right combinations of components hang together for purposes of more detailed analysis. We might ask at this point whether these findings imply anything about what physiologists should look for in the neural architecture of the auditory system. I am afraid that I am not very hopeful about drawing inferences from function to architecture. True, the auditory system does exploit these regularities. However, we should realize that a biological system might not go about this in the way that a careful computer designer might. We may not find a specific neural computation, for example, of the frequency change within each frequency band and then a second computation that sorts the bands into groups that show similar changes. As an example of the indirect methods of the auditory system, we have already discussed ways in which a peripheral auditory mechanism might turn a physical frequency fluctuation into a neural registration of an amplitude fluctuation. Or we might find, for example, that the reason that partials with synchronous onsets tend to fuse is that their onsets tend to mask one another and therefore cannot be heard separately.

Scene analysis, as I am discussing it, is a function, not a mechanism. It "takes advantage of" regularities in the input; it may never directly "mention" them. We may never find a single mechanism that does nothing but scene analysis. When nature evolves something, it often does so by using materials that were already in place for some other reason. The fins of the whale, for example, are adaptations of earlier legs, which, in turn, are adaptations of yet earlier fins, and so on. As I pointed out in chapter 1, neurological breakdowns may be the mechanism underlying functional accomplishments. We should not expect a direct mapping from function to mechanism. It may exist in some cases, and in those cases, science is fortunate. We should therefore not be dismayed if many of the accomplishments described in this chapter are found to be incidental byproducts of some well-known mechanisms, for this finding would not imply that they were not specifically evolved for scene analysis. Evolutionary selection favors the mechanism with the useful by-product over one that lacks it. Thinking in terms of scene analysis may not lead us to find new neural mechanisms. But it may help us to understand the purposes of the ones we know about.

Perceptual Results of Simultaneous Integration and Segregation

The last section was concerned with the factors used by the auditory system to decide which simultaneously present sensory components should be assigned to the same perceptual stream. The next section will discuss what we know about the use that is made of these grouped elements. Before even starting to look at the results of experiments, I would suspect that every analysis that can be made on a group of components heard in isolation can also be made on a subset that has been segregated out of a larger set: When we listen a particular sound in everyday life it is rarely the only one present and yet we seem to be able to assess its loudness, pitch, timbre, distance, direction, and so on. Many of these features are the results of analyses that must take into account a set of grouped acoustic properties. They pertain to the sound as a whole and not to its individual components. For this reason they can be called global properties. For example, the global pitch of a sound depends on the analysis of only those partials that have been grouped together. Presumably the global timbre does likewise.

In chapter 1, there was some discussion of emergent properties, properties that do not apply to the parts of a thing, but to the thing as a whole. A visual example might be the property of being a closed figure. Suppose we have a figure drawn using straight lines. None of the individual lines in it is a closed figure and descriptions of the individual lines will not be phrased in terms of this property. The property emerges when the interconnections of the lines are taken into account. It is a property of figures, not of lines.

When I speak of global properties, I am thinking of a closely related idea. For example, I have suggested that a global analysis of a fused set of partials might find a pitch appropriate to the set of partials as a whole, whereas if the partials were perceptually decomposed from the mixture, the partial pitches could be heard. Pitch is not a property that applies only to complex tones. It can be heard for partials as well. Therefore the word "emergent" is not quite right to describe the pitch derived from the whole set of partials. We need a word that means that a certain property, such as pitch, has been computed from all the components that are present and not from a subset. I have chosen the adjective "global" for this purpose.

The common idea behind the two concepts is that they describe features that have been computed on some grouped set of components. If the feature is emergent, it means that the lower-level components could not have this sort of property; an example is a closed figure. If the property is global, it means that the property was based on a grouped set of components, but there is no implication as to whether the lower-order components could have this type of property, an example being a global pitch. Since "global" is the more inclusive word, I will try to use it in the present discussion.

I sometimes use the word "partial" in expressions such as partial pitches, partial timbres, and the like. By this I mean to refer to the fact that less than the total number of acoustic components present are contributing to the perception of that property. By the term partial pitch, I am also usually referring to the pitch of a particular partial, since that is often what we can hear in an inharmonic tone.

Although the previous section focused on the factors that promoted the segregation of simultaneous frequency components, it was not possible to discuss this topic without mentioning some of its effects. After all, the only way to study the causes of segregation is to know that a segregation has taken place, and this requires us to at least have a good guess about the perceptual effects of such segregation. Therefore, rather than introducing something entirely new, the following section will simply try to list in one place the various perceptual effects that have been observed when a complex sound mixture is segregated into co-occurring streams by the auditory system.

Examples of Within-Stream Computation of Properties

Within-Stream Temporal Properties; Streaming Rules The most obvious effect that can be observed is that the mixture can be heard as two or more event sequences, each having its own independent temporal properties. A familiar example of this occurs when two voices are heard at the same time. The fact that we can often focus on just one of these and understand it implies that the sequential properties of each are kept distinct from the other. The interpretation of speech depends on the order of more basic speech events (perhaps phonemes) that occur within it. Therefore, if we can interpret the message of each voice separately, we must be able to form a sequence for that voice that excludes the other sounds.

An even more obvious case of the necessity for being able to register the within-stream order of events is in the recognition of melodies in music. Here we can fall back on data from an experiment that shows that it is possible to recognize a melody whose notes are being played in synchrony with the notes of two other melodies. In this experiment, the melodies were arbitrary arrangements of four pure tones, in the vicinity of 500 Hz, with the interfering melodies being more or less symmetrically placed, one higher and one lower than the target melody in frequency. The melodies were presented at a rate of 2.5 tones per second. The listeners had to distinguish between the test melody and an alternative one under conditions in which either one could be present as the mid-frequency melody in the three-melody mixture. The alternative melody contained the same tones as the test melody except that the temporal order of the middle two tones was reversed. In different conditions the masking melodies were at different frequency separations from the target. It was found that the melodies became easier to recognize as the frequency separation between the target and interfering melodies was increased. This recognition, moreover, clearly must have depended on the correct detection of the order of tones in the target.[425] The effect of frequency separation in promoting the segregation of different streams of tones resembles the effects of this variable that we saw earlier in our examination of the streaming phenomenon in rapid sequences of tones. The only difference was that in the stimulus pattern for the streaming phenomenon, the tones were never physically overlapped in time even though the listener sometimes interpreted the streams as existing at the same time.

Pitch Another property that depends in some way on the integration of simultaneous components is pitch. We have seen how the micromodulation in synchrony of a set of frequency components can isolate those and cause them to be the ones that contribute to the pitch analysis. An example of this that we have not yet discussed was provided by Stephen McAdams, who carried out an experiment in which he synthesized a mixture of three sung vowels, each on a different fundamental frequency.[426] Without any micromodulation, the listeners sometimes heard four to six pitches. But when the sounds were modulated, they tended to hear the three pitches, one for each fundamental. This suggests that the micromodulation might have encouraged the auditory system of the listener to put all spectral regions of the signal into a global pitch analysis. McAdams also reported that several other authors have noted that the "missing fundamental" pitches derived from certain stimuli are better heard when the complex is modulated coherently than when it is not modulated.[427] These all represent cases in which spectra are integrated by scene analysis so that a global pitch can be computed.

We have to be careful about generalizing from the results using micromodulation. So far I am aware of no demonstration that any other factor that promotes the grouping of components can affect the pitch computation. A plausible one to try would be the spatial separation of the components. Again, care must be taken in interpreting results. For example, it has been shown that two successive upper partials can be presented, one to each ear, and they will be perceptually grouped across the ears for the purposes of calculating a missing fundamental. This perception of global pitch is clear enough to allow listeners to recognize the musical interval formed by the fundamentals in a sequence of two such presentations.[428] This, however, does not show that spatial separation has no effects whatsoever on the pitch calculation. As we have seen, pitch is one of those properties that exist either for individual components of for subsets of components. In some cases, both the global and the partial pitches can be heard at the very same time; under some conditions the global pitch is strong and the partial ones weak and under others the opposite is found. The dominance of the global pitch over the partial pitches is not an all-or-nothing affair. Therefore in the experiment that I just described, we do not know whether the across-ear integration was weaker than it would have been if the pair of tones had been presented to a single ear. Actually the perception of the missing fundamental was fairly weak, and some of the listeners, despite previous musical training, had to be given up to an hour of training before they could hear it. In my own listening, I am never quite sure that I can hear the fundamental with such stimuli. To really know whether spatial separation reduces the integration of components for pitch computation, it would be necessary to do a study in which the strengths of the pitch percepts were compared in the across-ear and the within-ear cases.

Timbre What of timbre? We would expect two separate timbres to be able to be heard when two subsets of partials were segregated out of a mixture. We have seen one example of this in the sound that was created for musical use at IRCAM. When the odd and even harmonics of a synthesized oboe sound were segregated by location and by different patterns of micromodulation, the quality of the two separate sounds was not the same as the global oboe timbre that was heard when they were not segregated. Another example of scene analysis affecting the perception of timbre was mentioned when we discussed spatial location as a factor influencing timbre. There we saw that when one partial was sent to one ear and the rest of the partials to the other one, the listeners were not able to form the two into a single "spectral profile."[429]

Richard M. Stern has reported a related experiment on timbre perception. Synthetic trumpet and clarinet tones were presented in pairs, either at the same pitch or at different pitches.[430] When the two were at the same pitch the listener heard a single note that sounded neither like a trumpet nor a clarinet. But when the two pitches were different, a musically trained listener could tell which instrument was playing which note. Evidently the segregation of two sets of partials that were harmonically related to different fundamentals allowed an independent computation of timbre to take place on each set.

Vowels A perceptual property similar to timbre is the quality that distinguishes one spoken vowel from another. Both the distinction of one vowel from another and one timbre from another depend on the pattern of the amplitudes of different spectral components. If vowel quality is seen as an example of timbre, then research on the factors that makes two simultaneous spoken vowels distinguishable from one another is really research on the segregability of timbres. I plan to describe this research later when I deal more extensively with speech perception. For the moment it suffices to say that differences in fundamental frequency between the partials of two simultaneous vowels makes it much easier to identify the vowels.

In a way, research that uses vowel sounds as examples of timbres is easier to do than research with arbitrary timbres. It has the advantage that the listeners already have names for the sounds they are hearing and, for this reason, experiments that ask for identification of the components sounds are easier to set up. It has one disadvantage though. Since speech perception is highly overlearned, and may also make use of an innate mechanism that is specialized for speech, we cannot be sure whether the segregation that we observe is due exclusively to the basic scene-analysis capability of the auditory system. The only way to decide is by seeing whether the same set of factors that is known to affect the fusion or decomposition of other non-speech mixtures also affects mixtures of speech sounds. We will take up this issue in more detail in chapter 6.

Consonance and Dissonance Musical consonance and dissonance can be classified under the general rubric of "timbre" as well. It arises, acoustically, from the beating of certain partials in the mixture of two or more tones. Later, in chapter 5, we will see how the experience of dissonance that arises when two sounds are played together can disappear when the two sounds are segregated into separate streams.

The apparent ability of the auditory system to not hear the dissonance presents us with a theoretical dilemma. Does the auditory system not register the beating that occurs when two acoustically dissonant tones occur together? After all, beating is a phenomenon that is physically based. Surely the auditory system cannot overcome the physics of sound. What I am claiming is that although the beating of the partials of the two tones may be registered at some peripheral level of the auditory system, it is not assigned as part of the mental description of either sound because the auditory system can somehow tell that it is not an intrinsic property of either sound but, rather, an accident of their combination. It has been claimed by workers in visual information processing that the conscious experience of disembodied features is impossible. Features have to be assigned to a percept in order to be perceived.[431] Perhaps acoustic interactions between simultaneous events are picked up but not assigned to any stream and therefore remain outside the level of awareness.

In many preceding discussions I have described the allocation of a piece of spectral evidence to one stream or another as if this were an all-or-nothing effect. While it was convenient to talk that way for purposes of exposition the actual facts are not as clear cut. When we listen to a mixture of sounds, we may be able to perceptually segregate one of the components from the mixture, but our experience of this component is not exactly as it would have been if the segregated component were not accompanied by the other ones. The experience is somehow less clear and features of the remainder of the sound often "leak" through. This failure of all-or-nothing allocation means that some features are playing a double role: They are contributing to the description of the sound that we are focusing our attention on, but they would also contribute to the description of the background sound if we were to focus our attention on that one. It appears, then, that the principle of exclusive allocation does not operate as strictly as I implied in chapter 1. The failure of this principle leads to a phenomenon called duplex perception, in which a piece of acoustic evidence is used to construct two different percepts. Because this was first noticed in the context of speech research, it was taken as telling us something very special about speech perception. It is therefore convenient to discuss this whole issue in chapter 7, which considers the violations of exclusive allocation in speech perception.

Not all segregations are equally strong. We are not always equally capable of segregating a sound from a mixture. Some of this depends on our learned skills, but very often the signal itself imposes limitations on what we can do with it. These limitations come in two forms. One is related to certain limits on the resolving power of our peripheral apparatus. If two tones have frequencies that are too close together, rather than perceptually segregating the two tones, you will simply hear the pattern formed by their sum. A second limitation relates to whether or not the cues for segregation are unambiguous. Clarity will occur when a number of cues all suggest that there are two distinct sounds whose descriptions should be created independently. When some cues point in the other direction (as would happen, for instance, when two unrelated sounds happened to start and stop at precisely the same time) the segregation at the preattentive level would be less strongly created and this would make it harder for later processes, such as selective attention, to treat the two sounds as distinct.

What Is the Default Condition: Fusion or Decomposition? In this chapter, we have looked at a number of factors that lead the listener to either fuse or segregate a set of simultaneous components. Which is the default condition, fusion or decomposition? One could imagine two states of affairs. In one, the auditory system prefers to fuse the total spectrum at any moment and is prevented from doing so only if there is specific information that parts of it should be segregated. The alternative is that the auditory system tries to treat each frequency region separately unless it has evidence that it should group some of them into a more global sound. Is the total spectrum assumed to be innocent of internal structure until proven guilty or is it the reverse?

An observation made by Helmholtz is relevant to this point. He reported what happened when, using tones produced by bottles, he used a two-tone complex and started one tone (the higher) first. At first he could hear the upper partial, with its characteristic timbre clearly. Then it began to fade and become weaker. The lower one started to seem stronger and dominated the timbre, and the upper one started to sound weaker. A new timbre began to emerge from the combination. According to his description, he could hear out an upper partial of a complex tone whose two components were spaced by an octave; however,

> . . . I could not continue to hear them separately for long, for the upper tone gradually fused with the lower. This fusion takes place even when the upper tone is somewhat stronger than the lower. The alteration of the quality of the tone which takes place during the fusion is characteristic. On producing the upper tone and then letting the lower sound with it, I found that I at first continued to hear the upper tone with its full force and the under tone sounding below it in its natural [context-free] quality of *oo* as in t*oo*. But by degrees as my recollection of the sound of the isolated upper tone died away, it seemed to become more and more indistinct and weak while the lower tone appeared to become stronger, and sounded like *oa* as in t*oa*d. This weakening of the upper and strengthening of the lower tone was also observed by Ohm on the violin. . . . With the tones produced by bottles, in addition to the reinforcement of the lower tone, the alteration in its quality is very evident and is characteristic of the nature of the process.[432]

This observation seems to imply that the default is fusion since when the segregating effects of the asychronous beginning of the two sounds receded into the past, the tones tended to fuse. However, this interpretation fails to take into account that there was not only a cue for segregation in this situation but one for fusion as well. The cue for fusion was the harmonic relation between the two sounds, the upper one being an octave above the lower one. This would make the upper one the second harmonic of the lower. Therefore the asynchrony cue was not acting alone but was opposing a cue for fusion. Furthermore although the segregation cue could fade into the past, the fusion cue remained throughout. This may be why fusion ultimately dominated.

The question we have to address is whether we could imagine a case in which there were no cues at all, either for segregation or for fusion. That situation would seem to hold in a long burst of white noise (after the simultaneous onset cue for fusion faded away), since white noise, being the result of chance, would haphazardly contain fusion and segregation cues at random. One normally thinks of white noise as a coherent blast of sound. It is certainly not heard as a collection of separate sounds, each in its own frequency band. This would argue in favor of fusion as the default situation.

If we began by playing a narrow-band burst of noise, and then followed it by a wide-band spectrum that contained the frequencies of the first burst at the same intensities as in the narrow band, we would hear the narrow-band burst continue for a short time into the wide-band noise. But eventually we would hear only the wide-band noise. This implies that the default state is fusion.

There are also phenomena in music that point to the same conclusion but I shall defer discussing them until chapter 5.

Reallocation of Intensity and Timbre Information The observation from Helmholtz is relevant to another issue that we considered earlier. What happens to the properties of individual components when they give up their identities and become part of a mixture? Helmholtz's observation is valuable because he was able to observe the process as it slowly took place and to document the resulting changes in his experience. First, as regards loudness, he observed that when the high tone lost its separate identity, not only did it become weaker but the lower tone became stronger. Here is a puzzle: Why did the lower tone appear to get louder? After all, if the loudness of the high tone is to be allocated elsewhere, it should be to the global sound into which it it merging its identity. The lower sound is only another portion of the global sound. Why should it be given the loudness? I do not think that it was. I think this is a misinterpretation by Helmholtz of what he heard. It was the global sound that became louder, not the lower component. We have to remember that since the two sounds had the frequency ratio 2:1, they corresponded to the first two harmonics of a complex tone whose fundamental is equal to the frequency of the lower tone. Therefore this complex tone should have had a global pitch that was the same as the pitch of the lower tone (the fundamental) taken alone. For this reason it makes sense to believe that the lower-pitched tone that Helmholtz heard as getting louder was the global pitch of the now-unitary complex tone. This interpretation is supported by his report that the lower tone changed in quality as the fusion took place, which is what we would expect if the fusion of high and low sounds led to a computation of global quality of a single spectrum containing this combination of components.

Helmholtz's observation of the strengthening of the lower tone, with a concomitant weakening of the upper one, resembles my early observations with Rudnicky on simultaneous sequences of tones. As the reader may recall, we used two tones of different frequencies, each having its own rate of repetition. At certain points in the sequence, the high and low tones started exactly at the same time. At such points of synchrony, we noticed, as Helmholtz did, that the higher tone became weaker and the lower one stronger.

The agreement of the two sets of observations supports the following conclusions: (1) When a high tone loses its separate identity, its energy is allocated to the complex tone whose pitch is determined by the fundamental. (2) The perception of the high tone as a separate entity is traded off against hearing its contribution to the global tone; the stronger one interpretation is, the weaker is the other.

The Consequences of Simultaneous/Sequential Competition

Although I have presented the organization of sequentially and simultaneously presented acoustic components in separate chapters, it has been evident that they interact. When we consider how this happens some new questions arise.

One of these concerns the role of timbre. Different ideas that I have introduced about how timbre related to organization seem contradictory. I have said that timbre emerges when a set of *simultaneous* components was partitioned into subsets by processes of scene analysis. An example of this would be the listener's ability, when listening to a voice accompanied by a guitar, to know that two different streams were present, each with its own characteristic timbre. However, I have also shown that similarities in timbre are used to group sounds sequentially. An example of this would be the ability to follow the melody of the voice, even when the guitar and the voice crossed each other in frequency.

Timbre, then, is both cause and effect of perceptual organization. This is not a contradictory position as long as it can be assumed that the timbre is always formed first by spectral segregation and then, after being formed, affects sequential integration.

However the interaction between simultaneous and sequential organization is not always so simple. Often we segregate a part of a mixture, A + B, because we have just heard A in isolation. Do we use the timbre of A, derived when we heard it alone, as a way of detecting its presence in the mixture? How could we argue that we do this if we believe that the timbre of a subset of components is computed only after it has been segregated from the mixture?

Perhaps a way out of the dilemma is to distinguish between the *timbre* of a subset of acoustic components, which is a perceptual quality, and the *spectral composition* of that subset, which is a physical property. Then we can argue that when a sound, A, precedes a larger mixture, B, the thing that the auditory system tries to pull out of the mixture is not a timbre that matches A's (since timbre, a perceptual quality, has not yet been computed), but a combination of spectral components that matches A's. Then after the scene-analysis heuristics extract a subset of components, the timbre of that subset is computed. Timbre, according to this view, would be a perceptual description that was created after the parsing and grouping were done.

The timbre might be affected by the organization in even more complicated ways. For example, suppose that the presence of sound A1 before a more complex sound caused A2 to be extracted from the mixture. Perhaps A1 and A2 are not identical but are similar enough that A2 is extracted. It seems possible that the grouping of the components labeled A1 and A2 could affect the perceived timbre of both of them. If the auditory system thought that it was hearing only one long sound, the timbre assigned to A1 and A2 might be merged or averaged over time in some way. If A1 and A2 were truly parts of the same sound, this averaging would tend to correct errors in the calculation of the timbre of A2 that might result if it was not perfectly extracted from B.

The reader will have observed that the trick used to resolve the contradiction between timbre as cause and effect was to distinguish between physical properties and perceptual ones and to let the physical ones be the causes and the perceptual ones be the effects. This strategy leads us to the following question. Can a perceptual property such as timbre never be a cause of organization? Must we say that in sequential grouping, the auditory system looks always for a repetition of a physical pattern and never for a repetition of a perceptual effect? The only way to be able to decide this question would be to find different physical patterns that were heard as having the same timbre (the metameric timbres that we described in chapter 2). If two spectra, despite having metameric timbres, had different ways of grouping with other spectra, then it would be the physical pattern and not the timbre that controlled the grouping. If, on the other hand, patterns that had the same perceptual timbre always grouped in the same way with other sounds, we might have reason to conclude that the timbre itself was controlling the grouping.

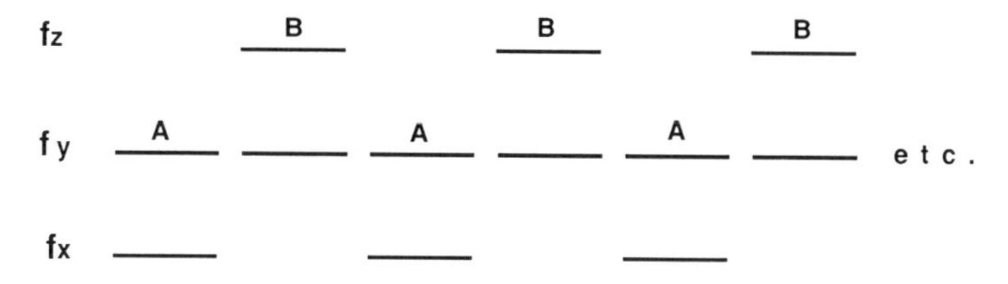

Figure 3.19
"Ternus" effect in audition.

Even in this case it might be whatever physical property caused the similarity in timbre, and not the timbre itself, that controlled grouping. The only indisputable way I can think of to prove that timbre, and not its physical causes, causes a grouping, would be to alter a perceived timbre through some manipulation of its prior context (but without changing its own spectral content), and then to show that it was the timbre, as altered, that governed its grouping with subsequent events.

We know that matches between the components in current and recent spectra can cause those components to form sequential groups and to be detached from the larger spectra of which they are a part. We saw this in the ABC experiment of Bregman and Pinker, where a sequential grouping AB was able to destroy the integrity of a complex tone BC. One would think that there should frequently be accidents in everyday listening in which components of two successive spectra, X and Y, matched one another by chance and were heard as separate sounds. Why do we never encounter such decompositions in everyday listening? Normal sounds seem to hold together.

One inhibiting factor in many cases would be the harmonic relations among the partials within X and within Y. These would oppose the sequential grouping. So would all the other factors that have been shown to affect spectral fusion. But even harmonicity might not always oppose inappropriate sequential integrations. Here is a laboratory example. Suppose we created an alternation of two tones, A and B, each formed of two harmonically related partials, and arranged it so that the bottom partial of the first one matched up with the top partial of the second one. Let us suppose that the frequencies were fx, fy, and fz as shown in figure 3.19. Let us also assume that the ratio between the frequencies fx and fy is the same as between fy and fz. This being the case, we can think of note B as an upward transposition of note A. Nevertheless, if fx, fy, and fz are far enough apart in frequency and the sequence is fast enough, the successive repetitions of the partials at fy will form their own stream. We would hear a continuous repetition of fy, accompanied by two additional streams, one consisting of fx and the other of fz. Here it is the partials rather than the complex tones as a whole that act as units. How is it that the constant harmonic structure does not fuse the partials of tones A and B so that we can hear a complex tone alternating between two pitches?

The reader who is familiar with the field of visual perception will have noticed the resemblance between this example and the Ternus effect. Think of the figure as describing the vertical positions of two dots as they change over time rather than the frequencies of two partials. In vision, the dots will sometimes be seen to move as a pair (the Ternus effect) or the middle one will remain stationary and the other one will alternate between a high position and a low one. One of the main determinants of the percept is whether the successive displays are separated by a time gap. If they are not, and the middle dot remains on continuously, it will tend to remain stationary while the other dot skips back and forth around it. With the time gap, the pair appears to move as a whole.[433] Apparently the continuous presence of the dot at the middle position is treated as an overwhelming cue that it has not moved. It is unlikely that it has been replaced by an accidentally corresponding part of a different object.

The factor of continuity is important in our auditory example as well. The interpretation of the partial at fy as a separate sound is made stronger if there are no silences between tones A and B (that is, where fy stays on all the time). Apparently the auditory system treats it as vanishingly unlikely that a harmonic of one sound would be exactly replaced by some other harmonic of a second one with no discontinuity.

Even with gaps, however, our laboratory example is sometimes not heard as two coherent sounds. Yet if we do not always hear A and B as coherent tones how can we hear a descending musical interval (say C-sharp followed by B-flat) as moving downward in an ordinary piece of music? If each harmonic of the first tone is searching for the nearest harmonic in the second to group with, there will be many cases in which this process will pair a partial of the first with a higher one in the second. It appears that instead of this piecemeal approach, the tracking of the note's movement is operating on the whole spectrum. The auditory system seems to be apprehending the motion of a global mass of sound upward or downward. In fact, as we shall see in chapter 5, a musical tone acts so much as a unit that we can usefully consider it to be describable by its fundamental frequency (let us just call it pitch). [This simplification allows us to show that there are parallels in music between the sequential and simultaneous organizations of pitches and the pure-tone grouping and segregation that we have observed in the experiments of the earlier chapters.] Why do the musical tones always function as units? There may be more than one answer to this question.

One is that all the factors that we have described as facilitating spectral fusion (correlated AM, FM, and so on) would be present internally in each tone, binding it together. Among these binding factors we might list spectral density. We should note the laboratory example that I have just described (together with many other products of the laboratory) is a spectrally sparse signal with few harmonics. We know that partials that are relatively isolated in the spectrum are easier to capture.[434] Therefore the spectral density of natural signals such as instrumental tones may prevent their being torn apart by sequential grouping of their partials. In sparse signals the individual harmonics may be able to act more independently.

Another factor that may contribute to the internal stability of musical tones is the fact that the formation of a sequential stream in a particular frequency region takes some time to build up in strength. An accidental coincidence of a subset of harmonics in two successive musical tones of different pitches is likely to be a brief event. Unless it occurs over and over again, the coincidence is likely to be discarded by the auditory system. It is probably this reluctance to form streams that prevents the helter-skelter appearance and disappearance of streams based on momentary matching of partials. In the experiments in which partials did group sequentially to break up complex tones, the alternation of the partial with the complex tone was repeated over and over to establish a strong sequential stream.

One requirement for a simple explanation of anything is that the explanation be free of contradiction. Some years ago, I argued that perception was a description-forming system that provided explanations of the mixture of evidence that reached the senses, and that one of its properties was the tendency to avoid contradictions.[435] I pointed out that consistency cannot be defined in its own right, but depended on higher order rules that controlled the kinds of descriptions that the system would allow to coexist with one another. An example of a consistency rule is that a region A in space cannot be both in front of and behind another region B at the same time. Different domains of experience were seen as having different types of consistency requirements.

Here is an example of an effect of the simplicity principle in auditory organization. It seems to embody a rule of consistency. The example is based on an experiment by Yves Tougas and myself at McGill University.[436] The pattern of tones that was used is shown in

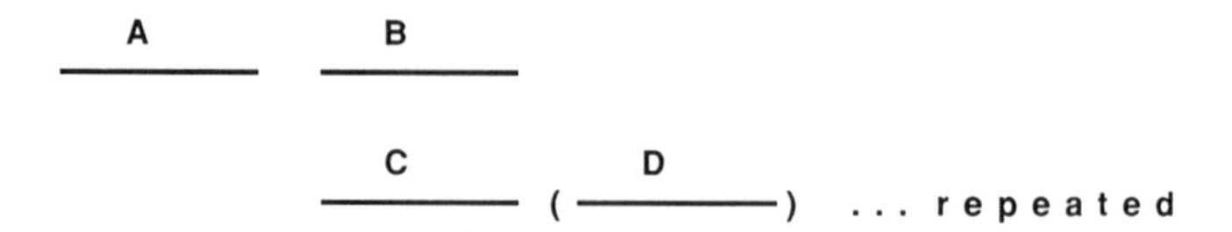

Figure 3.20
Competition of groupings. Tone D is presented only in some conditions.

figure 3.20. It was like the one used by Bregman and Pinker in that a tone, A, was alternated with a mixture of two tones, B and C. A was at the same frequency as B and was intended to capture it into a sequential stream, AB–AB–AB. . . . The only difference was that in some conditions there was a fourth tone, D, at the same frequency of C and following it in the cycle. In the conditions that had no fourth tone, a silence equal in length to tone D was added to the cycle in its place to ensure that the cycle always lasted for the same length of time. The pattern was played repeatedly to listeners who were asked to judge how clearly A and B could be heard as a repeating pair. They heard this AB grouping more clearly when D was present.

We explained these results by the following argument. D tends to capture C into a CD stream. This competes with the spectral fusion between B and C and weakens it. Due to this weakening, B is freer to group with A. We can use a metaphor to clarify this reasoning. Instead of tones, let A, B, C, and D, be Alice, Bob, Carol and Don, respectively. Bob and Carol are going together, but Alice is interested in Bob. Cleverly, she introduces Don to Carol. When Carol becomes attracted to Don, the bond between her and Bob decreases and Alice is more successful at persuading Bob of her attractiveness.

The results follow from the fact that spectral fusion competes with sequential grouping. The auditory system acts as if it is implementing the rule that a sound cannot exist in its own right with its own properties and at the same time give up its own properties to be fused into a larger organization. This consistency requirement can also be viewed as an example of the rule of belongingness or exclusive allocation that we discussed earlier. Later we will examine evidence that suggests that this rule is limited in two ways: First it is not all or nothing in nature, but quantitative. For example, when the grouping of B with A increases to some extent, B's grouping with C decreases to some extent. Second, the rule of exclusive allocation will not be followed when a component of sound fits in very well to two competing organizations (that is, when there are several cues favoring its inclusion in each organization). Sometimes instead of being apportioned to the two organizations, it is duplexed to the two. That is, it seems to be given almost completely to both.[437]

To the extent that the exclusive allocation rule holds, constraints on grouping can propagate to other frequencies and other times. The Gestalt psychologists would have called the frequency-by-time representation of sound a field and would have argued that it existed as a real field in the brain. The definition of a brain field is any analog of a set of relations in the outside world that acts in the way that a field does in physics. In a physical field, effects propagate from one part to another by crossing the intervening space. A local property of a field cannot affect something far away in the field without influencing things that are closer to it. Influences in a field are also usually stronger between elements that are closer together in the field. The pictures that I have constantly been drawing, showing time and frequency as the two axes, would, for the Gestaltists, be portrayals of actual fields in the brain. For them this would explain how constraints could propagate from one part to another of the frequency-by-time representation of our sounds, so as to exert their influences in favor of a consistent or simple organization.

There is an analogous idea in machine vision. In understanding a drawing, for example, a computer program could be trying to establish a label, such as "convex corner," for a particular junction of lines in the drawing.[438] Yet the information in the immediate vicinity of the junction (the local information) might be ambiguous and support a number of alternative labels. One approach to resolving ambiguity is to first create a description of the drawing in which we assign to each junction all the labels that the local evidence will support, and subsequently to compare pairs of adjacent junctions to see if their labels are consistent with each other.[439] When such comparisons are made, the number of possibilities for valid labels drops dramatically. This procedure will propagate constraints across the description, a decision about one line junction acting to force decisions about neighboring junctions. A generalized theory based on this method has been called "relaxation labeling."[440] Each local region of a pattern is assigned a set of labels. Associated with each label is a strength. An algorithm that allows labels to interact leads to the raising of the strengths of some labels and the reduction of the strengths of others.

Properties of relaxation labeling include the following:

1. Mutual support relations exist in the labeling of neighboring elements. In the foregoing auditory example, this type of relation might be in the form of a rule that says that if one tone is strongly attracted to a second, then the second should be strongly attracted to the first. In our example, "if C goes with B, then B goes with C."

2. Mutual antagonism relations exist among certain of the labels associated with a particular element. Hence in our auditory example, this would say that the following two labels on B would tend to interfere with one another:

—"B belongs with A in a stream whose base pitch is the pitch of A";

—"B belongs with C in a stream whose base pitch is the pitch of C."

I am assuming that because there are incompatible properties of the streams to which B is assigned by these two labels, if one label is asserted strongly this will weaken the other.

3. Certain physical relations between tones also affect the strength of labels. These are the properties that we have been calling heuristics of scene analysis. In our example, A will be attracted to B and vice versa by frequency proximity. So will C and D. B will be attracted to C by synchronous onsets and offsets.

In view of these rules, when D is added to the pattern the CD attraction (reflected both in the labels of C and D in a mutually supportive way) will enter the situation. By rule 2 (antagonism of labels) this will weaken the attraction of C toward B. By rule 1 (mutual support of labels) this will reduce the attraction of B toward C. By rule 2 (antagonism) this will strengthen the attraction of B toward A. By rule 1 (support) this will increase the attraction of A toward B. The perceptual effect of the last step is to favor the perception of A and B as a stream, which is what we find.

Admittedly sketchy, the above outline merely traces out a path of relationships whereby the presence or absence of D in the pattern could make a difference in the perception of A and B as a stream, and maps it informally onto a relaxation labeling system.

The experiment is interesting because its results are hard to explain by a filter theory of attention.[441] In such a theory, the formation of a stream in a particular frequency region is due to the tuning of a filter to that frequency. In our example, when A is heard in isolation, this tunes a filter to that frequency and when this filter subsequently encounters the BC mixture, it strips out B. The output of this filter then contains A and B, which are then perceived together as a pair. In a similar way, a second filter would become tuned to D's frequency by encountering it in isolation and, on the next cycle of the pattern, would act to strip C out of the BC mixture. This theory ought to find no reason why the high- and low-tuned filters should not act quite independently of one another, any later recognition process selecting the output of either one depending on its needs. Such a view would expect that when we are listening to the high stream, we are attending to the output signal of the filter that selects A and B and that the presence or absence of D in the low stream should not affect the clarity of this signal.

Although the effects of D are not consistent with a simple filter theory, the relaxation labeling model with which we have contrasted it is only one possible embodiment of a larger class of theories: field theories, in which large numbers of elements interact to determine a perceptual result and where consistency of interpretation is enforced in some way. Other embodiments of field theory might serve just as well.

The question of consistency of interpretation is related to the question of what happens to the residual when one portion of a mixture is extracted by processes of organization. If we start with a mixture PQ, and we extract P, what happens to Q? If P is now separate from Q, then Q should also be separate from P. Certain perceptual results should occur. The first is that Q should become freer to group on its own with other sounds. We saw that in the previous example. The second should be that it is heard as having the properties that are left behind when the properties of P are removed.

We can illustrate this second principle with a signal in which there is a repeated alternation of two sounds, A and B. A is a noise burst that is limited to the narrow band between 100 and 900 Hz. B is a wider band of noise limited to the band between 100 and 1,700 Hz. Acoustically, therefore, B includes A as a component band. I have tried to make a visual analog of this in figure 3.21, where the vertical dimension represents frequency. The A bursts are three units high and the B bursts are six units high. They are shown separately on the right. When A and B are alternated without pauses between them, instead of hearing an alternation of two bursts with different properties, we hear A as continuously present, with a higher pitched noise burst periodically accompanying it. The explanation is that the part of B that is identical with A tends to separate from the rest of B and group with A. This leaves the residual higher pitched part of B to be heard as a separate sound. If the pause between A and B is long enough, B will not be partitioned into A plus a residual.

The formation of separately audible residuals is an important part of the primitive scene analysis process, a property which, as we shall see in chapter 4, distinguishes it from schema-governed segregation.

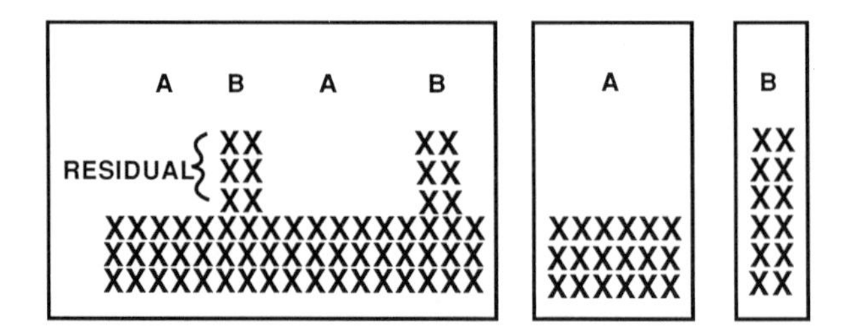

Figure 3.21
Formation of a residual.

Apparent Continuity and Contralateral Induction

We have seen that portions of a spectrum of sound can be separately allocated to different streams. One of the factors that led to the segregation of a particular part of the spectrum was the fact that a preceding sound was able to capture that part into a sequential stream. In this section, I would like to consider two phenomena that are examples of the same factor in operation but, because they are so striking, have been given special attention. They are both illusions, but the purpose of this section will be to show that they occur because basic principles of scene analysis are fooled by a sound pattern that would seldom occur in natural listening situations. Research on the two illusions is surveyed in a book by Richard Warren.[442]

One of them is a phenomenon that we looked at briefly in chapter 1. We can call it "the continuity illusion," although it has been given many other names. It is the illusion that one sound has continued behind a louder interrupting sound even when the softer sound is not really there during the interruption. A case of this, created by Gary Dannenbring, was illustrated in figure 1.15 of chapter 1.[443] In that example, a pure tone glided up and down repeatedly in frequency, but at a certain point in each glide, part of the tone was replaced by a silent gap. When that was done, the glide pattern was heard as having gaps in it. However, if the silent gaps were replaced by noise bursts, the gliding tone was heard as continuing through the noise and as not having any gaps. We saw that the effect was an auditory example of the perceptual closure effects that had been investigated by the Gestalt psychologists.

The second effect has been mainly studied by Richard Warren, using a consistent term, so I will use his name for it, "contralateral induction."[444] Here is an example. If, using headphones, we play a tone to the left ear, it will be heard on the left. However, if we play a loud noise burst to the right ear at the same time, the tone will be

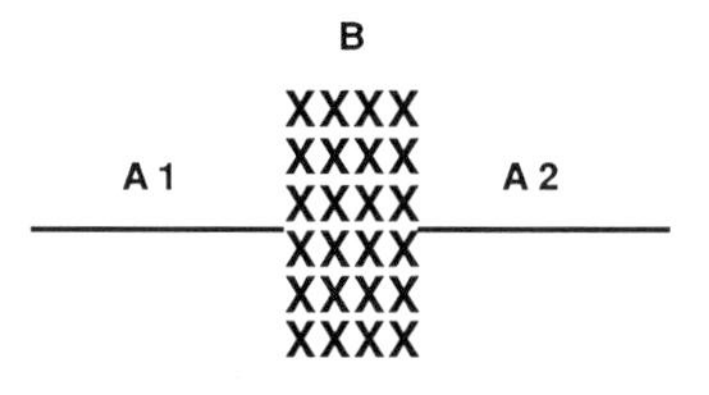

Figure 3.22
Labeling of the parts of the continuity illusion. A1 and A2 are parts of a longer tone A. B is a louder interrupting sound.

heard as closer to the midline of the listener's body. The contralateral noise will have induced an erroneous perception of the location of the tone.

I have chosen to put the two phenomena together, because both are cases in which spectral components are taken from one signal, A, and reallocated to a second signal, B, because they are assumed by the scene-analysis processes to be part of B. In the case of our example of the continuity illusion, a part of the spectrum of the noise has been allocated to the stream containing the tonal glide, supplying sensory evidence for the glide so that the latter is not perceived as having any gaps in it. We will have to explain both why the auditory system has detected a need for a subdivision of the noise spectrum and how it knows what to take out.

Our example of contralateral induction can be explained by assuming that a reallocation of spectral components has also taken place. In this case, scene analysis has assigned part of the inducing noise that arrives in the right ear to the same stream as the energy from the tone. Because of this, the tone is interpreted as having provided energy to both ears. Therefore it is heard as being located nearer to the midline of the body than it would have been if the contralateral noise had not been there. Again we have to explain how the system detects the necessity to reassign energy and how much of it to reassign.

The Continuity Illusion

I would like to begin with a discussion of the continuity illusion. The illusion has been investigated in many forms, but in every case, the experimenter deletes parts of a softer signal and replaces them with a louder sound, and the listener hears the softer sound as continuing unbroken behind the louder one. For our discussion, let us use the following terminology, illustrated in figure 3.22. The horizontal line represents an originally continuous sound whose center section has been deleted and replaced by a short, loud sound. The block of X's represents that interrupting sound. The continuous sound as a whole is called A and the interrupting sound, B. The part of A before the interruption is called A1 and the part after it is called A2.

Richard Warren has described and classified the known examples.[445] Perhaps the simplest case occurs when a soft noise burst seems to continue behind a louder burst that has an identical spectrum. In the most complex case, a spoken sentence appears to continue through a loud noise burst. This latter instance has been called "phonemic restoration" because when the noise burst replaces a phoneme in the speech, the brain of the listener will often restore the percept of a phoneme so that the partially deleted word seems complete.

The continuity illusion can be explained from the point of view of Gestalt psychology as an example of the general tendency for discontinuous perceptual events to exhibit closure if their properties match one another.[446] However I agree with Warren, who has done a great deal of insightful research on the continuity illusion, that we can understand it better by seeing it as a perceptual compensation for masking. In a natural listening environment when a sound is momentarily interrupted by a much louder one, the louder sound could totally mask the sensory information arriving from the weaker one. In such circumstances, it would be incorrect for the auditory system to interpret the weaker signal as having stopped during the interruption, especially if the weaker signal becomes audible again after the interruption. In Warren's view, the auditory system improves perception by restoring what it can infer as having been masked by the signal. While I do not think that the auditory system need know anything specifically about masking to achieve this task, I find Warren's view stimulating.

The auditory system, however, can never get something for nothing. If evidence is missing, you can never get more information by inferring what might have been there. According to a scene-analysis approach, the way that the auditory system improves the quality of its decision making in the case of an interrupting sound is by avoiding being fooled by the evidence that *is* there. For example, let us refer back to figure 3.22. At the transition between A1 and B, there is a sudden spectral change, a boundary, at the point where the interrupting signal starts. After this point, no specific evidence for the existence of A is present. Yet if this boundary were interpreted as the offset of A, the auditory perceptual process would incorrectly estimate the duration of A and describe A as a signal that had only those features that existed prior to the interruption. As a result, when processes of pattern recognition were applied to the signal, they would try to recognize a sound that had only those properties that occurred prior to the interruption and would not integrate those properties that occurred after the interruption as part of the description of the same sound. By interpreting A1 and A2 as two separate signals, the pattern-recognition process would come up with the wrong interpretation of the signal. We can get an idea of what such mistakes might look like from the following visual example of a printed sentence.

They should be*in the performance.

If the asterisk in the above sentence represented an inkblot that covered that position in the sentence, and if the absence of a visible letter at the position of the asterisk were taken as equivalent to a space, the reader would read the sentence as "They should be in the performance." But if the asterisk were treated as missing data, then the listener might go into his mental dictionary looking for a word of about five letters, starting with "be" and ending with "in", and find the word "begin". Similarly, in visual examples involving the recognition of the shapes of objects, when the outline of a shape nearer to our eye interrupts our view of a more distant object, the visual system will come up with two different descriptions of the distant object depending on whether it incorporates the shape of the occluding edge into the description of the more distant object or leaves it out. This problem was discussed in chapter 1 and an example was shown in figure 1.5.

The perceptual restoration of the word "begin" in the previous example would be correct if the word had actually been continuous through the inkblot. We should observe that the correctness of the interpretation of the sensory evidence that occurs on both sides of an interruption as evidence for a single object (or event) depends strongly on the correctness of the assumption that our view of the target has been occluded or interrupted. For this reason, the perceptual systems, both visual and auditory, must use a very accurate analysis of the structure of the sensory evidence to determine whether the parts separated by the occluding material show sufficient agreement with one another to be considered parts of the same thing or event.

As far as the continuity illusion is concerned, then, I would not only want to see it as a compensation for masking but would like to show that it is a part of scene analysis, and that the perceptual process that is responsible for it uses many of the same rules for scene analysis that we have already discussed.

I would like to start by proposing a set of principles that I see as governing the continuity illusion and then go on to illustrate them through examples taken from the research literature.

The account can be broken down into two parts. When the illusion occurs, the listener's brain must come up with answers to two questions, a "whether" question and a "what" question. In answering the "whether" question, it must decide whether the softer signal has stopped or continued at the point in time that the louder signal occurred. In this section we will see that primitive scene analysis makes a substantial contribution to this decision. This contribution can be made without recourse to learned knowledge that is concerned with the structure of the softer signal. By "learned knowledge," I am referring to such things as rules concerning the nature of the speech signal or the inventory of words in the language. The "whether" question is presumed to be answerable largely on the basis of purely acoustic cues that indicate that the softer signal has not ended but has merely been interrupted by another sound.

When the brain has determined that the softer signal did continue on behind the louder one, it must go on to answer the "what" question: What are the properties of the softer sound during the period when it was inaudible? For example, when the softer sound is a rising frequency glide of a pure tone both before and after the louder sound, and the two audible parts fit nicely together as parts of a longer glide, the brain concludes that the missing part was the middle portion of the long glide. As a second example, when the softer sound is a spoken sentence, it concludes that the missing part was the speech sound that is predictable from the parts of the sentence that were clearly audible. This question of what to restore is clearly based on a process of prediction that is able to use the audible portions to infer the nature of the missing parts. In the case of the ascending glide, the process must be able to interpolate along some dimension such as frequency. In the case of speech sounds, the restoration is clearly based on knowledge of the words of the language.

It is important not to confuse the two questions. I will argue that the "whether" question falls within the scope of scene analysis as we have described it previously. In deciding that A1 and A2 are parts of the same signal, the scene-analysis process is doing its job of assigning parts of the sensory input to a larger group that probably has all come from the same source. In doing so it alters the nature of the recognition process so that a sound that starts with A1 and ends with A2 can be recognized. Primary stream segregation is concerned with acoustic properties whose meaning is not yet interpreted. For this reason it cannot determine the specific nature of the missing material. The latter must be determined by a more complex process of pattern recognition. Therefore answering the "what" question depends on processes of a wholly different nature, which are outside the scope of this volume. We are employing a dichotomy here, between primitive and schema-based scene-analysis processes, that we will discuss in more detail in chapter 4. We are entitled to believe in a two-component process if we can show that the two components do different jobs and base their activity on different sorts of information.

Rules Governing the Generative Process

Let me begin by briefly listing the fundamental rules that govern the process of deciding whether a sound A has continued through an interruption by another sound B.

- There should be no evidence that B is actually covering up a silence between A1 and A2 rather than the continuation of A. This means that there should be no evidence that A actually shuts off when B starts or turns on again when B finishes.
- During B, some of the neural activity in the auditory system should be indistinguishable from activity that would have occurred if A had actually continued.
- There should be evidence that A1 and A2 actually came from the same source. This means that the rules for sequential grouping would normally put them into the same stream even if they had been separated by a silence instead of by B.
- The transition from A to B and back again should not be capable of being interpreted as A transforming gradually into B and then back again. If it is, the listener should not hear two sounds, one continuing behind the other, but simply one sound, changing from one form into another and then back again. The criterion for hearing "transformation" rather than "interruption" is probably whether a continuous change can or cannot be tracked by the auditory system.

In short, all the sensory evidence should point to the fact that A actually continued during the interruption and has not either gone off altogether or turned into B. Let us see how this works out in detail.

The "No Discontinuity in A" Rule

The first of the preceding rules said that there should be no reason to believe that there was not actually a silence between A1 and A2. We can refer to this as the "no discontinuity in A" rule. One source of evidence that is relevant to this decision is what happens at the bound-

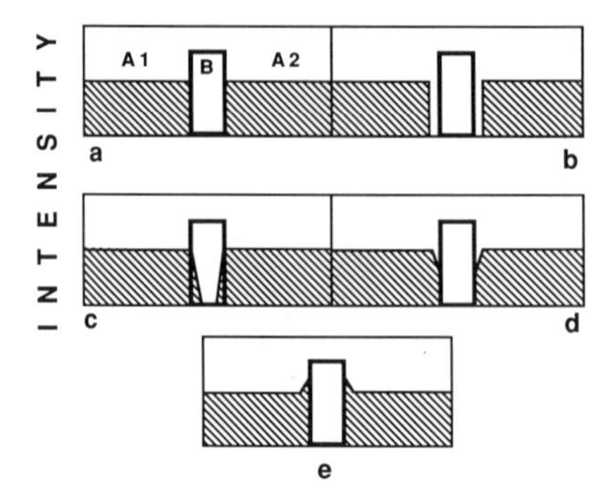

Figure 3.23
The effect of the boundary between sounds on the continuity illusion. (a) B is much louder than A and in the same frequency region. It masks the offset and subsequent onset of A. (b) There is a silence between A and B so that the offset and onset of B are audible. (c) B is not loud enough to mask the offset and subsequent onset of A. (d) A is perceptibly dropping in intensity just at the onset of B and rising just after B's offset. (e) A is perceptibly rising in intensity just before B and dropping just after B.

ary between A1 and B and between B and A2. It has been shown that if there are short 50-msec silent gaps between B and the two parts of A, then A will not be heard as continuing behind B.[447] This condition is diagrammed in part b of figure 3.23. I think the lack of perceived continuity occurs because the auditory system can hear A1 turning off before B comes on, and then, after B, can hear A2 turning on again. Even if the amplitude of B is sufficient to mask the offset of A1 and the onset of A2 its temporal separation from these two events prevents it from doing so. The idea that continuity occurs only when the auditory system cannot detect a drop in intensity when A turns off, or a rise when it turns back on again, is the essence of several theories of the continuity illusion.[448]

It is not necessary for the auditory system to detect a complete offset and onset before it becomes unwilling to hear A as having continued through the interruption. Gary Dannenbring and I did an experiment that did not insert silences between A1, B, and A2. Instead we introduced a 10-dB drop in intensity of A1 just before B occurred (matched by a 10-dB rise just as it reappeared after B). We found that the auditory system was less prepared to hear A continuing though B than if no such drop (and rise) had occurred.[449] This condition is shown in part d of figure 3.23. The utility of such a tendency should be obvious. If sound source A in the world is in the process of shutting off just as B appears, it should not be heard as continuing through the mixture. However, another result in the same experiment surprised us. In one condition, A suddenly began to increase in intensity just before B and then decreased in intensity upon its reappearance after B, as in part *e* of the figure. In this condition, too, there was a reluctance to hear A continuing during B. It seemed that any discontinuity in A, near the A-B boundary, interfered with the perceptual continuation of A, and that this discontinuity in A was interfering with the allocation of the A-B boundary to B.

Let me explain what I mean. In the case where A remains steady up to the A-B boundary, as shown in part *a* of figure 3.23, the spectral discontinuity at that boundary is attributed to B, not to A. It is as if the auditory system were saying (in the steady case) that the discontinuity marks the beginning of B, but has no relevance for the description of A. It resembles the exclusive allocation of properties discussed in chapter 1. We saw that in a drawing, a line might be interpreted as portraying the shape of the outline of a nearer object where it occludes a farther object from view. In such a case, the line would not contribute to the description of the shape of the farther object. Perhaps the temporal boundary between A and B is treated in a similar way; it is assigned to B and helps delimit its duration, but not A's. We still have to explain why sometimes it is assigned only to B, and why under other circumstances it is assigned to A as well. Perhaps, as a general rule, it tends to get assigned to the louder sound. However, if there is some indication that the softer sound is starting to undergo a change, the discontinuity can get assigned to the softer one as well and we will not hear it as continuing behind the louder.

Another example of the fact that boundaries tend to be assigned to the interrupting (louder) sound occurs in a demonstration created by Ranier Plomp.[450] A 1,000-Hz tone is frequency-modulated at 15 Hz. After every three modulations there is a white noise burst or a silence replacing the signal. In the case of a silence, the listener hears a series of triplets of warbles, as shown in part 1 of figure 3.24. In the case of the noise, shown in part 2, there is no experience of triplets. The sound is simply heard as a continuous sequence of modulations that is periodically interrupted by a noise burst. This means that the mere absence of the FM warbles was not sufficient to define the groupings that led to the perception of triplets. The triplets had to be separated by silence. The beginning and ending of an interrupting sound will define its own temporal boundaries but not the boundaries of the thing it interrupts.

The ability of the auditory system to detect a discontinuity in A may be involved in another fact about the continuity illusion. Suppose we start with a very weak A and a B of medium loudness and

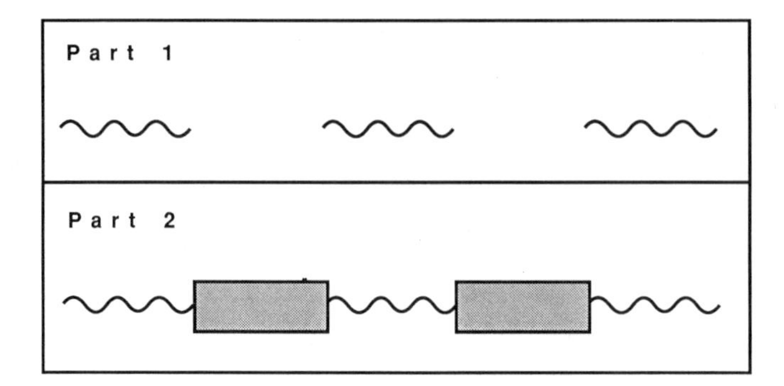

Figure 3.24
Part 1: bursts of a tone, modulated in frequency. Part 2: the same tone bursts alternating with noise bursts. (From Plomp 1982.)

alternate them repeatedly with no gaps. At these loudness settings, A will sound continuous. Suppose, then, that as the alternation proceeds we gradually increase the loudness of A. At a certain point, A will no longer sound continuous but will seem to be pulsing in loudness, dropping at the point where B turns on, and rising again after each B. This point has been called the pulsation threshold. (Obviously, when A becomes much louder than B the listener will hear A turning on and off repeatedly.)

The pulsation threshold has been interpreted in the following way: "When a tone and a stimulus S are alternated (alternation cycles about 4 Hz), the tone is perceived as being continuous when the transition from S to tone causes no perceptible increase of nervous activity in any frequency region."[451] In other words, the frequency receptors responding to A are allowed to be more strongly stimulated during the interruption, but not more weakly stimulated. The reason for this requirement is obvious if the auditory system is to infer that A did not turn off during the interruption.

We also know that the continuity illusion becomes less compelling when the weaker sound is presented to one ear and the more intense sound to the other.[452] This would also be expected if the louder sound is required to mask the offsets and onsets of the weaker before continuity may be heard. Sounds are less effective in masking others if they are presented to different ears.

The "Sufficiency of Evidence" Rule

The second rule said that during B, some of the neural activity should be indistinguishable from activity that would have occurred if A had actually been continued. This rule can be called the "sufficiency of evidence" rule. Warren and his colleagues have described it in this way: "If there is contextual evidence that that a sound may be present at a given time, and if the peripheral units [of the auditory system] stimulated by a louder sound include those which would be stimulated by the anticipated fainter sound, then the fainter sound may be heard as present."[453] This description can make sense of a number of effects that have been seen in experiments.

First, as we have already seen, if the interrupting sound is not sufficiently louder than the softer one, the softer may not appear to continue underneath the louder.

A second observation was made by Warren and his colleagues. As part of Warren's project to show that the continuity illusion was a compensation for masking, an experiment was done that compared two sets of conditions: those in which a louder sound would mask a softer one, and those in which the two sounds could be used to generate the continuity illusion.[454] Both the softer (A) and the louder (B) sounds were 300-msec sinusoidal tones. The authors expected that the frequency relations that allowed B to mask A would be the very ones that favored the perceptual continuity of A behind B. In the assessment of the continuity illusion, A and B repeatedly alternated with one another with no gaps. The listeners were told to adjust the loudness of A to the loudest level at which they could still hear it as continuous (the pulsation threshold).

The frequency of the louder tone was always 1,000 Hz, but the frequency of the softer one was varied in different tests for the pulsation threshold. The reason for this is that the masking of one pure tone by another depends on the frequency relations between them, and the experiment tried to determine whether this would also be found for the continuity illusion. The masking of the softer tone by the louder was also directly measured. In the masking test, the louder 1,000-Hz tone was kept on all the time while the weaker tone was repeatedly turned on and off. The masking threshold was the faintest intensity of A at which it could be heard going on and off. Again the frequency of tone A was varied on different tests. The results showed that the thresholds in both the continuity tests and the masking tests followed the same pattern. Let me describe it first for the masking. The masking by B was greatest when A had the same frequency and fell off with increasing frequency difference in either direction. However, this reduction in masking was not symmetrical, with A suffering more when it was higher than B in frequency. This is a typical finding and is referred to by the expression "upward spread of masking." The masking effects of a tone are greater upon frequencies higher than it than upon lower frequencies.

The results for illusory continuity were similar. Continuity was best when the frequency of A and B was the same, and declined (required A to be softer) as A's frequency deviated from B's. Furthermore, the same asymmetry in this effect was observed for continuity as for masking. When A was higher in frequency than B it could be made louder than it could be made when it was equally far below B in frequency and still be heard as continuous.

According to Warren's view the similarity between the two sets of results is due to the fact that continuity is a compensation for masking. The auditory system will restore the signal under just those conditions where, if it had really been there, it would have been masked. If this view were to be taken as literally correct, the auditory system would have to be equipped with a knowledge of which sounds can mask which other ones. As an indication of the complexity of the knowledge that it would have to have, consider another experiment that was done in the same series. Instead of using a tone as B, a broadband noise burst was used. This noise burst was filtered so that frequencies near 1,000 Hz were eliminated. Therefore it had a reduced masking effect when tone A was at 1,000 Hz. Correspondingly, it did not allow tone A to be heard as continuous unless it was very soft (and therefore capable of being masked by B). This would seem to point to a profound knowledge by the auditory system about the masking effects of a vast array of spectral patterns on one another.

There is, however, an explanation that does not require the auditory system to have such deep knowledge. This account says that rather than depending on a knowledge about masking, the continuity illusion depends in a very direct way on masking itself. Earlier we saw that if the auditory system detects onsets and offsets of energy in A at the points in time at which it abuts against B, it will not project A through the interruption. We can understand the close relation between continuity and masking by realizing that if these onsets and offsets are masked, the system will have no reason to infer that A has stopped and started again, and will therefore assume that A has continued through the mixture. The onsets and offsets of energy in a particular frequency region will be most effectively masked by a masker of the same frequency, and also more effectively by maskers below it in frequency than by those above it. The same idea will explain why a louder B is more effective in inducing perceptual continuity: It more effectively masks the offset and onset of A.

The idea that the discontinuities in A have to be masked also explains another observation. If A and B are tones, and there are gaps of silence between A1, B, and A2 (as in part b of figure 3.23) then the longer the gaps, the lower we must set the intensity of A in order for it to be heard as continuing through B.[455] This is consistent with what we know about the masking of a sound by another one that either precedes or follows it (backward and forward masking). The following two facts are relevant: (1) the nearer in time a target is to a masker, the more it is masked, and (2) the more intense the masker relative to the target, the greater the masking.[456]

It is interesting to remind ourselves of the details of the procedure that the experimenters employed to measure masking in the experiments that showed the connection between masking and continuity. B was the masker. It remained at a constant amplitude. It was accompanied by a less intense tone, A, that was periodically pulsed on and off. The main clue that a listener uses in deciding whether A is present in such a pattern is whether any periodic changes (discontinuities) can be heard in a particular frequency region. This procedure, therefore, was probably measuring the masking of these discontinuities. Therefore the correspondence between the results in the masking and continuity tests are consistent with the idea that the masking of the onsets and offsets of A are a necessary prerequisite for the continuity illusion.

This is not the only prerequisite. What we hear during B must be consistent with what we would hear if A were still present but mixed with another sound. Therefore the role of the spectral content of B is twofold. On the one hand it must be of a proper frequency and intensity to mask any discontinuities of A at the A-B boundaries, and on the other hand, it must be such as to sustain the hypothesis that A is indeed present in a larger mixture. That is, the peripheral neural activity that signals the presence of A when it is alone must be part of the neural activity during B.

We can easily see why the masking of the onsets and offsets of A is not sufficient. Suppose that A was a pure tone and B a white noise burst with a silent gap embedded in it. The onset of B would mask the offset of A1. However, if B lasted only briefly after masking A1, then went silent, then reappeared just in time to mask the onset of A2, we would surely not continue to hear A through the silence. Otherwise we would never be able to hear silences. This is the reasoning behind the second rule in our earlier list, which said that the neural activity during B had to be consistent with the case in which A was actually present.

Notice that the requirement applies to neural activity not to physical acoustic energy. The reason for making this distinction is that there may be cases in which there is no actual acoustic energy in B occurring at the same frequency as the energy in A and yet we will still hear the continuity. This will occur when the neural activity normally

Figure 3.25
Illustration of the principle of simplicity in the selection of energy from an interrupting sound to complete the signal that occurs before and after it.

associated with A is stimulated by B. B might have the wrong frequency but be very intense. We know that a strong stimulus leads to activity in neural pathways far removed from those that are primarily tuned to the arriving frequency. Therefore, this spreading activation might activate the pathways that normally respond to A.

One of the most interesting things about the continuity illusion is that the important thing is not the match of the neural activity during B to the activity present during A1 and A2, but the match of this activity to the activity that *would have occurred* if A had really continued behind B. B must provide the stimulation that would have been provided by that missing part. For a perhaps ludicrously simple example of this requirement, let us suppose that there are two frequency glides that are aligned on a common trajectory, as shown on the left of figure 3.25. The discrete A's in the figure are to be taken as signifying a continuous pure tone that descends along the trajectory that they outline. The B's are meant to show a burst of noise that briefly interrupts the glide. The noise is shown as containing frequencies that match the parts of the glide that occur before and after it as well as the part that would occur underneath it. The diagram shown on the right contains the same parts of A, but most of B has been erased. Only two parts remain, one that continues the first part of the glide (but reversed in slope) and one that connects up with the second. Those parts of the noise burst that remain correspond to a sound in which B consists of a pair of parallel ascending tonal glides. If we listened to the sound shown on the left, we would hear, if B was loud enough, a long glide passing behind B. Such effects have been observed by Gary Dannenbring and Valter Ciocca in my laboratory.[457] However, if we listened to the sound shown on the right, we would hear a high-pitched glide first descending and then ascending again, accompanied by a low-pitched glide that first ascends and then descends.[458]

Why is this not heard even in the example shown at the left? After all, the necessary frequency components are there! It seems that although the percept is obliged to use the sound that is present in the B interval, it does not select from it in arbitrary ways. The selected part of B seems not only required to be consistent with the audible parts of the interrupted sound, but to be the simplest sound that is consistent with those parts. The auditory system can apparently select a subset of the available stimulation to use for its restored percept, but it tends not to create percepts without a very strong base in the stimulation that is present before and after that stimulation. In the left-hand case, the required frequencies for reconstructing the full glide were actually present as part of the noise. In fact, you could argue that the glide itself was there, in the same sense that a statue is present in an uncut piece of stone. In the case of the auditory system, the process that acts as a sculptor, cutting the restored sound out of the available sensory stimulation, is the hypothesis that has been activated by the parts of the sound that occur on both sides of the interruption. The neural activity during the masker is not required to match the characteristics of the remaining parts of the interrupted sound themselves; rather it must match the properties of the missing parts of the hypothesized signal.

Further evidence that the perceptual restoration is required to be consistent with the neural stimulation in the B interval comes from experiments on phonemic restoration, in which a spoken utterance is interrupted by one or more bursts of louder sound. If the loud burst is fairly short, the listener does not perceive that any of the speech is missing; however, if the burst is removed and a silent gap is left in its place, the listener is aware of the gaps and their distorting effect on the speech.

It has been reported that the best restoration is obtained when the burst supplies the right kind of sound.[459] Richard Warren has argued that this happens "when the extraneous sound in a sentence is capable of masking the restored speech sound."[460] As I said before, I do not think that the auditory system needs to have an understanding of what would mask what. It would be sufficient for the system to simply know what sort of sensory evidence is needed to support the hypothesis that some particular sound, A, is present. This is a type of knowledge that it needs anyway if it is ever to recognize it. Then it would analyze the neural stimulation during the B interval for the sensory components signaling the presence of A. These components would always be present in B whenever B contained a masked A or even if B was composed only of a loud sound capable of masking A.

It turns out that the two explanations (masking potential versus hypothesis-confirming adequacy) are hard to distinguish empirically. The reason that the B sound would mask a speech sound is just because it activated those frequency-specific neural circuits that responded to that speech sound. Unless it did so, it would not mask the speech. Therefore, we know that the burst will create sensory activity that is characteristic of the missing sound (of course it will contain much more besides, as we argued with the metaphor of the uncut stone). As a result, it is hard to determine whether it is the masking potential of the signal or the fact that it includes hypothesis-confirming stimulation that enables the restoration to occur. I favor the latter hypothesis because it requires less knowledge on the part of the auditory system and because it is consistent with other examples of scene analysis.

If we assume that it is not the masking potential of B but its hypothesis-confirming content that is most important, the hearing of illusory continuity becomes just a particular case of hearing a continuing sound, A, when another sound enters the mixture. In all such cases we receive the sensory stimulation for A and then a mixture of the sensory effects of A and the other sound.

A simple case is one that we mentioned earlier: A band-limited noise burst, A, is alternated with a wider-band noise burst, B, that contains the frequency spectrum that is present in A (at the same intensity) as well as other frequencies, higher than those in A. If the two sounds are repeatedly alternated with no gaps between them, we will hear A continuing unchanged through B. In addition we will hear the higher frequency band of B, the part not present in A, as a sound that beats alongside the continuous A. In this example, we would not call the continuity of A an illusion. A is really present in B. The only reason for considering the demonstration interesting is the way in which we perceive the evidence coming from B. When B is played alone, it has the characteristic quality of a wide-band noise. However, we never hear that quality when A and B are rapidly alternated. Instead of hearing A–B–A–B–A–B– . . . , we decompose B, giving part of it to A and hearing the residual as a distinct new sound with its own high-pitched property. This result is really no different than what happens in any example of the continuity illusion in which a part of the stimulation received in the B interval is allocated to A. The only difference is that in most examples, we do not usually notice what happens perceptually to the rest of B when A is scooped out. This may be because the residual usually has no coherent structure of its own by which it can be recognized as different from the total B sound, or because it is loud enough that "borrowing" a bit of sensory evidence with which to construct the missing part of A makes little difference in the global quality of B.

The fact that a pure tone can continue through a noise burst tells us something about what it takes to confirm the existence of A inside B. The frequency component of the noise that will act as the continuation of B need not be a resolvable component of B. Indeed, if it were independently audible (as in the case where, in listening to B alone, we could discern a tonal component at the frequency of A) we would not think of the continuity of A during B as an illusion. It is because the component is not separately audible when B is presented alone that we think of the phenomenon as an illusion. Apparently the existence of A before and after B allows us to "scoop out" some of the energy of B as a separate sound. This is not unlike the examples that we saw earlier in which a complex tone, B, was alternated with a pure tone, A, whose frequency matched one of the harmonics of B. The alternation allowed the listener to hear out the embedded harmonic. Yet we did not think of it as an illusion.

If we look at the intensity of B that is required before restoration of A will occur, we see that the amount of energy that is produced by B in a single critical band is quantitatively sufficient to support the hypothesis that A is really present. For example, suppose we have a 1,000-Hz tone that is alternating with a band-passed noise that has a flat spectrum within the band. The critical band at 1,000 Hz is about 175 Hz.[461] Suppose the noise bandwidth is 3,000 Hz. That means that about 5 percent of the energy of the noise is received in this critical band. Converting to decibels, the critical band receives 13 dB less energy than the total energy of the noise. This means that when the tone is 13 dB less intense than the noise, the critical band at 1,000 Hz will get the same amount of energy from the tone and the noise. The intensity difference between the tone and noise that is used in experiments with these signals is typically about this size or larger.

The requirement that tone B must supply enough energy in the critical band occupied by A is equivalent to the requirement for perceived continuity that was stated by Houtgast: "When a tone and a stimulus S are alternated (alternation cycle about 4 Hz), the tone is perceived as being continuous when the transition from . . . tone to S causes no (perceptible) decrease of nervous activity for any frequency region."[462] Houtgast's criterion would also guarantee, by the way, that the offsets and onsets in A would not be audible, since sufficient energy at the frequency of A would continue right through B; in effect, there really would be no offset or onset "edges" of A.

Experiments that were done on the pulsation threshold by Houtgast are relevant to these issues. When a pure tone, A, is alternated with a much louder complex tone, B, with no gap between them, the pure tone seems to continue right through the complex one. If A is gradually raised in intensity, a point is reached at which it no longer seems continuous but seems to go off or be reduced in intensity during B. This makes A seem to pulse periodically, and is therefore called the pulsation threshold.[463] This can be thought of as the point at which the auditory system can tell that there was a reduction in intensity at the frequency of A when B came on.

If B has a harmonic at or near the frequency of A, then A will sound continuous up to a much greater intensity (as much as 20 dB higher) than it does if there is no matching harmonic in B. This makes sense. Since there is more energy in B at that frequency, the ear will not detect a drop in energy at the juncture between A and B. Therefore it will not hear A as dropping in intensity. The intensity of A will have to be raised before this difference will be detected. For this reason, the pulsation threshold can be used to study how well the auditory system resolves harmonics: If there is no difference in the threshold as A deviates more and more from the frequency of a particular harmonic of B, this means that as far as the ear is concerned the spectral regions near the harmonic in B have as much energy as the region that is right at the harmonic. In other words, the ear shows no frequency resolution in that range of frequencies.

What is interesting about this in the present context is that even when B has no harmonic that matches A, there is some soft level of A at which it sounds continuous through B. Which energy, then, from B is being matched up with A to create a perception of a continuous tone? Rather than thinking of matching energy at a particular frequency, we should think of matching neural activity. If there is spread of excitation from one basilar membrane region to another (whether this spread is mechanical or neural), then the auditory system, when it detects a certain level of neural activity at a particular frequency region, will not know whether this occurred because of stimulation by a signal at that frequency or because of spread of excitation from a stronger signal at some other frequency. Therefore when we say that tone A has captured a component of B we are being imprecise. We should actually say that the neural activity stimulated by A has captured some of the neural activity stimulated by B. In natural listening situations, this pattern of neural activity (a part of the activity at time B matching the activity at time A) will usually exist because the event that stimulated the neural activity during time period A has actually continued during time period B.

We should remember, however, that the neural activity in B that is "captured" out of it need not match A exactly. This is supported by one of Helmholtz's observations. I mentioned it earlier when I cited his argument that the perception of the matching component in B was not an illusion. The observation was that even if the component inside B did not match A exactly, it could be captured by A, yet the listener would be able to hear that A and the extracted component were different. The utility of this spread of capturing for scene analysis is that even if a sound changes slightly in pitch over time, it will be able to be tracked into a mixture.

The "A1-A2 Grouping" Rule

Another rule that I have proposed as governing the illusion could be called the "A1-A2 grouping" rule. This says that A1 and A2 will be treated as parts of the same sound only if the rules for sequential integration cause them to be grouped into the same stream. This means that they would have been grouped as parts of the same stream even if there were no B sound between them. Auditory stream segregation and the continuity illusion have been described in the literature as separate phenomena. However, both can be understood as arising from the scene-analysis process. Stream segregation occurs when the auditory system attempts to group auditory components into streams, each stream representing a single external source of sound. The continuity illusion occurs when the system interprets a sequence of acoustic inputs as the result of a softer sound being interrupted by, and masked by, a louder one.

An argument can be made that the illusion of continuity must depend on the processes that produce auditory stream segregation. It goes as follows: The continuity illusion depends on the interpretation that one sound has interrupted another. This means that A1 and A2 have to be interpreted as parts of the same sound but not as part of the same sound as B. Unless A1-A2 hangs together as a stream, there is no sense to the statement that B has interrupted it. Continuity through interruption is a special form of stream integration that occurs when it is plausible to interpret A1 and A2 not only as part of the same stream, but as a single continuous event within that stream. Therefore the requirements for the continuity illusion *include* those for stream integration.

There are two consequences of the assumption that restored continuity depends on stream organization. Since stream cues are part of the "interruption" decision and not vice versa, cues for continuity (or discontinuity) should not make a difference to stream segregation, but stream cues should make a difference to continuity.

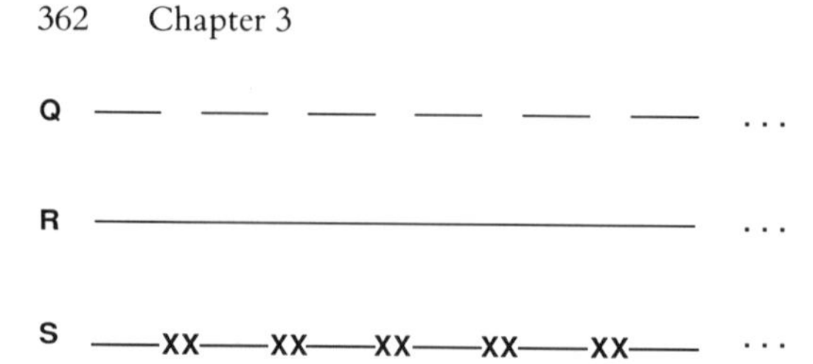

Figure 3.26
Streams, units, and continuity.

This means, for example, that adding a loud masking noise burst between two sounds, A1 and A2, should never affect the way that they enter into streams. If the stream-building process would have assigned them to different streams in the acoustic context in which they are situated, then the addition of a masking noise between them will make no difference and they will not be treated as two parts of a single sound. What, then, should the B noise do? According to this hypothesis, it should affect only those cases in which A1 and A2 would have been allocated to the same stream. But in those cases it should add the following element to the description: Not only have A1 and A2 been emitted by the same source but they are parts of a single sound from that source.

Figure 3.26 can clarify this. Let us distinguish three sounds, labeled Q, R, and S. Q is a tone that is pulsing on and off eight times per second, R is an unbroken 10-second-long tone, and S is the same as Q except that the silent gaps in the bursts of tone are replaced by loud noise bursts symbolized by the X's. In all cases, because all the parts of the tone are of the same frequency, the frequency-proximity rule for scene analysis will assign them all to the same stream. However, in Q the bursts will be heard as separate events within the same stream. The addition of the noise bursts in S makes us hear it like R, where all the segments of the tone are heard as one long event.

These sounds illustrate the fact that there are two aspects to the partitioning of a mixture of environmental sounds. One is to factor out of it the acoustic energy that arose from the same source. Another is to partition the energy of that source into separate events. An example of the first would be to group the sounds of a violin into a single stream, distinct from all co-occurring instrumental sounds. The second would involve hearing each note as a distinct event. Only by accomplishing both levels of grouping could we appreciate the rhythmic pattern of the notes. If the notes were strongly segregated into different streams, we would reject the rhythm as accidental. At the same time, unless there were distinct events starting at different

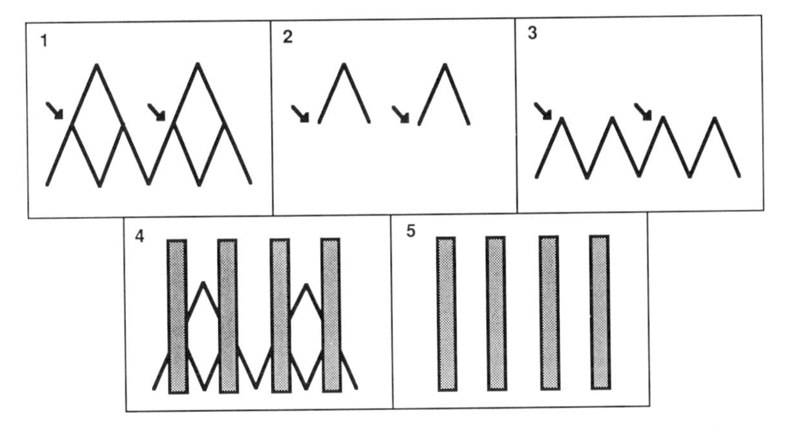

Figure 3.27
Pattern of glides used by Steiger (1980) to study the effects of perceptual restoration on stream organization.

times, there could be no rhythm in the stream. Music lends itself to convenient examples, but the situation is no different for everyday sounds. We could use a walker's footsteps in this example and draw the same conclusions.

In an informal experiment, Steiger created the acoustic pattern shown in part 1 of figure 3.27 in which a pattern of glides branches apart at what Steiger referred to as "decision nodes" (marked by arrows in the figure).[464] These patterns were segregated into two streams as shown in parts 2 and 3. Apparently when a stream reached the decision node it incorporated later material on the basis of frequency proximity rather than on the basis of "good continuation" of glide trajectories. Steiger asked the question as to whether the form taken by the stream segregation was related to whether the decision point was actually present or was, instead, created only by perceptual restoration. To answer it, he deleted the 20-msec portion just bracketing each decision point and replaced it with a loud white noise burst (part 4). The resulting streams sounded identical to those produced by the stimulus of part 1. There were three streams of sound. One consisted of the pattern of part 2, another consisted of the noise bursts shown in part 5, and the last contained the cycles of the lower stream, shown in part 3. Since this last stream did sound continuous, Steiger knew that perceptual restoration had occurred. However, it appeared that the restoration was not performed by extrapolating the glide from the the segment prior to the gap, but rather was based on information on both sides of the gap. The organization into two

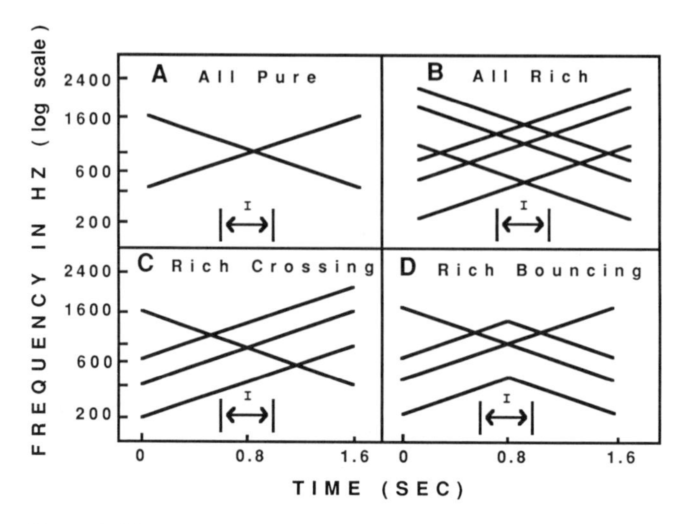

Figure 3.28
The four glide patterns (A–D) used by Tougas and Bregman (1985b). Interval I could be filled by glides (as shown), noise, or silence.

streams was the same whether or not the decision nodes were present or merely restored perceptually.

An experiment done by Yves Tougas and myself also showed that the perception of continuity through noise does not affect the organization into streams.[465] The auditory patterns that we used were the patterns of crossing glides that are shown in figure 3.28. Let us examine the perceptual results that occur when glides of this type are presented. In panel A we have an ascending and a descending glide. Each is a pure tone that is changing in frequency. Not surprisingly, this pattern will be heard as composed of two sounds. However, the two trajectories become ambiguous at the crossing point. Did the descending pure tone continue downward or turn around and go back up? One way that we hear this pattern is as a descending pure tone crossing an ascending pure tone. This is analogous to the way that our eyes tend to organize the diagram. It can be referred to as the "crossing" percept. The second way is to hear a higher glide falling to the midpoint and then "bouncing" upward again, accompanied by a lower glide that starts by gliding upward to the midpoint and falling downward again. This is analogous to visually dividing the figure into an upper V and a lower inverted V. It can be called the bouncing percept. The pattern in panel A tends to be heard in the bouncing mode because the principle of frequency proximity favors the grouping of glides that stay in the same frequency region.

In the pattern of panel C, the ascending glide is actually three related harmonics (the first, second, and third). We tend to hear this in the crossing mode because the auditory system fuses the ascending glide segments on the basis of their harmonic relations; therefore in the first half of the pattern it hears a pure descending glide and a rich ascending glide. Then at the midpoint, it seems to follow the same complex tone through the crossover point. The same seems to be done with the two parts of the descending pure glide. This grouping by harmonic complexity favors the crossing percept.

In pattern B, both the ascending and descending glides are formed of three harmonics throughout. Therefore the principle of grouping by the same harmonic pattern cannot favor either organization. The auditory system falls back on the tendency to group by frequency proximity just as it does in panel A. Again we hear the bouncing percept, this time involving two rich sounds.

In panel D, there is a very strong tendency to hear bouncing because the lower inverted V sound is enriched by added harmonics while the upper V is not. Therefore two tendencies favor the bouncing tendency—the tendency to restrict streams to a narrow frequency range and the tendency to group sounds with the same pattern of harmonics.

What does this have to do with the continuity illusion? There were two other sets of conditions based on the previous four patterns. One was made by deleting the middle 200-msec interval of each pattern (labeled I in the figure) and replacing it with a loud noise burst. These were called the "noise" conditions to distinguish them from the original "continuous" conditions. We were interested in the question of whether the perceptual grouping of these glides would be affected by what happened in the middle interval I. Another set was made by replacing the deleted material with a silence. These "silence" conditions were meant as a control for the fact that the noise condition differed in two ways from the continuous condition: by the absence of the gliding sounds at the crossover point and by the presence of noise. The silence condition differed from the continuous condition in only a single way.

The subjects were trained on the distinction between the crossing and bouncing interpretations of crossing glide patterns. Then they heard each of the experimental patterns and were asked to rate on a seven-point scale how easily they could hear either percept in that pattern. The major finding of the experiment was the striking similarity in the stream organizations regardless of the acoustic content of the interval I.

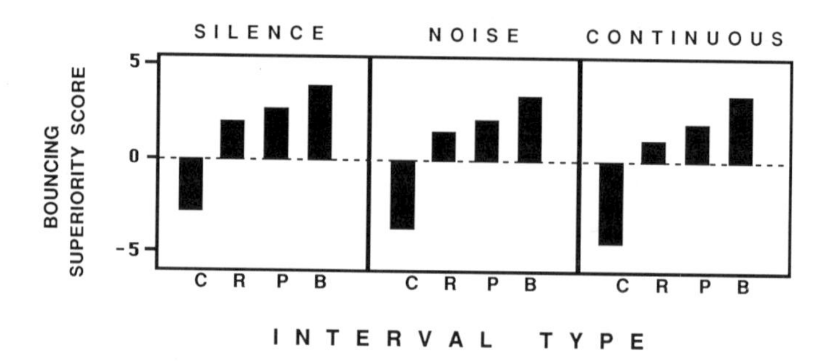

Figure 3.29
Data from Tougas and Bregman 1985b showing similarity of stream organizations despite illusory continuity.

Figure 3.29 shows the results, expressed in terms of a bouncing superiority score, which reflects the degree to which bouncing was easier to hear than crossing. Negative scores mean that crossing was the preferred percept. The three types of sound that occurred in the I interval (continuous glides, silence, and noise) yielded essentially the same stream formation and responded in the same way to the added harmonics. The only glide pattern in which there was a preference for the crossing percept (negative score) was the rich crossing condition (C) in which the added harmonics favored the crossing percept. The greatest preference for bouncing was shown in the rich bouncing condition (B) in which the added harmonics favored crossing. The conditions in which all glides were pure (P) or rich (R) showed a smaller preference for bouncing. The similarity of the results across conditions lends support to the idea that perceived continuity depends on the formation of streams and that the presence or absence of illusory continuity. The competition between grouping by harmonic pattern and grouping by frequency proximity resolved itself in the same way in all cases.

The results of this experiment appear to be explainable by a two-stage process. First, auditory streams were formed as a result of heuristics for grouping. Then, in response to cues for masking, a mechanism was activated to fill in the gaps in the already formed streams. According to this account, perceptual restoration works by the interpolation between events that lie within an already formed auditory stream and is a process that cannot affect the formation of such streams.

This experiment, by the way, and the informal demonstration by Steiger, are the only ones that have shown the perceptual restoration of the continuity of two streams concurrently. Furthermore, they have done so in a situation in which the two streams themselves were created by stream-forming heuristics. Remember that the glides occurred simultaneously. Their segregation into two streams was done on the basis of differences in frequency movement of the ascending and descending glides.

To understand the significance of this demonstration, we should remember that in natural listening situations several sounds are usually occurring at the same time. When a loud sound occurs, it often masks two or more of the weaker ones. When the loud sound disappears again we would not like to find ourselves listening to a different signal than we were before the interruption had occurred. And we should not want to recognize chimeric sounds created by grouping the earlier part of one signal with the later part of another. This is why the stream organizing processes must not be changed by the processes that restore continuity.

To repeat an earlier point: My account of the relation between stream segregation and perceived continuity implies two consequences. The first, supported by Steiger's demonstration and by the experiment that Tougas and I did, is that interruption by a louder sound, leading to continuity, should not affect the perceived groupings. The second is that the rules for grouping *should* affect the restoration of perceptual continuity. Effects of this latter type have been found in research done by Valter Ciocca and myself.[466] The pattern that we used was a gliding pure tone (A1), then a loud noise burst (B), then another gliding pure tone (A2). There were no silent gaps between A1, B, and A2. The listeners were led to believe, by a series of pretests, that sometimes the glide continued behind the noise and sometimes did not. They were asked in the main experiment to judge whether the glide continued behind the noise. They used a nine-point rating scale that ran from "very sure not present" to "very sure present." In actuality, the gliding tone was never present with the noise.[467] We varied the frequency placement and the slope of A1 and A2. For example, A1 could be an ascending glide and A2 could be its mirror image, beginning at the highest frequency that glide A1 had reached and gliding back down to the initial frequency of A1. This condition led to a good restoration of the missing glide, presumably because the two glide segments were in the same frequency region and therefore their perceptual grouping would be favored by frequency proximity. In another condition, both A1 and A2 were ascending, with A2 starting at the exact frequency that A1 would have reached if it had continued with a constant slope behind B. This condition was also judged as showing good continuity, presumably because the listener was able to project the trajectory of A1 through the noise. Other conditions, that were favored neither by frequency proximity nor by trajectory alignment, showed a weaker perception of continuity.

In this experiment, we found that two of the factors that are known to cause sequences of tones to be heard as a single stream also determined whether continuity would be heard. These factors are frequency proximity and alignment on a trajectory. Although the frequency proximity is always found to be effective in uniting sequences of sounds, alignment along a trajectory is not always found to do so.[468] In chapter 4, I have decided to consider the tracking of trajectories to be a process of schema-based stream segregation, involving attention to, and familiarity with, regular patterns of sound. Whatever the theoretical explanation for it, though, we know that in some cases, we can extract known or regular sequences out of mixtures more easily than unknown or irregular ones. Similarly, the restoration of the missing parts of sequences that display a regular pattern is widely found.

The presence of A2, appearing as soon as B has disappeared, seems to be of great importance to the continuity illusion; otherwise A tends not to be heard as continuing behind B. Giovanni Vicario has stressed the retrograde fashion in which the continuity illusion is controlled, with the mechanism deciding after the fact whether it heard the softer sound during the louder one.[469] This shows that the "whether" decision can be influenced by the sound that comes after the interruption.

The "what" decision is also influenced by material coming after the interruption. This has been demonstrated in phonemic restoration. When a speech sound is replaced by a loud noise, the sound that is perceptually restored can depend on material that comes after the noise.[470] For example, it has been reported that in the sentence, "It was found that the *eel was on the orange" (where the asterisk represents the sound of a loud cough that replaced a speech sound), the listeners would hear the incomplete word as "peel". If the final word was "table", then they would hear it as "meal". If the final word was "axle", the restored word would be "wheel".[471]

Obviously, from a logical point of view, the evidence in the B-A2 transition or in the material of A2 should be every bit as good as that during A1 or at the A1-B transition. However, we tend to believe that we hear a thing happening when it really is there rather than later when the evidence is all in. Our resistance to believing in retrospective effects partly arises from our belief that if some new element entered our experience sometime after the event, we would have to push our perception of everything after this element backward or else distort the timing relations. Perhaps a metaphor will help resolve this problem. Imagine a musician trying to transcribe a simple melody into musical notation as a person sings it. He is always operating with some delay and sometimes the delay can get longer than at other times. Despite this, the "score times" written on the paper can always be correct, regardless of the particular moment in "transcription time" that they happen to have been written. If the musician were transcribing a two-part melody, the corresponding notes in the two parts could be in correct registration on the score even if they were not written at the same moment. If we consider that the musician in this example represents our active perceptual processes and the score represents the final product of perception, we can see how our perceptual decisions can be made at variable periods after an event has occurred, but our perceptual record of the events need contain no distortions.

The "A Is Not B" Rule

So far we have shown how, in deciding about the continuity of sounds, the auditory system gathers evidence that a sound A has been interrupted by a second sound B. We have just argued that this interpretation of the acoustic pattern will not occur unless A1 and A2 are perceived as parts of the same sound. There is a also second requirement: B must not be interpreted as part of the same sound as A1 and A2. Otherwise we would hear A1 turning into B and then B turning into A2.

Both the interpretations "A transforming into B" and "A interrupted by B" are logically possible when we hear the acoustic transition between A1 and B. How could we decide which has taken place? I would propose that the interpretation that the sound has undergone a transformation requires the change to be slow and continuous. An example of a transition that could be interpreted either way, depending on the abruptness of the transition, is the transition from a soft sound to a loud one with the same structure and back again. From our everyday experience we know that it is possible to hear a sound get louder and then soft again. In such a case we do not hear the softer version as a separate sound continuing behind the louder one. Yet in the laboratory, we can alternate two sounds whose only difference is one of loudness and hear the softer one continue behind the louder.[472] But in this case, there is an abrupt transition between the softer and louder versions and back again. We also know that in the laboratory we can induce illusory continuity by alternating a soft pure tone with another pure tone that is louder and at a slightly different frequency.[473] Yet we know that if this transition were gradual, we would hear a single sound undergoing simultaneous frequency and amplitude changes.

We have observed a similar treatment of changes when we perceptually segregate tones that are alternating between different frequency regions into separate streams. When the high and low tones are joined by frequency glides instead of changing discretely in frequency, they are more likely to be incorporated into the same stream.[474] It is as if the auditory system does not believe that a sound can be transformed into another one instantaneously without going through intermediate stages.

If the preceding reasoning is correct, one of the crucial elements in the continuity illusion is that B should be segregated from A1 and A2 and put into a separate stream. This agrees with our experience of illusory continuity. The segregation of A and B into separate streams can be observed most easily in the version of the illusion in which a soft A and a louder B are repeatedly alternated; we hear B as a separate sound source whose bursts are superimposed on a continuous A.

It is likely that in the cases in which the continuity illusion occurs, a sudden change in intensity acts as if it were triggering two rules in the auditory system. Rule 1 is that the analysis of the current sound should be suspended and a new stream started. Rule 2 is that the new stream should be connected to some former stream if possible, and if the connection is successful, the analysis of that continuing stream should be resumed.

Rule 1 occurs at the boundaries between A1 and B and between B and A2. Rule 2 binds all the A's together and all the B's together. Since the changes in loudness of A at the boundaries is masked and some neural evidence for its continuation occurs during B, A is heard as continuous through B. However, since B is louder (and often spans a wider frequency range) its amplitude transitions are heard; therefore it is not perceived as a continuous sound but as a discontinuous series of bursts coming from a common source.

Let me make a brief digression. The idea that a sudden discontinuity induces the auditory system to begin a new analysis is supported by an informal observation that I made with the assistance of Pierre Abdel Ahad at McGill. We created a sequence of three tones with abrupt rises and gradual (exponential) decays. The decays were long enough that the notes overlapped one another substantially in time. When played in the forward direction, we heard a sequence of three tones with sharply defined pitches. However, when we played the sequence backward so that the notes had gradual onsets and abrupt decays, the sense of three definite and distinct pitches was lost and the pitches blurred together.

As another brief digression I would like to propose an experiment on the abruptness of spectral changes. It should be possible to set up a pattern in which a pure tone A turned continuously into a wide-band noise B by spectral widening and then back to A again. The B-A2 transition could be created by passing a noise burst into a resonator, and then feeding the output of the resonator back into itself recursively until it became a pure tone. The A1-B transition could be created by recording the A-B transition and then playing it backward. Splicing the two together would create an A1-B-A2 sequence that, if the theory is correct, would not yield illusory continuity of A.

The "Old-Plus-New" Heuristic

Earlier I argued that the continuity illusion was analogous to following a sound into a mixture of sounds and factoring it out of the mixture. This is a topic that we discussed extensively under the heading of spectral grouping. We saw that when a mixture is decomposed by the heuristics of primitive scene analysis into a continuing sound and a residual, this affects our perception of the residual as well. It appears to have properties that are determined by only the acoustic components that are left behind after the parts that match the continuing sound are taken away. This is what we called the old-plus-new heuristic. If illusory continuity is merely another example of this process of decomposing mixtures, it too should show these effects on the perception of the residual.

There is just one qualification to be added to this prediction. Later I will argue that the creation of a residual with its own properties will occur only when the mixture has been decomposed by primitive, as opposed to schema-governed processes of scene analysis. The primitive processes are conceived to be innate and not based on learned properties of the signal. Therefore, I would imagine that when an interrupting sound B is interpreted as having a part that matches A, this will give rise to a residual, with properties different from the total sound, but only in certain cases. The residual will be created whenever the decomposition has been based on primitive features of the sound, such as the feature of occupying a particular frequency region.

We have already examined two cases in which a definite residual is formed. One occurs when a soft burst of noise is alternated with another one that is much louder but has the same spectrum. We hear the softer sound continuing through the interruption, and hear the residual of the loud sound. We can show that a residual has been formed in this case because the interrupting sound seems less loud than it would be if it were presented alone; therefore some of its energy must have been allocated to the continuation of the softer sound. The second clear case of the formation of a residual occurs when a low-pitched narrow-band noise band is alternated with a wider band of noise that contains both the frequencies of the narrower band plus higher ones. We hear the residual as a series of high-pitched noise bursts accompanying the continuous lower-pitched noise. In both cases, not only is part of the weaker signal restored, but the stronger signal is heard differently. This shows that the restoration of continuity in the weaker signal is an example of the old-plus-new heuristic encountered in earlier examples of spectral decomposition.

In the cases that I have discussed so far, only the simplest characteristics of the weaker signal were used to extract it from the louder one. Yet there are other cases in which learned knowledge of the signal is involved in the extraction of the continuing signal from the noise. One example is the phenomenon of phonemic restoration, where a sentence is heard as continuing through an interrupting loud noise, despite the fact that the noise actually has replaced deleted phonetic material. Clearly in this instance the restored sound is not simply a copy of what went before the noise, but an extrapolation based on the listener's knowledge of what a speaker is likely to be saying. It is therefore based on schema-governed stream segregation and for this reason will not give rise to a distinct residual. There are other restorations clearly based on learned properties of signals. For example, it has been reported that musical scales can be restored when one note is removed and replaced by a loud noise burst.[475] We would not expect a separate residual to be formed in this case either.

Examples Examined in the Light of Theory

We have spent some time in arguing that the continuity illusion was the same process that is responsible for the decomposition of mixtures. It would be interesting now to use this approach to interpret the kinds of illusory continuity that have been observed. I will follow the order, from simple to complex, that is given in Richard Warren's presentation.[476] It appears that any sort of sound at all can be restored when a loud noise replaces a brief segment of it. We will see that in all cases, the neural stimulation that is characteristic of the restored sound can be found as part of the stimulation provided by the interrupting sound. This means that only a decomposition of this stimulation is required to restore the percept of the weaker sound.

The simplest case is what Warren refers to as "homophonic continuity."[477] This occurs when two sounds of different loudness but identical spectral content are alternated. One example that has been studied is the alternation of 300-msec bursts of 70 and 80 dB intensities of a one-octave-band burst of noise centered at 2,000 Hz. The weaker sound seems to be present continuously, continuing through the louder. Another example is obtained when two tones of the same frequency but of different intensities are alternated.[478] Again the softer one seems to continue through the louder one and to be present all the time. In these cases, it is obvious that the evidence required to create the weaker sound is embedded in the sensory stimulation arising from the stronger one.

A slightly more complex case occurs when the soft sound (A) and the louder one (B) are different in spectrum as well as in loudness. The earliest report was in 1950 by Miller and Licklider, who alternated 50-msec bursts of a pure tone and a broad-band noise, and reported that the tone seemed to be on continuously.[479] They called it the "picket fence" effect, drawing an analogy with our visual experience of seeing a scene through a picket fence. In the visual case, the scene appears to be continuous and to complete itself behind the obstructing parts of the fence. In a similar way, the tone completes itself behind the interrupting noise bursts. This effect was independently discovered by Giovanni Vicario, in Padova, Italy, who called it the "acoustic tunnel effect" by analogy with the visual tunnel effect.[480] In this visual effect, a moving body passes behind a screen (the tunnel) and, after a time delay, a second one emerges from the other side. If the speed of the two motions, the delay between them, and the positions at which they enter and exit from behind the screen are appropriate, the viewer sees one single object in continuous motion pass behind the screen and come out the other side. The difference between the picket fence arrangement and the acoustic tunnel was that in the former the interruptions were periodic while in the latter there was only one. However, in both cases, restoration was found, and since then the requirement that there be sufficient neural stimulation in the appropriate frequency region has been shown to apply in both cases.[481] This requirement is consistent with the assumption that it is spectral decomposition that restores the continuity.

In the cases that I have just mentioned the restored signal is contained in the frequency spectrum of the louder one. This, however, is not always true. In 1957, Thurlow found that continuity could be obtained when alternating a weak pure tone (A) with a louder one (B) of a different frequency.[482] He called this an auditory figure-ground effect, by analogy with the Gestalt principle whereby visual displays are organized into figure and ground, with the ground appearing to be continuous behind the figure. When tones A and B are of different frequencies, B does not contain the frequency content of tone A. However, if tone B is not of the same frequency as A its loudness must be increased to compensate for this difference in frequency. We know that the neural effects of a loud sound spread to adjacent frequency pathways in the auditory system and that this spread is greater with louder sounds. This leads to the conclusion that although B need not contain the frequencies of A, it must stimulate pathways that normally respond to A.

In the simpler forms of illusory continuity that we have just finished describing, the restoration can be thought of doing something fairly simple: continuing the perception of the sound that preceded the interruption in the exact form that it existed prior to the interruption. In the more complex form, however, the auditory experience that is restored must be thought of as a prediction from, rather than a continuation of, the interrupted sound. For example, we know that the missing parts of tonal glides can be restored. Gary Dannenbring, at McGill, created a pattern of alternately rising and falling glides.[483] We used this example in chapter 1. His stimulus pattern was shown in figure 1.15. The glides were interrupted by noise bursts either at the top and bottom vertex where the glides turned around, or else in the middle portion of each ascending and descending glide. Restoration was obtained in both cases.

We might imagine that this result suggests that the auditory system was extrapolating the glides into the noise. However, there is reason to doubt this conclusion. When the noise bursts replaced the center points of the ascending or descending parts of the pattern, the restoration was what you would expect, an illusory glide that joined the parts that were really there. However, when the noise burst was placed at the vertexes, replacing the turnaround point, the trajectory was not projected to the actual missing turnaround point. In one of Dannenbring's experiments, there was a sequence in which the noise replaced only the upper turnaround point. The listeners were presented with this as a test pattern that they were to listen to but were also given a second one that they could adjust. This adjustable pattern had a similar up-and-down gliding pattern, but no portions were missing, and the listeners could adjust how high the glide pattern swept in frequency (its lowest point was the same as that of the test pattern and its highest point had a brief steady-state portion of the same duration as the noise in the test pattern). They were asked to set the adjustable pattern so that it had the same highest frequency as the test pattern appeared to have.

The results showed that the highest frequency that the listeners heard in the test pattern was not the frequency that would have been there if the missing portions of the glides had been restored but was, instead, close to the highest frequency that *remained after the peaks were deleted.* The listeners never heard glides that appeared to have frequencies that were outside the range of the glides with which they were presented. That is why I said earlier that the restoration was based on interpolation rather than extrapolation. By following the slopes of the glides on both sides of the interruption, the listeners could logically have extrapolated what the frequency would have been at the missing vertex. However, they did not do so. Instead they simply interpolated between the frequencies before and after the noise burst. Another indication that the listeners did not extrapolate the glide trajectory into the noise was evident when Dannenbring and I were listening to some pretests of this pattern. What we did was simply to play the glide pattern over and over again, cutting away more and more sound on both sides of the peak and replacing it with noise. As we did so, the high pitch at which the glide turned around seemed to get lower and lower. If we had been extrapolating on the basis of the audible portion of the glide, this should not have happened. There was enough glide left in all cases for a successful extrapolation to the "true" vertex. A machine could have done it. Human ears, however, prefer to hear the high point dropping as more and more of the high-frequency portion of the pattern is deleted.

This result does not necessarily imply that the auditory system is incapable of measuring the slopes of glides. I have already described some of the work of Valter Ciocca, at McGill, who also studied the illusory continuity of glides through noise and found evidence that the auditory system could compare the slope of a glide that emerged from noise with what it had been when it entered the noise.[484]

Continuity of Words and Musical Scales

So far the process that carved out the missing sound from the neural pattern during the interruption could be viewed as a fairly primitive one that used general "knowledge" about the world of sound. It is reasonable to believe that this general type of knowledge could be wired into the auditory system. The examples of musical scale restoration and phonemic restoration, though, show that restorations can be based on prior knowledge of the stimulus.

Musical scale restoration works best when only a single note from an ascending or descending musical scale is replaced by a loud noise.[485] From this, you might think that all the auditory system would have to do is to simply insert a note halfway in pitch between the two notes on either side of the missing one. However, the notes of the major diatonic scale are not equally spaced on any physical scale; so this solution would not work. The pitch of the missing note must be supplied from memory.

The involvement of specific knowledge is clearest in the case of phonemic restoration in which the restored sound is a word that is appropriate to the context of the sentence. Phonemic restoration has been widely studied. The first study of perceptual restoration of sounds, done by Miller and Licklider, used lists of spoken words as well as tones. Their study compared speech that was interrupted by periodic silent gaps (about 10 times per second) to speech in which these gaps were filled by louder white noise. While the noise made the speech appear smoother and more continuous, it did not make the listener more accurate in deciding what the words had been.[486] However, other research has since found that filling the gaps by noise can actually improve the accuracy of recognition.[487] Why should this be? After all, the nervous system cannot supply information that is missing from the stimulus. It can only supply its best guess. Why could it not do that without the noise filling the gap? I have argued earlier that the noise eliminates false transitions from sound to silence and vice versa that are interfering with the recognition of the sounds.[488] In addition, because silences are interpreted as part of the speech itself and not as an added sound, the rhythmic introduction of silences is heard as a rhythm in the speech itself and disrupts the listener's perception of any natural rhythms that may have been in the original speech.[489]

The method of repeatedly interrupting a stream of speech has been used to show how the restorations depend on being able to develop a guess about the deleted sound from a consideration of the other nearby words. An experiment was done by Bashford and Warren in which three types of spoken material were used: lists of unrelated words, a magazine article being read aloud, and the same article with its words typed in the reverse order. Obviously listeners should be able to predict the missing sounds only when they could make sense of the sequence, that is, only with the second type of material. The listeners heard a continuous reading in which 50 percent of the speech was chopped out and either replaced by a silence or by a noise that was about 10 dB louder than the speech. The deleted portions were strictly alternated with the intact portions at a rate that was controlled by the listeners. At very rapid alternations, they could not tell whether any portions of the signal were missing. They were asked to slow the rate down to the fastest one at which they could tell that bits of the speech were missing. When the interruptions were filled with silence they could tell that there was missing sound even at rates of 9 or 10 interruptions per second, and the nature of the spoken material had little effect. However, it did have a strong effect when the gaps were filled with noise. With the newspaper material read in the normal order, they were unable to tell that material was missing until the rate of alternation was slowed down to about one interruption every 0.6 second. This was about twice as slow as the rate required for the other two conditions. Apparently the listeners were able to use the context to infer what the missing material was and once the acoustics told them that a restoration was justified, the inferred material was inserted into their percepts in a seamless way. I would guess that with unpredictable verbal material, only very weak hypotheses were generated and these did not give the listeners the same impression that everything was there. A later study from the same laboratory also showed that prediction of the speech sound was involved in perceived continuity. It was found that the maximum length that the noise burst may be before continuity is no longer heard depends on the rate of the speech, with slower speech tolerating longer interruptions. In slower speech, there is less verbal material to be predicted and restored.[490]

Although many of the studies have interrupted continuous speech repeatedly, others have introduced only a single interruption of a word or sentence by a loud sound. The early studies of this type were done by Warren and his colleagues at the University of Wisconsin in Milwaukee.[491] Generally the results have been the same as for periodically interrupted speech, but the method, focusing as it does on a single restoration, makes possible a more incisive analysis of the process. For example, one study that used this technique revealed the fact that while the listeners could hear both the speech material and the loud noise, they could not report accurately where in the sentence the interruption had occurred. Yet in the case where the gap was not filled with noise the listeners were able to accurately judge which speech sound had been deleted.[492]

The reader may recall that when rapid sequences of sounds are segregated into different streams, the listener is unable to accurately judge the temporal relations between elements of different streams. The perceptual loss of the position of the loud noise relative to the speech sounds indicates that the speech and the noise have been segregated into separate streams, a condition that I proposed, earlier in this chapter, as a prerequisite for stream segregation. On the other hand, when the silent gap remained the listener could correctly judge its position. Apparently the silence was not segregated from the sounds. This makes sense ecologically. Silence should not be treated as something that can interrupt a sound. There is no physical source in nature that can broadcast silences, superimposing them on top of other sounds so as to interrupt them.

The technique of looking closely at the effects of a single interruption has also revealed other effects. I have mentioned one of these already: Words that come after the interruption can affect how the listener restores the missing phoneme.[493] Another is that the restoration will be consistent with the specific nature of the neural stimulation provided by the interrupting sound (in the same way as in the nonspeech examples that we examined earlier).[494]

Integration as the Default Condition in the Auditory System

We can obtain evidence, from the illusion of continuity, that is pertinent to a question we raised earlier: Is the "default" condition in the auditory system to segregate concurrent auditory components or to integrate them? The evidence from the continuity illusion supports our earlier conclusion that integration is the default.

If we interrupt a tone by a noise burst and leave the noise on indefinitely, we may continue to hear the tone continue for some time but it will not last forever. Why is this important? In the continuity illusion, it is apparent that the segregation of the tone's frequency components from the noise can be attributed to a single factor—the presentation of the tone alone prior to the noise. There need be no properties of the spectrum of the noise itself that segregate those components. The fact that the perception of the tone gradually fades away suggests that the default condition is integration rather than segregation. When the segregating effects of the isolated presentation of the tone recede into the past, the default integration takes over.

We could have arrived at the same conclusion in a different way. If segregation were the default condition and if we listened to a simple long burst of white noise long enough, it would eventually fall apart into narrow-band frequency components. This would occur because the simultaneous onsets of all the frequency components at the onset of the noise, telling us to integrate all these components, would fade into the past and no longer be effective in opposing the default condition of segregation. We know that this result is never obtained.

Having integration as the default makes sense, since without specific evidence as to how to break down the spectrum into parts, an infinite number of subdivisions can be made, each equally plausible, with no principled way to choose among them. The conservative approach is to treat the spectrum as a unitary block except when there is specific evidence that this interpretation is wrong.

Duration of the Softer Tone

The continuity illusion, like most other organizational phenomena in audition, is not an all-or-nothing affair. Even under circumstances in which the interruption is too long to allow the softer one to go right through it, the softer sound may appear to travel a little way into the loud sound and to be heard again prior to the cessation of the interruption. This effect has been found when a 1-second sinusoidal tone was alternated with a 0.5-second burst of narrow-band noise.[495]

The length of time that a sound that is replaced by a louder one seems to continue on behind the louder one varies a great deal. Some sounds continue for quite a long time. There is an anecdote about a music teacher who gradually increased the intensity of a noise source that accompanied a recording of a musical performance and asked his class to signal when they could no longer hear the music.[496] Unbeknownst to them, when the noise became very loud, he switched off the music. Many members of the class reported that they heard the music long after it was switched off. Warren and his associates reported a laboratory observation of a case of long-lasting continuity. The softer sound was a $\frac{1}{3}$-octave band of noise centered on 1,000 Hz and the louder one was a band of pink noise extending from 500 to 2,000 Hz. They always had the same duration (D) and were alternated. However, in different conditions, D was varied so that each sound could stay on for quite a long time. All their 15 listeners heard the narrower-band noise continuing through when the loud noise lasted for several seconds, and six of them could hear it for 50 seconds.[497]

In most cases of illusory continuity (for example, with pure tones continuing through noise) the continuity lasts much less time than this, often less than a second. Perhaps the difference depends on how hard it is to imagine A inside B. Remember, first, that a long noise burst is not a sound with unvarying qualities. It is random, and we can hear different qualities of hisses, rumbles, pops, and so on, within it at different moments as we continue to listen. If A is a clear and definite sound like a pure tone, it may be hard to imagine it in the continuously varying noise. However, if A itself is a sound with constantly varying properties, we may be able to pick out some of these often enough, within a long B noise, to sustain the imagined presence of A. On this hypothesis, it should be wide-band irregular sounds that seem to continue the longest, since these offer the greatest array of different properties to search for in the louder noise. This account is consistent with the idea that the search for A inside B is not a simple process that takes place at peripheral levels of the auditory system but at higher sites in the central nervous system. Of course we already know that the higher sites are involved because they must surely be involved in phonemic restoration.

The "Roll" Effect
Another perceptual illusion related to illusory continuity was discovered by Leo van Noorden.[498] It also involves the alternation of a softer and a louder sound but is different from the continuity illusion in one basic way. There is a silent gap between the softer and louder sounds. Therefore, instead of the softer appearing to be continuous behind the louder, it appears first to go off (when it actually does), and then to come on again when the loud sound does. The effect has been found only with a very rapid alternation of two short sounds, the rate exceeding about 12.5 tones per second. Van Noorden used pure tones, A and B, that either were at the same frequency or at very close frequencies. To get the effect, you also have to make the two tones different in loudness and focus your attention on the softer tone, A.

Let us suppose that each tone is 40 msec in duration and there is a 10-msec silence between them. If the two are not very different in loudness, you hear a string of tones occurring 20 times per second. If A and B are very different in loudness, tone A disappears (through masking) and you hear only B occurring at 10 tones per second. The interesting effects occur at intermediate differences in loudness. Suppose, while alternating A and B, you start increasing the intensity of A from the point at which it is inaudible. When A first becomes audible, you will hear the continuity illusion. That is, a soft tone will be heard as being continuously present behind the 10 pulses per second of tone B. Then, as the intensity of A is raised further, you will begin to be able to hear pulsing at two different rates. If you turn your attention to the louder tone, you can hear it pulsing at 10 tones per second as before. However, if you turn your attention to the softer tone, it appears to be pulsing at twice this rate. It is as if the louder tone had split into two parts, one part contributing to the 10-Hz pulsation that you experience as a louder stream, and the other grouping with the 10-Hz pulsing of the softer tones to create a softer sequence with a 20-Hz pulse rate. This 20-Hz pulsation of the softer tone sounds like a drum roll; hence the name "roll effect."

There is another feature of the effect that is important. If you start with a condition that gives the roll effect and start to slow it down, eventually (say at rates slower than 12.5 tones per second), the extra pulses of the softer sound, A, will disappear and you will hear it pulsing at 10 Hz, the same as B. Furthermore, you can pick out either the soft tone stream or the loud tone stream by listening for one or the other.

A third basic fact about the roll effect involves the frequency separation between tones A and B. If adequate conditions for obtaining the roll effect are set up (say at an overall rate of 20 tones per second), and you begin to increase the frequency separation between A and B, the roll effect will start to disappear and both the A and the B tones will start to be heard as pulsing at their own 10-Hz rates.

The roll effect seems to be a version of the continuity effect that differs from it in that the softer tone, rather than sounding continuous, seems to be pulsing, the onsets of the pulse being determined by both the onsets of the softer tone and those of the louder one. Because part of this pulsing is derived from the onsets and offsets of the weak tone itself, this implies that its onsets and offsets are not being masked. This idea is consistent with the observation that we can convert the roll effect into the continuity illusion by merely decreasing the intensity of the weaker tone. Instead of hearing the weaker tone pulsing at a high rate, we begin to hear it as continuous. Evidently the reduction of the intensity of the softer tone allows the masking of its onsets and offsets by the louder, a condition that, as we saw earlier, is always required before illusory continuity can occur.

The roll effect seems to be a special case of the illusion of continuity in which the onsets and offsets are not completely masked but, instead, add the sensation of extra onsets and offsets. This idea of a close relation between the continuity and roll effects is supported by the observation that the two effects respond in the same way to the effects of the frequency difference between A and B and to the speed of the sequence.[499] In both effects, as the two frequencies are moved apart, the effect disappears in favor of a percept in which the A's and B's are perceived as separate sequences of distinct tones. In both cases, as well, when the frequency separation has destroyed the illusion, it can be restored if you speed up the sequence by shortening any silent gaps that may exist between the A's and B's. The effects of frequency separation have already been explained for the continuity illusion. As A moves further away from B in frequency, two things happen as a result of the decreasing overlap in the neural effects of A and B: The discontinuities of A are less masked and there is less evidence for the existence of A underneath B. Similarly, in the roll illusion, the frequency separation makes the onsets and offsets of the two tones more distinct from one another, and also decreases the evidence for A in the neural stimulation derived from B.

The effects of speed in overcoming frequency separation seem to be due to an increase in the masking of the discontinuities in the weaker tone. In the continuity illusion, we argued that silent gaps will allow a separate registration of the onsets and offsets of the two tones. Eliminating them makes the discontinuities less audible. In the roll effect, the discontinuities in the weaker tone apparently must not be too distinct either. When they are made so, either by shortening the silent gaps or by separating the frequencies, the effect breaks down and two streams of tones, pulsing at the same rate, are heard.

Under conditions in which we are completely unable to hear the discontinuities in the weaker tone, we hear it as continuous. If we hear the discontinuities as strongly segregated from those of the stronger tone, we simply hear two concurrent streams, soft and loud, pulsing at the same rate. There must be some intermediate status of our perception of the discontinuities, heard only under a very limited range of conditions, that yields the roll effect.

To summarize, the roll illusion, like the continuity effect, involves a perceptual synthesis of a second sound accompanying B. In both cases, the neural evidence required for the perceptually generated sound is actually present during the louder sound. In the roll effect, an onset of the weaker sound, accompanying the onset of the louder sound, is also added to the percept. In some sense the evidence for this onset is stolen from the evidence for the onset of the louder sound.

Comparison with Vision The role of the continuity illusion as a process of scene analysis can be clarified by examining both its similarities to, and differences with, some analogous phenomena in vision. The obvious analogy is a case in which one object obscures our view of a second one that is further away. Despite the fact that the visible parts of the further object are separated visually by parts of the nearer object they will be treated as continuous if their contours line up adequately and if they are similar enough, move in synchrony, and so on. If an object is moving, it can even be totally obscured as it passes behind another one and be experienced as continuously present to vision as long as the movement is continuous. This is the visual tunnel effect that we discussed earlier.

The similarities to audition are evident. The interrupter, whether it be object or sound, does not have the effect of dividing the interrupted thing into separate perceptual parts as long as the interrupter is seen as something distinct from the interrupted thing and if the separated parts of the interrupted thing fit together appropriately.

However, there are differences as well as similarities. They derive from the fact that most visual objects are opaque, but most auditory signals are transparent. Sounds are transparent because when two of them are active at the same time, their properties are superimposed. In vision, in the case of opaque objects, if a nearer object covers another, only the properties of the nearer one are present to the eye in visual regions in which the nearer one covers the more distant one. These differences in the effects of "covering up" lead to different requirements, in vision and audition, for perceiving the continuation of one thing behind another.

Let us designate the interrupted sound or visual surface as A, and consider it to be divided into A1 and A2 by B, the interrupting entity. We can describe the differences between vision and audition as follows. In audition, B must be louder than A, but in vision B must be closer than A. In vision there must be a direct abutment of the surfaces of the screening and screened objects. One object's surface must end exactly where the other begins and the contours of A must reach dead ends where they visually meet the outline of B. In the auditory modality, the evidence for the continuity occurs in the properties of B itself as well as in A1 and A2; B must give rise to a set of neural properties that contains those of the missing part of A. In vision, on the other hand, if the objects are opaque, there is no hint of the properties of A in the visual region occupied by B.

In the case of partially transparent screens in vision, in addition to the "bounding edge" requirement there is the same requirement as in the auditory case for continuing evidence for the screened object. However, in the visual case, the continuing evidence for the screened object tells the viewer not only about its own continued existence but about the degree of transparency of the screen. In sound, transparency is not a property on which sounds vary (they are all equally transparent); so the continuing evidence for the screened sound does not specify any property of the screening sound.

Contralateral Induction

Earlier in this chapter, two phenomena were introduced as a pair—illusory continuity and contralateral induction. They were grouped together because they both involved taking neural activity that was stimulated by one auditory event and reallocating it so that it helped to define a second one. In examining the continuity illusion, we saw that some of the neural evidence provided by the louder sound was interpreted as belonging to the softer event.

Contralateral induction has been briefly introduced earlier. It involves the following: If we play a sound (let us call it the target sound) to one ear, it will be heard on that side of the listener's body. However, if we play a loud sound, different in quality from the first, to the other ear at the same time (we can call this the inducing sound), the target sound will be heard as closer to the midline of the listener's body. The inducing sound will have induced an erroneous perception of the location of the target sound. In the example that I gave earlier, the target sound was a pure tone and the inducing sound was a noise burst. The explanation that I will offer, after presenting the evidence, is that if the neural activity stimulated by the inducing sound contains components that match those activated by the target sound, they will be allocated to the target sound. Since the target sound will now be defined by sounds arriving at both ears, it will be perceived as nearer to the center of the body than it was when unaccompanied by the inducer.

Why should we think of contralateral induction as a phenomenon worth mentioning? Aren't all cases of hearing with the two ears examples of contralateral induction? For example, if we played a pure tone of 1,000 Hz to the left ear of a listener, it would be heard on the left. Now if we played to the opposite ear, as the inducing tone, a pure tone of the same frequency, amplitude, and phase as the first, the target sound would now be pulled over to the midline of the listener's body. This simply follows from what we know about the interaural comparisons that take place in the normal localization of sound. Our special interest in contralateral induction seems to derive from the fact that the inducing sound is not the same as the target. If that is the case, how about the following example? We present a 500-Hz tone to the left ear and it is heard on the left. Then we play a mixture of a 500-Hz tone and an 1,100-Hz tone to the right ear. Depending on the intensity and phase of the 500-Hz component in the inducing tone, the 500-Hz sound will be pulled to the right (that is, toward the center of the body). At the same, the 1,100-Hz component will be heard as an isolated tone on the right. Again we are not surprised, because it follows from our belief that the auditory system can compare the neural activity at the two ears and find matches for individual frequency components. It need not treat the whole sound at each ear as a unit.

The novelty in contralateral induction is that there is no *specific* component or components at the second ear that have been inserted by the experimenter to match the target. Instead the match is due to some partial equivalence in neural activity at the two ears resulting from two sounds that we do not normally consider to have matching components. The extraction of some of the neural evidence activated by the inducing tone so as to match the target tone involves a decomposition of that evidence that would not have taken place if the inducer had not occurred at the same time as the target. For this reason, while we cannot really think of this matching as an illusion, we can be interested in it as a scene-analysis process.

Early reports of this effect used stimuli in which speech was pulled to the center by noise played to the second ear or in which a tone was pulled by another tone of a different frequency or by a noise.[500] Similar induction effects have been been created by presenting a tone as the target sound over a single headphone and presenting an inducing tone or noise over loudspeakers.[501] In 1976, Warren and Bashford named the phenomenon "contralateral induction" and developed a method for measuring it.[502] Their innovation was to repeatedly swap the positions of the target and inducing sounds. For a half second, the target sound would be in the left ear and the inducing sound in the right; then for the next half second, the positions of the two would be reversed. In this manner, every half second, the positions would switch. It would be expected that the images of both the target sound and the inducing sound should oscillate back and forth between the two sides of the body since the signals on which they were based did so. However, this occurred only under circumstances where the induction failed. If the induction succeeded, only the inducing tone would seem to move. The target tone would seem to be on continuously and to stay near the center of the listener's body, or perhaps move only a little way to either side of the midline.

The experiment allowed the listeners to adjust the intensity of the target tone while the sequence of switches continued. The amount of contralateral induction depended on the relative intensity of the two sounds. If the target sound was substantially softer than the inducing sound, the induction occurred and the target sound seemed to remain in a somewhat vague position near the middle of the listener's body. However, when it was increased in loudness, a threshold point was reached at which the induction failed and the target sound seemed to oscillate from side to side, just as it would have if the inducing sound had not been present. In short, the induction required the intensity of the target to be low as compared with the inducer. The listeners were asked to adjust the intensity of the target to the maximum level at which it still did not appear to switch from side to side.

This method was used with targets that were pure tones ranging from 200 to 8,000 Hz and inducers that were noise bands filtered in different ways. The results are shown in figure 3.30. The experiment found that the induction seemed to work via the frequency components in the noise that matched the tone. For example, when the frequencies near that of the tone were filtered out of the noise (band reject condition), the intensity of the tone had to be turned down in order for induction to occur. On the other hand, if the frequencies

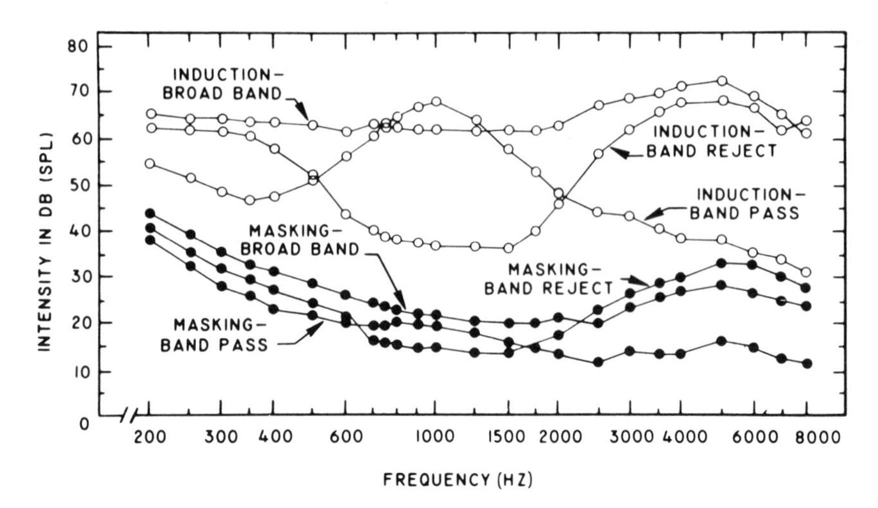

Figure 3.30
Upper intensity limit for contralateral induction of monaural tones presented with one of three contralateral 80-dB noises filtered as labeled on the graph (open circles). Detection thresholds in the presence of each kind of noise are shown as well (solid circles) (Warren and Bashford, 1976).

near that of the tone were retained but more distant ones were filtered out (induction band pass condition), the target could be turned up to a high level and still not overcome induction.

These effects resemble the continuity illusion in a number of ways. Let us adopt a terminology that helps to make this point. Earlier I referred to the tone that is heard as continuous in the continuity illusion as A but I used the word target when referring to the continuous tone in Warren and Bashford's version of contralateral induction. Let us call it A as well. Similarly, let us use the term B for both the loud interrupting sound in the continuity illusion and the loud inducing sound in contralateral induction.

The first similarity is that B must be much louder than A in both cases. Second, B must stimulate neural activity that is normally associated with A. Let us see what these two facts imply. In both cases, the auditory system is picking out from the loud sound, B, evidence that A is mixed in with B, and is finding this evidence because the neural response to A is a subset of the response to B. Therefore, both effects can be thought of as an attempt to deal with mixtures. Earlier the argument was made that one effect of the relative loudness of B was to mask the onsets and offsets of A. In Warren and Bashford's version of contralateral induction, there may be no need for this. There are two phases to the cycle that they used, one in which A is on the left and B on the right and one in which their positions are reversed. If the neural activity that is required to specify the existence of A (the softer sound) is received in both ears in both phases, then there are no onsets and offsets in the A evidence in either ear. Therefore the masking of discontinuities is not relevant in this case. This is just as well, because the masking of a sound by one in the opposite ear is not very effective.

There is a second similarity. The continuity illusion is actually playing a role in Warren and Bashford's contralateral induction experiment. Consider what is happening at one ear. It receives a sequence of sounds, A–B–A–B–. . . , that is exactly the stimulus for the continuity illusion: an alternation of a weak sound with a stronger sound that evokes a neural response that includes the response to the weaker as a subset. One would imagine, then, that there are two influences that are helping to segregate the A activity that is embedded in the B activity: the fact that A precedes and follows B as in the continuity illusion, and the fact that A is occurring simultaneously in the opposite ear. The twofold influence on the segregation of the A component of B should stabilize the perception of A as centrally located.

One observation about the perception of A in this experiment was that its perceived location, although generally at the center of the body, was not experienced as precisely located in space. Why should this be true if the neural activity derived from A was being matched by activity derived from B? Should this not have given a definite location? Remember that B was a noise burst. The particular frequency components that were present and the phase of each varied randomly from moment to moment. Therefore, although in the long term, the spectrum of B had the components that were needed to match A, these components existed with random phases and amplitudes. Since the relative amplitudes and phases of corresponding frequency components at the two ears are what tell the listener the location of a sound, this irregularity of interaural relations would specify not a single location but a distribution of locations, having a central position that is given by the average of all the matches. This argument, however, would seem to imply a much wider dispersion in the location of A than we actually experience in contralateral induction. It is possible that the dispersion is limited by a tendency of the auditory system to average across rapid changes in the estimates of the spatial location of a sound. We will see evidence for such sequential averaging in an experiment by Steiger and Bregman.

A pure tone of one frequency can serve as the inducing sound when another pure tone, of a different frequency but much softer, is used as a target. This follows from the fact that the neural effects of a loud pure tone will spread out to adjacent neural pathways that are responsible for the detection of other frequencies. Therefore the auditory system will be able to detect sites of neural activity stimulated by the inducer that match sites on the target side. Of course, other sites on the contralateral side will also be active, but these will be rejected as the effects of a different sound.

In one of their conditions, Warren and Bashford used, as the target (A), a burst of noise and, as the inducer (B), a noise that was 1 dB louder than the target and had the same spectral characteristics. Being an independent sample of noise, however, it was uncorrelated with the target. The listener experienced this condition as containing two sounds, a continuous noise diffusely localized around the medial plane of the body and a second very faint noise oscillating back and forth and always localized at the ear that was receiving the louder sound. This effect reminds us of the homophonic continuity effect that we discussed under the topic of illusory continuity. We should, therefore, call the present effect "homophonic contralateral induction." In both effects the operation of the old-plus-new heuristic is displayed quite clearly. B is treated as a mixture of A and another sound, X, and X is heard as a separate sound that has the energy that would be required if X and A were to add up to give the total energy present in B. In the present case, since B is only 1 dB louder than A, the residual, X, has very little energy and is heard as a very faint sound.

The decomposition of the inducing sound (B) to derive a part that matches A is not just determined by the fact that A and B are present at the same time. This is fortunate; although there are times, in a natural listening environment, when the segregation should be done, there are others when it should not. It should be done in the following case: A is a sound emanating from a source that is straight ahead of us and therefore provides inputs to both ears whereas B comes from a source very near our right ear, so that the B energy mainly comes to our right ear. Let us further suppose that B has a spectrum that includes that of A, so that A is not distinguishable in the right-ear signal taken alone. In this case, since A and B are actually two environmental sounds, the A stimulation should be extracted from the B stimulation. Otherwise we would think that the A energy is present only at our left ear and that it comes, therefore, from a source close to that ear.

In the next example, the A sound should *not* be extracted from the B sound: A really does come from a source near our left ear and B comes from a source near our right, and although there are frequency components in the right ear input that are the correct frequencies to have come from A, their source is actually not A. It just happens that B contains frequencies that match A. How can the auditory system tell which of these two real-world situations it is facing? The solution is to use the history of the sounds to decide.

As we have seen earlier in our discussion of the effects of stream organization on the localization of sounds, the perceived location of a sound does not just depend on the classical binaural cues. Continuity over time also plays a role in localization. Here is how we might use it in the present example. If A occurred alone close to our left ear and then, while it was continuing, B occurred at our right ear, a good strategy would be to continue to hear A at our left, despite the match of some of B's neural activity to A's. In other words we should use sequential grouping rules to group the energy arriving at the A ear so as to form a stream with what came earlier at that location rather than with what is happening at the B ear. In this way sequential grouping could correct the cases where binaural relations were deceptive.

Howard Steiger and I did an experiment to show that listeners could indeed make use of this sequential grouping strategy to prevent inappropriate contralateral induction.[503] The stimulus pattern included (in one time "frame") a pair of sounds, presented dichotically (one to each ear) over headphones as in the typical experiment on contralateral induction. The pair consisted of a pure tone at 1,024 Hz (the target) sent to the left headphone and a more intense one-octave noise band (the inducer), centered at 1,024 Hz, sent to the right headphone. The difference between this experiment and the typical one was that this frame alternated with a second frame in which there was only a single monaural sound, presented on the left. This monaural tone was called the captor tone because we expected it to capture the target tone out from within the dichotic tone so that it was no longer delateralized by the inducing noise. In other words, this sound was expected to tell the auditory system not to extract A from B's neural activity because A was merely a continuation of an earlier monaural event. The captor was always a pure tone which could vary in frequency.

The monaural and dichotic sounds were presented in a repeating sequence: the monaural sound for 100 msec, silence for 30 msec, dichotic sound for 100 msec, and then silence for 232 msec, the whole sequence repeated over and over. The listeners were asked to judge the left-right position of the target tone (and of the captor tone, in conditions in which it was present) by writing down a number from 1, representing the leftmost extreme, to 12 representing the rightmost.

In some conditions the captor tone was omitted from the cycle. When this happened, the listeners judged the target as being near the midline of their bodies; the induction occurred normally. However, when the left-positioned captor tone preceded the dichotic tone, the perceived position of the target depended on the frequency of the target. When the frequency of the captor matched that of the target it partially prevented the latter from being pulled over to the middle by contralateral induction. It was as if the auditory system had decided that the target was a reoccurrence of the captor and therefore preferred that its location not be too different in the two occurrences. However, as the frequency of the captor was made to differ more and more from the target's, it had less and less of an effect in preventing induction. We should not be surprised at this fact. We already have seen, in our discussions of sequential stream segregation, that the strength of sequential grouping of two tones depends directly on how close their frequencies are.

We have seen, then, how sequential stream segregation competes with the across-ear relations to determine how the sound received at each ear is to contribute to localization. Later we will see that the competition can occur even when the contralateral sound is exactly identical to the target. In some cases, the competition is so extreme that the result is duplex perception.[504]

It is easy to set up simple demonstrations in which the scene-analysis process treats the signals at the two ears as defining separate sounds rather than allowing one to induce displacement of the other. In one example, we begin with a case of contralateral induction. We play a continuous soft tone of 1,000 Hz at the left ear and a continuous white noise at the other. As we slowly raise the intensity of the noise, we hear the tone appear to move toward the center of the body. We stop raising the intensity when the tone is fairly well centered (and before we do damage to our right ear). Now without changing the intensity of the noise, we change it from a continuous to a pulsing sound (switching abruptly between 0.3 second on and 0.7 second off on each cycle). Now the tone remains on the left of the body. The scene-analysis system has decided, despite the fact that it is receiving bilaterally matched 1,000-Hz stimulation when the noise is on, that the left-ear part of it really belongs to a continuing tone at the left. In other words, it has used the old-plus-new heuristic. Part of the evidence it has used is that the onsets and offsets on the right are not matched by any changes at the left.

A second example is even more dramatic. Instead of using a white noise as the inducing tone at the right ear, we use a tone of 1,000 Hz, exactly matching the one at the left in phase. When it is continuous, as we slowly raise it in intensity from zero, we hear a 1,000-Hz tone move toward the center of the body (and even past it if the right-ear tone becomes louder that the one on the left). Now leaving the right-ear tone equally as loud as the left one, we set it to pulsing just as we did with the noise. (However, the proportion of "on" time to the whole pulse cycle must be less in this example than for the noise of the previous example.) Again the scene-analysis system decides that the balanced and phase-matched stimulation received, when the right-ear tone is on, really belongs to two sounds, one at the right and one at the left.

The astute reader will have noticed that we have already encountered an effect where sequential stream segregation and binaural relations were set into competition. When we examined the effects of spatial location on sequential grouping, we discussed an experiment, carried out by Deutsch, in which listeners were asked to identify a short melody whose notes alternated between the ears. This was difficult, presumably because of stream segregation by location. The task became easier when a constant drone tone was presented to the ear that was contralateral to the ear that was getting the current tone from the melody.[505] I interpreted this as occurring because the equalization of intensity at the two ears reduced the cues for localization of the melody's tones and accordingly reduced their tendency to form separate streams. Yet Deutsch's drone was not at the same frequency as the tone in the melody. We have interpreted Warren and Bashford's research as showing that the delateralization occurs only to the extent that the contralateral sound stimulates neural pathways that correspond in frequency to those activated by the target sound. However, if we reexamine their data, shown in figure 3.30, we see that with the filtered-noise inducers, even in frequency regions that lacked frequencies that matched the target tone, contralateral induction was obtained, albeit at low target intensities. It seems possible that although the exact matching of frequencies plays a role in allowing part of the contralateral neural activity to be used to specify the location of a target, it is not essential. This lack of frequency specificity as exemplified by Deutsch's drone experiment may be due to a spread of neural activation across frequency regions at some low level of the auditory system or to some effects of contralateral energy that are not frequency specific and occur higher up in the system.

Perhaps we can summarize the contralateral induction effect as a laboratory phenomenon that, like the illusion of continuity, shows us how powerful the auditory system is in finding frequency components that it is looking for even when this requires it to extract components out of mixtures. In the continuity illusion it is looking for frequency information that matches a previous signal, and in contralateral induction it is looking for a match to information received in the other ear. In both cases, it is able to carve what it needs out of the mixture, leaving the residual behind to be heard as a separate sound.

Our account of the phenomena of illusory continuity and contralateral induction has an important relation to the phenomenon of masking. Richard Warren has proposed that restoration will occur under conditions in which the interrupting or contralateral noise is loud enough to have masked the expected signal.[506] It has also been argued by many researchers that illusory continuity depends on the existence, during the interruption, of sufficient stimulation at the frequency of the expected sound to serve as evidence that the sound is really there. However, the two accounts are hard to distinguish because if a masker is to mask a target, then, in general, the masker must have about as much energy in the critical band (or bands) occupied by the target as the target itself has. An important point to remember is that in the stimulus for these two effects the evidence for the missing signal is not missing. It is simply part of a larger mixture of sound.

It is interesting to speculate about how this point relates to all other cases of masking. Auditory theory has usually considered masking to be a situation in which the masker has obliterated all neural evidence for the target. However, this may not be the best way to look at it. The better way may be to say that the evidence for the existence for the target has not been wiped out, but merely hidden. Let me offer an analogy. If you wanted to hide a red spot on a white canvas, the best way to do it would be to paint the rest of the canvas red too. The red spot would not be gone but the outline that formerly defined it against the white canvas would no longer exist. You can think of a masker as something that fills in the background in such a way that there is no longer any spectral shape defined against the white canvas of silence. The signal is still there, but it is camouflaged. Masking, then, is the loss of individuality of the neural consequences of the target sound, because there is no way to segregate it from the effects of the louder tone. If you introduce a strong basis for segregation, the signal can be heard as present. There are many ways that this could be done: You could expose the auditory system to earlier and later parts of the hidden sound as in the continuity illusion. You could expose it to sound in the other ear that matched part of the spectrum, as in contralateral induction. You could expose the auditory system to a prior copy of the hidden sound as in the experiment by Bregman and Pinker.[507] Or, you could give the hidden sound a different location than the masker, or a different pitch, or different amplitude or frequency modulation. In other words, you could employ any of the factors that increase spectral segregation. It is for this reason that (as Rudolf Rasch has suggested about musical performances) masking in natural listening situations is less of a hindrance than laboratory studies would suggest.[508]

Summary

This chapter began with a demonstration that the neural evidence that results from an incoming spectrum is inherently ambiguous with respect to environmental sounds. Does the evidence tell us that there was only one sound with a complex spectrum or a number of sounds with simpler spectra? The rest of the chapter described a number of heuristics that the auditory system uses to decide how the evidence should be decomposed.

One of the main rules that the system uses is that if the neural activity evoked by an earlier sound resembles a subset of the current neural activity, that subset should be interpreted as due to the continuation of the earlier sound. Then the difference between the subset and the whole neural activity should be treated as a residual-evidence pool. This is called the "old-plus-new heuristic." The residual may be heard as a sound in its own right or be further broken down. This heuristic was seen as responsible for many well-known examples from the research literature, including the ability to hear out a component of a complex tone, or to hear a softer sound continue through a louder one that masks it. It allows us to resist the masking effects of loud sounds upon weaker ones in mixtures (for example, in musical performances). Later we shall see how some rules of counterpoint in polyphonic music harness this heuristic for an artistic use.

The memory that the old-plus-new heuristic can use is fairly complex and is not just a record of a steady-state spectrum. For example, it can be used to extract a gliding pure tone that was heard earlier from a gliding complex spectrum that is currently being received. Its manner of activity is not simply that of a filter, because it makes some of its decisions after the complex mixture has gone by. For example, the continuity illusion is enhanced if the softer sound appears again at the termination of the louder one.

The relative intensity of various partials in a sound also affects the partitioning. A partial that is much louder than its nearby frequency neighbors is more likely to be heard as a separate sound. The auditory system also appears to treat as more "normal" a spectrum in which the higher partials are less intense. When this pattern is violated, the higher harmonics are easier to extract. Both these phenomena may be interpretable via long-known facts about the spectral spread of masking.

We have also seen that the harmonic relations in a spectrum are important. Partials that are in a common harmonic series are more likely to be treated as the spectrum of a single sound. This also holds when more than one harmonic series is present in the same spectrum; the spectrum is partitioned into more than one subset by means of the harmonicity principle. The separate perception of the spectral components of each subset is suppressed in favor of global qualities of the subset. The harmonicity principle in auditory scene analysis seems to be related to the pitch-extraction mechanism, but not to be equivalent to it.

Heuristics based on the Gestalt principle of "common fate" seem to be used as well. When different partials in the spectrum undergo the same change at the same time, they are bound together into a common perceptual unit and segregated from partials whose time-varying behavior is different. This principle applies both to changes in intensity and changes in frequency.

Spatial factors are also used. It appears that the auditory system is capable of estimating a separate spatial origin for different frequency bands in the spectrum and then grouping those bands into sets on the basis of a common spatial origin. Spatial origin is a strong cue for partitioning the spectrum but not an overwhelming one. It can be overcome by other factors. Indeed, even the spatial estimates themselves can be altered when in conflict with other cues; for example, other cues may tell the auditory system that two parts of the spectrum should be treated as parts of the same sound even though they yield different spatial estimates.

The cues for spectral grouping compete and cooperate until the scene-analysis system converges on the best estimate of how many sounds there are, where they are, and what their global properties are.

Chapter 4

Schema-Based Segregation and Integration

In chapters 2 and 3, we have studied the two types of primitive grouping, sequential and spectral, that help to solve the problem of auditory scene analysis. We have treated them as if they were fully explainable as automatic innate processes that act without conscious control. However, this cannot be the whole story about the organization of auditory signals. In many cases, hearing a signal in a mixture of sounds depends on conscious effort and prior learning.

In the present chapter, I would like to consider the contribution made by attention and knowledge in the perceptual analysis of signals. I will not be able to provide much of an account of the internal machinery of knowledge-based analysis. Little relevant research has been done. My main emphasis will be on trying to strip away the contribution of knowledge and attention in auditory scene analysis so that the workings of the primitive process can be seen more clearly.

The nineteenth-century physicist Hermann Helmholtz distinguished between analytic and synthetic listening to complex tones. Using analytic listening, he could hear out a partial of the tone. With a more natural, synthetic attitude he would hear the holistic properties of the tone. He argued that when listening for the partials of a complex tone, "the attention of the observer has generally to be drawn to the phenomenon he has to observe . . . until he knows precisely what to look for."[509] I do not agree that segregation is the product of attention while integration is the result of inattention. However, it does seem true that attention and learning can play a role when we extract some of the components of mixtures for the purposes of pattern analysis. The goal of this chapter will be to determine whether there is any basis for distinguishing between two classes of processes in auditory scene analysis—one automatic and unlearned and the other involving learning and attention.

I have argued earlier that recognizing the timbre of a signal when it is mixed with other ones depends on scene analysis. The auditory system must group all the components of that signal into the same perceptual stream. We saw that this was made possible by acoustic factors that bound the group of components together and at the same time distinguished them from the other ones that were present. However, J. O. Nordmark has described a number of situations in which the timbres of signals embedded in mixtures can be recognized despite the fact that there is no simple acoustic basis for segregating the partials of that signal from the mixture.[510] He has mentioned, as examples, mixtures of amplitude-modulated tones, square waves and filtered pulse trains, in which the pitch and intensity are held constant and there are no spectral or common fate cues to distinguish their partials from one another. The timbre of individual signals in the mixture is discernible. While Nordmark did not supply enough detail in his report to allow us to determine whether there was any acoustic basis for hearing out the component timbres, his examples are not the only ones that lead us to the suspicion that factors other than the ones surveyed so far are at play.

Other examples occur with speech sounds. Mixtures of two synthetic vowels can be created in which there are no spectral features that we know of that can group the harmonics or the formants into those that define the individual vowels. I have created the pair "ee" and "ah" in the laboratory. Both had the same onset and offset times, the same pitch at each moment of time, and the same loudness contour. Yet I was able to clearly hear the two individual vowels. More formal experiments using this sort of stimulus have been done by Michaël Scheffers, with similar results.[511] Scheffers fed either glottal pulses or white noise into a series of filters to create spoken or whispered vowels, respectively. In both cases, his listeners performed remarkably well in recognizing them. In the recognition test, since they had to choose the two vowels that were present in the mixture from a set of eight possibilities, the likelihood of guessing by chance was only 3.6 percent. Yet both vowels were correctly identified 45 percent of the time when the two were spoken and 26 percent of the time when they were both whispered.

There have been other cases where the auditory system has succeeded in putting spectral regions together for purposes of speech recognition despite the fact that there were acoustic cues telling it to segregate them. For example, James Cutting has synthesized syllables such as "da" by means of two formants and sent the different formants to different ears of the listener.[512] When the two formants had different fundamental frequencies, the listener heard two sounds. This occurred, presumably, because both the different spatial locations and the different fundamental frequencies indicated the existence of two separate sounds. Just the same, they heard the correct syllable (from among "ba", "da", and "ga"), an accomplishment that required them to integrate information from their two ears. Their recognition succeeded despite, rather than with the aid of, acoustic cues for grouping. A host of other researchers have found essentially the same effect—phonetic integration in the face of acoustic cues that favor the segregation of acoustic components.[513]

There is another case of auditory organization for which primitive segregation is not a sufficient explanation. The perceptual restoration of missing material in the continuity illusion does not lend itself to being explained by a scene analysis based on acoustic cues. For example, in phonemic restorations the restored sounds tend to be words that fit meaningfully into the sentence. Clearly the selection of the appropriate components from the noise burst must be based on something other than the immediately present sound because the restored material is not identical to what came either before or after the noise. It must depend not just on the sounds that are present, but the listeners' knowledge of their language.

Nature of Primitive and Schema-Based Organization

These examples all point to the fact that scene analysis can use a more sophisticated knowledge of the signal than what I have described earlier. I am therefore going to propose that there are two different processes in the construction of auditory representations, one that I will call primitive scene analysis and the other schema-driven construction of descriptions. The use of the word primitive is meant to suggest that the process is simpler, probably innate, and driven by the incoming acoustic data. The schema-driven (hypothesis-driven) process is presumed to involve the activation of stored knowledge of familiar patterns or schemas in the acoustic environment and of a search for confirming stimulation in the auditory input. This distinction is very much like the common distinction in information-processing theory between bottom-up and top-down processing.

Both processes are concerned with the decomposition of mixtures of information so that the right combination of information can enter into the description of an environmental sound. However, the primitive mechanism does this without reference to the recognition of specific familiar sounds, whereas the sophisticated ones select the right components as a part of the process of matching stored schemas for familiar environmental sounds to the incoming data.

Properties That May Distinguish the Two Systems

The approach that I plan to take is to assume that the primitive segregation process employs neither voluntary attention nor past learning. Therefore I will call the process schema-driven if it uses either of these capacities. In my definition of the schema-driven process, I may be accused of conflating two different processes. It is possible that the use of voluntary attention and the use of prior learning are not the same thing at all. However, I have two reasons for grouping them. First is, I am trying to strip away everything that is not part of the primitive process, to see whether some "pure" properties of the primitive process can be isolated. I feel that it is necessary to do so because there exist, in the research on perceptual segregation, some contradictions that can be resolved only by assuming that there is more than one process at work. Second, another way of describing voluntary attention is to call it programmed attention, or attention that is under the control of an inner process that is trying to find some particular pattern in our sensory input. Since I look at schemas as control systems that deal with patterns in the environment, it is natural to think of them as the ones that govern voluntary attention.

We know that both attention and prior learning can affect the process of extracting signals from mixtures. Let us consider these in turn and see how they function.

The concept of attention encompasses two distinct facts about the human mind. The first is that there are processes that can select part of the currently available sensory information for more detailed processing. Let me give an example: When you are asked to pay attention to sensations arising from your left foot, you will suddenly become aware of a set of experiences that were previously not part of your consciousness. This selective role of attention has been studied in audition mainly in a situation where a listener is trying to pay attention to one spoken message in the presence of a second one.[514] Many factors have been shown to affect the ability to do this. Among these are the acoustic differences between the two messages. For example, if the messages are spoken on very different pitches, as happens when one is spoken by a man and the other by a woman, it is easier for the listener to attend to one of these and not be interfered with by the other. Other differences, such as in location, can assist this segregation. The key factor that makes us think of this process as attention is that the listener is *trying* to hear one of the two messages. This notion of trying is central to the definition of attention.

Why, then, did I argue earlier that these experiments tell us about primitive perceptual grouping? Why are they not really experiments on attention? After all, the listener is usually trying to accomplish the task of hearing a subset of sounds as a separable pattern in a mixture. This is a difficult question. When we use a person as a subject in an experiment, the successful completion of the task involves a large constellation of capacities, including the ability to hear the signal, to understand the instructions, to sit still, to attend to the signals, to make some sort of judgment, to turn the judgment into words or numbers, and so on. If this is so, how do we know which process has been affected when the experimenter has manipulated some variable in an experiment? The answer is that we do not ever really know for sure, but we can make reasonable guesses based on common sense and on our prior understanding of these processes. For example, if it is easier to distinguish two voices when they are at different pitches, it is hard to see how the difference in pitches might affect the ability of the listener to sit still in the chair; we are not familiar with any mechanism whereby this ability could be affected by such a difference. On the other hand, if we attribute the influence of acoustic differences to their effect on our ability to pay attention to messages, this makes sense to us for two reasons: First, it agrees with our own experience outside the laboratory, and second, we can make up a plausible mechanistic story about how it could occur.

However it is more difficult to know whether to attribute the result of an experiment to attentional processes or to primitive processes that act independently of attention, because we do not have a very good understanding of either class of process. Therefore we cannot decide whether the effects of different stimulus variables are more consistent with what we know about one or the other. Perhaps one clue to the nature of the effect is the effect of *trying*. If trying harder makes a task possible, we will attribute the improvement to attention because this effect is consistent with our beliefs about attention. Unfortunately, we have no such touchstone for the primitive scene-analysis process. Suppose we found that some variable affected segregation independently of how hard a listener was trying to achieve segregation; are we to attribute this effect to a property of attention or to that of a preattentive process?

Apart from the role of effort there are other signs by which we recognize the presence of attention. One is that we have a more detailed awareness of things that are the objects of attention than of things that are not. This has led to descriptions of attention as a process that employs more of the mental resources of the listener than would otherwise be allocated to analyzing a sound.

Another sign is that we have trouble paying attention to too many things at the same time. This has led to the argument that there is a limited pool of resources that attention can make use of.

A third observation is that as we become highly practiced in a task, it comes to require less attention. For example, a person who is learning to drive feels swamped by all the things that must be attended to at once. However after a number of years, the driving process can become so automatic that the driver can drive while lost in thought about other matters. This has led to the view that attention is involved in the novel coordination of a number of separate skills. Although each skill, in itself, might already be highly practiced, the coordination is not; attention is no longer required when that coordination becomes a highly practiced skill in its own right. This view of attention implies that we cannot tell whether attention is or is not involved in a task by simply knowing what the task is. We have to know what resources are being employed by the person who is doing it.

We are left with a view in which attention is seen as an effortful process that coordinates existing schemas in a new task and in which the coordinating process (presumably some newly assembled schema) can control only a limited set of mental resources. The intimate connection between attention and learned skills (schemas) is one reason that I want to bundle attention and learning in a common package and distinguish them, as a pair, from primitive segregation.

An example of the role of attention in scene analysis is the intense concentration that it sometimes takes to be a good subject in an experiment in which you have to hear out one component of a mixture in which the acoustic conditions favor fusion. You must fix the sound of what you are listening for strongly in your mind and then try to hear it in the mixture. I find that in such cases if my attention is distracted by even a slight extraneous noise, I am no longer sure whether I can hear the target sound or not. I also find that I get better at it with practice. This improvement is not the mark of an automatic innate process.

The role of learning in the perceptual organization of sounds is easily demonstrated. In one condition of an unpublished experiment that I did many years ago, the listeners had to listen for a simple tune that covered a wide range of frequencies, and ignore other notes that were present in the same frequency range as the tune.[515] Under some circumstances the notes of the target tune were made much louder than the distracting tones. In this condition the listeners could hear the tune. But when the tones of the tune were of the same loudness as the distractors, most listeners could no longer hear the tune. In the course of running this experiment, I undoubtedly heard the tune thousands of times. Eventually I found that I could hear the tune even when it was no louder than the distractors. It was not as if I could avoid hearing the distractors as part of the stream, but I knew which tones were melody and which were distractors (since the distractors always were the same and situated in the same positions in the melody) and I could somehow mentally bracket the distractors and hear the tune. Jay Dowling also found that a familiar tune could be more easily extracted from interfering sounds than an unfamiliar one.[516] The role of learning can also be seen in the continuity illusion. For example, it is possible to obtain illusory continuity of a tune through an interrupting noise. However, this effect is stronger when the tune is more familiar.[517]

The characterization that I have given to primitive and schema-driven scene analysis has distinguished them in terms of the psychological mechanisms that are presumed to underlie them. It is also necessary to distinguish them by their effects on the process of stream formation.

First let us consider the primitive process that has been the subject of the preceding chapters. Its role is to employ heuristics that have been formed in the phylogenetic evolution of our sensory systems and to put together auditory features that have probably come from the same source. As clues to the correct grouping of features, it uses acoustic properties that tend to be valid in a wide variety of auditory environments, without regard for the specific meaning of the sounds. That is, the clues are the same whether we are listening to music, to speech, or to cars moving past us on the street. They include such things as frequency proximity, spectral similarity, correlations of changes in acoustic properties. These clues are the ones that form the basis for the so-called Gestalt principles of grouping. The Gestalt psychologists, mostly describing visual perception, argued that these principles were the expression of innate processes. They used two forms of evidence to support this argument. The first was the fact that even newborn animals showed these forms of perceptual organization. The second was the observation that, even in adult human beings, camouflage that was based on these basic principles of grouping could prevent us from recognizing even highly familiar shapes.

The schema-based process, on the other hand, makes use of knowledge about specific domains of experience. Before going into details, I want to clarify my use of the word "schema." This word is used by cognitive psychologists to refer to some control system in the human brain that is sensitive to some frequently occurring pattern, either in the environment, in ourselves, or in how the two interact. Many psychologists have speculated on the form in which the knowledge about such regularities is packaged in the brain, and the functional, and maybe even anatomical, structure that holds this knowledge in the brain has been given different names, such as cognitive structure, scheme, schema, frame, and ideal.[518] They all describe a computing structure that controls how we deal with one particular regularity in our environment. Such structures can be either very concrete in nature, such as the coordination of perception and movement patterns that is required to tie shoelaces, or extremely abstract, such as the coordination of grammatical and lexical patterns required to form a sentence. Often a convenient way to label these schemes is by the environmental regularity that they deal with. For example, the Swiss psychologist Jean Piaget studied the schema for causality.

When we perceptually analyze our auditory input, we can make use of schemas about recurring patterns in the world of sound. These patterns vary enormously in their degree of complexity and abstraction. My knowledge about the tonal glide that forms the song of the cardinal is both simple and concrete. Knowledge about the properties of a familiar word is more abstract because the word can appear in quite different acoustic forms when it is spoken by different persons or with different intonation patterns or speeds. Knowledge about a grammatical form (such as the passive) is even more abstract, because it is defined not in direct acoustic terms, and not even in terms of patterns of specific words, but in terms of the patterns formed by classes of words (nouns, verbs, auxiliaries, and the like). Yet patterns at all these different levels of abstractness are thought to be dealt with by schemas in the human mind.

Often the sound that we are listening to contains more than one pattern. If each pattern activates a schema, there will be a combination or pattern of schemas active at that time. Sometimes the pattern of activated schemas will form a larger pattern that the perceiver has experienced in the past. In this case the pattern of activity of schemes can evoke a higher-order schema. This occurs, for example, when individual items are recognized as different types of words, such as nouns or verbs, and their arrangement is recognized as a sentence.

There is considerable argument in psychology about whether any schemas can be innate (the nativism-empiricism controversy). We know that a vast number of schemas are learned. As examples we can cite the coordinations involved in all motor skills, the particular patterns used by our own language to convey different meanings, and the social patterns viewed as polite in our culture. The fact that these are learned is not disputed because they vary across individuals and cultures. The argument in psychology is mostly concerned with the complexity of the schemas that can be innate. Not even the most extreme nativists would deny that many schemas can be learned because they are aware of examples like the ones I have given. Similarly, no empiricist will deny that certain things are innate, such as learning ability itself or the tendency to extract or to group certain sensory inputs. The argument lies in how complex the innate schemas are in the human being. For example, are there ready-made ones that exist for the human face, for the sexual act, or for the basic structure of human language?

For the purposes of this book, it would not be necessary to decide such issues if we thought that schemas, whether learned or innate, worked in similar ways. I think that they do. One strong reason for thinking so is that they must collaborate smoothly.

Among the jobs that a schema must perform is to apply itself appropriately to a situation. This is what Piaget referred to as assimilation. Computer scientists refer to it as pattern recognition. Each schema must have its own particular methods of evaluating a sensory input to determine whether the pattern that it cares about is there. In the domain of sound, this evaluation has an inherent time dimension: The evaluation processes look for temporal patterns.

Schemas are scene-analysis processes by their very nature. Why? Because it is in the nature of a schema to analyze the sensory data for evidence for the presence of some pattern. Since it knows what the temporal patterning of the evidence should be, it can use this knowledge to extract the pattern from a mixture. If we grant that this is so, we are tempted to ask why we should have primitive scene analysis processes at all. We might argue that schema-driven scene analysis is more powerful because as we become more and more familiar with a pattern and build a more detailed schema for it, we can do better and better in extracting it from mixtures.

We can answer this challenge by remembering that schemas can only do the scene-analysis job on familiar patterns. Yet if we are to learn about patterns in the first place, so as to make them familiar by forming schemas for them, we need some primitive processes that are capable of extracting them from their acoustic contexts. Although the primitive processes probably always make a useful contribution to scene analysis, it is in the realm of unfamiliar patterns that they are absolutely essential.

Still, schema-driven analysis of acoustic input can be very powerful. One reason for this is that patterns extend over time. If four or five elements of a temporally unfolding pattern have already been detected (such as the first several notes of the national anthem), the schema enters a state in which it is primed to detect later elements. In this musical example it would find a note (and the listener would experience it) even if it were entirely obliterated by noise. We have already examined this phenomenon and others like it in our discussion of the continuity illusion. Notice that I have referred to this technique as powerful and not hallucinatory. The power resides in this: Because the evidence for the national anthem is of such high acoustic quality prior to and after the obliterating noise, the weakening of the criteria so that we may accept the obliterated sound as the missing note is quite well justified. By gathering evidence over an extended period of time, we are protected from damage to the quality of evidence at particular moments.

Some very simple examples of schema-based segregation can be found in the research of Charles S. Watson and his colleagues at the Central Institute for the Deaf in St. Louis. Suppose we play a sequence of several tones to a listener twice, but change the frequency of one of the tones (call it the target) on the second presentation, and test for the listener's accuracy in detecting the change. It is usually found that the accuracy can be up to 10 times worse than it would have been if the target and its repetition had been the only tones presented.[519] Apparently the tone becomes embedded in the sequence, and its own particular properties do not draw the attention of the listener. However, the accuracy goes up dramatically if the same sequence is used over and over again and the same position in the pattern is designated as the target on every trial, instead of using a new sequence and target position on each trial.[520] It also becomes easier when the target is marked out by increasing its intensity by 15 dB relative to the rest of the tones,[521] or by making its duration longer than that of its neighbors.[522] In all these cases, the listener is able to come to treat the relevant tone as different from the rest of the sequence. Yet the segregation is difficult, not usable by every listener, and benefits from training. I would argue that this segregation is based on a different mechanism than the one that would segregate it if it were in a wholly different frequency range from its neighbors. The latter mechanism produces a large and automatic perceptual isolation.[523] I believe that it is schema-governed attention that allows us to focus on the slightly longer or louder tone. A schema that describes the sequence can be learned and then used to select the target. This, I believe, is the mechanism for the analytic listening that Helmholtz described in 1859.

Even when schema-based recognition processes become strong, as when an adult listens for a familiar pattern, the primitive processes still play a role. If a schema-based integration could become entirely independent of primitive scene analysis, then camouflage would be impossible. Yet it happens all the time. We can make it hard for a listener to hear a familiar sound (such as a tune) by embedding it in a pattern of tones (even softer ones) in the same frequency region.

If the activation of a schema were designed to be independent of primitive scene analysis, it would have to occur even when the supporting evidence was not packaged in a single object. Schemas would therefore be very susceptible to errors resulting from inappropriate grouping. Parts of two people's voices could form a word that neither had spoken.

Our best guess at the present time is that the human brain has some method of combining the benefits provided by the two systems. We do not know whether we give more weight to the grouping decisions provided by one system or the other. Probably this varies with circumstances. It may be that the more practiced a schema-governed process is, the more weight is given to it in relation to the primitive scene-analysis process. This may be why speech perception can do two things that seem to violate the assumption that primitive scene analysis is dominant. One is that it can hear speech sounds even when it has to combine information across primitive groupings of sense data to do so. This achievement has been referred to as duplex perception and it will be the topic of discussion in chapter 7. Another thing that it can do is to hear two vowels out of a mixture even when there is no primitive acoustic basis for segregating the spectrum.

How Do We Know They Should Be Distinguished?

We have given some reasons for wanting to distinguish between a primitive and a schema-driven process, but that is not enough. We have to see whether there is empirical evidence for this distinction.

The first thing to mention is that there is confirmation that the primitive processes are unlearned. In chapter 1 we discussed the research of Laurent Demany who showed that infants aged $1\frac{1}{2}$ to $3\frac{1}{2}$ months of age showed evidence of auditory stream segregation.[524] Unfortunately, this is the only study that I know of on this important topic, probably because it is very difficult to do research with young infants. We can only hope that more studies will be forthcoming.

We are justified in distinguishing the two forms of scene analysis if we can distinguish two different patterns of causality in the evidence. One technique for doing this is to hypothesize that there are two different causal nexes and see whether this assumption allows observations to fall into simpler patterns.

In looking for a primitive and a schema-governed mechanism, we must remember that when we set a human being a task, the response that we observe is the result of the activity of the whole complex human being. When we do experiments, we have to hope that the variance attributable to the factor that we manipulate is due to its effects on only one mechanism, in this case, the primitive or the schema-based system for auditory scene analysis.

This approach is made difficult by the fact that the same sorts of acoustic properties that serve to segregate sounds through Gestalt-like processes of organization can also be the bases for recognizing these sounds. Therefore they appear in schemas. We can have a stored representation of a sequence of sounds that encodes the temporal pattern of its elements and their relative pitches; otherwise we would not be able to remember music. Our memory complex for changes in timbre over time is what enables us to distinguish one instrument from another. Yet we know that these same factors, pitch, timing, and timbre form the basis for primitive grouping as well. This makes it very hard to distinguish primitive from schema-based segregation. We can, nevertheless, make the attempt.

As an example let us look at the perceptual segregation of rapidly alternating high and low tones. Two factors that affect the degree of segregation are the frequency separation between the high and low tones and the rate of the sequence. However, Van Noorden has showed that the rates and frequency separations at which one gets segregation depend on the intention of the listener.[525] His findings were shown in figure 2.2 of chapter 2. The upper curve, the "temporal coherence boundary," showed the boundary between integration and segregation when the listener was trying to achieve integration. The lower curve, the "fission boundary" showed what happened when the listener was trying to segregate the streams. We saw that if the intention of the listener was to hear two distinct streams the frequency separation that was required was only about three or four semitones. Furthermore, this requirement was almost independent of the rate of the tones. This contrasted strongly with the case in which the listener was trying to hold the sequence together. Here not only did the separation have to be greater, but it depended strongly on the rate of the tones.

The dependence of the boundary on the frequency separation and rate of the tones in one case and not in the other is a clue that two different separation processes were at work. Why should frequency separation not affect the fission boundary? Remember that in this task the listener was trying to hear out one of the streams from the mixture and that furthermore the stream was very simple, the periodic repetition of a single tone. This meant that the listener could store a mental description of the sound and its periodicity and try to match that stored description to the sequence. This was obviously a case of schema-based attention, and it was very successful in analyzing the sequence. Since it did not depend on the relation between the target tones and the other ones, it was not sensitive to the frequency/time spacing between these two subsets. The lower limit of three or four semitones for the fission boundary, beyond which the listener could no longer pick up the tones of one stream without the intrusion of the others, may represent some physiological limitation on the sharpness with which our auditory attention can be tuned. It may not be a coincidence that the value of three or four semitones is about the same as the width of the critical band, the region within which a tone played simultaneously with another one will mask it.[526]

On the other hand, the temporal coherence boundary, where the listeners are trying to hold the sequence together, shows a strong effect of the proximity of the high and low tones to one another. A trade-off of frequency and temporal separations is evident; the faster the sequence, the less the listeners can tolerate a frequency separation between the tones. The organizational process opposes the conscious intentions of the listeners to deploy their attention in a certain way. Surely the up-and-down oscillation pattern is not an unfamiliar one to the listeners. Therefore a schema exists for that pattern. But the primitive organization into two streams opposes its application to the sense data.

A property that might be useful in distinguishing the two types of segregation is symmetry. When we cause a sequence of sounds to be segregated by increasing the frequency separation of subsets of tones, this improves the listener's ability to listen to either the higher or the lower sounds. The effect is symmetrical for high and low tones. This may be the mark of primitive segregation. When the segregation is by timbre, the same symmetry is found. If the difference in the brightness of the timbre of two interleaved sequences of tones is increased, both sequences become easier to isolate. If their spatial separation is increased, again both become easier to hear as separate sequences.

However, I do not think that the same thing occurs when the segregation is based on a schema for a familiar sound. As we increase the difference in familiarity between two sound patterns that are mixed together by making ourselves more and more familiar with just one of them, although we may become increasingly more skillful at pulling the familiar one out of the mixture, this does not, in itself make it easier to hear the unfamiliar one as a coherent sequence. Dowling did experiments in which the notes of two melodies were interleaved.[527] Some of them looked at the effects of pre-familiarizing his listeners with an arbitrary sequence of sounds that subsequently was mixed with another sequence. The listeners were able to detect a familiar sequence more easily than an unfamiliar one. However, in one experiment he prefamiliarized the listeners not with the target sequence itself but with another one that was to serve as the interfering background. After familiarizing his listeners with this background sequence, he interleaved another one with it and asked his listeners which of two possible sequences the new one had been. He found that familiarity with the background did not assist his subjects in isolating the target melody.

Here is another informal observation. In the course of running an experiment, I was obliged to listen to a melody that was interleaved with distractors in the same frequency range. Naive subjects could not hear the melody, but after hundreds of exposures I reached a point where I could. The distractors in this sequence never varied, so I became very familiar with them, too. The familiarity with the overall sequence of tones, melody tones interleaved with distractors, allowed me to hear out a part of it as the melody. The remaining tones were heard as adornments to the melody.

My ability to use my familiarity with the background contrasts with Dowling's results. In Dowling's case the listeners were prefamiliarized with the background taken alone, whereas I became familiar with target tones and background at once. I do not think I was segregating them in any primitive perceptual way, but was coming to deal with a primitively coherent sequence by using a schema to divide it into two parts. Dowling's listeners could not do this because they had a prior schema for only the background tones that they had been practiced on, not for the two parts together. We can conclude that having a schema for a background pattern does not help us to integrate a target pattern. A schema helps only if it contains either the target pattern itself, or both the target and background sounds.

It can be argued that the role of the primitive segregation processes is to *partition* the input, while the job of the schema-governed process is to *select* an array of data that meets certain criteria.

The existing experimental results on stream segregation by loudness differences may not be due to primitive segregation. They may be the result of a deliberate attempt on the part of subjects to focus their attention on the less intense or more intense set of sounds. I would remind the reader of my earlier discussion of research on loudness-based streaming in chapter 2. The conclusion was that the results of the research did not show the kind of symmetry of segregation that I am using as the hallmark of primitive segregation. This does not mean, of course, that primitive streaming by loudness does not exist, only that it has not been demonstrated yet.

The factor of speed may also help to distinguish the two kinds of constraints on stream segregation. In many, if not all, cases of primitive grouping, speed serves to increase the segregation based on acoustic factors such as frequency separation. On the other hand, when the segregation is based on the recognition of a familiar subsequence, the segregation may worsen with speed. This may happen because speeding up a familiar pattern distorts it or because the process of directing one's attention towards the sequence of components in turn may be less effective at higher rates.

The effects of speed on schema-based integration of sequences might be found if we were to do an experiment that used a task that has been employed by Diana Deutsch to study the recognition of melodies. Deutsch did some experiments in which simple familiar folk tunes were distorted by randomly deciding for each tone, independently, whether to move it up exactly one octave, move it down an octave, or leave it where it was.[528] Moving a tone by an octave keeps the chroma (note name) the same. That is, a C-sharp is still a C-sharp. However, scattering the tones into three octaves destroys the size of the changes in pitch height (roughly speaking, the change in frequency of the fundamentals of successive tones). It appears that pitch height relations are more fundamental than chroma relations in creating the perceptual organization that allows us to recognize a tune. Therefore the listeners could not recognize the distorted tunes. However, if they were told in advance what the tune was, they could hear it. Under these conditions it appeared to Deutsch that the listeners were mentally generating the tone sequence, abstracting the chroma of each note in turn, and verifying it against the corresponding tone in the auditory input.

My expectations about this task would be as follows: Recognition could be accomplished only at fairly slow rates of presentation, and it would not be achievable at six tones per second (whereas the original tune would undoubtedly be recognizable at this rate). At higher rates, recognition would be impossible for two reasons. The first is that primitive grouping by pitch height would increase at higher speeds, creating compelling patterns that were unfamiliar. Second, the complex control of attention and of testing hypotheses against the input would be too slow to keep up. The task that we have just discussed is a rather complex one, undoubtedly more intricate than the task of recognizing a familiar pattern of sounds in a mixture. Just the same, it would indicate that complex processes of directing ones attention to the individual elements of a sequence may be rate limited.

Another possible experiment would use a sequence in which a familiar tune was interleaved with distractor tones in the same frequency region. Assuming that at a low rate the listener could detect the familiar sequence in the mixture, we would expect that speeding up the sequence would cause primitive grouping by frequency to destroy the tune as a perceptual unit.

Because studies comparing the effects of speed on primitive and knowledge-based partitioning of signals have not yet been done, our expectations can only be conjectural.

I think that there is another difference between primitive and schema-governed segregation. Their temporal scope is different. The acoustic relations to which the schema-based processes are sensitive can span longer time intervals than those that the primitive processes look at. For example, in the phenomenon of phonemic restoration, when a sound in the middle of a word is obliterated by a noise, the word that the listener hears is one that fits appropriately into the framework of discussion and the current topic of discussion. This could depend on words that had arrived much earlier in the discussion. We already know that the subject of the immediate sentence can affect the restoration of words. Take, for example, the sentence "The *eel was on the ———", where the asterisk represents a noise burst and the blank represents the word that is in the last position. If the final word is "orange" the listeners tend to hear "*eel" as "peel", if the final word is "axle" they are more disposed to hear "wheel", and if the final word is "table" they favor "meal".[529]

Here the critical last word was very close in time to the target word (perhaps a second later). However, it is possible that it might be effective at a much greater distance if it preceded the critical word. Imagine a series of sentence such as this: "I have had a lot of trouble with the right rear wheel of my car. It seems to be very loose. It worried me a lot, so since I had a free day last Sunday I decided to do something about it. I looked at the *eel very carefully." Here, the topic of discussion is set up two sentences before the one with the missing phoneme, perhaps 5 or 6 seconds earlier. Yet I would expect to find a preference for restoring "wheel".

The effects of most acoustic variables on primitive scene analysis are much more local. If we alternate a sequence of high and low tones more slowly than two tones per second, no compelling segregation by frequency will occur. A 500-msec separation between tones of the same class seems to place them beyond the range of primitive interaction. There seems to be one exception to this time limit for primitive grouping. If you alternate high and low tone repeatedly at perhaps 10 tones per second, the strength of segregation builds up over a period of at least 4 seconds and perhaps longer. If the rate of alternation is slower, the preference for segregation can take as much as a minute to build up.[530] However, in this case, the hundredth high tone is not grouping with the first one but with the ninety-ninth and the hundred-and-first. The long exposure biases this grouping, but the grouping is still between nearby sounds.

In summary, we hope to be able to distinguish between primitive and schema-based scene analysis by the role of effort, the need for learning, the symmetry of the segregation, the interaction with speed, the time span over which they group material, and, in general, the different causal pattern observed in different tasks. With luck, the distinction between the two types of mechanisms will help us to understand some apparently discrepant results in the research literature.

Does Learning Affect Streaming?

Schemas can be acquired through learning. Therefore schema-driven scene analysis should be affected by learning. What evidence is there in the research literature about the effects of practice on our ability to integrate a stream of sounds and segregate it from a mixture?

Let us return to the research of Dowling on pairs of interleaved melodies.[531] We have seen that the subjects could not make use of their knowledge of the background melody to segregate the foreground melody if the two were in the same frequency range. But they could benefit from even verbal naming of the target melody itself. In one condition, he gave them the name of the melody and then played the mixture several times to them. Recognition was successful after an average of three to four presentations. Their ability to use the melody's name shows that familiarity can produce segregation in the absence of primitive segregation, but the fact that they required a number of exposures to the mixture even after they were told the name and that they detected the tune only with considerable effort suggests that the segregation process was not automatic, but that a schema-driven attentional process was involved.

Do Regular Patterns Form More Coherent Streams?

Cognitive psychologists think of schemas as descriptions of regular properties of the environment. It is natural, therefore, to ask whether regular auditory patterns form more coherent streams than irregular ones do. If the process that is responsible for the formation of streams is one that makes predictions about the properties of the next sound, regular patterns should afford better prediction, and therefore better integration.

Jones' Rhythmic Theory of Attention The role of certain kinds of schemas on the organization of sounds has been described by

Jones.[532] I have already briefly described the theory in chapter 2. Her research has concerned itself with the recognition and memorization of short melodic and rhythmic patterns. It has given evidence for the fact that human attention can be deployed in a rhythmic manner. According to Jones' "rhythmic theory" of attention, as we listen to a pattern of sounds, the process of attention is capable of anticipating the position of the next sound on the time dimension, the pitch dimension, and others as well. It therefore can prepare itself to pick up the next sound and connect it with the preceding parts of the sequence. A predictable sequence allows its components to be caught in the net of attention, while unpredictable elements may be lost.

Rhythmic attention, as described by Jones, is restricted to the use of certain kinds of rules; they describe the incoming sequence as a hierarchy of embedded units. A hierarchy, in the sense meant here, is formed when units serve as the parts of larger units and the latter, in turn, serve as the components of yet larger units. In her theory, any two sequential units that are grouped together to form higher-order units must have a particular type of relationship to one another. The later unit must be formed from the earlier one by repeating it after imposing a relatively simple transformation on it. This type of relationship is often found in music where repetition with variation is a common architectural principle. The theory describes rules for the encoding of pitch patterns and rhythmic patterns by rules of this type.

It is assumed that the attentional system tries to apply the rules on the fly to an incoming signal. If the rules do not apply, either because the sequence is irregular or because suitable rules have not yet been formed, some of the sounds may be lost from attention and not incorporated in the ongoing stream.

Jones offers an explanation of why a sequence of tones alternating between two frequency regions will tend to form separate streams if the alternation is rapid but not if it is slower. Her explanation, like that of van Noorden's,[533] depends on the assumption that attention cannot shift too rapidly along a sensory dimension. I have discussed the limitations of this explanation in chapter 2.

This theory sees auditory streaming as the result of the operation of a temporally extended process of attention. My own preference is to distinguish the schema-governed attentional process from primitive processes of grouping. In this dichotomy I see Jones' theory as weighted heavily toward the schema-driven process. It does not distinguish primitive from schema-driven bases for organization.

The theory has led to a number of studies, the results of which seem to suggest that a rule-based account of this type (which does not distinguish between primitive Gestalt-like grouping and grouping based on learned patterns) can be used to explain auditory organization. There are certain considerations that argue that the apparent success in explaining sequential integration by means of hierarchical pattern schemas cannot be taken at face value.

One is that the results of the experiments are often explained equally well by a primitive grouping mechanism as by a schema-governed attentional one. The reason for this is that the aspect of Jones' theory that predicts stream segregation, deriving from the idea that attention cannot shift too rapidly from one value of an auditory dimension to another, generally makes the same predictions about segregation that a Gestalt-like grouping account, based on proximities in frequency and time, would do.

In some experiments done by Jones and her collaborators, there are observed groupings of sounds that cannot be explained by her theory but are explainable by primitive organizational processes. For example, in one study by Jones, Maser, and Kidd, a subset of four middle-range pitches was found to form their own group despite the fact that the formal sequence-describing rules did not describe any particularly strong relation between them.[534]

There is another reason for not accepting the results at face value. While the theory proposes that it is perceptual integration that is assisted by the schemas, it has actually been tested most often with memory tasks, which are very sensitive to the activity of schemas. Therefore the results can be interpreted as effects on memory, not on perception. The listeners have been asked either to recall what they have heard (using some sort of written notation) or to compare two sequences that have been presented one after the other.[535] Cognitive psychologists have frequently described memorizing as the use of preexisting schemas to incorporate the study material or as forming new schemas that are appropriate to the material. Schemas, then, are thought to be intimately involved in the memorizing process. Therefore when a theory proposes that it is explaining a perceptual phenomenon, such as auditory streaming, by means of a process that involves the coding of the stimulus through pattern rules, it has to be careful not to use a task that is heavily dependent on memory or on conscious strategies for finding patterns by which the material can be more easily remembered. It is possible to find ways of minimizing the contribution of memory, for example by allowing the subjects to make their decisions about the stimulus while it is still present, by making the decision task as simple and overlearned as possible, or by using some measure other than description of the pattern (for example, asking how many streams there are or what the rhythm is).

Although the theory describes the use that attention makes of rhythmic schemas of the repetition-with-variation type, it does not describe temporal schemas of any other type. Yet many of the auditory patterns that we must deal with in daily life are not repetitious (or rhythmic) in this way. The theory seems to have been created in order to deal with the type of patterns found in music in which there are hierarchies formed out of discrete tones. I do not see how it could deal with the irregular time patterns that are found in many natural situations, as, for example, in the unique sound of an automobile braking to a stop or the modulating sound of a train whistle, or the long drawn out intonation pattern of the word "sure" that communicates irony. Yet we track such sounds over time and form schemas that describe their temporal properties.

A final point is that the theory does not address spectral organizational processes at all. Even if the theory is intended to account only for sequential integration, we know from the evidence that I presented earlier that there is a strong competition between spectral grouping and sequential grouping and therefore the accounts cannot be divorced.

In assessing the role of schemas in auditory scene analysis, however, it would not be wise to focus on the more specific statements of a particular theory. Instead it would be better to address some general assertions that any theory of Jones' type is likely to produce. First let me say what I think this type is. The class of theory that is involved is one that assumes that the organization of an auditory sequence into streams is not a consequence of the primitive process that I have described in earlier chapters, but is one that employs sequence-prediction rules. Certain statements follow from this assumption:

1. Learning will affect stream segregation.
2. Regular patterns will be found to form more coherent streams.
3. Streams are created by attention and by the search for regular patterns in the stimulus sequence.

The following sections will attempt to assess the truth of these assertions in the light of the available experimental evidence.

Any theory that bases the perceptual integration of a series of tones on the capacity of an attentional process to anticipate the position of the next tone in frequency and in time would seem to predict that a random sequence of tones (unpredictable by definition) can never be coherent since no rule can predict the properties of the next tone. However, I have listened to sequences of tones that occurred at a regular temporal spacing but at random frequencies. As these sequences are speeded up, groups of tones that happen to be near one another in frequency seem to pop out of the sequence and form a brief stream of their own. Since the sequence is random, these accidentally occurring groupings come and go in different frequency regions.

Van Noorden did a related experiment that bears on this issue.[536] He wanted to see whether the average frequency difference between successive tones would still predict the perceptual coherence of a sequence of tones when the observer did not know what the next tone would be. He constructed sequences in the following manner. Two decisions were made before the sequence began, a frequency for the initial tone (I) and an average frequency difference (D) between successive tones for that particular sequence. The first tone was at frequency I. Every subsequent tone was either higher or lower than its antecedent by either the frequency separation D itself, or by D plus or minus one semitone. The choice between higher or lower and between the three possible frequency separations was made at random. This kind of sequence can be called a "random walk" and if completely random can walk right outside the frequency range that the experimenter is interested in. So an upper and lower frequency boundary was imposed and when the randomly chosen frequency increment for the next tone would have moved it outside one of these boundaries, another one of the possible frequency changes was randomly chosen instead. On each run of the experiment, the average absolute deviation in semitones from one tone to the next was set at a particular value. The listeners adjusted the speed of the sequence to the fastest at which a single coherent stream could still be heard with no tones detaching themselves into a separate stream.

Van Noorden reported that at a very fast speed (20 tones per second) and at a small average frequency separation (one semitone), the sequence sounded like a ripply continuous tone because under these circumstances the separation is below the fission boundary. If the same sequence was played more slowly (about 80 msec per tone) the separate tones were heard but the sequence was still continuous in quality. At the other extreme, if the average frequency separation was 25 semitones, and the speed was high, no temporal coherence could be heard except for a few tones here and there that were not temporally adjacent but happened to be close in frequency to one another. Over a set of sequences with different frequency separations, as the average separation became larger, the speed of the sequence had to be slowed down more to maintain the experience of a single coherent sequence. The results closely resembled those obtained in experiments where high and low tones alternated in a regular manner.

When these results were plotted on top of results from the regular sequences, treating the average frequency separation in this experiment as analogous to the fixed frequency separation of the other experiments, the curves were quite similar. Van Noorden concluded that "previous knowledge of what tones are coming does not influence the temporal coherence boundary, and that listening for temporal coherence is probably not a question of moving the attentional 'filter' to and fro actively but of following the tone sequence passively." It is this passive process that I have called primitive scene analysis, and contrasted with schema-directed scene analysis.

Van Noorden's experiment does not prove that a prediction-forming process is *never* involved in auditory stream segregation. It merely shows that frequency separation is sufficient in itself to promote segregation without the participation of a rule-extrapolating process. Van Noorden's failure to find a difference between experiments that did and did not permit prediction of the next tone may derive from the particular nature of the tone sequences.

Does the Auditory System Track and Project Trajectories?

Let us now go on to ask whether there is any evidence that regular patterns are easier to integrate than irregular patterns and, if they are, what this implies about the importance of prediction in perceptual integration and segregation.

The first kind of regular pattern that we should look at is the regular trajectory. This is a smoothly ascending or descending change in frequency (or pitch) with time. In my discussion I will equate frequency with pitch, because in the experiments that have been done with trajectories, the two were never varied independently. In some cases, as well as being smooth, the change has been quantitatively regular: Each step in pitch was the same size on some plausible scale, such as the raw frequency scale, or the diatonic or the chromatic musical scale. If the trajectory were drawn on a graph whose dimensions were time and the chosen scale, it would always look like a straight line. Sometimes the trajectory was formed from a sequence of steady tones and sometimes it was a continuous glide.

According to any sequence-prediction theory of perceptual integration, an acoustic sequence of this type should be easily heard as an integrated whole. This follows because the rule that generates them is exceedingly simple. However, the coherence of simple trajectories might be expected on other grounds as well. The Gestalt approach to perceptual organization would explain the coherence of a tonal trajectory through the concept of good continuation. In visual displays, straight lines and smooth curves have this property.

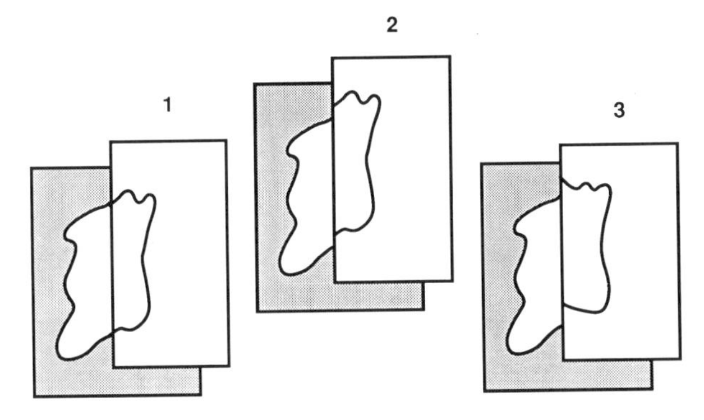

Figure 4.1
Left: an irregular figure that continues smoothly through a vertical line and is perceived as a unitary form. Middle: a discontinuity is created by displacing the right side vertically at the line, but the slopes of the lines on the two sides of the division are equal. Right: the slopes are not the same on the two sides of the line.

A visual example of the effects of smoothness and discontinuity on perceptual integration is depicted in figure 4.1. Panel 1 shows an irregular figure that passes smoothly through a vertical line that separates two surfaces; the continuity causes the figure to be seen as unitary, overcoming the fact that the two halves are drawn on backgrounds that make them appear to be on separate planes. In panel 2, the right side is displaced upward and the figure no longer looks unitary; its halves seem to lie on the separate planes. In panel 3, the contours on the two sides of the vertical line are made not to match in slope as they do in panel 2. This further dissociates the two halves. Despite the fact that there is no simple rule that can describe the shape of the curved figure, the continuity still has its effects.

In contrast with sequence-predicting theories, the Gestalt approach would not see this preference for smooth change as necessarily due to a process that tried to generate a rule to describe the whole shape. Instead, the preference would be based on the smoothness of transition of each part of the form to the next.

We can see that the integration of smoothly changing auditory figures, such as a smoothly ascending sequence, might be expected both from a sequence-prediction mechanism or from a primitive integration mechanism that preferred sequences that had low levels of discontinuity.

Evidence That the System Does Not Project Trajectories I will start reviewing the research on the subject of trajectories by describing some

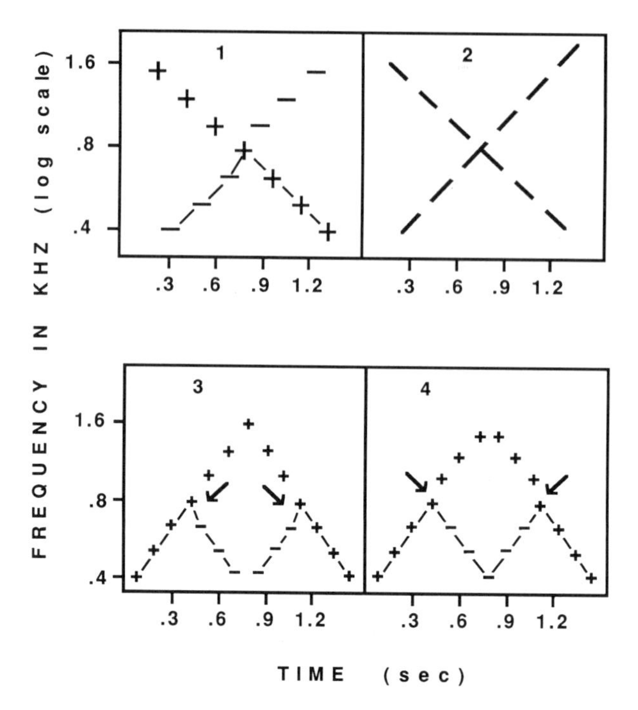

Figure 4.2
Competition between segregation by frequency region (the broken connecting lines) and by the following of a trajectory (pluses). 1: the crossing of an ascending and a descending pattern of tones. 2: crossing trajectories in which the individual tones are short glides and overlap in time. 3: the rhythm favors the trajectory. 4: the rhythm favors segregation by frequency range. (Adapted from Tougas and Bregman 1985a.)

experiments that failed to find evidence that the auditory system extrapolates trajectories.

A very common observation is that when an ascending trajectory of tones intersects a descending trajectory, as in part 1 of figure 4.2, it is very difficult to hear either the ascending or the descending trajectory crossing the other one. If you focus on the descending one, you tend to follow it down to the intersection, and then your attention is forced to shift to the second half of the ascending glide so that what you hear is the V-pattern that is formed by the higher tones. Alternatively you may hear the two lower halves as a pattern that ascends to the point of intersection and then descends again. The auditory system prefers to group sequences that are in the same frequency region than to follow a trajectory. The effect is compelling and is almost impossible to overcome by a voluntary attempt to follow one of the trajectories. A large number of experiments have studied how we perceive such crossing patterns and they have all come up with the same result.[537] The effect has been exploited in Diana Deutsch's scale illusion in which the tendency to group tones that stay in the same region can produce a failure to group all those tones that fall on a common trajectory or that come to the same ear.[538]

An experiment by Yves Tougas and myself tried in a number of ways to get the listeners to hear the trajectories as crossing.[539] One way was by the use of rhythm. Parts 3 and 4 of figure 4.2 show a simplified pattern: The pluses represent a rising and falling trajectory and the minuses show other tones that could group by frequency with the first part of the trajectory. When they did, the listeners heard two streams, one consisting of the tones joined by the short lines and the other consisting of the remaining pluses. These streams united tones that were in nonoverlapping frequency regions. The difference between parts 3 and 4 is that in the former, if the listeners group the tones that form the long trajectory (the pluses), they are selecting tones that are equally spaced in time and have a regular rhythm. However, when they group tones that are in the same frequency region (those joined by the lines), they are selecting tones that have an uneven rhythm. The arrows point to intertone intervals that are half the duration of the others. It might be imagined that the factor of rhythmic regularity would favor the integration of the trajectory, but it did not. In stimuli resembling those of part 4, the time intervals were rearranged so that homogeneity of rhythm favored grouping by frequency region, yet this made no difference. The stimuli of parts 3 and 4 were heard in the same way. The overwhelming organization was by frequency proximity with either rhythm.

Tougas and I tried to improve the likelihood of the formation of the trajectory-based organization by means of two other factors, shown in part 2 of the figure. We converted the tones into short glides that were aligned on the trajectory. We also introduced a temporal overlap of the tones of the ascending and descending glides so that if the auditory system were to group tones that were in the same frequency region, it would have to either backtrack in time, skip an interval of time, or break the unity of a tone. Neither of these manipulations of the pattern succeeded in causing the trajectory to be favored. There was only one manipulation that caused the grouping to be based on the trajectory. We took a pattern similar to the one in part 1 of the figure and enriched the timbre of the ascending pattern of tones. This succeeded in causing the listeners to hear two trajectories, one rising and the other falling. However, it is misleading to interpret these results as revealing a trajectory-based organization. Since we know from other research that tones that are different in timbre may form separate streams, there is no need in this experiment to attribute any influence at all to the trajectory.[540]

Another failure to find a trajectory effect in auditory grouping was obtained in an experiment done by Howard Steiger and myself.[541] This experiment was reported earlier in this volume and its stimuli illustrated in figure 2.17 of chapter 2. It employed a repeating cycle in which a pure-tone glide (A), acting as a captor, alternated with a complex glide BC containing two pure-tone glide components, B and C. It was possible for the captor to capture one of these components (B) out of the complex glide into a sequential stream consisting of two successive glides, A and B. This tended to happen when A and B had similar slopes and center frequencies. In one condition, A and B were aligned on a common trajectory. According to any theory that says that sequential grouping was the result of a prediction process, this arrangement should increase the likelihood that A would capture B, since the position of the beginning of C is predictable from the slope of A. However, no such increase was found.

This result is incompatible with what Valter Ciocca and I found when we studied the illusory continuity of glides behind a loud noise burst.[542] As reported in a later section of this chapter, the Ciocca-Bregman experiment found that the perceptual restoration of the missing portion of the glide was better when the glide segments that entered and exited from the noise were aligned on a common trajectory. However, there were many differences between the two experiments and it is hard to say which of them was critical. The tasks were different, capturing a component from a complex glide versus restoring a glide in noise. The durations of the glides were different, those in the perceptual restoration experiment being much longer (500 msec versus 130 msec). It is tempting to think that the fact that the experiment with the longer glides showed the trajectory effect means that it takes some time for the auditory system to measure the slope of a glide. However, we should recall that in the capturing experiment, despite the shortness of its glides, there was evidence that the auditory system could measure slopes. The capturing of B by A was best when they both had the same slope. Therefore we know that the slopes were registered. However it did not help to have the glides aligned on a common trajectory.

Another difference between the experiments was that the time interval between the end of the first glide and the onset of the second was different, only 20 msec in the capturing experiment and from 150 to 200 msec in the perceptual restoration experiment. Yet, contrary to what might be expected under the assumption that it is harder to extrapolate across a longer interval, it was the experiment with the longer interval that showed the trajectory effect. Maybe the longer intervals, together with the longer glides, permitted the listeners to use a schema-governed attentional process to group the sounds.

A final difference is that the interval was silent in one case and filled by noise in the other. Perhaps noise and silence give different instructions to the auditory system. Perhaps a silence tells it that the sound is now ended and that it can now terminate the following of the glide's slope, whereas a loud noise onset does not cause it to terminate the following of the slope in this way. With so many differences, we cannot really say why the results were different, but their difference casts doubt on the unqualified assertion that a primitive grouping process tracks trajectories.

Another failure to find a trajectory-extrapolating effect occurred in an experiment by Gary Dannenbring at McGill.[543] His stimuli were illustrated in figure 1.15 of chapter 1. A connected sequence of alternately rising and falling glides (linear on a frequency-by-time scale) was presented. In one condition, the peaks (where the ascending glide turned into a descending glide) were replaced by bursts of white noise. The listeners perceptually restored this turnaround point and experienced the glides as alternately rising and falling. To measure how the restored glide was experienced, they were asked to match the highest pitch that they heard in a second glide pattern (in which there was no interruption by noise) to the highest pitch that they heard behind the noise. These matches showed that the highest pitch that the listeners actually heard was not the one that the deleted peak would have had but was approximately at the highest pitch that the glide had reached before the noise (actually it was even a bit lower). Therefore the listeners did not extrapolate the pitch change into the noise, but simply interpolated between the pitches on the two sides of the noise.

Here is an informal observation of another failure of capturing by trajectory. The reader may recall the experiment that Alexander Rudnicky and I reported on the capturing of tones by a stream of tones of the same frequency.[544] The stimuli are illustrated in figure 1.7 of chapter 1. The listener's task was to recognize the order of the two highest tones (A and B). This was made hard by the presence of flanking tones (labeled F). However, the flanking tones could be captured by a series of captor tones (C) that was near in frequency to them. This made the order of tones A and B easier to recognize. When Rudnicky and I saw these results we wondered whether we could "tilt" the pattern and still get the same effect. We created the pattern that is illustrated in figure 4.3, hoping that the ascending

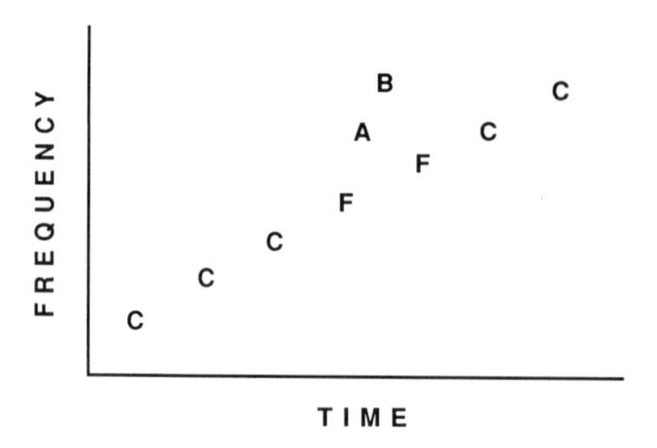

Figure 4.3
A modification of the stimulus pattern of Bregman and Rudnicky (1975) in which the capturing tones form an ascending sequence.

trajectory formed by the C tones would again capture the F tones so that they no longer interfered with the independent perception of A and B. However, we could find no evidence that this occurred and consequently abandoned the experiment.

Yet another failure to find a trajectory effect was found in an experiment that tried to capture a harmonic out of a speech sound. Researchers in Christopher Darwin's laboratory had done a number of experiments that showed that it is possible to capture a spectral component out of one of the formants of a short vowel and alter the perceived quality of the vowel. They had been able to do this by introducing, just before the vowel, a sequence of tones that were of the same frequency as the target component; however, they found that when they introduced, before and after the vowel, a sequence of tones that was aligned with the target partial to form a rising or falling sequence, the capturing showed no effect of the trajectory itself, but was entirely explainable in terms of the proximity of the frequencies of the nearer tones to that of the target.[545]

If a regular trajectory is a basis for the primitive grouping of sounds at all, it appears to be a rather weak one, easily overpowered by other factors. In chapter 2 we saw how the onset portion of a continuous long glide could be captured out of the total glide by being preceded by a short glide starting at about the same frequency. When this happened, the short glides and the initial portions of the long ones formed a stream of their own leaving the remainder of the long glides behind as a residual stream. The pattern was illustrated in figure 2.19 of chapter 2. Surely nothing can form a more regular trajectory than a glide that can be drawn as a straight line on log-frequency-by-time axes. Yet this did not prevent its being broken up by a frequency-based grouping.

The results of these experiments have led us to look for another reason for the findings of Dannenbring and myself, reported in chapter 2, and illustrated in figure 2.24.[546] In one condition of this experiment, the segregation of alternating high and low tones in a rapid sequence was reduced when the end of each tone consisted of a brief frequency glide pointing toward the frequency of the next tone. When we published this result we attributed it to a principle of grouping that makes use of the predictability of the position of the next sound (in a frequency-by-time space) from the final transition of the previous one. However, the results may not have been due to this sort of process at all. The presence of frequency transitions might simply have reduced the frequency separation between the end of one tone and the beginning of the next and the observed effect might have been entirely attributable to the principle of grouping by frequency proximity. If this were true, and if the time separation between the tones were to be reduced by speeding up the presentation rate of the sequence, splitting would be expected to eventually occur since increasing the presentation rate increases the segregation of sequences of tones that differ in frequency. We did observe this in informal observations.

We did some informal experiments in which we moved the tones closer together in frequency but pointed the transitions away from the adjacent tone. If the adjacent tone was lower in frequency, the transition went upward and vice versa. This arrangement did not reduce the integration of the sequence in comparison with the case in which transitions pointed to the next tone as long as the end point in the frequency transition was at the same frequency separation from the onset of the next tone in both cases. In fact, there was even a hint that the pointing-away transitions improved the integration. However, since this result did not accord with what we believed at the time to be a genuine trajectory pointing effect, we did not pursue this research to the point of publication.

Evidence That the System Projects Trajectories The preceding discussion has described a number of studies that failed to find that the auditory system extrapolated trajectories. However, this is not the end of the story. I am now obliged to review a number of research findings that seem to support the existence of an extrapolation mechanism. I will argue that there is an alternative explanation in every case.

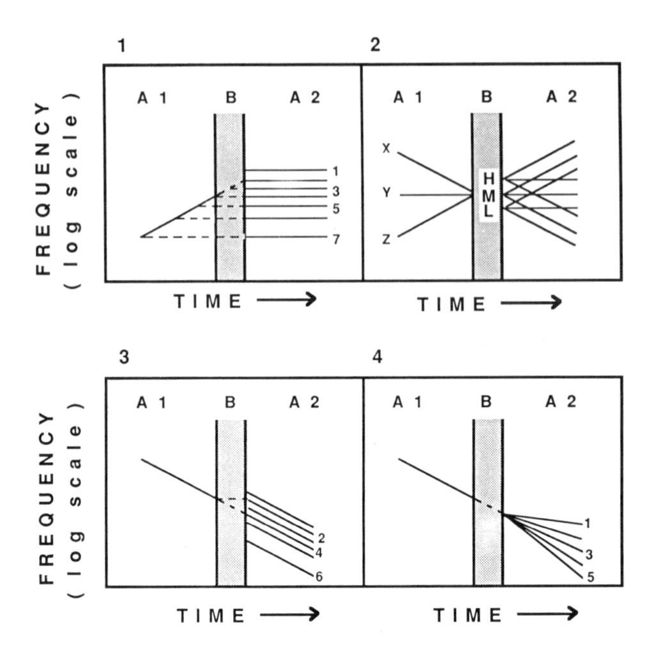

Figure 4.4
The alignment of glides and their apparent continuity. (From Ciocca and Bregman 1987.)

Trajectory-Based Integration of Streams Among the studies that seem to support a trajectory mechanism are a group reported recently by Valter Ciocca and myself on the continuity illusion.[547] Earlier Gary Dannenbring had shown that listeners could perceptually restore the continuity of a repeating pattern of ascending and descending pure-tone glides when a portion of the pattern was replaced by a noise burst.[548] However, Dannenbring never varied the alignment of the audible glide portions along a common trajectory, so there was no way to tell whether this alignment played a role in the continuity illusion. Ciocca and I used the type of stimulus illustrated in figure 4.4. It had three parts: a glide (A1) that preceded the noise, the noise itself (B), and a glide (A2) that followed the noise. A number of experiments were carried out in which the slopes of A1 and A2 were varied as well as the point in frequency at which they abutted the noise.

The listeners were pretrained on stimuli very like the ones in the main experiment except that in half of them, the glide actually continued underneath the noise at an audible level. They were trained to judge how sure they were that the glide continued through the noise.

In the actual experiment the listeners were led to believe that the glide continued through the noise but it never did. They were nonetheless asked to use a nine-point scale to rate how clearly they could hear the glide under the noise.

The figure illustrates the stimuli in a number of the experiments. Panel 1 shows an ascending glide (A1) followed by a noise burst, which in turn is followed by a set of possible steady-state tones (A2). One of these A2 sounds, the second from the top, began at just that point in frequency that the A1 glide would have reached by the end of the noise if it had been continuing underneath the noise. This predicted point of the exit of the trajectory from the noise is given the name "trajectory point" or T. The results showed that the A2 that gave the strongest impression of continuity was not the one at the T point, but the one that was at the highest frequency that A1 had reached before the noise. The more the other A2 glides departed from this best position, the less strongly they favored the perception of continuity.

If this experiment were taken alone, we would have to rule out the idea that the auditory system measures and extrapolates trajectories. However, others that we did seem to offer a different picture. The stimuli for the second experiment are shown in panel 2 of the figure. There were three versions of A1, ascending, descending, and steady, and there were nine versions of A2. Each A1 was combined with every A2 to create 27 different stimuli. One factor that distinguished the different A2 glides was whether or not they started at the trajectory point; the other was whether they were parallel to the A1 glide on a log-frequency scale. For each A1 there was one A2 that was exactly aligned with it on a log-frequency-by-time trajectory.

The results showed that for the falling A1 glide, the exactly aligned A2 glide was the best facilitator of continuity. The second best was the A2 glide that was the exact reversal of A1. This latter glide began at exactly the frequency that A1 had left off and rose to the frequency at which A1 had started. We can call it the "mirror-image glide". The other A2 glides did not promote perceptual restoration as well. In the conditions where A1 was rising, the rank of these two A2 glides was reversed. The mirror-image A2 glide was best and the trajectory-aligned A2 glide was second best. Finally, when A1 was a steady-state tone, the trajectory-aligned and the mirror-image A2 glides degenerate, by definition, into a common form, namely the A2 tone that is at the same frequency as A1. This A2 promoted continuity the best when A1 was steady-state.

Generally speaking, when A1 and A2 had the same slope, a trajectory effect was observed, the best continuity being obtained when they were aligned on a common trajectory. The continuity decreased as we moved the starting point of A2 away from the trajectory point. However, when the slopes of A1 and A2 did not match, the best continuity was obtained when the final frequency of A1 and the initial frequency of A2 were the same.

One way to explain the success of the mirror-image glide and the role of the similarity of the final part of A1 and the initial part of A2 in promoting continuity is by assuming that there is a preference for having the A2 glide as close as possible in frequency to the A1 glide. This is an example of the principle of frequency proximity. Presumably the nearest parts of A1 and A2 would have the greatest weight in this computation of proximity, but the superiority of the mirror-image glide to steady-state glides supports the idea that the more distant parts of the glides also count in the proximity calculation, the mirror-image A2 glide being best because it occupies exactly the same frequency region as does the A1 glide.

These results can be taken as further examples of the pervasive influence of frequency proximity in the sequential integration of streams. What is new is the apparent trajectory affect that seemed to be present whenever A1 and A2 had the same slope.

We went on to study this trajectory effect using stimuli that are illustrated in panel 3 of figure 4.4. In this experiment A2 always had the same slope as A1, but it could start at the trajectory point or above or below it. The A2 glides that started at or near the trajectory point (glides 3, 4, and 5) produced good continuity. For those that were nearer in frequency to A1 (glides 1 and 2) continuity was much worse.

Panel 4 shows the stimuli for a further experiment in which all the A2 glides began at the trajectory point but had different slopes. Of these, those that had the same slope or a more extreme one (glides 3, 4, and 5) gave good continuity while those with shallower slopes (1 and 2) did not.

The requirement of having A1 and A2 lie on a common trajectory was not precise. The exactly aligned glides were always good, but not always best. However this outcome is a reasonable confirmation of the occurrence of sequential grouping based on the alignment of trajectories. I can think of a possible explanation for the absence of more precise effects. We have no reason to believe that the log-frequency-by-time coordinates on which the trajectories can be described as straight lines are the ones that the auditory system uses to match up trajectories. The fact that we obtained any trajectory results at all suggest that this coordinate system is not too far off, but we do not know how far that may be.

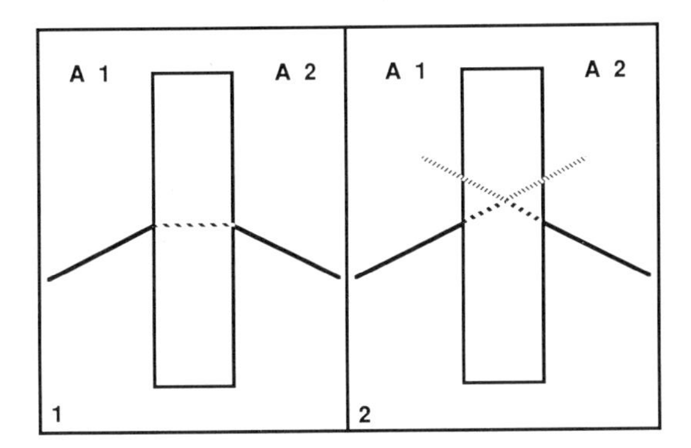

Figure 4.5
Illustration of two possible mechanisms for the restoration of glides through noise: interpolation (1) and extrapolation (2).

Clearly, this experiment supports the existence of a trajectory-extrapolating mechanism in perceptual restoration. However, we have to be very careful in interpreting it. There are two issues in the restoration of glides: One is the nature of the cues that are used to decide whether A1 and A2 are parts of the same glide. The present experiment supports the idea that A1 and A2 tend to be grouped whenever A2 has the same slope as A1 and when it exits from the noise at the trajectory point.

The second issue is the mechanism that is used to calculate what trajectory should be *experienced* during the noise. We could imagine the two mechanisms illustrated in figure 4.5. The first one, shown in panel 1 of the figure, works by interpolating a glide between the last frequency of A1 and the first frequency of A2. This mechanism treats restoration as analogous to stretching a rubber band between the last frequency estimate before the noise burst and the first one that follows it. The alternative mechanism for restoration, shown in panel 2, treats it as the extrapolation of a glide along a trajectory that is partially missing. The mechanism might be viewed as doing something analogous to placing a straight ruler along A1 and drawing a straight line forward past its end, then placing the ruler along A2 and drawing a line backward past its beginning until it reaches the line drawn from A1, then restoring, as the missing trajectory, the part of each line that does not extend past the other.

The experiments done by Ciocca and Bregman do not distinguish between these two alternatives. Although they show that alignment on a common trajectory may be the cue that promotes the grouping of A1 and A2, we could imagine either mechanism for restoration going along with this cue. It seems, no doubt, to go most naturally with a restoration mechanism that involves extrapolation of trajectories (the ruler method), since both the use of the cue for grouping and the method of restoration require the auditory system to extrapolate trajectories. The interpolation (rubber band) method of restoration seems, on the other hand, to go together most naturally with the frequency-proximity cue for integration, since neither requires the system to be able to extrapolate along trajectories. Even so, it is possible that the decision as to whether A1 and A2 are parts of the same sound is based on how well their trajectories lined up, but that the rubber band method is used to generate the experienced pitch trajectory.

The experiments by Ciocca and Bregman could not distinguish between different possible restoration mechanisms because they never measured *what* the listeners heard, but only *how clearly* they heard it. The only attempt to measure it was in an experiment by Dannenbring that was described earlier in this chapter. When the listeners restored the peaks in a rising and falling glide sequence they did not extrapolate the pitch to the missing peak but acted as though the auditory restoration process was stretching a rubber band between the nearest audible portions of the glides.

We must remember that the Ciocca-Bregman research showed that if glides are not aligned on a trajectory, the best matching is between mirror-image pairs. This mirror-image relation was, of course, the one that caused the grouping of the glides in the Dannenbring experiment. Perhaps it could be argued that if the glides are grouped by the frequency-proximity rule, the restoration will be by the rubber-band mechanism, and it is only when glides are grouped by their alignment on a trajectory that the ruler (extrapolation) mechanism will be used. However, the realization soon sinks in that in the case of aligned glides, the two proposed mechanisms will always give identical results. Therefore we have no need to ever postulate the existence of an extrapolation mechanism in the restoration of glides.

The only reason for believing in it is that the more complex forms of restoration seem to involve some sort of extrapolation. For example, we can restore the part of a word that has been deleted by noise, and this is obviously not achievable by an interpolation between the edges of the remaining portions of the word. However, this is not an acoustical extrapolation. Stored schemas for words are involved. The audible portions of the word are brought into contact with these schemas and one of these word schemas, selected by its acoustic match to the evidence and by its appropriateness to the semantic context, is perceptually restored. This is far from a simple process of

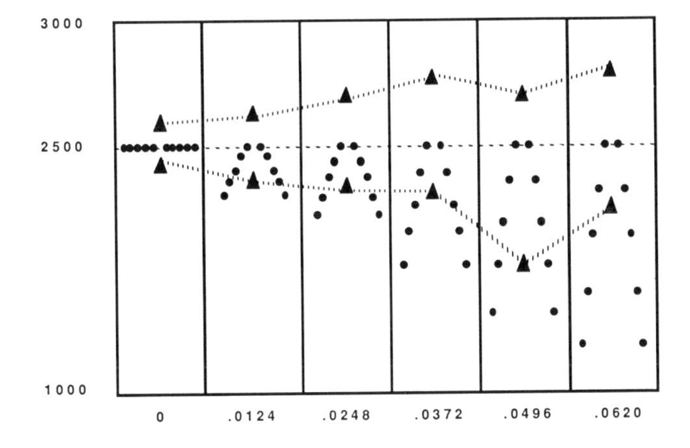

Figure 4.6
Six of the tone patterns used by Heise and Miller (1951). Circles: tones in the pattern. Upper triangles and lower triangles: mean values for the upper and lower limits for the adjustable tone.

extrapolation of an ongoing pattern and it clearly involves the use of stored schemas.

My best guess, then, is that glide trajectories are restored by interpolation unless a higher-order schema is responsible for the restoration. In the latter case, extrapolation can occur. Having brought schemas into the picture, however, it is tempting to ask whether even the trajectory-alignment criterion for whether to treat A1 and A2 as parts of the same glide derives from the learning of schemas. In other words, did the subjects in Ciocca and Bregman's experiments group the frequency aligned glides better because they had learned schemas concerning continuous forms of change? The data from this experiment cannot answer this question. However, we should remember that the stimulus was slow, and the listeners were making an effort to hear the sound. These factors would favor the use of schemas. It is even possible that the preference for the mirror-image continuation was based on a schema and was not just the result of frequency proximity.

An early experiment done by George Heise and George Miller has generally been interpreted as showing that trajectories can be extrapolated by the mechanism that creates auditory streams.[549] They presented listeners with a sequence of 11 pure tones, played at the rate of eight tones per second. Six of their sequences are shown by the circles in figure 4.6. These patterns form straight lines or inverted V's on log-frequency-by-time coordinates. The listeners could control the frequency of the sixth tone in the sequence (the middle tone). In each trial, a particular sequence was played over and over without pause while the listener adjusted the tone. If its frequency was set either too high or too low, it seemed to pop out of the sequence. This meant that it had been perceptually segregated from the sequence. The triangles superimposed on each pattern in the figure are the highest and lowest frequencies to which the listeners had to adjust the tone to get it to segregate. When the patterns were straight lines, as in panel 1, we cannot tell whether the "best position" for the tone is based on interpolation or extrapolation, since both mechanisms would give the same result, so let us examine the inverted V patterns. If we focus on the highest point of adjustment (the upper triangles) it appears that they fall on the point in frequency at which the trajectory would have reached a peak. Furthermore as the trajectories get steeper, the highest point gets higher as if trying to fall at the predicted highest point. This is the evidence for extrapolation.

However, you should not look only at the highest-limit adjustments but at the lowest-limit ones as well (lower triangles). The algebraic mean of the upward and downward adjustments made by the subject can be taken as an indication of the neutral point, the place where the tone fits in best. This value was not at the projected vertex. Instead it was at a point that was quite close in frequency to the tones that came before and after it, and in no case was this neutral point extrapolated outside the range bracketed by those tones. This suggests that the auditory system did not project the trajectory to the apex of the pattern but rather preferred a tone that lay within the frequency range of the pattern. But what of the tendency for the highest-limit setting to be higher when the trajectories were steeper? An examination of the figure shows that the lowest-limit results show a comparable effect. They get lower when the glides get steeper. This cannot be explained by the assumption that the best location for the adjustable tone is moving to a higher frequency. Instead, what appears to be happening is that the predicted point for the middle tone is getting less definite as the trajectories get steeper. That is, as they get steeper, they accept a wider range of tones as fitting into the pattern. A similar effect was found in the Ciocca-Bregman experiment that was discussed earlier.

An important fact in the results of Heise and Miller was that the tones following the adjustable one, and not just those preceding it, affected segregation. The best position for the adjustable tone in the ascending straight line patterns is higher than for the inverted V pattern despite the fact that the tones preceding the adjustable tone are identical in the two cases. This is because the later tones are higher in the straight line patterns.

To summarize, the results of Heise and Miller provide no evidence for a frequency-extrapolating mechanism that "looks for" a tone at the next predicted frequency. All of their results can be explained by the tendency to prefer a tone that lies as close as possible in frequency to the nearest neighbors on both sides of it, with perhaps a weak effect of its proximity to next-to-nearest neighbors.

Their results are different from those by van Noorden that we will describe later and will illustrate in figure 4.7. Perhaps the difference lies in the experience of the listeners. While those of Heise and Miller were graduate students in psychology, van Noorden served as his own subject at a time when he had been listening extensively to such patterns. It is possible that van Noorden formed schemas for the patterns and these were the source of the trajectory effect.

Order of Unidirectional Sequences Is Easier to Report The experiments that we have surveyed so far in looking for a trajectory effect have used a number of methods that were presumed to be sensitive to the streaming of tones. The ones I plan to look at now use a different method, the report of the order of tones in a sequence. They all show that the order is easier to report in smoothly ascending or descending sequences (glissandi) than in irregular ones. However, I plan to argue that these effects are not due to a trajectory-based principle of primitive grouping but to different factors.

Results Explainable by Other Factors The first factor that may be responsible for a number of these effects is memory. A sequence that continuously ascends or descends in pitch is probably easy to remember because of the simplicity of the rule by which it can be remembered.

An experiment by Nickerson and Freeman in 1974 found that the order of a sequence of sounds was easier to report when it followed a unidirectional trajectory.[550] However, as I have shown elsewhere in this volume, the detailed structure of their results shows that they were probably not due to stream segregation at all.

Warren and Byrnes also showed that it was much easier to report the order of sounds in repeating glissandi (of four 200-msec tones) than in irregularly ordered tone cycles.[551] However, the task that showed this effect most strongly was one where the listeners had to report their order verbally. This task is heavily dependent on memory. However, a second task was also used in which the listeners took four cards, each representing one of the sounds, and arranged them on the table to report the order of the sounds. This task reduces the memory load because the listeners can break up the task of reporting the entire sequence into one of relating each sound to the one that precedes it and inserting its card in the proper place. They need not remember the entire sequence at once. When the task was changed from verbal reporting to this card-ordering method, the superiority of glissandi over irregular patterns dropped from 110 percent to 21 percent. This suggests a strong contribution from short-term memory to the observed effects.

Another piece of evidence that the results were not due to primitive grouping was that the effect of frequency separation in this experiment was in a direction opposite to its known effects on primitive grouping: a greater frequency separation made order identification easier. If the difficulty of the irregular patterns came from their breaking into substreams, the task should have become harder when an increase in the frequency separation created more segregated streams. Another hint that higher-level cognitive processes rather than primitive grouping were responsible was that the effects occurred at a rate of presentation of five tones per second, a slow rate that, according to van Noorden, requires at least a 15-semitone separation between adjacent tones before compulsory segregation occurs.[552] None of the conditions of Warren and Byrnes employed such large frequency separations.

These observations suggest that the effect could be related to the problem of building a mental description of the event sequence, rather than simply grouping the events at a preattentive level. Therefore this experimental demonstration of the ease of reporting glissandi cannot be taken as evidence that there is a primitive process that tracks a trajectory and prefers to integrate its members into a single stream.

Stephen Handel and his associates at the University of Tennessee have found effects of trajectories in experiments on auditory patterns conceptualized in the framework of Gestalt psychology. McNally and Handel experimented with the effects of different patterns on streaming, using repeating cycles of four sounds, presented at the rate of five sounds per second.[553] Their listeners reported the order of the sounds by using a card-ordering task. One type of pattern was made by arranging the order of four tones separated by 100 Hz (750, 850, 950, and 1,050 Hz). Regular trajectories (four in a row ascending or else descending) were easier for the subjects than were irregular orders of the four tones. Although this result seems to show that the auditory system is extrapolating trajectories following a regular trajectory, there is an alternative explanation. The speeds and frequency separations that gave the reported effect with McNally and Handel's four-tone pattern suggest that stream segregation was not a compelling percept at all. The greatest separation (300 Hz) in this sequence was about six semitones. As I mentioned in relation to the Warren-Byrnes experiment, van Noorden's studies show that at five tones per second you would have to have about a 15-semitone separation to obtain compelling segregation. The separation between the highest and lowest tones used in McNally and Handel's experiment was closer to the separation at which van Noorden obtained compulsory integration, and the separations between the nearer pairs of tones were even closer to this value. So although the ability of the subjects to report the order of the tones may have been affected by an irregular order, the irregularity probably had its effects through another mechanism. I have suggested that this mechanism is memory.

In a different experiment, Handel, Weaver, and Lawson used the same rate of five tones per second but employed greater frequency separations.[554] In one of their sequences, four tones were spaced by octaves (750, 1,500, 3,000, and 6,000 Hz). On each listening trial, a particular arrangement of these four tones was continuously repeated for a minute while the subjects made their judgments. Two kinds of judgments were required. They indicated how the tones seemed to group perceptually by drawing lines to connect the tones in a picture that was similar to a musical score. On other trials, they were not told the order of the tones but had to judge it by arranging four cards on a table. In sequences in which the four tones were equally spaced in time, those orders that formed an ascending (1234) or a descending (4321) glissando were perceived as more coherent than other orders. That is, they were more often judged to be a single sequence and their order was more often judged correctly. But there is some discrepant data. Some of the irregular orders were also judged as forming a single stream on a substantial proportion of trials, up to 47 percent of the time in some conditions. This probably happened because of the slowness of the sequences. Again, because of the fact that the conditions were not those that led to a compelling stream segregation, we cannot rule out the participation of a more complex cognitive process, such as memory, in producing these results.

Although the slow rate in these studies makes their interpretation questionable, Pierre Divenyi and Ira Hirsh have observed superior performance on glissandi with rapid sequences of tones (1 to 30 msec per tone) where stream segregation would have been expected to occur.[555] The order of rapid unidirectional sequences of three tones has also proved easier to report than other orders of these tones.[556]

However, even if some or all of the superiority of glissandi in these studies really did result from a preattentive grouping process, the effect can be explained without resorting to an extrapolation of trajectories. The frequency-proximity principle alone would be sufficient to explain their results. I will offer the argument that in a glissando, some of the competition of groupings that are found in up-and-down sequences will not be present. This lack of competition may be responsible for the coherence of glissandi.

We should remember that frequency proximities in sequences of tones always compete with one another.[557] The grouping of temporally nonadjacent tones, as in the streaming phenomenon, occurs because these tones are closer to each other in frequency than adjacent tones are, and, in addition, are not very far apart in time. In a repeating glissando, however, there is never any tone that is closer to a given tone (A) in frequency than its sequential neighbors are, except for the next occurrence of tone A itself on the following cycle. Since a glissando is likely to include at least three or four tones, the successive occurrences of tone A itself are likely to be far enough apart in time to prevent them from forming their own stream. Hence A is most likely to group with its nearest temporal neighbors. This argument deduces the coherence of glissandi as a special case of the principle of frequency proximity under the assumption that proximities compete with one another.

There is, however, an observation by Leo van Noorden that cannot be explained by the competition of proximities. One type of stimulus that he made was an eight-tone sequence, presented at the rate of 10 tones per second and covering a range of one octave. The listener heard this sequence cycled repeatedly.[558] Several different patterns were used. Four of them are shown in figure 4.7. The difference between the two top patterns is that although the first high tone is equally far in frequency from its nearest temporal neighbors in both patterns, in the second pattern, the transitions before and after it seem to point to it. It is on a trajectory (roughly speaking) that is formed by the first three tones. When listening to these two patterns van Noorden found that the first high tone remained part of the sequence in the second stimulus, where the pointing was present, though not in the first. (The second high tone was perceptually segregated from the sequence in both cases.) The two patterns in the bottom panels of the figure were heard as integrated sequences. He explained this by saying that reversals in the direction of pitch change are infrequent in this sort of pattern. This explanation amounts to saying that the auditory system prefers to hear a pattern that continues a frequency change. It is as if, in a sequence of tones ABC, the frequency relation

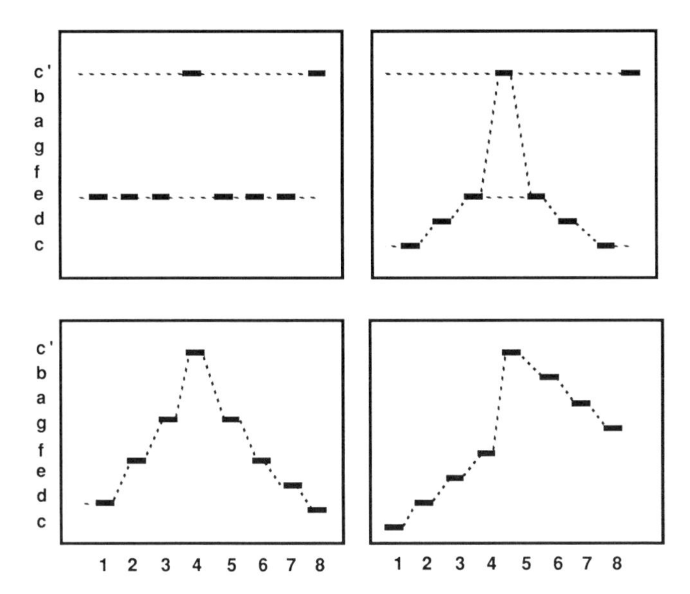

Figure 4.7
Four patterns used by van Noorden (1975) to study the effects of continuity of frequency change on grouping.

between A and B becomes part of the description of the pair and C is more readily integrated into the sequence if the relation BC is like the relation AB. If the relation between AB and BC is different, a drawing of this sequence would show a "corner" at B. Corners may tend to disrupt the integration of sequences. This, of course, is quite different from saying that the auditory system is making up a predictive schema for the sequence or is tracking a trajectory. Instead, it puts the source of the effect at a more primitive level of the auditory system, a process that forms a discontinuity when it detects something like a corner. This is reminiscent of the Gestalt principle of continuity that I described earlier and illustrated in figure 4.1. Guilford and his coworkers in the 1930s found that if listeners had to listen to two sequences of tones and judge whether the second was the same as the first, if the change was made by altering a tone at the apex of a V so as to decrease the sharpness of the V, it was usually not noticed, whereas if it increased the sharpness it was noticed more frequently.[559] This observation also suggests the existence of a system that detects corners and makes them more salient.

Whatever the process is that groups tones that fall on a common trajectory, it has different effects than the one that groups those that are near to one another in frequency. Let me illustrate this with a

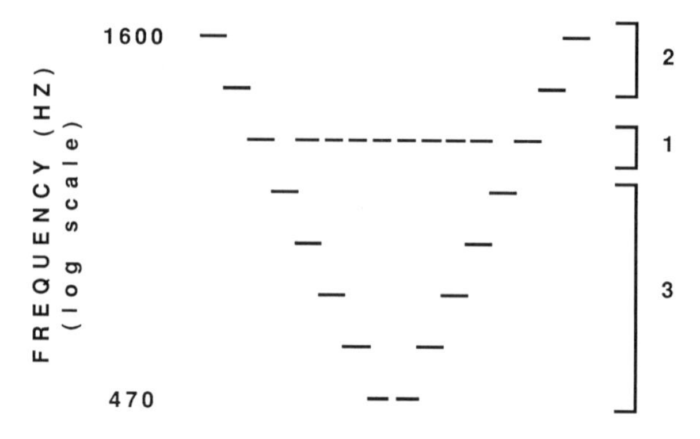

Figure 4.8
Pattern in which there is a competition between grouping based on trajectories and on the proximity of frequencies.

tonal pattern that I made a number of years ago. The pattern is shown in figure 4.8. In it, there are 24 short tones. This pattern was played repeatedly with no gaps between repetitions. Two speeds were used, a faster one of 15.6 tones per second and a slower one of 7.8 tones per second. Three parts of the sequence are separately labeled in the figure although they were not acoustically isolated in any way in the sequence. Part 1 is a set of tones that all have the same frequency and therefore would be expected to be grouped by frequency proximity. Parts 2 and 3 form the upper and lower halves of a pair of trajectories that together form an upright V. When the pattern was played repetitively at the higher speed, parts 1 and 2 formed a single stream on the basis of frequency proximity, leaving part 3 as a separate stream. This partitioning was done on the basis of frequency proximity and this organization became stronger with more repetitions.

When the slower speed was used, the organization became ambiguous. I could hear the frequency-based grouping as in the higher-speed sequence, but I could also hear, if I wished to, the long trajectories formed by perceptually connecting parts 2 and 3. However, I could never hear part 1 alone. The reader may recall that I have postulated that schema-based streaming is asymmetrical. Whereas the subset of sound selected by the schema becomes an perceptually isolated whole, the same does not happen to the "remainder" subset. This was what happened when I organized everything except part 1 by the trajectory principle but could not hear part 1 as a separate sequence. I also postulated that in a competition between primitive grouping and schema-based grouping, speed would favor the primitive grouping. The reader will recall that the frequency-based streaming was stronger with the faster pattern, suggesting that the trajectory-based streaming was based on a schema. I also noticed that the trajectory-based organization grew stronger with repetitions. Since learning will affect the strength of schemas, this effect of repetition points to a schema-governed process.

Experiments have been done that show that sequences of sounds can be made to be more coherent if frequency transitions are introduced so as to connect adjacent sounds. The one that I did with Gary Dannenbring has already been described in chapter 2 and illustrated in figure 2.24.

Some related experiments were performed by Ronald Cole and Brian Scott. They were aware of the fact that unrelated sounds in a rapid sequence tended to segregate into different streams. Why, they asked, did this not happen with speech? After all, consonants such as "s" and vowels are quite different acoustically. Why do they not form separate streams? To answer this question, they noted the fact that as the speech apparatus of a human talker moves from one speech sound to the next, the transition is not instantaneous and gradual changes are seen in the positions of the formants. They proposed that it was these transitions that held the speech stream together. Their first experiment observed stream segregation when a single consonant-vowel syllable was repeated over and over in a loop.[560] An example might be the syllable "sa". A schematic spectrogram of this syllable is shown in figure 4.9, on the left. In one condition, shown on the right, the brief portion of the syllable where the consonant turned into the vowel was cut out and the remaining portions spliced together. They reported that the resulting transitionless syllable sounded quite intelligible when played in isolation. However, when a tape loop was formed in which the syllable was repeated endlessly, after a few cycles the successive repetitions of the consonant (for example, the "s") formed a stream of their own as did the successive occurrences of the vowel. This segregation was, according to the researchers, reported immediately by all listeners. By way of contrast, when they made loops out of the full syllables, leaving the consonant-vowel transition intact, the segregation of consonant from vowel either was not reported at all or was reported only after a much greater number of repetitions.

Concluding that the formant transitions served to hold the stream together, they performed an experiment to determine whether the vowel transitions helped in the task of detecting the order of the basic sounds in a series of syllables.[561] They started with recordings of the syllables "sa", "za", "sha", "va", "ja", "ga", and "fa". Next they separated three components of each sound: the initial consonant, the

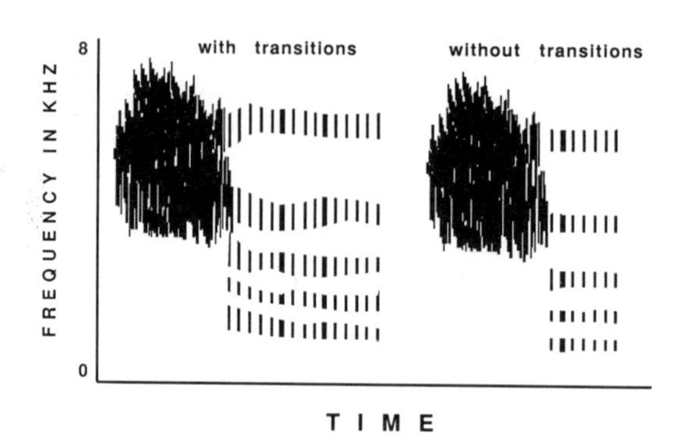

Figure 4.9
Schematic spectrograms of the syllable "sa". 1: with normal transitions. 2: with the formant transitions spliced out. (After Cole and Scott 1973.)

transition, and the vowel steady state. Then they made loops consisting of cycles of four sounds. For example, the formula for one such cycle was [s, sh, v, g]. This meant that the elements in the cycle were extracted from the syllables "sa", "sha", "va", and "ga", respectively. Three types of cycle were made from this formula. The first was composed only of the consonant sections of the four syllables, the second consisted of the four full syllables, and the third consisted of transitionless syllables made from these four syllables. The transitionless and full syllables were equated for duration by adjusting the length of the steady-state portions of the vowels.

The subjects were prefamiliarized with the individual sounds that were used in the loops. Then the loops were played to them and they were asked to write down the order of the sounds in them. They did worst on loops containing only the consonants. Next came the transitionless syllables. The best performance was on the full syllables that contained the transitions, apparently because each syllable was perceived as a coherent unit.

There are a number of ways to interpret these findings. The first is in terms of a trajectory effect. I would direct the reader's attention to figure 4.9. It is tempting to attribute the coherence of the normal syllables to the fact that the formant transitions point backward to positions of high energy in the consonant. To believe that this relation had any organizing value, one would have to suppose that the auditory system could follow a trajectory backward. Retrograde effects are not unthinkable; we have already encountered two examples in the continuity illusion. The first was in the restoration of obliterated words, in which words that come later in the sentence

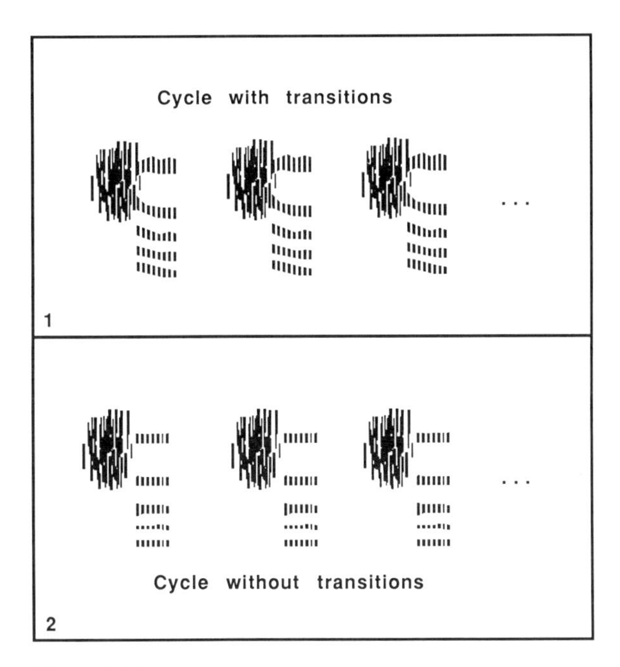

Figure 4.10
Schematic spectrogram of repeating cycles of the type used by Scott and Cole (1973). 1: sequence of normal "sa" syllables. 2: sequence of transitionless syllables.

could determine what the restored sound would be.[562] The second was in the illusory continuity of glides through a noise burst, where the restoration seemed to depend on the relations between the glide that exited from the noise and the glide that entered.[563] Therefore we might entertain the idea that the auditory system can tell that the backward extrapolation of the transitions leads to energy peaks in the consonant, and can conclude that they came from the same source.

A second interpretation of the results does not use the idea of trajectory extrapolation. It says simply that the existence of formant transitions avoids sudden discontinuities in the signal. Continuity is a form of frequency proximity, in which the position of spectral energy in each successive instant is close to where it was at the previous instant. This is an explanation based on continuity, not on the extrapolation of a trajectory.

A third possible explanation says that the elimination of the transitions did not directly affect the grouping of the consonant and vowel within each syllable but favored the grouping of vowels across syllables. To see how this could be so, we should examine figure 4.10, which shows a schematic drawing of a repeating cycle of "sa" syllables. Panel 1 shows this for a normal syllable and panel 2 for a transitionless syllable. I want to focus not on the role that the transition plays in connecting the vowel to the previous consonant but on its role in isolating successive occurrences of the vowel. When the transitions are present, the formant glides start at a different frequency value than the one that they attain in the steady state. Therefore each successive occurrence of the vowel starts with a spectrum that is different from the final spectrum of its previous occurrence. This difference in spectrum may reduce the vowel-to-vowel grouping that might jump over the intervening consonant. On the other hand, when the transitions are removed, since the vowels are now steady-state, each vowel has the same spectrum at its onset as it had at its previous offset, and this consistency may favor vowel-to-vowel grouping. This is an explanation in terms of the frequency proximity of the nearest temporal parts of successive vowels.

Finally, there is another explanation. The auditory system may be using its knowledge of human articulation to perform the integration. It may convert the acoustical input derived from the sequence of sounds into some representation of the sequence of vocal tract positions that might have produced them. Then, since the sequence is interpretable as the movements of a single speaker's vocal tract, it groups the parts of the syllable together. When the vowel transitions are absent, the hypothesis of a single speaker would be untenable since human vocal tracts cannot snap from one position to another instantaneously. This explanation bases the integration on a schema-driven interpretation of the signal as a speech event.

Although it is not possible to decide in favor of any of these hypotheses from the evidence at hand, the multiplicity of possible explanations makes it impossible for us to accept the data of Cole and Scott as unequivocal support for a primitive trajectory-following process in auditory perception.

In the preceding discussion I have put forward a number of possible alternative explanations that make it hard for us to determine whether the apparent grouping (when it occurs) of sounds that fall on a frequency trajectory is due to a primitive trajectory-following mechanism. Among them were the following:

1. The auditory system may simply detect local discontinuities rather than forming rules that predict the trajectory.
2. Unidirectional ascending or descending sequences may simply be easier for our memories to encode and recall than irregular sequences.

3. It is possible that there is a trajectory-following mechanism but that it is based on schemas and requires prior learning, and, in some cases, a conscious attempt to track the trajectory.
4. There is an absence of competition based on frequency proximity in glissandi.

Because one or all of these explanations may be true, it is hard to verify whether or not primitive auditory scene analysis automatically extrapolates trajectories.

Comparison with Vision The weakness of the trajectory effect in audition contrasts with its strength in vision. This can be seen by examining the phenomenon of crossing trajectories. In this chapter we have seen that if tones alternate between an ascending and a descending trajectory as in figure 4.2 of chapter 2, the listener will never hear the trajectories cross unless the tones on the two trajectories have different timbres. The situation is different in vision. André Achim and I created a visual analog to the trajectory-crossing experiment, substituting the vertical position of a visible spot for auditory frequency.[564] The viewer saw a spot rapidly alternating in position between points on an ascending and a descending trajectory. In other words, figure 4.2 could be used to illustrate the stimuli of the visual experiment if the *y* axis were relabeled "vertical position." As with tones, there was a streaming of the two trajectories, which we called visual stream segregation. The viewer saw an ascending and a descending trajectory of apparent motion happening at the same time, but in contrast with the auditory case, the trajectories crossed one another easily. We did not record whether the actual subjects in our experiment saw the trajectories as crossing or as drawing together and then bouncing apart. However, in our own viewing of the apparatus, we saw both percepts, with the crossing interpretation being at least as common as the bouncing one.

A similar tendency to follow visual trajectories has been reported by Ramachandran and Anstis.[565] The direction of apparent motion of a dot A is ambiguous when two different dots, B and C, are flashed immediately after it. However, they were able to bias the motion toward B rather than C by embedding the AB transition in a longer trajectory of flashed positions leading up to A so that the AB transition continued the direction of motion. They referred to this result as an illustration of "visual momentum" and explained it by the following argument:

> According to Newton's first Law of Motion, a physical object moving at uniform velocity in one direction will persevere in its

> state of uniform motion unless acted upon by an external force to change that state. . . . We have found that any object that moves in one direction will tend to be perceived as continuing its motion in that direction. . . . This might be regarded as a perceptual equivalent of Newton's first law . . . visual momentum may exemplify a prediction by the visual system that at least for small excursions the motion of a physical object is likely to be unidirectional.

This argument sees the existence of visual momentum as an evolutionary adaptation of the visual system to regularities in the physical environment in the manner described so elegantly by Roger Shepard.[566]

Can we formulate a similar argument in audition? I think not. The frequency changes in sounds do not have the same sort of momentum that the positional changes of objects do. One exception to this rule is the Doppler shift in frequency that rapidly moving objects exhibit. However, perceptible Doppler shifts are common only in our technological world with its fire engine sirens, train whistles, and the like, where we often hear very rapidly moving objects, and not in the forests and plains in which the human species took its present form. Also, there is no inertia in a vocal tract that makes it probable that a rising pitch will continue to rise. In fact, the opposite could be true. Since it is likely that the pitch range of the voice is limited, an ascending pitch change is likely to be followed by a descending one. Continuity of change in the voice in the very small scale, though, might be found because it probably takes fewer neural decisions to continue a change than to reverse it; however, the easiest change of all is probably to freeze a frequency transition and continue the sound at a fixed frequency.

Although this argument against pitch-change inertia does not rule out a primitive auditory process for tracking and extrapolating changes, it does not encourage us to expect one. However, human beings can do many things that they are not preprogrammed to do such as ride bicycles, read, and create works of art. These arise from the incredibly complex structure of schemas that must be learned anew by each member of our species. The ability to learn things of incredible complexity makes it possible for the species to adapt to an ever-changing environment. The value of following pitch changes in a world of music, sirens, and the like may well have led to the learning of ascending and descending pitch-change schemas.

"Is Auditory Attention Inherently Rhythmical?"

Another sort of regularity that we should look at is regularity of rhythm. We can ask two questions about it. One is whether there is a tendency for sounds that occur in a regular rhythm to be placed in the same stream by the scene-analysis process. We might imagine that such a tendency would be useful because there are many naturally occurring rhythmic processes in the world. The dripping of a melting icicle, the sound of a walking person, and the rhythmic croaking of frogs all fall into this category. Therefore a repetition of a sound at a constant period might usefully set up an expectation of another repetition of the sound after a similar period.[567]

Jones' theory takes this even further. For her theory, as we saw earlier in this chapter, the process that groups sounds does so by setting up a pattern of rules that predicts the sequence and by controlling the attention of the listener according to those rules. Furthermore, the rules are rhythmical, with the temporal description of inter-event times based on repetitions of a number of basic time periods. These time periods are presumed to be generated by regular oscillatory processes in the nervous system that are used, in combination, for matching the rate of incoming sounds when we are receiving them and for generating the expected rate of sounds when we are anticipating them.[568] For this reason it is claimed by Jones' theory that "attention is inherently rhythmic" and that "temporal predictability may be a prerequisite to the establishment of stream segregation based on frequency relationships."[569] In other words, even a strong segregating factor such as frequency separation would have no effect in segregating the notes of a temporally irregular sequence.

Thus there are three possibilities. One is that rhythmic regularity has no effect on the inclusion of sounds in streams. A second is that although regularity promotes inclusion in the same stream, it is not essential. A final possibility is that temporal regularity is so essential that there can be no stream segregation without it.

This last alternative seems to me to be unlikely, because there are many natural sounds that are not rhythmical that we must nonetheless segregate from other sounds. Examples are the dragging of an object along the ground, the crackling of a fire, and probably even the sound of a voice speaking (although the question of whether speech is or is not rhythmically regular is debatable). However, because Jones' theory takes this position we should consider it as a possibility.

Regularity of Rhythm: Does It Promote Segregation? Let us first consider the question of whether rhythm plays any role in the perceptual grouping of sounds. There is some evidence that it does.

Evidence That Rhythm Favors Segregation The main supporting evidence comes from the work of Jones and her colleagues at Ohio State University. For example, one series of experiments used a pattern of stimuli that resembled those that Alex Rudnicky and I had used earlier to study whether more than one stream can be active at once.[570] The pattern of tones was illustrated in figure 1.7 of chapter 1. In our experiment, the order of two target tones, A and B, was hard to detect in a sequence because the presence of two flanking tones preceding and following the target tones created the sequence FABF, which was hard to discriminate from the alternative sequence FBAF.

The task was made easier when a stream of captor tones (C), near in frequency to the flanker tones, stripped the latter away leaving the target tones in their own stream. In the following diagram we illustrate only the time intervals of the original Bregman-Rudnicky stimulus, not the frequency separations. The frequencies had a pattern similar to the one shown in figure 1.7.

C C C F A B F C C C C

However, Jones and her co-workers pointed out that not only were the captor tones close in frequency to the flanking tones that they were to capture, but they also were rhythmically related to the flankers such that the captors and the flankers considered together formed a slower isochronous sequence than the one formed by A and B. This can be seen in the preceding diagram. They argued that A and B might have been segregated by this difference in rhythm. Therefore they performed a number of manipulations of the time intervals between the tones so as to create other rhythms. For example, in one condition that can be roughly illustrated by the following diagram, the F's fell into an isochronous sequence with AB but not with the C's.

C C C F A B F C C C

In another sequence the entire pattern formed a single isochronous sequence:

C C C F A B F C C C

In both of these cases, the AB sequence was harder to isolate than it was in the original pattern. The researchers concluded that "temporal predictability may be a prerequisite to the establishment of stream segregation based on frequency relationships."[571] I interpret them as proposing that frequency differences would cause streams to segregate only if each stream could follow a regular, and preferably different, rhythm. Although these results did not really warrant such strong conclusions they did demonstrate some role of temporal patterning in the ability to attend to only some of the tones in a sequence.

Perhaps, rather than governing the process of primitive grouping, the rhythmic relations affected the ability of the listeners to ready their attention for the critical pair of tones whose order was to be judged. We should note that in Bregman and Rudnicky's experiment there were two influences at work. The first was the voluntary attention of the listener which was trying to select out the target tones, and the second was the involuntary primitive grouping of the tones, which was opposing the efforts of attention. It is this opposition that tells us that primitive grouping exists independently of attention. Rhythmic isolation may assist the selection process *directly* rather than indirectly through its effects on primitive grouping.

This conclusion is supported by the results of another study by Jones and her colleagues.[572] The listeners heard pairs of nine-tone auditory sequences, the second one transposed up or down as a whole relative to the first. In addition to the transposition, one of the tones in the second sequence was altered in pitch on half the trials. The listeners were required to judge whether the sequence was merely transposed or altered as well. At 3.3 tones per second, the sequence was slow enough that there would have been no compelling stream segregation. Yet the subjects could more easily detect the change of a note when their attention was guided there by the fact that the rhythm of the sequence placed an accent on this note. In this experiment it was probably the encoding or mental description of a sequence, rather than its primitive segregation, that was affected by the rhythm.

A similar conclusion about the effects of rhythmic grouping can be reached from the results of an experiment by Dowling.[573] His subjects heard a sequence composed of four phrases each consisting of five tones. They can be diagrammed as follows:

ABCDE FGHIJ KLMNO PQRST

The separation between the phrases was achieved by lengthening the last note in each one and adding a short silence (if the first four notes are thought of as quarter notes, the fifth can be thought of as a dotted quarter note which was followed by an eighth rest). Immediately afterward, the subject was presented with a test pattern of five tones and was asked whether it had occurred in the original sequence. The tests consisted of two types, one in which the tones consisted of a whole phrase from the original sequence (for example, FGHIJ) and the other in which the tones bridged phrase boundaries (for example,

IJ KLM). The test sequences that preserved the original phrasing were much easier to recognize. This result shows that an essential part of the memory for a sequence is its rhythmic pattern.

The question of whether rhythm affects the formation of streams was taken up by Stephen Handel and his fellow researchers at the University of Tennessee.[574] They manipulated the rhythm of a four-tone sequence, presented as a repeating cycle, by varying the positions of silences in it. If we represent the frequencies of four tones of increasing frequency by the digits 1 to 4 and silences by hyphens, the formula 12–34- would represent a sequence in which the two low tones and the two high tones were placed in separate groups, separated by silences. The formula 1–234- would isolate the lowest tone into a separate group. The experiment also varied the frequency separation between the tones. Each cycle of four tones (together with whatever silences were added) took 0.8 second, yielding an average tone rate of 5 per second.

This experiment is not really relevant to the question of whether predictability per se influences the formation of streams, because when a short sequence is recycled over and over, it rapidly becomes very predictable. In addition, any short repeating sequence can be described by a few rules and is therefore regular in Jones's sense. The study looked at the effects of particular forms of temporal grouping on the nature of the resulting streams.

The first finding of note was that the temporal grouping had little or no effect when the sequence consisted of two high and two low tones, where the high pair was separated from the low pair by a considerable frequency difference (400 and 500 versus 1,600 and 2,000 Hz). Apparently the frequency separation was the dominant influence on streaming.

When the four tones were equally spaced by octaves (750, 1,500, 3,000, and 6,000 Hz), the temporal grouping did matter. When the sequence was isochronous, the four tones tended to be heard as a single unsegregated sequence. When silences were added, tones preferred to group with others that were closest to them both in frequency and in time. Thus, rhythmic differences had an effect because they were really differences in temporal separation.

There was one exception to this general rule. There was a greater tendency to break up the four-tone sequence into separate perceptual streams when the resulting streams would be isochronous. If this should be borne out in future studies it means that a stream is stronger when its members are equally spaced in time and confirms Jones's hypothesis that rhythmic processes can be involved in the formation of streams. Notice, however, that this factor was evident only when large frequency separations did not force the streaming. Therefore these results do not lend support to the proposal by Jones and her associates that substreams will form *only* when they are rhythmically regular.

Segregation Occurs with Temporally Irregular Sequences Although there is some evidence that rhythmic regularity assists the formation of streams, there is enough evidence to reject the hypothesis that it is essential for their formation. It is not unusual to find, for example, a case in which an isochronous sequence breaks into two streams on the basis of frequency proximities, and neither of the two streams formed in this way is isochronous.[575] Another experiment that I reviewed earlier, by Tougas and Bregman, also showed that rhythmic regularity is not essential.[576] When a falling sequence of tones crossed a rising sequence, the listeners tended not to be able to follow either sequence across the crossing point, but switched over to the part of the other sequence that fell in the same frequency region as the earlier part of the one they had been following. There were two rhythmic conditions: In one, the sequence would remain isochronous if the listeners switched their attention to the other trajectory and in the other it would be isochronous if they continued to follow the same trajectory. The tendency to switch trajectories was unaffected by this rhythmic factor and seemed entirely governed by the principle of frequency proximity.

A recent experiment performed by Marilyn French-St. George and myself looked specifically for whether predictability in the pattern of pitches and time intervals would help a listener to integrate a sequence that was being segregated by frequency differences.[577] It found no such effect. The listeners were asked to listen to a 30-second sequence of pure tones, each of which was 40 msec in duration, with an average rate of about 11 per second. There were four main conditions.

In condition A the sequence was very regular. It was formed of a repeating cycle of eight tones, four lower ones and four higher ones. The onset-to-onset time between successive tones was always exactly 91.2 msec. The four higher tones were spaced apart by semitone separations, thus spanning a three-semitone interval, and the lower tones were spaced from one another in the same way. The high tones were interleaved with the low tones in the cycle. The listeners were told that during the 30-second presentation of the cycle they were to try to hold the tones together as a coherent sequence and to indicate when they were successful by pressing a key in front of them. On different trials, each lasting 30 seconds, the separation between the mean frequency of the higher and the lower tones was varied from

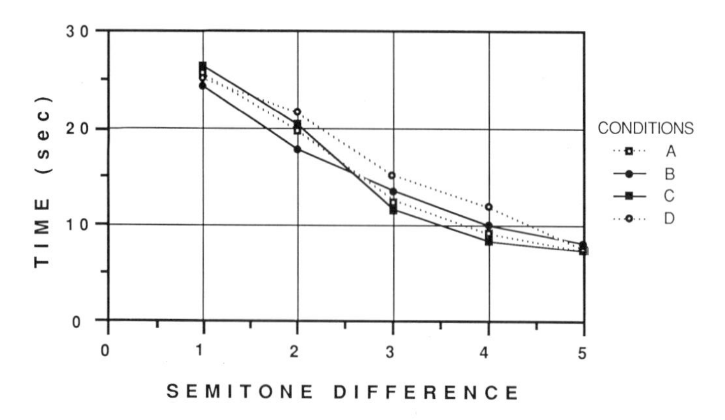

Figure 4.11
Results of an experiment by French-St. George and Bregman (1989) on stream segregation in which frequency separation and predictability were varied.

one semitone to five. In the one-semitone separation the two frequency ranges overlapped considerably, while for the four- and five-semitone separations they did not overlap at all.

In condition B the listener could predict when the next tone would come, but not what its frequency would be. In this condition, the same set of high and low tones was used as in the regular condition but the 30-second sequence was not a repeating cycle. The order of each successive eight tones was computed independently by shuffling the order of the high tones, shuffling the order of the low tones, and then interleaving them, so as to maintain the high-low alternation of the sequence. Again, the frequency separation between higher and lower tone sets was varied across trials.

In condition C the frequency of each successive tone was predictable, but the time between the tones was irregular. The sequence was a fixed repeating cycle of the original eight frequencies but the onset-to-onset time between successive tones was randomized between limits of 65.6 msec and 116.8 msec so as to keep an average rate of 91.2 msec. Again each 30-second trial had a different frequency separation.

In condition D we randomized the sequence of frequencies as in the B condition and the sequence of time intervals as in C.

In looking at the results, we found that that, in all conditions, the longer the listener listened, the less coherent the sequence became. This is in agreement with previous findings.[578] The results concerning frequency separation and predictability are shown in figure 4.11. In all four conditions we found, as expected, that the mean number of seconds, out of 30, for which the listener could hear the sequence as a single stream became less as the frequency separation between higher and lower tones became greater. Although Jones, Kidd, and Wetzel have proposed that stream integration is a prediction-based process and that the effect of frequency separation is restricted to cases where the sequence is predictable, we found no such restriction in our data.[579] Furthermore, the predictability of the sequence did not seem to help at all in holding the sequence together. The effects of frequency seemed about the same in all the conditions. If there was any condition that was different from the others it was D, the one in which both frequency and time were unpredictable; yet this sequence was easier, not harder, to hold together. The superiority of this condition, however, was not statistically significant.

It is still possible that predictability can help hold a stream together and that this experiment did not detect the conditions under which it does. For example, whenever the total stream was predictable, the substreams (high and low) also were. We do not know whether the predictability of the sub-streams helped them be heard as separate units, thereby counteracting the effects of the regularity of the global sequence (even though the listeners were asked to hold the overall sequence together). We need further experiments in which the regularity of the overall sequence and that of the within-substream sequence is varied independently. Another possible criticism of this experiment might be made: Due to the fact that the frequency separation changed on each trial, the listeners did not really become familiar enough with the regular sequence to take advantage of its regularity. In conditions with large frequency separations the sequence might have split before the hearer had a chance to learn it. Yet in certain intermediate separations, the listeners were able to hold on to the sequence as a coherent stream for a while, though not for the full 30 seconds. This should have enabled them to learn the regular sequence, yet there is no advantage for the regular conditions even at these intermediate separations. Another possibility is that the range of uncertainty in frequency and timing was too small.

Despite these criticisms, the experiment did succeed in showing that, at least within a certain range, neither a predictability in frequency nor in rhythm is a requirement for obtaining stream segregation effects.

The preceding sections have asked whether the regularity of a sequence, whether of pitch sequence or of timing, is responsible for holding it together. A number of observations have shown that while regularity seems in some cases to assist the attention in tracking a sequence of sounds over time, regularity is by no means a requirement for something to be heard as a coherent stream. Indeed, if it were, we would never be able to hear irregular sequences of sounds and we would be very surprised to discover that such sequences existed.

We have considered two elementary forms of regularity, simple trajectories and simple isochronous rhythms. Neither has a dominating influence on the formation of streams. Furthermore, it is not clear how to interpret the influences that do exist. Do they affect the primitive grouping process itself or some higher-level processes such as memory or attention?

"Are Streams Created by Attention?" Of course one could take the approach of denying that such a division existed and assert, instead, that all those phenomena that I have interpreted as arising from the activity of a preattentive process of primitive grouping arise instead from the activity of the attentional system itself. This approach would argue that a stream is simply that sequence of sounds that is selected by attention and that all the factors that are thought to influence primitive grouping are really influencing attention. This would imply that there is only one stream active at any moment, the one that we are attending to. However, the Bregman-Rudnicky experiment was done to examine this question and it concluded that streams were being formed among tones that were being rejected by attention and that this made it easier to reject them as a group (the "wrap up all your garbage in the same bundle" heuristic). I would refer the reader to the many discussions of this experiment elsewhere in this volume, especially the one in chapter 2, where we consider the question of whether there is only one stream active at a time.

Helmholtz might well have subscribed to the view that grouping is due to attention. For example, when he presented his method of playing a tone before a complex tone to assist a listener in hearing out one of the partials, he described it as a way of directing the listener's attention to the relevant partial. I have presented this method, on the other hand, as being derivable from a very general principle of preattentive grouping.

Could either Helmholtz or the author be wrong? To avoid such an outcome let me restate an earlier explanation that, while inelegant, has the virtue of preserving the honor of two scientists. There are both preattentive and attentional processes that can latch onto acoustic features as a method of attaining their ends. In the example of hearing out a partial, this process seems to involve effort and trying to hear the earlier sound in the mixture. This suggests a role for conscious attention. On the other hand, acoustic factors can make this attempt easy or hard. While it is possible that they affect the difficulty by denying the attention a clear criterion for latching onto the desired sound in the mixture, I believe that the existence of a primitive scene-analyzing process (supported by many arguments in this volume) is an attractive enough idea to be worth keeping.

There is merit in having redundant systems, a primitive one and another that is schema-driven. The primitive one can make early learning possible in a wide variety of environments and the educated one can sharpen up our listening in environments whose particular regularities we have learned to exploit. Let us think of a schema as a pattern of regularity in the world as it has been captured by some formula in the brain.

It might be instructive to ask ourselves what kinds of schemas are used by a listener who is trying to use an earlier sound to pull out a partial from a mixture. There are obviously all the myriad schemas by which we control our behaviors, including ones for decoding the language of the scientist who has sat us down to do this unlikely task. However, a crucial schema for doing this particular task is the notion of a "repetition." Without it we could not program ourselves to listen for something in the mixture that was a repetition of the earlier sound. I am not saying that we could not *hear* a repetition without a cognitive representation of the concept of repetition. I am saying, however, that we could not *listen* for one. That is, we could not govern our attention in a goal-directed way. The topic of schemas is far too rich to be dealt with in this book. I mean only to give a flavor here of what we would be looking for if we began to look for schemas that might help us to do auditory tasks.

I do not mean to imply that the two proposed processes, the one primitive and preattentive and the other schema-driven and attention-directing, always react the same way to the same acoustic variables. If this were true there would be no way to distinguish them. Sometimes they react differently. For example, when you are trying to hold on to a one-stream interpretation of a sequence of alternating high and low tones, the frequency separation of the tones and the speed of the sequence interact. At faster speeds a smaller frequency separation is required, presumably because a primitive process is trying to form substreams at faster speeds while the attentional process is trying to hold the sequence together. However, if you are trying to segregate the two streams, your ability to do so requires only a small frequency separation and is virtually independent of the speed of the sequence. Apparently when the primitive process wants to take the sequence apart, this hurts the voluntary segregation process. But even when the primitive process creates only a single

F A M I L I A R I T Y B R E E D S C O N T E M P T

F A M I L I A R I T Y B R E E D S C O NFTLEEMAPST

Figure 4.12
Extracting a set of letters out of a mixture by using the fact that they complete a familiar phrase.

stream, as when the frequencies are close together, it is still possible for the attentional process to take it apart by listening in a goal-directed way for either the higher or lower tone. These observations seem to show that it is easier to *select* a part of a sequence against the dictates of the primitive process than to *integrate* it against the workings of the primitive process. Attention does not operate with equal facility on any combination of sensory elements. Otherwise it would not be hard to select anything at all for attention. Hopefully we can use these conflicts between what we want to do and what we can do to clarify the nature of primitive grouping and attention.

I have taken the position that primitive grouping processes actually sort the signal but that the more sophisticated schema-based processes simply select what they need and do not leave a residual that is either diminished in any way or organized. In some sense they do not remove the evidence that they need from a mixture. They interpret it, but leave it there for other schemas to interpret too. It would be possible to design an experiment to test this view. It would be necessary to do an experiment along the lines of the one done by Bregman and Rudnicky that I described in chapter 1 and illustrated in figure 1.7.[580] In that experiment, a sequence of tones formed a stream and captured target tones out of a second stream in such a way as to make a judgment task on the second stream easier. This latter effect proved that it was a true capturing that leaves a residual that is simpler than it would be without the capturing. Now the experiment must be altered so that the target tones are not bound to their captors by frequency similarity, as they were in Bregman and Rudnicky's experiment, but by the fact that captors and targets together form a familiar pattern, one that would plausibly be united by means of a schema. It would have to be similar to the sequence that I have illustrated in figure 4.12, with sounds taking the place of letters.

Although I made up the example myself and the second line is the same as the first, I can extract the second word "contempt" from the jumble of letters only with effort, and I cannot detect the residual

C OPN ITGESM P T

Figure 4.13
Segregation of letters by the primitive properties of size and darkness.

word without an elaborate mental process of calculation. Look at the difference when the segregation is induced by the primitive factors of size and darkness, as shown in figure 4.13. The segregation is now effortless and both words in the mixed sequence are legible. I would expect the auditory experiment to show a similar effect.

Chapter 5
Auditory Organization in Music

Music is built out of sound. Therefore we should not be surprised if its perceptual organization is governed, at least in part, by the primitive scene-analyzing principles whose exposition has occupied the earlier parts of this book. Therefore, I plan to look at some musical phenomena from the perspective of these principles.

A musician might object that most of what is musically exciting has little to do with basic audition. Yet we cannot deny that we hear music through the same ears that provide us with the sounds of everyday life. I do not mean to assert that there is nothing more to music. Music builds elaborate structures of sound, but its esthetic tools are not merely the raw properties of the individual sounds. It also builds upon the scaffolding provided by a host of structural concepts such as scales, modes, and key relations and a variety of transformations that include transposition and repetition. The experienced musical listener makes use of a large number of musical concepts or schemas in listening to music. If this were to be a chapter on the psychology of music it would have to include some description of the role that musical knowledge plays when we listen to music. I would expect that topic to be as deep as the study of how we use linguistic knowledge when we listen to speech.

The discussion that follows, however, is on an admittedly narrower topic, the role of primitive organization in musical listening—not because the knowledge-based one is unimportant, but because its enormous complexity places it outside the scope of the present book.

I am not trying to recommend anything to musicians but merely looking for valid descriptions. An example of such a description might be one that shows that the auditory system assigns location labels independently to bands of energy at different spectral locations, and identifies the resolution with which it can do so. Naturally, I believe that if this is a valid description of the auditory system, it will have consequences for a number of human activities that involve the patterning of sound, including speech and music.

In my discussion of music in this chapter and speech in the next, the goal is not to find support for the principles themselves. This can be done only in highly analytic laboratory studies where unwanted influences can be equalized or randomized across conditions. If we tried to verify our principles by appealing to music, armed, as we are, with a number of different principles and the huge data base of music, we would easily be able to select cases that verify the principles. Rather, the goal is to speculate on, and try to understand, the use that is being made of these principles in complex cases of human audition.

Musical Scene Analysis

Traditionally, music is thought of as having a horizontal and a vertical dimension. This derives from musical notation in which the horizontal dimension stands for time and the vertical one depicts pitch relations. The choice of these two dimensions is not arbitrary and we find them not only in musical scores but in the scientist's spectrogram. Our standard western musical notation is not truly an analog for the raw sound of the music. For example, note durations are indicated by solidness or shape. However, because much of the pitch and timing information is translated into the two spatial dimensions of the score, many of the perceptual groupings that we see in the score correspond to groupings that we hear in the music.

Western musicians talk about the "warp" and the "woof" in music, a metaphor drawn from weaving, in which the woof, or the yarns that are placed lengthwise on the loom, represent the horizontal dimension, the successive sounds that form melodies, and the warp, or crosswise yarns, stand for the vertical dimension, the simultaneous sounds that form harmonies. When musicians speak of "musical texture" they are referring to how these types of threads go together, how strong the vertical ones are in comparison with the horizontal ones, how the horizontal ones change over time, moving together or independently, and so on. The choice of the metaphor of a woven cloth implies that the woof and warp are more than merely dimensions of the music; rather they are organizations that hold the music together in the same way that fibers hold a cloth together.

Some musical textures are said to be primarily horizontal or polyphonic in nature, the separate lines (melody for example) dominating over the harmonic dimension, and others are deemed mostly vertical, with the dominance reversed. For example, at cadences (note sequences that signal the ends of significant sections of the piece), the independence of lines is reduced and stream segregation is weakened.

The lines come back together again, signaling their unity as part of a single piece to the listener. There are degrees of finality, corresponding to the importance of the segment boundary that is being reached, and the degree of disappearance of segregation varies with the degree of finality (for example, ending with a pair of simultaneous notes spaced by an octave is more final than if they are separated by a musical third).

In much complex contemporary music we cannot talk about melodic lines in the traditional sense, but still there exist horizontal and vertical dimensions of organization. The total mass of sound may separate itself into layers that are distinct from others and persist for varying lengths of time. The way in which each of these layers continues and changes over time is the horizontal dimension. There can also be moments in the sound at which the different components fuse into a single global impression, such as at a crescendo or at the modern equivalent of a cadence, where the vertical organization is made to prevail.

The argument that I will make is that although these organizations can arise as a result of a particular musical style, they are based on general principles of auditory organization. To the extent that they are, the underlying principles transcend any musical style. If this is true, different musical styles simply give the underlying principles the opportunity to operate to greater or lesser degrees, but cannot change them.

Before beginning to apply stream organizing principles to music, we should notice that music often tries to fool the auditory system into hearing fictional streams. In natural environments, the principles that govern auditory scene analysis have evolved to build perceptual representations of the distinct sound-emitting events of our environment: the wind, a person talking, the train off in the distance, and so on. There are individual events in music too, sounds that occur when a particular string (as on a violin) or column of air (as in a woodwind), or other sound source vibrates. However, music does not always want these to be the basic units of our experience. Often, when a set of strings vibrates together, they are intended to be heard as a single source (as in the individual piano note). A set of different musical instruments may be used to create a chord or some other composite sound that is meant to be heard as a global whole. In order to get sounds to blend, the music must defeat the scene-analysis processes that are trying to uncover the individual physical sources of sound. Sometimes a composer wants a single physical source to be heard as two lines of melody as in the "virtual polyphony" that occurs when a single instrument rapidly alternates between two registers. To achieve this goal, the basic principles of auditory organization have to be exploited by means of voice leading and orchestration.

Although some parts of the crafts of counterpoint, orchestration, and construction of melodies are often codified into explicit rules, others are not, and the composer must learn through listening to music and through trial and error. A scientist would like to see all the principles written down. Many musicians assert that any principles that could be adduced, such as rules of counterpoint, would apply only to a particular form or style of music. As a scientist, I want to believe that this is not so, and that while many such rules will be specific to a style, if we dig deep enough, we will find universal principles of perception that can be converted to knowledge about orchestration. This belief is not unique to scientists. Many musicians espouse it; among them are composers and theorists of contemporary music such as Robert Erickson, who has argued that "we need a music theory that is not style bound, that is valid for world music, not its European, Chinese, or Indonesian varieties."[581]

I can imagine a description of orchestration that addresses issues such as the following: How can you make sounds fuse to create a single timbre? Which qualities of the individual sounds will contribute which aspects of this global timbre? How can multiple, simultaneous timbres be kept perceptually distinct from one another? What are the acoustic factors that are responsible for all these effects? Such a description would not be prescriptive, telling the composer what to do in the manner of traditional academic schools, but would simply say, "If you want this effect, do that, and here is the reason that it works." This chapter will not be that general description. It would have to be written by someone with a deeper knowledge of music.[582]

Although I have mentioned only the grouping of simultaneous events in this last description, I expect that sequential organization, which is responsible for the coherence of melodies, could be addressed as well. Contemporary music can have a particular problem in this regard because it cannot always fall back on traditional principles. It is possible, in such music, that the progression of sounds may have a sequential structure in the mind of the composer, that a written score may also show a sequential structure, but that there may be no such coherence in the mind of the listener. Pierre Boulez has complained that modern music often flies apart from centrifugal forces because there is no relation between the musical objects. For this reason, he argues, polyphony and homophony should be rethought.[583] I assume that by centrifugal forces he refers to the tendency of unrelated sounds to be heard in separate streams.

Before getting into greater detail I would like to introduce an idea that will be used throughout this chapter. This is that both sequential and simultaneous organizations actually *create* certain aspects of musical experience. Sequential grouping creates rhythms and different aspects of melodic form. Vertical organization gives us not only the experience of chords but also other emergent qualities of simultaneous sounds, e.g., timbre, consonance, and dissonance. These phenomena arise when certain acoustic components are perceptually grouped into the same vertical organization. It may seem strange to hear that dissonance arises from perceptual grouping, but, as we shall see later, there is reason to believe that it does.[584]

The sonic objects of music derive only in a very indirect way from the real instruments that are playing. We have to take into account the effects of both sequential and simultaneous organization in forming the streams that we hear and their emergent qualities.

Let me review what I mean by emergent properties. When elements enter into a higher-order organization, new properties are formed. For example, three straight lines, when joined in the right way, form a triangle. This triangle may be a closed form despite the fact that the none of the elements composing it is closed. "Closed" is an emergent or global property. In daily life, we can hone a knife until it is sharp, despite the fact that none of the molecules that compose it is sharp. Sharpness is an emergent property. Similarly, we can compose a sound that is voice-like, despite the fact that not one of the sine waves that compose it is voice-like. We can call this an emergent feature.

The things that we call emergent properties arise because the perceptual system does some of its analyses on larger-sized objects. The perceived boundaries of these larger objects, and hence the sensory materials that are considered to be part of each one, are governed by principles of grouping. In the day-to-day activity of the auditory system, their job is to create a description of the input so that the sensory effects derived from a particular sound source are grouped together into the description of that source, so that any emergent properties that arise will be characteristic of that sound source. I will call that a "natural" assignment and contrast it with a "chimeric" assignment. The Chimaera was a beast in Greek mythology with the head of a lion, the body of a goat, and the tail of a serpent. We use the word chimera metaphorically to refer to an image derived as a composition of other images. An example of an auditory chimera would be a heard sentence that was created by the accidental composition of the voices of two persons who just happened to be speaking at the same time. Natural hearing tries to avoid chimeric percepts, but music often tries to create them. It may want the listener to accept the simultaneous roll of the drum, clash of the cymbal, and brief pulse of noise from the woodwinds as a single coherent event with its own striking emergent properties. The sound is chimeric in the sense that it does not belong to any single environmental object.

To avoid chimeras the auditory system utilizes the correlations that normally hold between acoustic components that derive from a single source and the independence that usually exists between the sensory effects of different sources. Frequently orchestration is called upon to oppose these tendencies and force the auditory system to create chimeras. A composer may want the listener to group the sounds from different instruments and hear this grouping as a sound with its own emergent properties. This grouping is not a real source, however. Stephen McAdams has referred to it as a "virtual" source, perhaps drawing the analogy from the virtual image of optics, an example of which is the person who appears to look at you from the other side of your mirror each morning.[585] In order to create a virtual source, music manipulates the factors that control the formation of sequential and simultaneous streams. The virtual source in music plays the same perceptual role as our perception of a real source does in natural environments. It provides a sense of an entity that endures for some period of time (perhaps only briefly) and serves as a center of description. In a natural forest environment the individual sounds in a succession of frog croaks or footsteps are all treated as coming from the same source, and it is this idea of a common source that holds the succession together. Surely this must also be true for orchestral sounds, except that in the orchestral case the source is not a real one but a virtual one created by the acoustic relations in the music. It is the virtual source that is heard as having this or that quality, as being high or low, soft or loud, shrill or dull, staccato or legato, rapid or slow-moving. Experiences of real sources and of virtual sources are both examples of auditory streams. They are different not in terms of their psychological properties, but in the reality of the things that they refer to in the world. Real sources tell a true story; virtual sources are fictional.

There are two different kinds of vertical integration in multipart music. One is the actual fusion of sounds to create ensemble timbres. The other kind, not so strong, is the type of integration that causes the different "voices" to be experienced as parts of a single musical piece. This integration does not arise merely because the parts are played at the same time. If we were to hear, over a pair of headphones, a recording of a piano sonata by Beethoven in one ear and a violin partita by Bach in the other, this would not produce a sense of a single musical object for us. Therefore, within a single piece of music, which *is* perceived as a single musical object, the segregation of the parallel lines cannot be as extreme as the segregation of one piece from another or as the segregation of a voice from the sound of a car passing on the street.

Our scene-analysis process is not parsing the parts in a piece of music as wholly distinct auditory objects. Instead it is creating a hierarchical description, marking out the parts as distinct at one level of the hierarchy and the total composition as a unit at a higher level. This is like the visual example of seeing a mass of bubbles at the global level and individual bubbles at the lower level. The factors that make the lines of music cohere as parts of the same thing all fall into the category of lack of independence. If they were totally independent, as far as key, rhythm, pitch range, melodic material, and harmony were concerned, they would not be heard as parts of a single auditory event (although they might have some sort of conceptual relation). You would simply think that two groups of musicians were practicing. Even music of the type written by Charles Ives must have important musical relations between the parts; if this did not have to be true, we could create an endless fund of such music by simply combining the works of the existing repertoire two at a time, three at a time, and so on. It would be interesting to study what sorts of relations are required between two groups of sounds before they are experienced as part of the same higher-order event.

Unfortunately, the musical ways in which dependence among parts can be achieved are so numerous that any study of this question would be beyond the scope of this book. Furthermore, they are usually not based on primitive grouping principles. Therefore, while I acknowledge the importance of this hierarchical form of vertical integration, I will have to restrict my consideration of vertical integration to the more primitive type in which a number of simultaneous sounds fuse together and are heard as a single sound.

Melody

Let us first consider sequential (or horizontal) organization in music. We know from chapter 2 that both rate and frequency separation affects the integrity of perceived sequences. If they jump rapidly back and forth between frequency regions they will not be heard as coherent.

Coherence of Melodies

We know from a number of studies that the perceptual coherence of a sequence of pure tones depends on the rate of the tones and on their frequency separation. As the frequency separation becomes wider, we must slow down the sequence in order to maintain coherence. These experiments were done with pure tones; thus, the effects of pitch and frequency cannot be distinguished, because each tone contains only one frequency component. In the tones produced by instruments or by the human voice, each tone contains many frequency components, and the pitch depends on the fundamental frequency. Fortunately there is some evidence that the fundamental frequencies of complex tones act like the frequencies of pure tones in grouping sequences of tones.[586]

Van Noorden has commented on the fact that there is no principle of music composition that restricts the rate of tones as a function of their pitch separation.[587] We know that any piece of music is likely to have notes that span at least an octave. Why then are melodies not usually heard to fly apart as in the streaming phenomenon? One reason is that despite the absence of a specific rule, musicians have known for a long time that notes that were closer in frequency to one another stuck together better perceptually. As the composer Milton Babbitt has pointed out, this has become more evident as modern technology has allowed tone sequences to be controlled more exactly in electronic music.[588] Western music tends to have notes that are rarely shorter than 150 msec in duration. Those that form melodic themes fall in the range of 150 to 900 msec.[589] Notes shorter than this tend to stay close to their neighbors in frequency and are used to create a sort of ornamental effect.[590]

W. J. Dowling analyzed twenty recordings of Baroque music and found the median tone rate to be 6.3 tones per second.[591] At these rates, even with wide pitch excursions, it is very hard to get really strong segregation between subsets of tones. A second factor that favors coherence is that frequency transitions tend to be small. As a demonstration that music makes use of the fact that smaller steps in pitch hang together better, the psychologist Otto Ortmann counted the number of sequential (melodic) intervals of different sizes in 160 songs by Schubert, Schumann, Brahms, and Richard Strauss (about 23,000 intervals in all).[592] He found that the smallest ones were the most numerous, with the tabulated number of cases dropping off roughly in inverse proportion to the size of the interval, with small increases in likelihood for important harmonic relationships. The tendency for music to contain a preponderance of small melodic intervals has also been noted more recently by the musicologist Fucks.[593] Regarding the music of other cultures, anthropologists have reported that melodies of the world tend to have narrow pitch ranges.[594] It is possible that this may derive from the fact that music

Table 5.1
Musical fragments with compound melodic lines (Dowling 1967).

Composer	Selection	Index[a]	Artist	Instrument[b]	Recording	Tempo	T (msec)	Rank
J. S. Bach	Partita 3, Preludio	BWV 1006	Heifetz	Violin	Victor LM-6105	8.8	114	2
	Sonata 3, Fuga	BWV 1005	Heifetz	Violin	Victor LM-6105	5.9	169	12
	Partita 2, Ciacconna	BWV 1004	Heifetz	Violin	Victor LM-6105	4.6	218	16
P. A. Locatelli	l'Arte del violino XII, 1		Lautenbacher	Violin	Vox VBX-41	8.0	125	7
	l'Arte del violino XII, 2		Lautenbacher	Violin	Vox VBX-41	8.5	118	3
H. F. Biber	Passacagli in g		Lautenbacher	Violin	Vox VBX 52	3.1	322	20
J. S. Bach	Partita, Corrente	BWV 1013	Bobzien	Flute	Archiv-3226	8.2	124	5
	Sonata in E, Allegro	BWV 1035	Bobzien	Flute (cembalo)	Archiv-3226	7.2	139	8
	Sonata in b, Andante	BWV 1030	Bobzien	Flute (cembalo)	Archiv-3226	4.0	250	18
	Partita, Corrente	BWV 1013	Rampal	Flute	Epic LC3899	8.5	118	4
G. P. Telemann	Fantasia 6, Allegro		Rampal	Flute	Epic LC3899	4.9	204	15
C. P. E. Bach	Sonata, Allegro I		Rampal	Flute	Epic LC3899	6.4	156	10
G. P. Telemann	Fantasia 6, Allegro		Baron	Flute	Washington 402	4.0	250	19
A. Vivaldi	Sonata in a, Allegro		Baron	Flute (continuo)	Odyssey	5.0	200	14
	Concerto in C, Allegro I	P 79	Baron	Piccolo flute (strings)	36160012	6.2	162	11
	Concerto in C, Allegro I	P 79	Linde	Piccolo recorder (strings)	Archiv-3218	4.0	250	17
	Concerto in C, Allegro molto	P 79	Linde	Piccolo recorder (strings)	Archiv-3218	7.0	143	9
J. S. Bach	Goldberg variations, no. 8	BWV 988	Kirkpatrick	Keyboard	Archiv-3138	8.2	124	6
	Wohltemp. Klavier, Fuga 10	BWV 855	Kirkpatrick	Keyboard	Archiv-8211/2	5.3	189	13
	Wohltemp. Klavier, Prel. 3	BWV 848	Kirkpatrick	Keyboard	Archiv-8211/2	9.1	110	1

a. BWV, Bachs Werken Verzeichnis; P, Pincherle-index.
b. Accompaniment in parentheses.

may have its origins in singing, and that small jumps in pitch may be easier for the human voice. However, the effects of small pitch steps in holding the melody together perceptually may also have played a role, especially in music played on instruments.

It is possible for melodies to remain unified even if they occasionally employ large jumps in pitch. This is possible because frequency proximities are competitive. Even though a particular pitch transition (for example, from a low A to a high B) may be a large leap, unless the sequence leaps right back down to where it started from, the earlier tone, A, will generally not find another tone that is near enough to it in both time and frequency to be a better partner than the B. Therefore the melody will not skip over the B.

While musicians know how to make melodies coherent, they also know how to split them apart. In the Baroque period, composers such as Bach and Telemann often used a technique in which a solo instrument, by alternating between a high and a low register, would create the effect of two lines of melody being played concurrently. (Table 5.1 lists some musical fragments that possess this structure.) Later, the musicologists evolved names for this technique. If it involves rapid alternation between high and low tones (i.e., every other note being high)—as is commonly found, for example, in baroque solo violin music—it is called virtual polyphony. The more general technique, in which there is not strict alternation but the tones tend to alternate irregularly between high and low, is called compound melodic line, implied polyphony, or melodic segregation.[595] Robert Erickson has given a detailed illustration of stream segregation in Bach's finale from his C Major solo violin sonata.[596] He has also reported that informal experiments by students in his timbre seminar at the University of California, San Diego, suggest that it is difficult for a musician to maintain more than three streams in perception. This has led him to ask whether more streams could be created if all the resources of pitch, timbre, and melodic and rhythmic patterning were used. I suspect that more than three can be created, but not by a single musician playing only one note at a time. The techniques that are used to produce compound melodic lines in music do not give as strong a segregation between high and low streams as the laboratory examples that I have described in earlier chapters. The alternation of registers in a single instrument tends to produce a more ambiguous percept in which either the two separate lines or the entire sequence of tones can be followed. This is probably due to the fact that the human player cannot alternate between the high and low registers as fast as the 10 tones per second rate that I have used in many of my experiments; in addition, the frequency separations are probably not as high. It is not certain that the composers who used this technique would have called for such an unambiguous separation of musical lines even if the players could have achieved it. It is likely that the technique was not used simply as a way of getting two instruments for the price of one, but as a way of creating an interesting experience for the listener by providing two alternative organizations.

We should not, however, think of the number of distinct melodic lines that can be created by a single series of nonoverlapping tones as the limit to the number of streams we can maintain at the same time. The segregation of a number of simultaneously playing instruments is probably based on the same principles as compound melodic lines. Therefore, if we are capable of segregating any one of six instruments from an ensemble (and this could be made easy if the part-writing avoided correlations between the lines and if the selection of instruments was designed expressly to enhance segregation), we should consider each of these as giving rise to a perceptual stream. We surely cannot pay attention to all these streams at the same time. But the existence of a perceptual grouping does not imply that it is being attended to. It is merely available to attention on a continuing basis. Metaphorically speaking, it holds up its head to be counted but does not do the counting. One difficulty in hearing a particular instrument in a combination, assuming that you do not have any advance knowledge about the piece, is to know where in the spectrum to listen for it. The attention can be caught by a particular cluster of sensory data that has been formed by primitive scene analysis and may neglect the others. One way to get the attention of the listener onto a line is to let that line be audible alone during a gap in the others. We could probably compose a large number of distinct lines only under special circumstances, and these would probably be examples of rather poor music since a piece of music is probably not supposed to be heard as six different things at once. Therefore, the musical goals, rather than the auditory system, may be limiting the number of streams.

The role of frequency similarities in grouping musical tones was made explicit in a treatise by Otto Ortmann in 1926.[597] He argued that "the degree of association varies inversely as the pitch difference, or pitch distance" and that "*it is unbroken by any periodicity, such as octave-relationship, or fifth-relationship.*" The latter observation can be verified by looking at the observations of van Noorden on the temporal coherence boundary as illustrated in figure 2.2 of chapter 2.[598] There is no drop in the function at 12 semitones separation as you would expect if notes were somehow more similar to those an octave away than to those that were not quite an octave away. I have noticed the same absence of an octave effect in unpublished research done in collaboration with Gary Bernstein at McGill. This suggests that although the octave may be a privileged acoustic relation for tones played *at the same time*, and may have a privileged *musical* status when played sequentially, it occupies no position of acoustic privilege when the two notes are played in succession. It seems to be the mere size of the difference in log frequency rather than the nature of the musical interval that affects sequential integration.

Ortmann also noted the emergence of compound melodic lines when tones alternated between high and low ranges; he explained it by arguing that the proximity of frequencies within each melodic line created a strong enough association between them to overcome the association based on proximity in time that existed between the actually successive tones. He noted that the perceptual strength of the individual melodies that emerge from the segregation was strongest when the pitch variation within a component melody was small in comparison with the pitch distance between melodies.

We have noted the experiments of W. J. Dowling in chapter 2. Dowling did a number of studies in which he interleaved the notes of two familiar melodies played as a sequence of square-wave tones at the rate of eight tones per second and asked music students to recognize them.[599] When the fundamental frequencies of the notes in the two melodies overlapped, the overall sequence was heard as integrated, yielding an unfamiliar pattern of notes. However, in other conditions, over a series of repetitions he gradually transposed the notes of the one of the melodies upward until the fundamentals of the tones of the two melodies no longer occupied overlapping ranges. The task of the subjects was to name one of the melodies as soon as possible, and then to name the second melody whenever they could. They were able to do so fairly well when the ranges no longer overlapped and there was about a semitone separation between the two ranges. When a familiar tune was interleaved with random tones in the same fundamental frequency range, and the subjects knew which one they were listening for, they could often detect it. In another of Dowling's experiments, a short manufactured melody was presented to the listener. Then they heard the same or a similar melody interleaved with distractor tones and were asked if, apart from the distractor tones, the melody was the the same or different. This was much easier when the fundamentals of the distractors were separated in frequency from those of the melody. However, the isolation was never complete. Even with a 12-semitone separation an interleaved background produced interference. This research shows that stream segregation operated in a musical context in much the same way as it did in the experiments on simple repeating cycles of tones that we examined in chapter 2. It is reassuring to discover that the use of cycles in the laboratory, introduced for methodological reasons, did not produce a phenomenon that could not be seen in more natural circumstances.

Sequential organization is responsible for the perceived shape of melodies. We have already seen how a sequence of notes or a melody can be recognized only when it is sufficiently well segregated from potentially interfering notes with which it is interleaved. But what of cases in which there is no interference at all? Can our ability to organize a sequence of sounds have an effect on our ability to recognize it? Evidence that it does comes from research on sequences of sounds in which the listener's task is not to reject interfering notes as in the experiments of Dowling, but to *integrate* the entire sequence for purposes of recognition. In normal music, whenever it is possible to hear a melodic or rhythmic pattern this integration has taken place. But it is not always possible. For example, in rapid cycles of unrelated sounds (such as hiss, buzz, whistle, and voice) of the type used by Warren and his colleagues, it is very hard to recognize the order of the sounds.[600] The sequence seems formless. One reason for this has been mentioned earlier: The sequence may segregate into subsequences of related sounds. There may be another reason as well: We may mentally encode any sequence by the nature of the transformations that take place in it. When a succession of tones are all of the same type (for example, periodic sounds with similar timbres), we may encode it not by a categorization of the individual sounds but by an encoding of the changes or movements that take us from one sound to the next. I am not proposing a general theory of sequence encoding of the type proposed by M. R. Jones and described in chapter 4. I am making a much more limited claim, namely that the transformations constitute an important part of the encoding. Once encoded, a series of transformations is probably encoded again as a sequential form or melody. Because we know very little about how forms are represented in the brain, we cannot say much about this encoding of form except that it makes the sequence distinctive. The work of Jay Dowling and his colleagues suggests that the pattern of ups and downs and how these are embedded in a rhythm may be the most recognizable parts of these forms.[601] We know from extensive research on human memory that a unit is more memorable when it is embedded in a network of related units (in the way that facts are embedded in a story). It may be the same with musical sounds. Unless the sequence of sounds can be integrated into a sequential form, the sequence taken as a whole may not be memorable. The ability to encode acoustic transitions may depend on the same sorts of sequential similarities as primitive scene analysis depends on. Streaming may be only a more extreme effect of these similarities. When a sequence is formed of very different types of sounds, at high speeds the lack of integration may create separate streams, with each sound regrouping itself with those that are most similar to itself in preference to grouping with its nearest temporal neighbors. At lower rates the similar sounds may be too far separated in time to form separate streams, but the dissimilarity of adjacent sounds may still inhibit the formation of melodic forms, with the result that what we hear is a disjointed series of sounds—an extreme form of "klangfarbenmelodie." Except that it is not a "melodie" at all, since that would imply the presence of a sequential form. Rather than a form, we are left with a kind of perceptual granularity.

The distinction between an integrated sequence and an unintegrated one is both tricky and important. It seems likely that only when a sequence is integrated do we perceive it as a form, a coherent stream that changes its properties as it evolves over time, instead of as a sequence of unconnected sounds. Awareness of this fact can prevent composers from creating patterns that seem like musical forms in the score but are not heard as such. This pertains particularly to computer-generated music, because in the process of composing such a piece the composer may listen to a particular sequence of sounds dozens of times and may form a mental schema that describes its form. The composer's own schema-driven integration may be successful even when primitive grouping processes do not work. This can be misleading to the composer. It may be unrealistic to expect audiences to be prepared to listen to a piece dozens of times before they hear any form. Any composer who is too demanding in this respect may produce works that may be magnificent to the highly trained ear, but may never be shareable with a community of any size.

In nature, most sounds change in a fairly continuous way. Smooth slow changes allow us to incorporate the change as a transformation in the quality of a single object rather than a shift to a new one. However, in Western music the melodic shapes are formed not by continuous changes but by sequences of discrete steps along musical scales. This is not the same as hearing one continuous sound. Our ability to integrate such sequences may be related to the necessity to do so in natural environments. The natural cases that involve sequences of discrete sounds include footsteps, bird and animal calls, a person chopping wood, and so on. We may have to know that the discrete units are present (for example, to count them), but we also have to experience them as parts of a sequence that makes sense as a whole. Fortunately nature, having presented us with the necessity for hearing such units, has provided us with the means for doing so. We hear discrete units when the sound changes abruptly in timbre, pitch, loudness, or (to a lesser extent) location in space. A beginning is heard when the sound goes from a softer level to a louder one; an end is heard when the reverse is true.

The formation of boundaries in the visual system involves no such asymmetry. An outer edge of a form can be indicated by either a sudden drop in brightness (where the object is brighter than its background) or a sudden rise (where the background is brighter). By way of contrast, the end of a sound can never be indicated by a rise in intensity. This is because sounds are transparent. Therefore a nearer but softer sound can never occlude from perception a farther but louder one.

Even though certain discontinuities in their properties may put boundaries around individual sounds, their sequential similarity may bind them into a larger organization, the sequence of repeating sounds. We will be led to attribute the whole sequence to a common source. This will permit us to bring the successive sounds into relation with one another to discover the patterns that they make.

Transformations in loudness, timbre, and other acoustic properties may allow the listener to conclude that the maker of a sound is drawing nearer, becoming weaker or more aggressive, or changing in other ways. However, in order to justify such conclusions, it must be known that the sounds that bear these acoustic relations to one another are derived from the same source. Therefore only transformations that are computed among elements that have been assigned to the same stream should be treated as real. This strategy of allowing discrete elements to be the bearers of form or "transformation" only if they are in the same stream is the foundation of our experience of sequential form in music as much as in real life.

Leo van Noorden has pointed out a particularly strong case of sequential integration that occurs when there is only one or two semitones separating successive notes and the sequence is very rapid. He calls this fusion and describes it as a sort of melting of the successive tones into one another, yielding an experience of a glissando.[602] This permits us to use discrete-tone instruments to produce a sort of pitch glide, though it does not sound exactly like real pitch glides on string instruments. Van Noorden sees our experience of trills as an example of sequential fusion. Another example can be seen in Stravinsky's *Firebird*. At the beginning of the "infernal dance" movement, a rapid four-note run on the flute becomes a unified gesture, perceived as a glissando.

The timbre of notes affects the way they go together to form a melodic line. Similar timbres tend to group with one another, and this can either cement the melodic line or tear it apart, depending on whether the timbre similarities group the same notes together as the pitch relations do. Timbres seem to have been first conceived as the sounds of different instruments. In music that involved different instruments playing at the same time, typically a line of melody was given to a single instrument. Therefore each timbre was associated with a melodic line. Indeed our current concept of a melodic line which can, in principle, bounce back and forth between instruments is a rather sophisticated notion that has abstracted the concept of "melodic voice" out of the original "part played by an instrument." The traditional use of timbre (or instrument), then, has been to carry a melody. This has been referred to as the "carrier" function of timbre by Robert Erickson.[603] However, when the notions of instrument and melodic voice are distinguished from one another, the composer can create lines that are played first by one instrument (timbre) then by another. The transitions between one timbre and the next within the same line create an awareness of the timbres as such and they become, in their own right, what Erickson has called "objects." If these timbre changes are accompanied by large changes in pitch or of abruptness of note onsets, the objects become even more separated in perception. This grouping by timbre does not have to be all-or-nothing in nature. The composer can create conflicts between the groupings based on pitch and timbre. Such conflicts provide much of the interest in music by Anton Webern and Edgard Varèse. These composers are sometimes thought of as having used timbre as the major source of structure in their music, but, as Pierre Boulez has pointed out, neither composed purely by means of timbre. Rather, they used the "contradiction" between timbre and pitch to create musical form.[604] An interesting use of timbre for this purpose was made by Webern in his orchestration of the Ricercar from *The Musical Offering* by Johann Sebastian Bach.[605] Each of the parts is not assigned to a different instrument. Instead, a part is taken first by one timbre then another so that particular gestures and phrases in the music are outlined by the changes in timbre. The distinct timbres are created either by a single instrument or by a group of instruments whose sounds are pooled into an emergent timbre because they are moving together in close harmony. The result is unsettling, yet hauntingly beautiful. The smooth flow of the melody is replaced by a perceptual experience in which each phrase is placed under a microscope, as it were. The rates at which the timbres change (once every second or two) are not sufficient to totally break up the melody and we do not get the extreme sorts of segregative effects that we do in virtual polyphony. The effects are more subtle and intensify the musical meanings of the phrases. The experience of the Ricercar reminds me of the feeling that we get when looking at the pictures of faces in which the features are actually different sorts of vegetables or other objects. A number of these were painted in the late sixteenth century by the Milanese artist Giuseppe Arcimboldo.[606] Although we see the individual vegetables, we also get an impression of the whole face. The Webern example is not as extreme, however, and does not labor under the constraint of making the smaller parts appear to be recognizable fragments in their own right; therefore the Webern treatment supplements, rather than detracts from, our experience of the larger forms in the work of art. It differs from klangfarbenmelodie in that in klangfarbenmelodie the timbres are creating the forms, whereas in Webern's treatment they are merely making them stand out.

Phenomenal Dependency Based on Timing

Patterns of sounds create musical forms, but the properties that any individual sound will give to the form will depend on the other sounds that are present and the timing relations between them. A sound can contribute to the large-scale shape of the musical phrase or can merely be appended to another sound as an ornamentation.

Let us look at the contrast between a main form-bearing element and an ornamentation. The difference between the two seems to involve what Gestalt psychologists refer to as phenomenal dependency.[607] This phrase means that when a perceived structure has two parts, one can seem to belong to or be a part of the other. An example in vision is a person's nose, which seems to be part of the face as well as a thing in itself. An ornamental note, such as an acciaccatura (a type of grace note) or the upper note of a trill, is perceived in relation to another, more "stable" note. It does not in itself help to define the melody. Rather, it is perceived as a stylistic variation of the note upon which it is phenomenally dependent and it seems to lend qualitative properties to it. Musical devices such as these are picked out and given their own names in music theory because they are created by a sequence of notes played by the same instrument and are therefore recognizable in the score. However, there are other nameless techniques that occur in ensemble music where the dependent sounds are provided by instruments other than the one to which they are appended. A plucked string can provide the "attack" feature for a sustained sound that starts right after it. If the two are precisely the same pitch and of similar timbres, the listener may not realize that there were two notes at all. Alternatively, the two may be within one

```
Part 1:   A    B    C    D            E    F    G    H I

Part 2:            A BC   D E FG  H I

Part 3:   ABCDEFG  JKL
                 HI   MNO

Part 4:    B D  F G I K  M
          A C  E   H J  L NO
```

Figure 5.1
Sequential grouping of notes into within-stream "events."

or two semitones of one another. In this case the effect may be like an acciaccatura or grace note. The widespread use of phenomenal dependency in music raises the question of how we know whether a particular sound will be form-bearing or phenomenally dependent.

In any such dependency between a pair of notes, the two should be tightly bound together by primitive grouping. Therefore they must not be too far apart in frequency, time, or timbre. The closer the better. If their fundamental frequencies are not more than two or three semitones apart, and they succeed one another very rapidly, they will be in van Noorden's region of compulsory fusion.[608] Van Noorden discovered the size of this region using sinusoidal tones as stimuli, but it probably also applies to the complex tones used in music.

Second, they should be grouped into the same sequential unit. What do I mean by a sequential unit? Grouping can affect not only the formation of streams but of distinct events within those streams. An example of an event within a stream is a single note inside one of a pair of musical lines. Even such a simple thing as a note has to have been produced by grouping as a single perceived event the entire span of time for which it is on. A larger event might be a phrase in that line. Rules that describe primitive perceptual grouping are involved in forming these phrases.

The relative lengths of silence between moments of sound will be an important determinant of the groupings. However, we cannot simply name some duration of silence and say that any sounds that are separated by less than this amount will be part of the same group. As long as the sequence is not too slow (so that nothing groups with anything else), or too fast (so that everything forms one group), it is the relative, not the absolute, separations that count. For example, in part 1 of figure 5.1, C and D will be in the same group (ABCD). On the other hand in part 2, C and D, with the same horizontal separation as above, form parts of different groups. Apparently the temporal proximities compete with one another to form groupings.

Frequency proximities can also assist in this process of forming units. Even if the sequence is slow enough that a single stream is maintained, the sequence can be broken into successive groups by frequency proximity. An elementary case of this is seen in part 3, in which vertical position represents pitch. Here 15 letters clearly form four groups. Again, because of the competition of proximities, there is considerable flexibility in how far apart in pitch two tones may be and still be assigned to the same perceptual group. For example, G and H in part 4, with the same vertical and horizontal (pitch and time) separation as in the case above, are not so clearly part of separate groups.

The auditory system seems to form clusters by demanding that the within-cluster separations in pitch and time be smaller than the between-cluster separations. In addition to frequency and time separations, differences between successive notes on other dimensions, such as various aspects of timbre and whether the tones are steady or glide in pitch, can influence grouping. We have surveyed these influences in chapter 2. A number of experiments have been done on the perceptual unification of successive sounds in a sequence, primarily by Royer and his colleagues.[609] Some of these were discussed in chapter 2 under the topic of unit formation. While these experiments were not done with musical tones, they tended to confirm principles well accepted by musicians, such as the role of relative spacing in time.

Musically significant grouping can, of course, be strengthened by the rhythm of the music. The existence of a repetitive pulsation in the music causes the sounds to group around the pulses, and to be segregated sequentially from one another. Short notes that are off the beat tend to group with the stressed notes that precede or follow them.

None of the ideas that I have mentioned will be surprising to musicians. In fact the only criticism that they might make is that I have left out factors that seem obvious to them, such as the role of the listener's identification of a sequence of notes as parts of a familiar chord. However, I have tried to focus on primitive processes that I think are unlearned and that would tend to influence grouping in any style of music and to stay away from schema-based factors, such as knowledge of the musical system, that would apply only within a particular style. The problems of how musical schemas are formed and how they are used to integrate music are important and fascinating, but outside the scope of this book.

At this point we must come back to the central focus of the book and ask what role the primitive event-forming rules play in pattern recognition. Their role can be seen through an example. If, in figure 5.1, the G and the H are perceived as parts of the same event, we will go into our mental stockpile of sonic events, looking for one that has both a G component and an H component in it (think, for example of two notes in a familiar bird call). If they are not perceptually grouped, we will not search our knowledge base for a sound that has both qualities but will search for two different sounds, one with each quality. Therefore these rules are central in pattern recognition. I have made the same point about the rules that affect how sequences of sounds are taken apart into parallel streams. Indeed, the reader will have noticed that it is the same auditory similarities that influence both the formation of streams and the formation of sequential units inside those streams. The only difference is that when the components are put into different streams, the perceptual isolation between them is stronger and the different streams are interpreted not just as different sonic events, but as emanating from different sources of sound.

Effects of Melodic Absorption on Perceived Pitch

We have mentioned two ways in which a sound can become phenomenally dependent in music. One is by being appended as an ornamentation to another note. The other is by being grouped into a phrase. In one case, the dependent sound is subordinated to another sound at the same level (another note); in the other, it is subordinated to a phrase. In both cases, the result is a new pattern with properties that the parts contribute. Usually, in the process of amalgamating, the dependent parts give up, to some degree, the properties that they had as individuals. We saw a striking case of this in chapter 3 where the individual harmonics that form a complex tone give up their individual pitches completely. This process occurs to a lesser degree when sounds become parts of sequential units.

Sequential amalgamation can affect the perceived pitches of individual notes. The apparent pitches of the tones in a melody depend on the overall configuration. Guilford and Nelson found in the 1930s that when a melodic sequence was played and then played again with one note raised or lowered by a semitone, the surrounding unaltered tones were judged to rise or fall about a fifth of a semitone in the same direction as the altered tone.[610] Perhaps a more noticeable effect is that the phrasing of a sequence of notes makes some of their pitches less distinct.

Alex Rudnicky and I noticed this blurring of some of the pitches in a phrase in an experiment that is described in more detail in chapter 1. We asked listeners to judge whether a rapid sequence formed of two tones (2,200 and 2,400 Hz, at the rate of 65 msec per tone) was rising or falling in frequency.[611] The task was quite easy, but if the two tones, A and B, were embedded in a four-tone sequence, XABX, it became very difficult to report the order of A and B. This occurred despite the fact that the bracketing X tones (1,460 Hz) were far enough away in frequency from the target tones that little forward or backward masking should have occurred.

In normal musical performance and listening, pitches are very noticeable when they are at the points at which the pitch movement changes its direction, at the peaks and valleys of the melodic contour, or if they are at the ends of phrases, or are long in duration. Often the pitches of other notes are less distinct; performers who play continuous-pitch instruments, such as the violin, know that they do not have to be as careful about these notes, and that a slightly mistuned note in one of these less salient positions will rarely be noticed. The grouping into phrases, then, assigns central or subordinate roles to certain pitches. There is no really explicit theory from which to predict these observations, but the effects themselves are unmistakable.

Some of the effects must surely derive from musical knowledge. For example, the music psychologist Jamshed Bharucha has discussed the fact that a dissonance in Western music is usually followed by (resolves to) a tone that is more "stable" in the musical system.[612] This has the effect of providing a "melodic anchor." The dissonant tone is then experienced as perceptually subordinate to the anchor tone. He sees the stable note as a sort of cognitive reference point by which we assimilate the melody. A similar effect is heard when a player who has made a mistake covers it up by following it with a stable note that is near it in pitch so that the former is heard simply as an ornamentation. (Jazz improvisation has often been described as an ongoing accommodation of errors in this way.) Bharucha has shown that the anchoring is asymmetrical (a tone cannot be anchored by one that precedes it). The phenomenal dependency produced by melodic anchoring can affect our memory of the sequence. One of Bharucha's experiments involved a tone that is unstable in the key in which it occurred (because it is not in the triad that defines that key). The experiment showed that when that note was anchored by a stable tone, it was likely to be misremembered by the listener as being one of the stable notes of the key.

Figure 5.2
The "gruppetto". On the left, as it appears in a score; on the right, as it is usually played. (After Vicario 1982.)

Clearly the melodic anchoring effect is based on musical knowledge, since the listener must know which notes are stable in a particular key or mode. Just the same, the ability to anchor an unstable tone to a stable one depends on primitive processes of grouping. For example, the tones have to be near one another in pitch. The role of musical knowledge in the cognitive processing of musical sequences has been treated extensively in an excellent book by John Sloboda, so I will not attempt to do so here.[613] I will focus instead on the role of primitive scene-analysis processes.

Giovanni Vicario has given an example of how the particular quality of a musical sequence can be altered by manipulating primitive grouping.[614] Figure 5.2 illustrates the gruppetto, a sixteenth century Italian ornamentation. On the left we see how it usually appears in a score and on the right, how it is usually played. The first four tones of the ornamentation (the musical notes C, D, C, and B) can be divided into a first pair (CD) and a second pair (CB). Vicario created a laboratory version using 0.1-second tones as the notes and showed how the gruppetto could be perceptually embedded in what he calls the stronger structure of a longer trill by adding tones to its left and right. At the left he added one or more repetitions of the first pair and on the right repetitions of the second pair.

Figure 5.3 shows the four notes alone, (a), then below it two of the other conditions, (b) and (c), with different numbers of embedding tones. As the number of added pairs increases, the left half of the four-tone pattern is absorbed into the repetitive CD trill and the right half into the CB trill and the characteristic snake-like quality of the gruppetto disappears. The breaking up of the gruppetto is probably based, in this case, on a primitive process of grouping that responds to the fact that there has been an abrupt change in the frequency region occupied by the tones.

Vicario has also illustrated the perceptual grouping that occurs when a normal-length note is preceded by a short ornamental note. The latter is heard as an embellishment of the note that it precedes. Vicario has showed that the hearing of the note as an embellishment in this way depends on the length of the ornamental note.[615] He

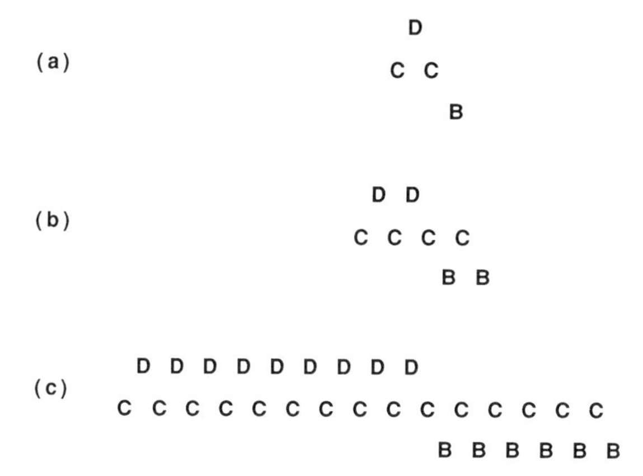

Figure 5.3
Breaking up the gruppetto. (a) Gruppetto alone (b) with a small number of additional embedding tones (c) with a large number of embedding tones. (After Vicario 1982.)

created a laboratory version of the effect by playing a 392-Hz tone preceded by a higher tone at 440 Hz. The second, or main, tone was always 1,600 msec in duration, but in different examples the duration of the first one ranged from 50 to 1,600 msec. When it was very short, its perceptual dependency on the long tone was marked, but as it became longer its dependency on the second one disappeared. The importance of relative duration is evident from these results. It is obvious from the argument that I have presented that before the durational difference could produce the dependency, the two tones would have to be perceptually integrated. The two-semitone separation that was used by Vicario falls within van Noorden's region of compulsory integration. If a large pitch separation had been used, the effect probably would not have been one of ornamentation of one note by another. There may be some exceptions for dependent notes to be very close in pitch. Stravinsky's piano sonata has a trill using a minor ninth (an octave plus a semitone). Since the tones involved are complex, it is possible that the higher note groups with the even harmonics of the lower, each harmonic of the upper being spaced by only a semitone from the nearest harmonic from the lower note.

Van Noorden also did some research that pertains to the perception of ornamentation in music. He looked at the perceptual integration of sequences consisting of two 40-msec tones.[616] The listener's experience of them depended on the rate and the frequency separation. Three important perceptual organizations tended to occur: (1) a sense that the two tones were simultaneous, (2) a clear perception of a jump in pitch, and (3) two independent, unrelated notes.

Simultaneity tended to be heard when the rates were very fast (less than 75 or 80 msec per tone) with the required rate getting faster as the tones drew closer together in frequency. The relation to frequency separation and speed shows that this effect is really the segregation of the two tones into separate streams, since we know already that in order to cause two streams to be segregated we must increase the speed if we reduce the frequency separation. When the tones of van Noorden's pair were less than about seven semitones apart, the experience of simultaneity could not be obtained.

The next experience, a clear pitch jump uniting the pair, could be obtained at the fast rate (about 70 msec per tone) when the tones had a separation of less than eight or nine semitones, but as the tones were slowed down the frequency separation could be increased so that at about 140 msec per tone even a 25-semitone separation could give an impression of a frequency jump between the tones. Finally the duration required to obtain a clear experience of unrelated tones was above 300 msec per tone at all frequency separations.

We see that the integration of two tones can take two forms, a first (in the region of compulsory fusion) in which they are experienced as being parts of the same sound, and a second (at intermediate frequency separations and speeds) in which they are experienced as being united by a frequency transformation. The first is the region of ornamentation and the second the region of melody. We will probably hear the first tone as an ornament when the onset-to-onset time is somewhere below 75 msec (less than a sixteenth note), and we will hear the phenomenal dependency of the first tone on the second when the second is longer than the first, long enough to prevent itself from becoming an ornament to its own successor.

Timbre (Cause and Effect)

Timbre as Cause of Segregation

Another important factor that can affect the perceptual grouping of music is timbre.

We know that sequential similarities in timbre can be used in the laboratory to promote sequential grouping of some sounds in preference to others, leading to stream segregation. This research was reviewed in chapter 1. But what of the real use of timbre-based grouping in music?

Similarities based on timbre can help the composer to define the structure of the melody. We have seen in chapter 2 how, in very rapid

Figure 5.4
(a) Measures 271 to 273 of the Credo from Palestrina's Mass *In te Domine speravi*.
(b) Piano reduction of the same measures.

sequences of tones, stream segregation can occur based on differences in timbres. But these effects occurred at rates that are a good deal faster than are usually found in music. Therefore we would not expect the segregation to be as strong in music. Nevertheless, at the slower rates characteristic of music, grouping by timbre similarity still plays a role. However, instead of causing nonadjacent sounds to group, as it might do in very fast sequences, it can cause some adjacent sounds to group in preference to others. This sort of function can be diagrammed as follows, where two different timbres are depicted by x and /.

xxxx////xxxx////

The x's form groups that are distinct from the slashes. This sort of grouping can serve to emphasize important divisions in the music. Webern, for example, used timbre changes to mark them. He often distributed a melodic sequence of notes to many instruments, allowing each to play a few notes at a time, as in his orchestration of the Ricercar from Bach's *Musical Offering*. However, the short sequence of notes played by an instrument was a significant motivic element in the music.[617] Boulez has pointed out that timbre can be used to break up a boring parallelism (parallel movements of two lines in a piece). If instruments with quite different attacks are available, for example, then having the instruments switch between melodic lines so that each of them first contributes a note to one line and then to another creates an illusion of a changing timbre, as in the Palestrina example given in figure 5.4.[618]

Musically significant grouping can, of course, be strengthened by the rhythm of the music. The existence of a repetitive pulsation in the music causes the sounds to group around the pulses, and to be segregated sequentially from one another. Short notes that are off the beat tend to group with the stressed notes that precede or follow them.

"Hocket" is the converse of "compound melodic line." The latter creates two or more lines of melody from a single instrument. Hocket does the opposite, creating a single melodic line by getting two or more instruments or singers to rapidly take turns in producing single notes or short groups of notes that together form a melody. This technique dates back to the polyphonic choral music of the thirteenth and fourteenth centuries. Numerous examples occur in Beethoven's late quartets and the technique has been extensively used by Anton Webern to achieve a disruption of the continuity of the melodic line. The segregation of the alternating sounds in hocket is much less than the segregation in compound melodic line since, in hocket, the pitch registers of the alternating members are not necessarily kept distinct. It is the timbre of the instruments or singers, and sometimes their spatial separation, that influences the segregation. Although this produces an antiphonal effect, it rarely creates a level of primitive segregation that is strong enough to force the listener to segregate the lines.

We have discussed ways in which timbres can be used to group sequences of sounds so that the pitch transformations (melody) that they form will be perceived, or to break them up so as to eliminate the experience of pitch transformation. But what about our experience of transformation between the timbres themselves? Musical patterns can easily be built out of transformations of pitch, loudness, and rhythm and it is these transformations that help to define the shape of the sequence.

So far we have been talking as if there were only two values that the relation between timbres could take—same or different. Two values can define only the simplest of forms, such as the kinds that I can build with a string of typewriter symbols of two types, such as ////xxxx////xxxx. With this description, grouping is all or nothing. This, of course, is not how pitch works. In pitch there is the notion of degrees of similarity. Some pitches are more similar than others. When changes occur, therefore, they define movements of different sizes and the succession of such movements defines shapes. There must be analogous degrees of similarity and difference among timbres. If we knew what they were, we could use timbre more effectively to control the grouping of musical sounds. Conceivably we could create sequences in which the listener heard changes in timbre as shapes evolving over time. We would also be able to know when a timbral change would be perceived as the same sound changing as opposed to a new sound starting and replacing the old one. That is, we would know what held timbral forms together.

The Description of Timbre

Dimensional Approach to Timbre One might think that an important step along the road of being able to predict the sequential grouping of timbres would be to know which ones sounded similar to one another for the human listener. After all, the factors described in chapter 2 as controlling sequential grouping were all similarities of one sort or another. When we begin to think about the similarities between things, we immediately realize that things can resemble other things in different ways. A child's ball might resemble some toys in being round, other toys in being red, others in terms of their sizes, and so on. One would expect the same to hold for sounds, a sound of a xylophone resembling a struck stick in having a percussive onset and a violin in having a fairly periodic waveform later in the note. The fact that a sound can resemble different things in different ways leads naturally to the idea of dimensions of similarity. To be more precise, one might propose that there are a limited number of dimensions on which every sound can be given a value, and that if two sounds have similar values on some dimension they are alike on that dimension even though they might be dissimilar on others. The desire to understand similarities leads us naturally, therefore, to investigate dimensions of sound. This sort of reasoning has been applied to the study of timbre.

The method of multidimensional scaling has been used by John Grey and his colleagues to discover dimensions of timbre. I refer the reader to the discussion of this research in chapter 2. Basically three dimensions were found. The first was correlated with the brightness of the spectrum, the second related to the simplicity of the behavior of the harmonics over the course of the note, and the third to the "bite" of the attack of the tone. We do not yet know whether similarities among tones in terms of these latter two features can affect their perceptual grouping.

The quality of brightness is based on only one fact about the spectrum of a sound, the relative balance of high and low frequencies. However, the relative intensity of spectral components may have

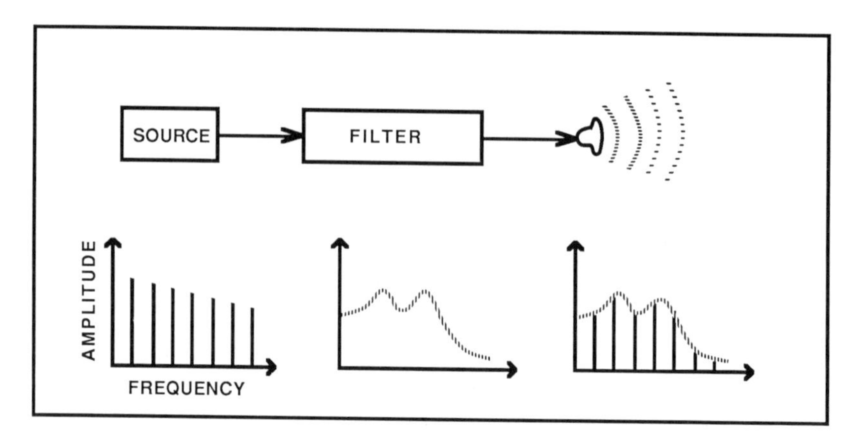

Figure 5.5
A model of speech production in terms of a source spectrum, a filter, and a resulting spectrum. This model also applies to many instruments. (From Slawson 1981.)

more complex properties. In particular, the spectrum may exhibit a number of peaks called formants. Figure 5.5 illustrates the fact that the generation of the formants in speech and in many musical instruments comes from resonances in the vocal tract of the speaking person or the body of the sounding instruments. The upper part of the figure shows this in schematic form and the lower part shows the spectral characteristics of each part. The leftmost component, labeled "source," represents the vibration that creates the sound (for example, the vocal cords of a person or the string of a violin). It produces a spectrum of a certain shape. The middle component represents the filtering characteristics of some resonators connected with the sound source, the vocal tract in the case of a person and the violin body in the case of that instrument. These resonators act as filters, reinforcing the sound in certain parts of the spectrum and attenuating it in others so as to create a pattern of hills (formants) and valleys, the formants being numbered from the lowest (F1) to the highest. Two formants are shown in the figure. The way in which the filter shapes the spectrum is shown below it in the figure. The output spectrum is the product of the shape of the original spectrum and the shaping properties of the filter. The pattern formed by the peaks and valleys may determine the timbre of a sound. For example, the distinction between different spoken vowels depends on the locations of the lowest three formants in the spectrum. The lowest two, called F1 and F2, are the most important, and if you set up a graph with the frequencies of

F1 and F2 as the *x* and *y* axes, and plot the different vowels on this graph according to the peak frequencies of their first and second formants, the vowels will be well spaced out with no two falling in the same position.

This has led Wayne Slawson to propose that this "F1-F2 space" is fundamental for timbre perception.[619] He has referred to the aspect of timbre that is affected by the formant structure of a sound as its color. Slawson has argued that as a sound is displaced along different paths through this space by altering its first and second formant, this corresponds to changes in different dimensions of color.

Slawson has attempted to show how a timbre sequence, in and of itself, can be a carrier of musical form. He has proposed that because these are natural dimensions of timbre, a sequence of modifications of a sound that is made by gradually changing the spectral positions of F1 and F2 will seem natural and we will perceive the sequence as a recognizable musical form rather than as an arbitrary set of changes. If a sequence of timbres that defines such a form is repeated in a new position in the space (by simply displacing it as a whole in the space), the new sequence will be heard as a transposition of the old one. Slawson has given rules for musically significant modifications of a pattern. Other suggestions have been made about how timbre must be handled before it can define musical forms. These have been set out by Stephen McAdams and Kaija Saariaho, and by Gerald Balzano.[620]

If the changing of timbre is used to create a musical form, it is important that the parts of the form should have a tendency to stick together. If the sequence that bears the form is interrupted in the middle by the abrupt entry of a brief sound it should tend to close itself through the interruption, that is to exhibit illusory continuity. Otherwise the discontinuity will destroy the intended form. Fortunately, there is evidence that closely related timbres will hold together. It comes from a number of sources. There is the research on the streaming of timbres that was discussed in chapter 2. It used sounds in which there was only a single spectral peak and therefore could be viewed as manipulating brightness. Therefore it is not directly applicable to timbres defined in terms of two or more peaks. However, there is also the research on the illusory continuity of vocal sounds that was reviewed in the section on illusory continuity in chapter 3. Since the formant structure of vowel sounds is the basis of Slawson's manipulation of vowel color, we could expect that his timbre patterns would be as cohesive as vowels are.

Some researchers who have been involved in computer-based acoustical research on musical timbre, such as Claude Cadoz in

Grenoble, have taken an entirely different direction.[621] They have argued that when we listen to a sound we are building a mental description not in terms of the qualities of the sounds that we are sensing but in terms of the physical properties of the source. Therefore when we hear a gong being struck, we do not mentally store the result in terms of the relative amplitude of different spectral components and how they change over time, but rather in terms of how hard the gong was struck. We build a model of the physical structure of the event, and when, in a succession of such sounds, we detect changes, we experience these as changes in the physical cause of the sounds. For example, if the gong player reduces the force with which the gong is struck, this may affect many individual features of the sound spectrum but we will hear it as a simple change in the striking force.

Gerald Balzano, following a clue from Gibson, has suggested that "the kinds of things we are capable of hearing that are important for timbre perception are events like pounding, blowing, plucking, rolling, whistling, screaming, and all sorts of physical processes that words can only hint at but which are nonetheless specified in the underlying dynamics of the signal."[622]

Much earlier W. H. Huggins proposed that two fundamental aspects of the behavior of sound-producing systems were (1) their source vibrations (as in the vocal cords of the human voice) and (2) the transformation imposed by resonances (as in the vocal tract of the human speaker). Furthermore, Huggins suggested that the human auditory system was capable of separating these two aspects of the sound.[623] This view differs from Balzano's in that it does not consider different *types* of sound, but different *aspects* of sound. Both these views might propose that when listeners hear a sequence of related sounds they track the changes in the perceived physical cause of the sound not in the sound's raw acoustic features. Therefore it would be smooth changes in the inferred physical cause that would define coherent sequences of sounds rather than smooth changes in raw acoustic qualities. This implies that if, over the course of a sequence of notes, a smooth change in the action of the player nonetheless creates a discontinuity of the raw properties of the sound, the listener should still hear the changes as coherent. For example, Balzano points out that if we create a synthetic timbre by copying the spectral envelope (the shape of the spectrum) of an oboe playing a middle C, and shaping the amplitude of the synthetic tone over time by means of a temporal envelope that is also derived from the same original, the result sounds like an oboe. However, if we synthesize a tone an octave above or below the original by using the original tone's spectral and temporal envelopes, the result will not sound as much like an oboe. This means that there are changes in the spectrum and dynamics of an oboe that are locked together with changes in pitch. Only when these changes are present do we identify a new note as also from an oboe. There are two alternative explanations of this fact. The sense of "oboeness" may derive from a raw perceptual invariance of the set of different oboe sounds (as proposed by Balzano) or from a learned schema that originates with our experiences with changes of pitch in the oboe. If the invariance is primitive, then there is something we know innately about what happens to an oboe when it is played at a higher pitch. Since it is unlikely that the human race was biologically evolved with oboes in mind, this alternative would be plausible only if the acoustic changes that occur in oboes when they are played at different pitches also occur with many other sound-producing physical systems. However, whether primitive or learned, the fact that we hear the notes as coming from the same source would be expected to help the listener to integrate the notes sequentially.

Despite the clarity of the difference in theory between sequential integration based on relatively simple acoustic dimensions and integration based on a continuity of physical source, it is difficult to distinguish these two theories in practice. To see why, let us examine the problem of tracking a sequence of sounds (that a composer wants you to consider to be a coherent line) through the interruptions and masking sounds that are introduced by other lines of sound. It is possible to think of this sequence in two different ways, in terms of the physical source of the sequence and in terms of its spectrogram. We will consider two models of sequential integration. In one, the spectrogram is used only to infer the physical properties of the source and if the change in the inferred source is not too rapid, the sound is sequentially integrated and easily tracked through the mixture. In the other, the smoothness and rapidity of changes in the spectrogram itself control sequential integration. The difficulty is this: I suspect that usually when a source's properties change smoothly, there will be a continuity of changes in the spectrogram. Only cases in which this correlation does not hold are useful for distinguishing the theories.

There are, of course, cases where, at first glance, the correlation seems not to hold. Anyone who is familiar with the variety of squawks and other sounds that can be emitted from a clarinet in the hands of a novice will know that small changes in the behavior of the player can lead to large qualitative changes in the sound. Suppose we had to follow a sequence of these through interruptions and were unable to do so. Would this not discredit the physical source model of perceptual continuity? Not necessarily. Its proponents could simply argue that while the behavior of the player may have changed in only slight ways, the mode of vibration of the instrument changed in large ways, and the physical model that we are using concerns the instrument itself and not the player. What this argument does is to make the two theories virtually indistinguishable, since any discontinuous change in the sound coming from a physical source must have to be caused by a discontinuous change in the acoustically relevant states of that source. The only evidence that would count would be a demonstrated ability to integrate a sequence formed of sounds that were radically different acoustically yet came from the same instrument. If a series of squawks and squeals from a clarinet *could* be fluently tracked when intermingled with the equally diverse sounds of a violin and a flute, both played abysmally badly, then this would argue that sequential integration was, indeed, based on a source model.

My own guess is that primitive sequential integration of the type that we use when we follow a sound through interruptions is based on a fairly simple set of raw acoustic properties and does not necessarily involve interpreting the sound or its changes in terms of a physical model of the source. For example, a fixed frequency sine wave never occurs in nature, and the listener has little sense if it being produced by an intelligible event of the type referred to by Balzano; yet it can be followed through interruptions fairly easily. On the other hand, I am quite confident that the way we hear two sounds of a particular instrument as being the same in its different registers is by knowing that both sounds are produced by that instrument. Whether we know that because we have learned an arbitrary association of each sound with the parent instrument or by some more profound analysis of the sound in the ways proposed by Cadoz, Balzano, or Huggins is not known. However, I think that any such interpretation of the sound is based on what I have called schema-based integration and not on primitive integration. We can use our knowledge that the sound is an oboe to listen for the oboe in a mixture, but this is not the only way we can integrate a sequence. This distinction is dealt with in more detail in chapter 4. So far as I know, experiments capable of distinguishing the contributions of raw acoustical properties and perceived physical causes in sequential integration have yet to be done.

Thus, even though the search for simple perceptual dimensions that are defined in terms of the sound itself may not tell us everything about how we interpret sequences of sounds, it may still have an important function. It is possible, even probable, that a fairly small number of perceptual dimensions actually controls sequential integration and perhaps these can be discovered by the scaling of similarity judgments. The assumption here would be that some subset of those features of sound that are responsible for judgments of similarity are the ones that control sequential integration. While this is by no means assured, it would be a reasonable hypothesis to start out with.

Another approach to finding the essential features by which we distinguish different sounds has been used by Jean-Claude Risset and David Wessel at the Institut de Recherche et Coordination Acoustique/Musique (IRCAM), a center for contemporary music founded by Pierre Boulez in Paris.[624] They call the approach "analysis by synthesis." In many cases, they take natural sounds, analyze them, and then alter them in some way to determine the effect on the listener. One of the goals of this research has been influenced by a requirement of computer music. That is to create natural sounding tones in the simplest way possible. A complete spectral analysis of a sound gives a set of parameters for the signal that can be used, in the reverse direction to resynthesize the signal. However, a fully detailed analysis will give a set of parameters that is as complex as the signal itself. It would be valuable to have some method of simplifying the set of parameters to be able to synthesize a plausible copy that is very similar to the original. Knowing what will work is an important step in understanding auditory similarity.

Various forms of simplification of instrumental sounds have been tried. One is to first subject the sound to a process that describes the amplitude of each frequency component as a function of time. For each individual frequency component the amplitude trajectory would consist of a first section that included the attack transient, a more or less steady section, and a section that included the decay. The intensity changes of a particular frequency component in each of these sections is complex. However, one can try to use a sequence of three to five straight line segments to represent the intensity changes of that component. This omits a large degree of complexity and yet gives a sound very like the original. This similarity means that the quality of the sound was determined more by what was left in than by what was removed. Gradually, by a process of repeated simplification and listening, it is possible to determine which changes make large differences and which make small ones.

A problem with this approach is that the listener's criterion is whether the tone still sounds like the original instrument. While this criterion serves the interests of computer music quite well, it is not equally valuable for the study of primitive grouping. It discovers only the features that distinguish one instrument from another. Therefore, what we end up studying, at least in part, may be *distinctive features of the set of instruments in the listener's culture*, not necessarily the dimensions that the brain uses for primitive organization. The process of deciding whether the sound heard in a mixture is a continuation of one that was heard in isolation 250 msec before may depend on features that are less specific than the ones that are essential for a convincing synthesis of a particular instrument.

There is an aspect of timbre that bears a certain analogy to things that affect grouping in vision. Let me first describe the visual case and then perhaps we can see how it might be analogous to something in audition. In vision, the grouping of two adjacent regions of an image can be affected by what is called their textures. The "granular" sounds that I described in the section on timbre in chapter 2 are the auditory analogy to visual texture. Stephen McAdams finds examples in modern music:

> Listen to the large sound masses played by the strings in Ligeti's *Atmosphere* or Penderecki's *Threnody to the Victims of Hiroshima* and ask yourself how many individual instruments are playing simultaneously in that section. Certainly you can identify that there are "many," but "how many" is difficult to determine because the sounds are all so closely related that they obscure one another and are not individually distinguishable.[625]

Such sound masses are analogous to the spraying shower or the flowing hair in vision. Though individual lines are not perceived, the granularity is, and the granularity of one piece can be quite unlike that of another.

In my earlier discussions in chapters 2 and 3, I suggested that "grain analyzers" in audition might be responsible for determining the particular form of granularity and that the latter could be one factor controlling the grouping of successive moments of time or different parts of the spectrum. This is a rich field for study and one that is still unmined in the laboratory. Therefore it would be particularly interesting to study examples drawn from the field of music in which it appeared that differences in granularity were responsible for grouping sounds across time or for segregating the component sounds in mixtures.

Timbre as the Result of Fusion

Up to this point we have seen timbre as a causal influence that can be used to affect grouping and other properties of music. However, timbre is not the automatic perceptual result of a certain acoustic input. Timbre is to some degree created by our processes of auditory scene analysis. This creates an odd paradox. Timbre influences scene analysis, but scene analysis creates timbre. (See the discussion in chapter 3.)

Therefore it is not sufficient for a composer to know what effects timbre will have on the music. The practical use of timbre involves the understanding of perceptual fusion. Let me explain. Once a timbre is available, it can be used in various ways, but where does the timbre come from? We are used to thinking of timbre as the quality that distinguishes one instrument from another. This definition will do in simple ensembles of one or two instruments, but as the ensemble grows, things become more complex. We start to experience emergent timbres that arise from a fusion of the effects of different instruments on the time-varying acoustic spectrum. For example, it was common in the classical period of European music to use the flute to double a violin melody an octave higher. The flute was not heard as a separate instrument; its effect was to brighten the sound of the violins. We sometimes call the timbre that comes from the sound of a number of instruments playing together "ensemble timbre." There is an important prerequisite to using it: To know how to compose sonic objects with desired timbres, composers have to understand what makes sounds fuse and in what form the properties of the constituent sounds are preserved in the timbre of the larger sonic object.

If timbre arises from the simultaneous organization of musical sounds, it is possible to see instruments in a new role. Pierre Boulez has argued that in the Baroque period, for example in the music of Bach, individual instruments had very distinctive qualities; these were used to identify pieces or movements or even to mark out the phrases.[626] However, according to Boulez instruments were gradually standardized and acquired less distinctive timbres. This corresponded with the growth of the orchestra in size. Now instruments have become generators of components of the timbre, and the orchestral timbre arises out of a fusion of these components. They act more like the individual oscillators in an electronic music studio. Simultaneous grouping causes large groups of instruments to fuse their effects to produce (in Boulez' words) "phantasmagoric instruments." Milton Babbitt has pointed out that when fusion is strong, as when there is a precise synchronization of attacks, there can be a complete misidentification of the instruments that are involved since their individual timbres are lost.[627]

Another form of timbre arises from a different dimension of grouping. In modern techniques such as "klangfarbenmelodie," as used by Schoenberg and Webern, the melody is carried by a succession of quite different instruments whose timbral shifts add interest to the music. In Webern's case it can introduce a sort of pointillistic quality to the music, where rapid changes of timbre interfere with smooth sequential integration.[628] The sparkling quality of the sequence is not a quality of any individual note but of the succession. If we can loosely refer to that sort of granularity in the music as a form of timbre, this is an example of the sequential laws of grouping creating new timbres by grouping or contrasting old ones. In both the cases that I have described, a new experience of timbre arises out of the global organization to which individual sounds are contributing.

We have stopped talking about timbres as the qualities that distinguish one instrument from another. Timbre has come to mean the qualities that distinguish one sonic object from another, where sonic objects can no longer be identified with single instruments and correspond more to what I have spoken of earlier as auditory streams.

Vertical Coherence and Counterpoint

Segregation and Masking in Musical Ensembles

We have seen earlier how the fusion of different simultaneous sounds in an ensemble can create new timbres. Yet in ensemble playing or choral singing we do not always want the result to be some enormous timbre for the whole group. We normally want certain lines to remain distinct from all the rest, be it the voice or instrument of a soloist, the baritone part in a choral piece, or whatever. This can be achieved through the practical use of the cues for perceptual segregation surveyed in chapter 3. These include competition among sequential grouping, spectral relations, parallel frequency and amplitude changes, and spatial differences.

Keeping the sounds of a soloist distinct from those of an accompanying ensemble is frequently an important requirement in music. Before mentioning anything very exotic in this regard, we should notice that the simplest way to keep them distinct is to have them sing or play notes that are different from the other parts. This is effective because the ear is trying to find a set of different fundamental frequencies to which the detected partials can be allocated. This search by the ear for related harmonics explains why instrumentalists, in order to avoid having their sounds blend with the others, will sometimes play slightly sharp. The effectiveness of this technique depends again on the auditory system finding a fundamental for the soloist's harmonics that is different from the other ones it is finding. We really do not know how large this mistuning has to be in order to work. The only available evidence is from research in which a single partial is mistuned from all the rest in an otherwise harmonic tone.[629] That research shows that the mistuning has to be from 3 to 6 percent before the mistuned harmonic is heard separately. If we recall that a 6 percent change is equal to a semitone, we realize that this degree of mistuning would never be acceptable on the part of a soloist. But because the research in question looked at the mistuning of only a single partial, and the instrumentalist is affecting an entire set of harmonics by playing sharp, the mistuning required for segregation may not be as great for the instrumentalist. James Cutting found that when parts of speech sounds are sent to different ears by means of headphones, a difference of as little as 2 Hz can prevent them from blending to produce a single sound. Instead, the listener hears two.[630] In Cutting's research, the dichotic presentation obviously contributed to the segregation as well, but without the 2-Hz difference the sounds tended to be heard as one. This suggests that even a small separation of fundamentals can make a big difference when there are other segregating factors as well.

Operatic singers use yet another method to maintain their distinctness from the ensemble. They alter the shape of their vocal tracts to produce what is called the "singing formant." Johan Sundberg in Sweden has shown that they enlarge the pharynx cavity and lower the glottis to alter their vocal spectrum and insert a broad bulge in the range 2,500 to 3,500 Hz.[631] This is a frequency range in which human hearing is very acute and yet in which it is unlikely that there will be a lot of energy from instruments. The listener can then track this spectral bulge over time, an accomplishment that was described in chapter 2.

Another method of separating soloists from the rest of an ensemble is to have them play at an extreme of the pitch range, say an octave or a fifth above the rest of the players, as, for example, in parallel organum. (I have heard a cantor in a synagogue use an octave separation quite effectively.) They also can violate the principles of common fate to keep their part distinct from the others. For example, their pitches should not move in a motion parallel to the others. Another application of this principle is to employ a rate of vibrato that is different from any other in the ensemble. A wide vibrato will keep the voice distinct. This is a lesson that has been well learned by opera singers. Rudolf Rasch, the Dutch researcher, has shown that imposing a 4 percent modulation in frequency on a note can improve its separability from a simultaneous one as much as by adding 17.5 dB to its intensity.

Onsets and offsets also play an important role. For maximum distinctness, the onset and offset of the notes of the soloist should not be synchronous with those of the rest of the ensemble. Rasch has shown that in ensemble playing, even when the notes are supposedly synchronous, their onsets can be asynchronous by 30–50 msec. This degree of asynchrony can make a part as separable as adding more than 30 dB to its intensity.[632] If the soloist exaggerates the asynchrony by judiciously departing from the notated metric positions (onset times) of the notes while everybody else attempts to play together, the part will stand out even further through this rubato performance.

In Rasch's research, the simultaneous notes were complex tones of different frequencies. Other research on the effects of asynchrony has been done with computer-synthesized instrument tones.[633] When the notes were played synchronously but at different pitches, listeners could identify the pair of synthetic instruments being used. This implies that notes segregated by means of different fundamentals carry their harmonics with them into two separate timbre calculations. The identification of the two instruments was impossible when the two tones were at the same pitch. However, if one of the two tones with identical pitches was started ahead of the other, the earlier (but not the later) timbre could be identified.

Finally, if the soloist can manage to be placed in a position in space that is separated from the other performers this will assist the segregation. Much of the work of the American composer Henry Brant, whose observations we shall discuss later, is based on this principle.

Although I have been describing these principles in the context of a soloist the same ones apply to the segregation of a subgroup of performers from the others while the parts within this subgroup remain blended. It is simply a matter of correlating the performances of the subgroup while decorrelating them from the others. In practice this will be difficult to achieve since, as Rasch has shown, their ability to synchronize exactly within their subgroup will be limited. Spatial separation or pitch differences are easier to achieve.

An interesting side issue has to do with how synchronously performers have to be playing before a listener hears them as being "together" (attacking notes at the same time). Musicians have noticed that as the size of the ensemble increases, the synchrony requirement becomes less stringent. Robert Erickson, in a challenging article on the psychology of music, has set this out as a problem to be explained.[634] I can think of one assumption that would make sense of it. Perhaps it is not the synchrony that is important, but the asynchrony. If the listener can hear distinctly different onsets, the attack will seem ragged. In the case of the large ensemble of musicians, the large number of slightly asynchronous onsets will create a blurring of the onset and so make the actual starting time of any individual player undetectable. Therefore the evidence for asynchrony will be unavailable and there will be no experience of an individual starting ahead of any other individual.

There is another related musical phenomenon. Niklaus Wyss has mentioned to me that he has noticed, in his conducting of symphony orchestras, that the perceptual definition or clarity of a foreground line could be made better by improving the precision of the background. This could mean that even though the instruments in the foreground part are well synchronized, the foreground is not picked out as a separate stream unless it has a temporal pattern distinctly *different* from the background. If the temporal properties of the background are not clear, as a result of imprecise playing, the foreground pattern, though sharply defined in itself, will not have a sharply defined *difference* from the background pattern. If well-defined differences in onset are required before segregation takes place, this would explain the effect.

An important factor in keeping different musical lines or parts from blending together or interfering with one another is spatial separation. I have found it easy to convince myself of this by doing simple experiments with a stereophonic music reproduction system. While listening to a dense orchestral passage, I switched the system back and forth between monophonic and stereophonic modes. My focus of attention was not on whether I could discern the spatial locations of the different instruments but on how clearly and distinctly I could hear the different parts or instruments. The difference between mono and stereo in the "definition" of the music was surprising. People often think that it is the awareness of where the instruments are that is the most important advantage of stereo reproduction, but this localization depends strongly on the correct placement of the loudspeakers with respect to the listener. However, the increased segregation of different instruments is much less sensitive to speaker location. As long as the different instruments have different phases and loudnesses at the two ears, they can be segregated. I have also done some informal experiments while listening to a concert hall performance, first listening with two ears and then covering one. With one-ear listening, the sounds were more mushed together and the parts had much less definition than they had with two ears. Again this was surprising because at the location at which I was sitting there was a considerable amount of reverberation and much of the sound that I was hearing was reflected off many surfaces. It is possible that the segregation was based only on the direct (unreflected) sound, but it is conceivable that the phase alignment of the frequency components is capable of telling the ear that all the members of a set of frequency components have come from the same place, even when there have been one or more reflections of the sound. I would think that there are some rich possibilities for research here.

Counterpoint

The purpose of this section is to show how the principles of primitive auditory organization have been used by composers to achieve musical goals involving segregation and fusion. We have some clear examples in the practice of counterpoint. "Counterpoint" is the name for the technique of composing the various parts in polyphonic music. I will be mainly referring to those used in the Palestrina style.[635] The principles of counterpoint embodied in this style seemed to have served a number of goals. The first was to have more than one part sounding at the same time and in a harmonious relation to one another. However, this was not the only one. They also served the purpose of having each part make a separate contribution to the musical experience by being perceived as a melody in its own right. At times, the different parts would become partially independent in perception, but they would be tied firmly together again by good harmonies at key points, such as at the ends of phrases or passages. At the points at which the parts were to be independent, two things had to be arranged. The first was that they had to be prevented from fusing with the other parts and the second was that sequential integration had to be strong within each part. I think that some of the compositional principles that achieved these purposes did so because they corresponded to principles of primitive auditory organization. C. W. Fox, a music theorist who was influenced by Gestalt psychology, saw counterpoint as a set of principles that were relevant to contemporary music. In his article "Modern Counterpoint" he argued that "the art of counterpoint is essentially an art of segregation of melodic lines."[636]

The goals of harmony and of having good melodies were not always compatible with one another, and in order to create a good melody in an individual part certain notes would have to be introduced that were dissonant with a note that occurred at the same time in another part. Because polyphonic musical style, especially in its early stages, found "uncontrolled" dissonances undesirable, certain techniques were introduced to control the dissonance. Dissonance was permitted only in certain places. Again I plan to explain some of these restrictions as the practical use of certain of the cues that we have already discussed in other chapters. They were not just the arbitrary dictates of a particular style of music. The goals were the goals of that style, but many of the methods made use of universals of auditory perception.

The vertical links were made through the harmonies of triads, such as the major triad. The major triad built on a given note consists of the note itself (the tonic), the note that is four semitones above it, and the note that is seven semitones above it. When one of these notes is played together with the tonic, the simultaneous combination is called a *harmonic interval*. Therefore the three notes in the triad generate the following intervals: the unison (the same note played with itself, say on two different instruments), the major third, and the perfect fifth. They correspond to the separation between the first note itself and the first, third, and fifth notes of the major diatonic scale (for example, C, E, and G in the key of C)—hence the names "third" and "fifth."

Considering these pitch separations in terms of their fundamental frequencies, the upper note of the third bears the frequency ratio 5:4 to the lower note (for example, E versus C), and the upper note of the fifth bears the ratio 3:2 to the lower (for example, G versus C). Accordingly, the upper note of the fifth bears the ratio 6:5 to the upper note of the third (for example, G versus E). As I said, the lowest tone is considered to have the relation of unison to itself (played by another player). In addition to these three harmonic intervals, the unison, the third, and the fifth, we must mention the notes one or more octaves above or below each of them, since these were considered to be equivalent to their octave-separated counterparts. When two notes are separated by an octave, of course, the higher note has the frequency ratio 2:1 to the lower.

In Palestrina counterpoint, one part, designated the "cantus firmus," was the basic melody, sometimes progressing very slowly (say in whole tones), and there were, in addition, one or more parts written above or below it. Let us imagine that the parts were written separately, first the cantus firmus, then the second part, then the third, and so on. In writing the second part, there would be certain points in a phrase at which a note had to be chosen that was consonant with the cantus firmus. To be consonant it had to be separated from it by the ratios 2:1, 3:2, 5:4, 6:5 (or their inversions 1:2, 2:3, 4:5, 5:6) or by double these ratios (their octave-separated equivalents).

When notes whose fundamentals bear simple ratio relations to one another are sounded at the same time, their combination is not experienced as perceptually rough. (We shall examine the reasons for this in a later section.) In the Western musical tradition, the chords formed from the major triad and from their octave compounds are therefore viewed as harmonious or consonant. What is important from the perspective of perceptual organization is that these chords have a primitive tendency to partially fuse in perception (although musical contexts can introduce other tendencies). The fusion in chord perception is not as strong as the fusion of the partials of a single note or as weak as in the perception of unrelated sounds, but falls somewhere between these two extremes. Perhaps we ought to call it vertical grouping rather than fusion. This vertical grouping contributes to the experience of chord perception in which the chord, rather than the individual tones, becomes the acoustic object that we hear. Thus, consonant pitch relations may be one of the bases for the vertical links between parts that hold the piece of music together. We shall see that other factors strengthen these vertical links as well; so harmonicity may not be critical for chord perception.

Distinctness of Voices However, in counterpoint the goal was not simply to promote the perception of the harmony of the chords, but to induce the perception of multiple, concurrent parts. Therefore the vertical ties between the parts that were produced by rules of harmony were balanced by other rules that were used to keep the parts distinct. I will go over some of these and show how they make use of principles of primitive auditory organization.

The goal of segregation was approached in two ways. One was to strengthen the horizontal bonds between notes and the other was to weaken the vertical ones. I ask the reader to recall that I am only going to try to discuss the role of primitive scene-analysis principles, principles that might be presumed to be effective in any musical style. Therefore I will have nothing to say about such matters as musical expectations, as they occur, for example, in cadences (sequences of notes that signal the end of a phrase or section in Western tonal music) or other chord progressions. These expectations, and the rules of composition that set them up, are specific to musical styles and are based on cognitive schemas, not primitive perceptual organization.

One way to keep the concurrent melodic lines distinct from one another is to make sure that the notes within each line are bound strongly together into a sequential grouping. This could be accomplished by using small steps in pitch rather than large skips, for reasons that I have described earlier. Since the vertical grouping of notes competes with the horizontal grouping, if a note in a melody departs too much in pitch from its predecessor, it risks being captured by, and fused with, a tone in one of the other parts that occurs at the same time. This risk is reduced if both the tone itself and the one in the other stream that might fuse with it are both strongly bound into their own respective streams.

The distinctness of lines is also favored by avoiding the synchronous onsets of notes in different parts. Therefore the strongest separation will be obtained if a note in one part is held as a note in another part changes pitch, or if there is a rest (silence) in one part while there is a note onset in another. On the other hand, we will favor vertical grouping if we allow two notes to onset at the same moment. And the vertical grouping will be strongest when each of them deviates quite a lot in pitch from its predecessors in the same part, since this will weaken their horizontal grouping. (Such large movements in pitch are called "leaps" by musicians.)

Van Noorden's work bears on another method of getting concurrent lines to be perceived as independent of one another: giving them different rhythms. When trying to demonstrate stream segregation in the laboratory, it is helpful to use the repeating pattern that is shown in figure 2.26 of chapter 2. When the frequency separation between the higher (H) and lower (L) tones is small, the sequence is heard as a single stream in which we hear a pattern of HLH triplets that sounds like a galloping rhythm, as suggested in part 1 of the figure. However, when the frequency separation increases, segregation occurs and each stream consists of an isochronous sequence of tones, but at different repetition rates, as visually suggested in part 2. This difference in rhythm makes it easier to focus on the parts individually.[637] This particular example concerns a sequence in which no two notes ever start at the same time. I imagine that in polyphonic music, where notes can occur at the same time, the use of different rhythms in different parts can have an even stronger segregative effect. The increased effect would derive from the fact that having different rhythms in two parts guarantees that there are always some notes in one part that do not have a synchronous onset with notes in the other part. If the two parts always have synchronous onsets, as in the "note against note" style of counterpoint, the vertical organization of the parts increases. Therefore, in composing in this style, more attention has to be given to the use of the other cues that can segregate the melodic lines. In other counterpoint styles, differences in rhythms were used to keep parts separate. The use of rhythms is a clear example of the use of onset asynchronies in promoting segregations. We saw in chapter 3 that onset asynchrony is an effective cue for primitive segregation mechanisms. Rasch's work, mentioned earlier in this chapter, showed its effects in ensemble playing.

When the composer of counterpoint wanted a listener to be able to follow a single melodic line, another technique was to refrain from having this line of melody cross the other ones. Otherwise the listener would tend to follow this melody to the crossover point and then start tracking the other part that it was crossing. The tendency for the listener to lose the continuity of crossing lines occurs because there is a very strong tendency to perceptually group tones whose fundamentals are close in frequency to those of their predecessors. This usually overrides the tracking of an individual part unless it is carried by a voice or instrument whose timbre is quite different from those of

Figure 5.6
A tonal pattern used by Wright (1986) to demonstrate the effects of frequency proximity, continuity, timbre similarity, and repetition.

the parts that it is crossing. The experimental evidence for such a statement is quite clear.[638] The musical use is also widespread. Crossing of lines was usually avoided in counterpoint. An exception is in the organ trio sonatas of J. S. Bach. However, the parts were required to be played on different organ manuals or pedals having quite different stop settings. This guaranteed that the lines would have different timbres and that listeners would be able to follow a line as it crossed another just as they were able to do with the laboratory stimuli used by Yves Tougas and myself.

A number of these principles were studied by James Wright in an informal experiment with a musical sequence.[639] The pattern is illustrated in figure 5.6. Three different "orchestrations" were used for this pattern. In the first, all the tones had the same timbre. This led them to group into two streams, one consisting of the two lowest tones (G and A) and the other including the remaining tones. The tones with the X-shaped note-heads formed an ascending and descending scalar figure that cut through the other lines. Despite its smooth trajectory and regular rhythm, this pattern was very hard to hear; a naive listener could not hear it at all because it attempted to cross the streams that had been set up by the grouping of the higher and lower notes by frequency proximity. In the second orchestration, the two streams that tended to occur spontaneously in the first orchestration were reinforced by giving different timbres to the two subsets of tones. When this was done it was almost impossible for even a trained listener to hear the crossing scalar figure. Finally, a third orchestration was used in which the tones of the scalar figure were given different timbres from the rest of the tones. Wright described the resulting experience: "In this case, the scalar figure was heard, clearly delineated, crossing back and forth between the frequency regions that had determined the grouping in the first and second orchestrations. All the other tones sounded like random sounds bracketing the salient scalar figure, and not themselves forming any continuous stream, since the scalar figure was breaking them up."

He pointed out that the second orchestration is typical of conventional eighteenth and nineteenth century orchestration in which instruments (and therefore timbres) were assigned to different lines of music that were "good Gestalten" even without any reinforcement by a shared timbre and therefore would have been heard as separate parts anyway, even in piano transcriptions. The timbres simply colored the already separate lines. According to Robert Erickson, this approach simply uses timbre to carry melodies that are already well defined by frequency relations.[640]

Another important factor that fuses parts is the parallel movement of different parts moving up and down together. We know from our discussions of common fate in chapter 3 that parallel frequency modulation favors the fusion of frequency components that are present at the same time. This was recognized in counterpoint theory by the fact that certain cases of parallel movement were discouraged. The prohibition was strongest for parallel movements in which two parts maintained either the frequency ratio 2:1 (parallel octaves) or 3:2 (parallel fifths), possibly because these simple frequency ratios already had a strong tendency to cause the parts to fuse perceptually because of their harmonicity. Even so, the rule is not absolute. The use of timbre differences can make it possible to overcome these unwanted effects of the parallel movement. For example, if use is being made of voices or instruments with different timbres, it is possible to permit the use of a rising or falling series of parallel chords (in which the same harmonic interval is held from chord to chord) providing that the timbres break up the parallelism. As the sequence progresses, each of the distinct timbres crosses to a different position in the chord. As an example of this, the music theorist Knud Jeppesen cited the passage, shown in figure 5.4, from the Credo of the Palestrina four-part mass, *In te Domine speravi*.[641] It might be useful to look first at the piano reduction shown in part b of the figure. The parallel chords in the second measure are easy to see in this version. Part a, in which the parts sung by the soprano (S), alto (A), and tenor (T) are notated separately, shows how the parallelism was broken up by the assignment of the notes to the soprano and alto voices. Jeppesen argued that the crossing of the voices was not just a trick for evading the letter of the rule that prohibited parallel fifths, but that in perception there was no longer any parallel movement of parts because the ear tended to follow the individual voices. According to Wright, a naive listener is still quite dominated by the parallelisms, and it takes careful listening to hear out the alto part, for example, as a separate melody. Nevertheless, the crossing over does reduce the sensation of a single musical object simply moving upward in pitch. If we accept Jeppesen's contention that the parallelism is not perceptually salient, we can see, in this example, how the goal of distinctness of parts could be satisfied while one of the rules that normally served this goal was violated. I think that this shows that it was the effort to satisfy the goals of the style (one of which was distinctness of parts), coupled with an understanding of how factors such as timbre influenced the perceptual organization, that allowed composers to violate the basic rules in appropriate circumstances.

A recent set of unpublished studies carried out by David Huron as part of a doctoral thesis in progress in the department of music of the University of Nottingham bears on the separation of voices in counterpoint. The studies have shown quantitatively that J. S. Bach did use the stream-segregation factors that I have been discussing to ensure the perceptual segregation of parts. Huron has statistically analyzed a considerable body of Bach's keyboard music and found that an increase in the number of voices in the music is accompanied by an increase in the number of uses of stream-segregating techniques such as separating the pitch ranges of the parts, having tones in different parts come on asynchronously, using small within-part pitch changes, and having the musical lines in different concurrent parts undergo different directions of motion.

Spatial Separation Spatial separation can also be used to keep parts perceptually distinct. Although I have not found any formal research on this topic, I was delighted to find that the American composer Henry Brant had written a report on the effects of spatial separation in music. It summarized years of practical experience in composing, experimenting with, and conducting music in which different performers, or groups of performers, were placed at different locations in a hall and in which "the spatial distribution of the performers throughout the hall is a planned, required, and essential element of the music."[642] The effects of spatial separation that he reported turned out to be exactly what might have been expected from the principles of scene analysis that were developed in the previous chapters. To oversimplify his findings a little, the further apart performers are in space (horizontal angle), relative to ourselves, the more independent we will hear their lines to be. (This is an oversimplification because the room acoustics have to be taken into account as well.) The effects that were observed by Brant can be summarized by means of a simple contrast between a hypothetical pair of widely separated players and an equally hypothetical pair of players who are in exactly the same location. We can take, as the example of separated performers, a case in which there are two instrumentalists, one at the center of the right wall of a hall and the other at the center of the left wall, with the audience seated in between. For an example of nonseparated players, we place them side by side at the front of the hall (the conventional position for performance).

The first influence of spatial separation is on melodic segregation, or clarity. With the players in the same location, if the players are playing in the same octave, it is impossible for the listener to keep the parts distinct from one another, especially when the performers converge on the same note. However, for the separated pair the melodic lines keep their independence, even when the pitches come close together. This means that the composition can maintain clarity without having to keep the different parts in nonoverlapping pitch ranges. Brant puts it this way:

> The total impression of spatially distributed music, in its clarity of effect, . . . is to some extent equivalent to setting up the performers close together on a stage, as usual, but writing the music in such a way that each texture remains in its own octave range, with no collision or crossing of textures permitted. The spatial procedure, however, permits a greatly expanded overall complexity, since separated and contrasting textures may be superimposed freely over the same octave range, irrespective of passing unisons thus formed, with no loss of clarity.

Thus, the composer has an additional dimension of separation to work with. By separating lines in both pitch and space, a larger number of them can be kept distinct from one another.

A similar effect is experienced with rhythms. We saw earlier how increasing the pitch separation between the simple component rhythms of a complex polyrhythm allowed the listener to hear out the component rhythms. Brant reports that spatial separation has a similar effect. For example, suppose two players are playing unrelated rhythms. Then as they are separated further and further in space, the listener finds it easier to hear out the individual rhythms and not hear them as an incoherent blend.

In his article Brant makes the point several times that not only do the separated parts appear clearer, but also louder and more resonant. Perhaps this is because both the direct sounds and the reverberant sounds of the separated instruments are kept in perceptually distinct packages, one for each location, and hence do not mask one another. We have seen in chapter 3 how factors that enhance perceptual segregation can minimize the effects of masking.

The segregation that arises from spatial separation is not without its costs. One musical goal of a composer is to keep lines distinct, and, in this, spatial separation succeeds admirably well. But another goal is to have rhythmic and harmonic relations between the parts. These relations are, to a large degree, lost in the case of the separated players. It is, for example, hard to hear the harmonic properties of a chord when its components are originating at widely different places. This illustrates the fact that "vertical" global properties, such as harmony, are computed within streams. Only to the extent that sounds enter a common stream do we hear their harmony. Similarly, it is hard to hear any connection between the rhythmic patterns coming from widely separated players. One solution to this musical problem is to have several players in each location and to compose the music in such a way that the harmonic and rhythmic relations are important only between instruments that are at the same place. The parts at different locations are composed so that "no exact rhythmic correspondence is intended between the independent groups." Brant has used such techniques in many of the pieces that he has written. The result is "spatial counterpoint."

Counterpoint and Dissonance

One of the goals in early counterpoint was the control of dissonance. Before developing this claim, and because dissonance is a tricky concept, I would like to draw a distinction that will be useful in the following discussion, the distinction between "musical dissonance" and "psychoacoustic dissonance" or roughness.

Musical dissonance is a role that certain musical intervals or chords play in the structure of Western tonal music. Certain harmonic intervals (combinations of two notes played simultaneously) are designated as dissonant and others as consonant. They are given contrasting roles in musical sequences. The consonant intervals are viewed as marking stable points in the music whereas the dissonant intervals function as deviations from stability that are temporary moments of tension and must be followed by a return to stability.[643] The dissonance referred to in this contrast is what I will call musical dissonance. It depends on a categorization that assigns particular types of sounds to roles in the musical style. At various times in history, the decision as to which intervals should be treated as consonant and dissonant has changed. For example, in the tenth century the fifth was not considered consonant, but by the sixteenth century the fifth was considered almost equal to the octave as a consonant interval.

By psychoacoustic dissonance I am referring to a quality of roughness that certain tones have when they are played together. This should not change with musical style or with the passage of time. Psychoacoustic dissonance is not a division of chords into two categories, consonant and dissonant, but is a continuously variable quality that varies from very smooth to very rough. The quality of being relatively smooth probably was what prepared the way for the octave, the fourth, and the fifth to be assigned the role of musically consonant intervals in different historical periods. If this is so, then, as Wright and I have phrased it, "in their origin, the role of many of the pattern principles encountered in contrapuntal theory was to control the sensation of roughness associated with the dissonances and . . . it was only later, when these principles became embodied in musical styles, that they acquired a syntactic role."[644]

By now the musical dissonance has diverged so far from psychoacoustic dissonance that it is possible to imagine a musical style that uses smooth intervals so rarely that they stand out as deviant when they occur and by this fact become musically dissonant. Let me make it clear, then, that I am going to attempt to show, in the use of certain rules for the control of dissonance in counterpoint theory, the traces of perceptual principles that affect the experience of psychoacoustic dissonance or roughness. These musical practices were probably introduced at a time when there was a closer relation between psychoacoustic and musical dissonance than there is now.

Physical Causes of Dissonance In looking, then, at the causes of psychoacoustic dissonance, I plan to explain a fact that musicians have known all along, namely that the perceived dissonance of a simultaneously sounded pair of tones depends not just on the pair itself but on the context of other sounds. However, although the musician offers explanations through a description of the context in terms of music theory, and although that description of the context may well be important, I will offer an explanation based on a nonmusical description of the pattern. To anticipate, I will propose that when the two potentially dissonant tones are experienced as being in *separate streams*, the experience of roughness or psychoacoustic dissonance is suppressed, and that certain practices in counterpoint make this perceptual organization more likely to occur. But before I do this, let us look at the more traditional explanations of psychoacoustic dissonance. In the following account I am indebted to a comprehensive unpublished review by Linda Roberts.[645]

The Pythagoreans in the fifth century B.C. discovered that two notes produced by stretched strings were consonant (that is, they sounded smooth together) when the ratios of the lengths of the strings were formed out of low integers, such as 2:1 (the octave), 3:2 (the fifth), and 4:3 (the fourth). With the advent of modern physics, it became apparent that the effect of shortening the string was to raise the frequency of vibration of the string by the same proportion. The rule was rephrased to state that the most consonant tonal combinations involve simple ratio relations between frequencies.

The explanations of why certain frequency relations create dissonance have fallen into two categories: (1) those based on unconscious calculations of the brain about the frequency ratios (with the brain liking simpler ratios better) and (2) those based on acoustic properties of the mixture. The latter type of explanation now prevails.

The theory that is best accepted today originated with the nineteenth-century German physiologist and physicist Hermann von Helmholtz. It blames the roughness of dissonant tones on the perception of beats.[646] Helmholtz espoused a theory of hearing that argued that the auditory system resolves complex tones or mixtures of tones into individual spectral components (partials). When two partials are too close in frequency for the auditory system to resolve them, it hears the beats (periodic fluctuations in intensity) created by their summation. The frequency of the beats is equal to the difference in frequency between the unresolved partials. To this theory has been added the more modern notion of the *critical band*, which is defined as a certain frequency separation (called the width of the critical band) within which partials are not fully resolved by the auditory system and therefore interact to produce phenomena such as masking or, as in the present case, beats. The critical band represents some limitation in frequency resolution and its width is different in different frequency regions. At 1,000 Hz, the width of the critical band is something like 150–180 Hz (about three semitones). When the frequencies of the partials rise above 1,000 Hz, the critical bandwidth grows in rough proportion to the frequency range occupied by the two partials, so that it stays under three semitones all the way up to 10,000 Hz. However, if the pair of partials is moved below 1,000, the width of the critical band does not decline in direct proportion to the frequency and it never becomes smaller than about 100 Hz.

When a single tone, whose partials are all harmonically related, is played, all the consecutive partials are spaced by the same frequency, the fundamental (since they are all integer multiples of that frequency); therefore, any pairs of consecutive harmonics that are not resolved by the ear will beat at this frequency, causing the beat frequency to reinforce the pitch of the fundamental. On the other hand, when *two* different complex tones are presented at the same time, the nearest neighbor in frequency to a particular partial need not be from the spectrum of the same tone, but may be from the other one. Therefore the frequencies of the beats that we hear will depend on the relations between the partials of the two tones.

Lower tone alone:	1f	2f	3f	4f	5f	6f	...
Higher tone alone:		2f		4f		6f	...
Both tones together:	1f	2f	3f	4f	5f	6f	...

Figure 5.7
Correspondence of harmonics in octave-related tones.

Let us consider why an octave is so smooth. The frequencies of the partials of the lower-pitched tone can be represented as in the first line of figure 5.7. Those of the higher tone are related to a fundamental that is twice as high as the first and can therefore be represented as in the second line of the figure. We should notice that the harmonics of the higher tone correspond with the even harmonics of the lower one. If the ratio between the two fundamentals is very close to 2.00, the frequency of the beats of corresponding harmonics from the two tones will be about zero and the beats of successive harmonics in the mixture will be at exactly the frequency f, just as they were with the lower tone alone; these beats, therefore, should be absorbed into the pitch of the lower tone. The correspondence of harmonics occurs because of the simple ratio between the two fundamentals.

In general, if the ratio between the two fundamentals is $m:n$, and m and n are integers, every nth harmonic of the first fundamental will correspond in frequency with every mth harmonic of the second. Therefore, when the ratio can be expressed in terms of small integers there will be many exact correspondences of frequencies. Even if the ratio is not exactly 2:1 or 3:2 or another such ratio, but is near these simple ratios, the partials that would have the same frequency in the exactly tuned case will be quite near to one another in frequency. Hence, the frequency of the beats between corresponding harmonics will be quite near zero and will not be unpleasant. Such near misses, rather than exact correspondences, occur frequently in the equally tempered scale of modern Western instruments.

In the case of simple ratios other than 2:1, the beats between the successive interleaved harmonics will be related to the frequency of another lower tone (the "fundamental bass") of which both fundamentals are simple multiples. The beats will be either at the fundamental frequency of that tone or at one of its lower harmonics. Because of the simple ratio between the two simultaneous tones, this fundamental bass tone will be another audible tone, harmonious with the other two. As an example, if the fundamentals are at 300 and

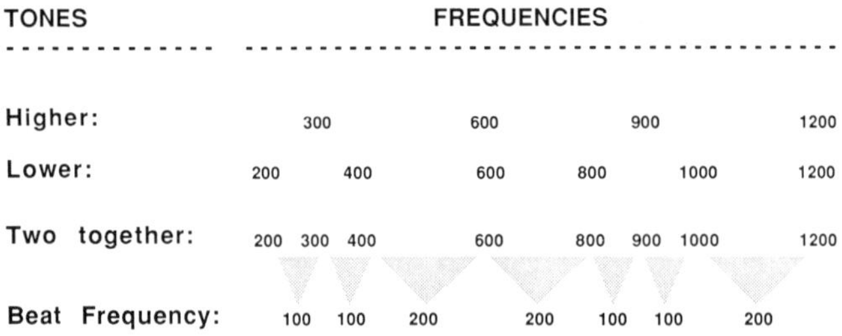

TONES	FREQUENCIES
Higher:	300 600 900 1200
Lower:	200 400 600 800 1000 1200
Two together:	200 300 400 600 800 900 1000 1200
Beat Frequency:	100 100 200 200 100 100 200

Figure 5.8
Correspondence of harmonics of tones that are a fifth apart.

200 Hz, where the ratio is 3:2, harmonics will occur as shown in figure 5.8. Beat frequencies between nearest pairs of partials are also shown, below and between the pairs of partials that are causing them. The beat frequencies are always at multiples of 100 Hz as are the two tones themselves. Therefore there are a few dominant beat frequencies, and they are all harmonically related and likely to be absorbed into the pitches of the two simultaneous tones or the pitch of the fundamental bass. Furthermore, some of the beats generated by the lower harmonics, while legitimately computable from the properties of waves, are generated by partials that are more than a critical band apart. They will therefore not result in perceived beats (which are due to the reception of two different partials in the same critical band). The relations that I have been describing in this example will all occur among the tones of the major triad, the chord that is central for harmony in Western European music.

By way of contrast, when two notes that are heard as dissonant are presented (for example the ratio 25:12, which is not much different from an octave but has a much more complex frequency ratio), very few harmonics will correspond, and the spacing between the partials of one tone and their nearest neighbors in the second tone will vary quite a lot, yielding a cacophony of different beat frequencies. If certain rates and irregularities of beating are heard as unpleasant, this mixture will be likely to provide them.

One advantage of the theory of critical bands is that it explains the observable fact that harmonic intervals formed of pure tones are not psychoacoustically dissonant (rough). As long as two pure tones are more than a critical bandwidth apart, no beats will be registered in the auditory system, since beats are the result of the interaction of tones in the same critical band. Since pure tones have no higher harmonics, if the pure tones themselves do not beat, there is nothing else that can beat. Although a musician may be aware that the tones are considered to be musically dissonant in traditional diatonic music, they will not sound rough together.

Difference tones are another auditory phenomenon, caused by distortion in the middle and inner ear. Although they have a different cause from beats, they, like beats, have a frequency that depends on the frequency differences between partials. For this reason, they are most audible when the ratio between the fundamentals of two tones is complex. Helmholtz assigned a lesser role to these difference tones in perceived dissonance.

In summary, simultaneous tones give rise to an interaction between partials that is more complex and irregular when the ratio of their fundamental frequencies is not close to a simple ratio of integers.

Carl Stumpf, a German psychologist and philosopher of the late nineteenth century, connected the ideas of fusion and dissonance.[647] He thought that sounds were consonant if they fused. For Stumpf, the term consonance was a measure of the tendency of two tones to fuse, and it was the resistance to this fusion that we perceived as dissonance. A recent experimental study by Lucinda DeWitt and Robert Crowder has confirmed that the more consonant musical intervals tend to fuse more strongly.[648] How do these ideas relate to ideas about scene analysis?

We have already mentioned that the fusion of complex tones is better when their harmonics coincide. This is due to the activity of a scene-analysis mechanism that is trying to group the partials into families of harmonics that are each based on a common fundamental. If the right relations hold between an ensemble of partials, they will be grouped into a single higher-order organization that will be given a single description (certainly in terms of pitch and probably in terms of other auditory qualities as well). The greater fusion of consonant harmonic intervals may occur because concurrent pitch analyzers will not find three totally distinct series of harmonics, owing to the close mathematical relations among the partials.

It is this fusion, in most cases incomplete, that contributes to the experience of chord perception in which the chord, rather than the individual tones, becomes the acoustic object that we hear. We can think of a chord as a global entity that has its own emergent properties. If tones belong to the chord they contribute to a sonic shape, rather than "sticking out" and being clearly understood not to be part of the shape at all. In some theories of harmony, that of Schenker, for example , dissonant tones were not supposed to be able to form a true chord.[649] Perhaps this was because dissonant combinations are less likely to fool the scene-analysis process into assigning them to the same perceptual object. Consonant combinations of tones, on the other hand, may partially fuse and therefore provide one sort of vertical link that holds the melodic lines together as parts of a coherent piece of music. We shall see that other factors can strengthen these vertical links as well.

It is my opinion that there are two perceptual effects of simple harmonic relations that are independent of each other. The first effect produces psychoacoustic consonance and dissonance, and the second controls fusion. The fusion depends on fooling the scene-analysis process, and the dissonance is the result of the beats and difference tones. Therefore, the so-called instability of dissonant intervals in music may depend on two quite separate facts. The idea that dissonant tones are unstable because they are not truly able to form a chord that holds different musical parts together really depends on the fusion properties of tones. On the other hand, the idea that they are unstable because they have a rough quality depends on the quite separate fact that they lead to complex acoustic patterns. Stumpf thought that the fusion was the real psychological cause of the dissonance. In this, I think, he failed to properly distinguish between "heard as one" and "heard as smooth." You can hear a burst of static as rough even though the static is heard as a single sound. Conversely, we often fail to hear any roughness in a combination of two sounds even though we do not fuse the components. For example, with dichotic presentation of two pure tones of different frequencies or monaural presentation of two pure tones of somewhat greater differences in frequency, we hear no roughness but we do not fuse the tones.

The theory that I shall propose will relate psychoacoustic dissonance to fusion but in a different way than Stumpf did. It will argue that the perception of dissonance can be suppressed when the tones that form the dissonance are perceived as belonging to different auditory streams.

In a dissonant combination of tones, the dissonance is a property of the combination. Each tone taken alone is not dissonant. We must remember that the goal of the auditory system is to sort out the available evidence so that it can build global descriptions of distinct objects. Therefore, if the auditory system were always successful in this task, whenever it heard a dissonant combination of tones it would build descriptions of the two separate nondissonant tones and discard the combination as the result of an accidental co-occurrence, a chimera as it were. However, music deals in chimeras. The chord is a case in point. Although the chord is a structure formed out of separate tones, it is treated at least partly as a global whole in perception, with the result that global properties are derived by our auditory systems. These global properties give the different types of chords their characteristic qualities. I think the same thing happens with combinations of tones that are dissonant. (There is a controversy, which I shall avoid, as to whether to call such combinations "chords.") When cues that favor vertical integration are present, the auditory system treats the combination as a unit, and whatever properties are extracted are assigned as global descriptions of this unit. When the cues favor segregation, the combination is treated as accidental and only the individual, nondissonant tones are perceived. Under these circumstances the dissonance is discarded from awareness.

There is a conceptual problem that results from this way of arguing. If we truly believe that the roughness is the direct result of physical events, such as beats, how is it possible not to hear them as part of the sound? In order to clarify this issue, it is necessary to make yet another distinction: that between a potential dissonance and a perceived dissonance. The physical circumstances that give rise to a complex and incoherent pattern of beats at certain rates provide the condition under which one can potentially hear dissonance. We can even take it for granted that the registration of these beats by the peripheral auditory system must obligatorily take place. Yet this registration is not in itself equivalent to perception. The potential is there, but the perception has not yet taken place. This situation can be called a potential dissonance. Actual perception occurs when the sensory information is translated into a quality of roughness and assigned to one of the auditory events whose description is being built. Then we have a perceived dissonance.

Following up on this argument, we can ask what will cause the combination of tones to be treated as a unit by the auditory system. The answer is, "any of the factors that were shown in chapter 3 to promote the fusion of spectra." These include spectral proximity, harmonic concordance, synchronous changes, freedom from sequential capturing, and spatial proximity. We shall see that a number of these can be used in music to control perceived roughness.

This way of looking at the perception of dissonance has an unexpected implication. Psychoacoustic dissonance (or roughness) should be heard more strongly when tones are fused. We should notice that this statement is in some sense directly opposite to Stumpf's view of dissonance, in which dissonance was equated with *lack* of fusion. It should be mentioned, however, that my view is not unknown among musicians. Victor Zuckerkandl used the expression "tonal coalescence" to describe the fusion of sounds and mentioned that he thought this coalescence could produce dissonance.[650] I would like to reconcile the opposition between Stumpf's view and my own by the following argument. Many factors, including bad harmonic relations, will act to prevent the fusion of tones. To the extent that they succeed, we will not hear dissonance. But they will not always succeed. If I sit down at an electric organ and press two keys at the same time and release them together, although their bad harmonic relations should act to keep them distinct, the fact that their onset is simultaneous, their duration is the same, and they are coming from the same location will tend to keep them fused. To the extent that they are fused, a listener will experience the dissonance. Because there are many factors that affect fusion, not all co-occurring tones will be equally well fused. Furthermore, there is no reason to believe that fusion is an all-or-nothing phenomenon. There can probably be different degrees of fusion, and these may result in different degrees of perceived dissonance.

I ask the reader to always bear in mind that we are talking about psychoacoustic dissonance, not musical dissonance. The distinction, however, needs some qualification. I have been talking as if psychoacoustic dissonance, or roughness, lived in a completely different world than musical dissonance. That surely cannot be the case. Even though the musical categorization may not exactly correspond to the degree of roughness, there has to be some relation. It is hard to imagine that the musical categorization would be utterly independent of the psychoacoustic factors.

The interaction probably takes two forms, historical and immediate. Historically, there must have been a reason why certain intervals were considered consonant, were used more frequently, occurred with longer durations in the music, and were considered points at which the music ought to come to rest. There were probably two distinct reasons. One is that when certain notes in different parts were sounded together they tended to fuse the different parts into a coherent whole; the other is that they sounded smooth and pure. Dissonances, by contrast, were disruptive and rough. These raw properties undoubtedly lay behind the assignment of the musical roles of stability and instability to the consonant and dissonant intervals.

The second connection between the psychoacoustic and musical domains is more immediate. Although the inner dynamics of musical thought may take the listener into structures and experiences that are not expressible in psychoacoustic terms, music is still heard with the ears. The property of dissonance as roughness must enter into the experience at some level. Furthermore, this roughness will sometimes be desirable and sometimes not, depending on the musical goals of the composer. This situation requires the composer to control the experience of roughness as part of the crafting of the music.

Early in the evolution of polyphony, musically dissonant combinations were never allowed, but later, the goals of composers changed. They began to want to create separate parts that contained melodies that were at the same time good melodies and also separable from one another. This made it harder to avoid dissonance. At the same time they began to use dissonance to add variety to the music. It seems plausible that they discovered that they could introduce musical dissonance while partially suppressing the psychoacoustic dissonance, and that this evolved into "rules" for the "control of dissonance."

How the Control of Roughness Can Be Accomplished

Composers can attenuate the perceived degree of roughness in the same way as they can attenuate the perception of any sort of global property of a mixture, by ensuring that the simultaneous sounds are not assigned to the same auditory stream. Earlier, in chapter 3, we saw that simultaneous auditory components can be prevented from contributing to an overall timbre by such a segregation. What I am saying here is that roughness is just another form of timbre and that it can be controlled in the same way. Because the composers of the polyphonic style wanted to keep the parts distinct at certain points (for reasons unrelated to the control of dissonance), they had to set up a number of parallel auditory streams anyway. The acoustic separation of these streams may not have been as extreme as that created in the laboratory, but at least it offered the listener the possibility of segregating them without too much effort. One way to control psychoacoustic dissonance was to ensure that the potentially dissonant combination of notes occurred only at moments when the streams were maximally segregated. This strong separation could be ensured in the same way as the distinctness of the polyphonic lines was being preserved in general: by capturing notes into the same stream by similarities of pitch and timbre in the same part, and by avoiding between-part synchronies and parallel changes.

Figure 5.9 shows some examples of patterns of notes in which dissonant intervals were permitted in the Palestrina style. They all had the following in common: they avoided the simultaneous attack of potentially dissonant notes, and they arranged it so that at least one of the dissonant notes was captured sequentially into its own stream in a strong way.

The first of these, the *passing tone* is illustrated in part a of the figure. A passing tone (labeled P) is a note inserted between two harmonic notes (notes that are part of the harmony). In this example, the interval formed by the passing tone (the D in the upper staff) with the E in the lower staff is a seventh (labeled with the 7 marked

Figure 5.9
Examples of note patterns for the control of dissonance. (From Wright and Bregman, 1986.)

below the staff). The interval is dissonant, but it is permitted in this pattern. Let us examine the pattern from the perspective of stream segregation. The passing tone is placed between two tones that are already quite close to one another in pitch, and it improves the continuity between them. The passing tone, therefore, improves the coherence of the stream of which it is a part. By the same token, the passing tone is strongly bound into that stream. Another fact about it is that its onset is asynchronous with the whole tone in the lower staff with which it is dissonant. The whole note has come on already and is not changing as the dissonant passing tone begins. This asynchrony of onset will segregate the two tones. Part b of the figure shows a similar example in which the passing tone is accented by the rhythm. Part c shows a *neighbor tone* (labeled N), also called an auxiliary tone. Again it is a dissonant tone, in our example a B played against an A (a two-semitone interval or major second). It is a single semitone step downward from its neighbors on both sides. The neighbor tone is closer in pitch (measured in semitones) to its neighbors in the same stream than to its predecessor and successor in the lower stream. The difference is not large, but the preference for

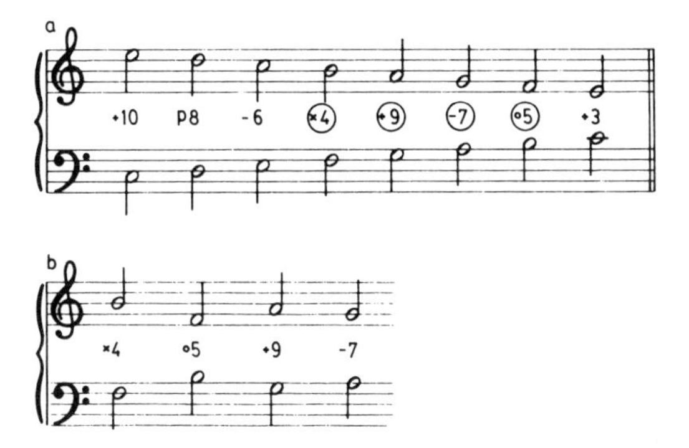

Figure 5.10
Melodic trajectory. (a) Scales in contrary motion form a series of dissonances that are not perceived as such; (b) the same series of dissonances extracted from context and rearranged. (From Wright and Bregman 1987.)

grouping this tone into its own stream (the upper one) would be promoted by the relative shortness of the step and also by any timbre differences between the voices or instruments performing the two parts. The example that is given here is extreme in terms of the closeness of the parts. Often they would be more separated, allowing the neighbor tone to be much closer to its own stream than to the other stream. The other observation about neighbor tones is that, like passing tones, their onset occurs at points in the music at which there is no onset in the other stream. The half note in the lower voice continues as the quarter-note neighbor tone begins.

Part d shows what is called an *anticipation* (labeled A)—a dissonant note which is identical to the note that follows it in the same part and which is therefore tightly bound into its own stream by pitch similarity. Once again, its onset occurs while the note in the lower stream is held.

The pattern in part e is called the *suspension formula*. It consists of three notes: the preparation (P), the suspension (S), and the resolution (R). The S is dissonant with the whole note that lies below it. In the upper part, P and S are notated as separate notes, but the fact that they are the same pitch and tied together means that they are played as a single long note. The horizontal line shows the length of this note. Similarly, in the lower staff, the horizontal line shows the duration of the whole note which is dissonant with the tone labeled S above it. What can be seen by comparing the two horizontal lines is that the two notes that form the dissonance neither come on nor go off at the same time. This double asynchrony would have a strong segregating effect on the dissonant tones. As before, this is assisted by the fact that each of the dissonant tones stays as close as possible to its neighbors in the same stream.

Other methods are also available to control the segregation of lines from one another. They involve strengthening the horizontal organization of notes. For example, trajectories can be used to group the notes. In chapter 4 we saw that there is some uncertainty as to whether the grouping by trajectories is a primitive or a schema-driven process. We can leave that issue open here. Whatever its basis, a trajectory in one part seems to reduce its integration with other parts, thereby reducing the perceived dissonance. If it is a schema-dependent process, it probably works by directing the attention of the listener to the schema-governed trajectory and away from the dissonance of the individual notes. If it is a primitive process, it probably blocks the assignment of the dissonance to the description of the streams at a more basic level. Wright and Bregman offered the example shown in figure 5.10.[651] Part a of the figure shows two scales in contrary motion, which when played on the piano do not lead to an experience of dissonance. Yet, as shown by the letters that are marked below them, four of the intervals are dissonant. When we extract these chords from their context, rearrange them to destroy the trajectories, and play them again, their dissonance is clearly audible. Somehow the embedding of the dissonances within scale trajectories has suppressed the perception of the dissonances.

There is one uncertainty with this musical demonstration: Playing the chords in the wrong order changes not only the within-voice trajectories, but also the within-voice frequency proximities. Tones aligned on a trajectory are not only parts of a simple pattern, they also are near in frequency to their within-voice neighbors. Careful laboratory studies would have to be done to find out whether the alignment of notes on a trajectory had an effect over and above the effect that this has on their frequency proximities.

It is also possible to strengthen the sequential organization through repetition. The repetition of a short pattern of notes over and over again is known in music as *ostinato*. The repetition has the effect of perceptually unifying the repeated sequence, and the notes that form part of it are not perceived as isolated notes but as parts of the larger unit. By being absorbed into the melodic unit, which is a horizontal pattern, their vertical groupings seem to be weakened and they produce less roughness than they would otherwise do. The perceptual effects of the ostinato have not gone unnoticed by music theorists. C. W. Fox, in a passage that has been cited by Wright and Bregman, expands on the notion of a prepared note (one that is preceded by a

Figure 5.11
Polyostinato from Bartok's *Fourth String Quartet*, measures 14–18.

copy of itself—a situation that seems to free it from vertical influences). He argues that the idea of preparation by means of prior exposure can be extended from single notes to groups of notes, and this will have similar effects on vertical integration: "A prepared ostinato, some or all of the notes of which conflict harmonically with the other voices, is the clearest example in modern music of a prepared melodic unit. . . . If a melody, short or long, is repeated immediately even only once, it may be segregated as an independent line against the other voices."[652]

Ostinato was a device used in polyphonic music as early as the thirteenth century. Many twentieth-century composers have used it to increase the segregation of parts from one another so that musically dissonant combinations of notes could be used without too much perceptual roughness occurring. This has often taken the form of polyostinato, in which repetitions of note patterns occur in more than one part at a time. The ostinatos in different parts have different lengths (periods). This has the effect of breaking down the correlation between the directions of motion in the different parts so as to indicate to the auditory system that it is not merely listening to repetitions of a single musical object. The resulting increase in the segregation of the lines allows a greater freedom in combining dissonant notes. This permits the "reckless counterpoint" (rücksichtsloser kontrapunkt) of twentieth century composers such as Stravinsky, Hindemith, and Prokofieff.[653] An example of the reckless counterpoint in Bartok's *Fourth String Quartet* is given in figure 5.11. The example shows polyostinato in which the repeating patterns are of different lengths in the different parts.

The buildup of a stream when a pattern is repeated may be related to the laboratory phenomenon in which sequential integration be-

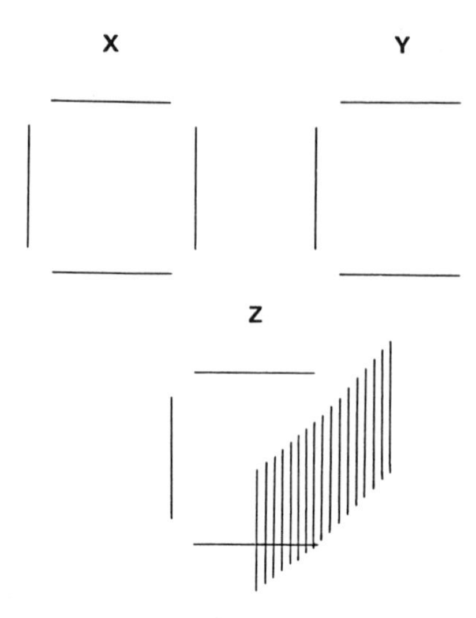

Figure 5.12
Visual ostinato. Pattern Z has embedded within it the whole of X, yet it looks like Y plus an additional set of lines. (From Wright and Bregman 1987.)

comes stronger with more repetitions of a cycle of tones.[654] I have interpreted this effect as the result of learning that a certain frequency region contains a stream. The effects of the repetition of a short pattern of notes are probably based on a slightly different sort of learning that involves the evolving of an expectation that a unit will be repeated. Then, through this learning, each note groups with the others in its own unit and each repetition of the unit groups horizontally with the previous ones, weakening its grouping with the simultaneous notes in a different part.

The effects of repetition that are observed in ostinato are not unknown in other domains of perception. An example of a visual ostinato is seen in figure 5.12.[655] Pattern X is seen as a square with its corners missing. Pattern Z contains within it the whole of pattern X; yet no square is seen in it. It looks like pattern Y with a set of parallel lines added to it. The repetition of the parallel lines captures the right-hand vertical line in pattern Z that would have formed the side of the square. Instead of forming part of a square the critical line becomes part of the unit formed by the group of parallel lines. The analogy with ostinato is fairly close, the critical line in the visual case corresponding to the auditory case of a note that is potentially dissonant with a note in another part. In both cases, the critical element is prevented from entering into a potential grouping (the square or the

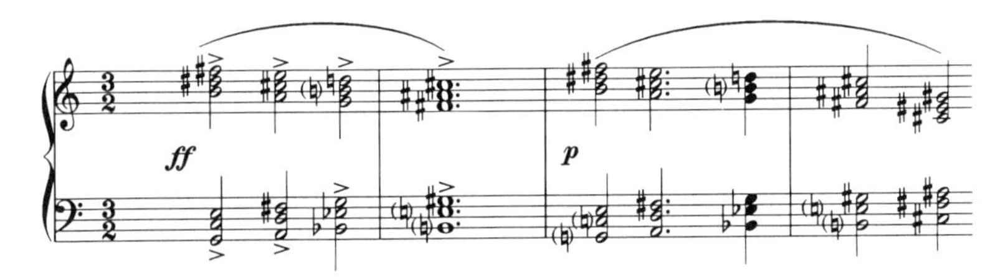

Figure 5.13
Polytriads as used by William Schuman. (From Wright and Bregman 1987.)

dissonance) by being captured into a larger organization (the group of lines or the ostinato). In both cases, repetition is responsible for the capturing.

In chapter 3, we examined an experiment by Bregman and Pinker in which co-occurring pure tones, B and C, might or might not fuse depending on whether B was captured by an earlier pure tone into a sequential stream. I was surprised by the fact that the resistance of B to being captured was unaffected by whether or not B and C were harmonically related. As a rather ad hoc explanation, I suggested that it took a number of harmonics to establish strong evidence for a harmonic series and only when it was established would the nonfitting harmonics be rejected from the group. This explanation, although never tested directly, made sense of the results of other experiments as well. While this was a hypothesis introduced to explain a laboratory finding, it seems to account for some musical examples. Let us examine figure 5.13, which shows measures 1 and 2 from the second movement of William Schuman's *Three-Score Set* for piano solo. The texture is composed of two streams, a higher and a lower one, each consisting of a sequence of major triads, those in the bass being in the second inversion. Within each stream, there are no dissonances, the major triad being the very model of consonance. However, there are strong potential dissonances between the notes in the upper and lower triads. These are, however, largely suppressed perceptually. There are two reasons for the perceptual segregation that reduces the dissonance. The first that a musician will give is the fact that the pitches of the two simultaneous triads are well separated, usually by more than an octave. We have seen in chapter 3 that the existence of large frequency separations between pure tones tends to reduce their fusion. Apparently an analogous effect occurs with complex tones, large separations between their fundamentals reducing their tendency to fuse. The second reason is the tight binding of the tones within any triad as a result of simple harmonic relations.

We should notice that the sequence of chords in each clef maintains a *real parallelism* rather than a *tonal parallelism* with one another. In what I am referring to as tonal parallelism, the notes of the chord would stay an equal number of *diatonic scale steps* away from one another as the chord moved up or down. However, due to the fact that the degrees of the diatonic scale are not equally spaced in log frequency from one another, the notes would not retain their harmonic relations to one another as the chords moved. What I am calling real parallelism, on the other hand, requires the tones to move in parallel on the *tempered chromatic scale*, whose degrees do maintain a constant separation in log frequency. Parallel movements on this scale, as a result, do maintain the harmonic relations between the notes of the chord (at the cost of having the succession of chords move into different keys). In real parallelism, then, the notes of the triads benefit not only from the factor of common fate, the fact that they are moving in parallel, but also from the maintaining of good harmonic relations. The resulting vertical integration apparently leaves them less available to group with tones outside their own triad. If this is a valid explanation, it suggests that vertical groupings can compete with one another in the same sort of way that sequential ones can. We saw in chapter 2 that a tone that was strongly bound into a sequential organization was less available to be grouped sequentially with other tones. Perhaps the same sort of exclusive allocation can occur in the fusion of sets of acoustic components that occur simultaneously.

The blending of tones by real parallelism can be used to create an experience of a single richer tone. There is a clear example of this in the design of the pipe organ. In order to increase the richness of the tones, a method is used in which two or more pipes are sounded at the same time. The method is named the *stop* after the mechanical device that controls it. Some stops, called *foundation stops*, involve activating two pipes an octave apart. These blend easily into a single experience. In others, called *mutation stops*, the fundamental of the higher pipe is not tuned to the octave, but to one of the other harmonics of the lower pipe. This method can reinforce some of the higher harmonics of the resulting sound and give the impression that a tone with the pitch of the lower tone is present, but with a richness that is supplied by strong higher harmonics. Some care must be taken with these mixtures to avoid the impression of two separate pitches. This can be done by ensuring that the lower-pitched pipe is sounded much more intensely than the higher one. In "mixture" or "compound" stops, three or more pipes with different pitches are used.

Figure 5.14
Measures 149–150 from Ravel's *Bolero*. (From Wright and Bregman 1987.)

In some cheap pipe organs, two pipes with an interval of a fifth (frequency ratio of 3:2) are used to simulate a longer pipe whose fundamental is an octave lower than the lower of the two actual pipes. This is the fundamental bass that I described earlier in this chapter. Its fundamental is a frequency for which the lower actual pipe is the second harmonic and the higher one is the third.

In all the organ stops, the impression of a single tone is assisted by the fact that the mechanical linkage ensures that the pipes that are involved in the stop will all be activated at the same time. As we have already seen, this is a cue to the scene-analysis system that it should group the partials as a single sound.

The fact that you can get a rich but coherent tone from the organ stops suggests that the strategy of tuning the fundamentals to simple integer ratios is a good one. It appears to work because it ensures that a certain number of the harmonics of the two notes will coincide, a factor that was discussed above when we saw that dissonant tones fuse less well than consonant tones.

Naturally, when a succession of notes is played, the linked pipes always maintain a fixed frequency relation to one another; so if they were considered as separate "voices," they could be seen to be in "real" parallel motion. This parallel motion may also play a role in the blending of the pipes.

Notes that have good harmonic relations to one another and move in real parallel motion will tend to undergo vertical grouping. This grouping may or not be desirable. In the case of our polytriad example, the within-triad integration was desirable because it helped to prevent notes from grouping with ones that were outside their triad; this permitted potentially dissonant note combinations to be used more freely. In the case of the organ, the blended notes could be used as if they were a single note with a richer timbre. However, in the case of the polyphonic textures that were created by rules of counterpoint, certain types of real parallel motion (of fifths and octaves) were prohibited because the merging of parts that they would have caused was not desired in the style. It was not emergent timbres but separately moving lines of melody that were valued.

When musical goals changed, parallel moving chords were used to create ensemble timbres. An example can be found in Ravel's ballet *Bolero*, in which many techniques that we discussed in chapter 3 are used to promote the fusing of the parts, In measures 149–150, shown in figure 5.14, subgroups of instruments are yoked together by the fact that their parts move in real parallel motion and their notes go on and off together because of an exactly duplicated rhythm. The blending is further assisted by having the instruments that play the higher parts in these yoked groups play less loudly. This may be making use of a fact that we observed in chapter 3: Higher partials would fuse better into a complex tone if their amplitudes were less than those of the lower partials. The attenuation of high components occurs both because of the instruments used, flutes and celesta, and because the score is marked *pp* (which means very soft) for the flutes and *p* (soft) for the celesta. The only instrument marked *mf* (moderately loud) is the french horn (marked "cor"), which is playing much lower notes. Another factor that promotes fusion in the Ravel example is the vertical spacing of the notes, which replicates the harmonic series. In all these respects, the simultaneous notes act as if they were all harmonics from the same phantasmagoric instrument, and by doing so induce our scene-analysis processes to combine them for purposes of computing its timbre.

We have seen how the goal of having separate musical lines prohibited the use of parallel movement of consonant combinations of tones in the Palestrina style of counterpoint. However, consonant intervals do not only have the musical job of binding lines together vertically. They also have their own special qualities as sounds. Yet consonance is as much an emergent property of a combination of tones as is dissonance. I think that if we were to hear, over headphones, a violin partita by Bach in one ear and a piano sonata by Beethoven in the other, and if these were well segregated perceptually, a combination consisting of one note from the Bach and one from the Beethoven would be neither consonant nor dissonant. They would simply not be registered as a perceptual simultaneity. Therefore, when we describe the qualities of musical intervals, consonance and dissonance are not simple opposites; there is a third possibility—nonconnection, or what Wright has referred to as a dead interval.[656] What, then, is consonance if it is not simply the absence of dissonance? First, it is the smooth and harmonious sound that I have called psychoacoustic consonance. It is also the awareness of musical consonance, the fact that the interval or chord is composed of notes that have a privileged relation in our musical system. The prohibition against a succession of parallel consonances might have been an attempt to prevent the repeated quality of consonance from making the music too bland. Since one alternative to consonance was dissonance and that was also to be used sparingly, the third alternative, vertical disconnection through nonparallel motion, was chosen.

We have reviewed a number of factors used by composers to control dissonance. But if any factor that will increase the segregation of simultaneous sounds will also suppress the perception of dissonance, then the other factors that were described in chapter 3 should also be usable. For example, since we know that spatial separation is a basis for segregating signals we should be able to suppress the dissonance between two tones by placing their sources in quite different spatial locations. So far as I know, there has not yet been any formal research on whether this is actually possible, but the composer Henry Brant, whose writing about spatial separation we discussed earlier, has told me that he has noticed this reduction of dissonance in his experimentation with spatial counterpoint.

Another way in which it should be possible to reduce their dissonance is to impose uncorrelated vibrato on them. Because uncorrelated vibrato is the usual case for two instruments played by different players, we should study the effects of vibrato on perceived dissonance by trying to *enhance* dissonance through the imposition of an exactly synchronized vibrato on two potentially dissonant tones. Although instrumental music, due to the limitations in the players' capabilities, would not be able to use exactly synchronized vibrato, computer-generated music could take advantage of this factor for both suppressing and intensifying perceived roughness.

We have looked at rules that in the sixteenth century had the effect of suppressing psychoacoustic dissonance by inducing the potentially dissonant tones to fall into separate streams. These rules are not sacred. They were simply the means used to achieve a goal. When the goals changed, the methods changed. Gradually the dissonance came to be increasingly valued for the variety and tension it gave to the music. Accordingly, by degrees, some of the rules for its containment were relaxed. James Wright has drawn an interesting schematic that summarizes characteristic changes in the control of dissonance that took place over time.[657] Figure 5.15 is an adaptation of it. Along the x axis, we get decreasing sequential integration due to a relaxation of the rule that dissonances had to be approached and left by a whole or half tone step. Ascending the y axis we get an increasing spectral fusion, due to a relaxation of the restriction against synchronous onsets and offsets of potentially dissonant tones. The line that runs upward and to the right represents increasing levels of psychoacoustic dissonance and the lines that cross it represent possible tradeoffs between the two factors that hold dissonance at about the same level. Also shown on the surface are the positions of several composers, which have been determined by examining particular fragments from their compositions. Although the fragments were not chosen in any systematic way, I find the graph quite interesting. I take it as a provocative hypothesis about historical changes that have occurred.

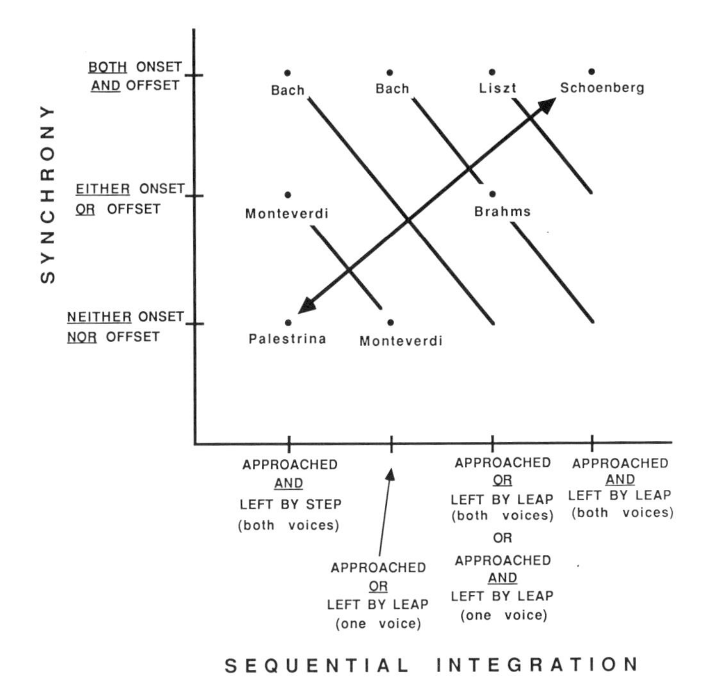

Figure 5.15
The salience of perceived dissonance, shown as a competition between factors favoring sequential integration and spectral integration. (From Wright 1986.)

Polyrhythm In chapter 2 we found that scene-analysis principles affected the ability of a listener to hear the separate rhythms in polyrhythmic textures. The perceptual problem of discarding the composite rhythm (the global rhythm that emerges when the separate rhythms are not segregated from one another) in favor of the component rhythms is the same as that of hearing separate melodies in two parts. Therefore we will not be surprised to learn that the same factors influence the listener's ability to isolate both rhythms and melodic lines. We have just seen that a major factor in segregating polyphonic parts is the asynchrony of onsets and offsets. However, this factor is less important when we want to compare the listener's ability to hear polyrhythms in different pieces. The asynchrony in different parts is usually guaranteed by the difference in rhythm. This means that other factors will play a larger role in making the component rhythms easier or harder to hear. The asynchronies will usually do a good job in breaking down the spectral integration of the parts; so fusion will not be a problem. The real difficulty will be that the listener will tend to integrate the notes of the different rhythms into a single composite rhythm. Therefore the composer's problem is how to promote sequential segregation (streaming) of the separate rhythms. Any factor that affects sequential integration should be useful for this purpose. We could expect the rhythms to be easier to segregate when the different rhythms were carried by instruments that occupied different pitch ranges, and given that a substantial difference in pitch was present, the rhythms should segregate better at higher speeds. Segregation should also be favored by different timbres, different spatial locations, and by within-note glides (note bends, or portamenti) that go in different directions in the different rhythms. Differences in loudness would assist us in picking out the louder rhythm, but probably not the softer. Unless there were also differences in other acoustic factors between the component rhythms, the loudness difference would simply cause accents to appear in the composite rhythm on the loud beats. Although some of the preceding statements are nothing more than extrapolations from what we know about stream segregation, others are well supported by research on the perception of polyrhythms.[658]

Polytonality We have discussed two "poly" forms of music: polyphony and polyrhythms. There is a third: polytonality. It is defined as the use of two of more keys at the same time, each occurring in a part or voice in the piece. When clearly perceived by the listener, it offers what Piston calls a counterpoint of keys.[659] Carol Krumhansl and Mark Schmuckler at Cornell University have looked at the question of whether a listener can perceptually separate the experience of the two keys.[660] They used as their stimulus material two excerpts from Stravinsky's *Petroushka*, in which there are two melodic lines. A slightly higher one consists of notes that are drawn primarily from the major triad of the key of C; a lower one contains notes that are drawn primarily from the major triad of the key of F-sharp. They tested the listener's sense of key by playing the passage to them and following it by a single note, the "probe tone." The listeners were asked to rate the probe tone as to how well it fit into the musical context established by the tones of the passage that preceded it. Earlier experiments that had used the probe tone technique had shown that different probe pitches fit into the context with different degrees of goodness, depending on their prominence in the key that had been established by the earlier notes.[661] By using this technique it is possible to tell which key context is established by any sequence of notes. In some conditions of the Krumhansl-Schmuckler experiment, the two melodic lines, each in a different key, were played simultaneously, but to different ears or in different timbres, and the listeners were asked to listen only to one of the lines. Despite the difference in location or timbre, the listeners were unable to reject the influence of the second key. The researchers explained this by appealing to principles of perceptual grouping. They pointed out that the notes in the two parts had exactly synchronous attacks, having been produced by a computer-controlled synthesizer, and were close together in pitch. Both of these cues were known from earlier research to strongly favor perceptual integration. It should be pointed out that under some conditions orchestral musicians who had recently performed the piece showed the same inability to attend to only one of the parts. This suggests that familiarity with the individual parts (and keys) does not allow listeners to select only a subset of materials when primitive principles of scene analysis are opposing this selection.

Potential Offered by Synthesis Techniques This chapter has mainly been about the music that has been created for mechanical instruments. We have been concerned with how sequential and spectral groupings can be controlled. However, it should be obvious by now that we know enough about the acoustic factors that cause these forms of grouping to be able to control the groupings with greater precision than these instruments permit. This offers a unique opportunity for computer music, in which the acoustics can be controlled exactly. For example, it would be possible to control the blending of two parts with one another on a very short temporal scale. A sound could be part of another sound, then briefly have its own identity, then merge back with the larger mass, all within the space of a few seconds. Jean-Claude Risset does a similar thing in his composition *Inharmonique*, and John Chowning's *Phone* contains changes of timbres into chords and vice versa. This poking out of sounds from the mass could be used to "teach" the listener the structure of the mass so that schema-based processes of scene analysis could take over the task of parsing the mixture.

This type of rapid binding and unbinding of the parts could simply not be done with conventional instruments, at least not in as many ways. Using these instruments, the composer is usually restricted to the use of the factors of synchrony, pitch separation, and timbre differences to achieve this. Computer-generated sound offers a wider set of factors, particularly those depending on rapid synchronized changes in the sounds (AM and FM), on harmonic relations among sounds, and on perceived spatial positions. For example, the computer music composer and theorist John Chowning has described how to synthesize sounds that appear to move in space.[662] The method simulates the amount of direct and reverberant sound that a listener would be receiving from each direction as well as the Doppler effect when the sound moves. We know from earlier chapters that spatial locations can be used to control both sequential and spectral integration. Therefore, if the parts were moving through space as well as varying in the more traditional ways, they would tend to bind together as they reached common locations and be more segregated when their spatial locations were distinct. Two parts that darted around in space together but sometimes took their own independent trajectories would have the same balance of dependence and independence that is achieved in conventional polyphonic music by synchronies and by independent and dependent pitch changes. Or a tone could be part of a chord at one spatial location, fully fused with it by a synchronous micromodulation, then depart from that chord, move through space, and become part of another chord at a different location.

The possibilities inherent in the use of spatial cues, in conflict and cooperation with other bases for segregation and integration, seem boundless. Conflicts between groupings based on different factors could be resolved temporarily in favor of one cue or another by simply enlarging the size of the contrasts on one factor (such as spatial location) and reducing those on another, then shifting the balance to favor grouping based on the second one. It would be hard to enumerate all the conflicts between cues that can be used. I would simply refer the reader to all the cues for sequential and spectral integration that were covered in previous chapters.

Computer synthesis could also be used to create superdissonances, psychoacoustic dissonances that are beyond the capacity of normal instruments to produce. Every known cue could be employed to tell the auditory system that all the acoustic components were from the same vibrating source and to thereby induce it to compute a single global quality for the combined sensory input. On the other hand, it is to be hoped that the holders of this great power would never exercise it, restrained by compassion for their audience.

Automatic Recognition So far we have seen how an understanding of perceptual principles can help us understand certain aspects of the composition and performance of music. However, there is another area in which such knowledge can help. Some contemporary music researchers have undertaken to program computers to transcribe music. The sounds of a musical performance are converted into a numeric representation of the waveform and then stored as a file in the computer. The goal is to write a program to convert this acoustic description into a description in terms of pitches, note values (such as quarter note or eighth note), key signatures, time signatures, and so on. There is a great deal of complexity in this process that we cannot hope to even mention here, but one of the fundamental questions is related to the issue of scene analysis. How many notes are being played at a certain moment and what are their individual acoustic descriptions? Solving this problem is an essential step on the way to a more abstract description framed in terms of the concepts of music. Some promising beginnings have been made in this direction by Christopher Chafe, with the collaboration of David Jaffe, Bernard Mont-Reynaud, and others at Stanford University's Center for Computer Research in Music and Acoustics (CCRMA).[663] They have started with the analysis of a recording of a natural piano performance of a Frescobaldi toccata. The techniques that they have used for segregating concurrent pitches work on a number of assumptions about instrumental sound. The first is that significant events are marked by sudden changes in amplitude. The program first detects sudden changes, both in the sound as a whole and in separate frequency bands, and then analyzes the more stable periods between changes. A second assumption is that each significant event will have a harmonic structure. It uses the set of detected partials and suggests candidates for a set of fundamentals. It deals with the problem of coincidence of harmonics from different fundamentals by assuming that a frequency component formed from summed partials will have a higher amplitude than individual partials. These summed partials are detected by assuming that the harmonics of a natural tone will fall off in intensity with increasing frequency. When the program finds a possible fundamental, it takes the energy from each frequency band that could be a harmonic of this fundamental, subtracts out a fraction of its energy, and treats it as the harmonic of that fundamental. As the frequency of the harmonic goes up, the program allocates a smaller and smaller fraction of the amplitude. Another assumption is that notes endure over time. Therefore the spectrum has to show a good fit to a proposed harmonic series for a minimum length of time. There is some specific tuning of the algorithm to piano tones. For example, the "harmonics" that it looks for are those of the piano, which are a little farther apart in frequency than mathematically exact harmonics would be. There are other assumptions that take advantage of the fact that the music is being played in western tuning. For example, the pitch estimates are rounded to the nearest pitch in the tempered scale. The program is quite successful (perhaps 95 percent of the time) in detecting the notes that were actually played by the pianist. Many of the assumptions built into the program are the same as those made by the human auditory system. In earlier research at CCRMA on the problem of transcribing polyphonic performances, Andy Moorer built into his program other assumptions used by the human auditory system.[664] For example, in deciding which voice a given note should be assigned to, the program used a simple frequency difference between successive notes in the voice as a measure of the goodness of the assignment. This is equivalent to the principle of frequency proximity in perceptual grouping. The program also assumed that voices do not cross in pitch. The researchers at CCRMA believe that further progress will be made by incorporating more of the cues used by the human listener into such programs. An expansion of the range of cues will make necessary the development of algorithms that employ voting schemes by which different cues can be made to cooperate and compete.

Summary

This chapter has illustrated the effects of primitive processes of scene analysis in music. We have seen how properties of musical sound could emerge from the perceptual integration of acoustic components over time and across the spectrum. The integration affects the coherence of melodies, the hearing of rhythms, the isolation of one musical voice from another, the perception of timbre, and the awareness of roughness. I have argued that the primitive processes of auditory organization work in the same way whether they are tested by studying simplified sounds in the laboratory or by examining examples in the world of music. The processes seem to be the same ones that deal with the acoustic environments of everyday life. We have seen how the major ideas of the theory of scene analysis map onto important concepts in music theory.

In the course of examining musical examples, new demands for laboratory research have emerged. For example, it needs to be shown in well-controlled studies that the segregation of streams really suppresses the awareness of the dissonance that occurs with certain note combinations. This illustrates the fact that the flow of influence between scientific research and music can move in both directions.

Chapter 6
Auditory Organization in Speech Perception

I now want to examine the role of the primitive scene-analysis processes in the perception of speech. As the discussion proceeds, however, we will see that the contribution of primitive processes is obscured by the contribution of speech schemas. I described some general properties of schemas in chapter 4. Among them was the property of being able to extract what is needed from mixtures. Since both primitive grouping and schema-based grouping operate at the same time, it will be difficult to know what is primitive and what is not. The strategy that I will follow is that when the organizational processes are the same in speech as in simpler signals, I will assume that they derive from primitive processes, whereas when particular capabilities for perceptual isolation are found in speech, I will assume that these are schema-based. However, I will not take any position on which schemas are innate and which are learned.

In 1953, Colin Cherry, a British researcher working at the Massachusetts Institute of Technology, reported research on what he called "the cocktail party problem."[665] How can we select the voice of a particular talker in an environment in which there are many others speaking at the same time? He did a number of experiments in which a person, listening over headphones, had to report what a recorded voice was saying when it was accompanied by a second recording made by the same talker. He found that two factors affected the ease with which this could be done. The first was whether the recordings were sent to the same headphone or to the opposite one. It was much easier to follow one voice when the other was sent to the opposite ear. The second was that when the two recordings were sent to the same ear, it was easier to follow one of them when the next part of what it was saying was predictable from the previous part. When this predictability decreased, the listener often switched attention to the other recording. The act of segregating and following one of the two recordings was called "filtering."

Cherry proposed other factors that would make it easier. He mentioned the assistance offered by cues such as differences in the quality of the two voices, differences in their mean speeds or mean pitches, differing accents, and even visual cues such as lip reading. Other researchers showed that when Cherry had made segregation easy by sending the messages to different ears, it was not the fact that each ear got only one signal that was important, but that the perceived spatial origins of the two sounds were different.[666] The same researchers showed that high-pass filtering one message above 1,600 Hz and low-pass filtering the other below that frequency also allowed an easy segregation of the messages.

Cherry mentioned several factors that he thought would help us to segregate voices. Some were raw physical qualities, but others had to do with the ability of the listener to predict the next moment of speech from the previous one. It is not clear whether this ability to predict is really used in segregating the message from others at the basic scene-analysis level or is only used in matching the sound to memories of words, phrases, and so on. However, there is no doubt that it is governed by the listener's knowledge of speech and language—a property that labels it as schema-based integration and therefore excludes it from the present discussion. I want to focus on an examination of the role of primitive scene-analysis processes in the separation of speech sounds.

A great number of theories were invoked to account for the selective attention demonstrated by Cherry. However, they were all similar in certain ways. They all mentioned that the physical properties of one of the voices could be used by the listener's attention to select that voice, and they all seemed to presuppose that factors such as location, pitch, timbre, and loudness were simple and easily available. Yet if we made a stereophonic tape recording at the position of the listener's ears at a cocktail party and then made a spectrogram from each channel of that recording, the resulting pictures would look very unlike the patterns that phoneticians have come to associate with speech sounds. Nor would the pitch and timbre of individual speakers' voices or their locations be obvious from an inspection of the pictures. Yet these were the "physical factors" that were assumed to be the strongest bases on which the process of attention could separate the mixture and track the desired target.

It is clear that we must introduce scene analysis as a preliminary process that groups the low-level properties that the auditory system extracts and builds separate mental descriptions of individual voices or nonvocal sounds, each with its own location, timbre, pitch, and so on. Only then does it make sense to say that our attention can select a voice on the basis of one of these qualities.

What I am arguing is that factors such as pitch, timbre, and location are the *results* of segregating the mixture, not the *causes* of its segregation. "But," one might reply, "is it not true that a particular voice has its own spatial location, fundamental frequency, and so on, and that it is these properties that allow us to select it from the mixture?" The apparent contradiction, as in other cases that we have examined, is resolved by drawing a distinction between the physical and psychological realms. It is true, for example, that every signal at the cocktail party has a physical place of origin, but this does not guarantee that this origin is represented in the perceptual domain or that all the information that has been received from that origin will contribute to the appropriate mental description. For example, in certain illusions, the evidence received from one part of space is assigned to a perceptual sound that is heard as being at a different location.

A more exact account of causes and effects would be to say that the physical place of origin may be responsible for some physical properties that the received signal has, and if this evidence is used correctly, the perceptual image of the sound will have a mentally represented place that corresponds to the physical place and a set of perceived qualities that adequately represent the physical properties of the source. Until this is accomplished, however, there is no mentally integrated sound with its own location label that can be selected by higher mental processes.

If we look at the spectrogram of a mixture of sounds such as figure 1.4 of chapter 1, we see that there are two dimensions on which acoustic information must be grouped. The first is over time, to reconstruct the temporal pattern of the sound. The second is over the spectrum. Without the partitioning of evidence that is accomplished by such grouping, the evidence for particular speech sounds can be invisible. Christopher Darwin has given a nice example to show that the array of sound will be heard as having the phonetic patterns that we are familiar with only after it is partitioned into streams:

> Knowledge about the properties of phonetic categories [such as the phoneme "b"] must be represented by properties of the sound produced by a single . . . speaker. Yet properties that are apparent in the raw waveform are not specific to a single speaker or sound source; they are properties that are due to whatever sound sources are present at the time. For example, the silence necessary to cue an inter-vocalic stop consonant [such as the "b"

in the word "about"] is silence of a single sound source; there may be no actual silence present in the waveform.[667]

We want to understand the segregation of speech sounds from one another and from other sounds for many practical as well as theoretical reasons. For example, current computer programs that recognize human speech are seriously disrupted if other speech or nonspeech sounds are mixed with the speech that must be recognized. Some attempts have been made to utilize an evidence-partitioning process that is modeled on the one that is used by the human auditory system. Although this approach is in its infancy and has not yet implemented all the heuristics that have been described in the earlier chapters of this book, it has met with some limited success. I will describe a number of these approaches in this chapter.

Sequential Organization of Speech Sounds

In this section we will look at the sequential integration of the speech signal. The rapid sequence of different types of sounds coming from a particular talker has to be held together into a single stream and, at the same time, must not connect up sequentially with the sounds coming from a different talker.

At the very microscopic level, even the identification of many of the speech sounds themselves depends on the relevant information being assigned to the same perceptual stream. For example, in the phrase "say chop", there is a brief silence before the "ch" noise burst that tells the listener that it is "ch" rather than "sh". The silence tells the listener that there has been a closing off of the air flow of the talker's voice. Yet the listener must interpret the silence as occurring between speech sounds made by the same voice. If one voice stops and another one starts, this does not signal a closure. An experiment done by Michael Dorman and his colleagues shows that the heuristics of scene analysis can contribute to the correct interpretation.[668] If the pitch of the voice changes suddenly from that of a male to that of a female between the two words, the perception of "chop" does not occur. Listeners will hear "shop". The dip in intensity signals "ch" only when it is interpreted as a within-stream dip and not the product of an accidental concatenation of two distinct sound sources.

Sequential integration also has to operate on a longer time scale. In the early observations by Cherry, in which a person was asked to shadow one verbal message while ignoring a second, whenever the acoustical basis for segregation was not good (for example, when the two messages were spoken by the same talker and not spatially segregated) the listener would frequently switch from tracking one message to the other. The problem did not seem to be one of segregating the simultaneous sounds; otherwise the listener would not have been able to track either message. It seemed, instead, to be a problem of the sequential grouping of the words from a single talker.

The need for sequential integration of speech sounds introduces a serious problem for primitive scene analysis. Speech is a succession of qualitatively different sounds. For example, an "s" is a type of noise burst whereas an "o" is a type of tone with a harmonic structure. We know that a noise burst will sequentially segregate from a tone; so why do the sounds of the speech stream hold together?

The basic building blocks of speech are usually described as phonemes, which are divided into vowels and consonants. For our rough purposes here, phonemes can be thought of as the simple sounds that are indicated by single letters or pairs of letters in writing. Examples are "s", "b", "ee", "sh", and "th". Phoneticians view these as the basic elements out of which the words of a particular language are built. Richard Warren gives the average rate of phonemes in normal speech as 10 or more per second.[669] We ought to recall that at these rates it is easy to get stream segregation of alternations of high and low pure tones. Yet Warren points out that speech is intelligible at much faster rates. Machines have been constructed that can speed up speech without altering its pitch. It has been reported that listeners can be trained to comprehend speech at a speed of about 30 phonemes per second without temporal order confusions.[670] Speeded-up speech remains partially intelligible even at four times the normal rate.[671] At these rates, if we listened to an alternation of high and low tones, substreams would form and would seem utterly unrelated. It is evident that speech is more cohesive than such tonal patterns. Still it is not utterly resistant to segregation. Van Noorden has reported that when speech is speeded up by a factor of 2.5 or more it tends to segregate into substreams.[672] Presumably the ability to perform at higher rates than this requires some training to allow the schema-based recognition process to overcome the effects of primitive segregation.

Warren has been struck by the inconsistency between peoples' performance on two tasks.[673] On the one hand they are able to understand a rapid sequence of speech sounds; on the other, they are unable to report the order of unrelated sounds (for example a hiss, a buzz, a whistle, and a vowel) in a short cycle. Yet the rate of sounds in the cycle of unrelated sounds may be much slower than the rates of phonemes in speech.

It would seem that in order to understand speech, the listener would have to be able to determine the order of its sounds, because the same sounds in a different order would have a different meaning (for example, "serve" and "verse").[674] In an attempt to reconcile this contradiction between performance on speech and nonspeech sounds, Warren argues that listeners to a cycle of unrelated events have to decompose the signal into constituent parts, recognize each part, and then construct a mental representation of the sequence. Listeners to speech do not have to go through this process. Rather they can do some global analysis of the speech event and match it to a stored representation of the holistic pattern. After all, Warren continues, children can recognize a word and often have no idea of how to break it up into its constituent phonemes.

Even if this explanation were true, however, it would not solve the problem of stream segregation in speech. It seems that even direct recognition of holistic patterns should require that the parts of the sound that enter into the same analysis be part of the same stream. We have seen in chapter 2, for example, that listeners who are listening for a pattern that they have just heard have a great deal of difficulty if the tones that form the target pattern are absorbed into separate streams. The converse is also true; if irrelevant tones are absorbed into the same stream as the target pattern, they camouflage it.

Furthermore, only tones in the same stream enter into our recognition of another holistic property of a stream, its rhythm. It is likely that when we listen for a familiar melodic pattern or rhythm in a sequence, we can recognize it only if we can perform a global analysis on the pattern isolated from co-occurring ones. This was true, for example, for the familiar melodies studied by Dowling. As the reader may recall from chapter 5, if the notes of two familiar melodies were interleaved in time, there had to be a segregation of the tones of the two melodies into two separate streams, each containing the notes of one melody, before recognition was possible. These facts about the recognition of tonal patterns for which recognition schemas are already available suggest that the recognizability of speech sounds as global patterns would not, in itself, exempt speech sounds from the effects of primitive grouping.

If speech holds together better than sequences of arbitrary sounds, it may not simply be due to the fact that schemas exist for the speech. Some years ago I became interested in how an infant who was in the process of learning language by being presented only with continuous streams of speech could discover what the component words were. Chapter 2 contains a description of the experiment I did. To briefly recapitulate, I simulated the baby by using myself as a subject. I made a tape recording of a small number of words repeated many times in a random order without pauses. I played the tape backward to destroy the familiarity of the sounds (that is, their fit to preexisting schemas). After listening many times I was eventually able to discover (but not identify) a number of the backward words. However, I was not able to do the same thing with a similar tape that I made out of nonspeech sounds. I had created this by making artificial words that had 0.1-second mechanical sounds substituting for phonemes. In this sequence, the sounds did not cohere sequentially and I could not discover the repeating artificial words. Evidently there was something very different between a speech sequence and a sequence of artificial sounds.

People have tried to examine the extent to which speech sounds hold together by listening to rapid repetitions of short cycles. I have made some informal observations in my laboratory using synthesized vowels ("ee" and "ah") having the same fundamental frequency. I found that a rapid sequence in which the two occur in alternation split readily into two streams, one containing each vowel. This segregation may have been due to some simple factor such as brightness differences or to the fact that peaks in the two vowel spectra were at different frequencies.

Some of the research with cycles of speech sounds was stimulated by the finding of Richard Warren and his colleagues that listeners had a great deal of difficulty in reporting the order of events in a rapid cycle of unrelated short sounds, but could report the order more easily if the short events were spoken digits, each recorded separately and then spliced together to form a cycle.[675] Cycles that consisted of four different tape-recorded natural vowels, played at a rate of 200 msec per component, were also studied. It was very difficult to report their order if the individual 200-msec segments were chopped out of the steady-state portion of a longer vowel and the segments abutted against one another to form the cycle; it was easier if each individual segment was reduced to 150 msec and a 50-msec silence was introduced between segments; it was easiest of all when each segment was a full vowel with its own natural onset and decay. Further studies were able to detect some slight ability to report the order of steady-state vowel segments even when the segments were as short as 100 msec per segment provided there were brief silences between them.[676] This should be contrasted with two facts. First, it is much better than performance on a cycle of wholly unrelated sounds (such as hiss, buzz, and tone) at these rates. Second, it is much worse than the ability to integrate phonemes in rapid connected speech.

The superiority in detecting the order of vowel sequences, as compared with unrelated sounds, may come, at least in part, from the ability of the listeners to encode a cycle of vowel sounds through the use of language skills. It is possible that they can hear the cycle as a four-syllable verbal utterance and use their verbal skills to remember it. In the case of cycles of fully meaningful words such as digits, verbal skills would be particularly effective. Verbal encoding would help account for why having natural beginnings and endings on the vowels makes the cycle easier and would explain why other researchers, using recycled sequences of vowels or vowel syllables, have found that the best performance occurred when the sounds were closest to those in normal speech.[677]

James Lackner and Louis Goldstein did an experiment to find out whether the existence of stop consonants (such as "b" and "p"), which introduce brief silences and rapid spectral transitions between the vowels, might assist in the detection of the order of sounds in a cycle.[678] They expected that it would be easier to distinguish the order when vowel (V) syllables such as "oo" were alternated with consonant-vowel (CV) syllables such as "bee" than when the cycle was formed entirely of vowels. The syllables were each 200 msec in duration. To their surprise, the hardest case was when two CV syllables, both of which started with the same consonant, alternated with two different V syllables (for example, "dee-oo-bee-ah-dee-oo-bee-ah-. . .").

The level of performance on such cycles was below chance. This occurred because the CV syllables formed one stream (such as "bee—dee—bee—dee—. . .") and the vowels formed another stream (such as "oo—ah—oo—ah—. . ."). They interpreted this as an example of stream segregation. In support of this, they reported that the listeners usually described the order of the cycle in a stream by stream order, first one of these two classes and then the other. Apparently the onsets of the consonants, rather than merely inserting convenient marker points into the sequence, had the effect of labeling some of the syllables as similar and causing them to group. This suggests that the onsets of sounds may play a role in grouping them over time, those with sudden onsets (such as syllables formed of stop consonants and vowels) segregating from those with smoother onsets. In nonspeech sounds, such a tendency would help to group a succession of events that had a common physical cause, such as the successive cries of the same bird or animal. Lackner and Goldstein also found that if recordings of the same syllable spoken by a male and a female were alternated, the two syllables formed separate streams. This segregation

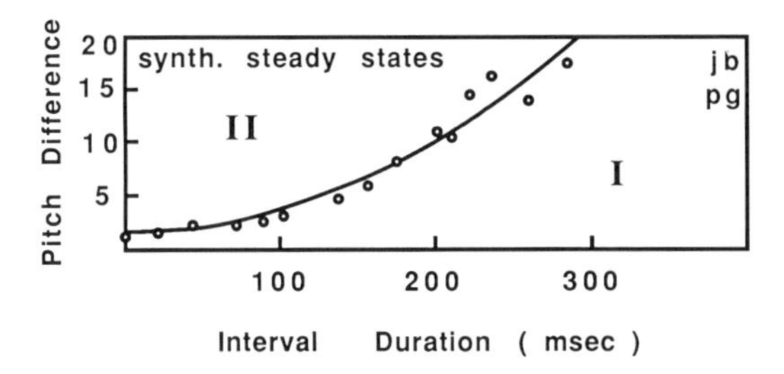

Figure 6.1
Stream segregation of vowels of alternating high and low fundamental frequencies. The horizontal axis shows the length of silence between the 100-msec tones, and the vertical axis shows the pitch difference in semitones. In region I, the listeners definitely hear one stream of vowels. In region II, they definitely hear two streams. (From Noteboom, Brokx, and de Rooij 1978.)

was probably based on differences in fundamental frequency, but since the syllables were recordings of natural speech, there may have been other differences as well.

Noteboom and his colleagues at the Institute for Perception Research in Eindhoven systematically studied the effects of differences in fundamental frequency on stream segregation of vowels.[679] They presented subjects with a sequence of nine artificially synthesized vowels. The vowels had steady pitches as though they had been sung. In the sequence of nine vowel sounds there was an alternation between a higher and a lower pitch. They varied the separations of the high and low fundamentals between 0 and 20 semitones. The duration of each vowel was 100 msec, but they also inserted silences ranging between 0 and 400 msec between successive vowels. When the jumps in pitch (fundamental frequency) were large and the silences short, the vowels segregated into two different streams as if sung by different singers.

The streaming of these vowels showed exactly the same pattern as the streaming of pure tones that we encountered in chapter 2. The results from two listeners are shown in figure 6.1. There was a tradeoff between pitch separation and temporal separation. It took less pitch separation to segregate the vowels if the sequence was more rapid.

Continuity of the Fundamental

When one takes either natural or synthesized vowel sounds and splices them together either with or without an intervening silence, there is more than one kind of discontinuity. The pitch may be discontinuous but so are the peaks in the spectrum. There are also overall discontinuities in loudness when silences are introduced into the cycle. Therefore, when we observe that pitch differences can cause segregation, we wonder whether this would have happened if the other discontinuities had not also been present. It is possible to answer this question, but not with isolated vowels. We can use natural speech or an elaborate method that employs speech synthesis.

Although the vowels are not exactly complex tones, they are quasiperiodic, each repetition of the waveform being almost, but not quite, like the one before it. From here on, I will refer to the vowels as periodic sounds and let the reader supply the prefix "quasi" as desired. Because of the periodicity of vowel sounds, the human auditory system can hear them as having a pitch. This pitch will change over time, and the resulting *pitch trajectory* is experienced by the listener as a pattern of intonation. This pattern is governed by at least two constraints. The first is that the pitch of a voice changes relatively slowly. The second is that it follows the melodies that are inherent in the patterns of grammar and meaning that are part of any language. The first constraint is more general; the second is specific to a particular language. We know that the human listener takes advantage of both constraints to follow a voice over time.

Darwin used natural voices to study the effects of pitch continuity on sequential integration. His experiment was stimulated by an experiment reported in 1960 by Anne Treisman, who had asked listeners to shadow one passage of continuous prose while ignoring another simultaneous one.[680] In her experiment, the target message was sent to one ear over a headphone while the competing message was sent to the other. The listeners were asked to shadow the material that was sent to one ear (the "target ear"). At some point in the passage, the channels were suddenly switched so that the two passages continued on smoothly but in the ears opposite to those in which they had started. As a result, the listeners sometimes repeated the first few words after the switch from the nontarget ear. This showed that they could not prevent their attention from switching ears with the passage that they had been shadowing, even though they had been instructed to follow an *ear*, not a passage. Treisman used this result to argue that the tracking of voices in mixtures could be governed by the meaning content of the message.

Fifteen years later Darwin pointed out that when one of the passages was switched from the left to the right ear, not only did the material in the right ear continue the meaning of the passage that was formerly in the left, but it also continued its pitch contour.[681] He set about separating the effects of these two kinds of continuity. Like

Treisman, he sent different passages to the two ears of listeners and asked them to shadow the material sent to one of their ears. The material sent to the two ears was read by the same female speaker, but for convenience of explanation I will refer to the material in the two ears as being from two different voices. In one condition he introduced the semantic switch without any within-ear discontinuity of pitch. That is, at the switching point the voice in each ear took over the passage that had previously been spoken by the other voice but did so without a break in the pitch contour. In another condition, he introduced a pitch contour switch without any break in the semantic content. Another condition replicated Treisman's condition in which both semantic content and pitch contour changed together. Finally there was a control condition in which there was no switch at all.

Both kinds of switches induced the listeners to make errors, but the type of error seemed to depend on the type of switch. When the semantic content switched, the listeners were likely to miss some words from the ear that they were shadowing (presumably because the new words in that ear did not continue the previous ideas and therefore were unexpected) but they did not usually report words from the other ear. On the other hand, when the pitch contour suddenly was switched to the other ear, this often caused the listeners to report a few words from that ear. Apparently the continuity of pitch contour was controlling their attention to some degree.

In Darwin's experiment, the sequential integration was shown to be affected by both factors. It appeared that a primitive pitch-following process seemed to work in concert with a more sophisticated one that dealt with meaning. Since this book is about the primitive process, I will have little further to say about the more sophisticated one.

Very striking examples of the role of the continuity of the fundamental frequency in speech perception can be created by artificially synthesizing speech. Speech can be synthesized in two stages: The first stage simulates the creation of acoustic energy in the vocal tract and the second simulates the filtering of this sound by the shape of the vocal tract (the throat, mouth, and nose).

In the first stage, the initial sound takes one of two forms. The first is turbulent hissing noise created by forcing air through a constriction. This happens, for example, when we say "s". The second form is the periodic (pitch-like) sound that is created by our vocal cords, for example when we say "ee". The periodic sound is present whenever our vocal cords are active—that is, whenever there is voicing. For example, all vowels are predominantly periodic. Some consonants, such as "w" or "l", are also voiced. Consonants such as "s", "f", "sh", and "t" are created entirely from turbulent noise without any presence of vocal cord sound and are therefore called "unvoiced." Some sounds, such as "z", involve both periodic sound and turbulent noise.

The pitch of speech is created at the sound-creation stage by the fundamental frequency of the voicing. The pitch contour is imposed at this stage by changing the fundamental frequency of the voicing over time.

At the second stage, the turbulent or vocal cord sound undergoes filtering that represents the effects of the changing positions of the throat, mouth, and nose on the signal. The filtering enhances certain bands of frequencies and imposes a pattern of peaks (formants) and valleys onto the spectrum. This pattern tells the listener which particular shapes have been assumed by the vocal tract of the speaker and hence which vowels and consonants have been spoken.

The vowels are distinguished from one another by their patterns of formants. A good replica of a vowel may be synthesized by starting with a periodic waveform that is rich in harmonics, with its higher harmonics less intense than its lower ones, and then passing this periodic sound through a series of resonators that simulate the filtering effect of the vocal tract. If the periodic sound that is fed into the resonators has a steady fundamental frequency, the resulting sound is experienced more as a tone than as a vowel. To make it more like a vowel, its fundamental frequency should be modified in two ways: (1) It should be jittered randomly by less than 1 percent to simulate the fact that the successive periods of the human voice are not all identical. (2) It should vary slowly in frequency to emulate the larger pitch variations of the human voice. Another variation that occurs in the spectrum of a vowel over time is in the position of its formants. Because the vowel is spoken in conjunction with other sounds, the movement of the speech apparatus from one sound to the next introduces movements in the formants.

The second stage, being purely a filtering operation, does not change the fundamental frequency of the periodic portions of the sound. Therefore it does not change the perceived pitch of the voiced sounds to any appreciable degree.

To summarize, the pitch of a vowel or voiced consonant is determined entirely by the fundamental frequency of the vocal cord vibration, while the identity (which phoneme it is) is determined by the filtering in stage 2. This means that in a two-stage synthesis of artificial speech, the pitch can be changed in stage 1 without changing which phonemes are heard.

It has been noted that when individual words are prerecorded and then a sentence is made by splicing the individual words together, the resulting speech is often unintelligible. It sounds garbled. Listeners often report hearing the speech coming from different directions or different speakers and they often mistake the order of sounds.[682] It was thought that it was the discontinuity of fundamental frequency that caused the perceptual failure to integrate the sequence. Darwin and Bethell-Fox investigated this hypothesis. But rather than splicing different sounds together, a technique that introduces discontinuities in other properties as well as in pitch, they used the method of speech synthesis to demonstrate a dramatic effect of a sudden discontinuity in the fundamental frequency.[683]

Their stimulus pattern was a voiced spectrum that had a number of successive parts. In the middle section was the formant pattern that is characteristic of the vowel "a" as in "cat". It was held steady for 60 msec. Before and after the "a", and separated from it by 60-msec spectral transitions, were formant patterns that were characteristic of another vowel (for example, "u" as in "put"). That is, the first and third vowels were the same (and were not "a", of course). The spectrum of the two flanking vowels also stayed steady for a brief period. The parts that lay between the "a" and the flanking vowels were transitions of the spectrum that smoothly shifted the position of the formants from those of the first vowel to those of the "a" and from the "a" to those of the third. Each of these two transitions lasted for over a period of 60 msec. For example, the sequence might be represented as "u". . . "a". . . "u", with the dots representing the transitions.

Recall that these spectral patterns are due to the filtering stage of the synthesis and are independent of the fundamental frequency (pitch) of the voicing. When the pitch was held constant throughout the stimulus (at 130 Hz), the listeners heard not a sequence of three vowels (such as "u-a-u") but a syllable such as "wow" in which the "u" sound becomes a "w". Some consonants (for example, "w") simply involve a smooth change in the spectrum from a value that is sometimes used for a vowel ("u" in the case of "w") to the spectrum of the vowel that is adjacent to it. Such consonants are called sonorants and include "w", and "y", among others. The "wow" in our example was heard because the "u" and its transition were perceptually integrated with the vowel "a".

In another condition, the pitch had two different values, a high and a low one (101 and 178 Hz), and an abrupt shift was made from one to the other halfway through the transition on each side of the "a". For example, the pattern could be high-low-high, the pitch shift from high to low occurring halfway through the "u-a" transition and the shift back up again occurring half way though the "a-u" transition This prevented the listeners from integrating the total formant pattern into a single syllable. Instead they heard (in our example) two low-pitched syllables and a high one. Apparently they began to hear a new voice at each place at which the pitch changed. When they were asked what consonant preceded the "a" they reported ones such as "b". Apparently they heard the short spectral transition (the part that adhered to the "a" when the longer transition was split in half by the pitch change) and interpreted it as the one that normally occurs at the onset of stop consonants such as "b", "g", and "d". The strong role that the smoothness of pitch change plays in holding natural syllables together is illustrated by the dramatic dissociation of the parts of the sequence when this continuity is violated.

It is easy to see why the voiced sounds of normal speech hold together during periods of spectral continuity. But we also have to account for why they hold together at moments when the spectrum undergoes a sudden discontinuity, as it does when a stop consonant such as "p" is interpolated between two vowels as in the word "repay". One obvious source of continuity is that the pitch contour of the sentence usually travels right through such interruptions, smoothly changing in pitch. But this holds only the two vowels together. What holds the intervocalic consonant in with them? Partly, this may be due to the fact that the air-stopping gesture of the vocal tract also introduces smooth transitions in the formants of the voiced sound just before and after the stop closure. These parts of the consonant may be integrated with the steady-state vowel formants as a result of smoothness of spectral transition. But what of the other parts, the silence that occurs during the brief closure of the "p" and the brief burst of noise as it is released? How does the pitch continuity affect our perception of these?

Suppose one synthesized a word in which the pitch that followed the silence was quite different from the pitch that preceded it, with no smooth transition to unite them. Extrapolating from the results of Darwin and Bethell-Fox, we would guess that the two pitches would be heard as separate voices.[684] It is possible that the silence would no longer be heard as a stop consonant embedded between two vowels. Indeed, it might not be registered as a silence at all, because its beginning would be interpreted as the end of voice A and its end as the onset of voice B. This example suggests that it is the continuity of pitch across a silence that allows it to be perceived as a closure of the vocal tract or even as a silence.

An experiment on this issue was done by Michael Dorman and his colleagues.[685] It used a brief silence to cue the distinction between "sh" and "ch". In the sentence "Please say shop", if a silence of 50 msec or more was introduced before the "sh", the listeners tended to hear "Please say chop." However, if the words "Please say" were in a male voice and "shop" in a female, listeners heard "shop" despite the presence of the silent interval. The dip in intensity signaled "ch" only when primitive scene analysis decided that it was a within-stream dip and not the product of an accidental concatenation of two distinct sound sources.

Spectral Continuity

The acoustic nature of speech is commonly portrayed by means of a spectrogram. Figure 1.3 of chapter 1 showed a spectrogram of the word "shoe" spoken in isolation. The spectral peaks (formants) that continue over time are shown as dark streaks that run in a generally horizontal direction. Often a person viewing these formants thinks of them as if they were tones with their own pitches. However, formants are not pitches. In voiced sounds, where the formants are most noticeable (as in the vowel part of "shoe"), they are the groups of harmonics, all related to the same (much lower) fundamental, that happen to be emphasized by the vocal-tract resonances. In unvoiced sounds, which are turbulent noise (as in the "sh" part of "shoe"), the formants are enhanced bands of frequencies in the noise.

Since the formants are caused by the filtering that comes from the shape of the vocal tract, and this tract does not snap instantly from one setting to the next, the formants in successive sounds tend to be continuous with one another. This is most easily seen when the two successive sounds are both voiced, as in the syllable "you" shown in figure 6.2.

However, we do not always see continuity between the formants in noisy consonants such as "f" and the surrounding vowels. The formants in the noisy parts will be similar to those in the voiced ones only when the noise and the voiced sound have both been filtered in the same way. This will happen whenever both have traveled through the same cavities in the vocal tract on their way to the outside world. Since the voiced sounds are created in the vocal cords, and these are below the resonant cavities, voiced sounds travel through the whole system of cavities. However, different noisy sounds are created at different places. For example, the "h" in the word "aha" is created below all the cavities of the mouth and nose and therefore is filtered in the same way as a vowel. For this reason it will have formants that are continuous with those of adjacent vowels. On the

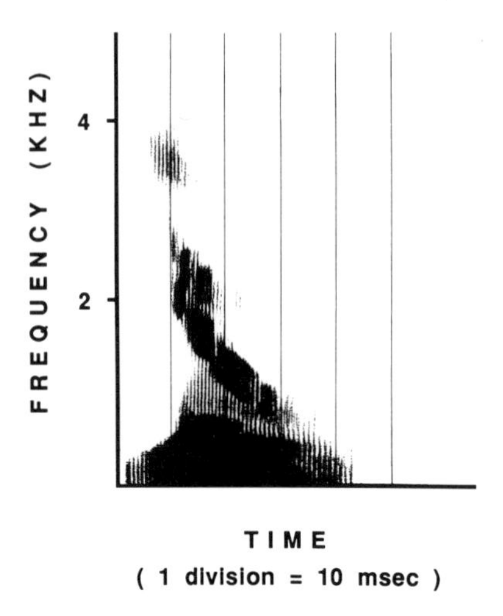

Figure 6.2
Spectrogram of the word "you" spoken in isolation.

other hand, the spectrum of "th" in "thaw", which is formed at the front of the mouth, will be affected only by the cavities in the very front of the mouth and will not have a formant structure that is strongly related to the "aw" that follows it. As the mouth moves between the positions that create the "th" and the "aw", that motion will be visible in the spectrum, but not always as the movements of clearly distinguishable formants. To summarize, the transitions between many speech sounds, but not all, will be visible in the form of continuous changes in the peaks visible in the spectrum.

Recall that I have been discussing formant trajectories and not trajectories in the pitch of the speaker's voice. Formant changes and pitch changes are separate acoustic phenomena. We have already seen how powerful the continuity in the fundamental of voiced speech sounds can be in holding them together. We can go on to consider the entirely separate question of whether continuity in the pattern of formants has a similar effect.

It was first reported by Peter Ladefoged that if a click was superimposed on a sentence, listeners could not tell where in the sentence it had occurred.[686] Our knowledge that the formation of separate streams can cause a loss of between-stream temporal relations leads us to believe that the click must have been heard in a separate stream from the speech. A similar effect occurs in the phonemic restoration phenomenon.[687] When a noise burst replaces a speech sound in a sentence, there are two effects on listeners. The first is that they will often hear the partially obliterated word without any sense that part of it is missing. This is the actual phonemic restoration. The second is that the listeners will not be able to report, with any great accuracy, where in the sentence the noise burst has occurred. Again this is evidence for stream segregation. One is inclined to explain both these cases of segregation by appealing to the fact that there is a sudden change in the spectrum when the click (or noise) occurs, the spectrum of the click or noise being quite unlike that of neighboring speech sounds.

How, then, can speech sounds that resemble noise bursts or clicks remain coherent with neighboring speech sounds? For example, noise bursts such as "s" or "sh" occur in English, and clicks occur in African languages such as Xhosa. Since the meaning of words in these languages depends on the location of these clicks and noises in the words, the listener must not sort them into separate streams. The ability to hold the speech stream together may be partially due to learning; there are studies that suggest that stream segregation may be affected by practice. However, there may be subtle properties of the acoustic sequence that allow primitive organization to hold the stream together. I once tested myself by listening to a speaker of Xhosa (a click language that I do not understand at all) and experienced no difficulty in locating the position of the clicks relative to the other sounds in her sentences. This was done without visual cues and was verified as correct by the speaker.

It is worth noting that when a click is produced by speaking, it has a different acoustic relation to the surrounding speech sounds than it would if it were simply superimposed arbitrarily onto the speech stream. The spoken click occurs as a result of a consonantal gesture. The motion of the articulators that stops or releases the consonant will also have effects on the spectrum of the voicing that is going on. The voicing will therefore undergo major changes at the same time as the noise or click appears and disappears, and this synchronization of changes may tell the auditory system that the two effects are related to each other. A mechanically superimposed click, on the other hand, will often be placed so as to overlap a voiced sound (for example, in the middle of a vowel); so the normal covariation of changes will not occur.

The mere fact that one sound goes off at the same moment as another goes on, the situation that occurs at the boundary between speech and noise in the phonetic restoration stimulus, is not enough to tell the auditory system that the two sounds are related, nor should it be. The replacement of one sound by another of a different type often occurs when a loud sound masks a softer one coming from a different physical source. We have already discussed the cues for the masking of one sound by another in the section in chapter 3 on the continuity illusion. Such cues cause segregation, not unification. The auditory system seems to be prepared to integrate two sounds only when the cues for masking are not present. If the transition can be interpreted as the beginning or end of masking, the replacement of one sound by another does not count as evidence that the two were affected by the same cause. However, when there are changes in the two sounds near the temporal boundary between them, such as sudden movements in the spectrum, these may be used as evidence that the disappearance of one sound and the beginning of another may have arisen from a common cause.[688]

There are a number of reasons for our interest in formants. One is that they are affected in fairly direct ways by the resonances of the vocal tract. Another is that, being compact frequency bands, they are readily discernible to our eyes as we look at speech spectrograms. We therefore expect them to be important for our ears as we listen to speech. Furthermore, their frequencies or frequency trajectories seem to be sufficient to allow us to discriminate many phonemes from one another. Therefore the formant seems to be a plausible unit for the auditory system to be using for scene analysis. Accordingly, there have been experimental investigations of the role of formant trajectories in holding speech sounds together.

Dorman, Cutting, and Raphael studied the effects of spectral continuity in synthesized speech sounds.[689] They wanted to find out how formant transitions contributed to the sequential integration of syllables. They excluded those speech sounds that lack significant formants (such as the noise bursts that occur in consonants such as "s"). A number of different types of cycles were created, each containing four synthesized vowels ("ee", "a", "uh", and "oo"), all with the same steady fundamental frequency and each having three formants.

The different types of cycles are illustrated in figure 6.3. The first type (long vowels) contained 120-msec vowels with instantaneous transitions from one to the next. This type was intended to simulate the stimuli of the experiments, described earlier in this chapter, in which steady-state portions of natural vowels were spliced into cycles. The second type consisted of consonant-vowel-consonant (CVC) syllables in which the consonant was "b" (for example, "boob"). The consonant "b" was used because it can be convincingly synthesized using only formant transitions. A listener will hear an initial "b" when there are rising formant transitions leading into the beginning of the vowel's formants and a final "b" when there are falling transitions at the end. In these CVC stimuli, the durations of the steady-state vowel portions were 30 msec and those of the transi-

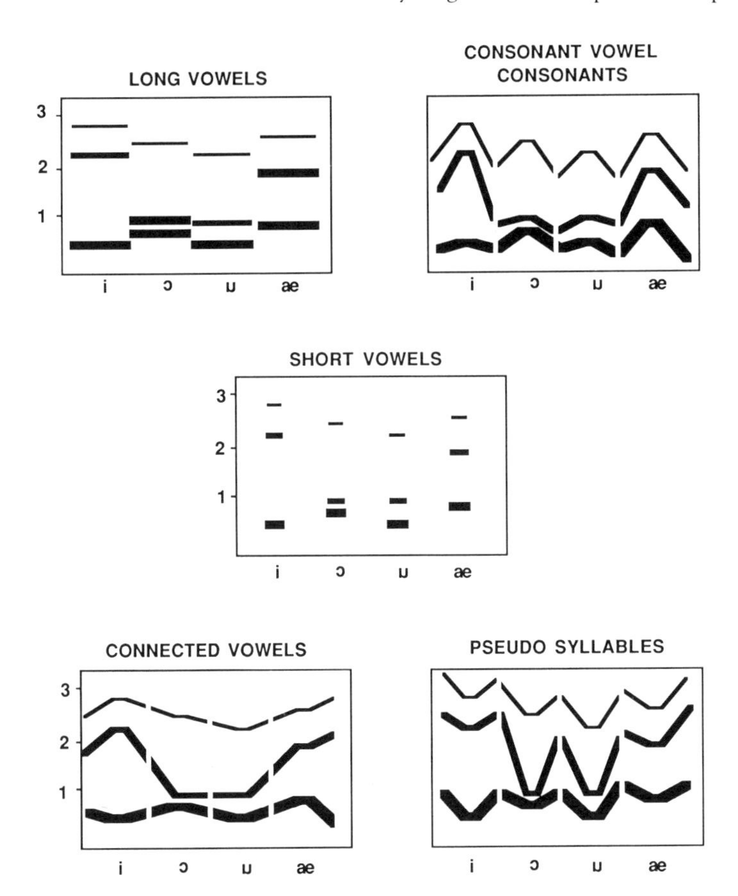

Figure 6.3
Schematic spectrograms of the five types of stimulus sequences used by Dorman, Cutting, and Raphael (1975).

tions were 45 msec. In a third type (short vowels), only the 30-msec steady-state vowels from the CVC syllables were used, the transitions being replaced by silence. In the fourth type (connected vowels), the formants of successive vowels were connected directly to one another by formant transitions. The final type was made out of sounds that the experimenters called pseudosyllables. These were created by extending the formants of the steady-state vowel formants upward in frequency for 45 msec on both sides of the 30-msec steady-state portion rather than downward as in the case of the "b-vowel-b" syllables. No real consonant can be synthesized by such upward transitions, and, according to these researchers, there is no movement of the vocal tract that will produce such transitions.

The task of the listeners was to write down the vowels in their order of occurrence in the repeating cycle. We have to collect the results across a set of experiments in a sort of intuitive way, because no single experiment compared all the types of cycles and the results were not fully consistent with one another. Nonetheless, it is clear that there were two conditions that were relatively easy: the one with the vowels connected directly to one another by formant transitions and the one with the CVC syllables. Those consisting of the vowels that were not connected by smooth transitions were substantially worse, and those consisting of pseudosyllables, in which the transitions were unnatural, were the worst. The research also showed that the smooth transitions of the lowest formant were most effective in holding the sequence together and those of the highest formant were the least effective.

The subjective impressions of the sequences, as reported by the experimenters, suggested that these results were due to differences in the degree of perceptual integration. In the unconnected vowel sequences, the listeners often heard two streams of vowels, with "ee" and "oo" in one stream and the other two in a second.

The perceptual integrity of the sequences in which vowels were directly joined by transitions is explainable as a continuity effect analogous to the one found by Bregman and Dannenbring with alternations of high and low tones joined by frequency glides.[690] But the advantage of having "b" consonants between the successive vowels cannot be explained in this way. Rather than joining the formants of successive consonants by a direct frequency transition, the consonant introduces a frequency change (a dip and then a rise) in all the formants. There is some continuity; if the listeners tracked the frequency transitions they would never be faced with a sudden discontinuity as in the case of the transitionless vowels. However it is not apparent why the CVC condition should be as good as the condition that introduced direct and smooth transitions from one vowel to the next. Perhaps the listener's knowledge of language played a role in the success of the CVC condition. This is suggested by the failure of the listeners to derive any benefit from the unnatural transitions in the pseudosyllables. However, it is also conceivable that the acoustic organizing principle involved here is a primitive one rather than one that depends on the structure of language. We will know only when we have done experiments on nonspeech cycles (perhaps sequences of tones) in which successive tones are connected by brief dips in frequency, as the CVC formants were, or by brief rises in frequency, as the pseudosyllable formants were.

Earlier we saw that an experiment that shifted the fundamental frequency of a voice before and after a silence prevented the silence from being interpreted as a stop consonant closure. However, the absence of continuity in the fundamental can be compensated for by a continuity in the spectral peaks. Silence retains its effectiveness as a cue for closure despite a shift from a male to a female voice across the silence, as long as the general articulatory pattern is continuous across the two speakers.[691] This confirms the findings, described in chapter 2, that fundamental frequency and spectral peaks are independent contributors to sequential integration.

The research of Cole and Scott, which has already been described in chapter 4, did employ, in addition to vowel sounds, unvoiced sounds such as "s" that are not normally thought of as having formants.[692] To briefly summarize their procedure, they took consonant-vowel syllables such as "sa", spliced out the formant transitions leading from the consonant into the vowel, and created rapid cycles of transitionless syllables. Their listeners had more difficulty in judging the order in cycles formed of these syllables than in cycles formed out of normal syllables, which presumably were heard as coherent units. The researchers interpreted the perceptual coherence of the normal syllables as due to the fact that formant transitions in the vowel pointed to important spectral regions in the noise burst of the consonant, and related this to the findings of Bregman and Dannenbring on spectral continuity in cycles of tones.[693] In chapter 4, I offered three other explanations of the findings of Cole and Scott. Regardless of which of these is correct, the experiment shows that formant transitions can affect the grouping of successive sounds. This is, however, somewhat mysterious because there was no marked formant structure in some of the consonants that they employed.

It is difficult to explain why noise bursts (such as the "s" in the word "essay") will group with adjacent voiced sounds. Even if the voiced sounds group with one another because of pitch continuity, why is the interrupting frication noise not rejected into a separate stream and the vowel extrapolated right through it as in the case of the continuity illusion? Part of the evidence that prevents the perception of the two vowels as a single sound is the change that the formants undergo just before and after the "s" occurs. This change takes the form of formant transitions that are caused by the fact that the mouth has to move to a new position to produce the "s". In an earlier chapter on the continuity illusion I described the "No discontinuity in A" rule (where A is the sound that occurs before and after the interruption). Violating this rule by introducing a change in sound A just before and after an interruption by sound B can reduce the perceived continuity of A.[694]

Applying this rule to speech, the auditory system may have a choice between integrating the noise or rejecting it as an interruption. The discontinuity of the voiced sound before and after a consonantal noise may inhibit its rejection into a separate stream. This explanation implies that clicks or bursts of noise that are spliced into a speech stream at arbitrary points (so that they do not fall between two discontinuities in the voicing) will probably be rejected as extraneous sounds. The research on inserting clicks or noise bursts into sentences generally shows that the speech is heard as continuing behind the added sound, which is merely perceived as an interruption. As far as I know there has been no examination of whether there are alterations in the placement of the click or noise that will cause it to be integrated into the speech stream rather than heard as an interruption.

We might suspect that the loudness of the noise burst would play a role. If the noise is really masking a continuous voiced sound, it should be loud enough to do so. To obtain the continuity illusion the interruption has to be a good deal louder than the ongoing sound. People who have tried to synthesize speech sounds have noticed that if the consonant noise bursts are too loud they do not become part of the speech. Perhaps this is explainable by the preceding argument.

Another fact that may be related to the sequential integration of different types of sounds is that the onsets of many instrumental sounds, such as those of the struck or plucked instruments (guitar, piano, and the like), are very noisy. That is, the sound is not periodic at the onset but gradually evolves into a periodic sound. Yet this noisiness is integrated with the sound that follows it and is heard as a quality of the onset of the sound (as, indeed, it is). We do not understand how the auditory system registers this transition, but I know from my own experience in synthesizing sounds that it is not sufficient to splice a bit of loud noise onto the beginning of a periodic sound for the noise to be heard as a noisy onset of the second sound.

Typically it is rejected as a separate sound. Again, we do not know why this happens, but it bears a suspicious resemblance to the case of integrating consonant noise bursts with voiced sound that precedes or follows them.

Obviously we need fundamental research on the sequential grouping of voiced and unvoiced sounds. For example, it would be useful to know whether imposing a formant pattern onto an unvoiced sound would help it to group with a voiced sound that followed it. We would not necessarily want to use real consonants in studying this problem, but could pass a wideband noise through filters that imposed formants on it that matched those of a similarly filtered complex tone. If such a filtered noise were alternated with the tone in a cycle, we could compare the perceptual integration in this case to what would be obtained if the noise had no formants or if the formants were less sharp or did not match those of the tone. To the best of my knowledge, nobody has carried out such research.

I have also been told by researchers who are trying to get computers to produce intelligible speech that a continuity problem arises when they try to generate a continuous speech stream by concatenating stored segments. Apart from the discontinuity of the fundamental frequency and of the formants at the segment boundaries, there is a problem with formant bandwidth.[695] If one of the segments has formants that have a different bandwidth than its predecessor, even though the center frequencies of the formants may match up correctly, the spectral discontinuity tends to be heard as the intrusion of a new speaker. A difference in bandwidth means that at the moment of change there will be an abrupt drop or rise in the energy in certain frequency regions. Therefore the change can be viewed as one of loudness instead of one of bandwidth, and it makes us suspect that a sudden change in the intensity of any spectral region may disrupt the perception of a single stream.

Spatial Continuity We have seen how continuities in the fundamental frequency and in the formants are important in keeping speech sequences integrated. Both these forms of continuity derive from the fact that they are produced by gradual changes in the speaker's articulation; the human vocal tract cannot snap instantaneously from one setting to another. There is another continuity that derives from a property that speakers share with inanimate sound sources: the fact that they tend to stay in the same place or to move relatively slowly through space. As we have seen in chapter 2, sounds that are alternated rapidly between the ears often group themselves into different streams, each localized at a different ear, and this makes it hard to integrate the entire sequence. This difficulty of integration has been shown to apply to speech as well as nonspeech sounds. When successive segments of continuous speech were presented to alternate ears, the capability of recognition broke down.[696] Later it was shown that this happens because the residual portion at each ear is treated as if the material sent to the other ear were missing; that is, the switch of the material to the other ear leaves a perceptual gap that acts as a silence, creating a false segmentation of the signal.[697] We can conclude that if discontinuities in spatial location act to disrupt the integration of speech then the spatial continuity that is found in normal circumstances must be holding it together.

The breakdown of identification when material is switched from one ear to another is also due to the loss of information about individual phonemes. When, in a nasal-plus-vowel syllable such as "me", the "m" is sent to one ear and the "e" to the other, listeners find it very hard to identify the "m". Apparently the sudden increase of the bandwidth of the spectrum is what signals the release of a nasal consonant, and this increase can be assessed only by comparing the successive spectra. When primitive scene analysis favors the interpretation that the two spectra are in separate streams, this comparison of spectra is not carried out.

Are These Acoustic Continuities Enough? We have seen that a number of acoustic factors influence the integration or segregation of speech sounds. Most of these are concerned with similarities or continuities of one sort or another. Do we have enough in these acoustic factors to explain why normal speech holds together sequentially? After all, the segregation of unrelated sounds, such as noise and tone, presented in cycles in the laboratory is quite strong. There are different points that can be made in addressing this question.

One is that the use of cycles in the laboratory creates a much stronger segregation of sounds than is normally obtained. This is true for two reasons: The repetitive nature of the alternation allows the evidence for separate streams to build up over time, and the competition that occurs in cycles can promote the segregation of sounds. Let me explain. In a short cycle, there will be only a short delay between successive occurrences of the same sound. Therefore, if the grouping process must choose between integrating a successive pair of sounds of different types (A and B) or waiting only a bit longer and integrating two sounds of the same type (A and A), it will skip over the different tone, B, and group the two A's, causing the B tone to be rejected from the stream. Happily, the B tone will have repetitions of itself to group with. If the cycle is slowed down, the choice of waiting a long time to group two tones of the same type or grouping each tone with the next is resolved in favor of grouping unrelated tones. The competition between grouping by temporal proximity and grouping by similarity is always part of the stream-forming process.

In speech, in contrast with artificial cycles of sound, even though two sounds of different types, A and B, are next to one another, it is unlikely that there will be another occurrence of an A-type sound for the A to group with (and a B-type sound for the B to group with) in the short time interval in which the qualitative similarity can dominate the grouping process. Also, even if this does happen once, it is unlikely to be repeated immediately again and again so as to permit the formation of separate streams containing the two types of sounds. It is not that normal speech sounds are immune from segregation. The experiment by Cole and Scott on the repetitive looping of single syllables showed that they are not.[698] Even when the normal formant transitions were left in the syllables, syllables such as "sa" would eventually split into two streams, one formed of unvoiced sounds deriving from the "s" and the other of voiced sounds deriving from the "a".

Another factor that may affect the tendency of speech sounds of different types to be integrated sequentially may be their grouping into larger units such as syllables. While it is possible that this is accomplished by schemas (for example, schemas for familiar syllables or schemas that represent the way that syllables are produced), it is also possible that this grouping could also be derived from primitive scene-analysis principles. The second syllable of the word "repay" may hold together as a unit, with the brief noise burst caused by the release of the "p" being heard as an onset property of the syllable "pay" rather than a separate acoustic event. The acoustic factors that cause this might resemble those that unite the noisiness at the onset of the plucked string of a guitar with the later, more periodic part of the note. One such factor might be a sudden rise in intensity followed by a slower decay. It may be that a brief noisiness that accompanies a sudden rise in intensity tends to be grouped with the loud (but decaying) sound that follows it. This might be a primitive, unlearned grouping tendency. Its role in nature would be to hear as single units the events created by impacts, where the onset is determined by the brief period of energy transfer in which the sound is never periodic, followed by the vibration of the struck body, which may or may not be periodic depending on the nature of the struck body. The perceptual formation of syllables in speech may be accomplished by the same primitive process.

Of course it is hard to distinguish whether this form of integration is based on specifically speech-related schemas, more general *learned* schemas (such as one for an impact), or primitive unlearned grouping tendencies. We might think it possible to find out through the study of newborn infants, but studying the perceptual grouping of sounds in such young babies is difficult, if not impossible. Perhaps we could achieve the more limited goal of finding out whether the grouping was determined by knowledge of one's own specific language if we studied the grouping of unfamiliar sounds in unfamiliar languages, such as the phonemic clicks of Xhosa.

As I hinted above, another way to account for the integration of speech is to move to a wholly different approach that argues that it is our learned knowledge of speech sounds that allows us to integrate them. This knowledge might take a more specific form, such as memories of specific words, or a more general form, such as stored records of the inventory of the different sounds of our language and the probabilities with which they follow one another. Encountering a familiar word pattern or a highly probable sound transition, we would integrate the sequence of sounds.

There is even a more profound type of knowledge that a listener might have: a mental model (but not a conscious one) of the vocal tract of the human speaker, together with some methods of deriving the possible sounds and sound sequences that it could make. Then any incoming sequence would be passed through the model, and if any subset of the acoustic components could have been produced by a single speaker it would be grouped and labeled as such. Once again the theories may take two forms, divided along the nature-nurture dimension. One version would hold that the model is formed largely through learning. The more provocative view is that the perceiver's model of the human vocal tract is innate. This latter is the approach that has been taken by Alvin Liberman and his associates at Haskins laboratories, and we shall examine its properties later in more detail.[699]

Integration based on any of these types of knowledge would fall into the category of schema-driven integration discussed in chapter 4. A plausible candidate for this form of integration is the fricative-vowel sequence (as in the word "say"), because of the lack of spectral similarity or continuity between the fricative and vowel portions. Indeed, persons who try to synthesize speech with machines have found that unless the balance of spectral components and the loudness of fricatives are tuned just right, the fricative is experienced as an added sound and not as part of the speech. It is possible that the requirement for an exact replication of the natural spectrum and loudness of fricatives stems not from requirements imposed by primitive grouping processes but from our knowledge of the acoustical patterns of speech (as stored in our speech schemas).

The process of sequential integration of speech is involved in the perceptual restoration of speech when some of the sounds in a speech sample are deleted and replaced by noise bursts. Particular cases of this, called phonemic restoration or the "picket fence" effect, have been discussed already in chapter 3. I will not repeat that discussion here except to point out that the integration of speech sounds before and after an interruption should depend on the same principles of sequential grouping that hold speech together even when parts of it are not obliterated. For example, suppose we were to do an experiment on phonemic restoration in which the part of the sentence that preceded the loud noise burst was heard as coming from a female speaker to the left of the listener and the part that followed the noise was heard as coming from a male speaker to the right of the listener. Even though the two parts went together quite well to form a meaningful sentence, I would not expect the two parts to be integrated or the missing phoneme to be perceptually restored.

I would like to draw a comparison between the laboratory examples of sequential stream formation and the examples that occur in speech. In the basic laboratory demonstration of streaming the tones are discrete and often separated by silences. In speech, on the other hand, the sounds are continuous; so how could a tendency to group sounds that were separated in time be useful? One way is to group speech sounds that have been interrupted by a masking sound. The similarity of the sounds before and after the masking sound would be grouped by their similarity and this, in turn, would activate an analysis of the spectrum during the interrupting sound for evidence of the continuation of the interrupted sound. I have already described this in chapter 3.

Often, however, an added sound does not really mask the underlying sound, but simply creates a jumble of properties. Think, for example, of what happens when the voices of two speakers are mixed. Due to the natural stopping and starting of speech and its variations in intensity, there are moments when the spectrum mainly reflects the properties of one of the voices. There are other moments when the spectrum is mainly shaped by the second speaker. Clear acoustic properties may be ascertainable in both cases. There is a third class of moments in which the sounds can be easily segregated by the use of primitive principles such as grouping by differences in fundamental frequency or in spatial origin, or by asynchrony of onset. We can think of these three types of moments as yielding "high-quality" data. However, there are times when the mixed spectrum is very complex and the primitive scene-analysis processes cannot decompose it. We can think of these as regions of "low-quality" data. It would be appropriate to treat the low-quality moments in the same way as we treat an interrupting noise burst. We would simply group the events on both sides of it according to their similarities and then look for continuations of the high-quality sounds in the low-quality regions.

I can think of two ways of doing this. The first would be to have a test for the quality of data in a temporal region so that when the region was judged as high-quality the horizontal grouping process would use its properties to establish sequential links and favor the formation of one or more streams. This process would make use of the brain's proven capacity to link discontinuous but related sounds, as in the streaming phenomenon. Then the low-quality areas would be analyzed for the presence of properties that matched those within one or another of the primitive groupings of evidence (perhaps we could call them "protostreams") that had been established through the organization of the high-quality data.

Another approach would be for the auditory system to always look for continuations of the previously detected regions of spectral activity. The system would look for matches even for the accidental spectral patterns arising from the mixture of two voices but would not find any sequential material to link it up with, so the memory for these patterns would disappear. However, patterns that were parts of individual voices would find matches in subsequent time periods, and the streams of which they were a part would be strengthened. This method would not need to make a decision about the quality of regions of data, but would require more memory to carry along the often meaningless patterns that were derived from mixed data. Since we do not know much about the memory capacity of the auditory system, we do not know how plausible this alternative might be.

Simultaneous Organization

So far we have looked only at the grouping and segregation of speech sounds that arrive at different times. However, it is obvious that there must be principles that group and segregate the acoustic components of speech that arrive together. These principles must involve both segregation and grouping. They must segregate the acoustic components that belong to different voices so that we do not hear sounds that are the accidental composite of a number of voices. They must also integrate the components that come from the same voice so that we do not hear, as separate sounds, the formants or the harmonics of the individual voice. Part of the integration of harmonics can be accomplished by the limited resolution of the auditory system, especially with respect to the higher harmonics, but its resolution is perfectly adequate to register the lower harmonics separately.

If we assume that the first stage of the auditory system creates something that resembles a neural spectrogram, then to detect and recognize the sounds made by a particular voice, when they are part of a mixture, the auditory system must allocate each spectral component either to that voice or to some other sound. We have seen, in our examination of nonspeech sounds, that simultaneous components can be segregated by a number of factors, including spectral region, pitch, spatial location, and independence of changes. We should examine the role that each of these factors plays in the segregation of speech sounds. Part of the motivation for doing this is to find out the extent to which such primitive acoustic differences play a role in the parsing of the neural spectrogram so that we will know the extent to which they have to be supplemented by schema-based processes of grouping.

In trying to decide this issue, it is necessary to have at least a rough idea of how the primitive processes and the schema-driven ones are different in their modes of activity. I am going to try to propose such a difference.

I would like to propose, as I did in chapter 4, that they differ in the way in which they partition a mixture. Primitive segregation acts in a symmetrical way to partition a signal. If the signal is partitioned into two parts on the basis of a difference in location, for example, both of the parts are equally accessible to more sophisticated analysis. Therefore we can say that the primitive process *sorts* the signal. Schema-driven processes select and integrate material from the signal rather than sort it. They look for certain patterns in the data, and when they find them they extract them. The residual that they leave behind is not organized or coherent in any way. Schema-driven processes create a figure and a ground (in Gestalt terminology). Primitive processes do not; all the partitioned streams have equal status.

Segregation and integration have been treated as if they were opposite sides of the same coin. Perhaps they actually are for the primitive processes, which perform a sorting function: what they do not segregate they integrate. But the schema-driven functions do not have this property of sorting, or of creating a symmetry between segregation and integration.

Second, I think that the primitive processes will be found to be sensitive to variables to which the schema-governed ones are not sensitive. For example, the fundamental frequency of a set of harmonics will turn out to be very significant to the primitive processes and less so to the schema-governed ones.

I am not going to say very much about the schemas that are involved in the interpretation of speech. Doing so would require not just a whole book, but a library. I am hoping that despite the large number of schemas of different types involved in the understanding of speech, there are some ways in which their modes of operation are similar enough that we can determine when they are involved in a perceptual process.

The research on the grouping of simultaneous components has mainly been concerned with the grouping of formants. The apparent reason for choosing the formant as the unit of analysis is that the pattern of formants is what defines a vowel sound. The pattern of change in the formants also provides a strong cue for the identity of stop consonants.

There are other reasons for the choice of formants as materials. The theory of how they are produced is fairly well worked out. Also, they are fairly simple acoustic phenomena and are therefore easy to synthesize well enough to create plausible-sounding vowels or voiced stops.

A final reason is that they are sustained events and therefore can be heard as speech even without the participation of other types of spectral events. By way of contrast, the noise burst that defines a fricative, if produced in isolation, will simply sound like a burst of noise.

We do not know whether formants are meaningful perceptual entities in themselves. Most scientists who work in speech research believe that they are, and that the auditory system assesses the frequencies of these spectral peaks and tracks their changes over time as a partial step on the way to recognizing speech. We may, however, just be fooled by the prominence of the formants in the spectrogram. The eye of the observer certainly treats the formants as separable features of the spectrogram. Whether the ear does so too or whether the cue value that we attribute to the formants themselves is really the result of a different form of analysis will have to be decided by future research. (There are researchers who doubt whether formants play a central role. They think that the formants are merely the acoustic basis for the perceptual analyses of global qualities such as the compactness and tilt of the spectrum, or the rapidity of spectral change.[700])

Role of Harmonic Relations and F0

Everyday observation tells us that we can hear two separate pitches when tones of different fundamental frequencies are played. The segregative process that makes this possible also helps us to sort out a mixture of voices. Effects of pitch have been found in the studies of selective attention that I mentioned earlier, in which listeners are asked to shadow one of a pair of voices. It is easier for them to do so when voices of two different pitch ranges, such as a male and a female voice, are used than when the two voices are in the same pitch range.[701] It also helps to have the spectra of the two signals restricted to different ranges by filtering.[702] These studies of selective attention used natural voices reading connected materials, and so the acoustic situation in these cases was very complex. The studies that I shall describe in the following pages were more analytical from an acoustic point of view.

Two-Voice Research

The auditory system faces a serious problem in using the different fundamental frequencies of two voices to segregate them from one another. At each moment of time, the auditory system must not only detect that there are two fundamentals and use this to derive two different pitches but must somehow form a separate view of the two different spectra. Each view must consist of a description of not only the harmonics that belong to each voice, but (in the ideal case) the intensities of each of them. This is necessary because the identity of the voiced sounds depends on the relative intensities of the different harmonics and how they change over time. To decide which vowel is present in each of two voices, the complex pattern of intensities that is registered in the neural spectrogram must be decomposed into two separate formant patterns.

First, of course, it is necessary to show that the auditory system can use information about the existence of different fundamentals to segregate voices. Relevant experiments have been done by Brokx and Noteboom at the Institute for Perception Research at Eindhoven in the Netherlands.[703] In one experiment listeners were asked to repeat aloud a series of nonsense sentences that were heard mixed with a second voice that was reading a story.

In an ingenious experiment, a male speaker was trained to produce high-pitched imitations of the same sentences spoken by a female speaker using the female's pattern of intonation (pitch variation). His imitations yielded sentences spoken by a male voice but with a high average pitch (about 160 Hz). To obtain a contrasting set of low-pitched sentences, he simply spoke them in his normal voice. Each of the resulting two sets of sentences was mixed with the same interfering speech, a story spoken in his natural pitch range. This yielded two test conditions, one in which both voices in the mixture (test sentences and interfering story) were low pitched and one in which the sentences were high but the story was low. As might be expected, the sentences were harder to perceive when they were in the same pitch range as the interfering story.

In another set of conditions, the pitch of the test sentences was controlled more exactly. They were recorded by the same indefatigable male speaker, who was now trained to speak in a monotone at the same pitch as a tone that was provided to him through earphones. Two versions were made of his sentences, one at a fundamental frequency of 110 Hz and one at 220 Hz. The story that was used to mask the sentences was spoken in his natural voice, which, though it varied normally in pitch, had an average fundamental of about 110 Hz. The listeners made more mistakes on the low-pitched sentences, which were nearer to the pitch of the masking speech from the story, than they did on the high-pitched sentences.

To be even more precise about the fundamental frequencies that were used, another experiment was done in which a digital signal processing technique was used to produce speech with an absolutely constant pitch.[704] The interfering story was produced with a fundamental frequency of 100 Hz. The test sentences were generated on different fundamentals in different experimental conditions. As the fundamentals were separated in frequency, the number of errors decreased. They dropped from about 60 percent when the fundamentals were the same to about 40 percent when they were three semitones apart. When the mixed voices were exactly an octave apart, the number of errors went up again, presumably because there are so many overlapping harmonics in spectra in which the fundamental of one is exactly double that of the other. (The reader is referred to the discussion of dissonance and perceptual fusion in chapter 5.) The amount of separation in fundamentals that is needed before listeners hear two separate voices is not large. The experimenters reported their own impressions as follows: "Whereas at zero semitones [separation] one definitely hears only a single auditory stream of garbled but speech-like sound, at one half semitones [separation] one hears very clearly two voices, and it is possible to switch one's attention from one to the other." In normal speech, the pitch keeps changing all the time and it is therefore unlikely that the fundamentals of two simultaneous voices in a natural situation will remain within half a semitone of one another for more than a brief moment at a time.

To examine the effects of fundamental frequency even more precisely, Michaël Scheffers, working at the same laboratory in the Netherlands, carried out a series of experiments in which listeners were asked to identify pairs of synthetic vowels presented simultaneously.[705] Such stimuli are ideal for studying the effects of differences in fundamental frequency. A first reason is that the vowel can be recognized even when its spectrum is unchanging. A second is that it can be created from a wholly harmonic spectrum. Finally, the use of mixtures of single vowels, rather than whole sentences, excludes the sequential role of pitch continuity in uniting a sequence of syllables as part of the same message.

In one study Scheffers used a computer to synthesize eight Dutch vowels, each 200 msec in duration.[706] Six different separations in fundamental were used: 0, $\frac{1}{4}$, $\frac{1}{2}$, 1, 2, and 4 semitones. The two fundamentals in a mixture were always placed symmetrically above and below 150 Hz. The subjects were asked to identify both vowels in each mixture. Performance was better when the fundamentals were different, but virtually all the improvement, from about 68 percent to about 79 percent correct, was caused by changing separation of the fundamentals from 0 to 1 semitone. In fact, an earlier study showed that the percentage correct dropped when the vowels were separated by 8 or 12 semitones. At these separations, the performance was considerably worse than when the vowels had the same fundamental.

Scheffers interpreted his results as consistent with the "harmonic sieve" model of pitch perception, developed in the same laboratory.[707] It is an example of the class of pattern-recognition models of pitch perception discussed in chapter 3. The auditory process of finding the fundamental of a set of harmonics is thought of as analogous to a sieve. The sieve for any given fundamental has "holes" in it that are spaced apart such that only the harmonics of that fundamental can "fall through." Others are blocked. If the harmonics of a second vowel are mixed with those of a first, the sieve that is responsible for detecting the first fundamental will block the harmonics of the second (except for the occasional one whose frequency happens to be near one of the harmonics of the first). If, at any given moment, there are two subsets of harmonics (belonging to different harmonic series), they will be detected by two different sieves. We can suppose that the harmonics that fall through the same sieve will tend to be grouped together for purposes of vowel recognition. Scheffers' finding suggest that the sieve mechanism can block unwanted partials that are as little as one semitone away from the harmonics that do fall through the sieve. Other research has given similar results.[708]

In research carried out in our laboratory, Magda Halikia (Chalikia) included some conditions that were like those of Scheffers but did not find any anomalies at large differences in fundamental frequency.[709] Her stimuli, however, were different. They were four different English vowels rather than the eight Dutch ones of Scheffers, and her synthesis of each vowel used only three formants rather than the five that Scheffers had used. It also appears from the spectra that were published by her and Scheffers that the bandwidths of her formants were larger. Whatever the reason, her results were much simpler. Averaging over three of her experiments, we can derive the following percentages of correct responses for separations of 0, 0.5, 3, 6, and 12 semitones (one octave): 58, 83, 84, 86, and 73 percent. (Note that the chance probability in her experiment would be 50 percent, on the average, if the subject made two guesses on every trial.) In one of her experiments, in which a 9-semitone separation was included, the percentage correct for this separation was the same as for the 6-semitone separation. These averaged results were also quite representative of those for the individual experiments. Each one showed a striking improvement between the 0-semitone separation and 0.5-semitone. The only drop at higher separations was at the octave, and even there performance remained quite high. Apparently the exact coincidence of harmonics in the two vowel spectra in the case of the 0-semitone separation makes them much harder to segregate and the coincidence of every second harmonic at the octave introduces a lesser difficulty.

Split-Formant Research

So far, in our discussion of the role of harmonic relations in segregating voices, we have proceeded ever more analytically, from mixtures of natural voices to mixtures of synthesized vowels. The next step is to see what happens when parts of the spectrum that are smaller than an individual vowel are given the same or different fundamentals. Being in different parts of the spectrum, the parts cannot actually contain the fundamental itself but can contain harmonics whose frequencies are multiples of the same fundamental. Most of the experiments that I shall discuss synthesize formants separately, using harmonics related to a chosen fundamental, and then mix these formants for presentation to a listener.

In 1955, Donald Broadbent published a brief report of some research in which the two ears of a listener received signals that were filtered differently.[710] The signal sent to one ear was high-pass filtered at 2,000 Hz and thus contained the higher frequencies. The other ear got the lower ones, resulting from low-pass filtering at 450 Hz. Because the filters were not very sharp, there was some overlap of frequencies at the two ears.[711] When normal speech was used, a large majority of the listeners reported that they heard only a single voice despite the division of the two frequency ranges. Broadbent attributed the fusion to two factors: first to the synchrony of onsets of energy in the two channels that occurred as consonants were released, and second to a common amplitude modulation in the two divided spectral regions. He was referring to the amplitude pulsation at the period of the fundamental that is seen as vertical striations in spectrograms such as the one shown in figure 6.2.

Two years later Donald Broadbent and Peter Ladefoged did a related experiment, but this time the signals were synthesized.[712] They were the first to raise the issue of the correct grouping of formants when the ear of the listener was presented with a mixture of formants. How, they asked, could the auditory system know which combination of formants to group to form a vowel? They proposed that it could be done on the basis of similarities within subsets of formants, and one similarity that they proposed was the factor that Broadbent had noted earlier—the overall repetition rate of the waveform. This rate would be determined by the fundamental of the voice, and would be visible in each formant as a pulsation (the vertical striation referred to earlier). Formants in which there were identical repetition rates would be grouped as parts of the same speech sound.

They produced a simple sentence—"What did you say before that?"—by speech synthesis. They created the voiced sounds as follows. They fed the pulse train from an electronic sound generator that was meant to simulate the vocal cord pulsation—and therefore to provide the fundamental frequency (F0)—into a set of resonant circuits that created formants. Sometimes the same F0 generator was used to create formants 1 and 2 and sometimes a different generator was used for each. In the latter case, the fundamental frequencies would be different. Either the resulting formants were both sent to the same ear of the listener, or else formant 1 was sent to one ear and formant 2 to the other. Their listeners were asked whether there were one or two voices and whether they were in the same or different spatial positions.

When the same F0 generator was used for both formants, either varying the pitch in a natural way or creating a monotone, the listeners usually heard only a single voice, even if the formants were sent to different ears. (Later research showed that the voice was heard at whichever side of the head received the lower formant.[713]) Having the same fundamental seemed to bind the formants together. However, when a different fundamental was used for each formant, the listeners usually heard two voices. For example, if one of the generators (say the one feeding the first formant resonator) was programmed to give a natural pitch contour to the sentence, but the other was programmed to stay 10 Hz higher than the first one at every instant, the listeners usually reported two voices, even when the two formants were mixed and presented to both ears. A particularly interesting condition was one in which there were two generators, one for each formant, both programmed to follow the same pattern of F0 over time. Due to slight inaccuracies in the equipment, the fundamentals tended to go in and out of phase randomly as one got slightly ahead of the other. In this case the binding of the two formants was weaker and they could no longer be fused if they were sent to separate ears. This suggests that a great precision in timing is needed to induce the maximum fusion of different spectral regions and that just having harmonics that are related to the same fundamental is not as powerful.

In a second experiment by these researchers, simpler sounds were used—just two formants, sustained without change for 15 seconds. Lacking the normal variations of a voice, these were heard as buzzers rather than as vocal sounds. As before, when the two fundamental were the same, the listeners tended to hear one sound, and when they were different to hear two. I think that the most important result, and one which agrees with data from other studies, was that even if the two resonances (formants) were centered at exactly the same frequency in the spectrum, and hence were totally overlapped spectrally, if they had different fundamentals they were heard as two voices. This illustrates the role of the pitch-detection mechanism in segregating two overlapping periodic sounds.

These experiments are important in that they gave exactly the same results for speech sounds in sentences and those that were not even heard as speech. But we must be careful to remember that in these experiments the listeners were only asked about the number and location of the sounds. They were not required to recognize what was being said.

James Cutting studied the effects of fundamental frequency in binding together formants that were presented to different ears.[714] The formants sometimes carried complementary and sometimes contradictory information about the identity of a syllable containing a stop consonant and a vowel. Such syllables can be convincingly synthesized using only two formants. The first result was concerned with the number of sounds heard. Even when the same pair of formants (the syllable "da") was sent to both ears, if the left and right ear signals were synthesized with different fundamentals, they were heard as two separate sounds. There was a striking difference in the percentage of times that the listeners judged that there was only one sound present when they both had the same fundamental (100 percent) to when their fundamentals were separated by only 2 Hz (nearly 0 percent).

When one ear got one formant of a syllable such as "da" and the other ear got the second, again the listeners were much more likely to report two different sounds when the formants had different fundamentals, but this segregation did not prevent the listeners from being able to recognize that it was "da" that they had heard and not "ba" or "ga". This result is remarkable. The listeners could combine the left and right ear information to derive the identity of the speech sound. At the same time, they appeared to segregate them to derive independent percepts that included their locations and pitches. This sort of result has occurred in many experimental contexts. It has been used as the basis of a claim by Alvin Liberman that ordinary principles of auditory analysis do not apply to speech perception. Because it is so important, I will discuss it in more detail later.

Christopher Darwin, together with a number of collaborators at the University of Sussex, has tried to show in a number of ways that the perceptual fusion and segregation of speech sounds are governed by the principles of auditory scene analysis and that this fusion affects the perceived identity of the sounds.

Darwin, in 1981, reported a series of experiments which, like those of Broadbent and Ladefoged and of Cutting, synthesized formants with different properties from one another and looked at the extent to which the listener recombined them perceptually into a single sound.[715] While he manipulated several properties of the formants, I shall mention only their fundamental frequencies here. In every case in which a speech sound was created by combining formants that had different fundamentals, the listeners tended to report hearing more than one sound. At the same time, there was usually no tendency for a difference in the fundamental to inhibit the perception of the phoneme that resulted from the combination of those formants. In short, the listeners did segregate the formants, in the sense of hearing more than one of them, but at the same time combined them to derive the correct speech sound.

There was one exception to this general pattern. One of his experiments used the pattern of formants shown in figure 6.4. One combination of these, the formants F1, F2, and F3, if heard in isolation, will give the syllable "roo"; another combination, F1,F3,F4, will be heard as "lee". It is important to notice that the first and third formants appear in both syllables and therefore there is a competition for the belongingness of these formants. Unless formants are used twice, the listener cannot hear both syllables. With this setup, the listeners

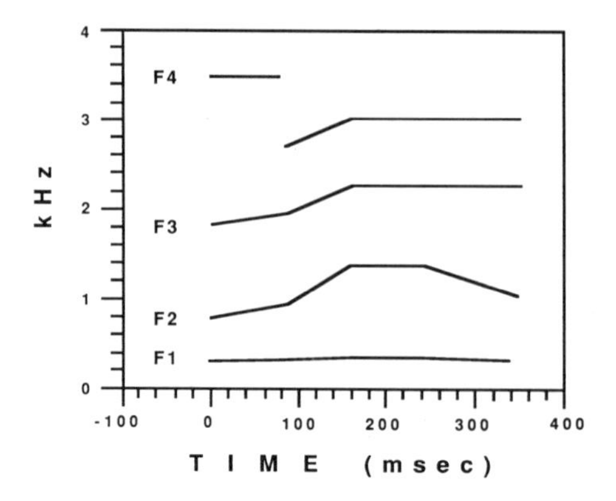

Figure 6.4
Frequency tracks of the formants used to synthesize the syllables "lee" and "roo". (From Darwin 1981.)

tended to hear the syllable whose component formants were labeled as going together by all having the same fundamental frequency. Nonetheless, in the alternative condition, where the formants were broken up by not being labeled with the same fundamental, the syllable was still heard on a significant number of occasions in a series of tests. This suggests that while a common fundamental *can* contribute to the perceptual decision of how to group formants to get a speech sound, its effect is seen only in situations in which there is a competition between speech-recognition schemas.

The conclusion that we can draw from the studies of both Cutting and Darwin is that the phoneme-recognition system, a schema-based process, has some way of selecting what it needs out of a mixture of sounds without the assistance of primitive scene-analysis processes that operate on the acoustic similarities. The results tend to show, however, that the schema-based ones can improve their performance in difficult situations by using the information provided by primitive grouping.

Harmonics in Nonoverlapping Frequency Ranges We have now reviewed research that has tried to manipulate the perceptual segregation either of whole voices or of individual formants. We should note one important difference between the two cases. With whole voices the material to be segregated is in overlapping frequency ranges, and we find that the segregating effect of different fundamental frequencies in the two voices (and presumably the integrating effect of all the spectral components from the same voice having the same fundamental) plays a very important role in segregating the voices. On the other hand, in the case of manipulation of individual formants, the main energy of each formant is usually in a fairly distinct frequency region. In this case the phonetic integration is not usually very sensitive to the relation between the fundamentals of the formants.

This points to the possibility that in normal speech the main use of the fundamentals in scene analysis is to disambiguate cases in which a number of alternative phoneme recognitions are supported equally well by the mixture (as in whole mixed voices). It appears that each phoneme-recognizing schema can look for the formant patterns that it needs, and if crucial evidence is not simultaneously being claimed by another phoneme recognizer, the fundamental frequencies in different parts of the spectrum will have no effect on the identity of the derived phoneme. This latter description probably tells us what happens in natural listening to a single voice and in the formant-manipulating experiments in which there is no competition among phoneme schemas.

Scene Analysis in the Defining of Formants

So far we have looked at the process of segregating voices and grouping of formants. But formants are not the only sounds in an environment. Other sounds can interfere with the extraction of the peak frequencies of the formants, a value that listeners may need on the way to arriving at a description of the speech sounds. Most linguists believe that the description of a formant that is most relevant to phoneme recognition is this peak frequency. It is not a direct property of the formant itself but something more abstract, a peak in the spectral envelope. The latter is an imaginary smooth line that represents the intensity that each harmonic *ought to have* if it occurs in a spectrum that has been filtered in a certain way.

The issues can be clarified with the help of figure 6.5, which shows the spectrum of a spoken vowel with an extra pure tone added near one of the peaks. The vertical lines represent the intensities of different partials that are present in the spectrum. The dotted line represents the relative intensities that the harmonics *might* have had if they had been at different places along the spectrum. The peaks in this envelope are important because they come from resonances in the vocal tract of the speaker; therefore they tell the listener about how the speaker's tongue, jaw, and so on are positioned. The line labeled T represents an additional nonspeech tone that has been mixed with the speech sound. If we focus on the first formant, labeled F1 in the

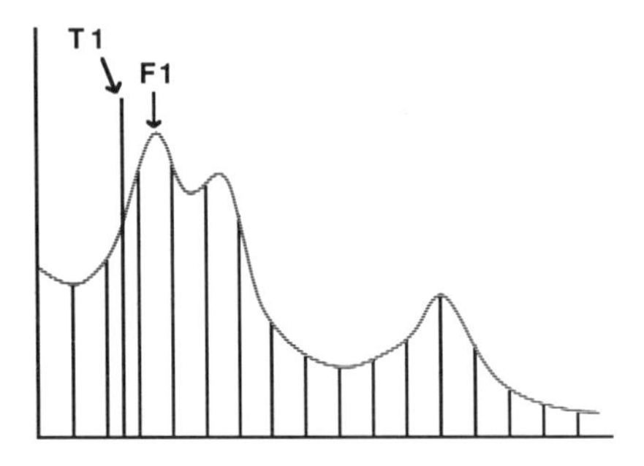

Figure 6.5
Spectrum of a vowel mixed with a pure tone in the region of the first formant. T1: pure tone. F1: first formant peak.

figure, we see that the point that defines it is not the frequency of the most intense partial in the region, because this partial is the added tone. It is not even that of the second most intense, which is part of the voice but is not at the resonance peak. Depending on the fundamental frequency, it will often be the case that there is no harmonic exactly at the resonance peak. Somehow two results have to be achieved. The added tone must be rejected and the remaining partials used to estimate the frequency of the peak. The first of these two involves scene analysis, and Darwin and his colleagues have examined how principles of auditory grouping can help the listener to achieve it.

Darwin and his associates have investigated a number of heuristics whereby the auditory system could determine that the tone did not belong to the vowel. Their general method has been to use a vowel spectrum that yields a sound that is intermediate in quality between two standard vowels, say the "i" in "bit" and the "a" in "bate". Then they introduce an extra tone in the region of the first formant. If the tone is accepted as part of the spectrum of the vowel, it shifts the identity of the vowel toward one of the two standard vowels. To the extent that it is rejected, the shift is smaller or nonexistent.

One experiment by Darwin and Gardner examined the factor of harmonicity.[716] It was based on the premise that the tone can be rejected if it does not fit into the harmonic series defined by the spectrum of the vowel. This expectation was derived from the harmonic sieve model of pitch perception that I described in relation to the research of Scheffers and also in chapter 3. The experiment mixed a vowel spectrum with a pure tone whose frequency was mistuned by varying amounts from one of the harmonics of the vowel. With about 8 percent mistuning, the tone was effectively segregated from the vowel so that the vowel's identity was affected very little by its presence. The effect has nothing to do with the fact that one of the sounds was a vowel. In Brian Moore's laboratory the same amount of mistuning was found to be sufficient to cause a mistuned harmonic in a complex tone to stand out as a separate sound.[717]

Earlier we saw that when only one synthesized sound was present, the mistuning of different formants relative to one another (in the sense that their harmonics belonged to different fundamentals) did not prevent their integration into a single speech sound. We attributed this to the fact that a phoneme-recognition schema was capable of simply looking for energy in the spectral regions in which it expected it, and could overcome the segregating effects of scene analysis. Yet we saw in Darwin and Gardner's research that the phoneme schema does not seem to be able to overcome scene analysis when a tone is added to a formant. Why the difference?

One possibility is that it arises from the sorts of evidence that the phoneme-recognition schemas can use. These schemas, while they map patterns of formants onto particular speech sounds, and are therefore capable of taking what they need from mixtures, may contain no definition of what it means to be a formant. So they may be fully dependent upon more primitive processes for this decision.

A second possibility is that primitive scene analysis may have a more dominant role in spectral grouping when the sounds that are to be separated occupy the same spectral region. Recall that in the experiments on the spectral grouping of synthesized formants, where scene analysis did not affect the phonetic interpretation, the mistuned formants mainly occupied different spectral regions.

The effects of the similarity in fundamentals of co-occurring formants must depend upon a neural mechanism that can calculate whether or not one or more partials are multiples of a particular fundamental (F0). One proposed method is the harmonic sieve. Since this method involves measuring the frequency of each harmonic to determine whether it is close enough to qualify as a multiple of some particular F0, it will succeed only if the frequencies of the harmonics are separately resolvable by the auditory system.

An alternative view is that the F0 can be assessed without having to resolve the harmonics on which it is based. This can be done by responding to the pattern of timing in the neural impulses activated by the sound. We have examined this theory in chapter 3.

Often, in psychology, when you ask whether the nervous system does it this way or that, the answer is both. The methods of the nervous system are highly redundant so that it can continue to do a reasonably good job when particular types of evidence are missing. Basilar-membrane place analysis may be carried out to determine the fundamental or fundamentals in spectral regions in which the harmonics are resolved, and periodicity may be used where they are crowded too close together.

Computer Models for Segregation of Two Voices

Attempts to segregate simultaneous voices by their fundamentals have used one or another of these methods. Thomas Parsons chose the approach of analyzing an incoming spectrum to find harmonics from two different fundamentals; Mitchel Weintraub chose to use the timing information that is located within narrow spectral regions.[718]

Parsons' program used Fourier analysis to derive a spectrum for the mixture in successive 51-msec segments. It then examined the peaks in the spectrum and used some tricks to decompose them into separate partials. Next it looked for the fundamental (F0) that would best account for the set of detected components. It then put aside all the harmonics that were accounted for by this F0 and tried to find another one for the partials that remained. If it succeeded, it treated the harmonics associated with this second F0 as a second set.

Next it had to decide how to group the discovered sets of harmonics over time. It did so by assuming that the pitch of each voice would not change radically from one analyzed segment to the next. For each voice, it predicted the F0 in the current segment from the pattern of F0's found in previous segments and accepted the one that best matched this prediction. It therefore used sequential grouping based on F0 similarities and trajectories. This method allowed certain F0 estimates to be rejected as erroneous.

I have argued earlier that the purpose of auditory segregation is to make subsequent recognition easier. However, rather than passing these separated sets of harmonics on to a speech recognizer, Parsons' program used them to resynthesize each voice so that a human listener could judge how well the two had been segregated by the procedure.

It is obvious that Parsons' program is not suitable for unvoiced sounds (which have no F0) and therefore cannot be a general method for voice separation. However, when it was tested on sentences consisting mainly of voiced sounds ("Where were you a year ago? We were away in Walla Walla."), each of the resynthesized versions of each voice was relatively free of intrusions from the second original voice. The quality tended to be poorer when the unwanted voice was louder than the target voice.

Weintraub's program also used the fundamental frequencies of the speakers' voices to segregate speech. The speech was from two talkers, a male and a female, speaking sequences composed of digits. Unlike Parsons' program, it assessed the two fundamentals by analyzing the pulsation of the signal within narrow spectral bands. As its first stage of analysis, it employed the cochlear model of Richard Lyon that we discussed in chapter 3.[719] A sample of one of Lyon's cochleagrams was shown in figure 3.10 of that chapter. A computer implementation of Lyon's model transformed the incoming signal into a temporal pattern of pulsations in each of 85 frequency channels. Then Weintraub's program looked for regularities in the pulsations in each channel. It combined these across channels to find two different periodicities in the timing information. These were treated as the two fundamentals. Like Parsons' program, but using different methods, it linked successive estimates of pitch into two F0 tracks, each representing the successive F0's in one of the voices over time. Then it allocated the spectral energy in each frequency region, giving all or part to each voice. Unlike Parsons' program, it did not segregate individual harmonics, and therefore it had more difficulty with the problem of partitioning the spectral energy in each frequency band to the two voices (Parsons just gave the total energy from each harmonic to the voice spectrum to which that harmonic was assigned.) Like Parsons' program, Weintraub's assessed the degree to which it had been successful by reconstructing the two separated voices.

The programs were successful enough that they established the plausibility of estimating the fundamentals in an incoming signal and the utility of using them to segregate different voices. Yet each had only a limited degree of success and purchased that by restricting the signal to a mixture of only two voices speaking primarily voiced sounds. Obviously the use of F0 to segregate voices applies only to those speech sounds that have harmonically related partials, not to any others. To make it worse, the possibility of finding different fundamentals gets harder as the number of voices goes up. How does the human deal with complex mixtures of voices? Not, I think, by improving on the computer's ability to use F0 for segregation, but by increasing the number of scene-analysis factors that it uses.

Energy that "sticks out" inappropriately from a spectrum may also tend to be segregated. Darwin drew this conclusion from an experiment in which he used his method of mixing a tone with a synthesized vowel.[720] The tone was at the exact frequency of one of the harmonics in the first formant and started at the same time as the vowel. The only thing that was altered was the intensity of the added tone. At lower levels of intensity, the tone was incorporated into the vowel, affecting its identity, but at higher intensities some of the energy from the added tone was rejected from the perceptual computation of the vowel's identity. Darwin attributed this to some ability of the auditory system to reject tones whose intensity could not fit into a speech spectrum (or perhaps, more generally, one that was shaped by a system of resonances). It was not apparent whether this implied that the auditory system had a special method for processing speech sounds or whether it was using a more general method for rejecting spectral energy that sticks out too far from the spectrum. If it is truly the result of a specialized analyzer for speech, then that analyzer must have a property that I have so far attributed only to primitive scene-analysis processes and not to schema-governed ones. This is the property of being able to partition a spectrum. To do this, a process must be able not only to find, in a dense spectrum, components that it is looking for, but also to remove this set of components and leave behind a coherent residual from which the components have been removed. The evidence that I cited in chapter 4 suggested that schema-based segregation did not make a coherent residual available to other pattern-recognition processes.

Common-Fate Cues

Summary of Findings with Nonspeech Sounds

The next class of cues for segregating speech sounds involves correlated changes in different parts of the spectrum. In chapter 3, these were called common-fate cues. They included changes in both frequency and amplitude.

As far as frequency was concerned, we saw that parallel changes of partials (in log frequency) in different parts of the spectrum promoted the grouping of subsets of harmonics. These changes included slow glides in frequency as well as micromodulation. There was some uncertainty, however, as to whether the effects could not be attributed to an explanation that had nothing to do with a common-fate heuristic (such as the fact that a subset of partials, changing in parallel, will maintain their harmonic relations).

The major use of amplitude differences was to segregate sounds that started at different times. Associated with this factor was the old-plus-new heuristic that tried to subtract the effects of an earlier-starting tone out of a mixture. We saw also that a sudden change in the amplitude or phase of a certain spectral component in a mixture tended to segregate that component from other components that did not change. Sudden sharp rises in the intensity of a number of frequency components, all at the same time, tended to cause them to fuse. Another form of amplitude change that was shown to be important was the rapid changes in amplitude that occur throughout the spectrum when adjacent harmonics beat with one another at the fundamental frequency of the harmonic series.

Correlated Frequency Changes

Frequency Modulation of Harmonics Let us begin by looking for evidence that parallel frequency changes are involved in the segregation of speech sounds from one another. One would imagine that they should be. The human voice changes in pitch over time. This causes the harmonics that are parts of the same voice to move in parallel on a log-frequency scale. As the fundamental glides up in frequency by 25 percent, for example, each harmonic also goes up by 25 percent. When two people are talking at the same time, it is unlikely that their fundamentals (perceived as pitches) will be changing in the same way at the same time. A betting man would wager that any harmonics that were moving up or down in parallel and maintaining their harmonic relations to one another all belonged to the same sound.

In chapter 3, we found some evidence that our ears bet in the same way. Different frequency modulations of two sets of partials cause them to be segregated and grouped into two sounds. But it was not clear whether this grouping merely told the auditory system that there were two sounds or also partitioned the two spectra well enough to permit separate descriptions of their two timbres. Speech perception provides a good vehicle in which to study this question because you can ask the listeners not only whether they hear more than one sound but also what the identities of the speech sounds are. If recognition is possible, the segregation must have been sufficient for the building of a description of the individual spectra.

However, there is a phenomenon called "the tracing out of the spectral envelope" that makes research on this subject hard. Earlier in this chapter we saw that formants are defined by peaks in the spectral envelope and that most theories of speech recognition require the auditory system to estimate where the peaks are. This estimation may be very hard when the harmonics are widely spaced. This occurs when the fundamental is high, since successive harmonics are separated from one another by the fundamental frequency. An example is the spectrum of a female voice. Part 1 of figure 6.6 illustrates a typical vowel spectrum and shows the spectral envelope (E1) that results from a momentary setting of a speaker's vocal tract. Part 2 focuses on the region of the second formant. The curve labeled E1 is the true spectral envelope created by the vocal resonances of the speaker.

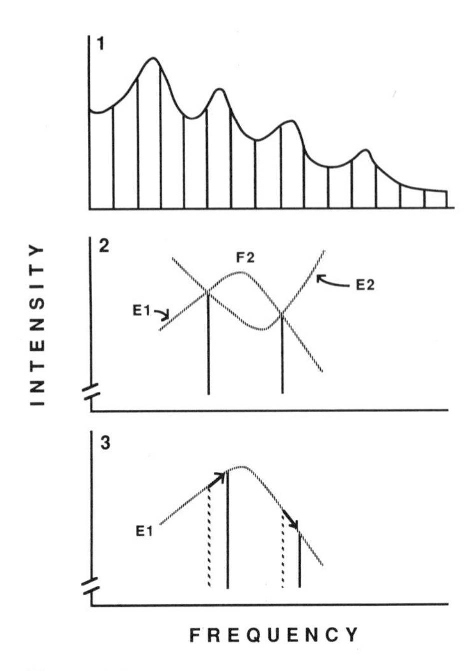

Figure 6.6
Illustration of "the tracing out of the spectral envelope" by a moving partial. 1: spectrum. 2: two possible spectral envelopes that fit the same harmonic intensities. 3: evidence for the local slope of the envelope as the harmonics go up in frequency.

However, as E2 shows, there are other envelope shapes that are equally consistent with the intensities of the two nearest harmonics. Part 3 shows what happens when there is a rising pitch and the frequencies of all the harmonics move upward. The dotted lines show the original harmonics and their intensities, while the solid lines show their new frequencies and intensities. Stephen McAdams and Xavier Rodet have argued that if the evidence provided by these movements and changes in intensity is taken into account, alternative envelopes such as E2 can be ruled out. Rodet has demonstrated that this information can be used by computer algorithms to achieve better estimates of formant peak frequencies, and McAdams and Rodet have shown that human listeners seem to employ this type of information in deciding on the identity of a vowel.[721]

If people used this information it would make it harder to determine the contribution of the parallel movement of harmonics in segregating them from a mixture. If we use, as our criterion, the identification of a vowel in a mixture, any improvement that is found to result from moving all the harmonics in parallel may be the consequence of tracing out the spectral envelope rather than segregating the right subset of harmonics.

The reader might be inclined to ask at this point how the listeners could benefit from a better estimate of the spectral envelope if they could not even segregate the correct subset of harmonics. The answer to this question depends upon how the evidence furnished by spectral tracing is used by the human brain. One possibility is that it is used by schemas for speech recognition. We must recall that there is evidence to suggest that the speech sound schemas can extract what they need from a mixture even without the assistance of primitive scene analysis. The tracing out of the spectral envelope could help these schemas to confirm that certain formants were present.

The second possibility is that the envelope tracing is used by processes more primitive than those of speech recognition. The auditory system may be built to make use of the fact that it is often dealing with acoustic sources whose resonances are either stable over time or are changing fairly slowly. If changes in the intensities of certain harmonics accompanied changes in the fundamental in a way that was consistent with their all being passed through the same resonance system, this might contribute to their being grouped together. For example, if there were two speakers or two musical instruments present in a mixture, the auditory system might be able to build up a picture of the two sets of resonances and then, at later moments, assign to each resonance the harmonics that were consistent with it. How this could be done is not clear at the moment, but we cannot say that it is impossible.

To establish the role of common fate in frequency in binding harmonics together, it is necessary to test the effects of *covariation* in the movement of harmonics and not just the effects of movement itself. The simplest way to do this is to have two sets of harmonics. The changes in each set must be parallel but the changes in the two sets must be independent. We must compare this with the case in which the movements of all the harmonics are parallel.

Even when speakers think that the pitch of their voices is perfectly steady, it jitters slightly from moment to moment. I described this in chapter 3 as micromodulation. John Chowning has shown in acoustic demonstrations that adding this jitter to a synthesis of the human singing voice makes it sound much more natural and causes the harmonics to fuse into a speech sound.[722] Stephen McAdams carried out experiments with a mixture of synthesized voices.[723] He wanted to find out whether imposing independent micromodulation patterns onto the fundamentals of the different voices would cause the listener to fuse the subset of harmonics that defined each voice and to segregate the subsets that defined different voices. The micromodulation that he used was a mixture of regular vibrato and random jitter. He synthesized the vowels "ah", "ee", and "oh" in a male singing voice and presented them in mixtures, each vowel at a different pitch (five-semitone separations between adjacent pitches). The listeners knew which three vowels could be present and were asked to judge the salience of each of these or their certainty that it was present. Sometimes none of the vowels had any modulation, sometimes only one did, and sometimes they all did. When they all did, either they all had exactly the same pattern or else two of them had the same pattern and the third had a different one.

Generally a vowel was heard better if it was modulated than if it was not. However, it did not matter whether the other vowels were modulated or not. Nor did it matter, when the vowels were modulated, whether the modulation was parallel or independent in different vowels. It appears, then, that the segregation of the vowels was not assisted by the independence of the modulation patterns. This result was subsequently confirmed in an experiment by Cecile Marin.[724] Nonetheless, McAdams did notice one effect of the modulation that was not just due to tracing out the spectral envelope. This is that often, when the harmonics were steady, many of the listeners heard more pitches than the three they were supposed to hear. Apparently, the accidental harmonic relations in the mixed spectrum fooled the pitch-detection system into computing extra pitches. However, when the harmonics were being modulated, there was a clear perception of three pitches.

Marin extended the research of McAdams by asking whether it was the listeners' sensitivity to tracing out of the spectral envelope that strengthened the perception of modulated vowels as compared with unmodulated ones. She designed two forms of modulation. In the first, the listener could use the modulation to get a "fix" on the spectral envelope. In this form of modulation, the spectral envelope was fixed and the amplitude changes in the moving harmonics traced it out. In the second type, the spectral envelope that defined a given vowel moved up and down in frequency with the harmonics. This meant that the harmonics remained constant in intensity and there was no fixed spectral envelope. The two forms of modulation strengthened the perception of the modulated vowels equally well. This means that it is not the tracing of formants that makes modulated vowels clearer. Perhaps the modulation simply evokes a stronger response in neural systems that are computing the vowel quality.

We know from a large number of demonstrations that concurrent sets of harmonics that have different modulation patterns will be given separate pitch analyses. Therefore there is a contrast between the effectiveness of micromodulation in giving separate pitch identities to subsets of harmonics and its ineffectiveness in affecting the recognition of speech sounds. This is not the first time that we have encountered this lack of correspondence between the effects of primitive grouping and the identification of speech sounds. As we shall see, the absence of effects of scene analysis on the recognition of speech sounds is one of several pieces of evidence that has encouraged Liberman and his colleagues at Haskins Laboratories to argue that the brain's system for speech identification *never* makes use of primitive scene-analysis processes.

There is, in addition to micromodulation, another form of pitch change that takes place in the human voice. As we talk, our intonation rises and falls over the course of words, phrases, and sentences.

Magda Halikia (Chalikia), in our laboratory, studied the segregation of simultaneous pairs of synthetic vowels whose pitch was moving in this slower way.[725] She used various mixtures involving the vowels "ee", "ah", "u" (as in "put"), and "e" (as in "bed"). The listeners were asked to identify the two vowels in each mixture. Halikia studied two aspects of the role of fundamental frequency in the segregation of the vowels: the frequency separation of their fundamentals and how the fundamentals changed over time. The conditions are illustrated in figure 6.7. The frequencies of the fundamentals were either steady or else moved in either parallel or crossed trajectories over a 1-second period. Figure 6.8 shows the results.

I have already mentioned Halikia's findings on frequency separation so I will say no more here. The effect of the movement of the fundamentals was interesting. Both crossing and parallel gliding helped the listeners to identify the vowels. The help from the parallel gliding could not have been due to the segregation of partials based on different patterns of movement. Halikia attributed it to the tracing of the spectral envelope as the spectra moved. There was a small additional benefit to having the fundamentals move in different directions, but the difference was generally not significant. The one strong effect was at the octave separation of the fundamentals, where the different direction of modulation in the crossing condition prevented the continuation over time of a fixed octave relation between the two fundamentals. This continued relation tended to fuse the vowels when they were steady or moving in parallel.

Although the assistance from the crossing of the fundamentals was not, on the whole, better than from their parallel movement, we

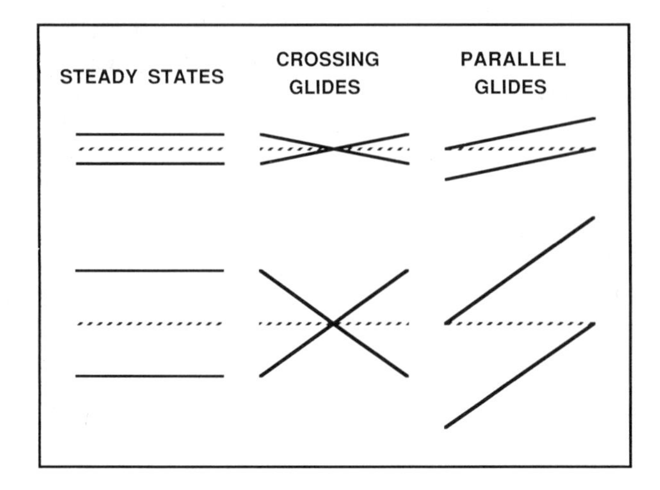

Figure 6.7
The pitch transitions in a pair of mixed vowels: steady states, crossing glides, and parallel glides. Top: small frequency separation. Bottom: large frequency separation.

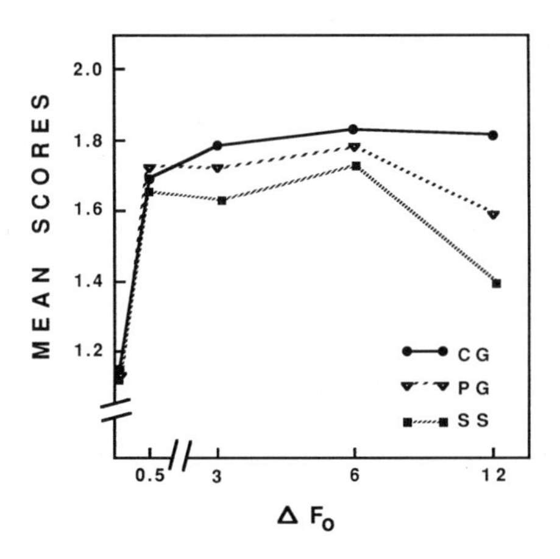

Figure 6.8
Mean identification scores for pairs of vowels with steady-state pitches (SS), parallel glides (PG), or crossing glides (CG). (From Halikia 1985.)

should take into account how the three kinds of patterns, steady, parallel, and crossing, were equated on the frequency separation of the two fundamentals. It was done by equating their maximum separations. This penalized the crossing pattern. For the other two, the maximum separation continued for the full 1 second. For the crossing pattern, it defined only the separation at the beginning and end. Between these two points, the separation was much less. We can see in figure 6.8 that frequency separation was the largest single effect, so the penalty paid was large; yet the crossing fundamental was still always easiest. This suggests that the crossing patterns are easier than parallel ones when the effects of frequency separation are removed. This additional advantage, if real, cannot come from envelope tracing, since both kinds of movement would have done this. It would have been due to common fate, the independent movement of the different subsets of harmonics in the mixture.

The idea that the partials of a voice can be segregated from partials that are unrelated to that voice if the two sets of partials have different patterns of motion was supported by another of Halikia's observations. She mixed a steady-state vowel with a gliding nonvowel tone. The latter sound consisted of a large number of partials of equal amplitude, covering the frequency range of the partials of the vowel. This tone was either swept in fundamental frequency or steady. If it was swept, it started at a fundamental frequency that was three semitones in frequency above or below that of the vowel and ended at the same frequency as the vowel. If steady, it remained three semitones above or below the vowel.

We already know that a separation in fundamental frequency favors the segregation of two sounds. On this basis, the gliding tone should have hurt the identification of the vowel more than the steady tone, since it moved nearer to it in fundamental frequency. However, the opposite results were found. The vowel paired with the gliding tone was more intelligible. Since the vowel remained steady, the results cannot be attributed to the tracing of the spectral envelope. A genuine segregation based on differences in the motion of the two fundamentals must be involved. Of course it is possible that steady-state motion is not really a type of motion at all, and that rather than dealing with nonparallel frequency motion we are dealing with a difference between two entirely different sorts of beasts—moving harmonics and steady-state ones—with a tendency to segregate from one another.

The results of an experiment by Gardner and Darwin suggests that common fate in FM may not be effective in segregating speech sounds from other ones.[726] These researchers followed a technique pioneered in Darwin's laboratory: They altered the perceived identity of a vowel by inducing some of the energy in the spectrum to be perceptually isolated from the vowel spectrum. They first added a tone to the spectrum of a vowel at one of its harmonic frequencies. This caused it to sound more like a different vowel. Then they tried to induce the auditory system to isolate the added tone so that the vowel would sound more like it was before the tone had been added. The acoustic cue that they used in this experiment was correlated FM. The added tone was modulated either in parallel with the harmonics of the vowel or at a different rate or phase. The frequencies were varied by 2 percent and at rates of 6 or 10 times per second. All to no avail. Perceptual segregation was induced, but it did not affect phonetic identity. That is, the listeners heard an extra sound source, but the modulated partial still contributed to the vowel's quality.

The report of an extra sound source in this speech sound resembles a finding of Stephen McAdams with nonspeech sounds.[727] McAdams studied the perception of complex tones (built out of 16 equal-intensity partials) in which all the partials were subjected to micromodulation. In some tones the modulation was identical for all the partials (coherent modulation), and in others one partial was modulated in a different temporal pattern from the others (incoherent modulation). On each trial the listener heard one signal of each type and was required to judge which one seemed to contain more sound sources. McAdams found that when the tones were harmonic the choice of the incoherent tone as having more sources increased with the depth of the modulation (the variation in frequency caused by the modulation) and was greater when the independently moving partial was a higher harmonic. Since higher harmonics are *less* resolvable from their neighbors by the auditory system, this latter result suggested to McAdams that the multiplicity of the sound, in the case of the higher harmonics, was being judged not by being able to really hear out the partial but by the fact that incoherent modulation created the sort of phase rolling or chorus effect that is heard when slightly different sounds are played at the same time. On the other hand, when one of the first five harmonics was uncorrelated with the others it sounded like a separate sinusoidal tone. Since the harmonic that Gardner and Darwin had modulated in a speech sound was one of the first five, their discovery that it was heard as a separate sound agrees with McAdams' result.

In all these results on differential modulation of subsets of partials, there was a kind of segregation that clearly affected the perceived number of tones. However, it is doubtful whether the segregation improved the assignment of a separate phonetic identity to one of these subsets.

More recently, however, unpublished research by Chalikia and Bregman on mixtures of two vowels with gliding fundamentals has demonstrated a clear superiority of the crossing glides over the parallel glides even when their maximum separations were equated. But this superiority was found only when the spectrum of each vowel was *inharmonic*. The inharmonicity was designed by taking a harmonic spectrum and deriving a new spectrum from it by displacing each partial upward or downward by a random amount, keeping it within one-half a harmonic spacing of its original frequency. When this spectrum glided, it did so in a way that maintained the ratios among its partials over time. To create an inharmonic vowel, the resulting inharmonic spectrum was passed through filters that created the vowel-defining formants. The superiority of the crossing movement over the parallel movement in separating the vowels was greater when they had these inharmonic spectra than when they had normal harmonic spectra. Apparently it becomes more helpful to unify a spectrum by giving it a distinct pattern of movement when it is not already being unified by the property of harmonicity.

Segregation by Independent Movement of Formant Center Frequency? There is another kind of change that can occur in voices and that we might expect to be used in segregation. This is the movement of formants. It is caused by the changing resonances in the speaker's vocal tract as the sizes and shapes of the cavities change over the course of an utterance. If we used this cue, however, to segregate formants that were not moving in parallel, we would just as often be segregating the formants of a single voice from one another than the formants of different voices.

When we look at a spectrogram of a single person talking, we see that the formants of the voiced segments act somewhat independently of one another, often moving in different directions. For example, in the word "yaw", a schematic spectrogram of which is shown in figure 6.9, the first formant moves up as the second one moves strongly downward. Why does this not cause them to segregate from one another so that they are heard as separate whistles? It is probably their harmonicity that holds them together. We must remember that a formant is merely a group of adjacent partials in the spectrum of a complex tone that has been enhanced through resonance. When we speak of a formant as moving down in frequency we mean that the region of enhancement has moved down, not that the partials themselves have moved down. Indeed, if the pitch of the voice was rising

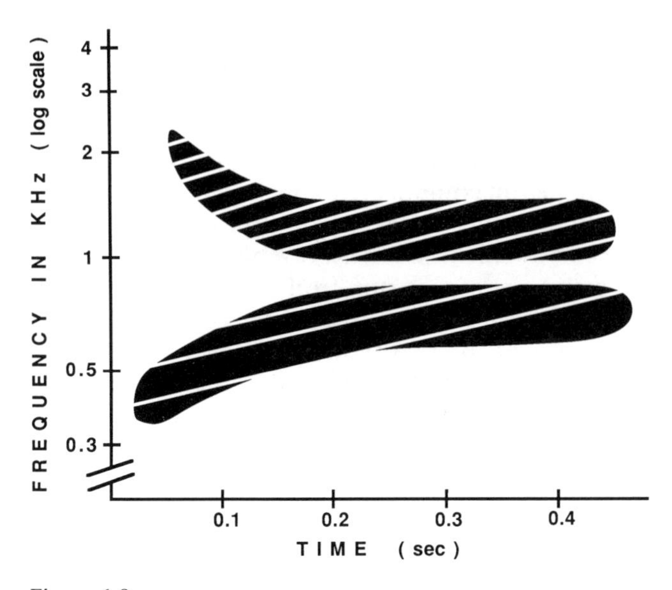

Figure 6.9
Schematic spectrogram of the word "yaw" spoken with rising pitch. The thin rising lines represent harmonics of a rising fundamental and the darkened regions represent formants.

during the word "yaw", all the individual partials would rise in concert. Therefore the second formant could be dropping as all the partials were rising. As the formant dropped it would enhance different (rising) partials. This effect is shown in figure 6.9, where the thin rising parallel lines represent partials and the larger outlined regions represent formants. If it were subsets of partials that were moving in two different trajectories, as would occur if they were coming from two different voices, their independent motions would guarantee that within each subset the harmonic relations would be preserved but that there would be no sustained harmonic relations that held across the two subsets. In such a case we would expect segregation to occur. However, we can see in figure 6.9 that when formants move in different directions, the change maintains the parallelness of the partials, and therefore their harmonicity.

If we think back to the experiment done by Dorman, Cutting, and Raphael on cycles of synthesized vowels, we can recall a condition in which they joined adjacent vowels by connecting the corresponding formants by formant transitions.[728] Their interest was in the fact that the vowels were now more sequentially integrated. But they did not comment on the fact that the high level of identification of the order of the vowels by the listeners suggested that the vowels were well integrated *spectrally* as well, despite the fact that the formant transitions were not moving in parallel.

We should think a bit about the ecology of such matters. Since formants are resonances imposed on a single spectrum, their independent motion does not represent the existence of different sound sources, but tells us about changes in the dimensions of the chambers in which the sound is resonating. We would want to read this as a single sound source with changing properties or moving through changing enclosures.

On the other hand, it is not entirely impossible to segregate the formants that have been imposed on a single harmonic spectrum. For example, if we take a complex tone with only a few lower harmonics (tone A) and repeatedly alternate it with a complex tone (B) that has all the harmonics of A as well as some additional higher ones, in such a way that there is no break between the tones, tone A will be heard as continuous, and a second sound (the extra harmonics that are present in B) will be heard beeping in the background. B will get decomposed into two parts. A sound pattern like this would correspond in the natural world to two unrelated sounds that happened to have the same fundamental frequency but had different harmonics. This would be a rare occurrence but it can happen, at least for brief moments.

Notice, however, that the heuristic being used in this last example is not the independent changes of the *frequency* of the resonance peaks but a large asynchrony in their onset. The latter is much stronger evidence for the existence of two voices. Apparently the independent movement of formants does not constitute such persuasive evidence for the auditory system.

Nonetheless Stephen McAdams has reported that Jean-Baptiste Barrière, in a computer music piece, manipulated the way the individual formants changed over time to make the spectral forms coalesce into vowels or disintegrate into the several formants as individual images. McAdams has also reported synthesizing an example of Tibetan chant, a musical form in which vocal resonances are caused to move over time in a nonspeechlike manner. In his example, the voices are slowly made to disintegrate by decorrelating the formant movements.[729] Why does this not happen to all voices, since, as I pointed out earlier, their formants will often move in different directions at the same time? This requires more research. Possibly the synthesized formants moved over wider ranges than do normal speech formants or perhaps other factors that normally favor the integration of the whole spectrum were weaker. For example, in Tibetan chant, the perceptual segregation of the formants, as they move in different patterns, is assisted by the fact that the fundamental frequency is held constant. This would eliminate the coherence that is contributed by the parallel movements of all the harmonics. Also in Tibetan chant, the movement of the formants is much slower than in speech. Clearly, then, the existence of the two contrasting cases, speech and Tibetan chant, opens up opportunities for research.

Correlated Amplitude Changes

There are two other facts to mention about the duration and timing of sounds. The first is that unrelated sounds tend to go on and off at different times. This property of the world is exploited by a tendency of the auditory system to segregate sets of partials or parts of the spectrum that start at different times. The second is that often a sound will continue or be repeated as a second sound joins it. The auditory system exploits this fact by extracting from mixtures any components that are close in frequency to sounds that were heard in isolation just prior to the mixture. In chapter 3, we called this the old-plus-new heuristic. That chapter gave a number of examples of the perceptual results of these two facts.[730] It is possible that a part of the tendency to segregate mixed components that start and stop asynchronously may be an extension of the old-plus-new heuristic, because the auditory system gets a good look at the components that start earlier and therefore knows what to look for in the mixture. However, it cannot explain why components that end asynchronously will be segregated.

Sequential Capturing (Onset and Offset Asynchrony) Asynchronous changes in the amplitudes of formants can occur in natural speech. For example, sometimes in a long nasal sound, such as the "n-m" sequence in the phrase "in Maine", the higher formants are quite attenuated during the nasals and start up again quite strongly when the following vowel begins. One would think that this asynchrony would cause the spectral bands to segregate so that the components that were heard in the nasals would be experienced as continuing past the onset of the vowel, with the added formants coming from the vowel's onset sounding like the beginning of an accompanying sound. Actually I think that there is some tendency for this organization to occur. If you say "mamamama . . .", continuously to yourself, you will be able to hear a continuous tone with a repeating tone accompanying it. However, the segregation is not strong because the sounds are held together by the continuity of the fundamental frequency. We need experiments to measure the extent to which such asynchronies affect the integrity of speech signals.

The factor of asynchrony has been used to explain why, in musical ensembles, there is so little masking of one note by another. Asynchrony has similar effects in speech. Scheffers made an interesting observation when he was in the process of designing his experiments on the segregation of two synthesized vowels by differences in fundamental frequency. (We discussed these experiments earlier.) He noticed that if the target vowel started some tenths of a second later than the masking vowel, the recognition of the target was virtually as good as it would have been in the absence of a second vowel.[731] Furthermore, the ability to recognize it no longer depended upon the differences in fundamental frequency. It is interesting to compare these results with conclusions drawn by Rasch on the asynchrony of musical tones.[732] He attributed the value of asynchrony to the brief opportunity for the auditory system to hear the target unaccompanied by the masker. This would not account for any advantage of turning the target on second; yet Scheffers found such an advantage with vowels. His result resembles that of Kubovy, who found that changing the intensity of a component tone inside a mixture caused that tone to be perceptually segregated from the mixture.[733] In natural speech such sudden changes of energy would occur at the beginning of syllables such as "ba" or "ga", making such syllables resistant to masking.

Earlier in this chapter, we discussed the work of Darwin and his colleagues on the segregation of a pure tone from a vowel spectrum with which it was mixed. We saw how the auditory system could use the harmonic relations between the tone and the spectrum to decide whether they should be segregated. The same research showed that the system could also use the asynchrony of the onsets of the tone and vowel.[734] The added pure tone was made to coincide exactly with one of the harmonics of one of the formants in the vowel spectrum so that the only factor that allowed the auditory system to segregate the tone was its asynchrony from the rest of the harmonics. The results showed that when the tone was added synchronously with the rest of the harmonics, its energy was incorporated into the perceptual estimation of the frequency of the formant. If it started earlier it was increasingly rejected as its asynchrony became greater and greater, until at an asynchrony of about a quarter of a second, its energy had no effect at all on the perception of the vowel.

The effect of asynchrony can also be viewed as sequential capturing of the part of the tone that is mixed with the vowel spectrum by the part that precedes the spectrum. This perspective is more obvious when a silent gap is left between an earlier portion of the tone and the tone-vowel mixture. Then we can think of the earlier part of the tone as a captor analogous to the captor tone in the experiment by Bregman and Pinker discussed extensively in chapter 3. In the research of Darwin and his co-workers, when a 1-second captor tone preceded the tone-vowel mixture, its effect depended on how close it was in time to the mixture. When it was continuous, the extra sound was rejected completely and, at the other extreme, when it was separated from the mixture by a 300-msec silence, it had no ability to capture the added tone out of the mixture. An intermediate separation gave intermediate results.

If a sequence of captor tones preceded a short tone-plus-vowel mixture, the capturing became greater as the number of capturing tones was increased and was also improved if the tone sequence continued after the vowel. Capturing was also found when the preceding and following tones could be grouped with the tone in the mixture to form a sequence that descended smoothly in frequency. But it was found that it was not the trajectory itself that was responsible for the capturing, but merely the fact that the two tones that immediately preceded the mixture were near in frequency to the target tone.[735]

A first attempt to explain these results might be to argue that the preceding tone had habituated the auditory system and made it less sensitive to that frequency. The experimenters pointed out that this theory could not account for a second observed fact. When the tone started at the same time but ended later, it tended again to be rejected from the spectrum of the vowel. Although this offset effect was not as strong as when the asynchrony was at the onset, the fact that it occurred at all is not explainable by a habituation theory. Incidentally, this asymmetry between onset and offset asynchrony is not unique to tone-vowel mixtures. It was observed earlier by Dannenbring and Bregman in the perceptual isolation of a harmonic from a complex tone.[736] Evidently although retrospective grouping effects do exist, they are weaker than forward capturing. Perhaps a better refutation of the idea that the captor tone works by desensitizing the auditory system to a particular frequency is that the tone that is part of the mixture is not heard *less well* than it would have been if it had not been preceded by a captor; it is actually heard *better*, but it is heard as a separate sound, not as an undifferentiated part of the mixture. The effects on perceived loudness are more like one would obtain by adding some energy to the target tone rather than by subtracting some.

To further demonstrate that the effect of the preceding tone is one of grouping, not habituation, Darwin and Sutherland did an experiment in which the preceding tone was itself captured into a mixture so that it was less free to group with its counterpart in the tone-vowel mixture.[737] The sound pattern that they studied was constructed as follows: There was a mixture of a pure tone (tone A) and a vowel as before, and again the tone started before the mixture. However, another pure tone (tone B), an octave higher than tone A, and therefore harmonically related to it, started at the same time as A, but stopped just as the vowel came on. It was expected that tone B, starting at the same time as A and harmonically related to it, would group with the leading part of tone A and prevent it from grouping with its own tail end that was accompanying the vowel. The tail end should then be free to be interpreted as part of the vowel. By being an octave above A, tone B would be too far away to mask or suppress it by any mechanism that is known to exist in the peripheral part of the auditory system, and therefore its effects would have to be attributed to grouping. The results showed that while the presence of tone B did not completely nullify the effect of starting tone A ahead of the mixture, it did reduce it by about a half. That is, the leading part of tone A was less able to capture its own later part out of the tone-vowel mixture. Consequently the vowel identity was more altered by the part of A that was within the vowel.

Asynchronous Onsets Can Be Integrated The experiments described so far in this section have shown that asynchronous onsets or antecedent capturing tones can promote the perceptual segregation of parts of the spectrum. This has been found in two contexts, Darwin's studies of the isolation of a partial from a formant and Scheffers' studies of the segregation of two mixed vowels. However, the findings are more complex when the experiment is concerned with the fusion or segregation of two separately synthesized formants. Cutting found that when the first and second formants of a two-formant synthesized stop consonant were played to different ears, listeners could still identify the consonant with over 90 percent accuracy, but when an onset asynchrony was introduced between the two formants, the accuracy got worse as the asynchrony increased, dropping to about 50 percent at an asynchrony of 160 msec (the chance value was 33 percent).[738] Actually this level of accuracy is not bad when you consider that the consonant is defined by a short 50-msec spectral transition at the onset of each of the formants. However, if the recognition process has to pick up the *pattern* formed between the transitions in the two formants, then, when the formants are asynchronous it must not actually fuse them, in the sense of remixing them. Instead it has to *coordinate* the evidence derived from the two. Therefore it is not certain whether the result should actually be described as fusion, in the sense of losing the identities of the individual components in favor of the computation of an emergent property of their combination. Perhaps the word coordination would be better.

The ability to coordinate the evidence from the two formants was disrupted much less by differences in fundamental frequency than by asynchrony. This should not be surprising since the temporal course of the evidence for the consonant's identity is not distorted. Indeed, we should think of the effect of asynchrony in the case of two formants as not doing its harm by damaging the coherence of the consonant but by distorting the evidence for it.

Darwin also looked at the power of asynchrony to prevent the integration of formants but did it a little differently.[739] He used vowels synthesized from three steady-state formants. The correct guessing of the identities of these vowels was only minimally affected (between 5 and 10 percent drop) by asynchronies of as much as 200 msec between the onsets and offsets of the first and third formants. Yet at the same time, these asynchronies led the listeners to report that they heard more than one sound. We saw a similar pattern of results earlier when I described Darwin's manipulation of the difference in fundamental of the different formants. The listeners heard more than one sound, but still could identify the phoneme.

In a different experiment Darwin did find an effect of asynchrony of onset on phonetic identity.[740] This occurred under conditions when four formants were mixed. The perceptual result, either the syllables "lee" or "roo", would depend upon which three formants were grouped by the auditory system. One can think of the situation as involving two syllable descriptions that compete for the formants. If Darwin lengthened the second formant so that it started 300 msec ahead of the 330-msec mixture, the auditory system tended to remove this formant from the computation of the identity of the syllable so that the description that used the other three would win. However, the removal was not complete.

Taken overall, the effects of asynchrony seem to be the same as those of differences in fundamental frequency in speech sounds. Whole speech sounds are strongly affected, with asychronous ones much easier to segregate. Asynchronous tones are separated from speech sounds more easily. Finally, asynchronies do segregate formants from one another but the segregation does not prevent the recognition of the phonemes, except where alternative descriptions are competing for the possession of a formant.

We have talked about the asynchronous onset of signals. Another acoustic phenomenon that produces synchrony of amplitude changes in the voice is the beating among its partials. If you look at a wide-band spectrogram such as was shown in figure 6.2, you see small vertical striations that occur in all voiced regions. These all occur with the same period, the period that the fundamental of the voice has at that moment. The reason for their occurrence is that in a wide-band spectrogram the filters are not narrowly tuned. Therefore, instead of responding to (resolving) separate harmonics, they respond to the interaction between the nonresolved ones. This factor was thoroughly discussed in chapter 3, so we will not repeat that discussion except to note that any ability of the auditory system to integrate spectral regions that were showing a common periodicity would contribute to the separation of mixed voices.

It should be pointed out that this striation is a good source of information about the fundamental frequency of the voice and that this can supplement the information contained in the spacing of the harmonics. The latter is useful only in lower frequency regions where (due to the structure of the human cochlea) the harmonics are more resolvable and it is easier to estimate their individual frequencies. The amplitude fluctuations that the auditory system receives, on the other hand, occur most strongly in higher regions of the spectrum where the ear's frequency resolution is much lower. We should not be misled by the fact that ordinary spectrograms show the striation equally well throughout the spectrum. This happens because the computations that create a spectrogram do not have the human ear's decreasing ability to resolve higher frequencies. Lyon's cochleagram (figure 3.10 of chapter 3) shows this change in sensitivity with frequency much better. Weintraub's computer program to segregate mixed voices uses the amplitude fluctuation to estimate two fundamentals at any given moment, one for each voice.[741] However, it does not use the actual *synchrony* of the fluctuations as a way of deciding which frequency regions should go together.

It may seem as though this amplitude fluctuation is helpful only in the voiced components of speech which are constructed out of harmonics that can beat together. However, a matching amplitude modulation can also help the listener to integrate certain kinds of noisy spectral components with harmonic ones. For example, the "z" sound in the word "zoo" is formed when the periodic variation in pressure coming from the vocal chords is used to drive air through a constriction at the front of the mouth. Therefore the "z" has both periodic properties and noisy ones. In a simple *mixture*, noisy and periodic sound tend to be perceptually segregated, but the "z" is not a mixture. The periodicity is present both in the "tone" (harmonic sound) coming from the vocal cords and the noisy sound that is created in the front of the mouth. If it were possible to subtract the harmonic sound out of the "z", a periodic amplitude modulation of the noise would still be seen, since the harmonic and noisy sounds are not simply additive but also multiplicative. In the "z", the noise has the periodicity of the vocal chords imprinted on it. This could assist in the perceptual fusion of the harmonic and noisy components of the sound. It would be important to verify the role of AM in the fusion of harmonic and nonharmonic sounds using synthetic stimuli in which the AM of the noisy sound could be controlled separately from the frequency of the harmonic sound.

To summarize, we see that correlated amplitude changes in different parts of the spectrum can contribute to the assignment of the right spectral components to a perceived source. Such correlations occur at the stopping and starting of environmental sounds and, at a more microscopic level, when groups of nonresolved harmonics beat with one another at the period of their fundamental. In speech, the period of the fundamental also affects noisy sounds that are being formed at the same time as harmonically structured sounds.

Spatial Location Cues

In chapter 3 we saw that a major factor in the segregation of simultaneous sounds is their separation in space and in chapter 5 we found that "vertical" relations in music are suppressed if the participating notes come from quite different spatial positions. The contribution of spatial separation to auditory scene analysis applies equally well to speech sounds. For example, people who lose their hearing in one ear report having a difficult time in picking out a single conversation from a mixture of conversations. The fact that differences in spatial origin can, in principle, serve as powerful information in segregating voices is illustrated in the reasonable degree of success that engineers have had in programming computers to segregate co-occurring speech signals by their locations (see chapter 3).

The research in the 1950s in which listeners were asked to shadow one speech stream in a mixture of two showed that it was enormously easier to do this when the voices came from very different positions in space. In fact, it was so easy to concentrate on one voice when they were spatially separated that often the listener did not even notice what language the other voice was speaking.[742]

Nonetheless, some later research of a more analytical type found only modest effects of spatial separation. Schubert and Schultz played pairs of voices to listeners over headphones. Each ear got both voices but the interaural phase relations for each voice were adjusted so as to suggest different origins in space. Such phase-altered mixtures were compared to simple mixtures of two voices presented to both ears. These researchers found that the ratio of intelligibility scores of phase-altered to unaltered signals ranged from about 1.00 to 2.00 and the benefit from altering the phase was stronger when the distracting sounds were broad-band noise than when they were voices.[743] There are obvious differences between the techniques of the earlier studies (one voice to each ear) that found strong effects, and the later ones (phase manipulations) that found weaker ones. Notice that the phase-altering technique does not allow the individual voice to have a different intensity in the two ears, while the presentation of a separate voice on each headphone maximizes the intensity difference. It is likely that the cocktail party effect depends in some important way on this intensity difference. One possible explanation is that the intensity difference merely improves the estimation of separate spatial locations for the various frequency components of each sound. In this case, the segregation is based on improved grouping of spectral components by spatial origin. Another possibility is that the ear nearer to the target signal (or exclusively getting it, in the case of dichotic presentation) simply benefits from the enhanced signal-to-noise ratio and the reduced masking within that ear. It is also possible that the problem with mixed voices in the Schubert-Schultz study was not primarily due to an ambiguity of spectral grouping but to a raw masking of one voice by energy in the other. Scene analysis may not be able to contribute as much in such cases.

Because so many factors could be operating when the task is to segregate signals coming from different locations, this is not, perhaps, the best test for whether or not the auditory system uses spatial location as a basis for partitioning of the spectrum. Perhaps the best test would be a situation in which differences in spatial origin *prevented* the auditory system from putting the information from different spatial locations together. Unfortunately, we rarely obtain this compelling segregation effect with speech because of the existence of schemas for the recognition of speech sounds. These schemas appear to be very powerful and not to care about the spatial origins of acoustic components.

Here is an example of the fact that spatial separation does not compel segregation of speech components. Donald Broadbent presented the high-frequency components of speech to one ear and the low-frequency components to the other.[744] The listeners fused the two signals and reported hearing only a single sound. Yet this fusion was not due to the destruction of the information that was needed to segregate the two signals. Two things point in this direction. First, there is evidence that spatial location can be assessed independently in different frequency bands (see chapter 3). Second, the signals sent to the two ears in Broadbent's experiment were in different frequency regions, making an independent assessment of their location quite possible.[745] The fusion was probably a scene-analysis decision. If you give the auditory system sufficient information that the signals at two ears derive from a common source, the brain will fuse them. In the Broadbent example, there would have been a number of commonalities: fundamental frequency, synchrony of starts and stops, and so on. Broadbent himself attributed the fusion to these. I conclude that the existence of separate spatial estimates for different frequency bands is only one factor among many that lead to the grouping and segregation of components of signals.

Segregation of Formants

Other studies have looked at the tendency of the brain to fuse parts of speech signals whose formants are presented to different ears.

James Cutting carried out a series of experiments on the fusion of phonetic information from a two-formant synthetic syllable with the formants presented to different ears.[746] It is interesting to note that this dichotic presentation still allowed the syllable to be identified between 75 and 100 percent of the time as long as the two signals were properly synchronized. This happened even when the two formants had different fundamentals.

The results were different when listeners were asked how many different sounds they heard. When the two formants had the same fundamental, they were still heard as a single sound 60 percent of the time, even though presented to different ears. This shows that segregation by location is not obligatory. But when the fundamentals were only 2 Hz apart (100 and 102 Hz), the formants were almost always heard as two sounds. Since this difference in fundamentals was only one-third of a semitone, it is unlikely that the listeners experienced much of a difference in pitch. This pitch difference alone would probably not have been sufficient to segregate the two sounds if they had not been in separate ears.

It is possible that differences in location and in fundamental frequency act in combination to produce a segregation that is stronger than the sum of the individual effects. To quote Christopher Darwin:

> . . . in speech . . . it is common to find the higher formants predominantly noise-excited and the lower ones predominantly excited by a periodic source. . . . An heuristic that grouped only harmonically related tones together would fail to include components from the same speaker for a substantial proportion of what

> is conventionally regarded as voiced speech as well as for all whisper, friction and aspiration. It is perhaps not surprising that the auditory system is prepared to tolerate differences in harmonic structure provided that they originate from a common location; and since even prolonged listening to dichotic formants on the *same* pitch failed to abolish the fused percept, the auditory system is also apparently prepared to tolerate a difference in location if sounds share a common periodicity.[747]

We must note, as we have many times before, the discordance, in Cutting's findings, between the increased number of sounds that the listeners experienced (when dichotic presentation was combined with pitch differences) and the apparent lack of effect on the identification of speech sounds. Similar effects were found by Darwin with dichotic presentations.[748] Yet even the phonetic fusion can be broken down if dichotically presented syllable patterns are repeated over and over, with the end frequency of each formant in one repetition being the same as its starting frequency in the next repetition, and with the two formants on different fundamentals in the two ears. The sequential grouping of the separate formants causes two separate streams to form, one for each ear, and the phonetic identity of the syllable pattern changes, suggesting that phonetic integration has been prevented. This happens when the two sounds are differentiated both by location and by fundamental and does not occur when only one of these factors distinguishes them.

We are led to this conclusion: if you increasingly pile up cues that suggest that the two signals that are being presented to different ears are actually from different environmental sources, the first effect is that the perceived number of signals increases, and then with more evidence, the phonetic integration is disrupted. The phonetic integration probably requires more evidence to disrupt it because of the participation of speech-sound schemas. It seems plausible that such schemas work by detecting energy in certain parts of the spectrum with certain temporal relations. If the schema that is looking for a particular speech sound is able to find the pattern of evidence that it is looking for, this may vote heavily in favor of that speech sound. The relative insensitivity of the phonetic schemas to factors such as perceived location and fundamental frequency is probably due to the fact that neither of these factors is probably used by the recognition schema since neither is involved in the definition of a speech sound. Since the time-varying spectral pattern does form part of the definition, we would expect any factor that distorted it to retard recognition. As for the links between the bits of evidence that are supplied by scene analysis, these may be decisive in governing the recognition only in competitive cases in which more than one speech-sound schema can fit the undifferentiated spectral pattern.

A striking example of the power of speech-sound schemas to integrate spectral information without the assistance of scene analysis occurred in an experiment by Scheffers.[749] Pairs of vowels, synthesized with a fixed fundamental, were presented to listeners to determine whether the difference in the fundamentals of the two vowels helped in their segregation. It did. I proposed that the difference in fundamental frequency allowed the auditory system to group the set of harmonics for each vowel and thereby "see" its spectral shape. Otherwise, I assumed, the formants from the two vowels would be grouped inappropriately to create illusory vowels. However, there was a striking result in Scheffers' experiment that opposes this idea. Even when the two vowels had exactly the same fundamental frequency and spatial location, and had synchronized onsets and offsets, they were guessed correctly 68 percent of the time.

The only explanation for this astounding success is that there must be schemas that, if activated, are capable of taking what they need from a dense mixture of sound. This should not surprise us. A similar effect was illustrated in chapter 3 in the case of phonemic restoration. A sentence, interrupted by a loud masking sound, can be heard as continuing right through the interruption even if the part of the sentence that coincides with the masking sound has actually been physically removed. I pointed out that the neural stimulation that corresponded to the missing sounds was actually present, having been activated by the masking sound. Therefore the speech-sound recognizers must have been extracting the evidence that they needed from the complex neural activity stimulated by the masking sound.

Chapter 7

The Principle of Exclusive Allocation in Scene Analysis

In a number of cases that have been discussed in chapter 6, we have seen apparent violations of the principle of belongingness. The reader may remember from earlier chapters, particularly chapter 1, that this was a principle of Gestalt psychology that I translated into scene-analysis language as "exclusive allocation." It was discussed with reference to the familiar vase-faces ambiguous figure of the Gestalt psychologists, shown in figure 1.6. When we are aware of the faces, the edge that separates a face from the vase is seen as the boundary of the face. When the vase is seen, that same edge "belongs" to the vase. It seems that the same piece of sensory evidence (the edge) cannot be allocated to both the face and the vase at the same time. In audition the principle says that if a piece of sensory evidence (such as a tone) is allocated to one perceptual organization (such as a stream), it cannot, at the same moment, be allocated to another. This principle has been found to hold true in a number of experiments; it makes it possible to capture a tone out of one stream by introducing some additional sounds with which it prefers to group.[750] If no rule of exclusive allocation existed, the tone would be able to be in both streams at the same time.

In chapter 1, it seemed as though the exclusiveness was a natural result of allocating evidence to distinct environmental causes and that unless the mixture of evidence was parsed in this way, processes of pattern recognition would attempt to recognize bundles of properties whose cooccurrence was purely accidental; they would therefore come up with chimeric percepts. Therefore, the rule of belongingness was not merely some incidental property of perception but was central to the attempt to sort evidence out.

However, in chapter 6 we have seen many examples in which some manipulation of the relations between parts of the spectrum, such as putting them on different fundamentals, had two contradictory effects: It caused them to be heard as separate sounds while at the same time they were taken in combination as specifying a particular speech sound. This discrepancy in grouping appears to violate the principle of exclusive allocation. Parts of the spectrum that were segregated by primitive scene analysis seem to have been put back together again for speech recognition. This seems to imply that the primitive processes have no real function in speech perception.

Claims and Facts about Duplex Perception of Speech

In the following pages I would like to focus on, and try to understand, one of the cases in which speech perception seems to ignore the dictates of primitive scene analysis. It has been called the duplex perception of speech (DPS).[751]

DPS was first reported by Timothy Rand of Haskins Laboratories in New Haven, Connecticut.[752] Here is a simple demonstration of the phenomenon.[753] It is based on the well-known fact that recognizable acoustic sketches of speech can be constructed from simplified sounds. These simplifications have been used to study the cues for speech recognition, much as simplified drawings have been used to study visual recognition. For example, as shown at the top of figure 7.1, the syllables "ga" or "da" can be conveyed to a listener by the use of a three-formant sound. The distinction between the two syllables can be made to depend, in this auditory sketch, on the slope of the transition at the onset of the third formant. If the transition falls in frequency as it approaches the steady state, it specifies a "d"; if it rises, it specifies a "g". Intermediate values will give a range of sounds that are sometimes heard as "d" and sometimes as "g".

Now the trick of the demonstration is to divide the signal into two distinct acoustic channels, such as the two channels of a stereophonic tape recorder. One channel, shown in the lower left panel of the figure, contains what is called the base. It contains everything but the crucial third formant transition. Alone it sounds like a stop consonant that tends to be heard as "da". The other channel, shown at the lower right, contains just the crucial formant transition. Alone, it sounds like a chirp. When the two channels are mixed electronically, the formants are integrated and the mixture will sound like either "da" or "ga", depending on which formant transition is used.

The duplex percept occurs when the formant transition is sent to one ear of the listeners and the base to the other. At the ear that receives the base, a syllable is heard that sounds like "da" or "ga", depending on which formant transition has been sent to the opposite ear. This suggests that the two channels have been integrated as in the case of electronic mixing of the channels. However, at the ear that receives the isolated formant transition, a chirp is heard, just as if the formant transition had been presented in isolation. This suggests that

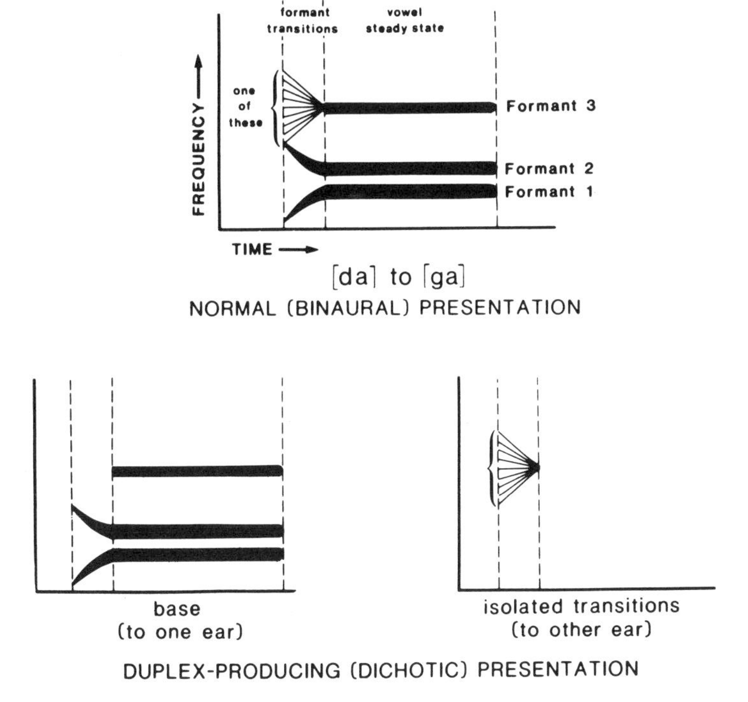

Figure 7.1
Schematic representation of a stimulus pattern used to generate duplex perception by Mann, Madden, Russell, and Liberman (1981). Top: the formant pattern used to represent "da", "ga", or sounds in between them. Lower left: the base. Lower right: the consonant-distinguishing formant transition. (From Liberman 1982.)

the two channels have been segregated by the listeners. The duplexity about the percept is that one and the same bit of acoustic information, the formant transition, is being heard simultaneously in two distinct ways. As part of the speech sound it is signaling the distinction between "da" and "ga". At the same time it is being heard as a distinct nonverbal sound, a chirp. In other words, the rule of exclusive allocation has failed. If the rule had been obeyed, the information from the formant transition would either have been segregated from the base and heard as a separate chirp or else it would have been fused with the base to contribute to the syllable percept. It should not have contributed to both experiences at once.

Experiments have shown that the phonetic integration (integration of the formants to derive a speech sound) in DPS is really a genuine pulling together of information and not merely a case in which listeners use the quality of the chirp to guess which speech sound was the correct answer. It seems that the formant transition is integrated in exactly the same manner as it would have been if the two sounds had been electronically mixed and sent to a single ear.[754] The binaural event is being judged as a speech sound and not on the basis of its raw acoustic characteristics. For example, it is perceived categorically, as speech sounds are.

It is thought that the basic sounds of language are the phonemes. Examples include "b", "d", "a", etc. Each language is considered to have a small number of such phonemes (perhaps 20 to 30) from which larger units, such as words, are constructed. The phonemes can be thought of as categories rather than as unique sounds because there are a number of possible ways of saying each of them, yet as long as the variations remain within certain limits (called the category boundaries), the listener still hears the intended phoneme. In other words, any variations that stay within the category are unimportant for the purposes of phoneme identification. It follows, from this description, that phonemes are perceived categorically. One of the signs of this categorical perception is that when an acoustic difference between two speech sounds is crucial in placing them into different categories, it will be accurately discriminated, whereas if there is an equally large difference that does not affect the category of the sounds (for example, where both are acceptable versions of "da"), it will be less accurately discriminated.

Research of the Haskins Laboratories group has demonstrated that the perception of the speech sound side of the duplex percept (the "da" or "ga") shows this property of categorical discrimination whereas the perception of the chirp side does not.[755] That is, when the listeners are presented with the whole base-plus-transition signal but are asked to listen to the signal that sounds like a speech sound, even if the acoustic signal is intermediate between the ones appropriate for "da" and "ga", it tends to be heard as either one or the other. Furthermore, a pair of intermediate examples whose members straddle the category boundary (where one is heard as "da" and the other as "ga") will be more readily discriminated from each other than a second pair whose members both fall on the same side of the boundary (both heard as "da", for example). This will happen even though, in some raw physical sense, the members of the two pairs are equally different from one another.

The situation is different if the listeners are asked to focus on the chirps. Despite the fact that they determine whether the opposite ear's signal is heard as a "da" or a "ga", they are not, themselves, perceived categorically, but as sounds that vary continuously in quality. This shows that the speech-sound percept is processed by our speech-recognition schemas and that the chirp percept is not. The fact that the two types of percepts can exist *simultaneously* has been considered by Alvin Liberman to be of central importance. It shows, according to his argument, that the brain process that underlies the perception of speech sounds is biologically distinct from, and independent of, the processes that handle the perception of nonspeech sounds. If they were not separate modules, the argument goes, they would interact and produce a consistent percept. This argument is part of a more general one that Liberman has offered to establish that language is organized as a separate module of the brain that has only a very limited commerce with other brain modules, such as the one for general auditory perception.[756]

DPS, like the other examples of the violation of the principle of exclusive allocation, poses a difficulty for the theory of primitive scene analysis. It is obviously the primitive grouping processes that are responsible for the segregation of the chirp from the rest of the sound. Yet if scene analysis is to do any good, why does it not dictate which grouping of acoustic evidence the phonetic recognition schemas should look at?

Before attempting to deal with this challenge, let us look at some of the experimental facts about DPS. The effects of acoustic relations between the base and the formant transition have been studied. Rand, in the first experiment on DPS, attenuated the transition by as much as 40 dB and found that identification was largely unimpaired.[757] Cutting also found this insensitivity to the amplitude of the transition.[758] In addition, he found that advancing or delaying the transition relative to the base led to a gradual decline of phonetic fusion as the onset disparity increased, showing a significant decline (to about 75 percent fused responses) by 40 msec. Overall, the sensitivity to asynchrony was real enough, but not large.[759] I mentioned earlier that it could easily be explained not by assuming that asynchrony was preventing fusion but by assuming that it was simply destroying the temporal relation between the transition and the base that defines the syllable. Again a factor that is known to affect primitive grouping has been shown to have little effect on phonetic integration.

Cutting also studied whether the phonetic fusion was affected by the tuning between the transition and the base. Recall that the transition and the base are both composed of sets of harmonics, not individual ones. In the formant transition, it is not the frequencies of the individual harmonics that are changing. The transition is a change in the position of a spectral peak, that is, a change in which harmonics are being strengthened or weakened. The frequencies of the harmonics can be held constant through formant frequency changes. Cutting compared cases in which the harmonics in the base were related to either the same fundamental (F0) or to different ones. There was no effect on phonetic integration. However there was also no affect on whether the listeners heard one versus two sounds (primitive segregation). This seems to contradict earlier findings that the fusion of two formants is affected by whether or not the formants are on different fundamentals.[760] A hint as to why F0 is unimportant may be found in Cutting's observation, in the same series of experiments, that if an entire formant for a syllable is fed to one ear, and not just the initial transition (the so-called chirp), the fusion of that formant with another presented to the opposite ear *is* affected by the difference in F0. Probably the reason for the discrepancy lies in the fact that the auditory system does not get a good estimate of fundamental frequency from the transition, either because it is too short or because it is sweeping across the spectrum too quickly. There is evidence from other research that the longer a synthetic formant is, the more its F0 will affect its grouping with other spectral components.[761]

When we look at figure 7.1, we see that the end of the formant transition of the chirp stimulus joins up in frequency with the beginning of the third formant (F3) in the base stimulus. It is tempting to think that this continuity is somehow involved in the ability of the brain to integrate the transition and base to derive a speech sound. Repp and Bentin have shown that this is not so.[762] They found, for instance, that it was possible to replace the chirp (the normal formant transition derived from analyses of the spectrograms of real speakers) with a simpler sound and still obtain the distinction of "da" versus "ga". They showed that they could use a 50-msec steady-frequency segment of a formant at 2,800 Hz instead of the descending "d" transition, and a steady 1,800 Hz segment instead of the rising "g" transition. Neither of these joined up in frequency with the remainder of F3 in the base. Yet this spectral discontinuity did not prevent the listeners from distinguishing between "da" and "ga", although it did reduce their accuracy a little. The loss of accuracy was small enough that we can blame it on the distortion of the normally found information about the consonant's identity rather than on a failure in integration, since the deterioration was found even when the steady segment and the base were presented to the same ear.

In another variation, they included the transition in one ear but deleted the remainder of the third formant from the base in the other ear, so that, again, there could be no spectral continuity across the ears in the third formant. This, too, had little effect on the listener's ability to discriminate "ga" from "da". We see from the results of this experiment that the spectral continuity of the transition with the base is not a prerequisite for obtaining the phonetic integration.

Despite all these negative findings there is one suggestion that primitive grouping is playing some role. Cutting did find that the phonetic fusion that he obtained with the dichotically presented transition and base was not as great as when he mixed them electronically and presented the mixture to the two ears (81 percent versus 100 percent). Data obtained by Repp and Bentin seem to support this result by showing that if the transition in the electronically mixed presentation is protected from being masked by the lower formants by starting it 20 msec before the base, this form of presentation allows perhaps 10 percent better recognition of "da" and "ga" than the dichotic presentation does.[763] These results seem to show that the phonetic integration *is* being affected by the spatial cues that specify separate sources of sound, but not to a large degree.

The general drift of these findings is that the phonetic integration of the chirp and the base does not depend very much on variables that affect primitive grouping. This could have been surmised from the basic fact that the dichotically presented signals were heard as two and not as one. This means that the factors involved in primitive grouping supported the segregation of the two sounds, and yet, at the same time, the integration of the evidence to support the derivation of a single speech sound occurred. The research on the effects of F0, asynchrony, and spectral continuity support the same conclusion about the relative insensitivity of the speech sound integration to the primitive factors.

There is an important fact about duplex perception that Liberman and his associates have stressed: It is precisely *duplex*, not *triplex*.[764] To see why this is important, let us examine one possible account of the recognition process. The primitive scene-analysis processes seemed to be indicating that there were two sounds, one on either side of the head. Quite separately, and in addition to this, the speech-perception process found it convenient to integrate the two pieces of evidence and assign a phonetic identity to their combination. Why could we not have experienced three aspects to the sound: a chirp, clearly on one side; the base, heard as it would be without the integrated formant transition, clearly on the other side; and an awareness that the two together made up the syllable "da"?

This organization would not have violated the principle of exclusive allocation. Let me explain why. Our perception of the world is at multiple levels. We can see a finger shape as a part of a hand, and at the same time see it as part of the body of a woman. The body, in turn, can be seen as one part of a couple that is dancing, the couple being perceptually segregated from other nearby objects by their proximity and shared motion. We often refer to such an organization of parts within parts as a hierarchy. It is not a violation of any rule of exclusive allocation to say that a finger shape is part of a hand and part of a body at the same time, although it would be more correct, perhaps, to say that the finger shape is allocated to the hand, and the thing that gets allocated to the body is the hand as a whole, rather than the smaller finger shape.

The same argument can be applied in audition. It would not necessarily be contradictory to hear two sounds, one on each side of the head, as well as perceiving the two of them as constituting an entity at a higher level, a syllable of speech. There would be no organizational conflict in this case. Of course the chirp would be heard as a separate sound and as part of a larger entity at the same time, but this would be consistent with how we always experience things that fall into hierarchies.[765]

However, the duplex percept is not hierarchical. The chirp is simply not experienced as a part of the speech sound. Our experience attributes the entire responsibility for the "da" or "ga" to the base. This misattribution has to be accounted for; it cannot be explained by the idea of hierarchy.

Liberman views the violation of exclusive allocation, and the fact that this violation is also inconsistent with a hierarchical organization, as evidence that two systems of organization must be operating at the same time. He refers to these as two modes of perception, a phonetic mode and an auditory (or non-speech) mode.[766] I prefer to name them differently. Modes are thought of as alternatives to one another. However, I think of "phonetic" and "auditory" not as alternative modes of perceiving but as aspects of the mental description (the percept) that are conceptually distinguishable from one another and that result from different description-building processes. When a sound is heard as a speech and a nonspeech sound at the same time, the phonetic aspect of the percept is contributed by schemas that incorporate our knowledge of speech, and the sounds-in-space aspect is contributed by primitive scene-analysis processes. What I have described as the sounds-in-space aspect of the representation is identical to what I have referred to throughout this book as the perceived streams. They represent sounds as distinct in some basic way (not always spatial) from other ongoing sounds. The streams are the perceptual objects to which other attributes, such as "voice" and "da", cohere. In DPS, the "voice-saying-da" description is given to only one of the two perceived streams, not to a higher-order combination of the two.

I will take no position on another claim of Liberman—that the ability of two systems to act at cross-purposes shows that they are biologically distinct and that the speech process, in particular, is an innate and distinct mental module. Like Liberman, I view the speech recognition schemas as distinct from the primitive organizational processes, but for my purposes it is sufficient to note that they deal with different regularities. For the purposes of the present discussion, it is not necessary to speculate on how this specialization is achieved biologically, whether by innate "wiring" or through learning. Primitive scene analysis deals with those regularities that arise in an auditory input when a subset of components have arisen from a single source of sound with its own particular spectral properties and spatial location. Its result is to link the components into wholes. Phonetic schemas, on the other hand, deal with the regularities in the structure of speech sounds, and one of their results is to assign a phonetic identity to a sound.

The advantage of having an architecture in which different subprocesses can specialize in detecting different regularities in the sensory input is that each individual process is not required to know about all the regularities in the world. Knowledge can be specialized and modularized. The overall product of the activity of these subprocesses is a mental description of the world in which regularities of different types are coordinated with one another. "Coordination" is the key word here. For example, in the overall description, a "da" is not just a speech sound; it usually has a pitch, a loudness, and a spatial origin, is spoken by a particular individual, is possibly humorous, and so on. How the different aspects, calculated by specialized systems, are coordinated and made into a consistent whole is the ultimate mystery of human perception. It is the appropriateness of the coordination that seems to fail in the case of duplex perception, as it seems to do in many other illusions. I have discussed this problem of coordination in more detail elsewhere.[767]

Having said all this, my final point will be that many of the specialized schemas must surely be innate and others learned. The one that uses cross-ear comparisons of time of arrival and intensity to infer the spatial location of sounds is probably innate. The ones that use the shapes of black marks on a white page to infer that one is reading a description of mathematical concepts are obviously learned. Yet the unlearned ones, such as spatial localization, may be capable of profiting from learning; for example, since the head of a child grows, the interaural phase difference that specifies a particular angle of incidence of the sound will also change, and some learning mechanism must compensate for the change. Conversely, the learned schemas must obviously make use of primitive unlearned abilities (or else there would be nothing from which to build up the learned abilities). Therefore it is difficult to draw absolute distinctions between native and learned capacities. Fortunately it is not always necessary to do so in order to carry out a functional analysis of perception.

I will not address Liberman's claims about the biological specificity of phonetic perception; they lie outside the scope of this discussion. However, the DPS illusion and the other examples of violation of exclusive allocation present a serious problem for the idea that general purpose scene-analyzing processes make it easier for us to deal with all sorts of pattern recognition, even speech. One might think that the recognition occurs as a sequence of events: first the primitive process does some grouping; then it hands the groups along to a specialized recognizer, such as a speech system. Duplex perception shows that this idea is too simple-minded.

Indeed, a paper by Mattingly and Liberman has argued that the order of processing is exactly the reverse: the speech system gets the acoustic information first, extracts what it needs, then passes on the signal, with the speech-relevant components removed, to the nonspeech processes.[768] That is, after certain acoustic components are interpreted as speech sounds, they are made unavailable to further processes. This view of the order of processing has been named the "preemptiveness" of speech by the authors. The speech interpretation process is viewed as leaving a residual, a process that I have hypothesized earlier cannot be carried out by schema-based processes.

There is a phenomenon, observed at Haskins Laboratories, that has been interpreted as supporting the preemptiveness argument.[769] First a device called the Pattern Playback was used to convert a schematized drawing of a speech spectrum into sound. It sounded (more or less) like the sentence "Alexander's an intelligent conversationalist." Then the researchers tried to disguise this sentence by adding to the drawing extra streaks at different angles so that the original patterns that represented the speech were hard to see. When the altered drawing was again passed through the Pattern Playback machine, two things were heard, a phonetic message much like the original one and a set of whistles and chirps. It might be argued that the speech recognition took what it needed out of the spectrum and the residual set of disconnected formant transitions was interpreted as nonspeech sounds. (Another interpretation, of course, is that the rules of camouflage are different in audition and vision and that primitive processes isolated many of the added formants.)

There is one difficulty with this theory. The duplex perception phenomenon argues against the ordering of speech and nonspeech recognition in the way proposed by the preemptiveness idea just as strongly as it does for the reverse ordering. That is, in DPS, since the speech system accepts the formant transition as defining a speech sound, then it should become part of the same package as the base. No chirp should be heard because the formant transition has been "used up" as part of the speech. We must assume a using-up process of this type if we are to explain the extra chirps in the "Alexander" sentence as being the ones that were not used to derive the phonetic sequence. Indeed, DPS argues against *any* absolutely fixed order in which primitive scene analysis and speech processing affect the bundles of evidence that the other can get access to. If scene analysis controlled the bundling, the phonetic integration in DPS would be impossible, and if speech did, only one sound would be heard.

Problems with the Claim that Speech Is Exempt from Scene Analysis
Perhaps a weaker version of the Haskins claim would be that the two systems act concurrently and independently and that the speech recognition system is exempt from any constraints imposed by primitive scene analysis. We can call this the "independence" theory. It would explain why the primitive perceptual segregation of formant transition from base in DPS did not prevent their integration to form a speech sound. A number of arguments make this theory not very appealing.

The first can be called the argument from design. Given that evolution has designed the human auditory system, it seems that it would be unwise to have designed it in the way proposed by either the preemptiveness theory or the independence theory. In support of the preemptiveness design, Mattingly and Liberman have contended that human utterances constitute a class of sounds of primary importance to our species, that we must be able to filter them out from other sounds with which they are mixed, and that our built-in speech knowledge ought to be used for this purpose.[770] There is no doubt that we do use it in this way. We can even carve speech sounds out of solid noise as we do in phonemic restoration. But this ability need not be purchased at the cost of jettisoning primitive grouping processes.

A speech message comes from a distinct spatial location; its components are, to a large degree, harmonically related; they tend to be spectrally and spatially continuous over time; they tend to start and stop together, change in frequency together, and so on. If speech perception were to do without the help of primitive grouping factors, it would have to segregate speech sounds without the use of these factors, with a resulting loss in power, or else would have to have its own skills in dealing with them, separate from those of the primitive processes.

The latter solution would not be any better than accepting the aid of primitive scene analysis, because the problem of order of computation would just be moved into the interior of the speech system. This system would still have to determine an appropriate order for the application of the two kinds of constraints on the interpretation of incoming auditory events: constraints found when sounds are produced by coherent events, and those that are found when they are speech. It would still need specialized processes (such as pitch detectors and binaural asynchrony detectors) to detect different properties. There is no biological advantage in replicating all these processes for the private use of the speech system, and it violates a good architectural principle for systems: that each specialized process should not have to know everything that all the others know. (Imagine a large city where the mayor had to know the detailed job of every civic employee.) The processes that encapsulate the knowledge concerned with the structure of the speech signal should not have to know how to carry out a spatial analysis any more than our ability to judge whether an act is friendly has to do so. Yet it should be able to benefit from the results of those analyses.

Perhaps the following account of our complex perceptual system might come close to the truth. It seems likely that as a particular act of perception unfolds, specialized processes carry out their separate computations and then coordinate their results in a way that benefits from their consistency. The separate computations are used to build highly articulated descriptions of events. For example, a sound is heard as a voice, as being at some location, as saying a certain word, and as a person sounding earnest, and these are all part of a single, but highly articulated, description. The architecture of a system capable of flexibly building up such descriptions is still an utter mystery, but the solution will not be obtained by having the separate knowledge sources refuse to cooperate.

A more down-to-earth argument against the idea that speech recognition is exempt from primitive scene analysis is that several pieces of empirical data show that it is not. We have only to point to the research done in Darwin's laboratory that was reviewed in chapter 6. It has shown that when phonetic interpretations are set into competition the winner can be determined by the pattern of formant grouping that is imposed by scene analysis. It has also shown similar influences on the grouping of partials in a spectrum to derive a vowel identity. We have also reviewed cases of differences in fundamental frequency helping us to segregate vowel sounds, continuity of fundamental frequency helping us to integrate a succession of vowel sounds, and a host of other illustrations of the roles of primitive scene analysis in dealing with mixtures of speech sounds. The occasional failure to find a clear effect of these grouping principles should not blind us to the successful cases. We should not focus narrowly on the apparent failures of the primitive processes to impose an exclusive allocation of components that speech recognition cannot override. Instead, we should try to look more closely at the cases that do and do not show this pattern of results, in order to come to a better understanding of the interaction between the analyses of auditory input as sources in space and as speech.

When Is Exclusive Allocation Violated?

Examples Involving Speech

First we must look at the relation between violations of exclusive allocation and the existence of spatial disparity between parts of the signal. We will find that such disparity is neither a necessary nor a sufficient condition for the violation.

It is not automatically true that spatially separated acoustic stimuli will be segregated for purposes of hearing sounds in space but integrated phonetically. The earliest experiment on the splitting of formants between the ears reported by Broadbent and Ladefoged found that when the fundamental of the two formants was supplied by the same generator so that the same natural pitch contour was followed by both of them, not only was there phonetic fusion, but the sound was heard in one place.[771] Apparently when the cues for fusion are strong enough, both spatial and phonetic fusion can take place. But even this earliest study noticed that when the fundamentals were supplied by different oscillators, either on a different fundamental or even following the same natural F0 contour, but shifting randomly in and out of phase, the two formants would segregate spatially. These observations show that before the auditory system will impose a definite segregation of dichotically presented formants, it needs additional information favoring segregation (such as different fundamentals or shifting phase relations) to supplement the fact that the two formants are presented to different ears. This requirement is necessary even for the purposes of deciding the number of sounds and their locations. Apparently, starting and stopping together tend to promote fusion despite the dichotic presentation. In DPS, the isolated formant transition is both short and rapidly changing; this probably prevents the binaural system from obtaining a good estimate of its fundamental so as to bind it to the base as a single sound.

In chapter 6, we noted Darwin's finding that presenting formants dichotically can reduce their ability to unite to form a speech sound if they are presented over and over in a cycle and their trajectories are continuous across cycles. The fact that it takes a number of cycles for the segregation to occur shows that the failure to unite does not result from the fact that the stimulus does not sound like speech (although this may contribute), but from the building up of grouping tendencies according to the principles discussed in chapter 2.

It seems that when there is strong evidence pointing to either integration or segregation, it governs both the sounds-in-space and the phonetic interpretation, but when the evidence is not of high enough quality, the two interpretations can be inconsistent.

Another important point is that separation of spatial origin is not necessary to obtain DPS. Darwin presented groups of formants that together formed speech in a mixture that was presented to both ears over headphones.[772] When each formant had a different fundamental (F0), listeners often reported the presence of more than one sound but, at the same time, integrated the formants to derive the speech sound. The sounds-in-space segregation is quite strong with a small difference (under a semitone) in F0, whereas a larger difference (four semitones) is needed before there is a maximum effect on phonetic identification.[773] This means that when F0 differences are either very small or very large both the phonemic and the sounds-in-space interpretation may be affected in a consistent way, but that at intermediate differences the effects may be inconsistent. (This constellation of results is found when there is competition among phonetic schemas.)

When segregation occurs by F0, assisted by differences in spatial origin, the speech sound tends to be heard as coming from the lowest formant or set of formants that is heard as a separate sound (the one in the lowest frequency band, not the one with the lowest F0), probably because this sound is the one that, when played in isolation, sounds most like speech. In the classic DPS demonstration of the Haskins group, it is the base that occupies the lower spectral region.

The speculation has been offered that the isolated formant has to be of short duration in order to yield duplex perception.[774] This is perhaps encouraged by the fact that in the Haskins DPS example the isolated formant is just a short transition. However, it appears from the work of Cutting and of Darwin and his associates that when F0 differences are added to spatial differences the isolated formant can be long. Indeed, when its F0 is different, the longer it is, the better it seems to contribute to segregation.

DPS can also be obtained by manipulating the relative onset times of synthetic formants that are mixed and presented to both ears. If the formant transition precedes the base, it is heard as an isolated non-speech event *and* it contributes to the phonetic identity of the consonant.[775]

Another manipulation can also produce duplex perception without any spatial separation of the sounds. The formant transition in this example is replaced by a sinusoid whose frequency glides along the path of the formant. At low intensities the frequency transition contributes to the perception of either "da" or "ga" but is not heard as a separate sound. At higher intensities, it is heard as a separate sound but still continues to contribute to the perceived distinction between "da" and "ga".[776] The authors argue that the speech recognition system needs only a little bit of the signal to form the phonetic percept. When more than this is present, the remainder is heard as a nonspeech sound. This is another phenomenon that is thought to illustrate the preemptiveness of speech perception.

Apparent violations of exclusive allocation can be produced for synthetic vocal sounds in ways other than by causing formants to segregate from one another. McAdams has described a synthetic voice-like sound created by Alain Louvier at the Institut de Recherche et Coordination Acoustique/Musique (IRCAM) in Paris.[777] The sound was created by first analyzing natural speech by computer and then resynthesizing an altered version of it. There is a method for analyzing speech that separates the contribution of the source vibration (the buzzing of the vocal cords or the hissing of air in parts of the mouth) from the contribution of the filtering that is imposed by the changes in the resonances in the vocal tract that occur during speech.[778] The pattern of resonances is treated mathematically as if it were a complex filter. This source-vibration-plus-filter analysis of speech is very useful because it makes it possible to resynthesize the speech in a way that changes some, but not all, of its properties. For example, the source vibrations that normally come from the vocal cords can be changed without changing what the filter is doing. This will change the pitch or quality of the voice without changing the identities of the speech sounds. For example, if the vocal cord vibration is replaced by aspiration noise of the type found in the sound "h", a spoken word will change into a whispered word. Louvier, rather than replacing the source vibration by a simple sound, replaced it with complex mixtures of sounds. This gave the effect of a voice with several distinct components in it, but saying recognizable words. The voice was multiple but the words were coherent. It is not clear whether this is an example of duplex perception or of what

Liberman calls triplex perception (hierarchical organization). It all hinges on whether all the unfused sounds were considered part of the voice. Hierarchical perception in this case is not hard to imagine. Probably if you could get a baritone and a soprano, each singing a different pitch, to synchronize their articulation of identical words with an inhuman precision, you could obtain the sense of a single stream of speech generated by more than one stream of pitch.

Earlier, I proposed the idea that speech and nonspeech are not separate modes, in the sense of being alternatives to one another, but are processes that recognize different aspects of sound so as to build a description that contains all of them. I am reminded of an engaging example of a sound that had both speech and nonspeech properties at the same time. As a boy, I used to hear a radio commercial put out by the Bromo-Seltzer company. It consisted of a commercial message "spoken" by a steam powered train. First the whistle called out a slogan and then the name of the product was repeated over and over by the sound of the steam engine as it picked up speed. The sound of a train was perfectly represented and so were the words. I presume that it was done by recording the train sounds, and then piping them into the vocal tract of a person while the words were being mouthed. The effect was the same as in the IRCAM example, the glottal pulse of the speaker being replaced by an arbitrary sound. The result was that listeners heard this as an environmental event (a train starting up) and a verbal message at the same time. The effect was not hierarchical, in the sense of sounds distinct at one level combining to create a voice at a higher level. Rather the hierarchy was upside down. A single sound provided the acoustic evidence for two higher-level descriptions, a train and a voice. This example shows that many kinds of relations, not just hierarchical ones, can be created between verbal and nonverbal components in our mental representations of events.

Multiple Allocation of Evidence with Nonspeech Sounds

The violations of the rule of exclusive allocation that I have presented so far all involved speech. It is important to ask whether speech perception is always involved when such violations occur.

Music There is evidence that multiple allocation of evidence also occurs in music. An experiment was carried out on duplex perception of musical sounds by Richard Pastore and his colleagues in Binghamton, New York.[779] Dichotic presentation of musical tones was used. The intention was to induce a duplex percept in which a full chord was heard at one ear while, at the same time, one note of the chord was heard at the second ear. The listeners were asked to decide whether they were hearing a major or a minor chord. The two types of chords share two notes, the tonic and the fifth. These two were always presented together to one of the listener's ears. Listening to that ear alone, the listener could not tell whether the chord was major or minor. Major and minor chords differ in the middle note of the chord, with the major chord containing a major third and the minor chord a minor third. This distinguishing note was sent to the second ear. Many of the listeners reported hearing a complete chord (major or minor as appropriate) in one ear and, in addition, a single note in the other. Judgments of the chord and of the tone showed different patterns of accuracy, as in the examples of DPS.

This experiment was replicated and extended by Collins.[780] Her subjects were all trained music students. In addition to judging the type of chord that was presented, they also had to report how many notes had been presented to each ear. With the standard dichotic form of presentation, only 3 out of 30 subjects reported duplex perception. In a second condition the starting time of the distinguishing tone was advanced or delayed relative to the other two tones. Synchronized presentation improved judgments of minor/major. Asynchrony increased the overestimates of the number of notes but did not alter the fraction of the overestimates reported as duplex. Only 5 out of 20 subjects in this condition consistently reported hearing 4 notes in a duplex way.

In the two experiments on the duplex perception of musical tones, results were not always consistent, but there were, in both cases, a certain number of listeners who heard the duplex percept. I do not think the exact numbers matter. Perhaps they depend on acoustic factors such as the exact nature of the tones that were used (for example, the sharp attacks of the recorded piano tones used by Pastore and co-workers). Whatever the case, we can still conclude that some listeners under some conditions will violate the rule of exclusive allocation of evidence when faced with conflicts in the cues for the grouping of musical stimuli.

The idea that we can consider these musical examples as duplex perception has been criticized by arguing that the listeners were hearing the tones in a hierarchical manner, two tones at one ear forming one stream, the tone at the other forming a second stream, and the two streams, taken together, as defining a chord.[781] But to offer this explanation is to simply assert that either the researchers were misrepresenting their findings or the listeners could not describe what they were hearing. Pastore and his colleagues say "All of our subjects reported hearing a single note in one earphone and a complete musical chord in the other earphone."[782]

Perhaps those who have offered this criticism have been led to their interpretation by the fact that in normal listening there is usually an important difference between the perception of a syllable and the perception of a chord. Both involve the integration of the properties of acoustic components. However, when the individual notes are integrated to perceive the chord, you can still hear the individual notes if you listen carefully enough. This is probably due to the fact that three fundamental frequencies are detected. The situation with syllables is different. Listeners are not usually able to perceptually pick out the individual formants of which it is formed. It is true that they can be helped to do so by special tricks, such as the playing of an isolated formant just before playing the complete speech sound. However, in the normal occurrence of speech, the syllable is experienced as a single integrated sound. Despite these considerations, we should remind ourselves that the dichotic listening situation is highly unnatural and could well have evoked a true duplex perception of chords.

Accepting the possibility that chords can be heard in a duplex way, what sort of perceptual conflict might caused this experience? Those who argue that DPS is due to the conflict between two biologically distinct modes of auditory perception (speech and nonspeech) could argue that the conflict in the musical case is between a biologically distinct musical mode that was trying to integrate the sounds and the primitive scene analysis that was trying to segregate them. The case for a biological specialization for music in the human brain might be supported by the observation that brain damage can produce disabilities not only with respect to speech (aphasias) but with respect to music as well (amusias). Reasoning in this way would lead us to conclude that violations of exclusive allocation would be restricted to cases in which major biologically specialized subsystems of perception are in conflict with one another.

Violations That Do Not Involve Competition among Major Subsystems
Of course the validity of this argument depends on what you are willing to count as a major specialized subsystem. To refute the idea requires cases in which the two interpretations that are in conflict are obviously not derived from different major subsystems. I am going to discuss two kinds of cases, one in which the two interpretations both lie inside the system that recognizes familiar environmental sounds and another kind where the conflict is within the scene-analysis system as it applies to simple tones.

The first case is a violation of exclusive allocation in the perception of natural environmental sounds. Carol Fowler and Lawrence

Rosenblum recorded a metal door closing.[783] Then they separated the higher frequencies from the lower ones and recorded them on separate channels. When the complete version was played to listeners, it was readily identified as a closing metal door. But the version composed of only the lower frequencies was identified as a closing wooden door. When the low frequencies were played to one ear and the high ones to the other, the listeners heard two sounds, a *metal* door in the ear that was receiving the low frequencies and a high rattling sound in the ear receiving the high frequencies. Evidently the two bands of frequencies were integrated to reconstruct the percept of the metal door and, at the same time, the higher band, taken alone, was heard as a distinct high-pitched rattle on the other side of the head.

Here we have a violation of exclusive allocation in a case in which all the percepts (metal door, wooden door, and rattle) belong within the same domain: natural sounds. It is unlikely that the human would have evolved specialized biological mechanisms for the recognition of recently invented technological artifacts such as doors. It is safe to say that general-purpose recognition processes are susceptible to duplex perception.

Violations with Pure-Tone Stimuli A second group of cases involves simple, meaningless sounds. The first example is not really about duplex perception but illustrates the creation of multiple images through an unusual use of auditory evidence. It occurs when conflicting cues for spatial localization of sounds are created in a laboratory situation. Spatial localization in the horizontal plane is largely determined by two cues. The first is the relative intensity of the signal at the two ears (intensity cue) and the second is the delay of the signal at one ear relative to the other (timing cue). Suppose we put the cues into conflict. The intensity cue is set up to specify a signal source to the left of center, while, at the same time, the timing cue is made to specify a source to the right of center. If the spatial discrepancy between the positions signaled by the two cues is not too large, the listener hears a single tone located at an intermediate position. However, when there is a large discrepancy, instead of averaging the two positions the auditory system often reports two sounds, one at the position signaled by the intensity cue and the other at the position signaled by the timing cue.[784] This generation of multiple images is analogous to duplex perception; information that is usually combined to create a single description of the sound is being separated to produce two. It is obviously not occurring as a conflict between a higher-order auditory system and a lower-order one. The conflict is between two cues (perhaps they might be called mechanisms) that are involved in the low-level process of spatial localization.

This is not a case of duplex perception. There is no single source of information, analogous to the formant transition in DPS, that is supplying all the properties for one stream as well as supplying some of the properties for a second stream. However, it is a case in which a double image is being formed on the basis of evidence that is usually used to create only one.

Perhaps a better example of the formation of extra images is one discovered at McGill by Howard Steiger in his doctoral research.[785] It again involves a conflict between two cues for spatial location. The first is a binaural cue: the fact that two identical signals are being received in synchrony at the two ears, thus specifying a tone that is in the middle. The second is a context cue: the fact that just before the current binaural input, there was a monaural tone that was very similar in frequency to the current binaural tone. The earlier monaural tone apparently sets up a tendency to hear a stream in a certain frequency range (similar to the tone) and in a similar location (at the side of the head). This expected position conflicts with the location cues set up by the binaural tone, which specify a centered tone.

In experiment 8 of Steiger's thesis, the stimulus was a rapidly repeating cycle containing a 100-msec monaural pure tone, a 100-msec binaural pure tone, and a 394-msec silence. The cycle was presented in either the order *binaural tone, monaural tone, silence, . . .* (binaural first) or the order *monaural tone, binaural tone, silence, . . .* (binaural second). The monaural tone was either near in frequency to the binaural tone (75 cents) or far from it (2 octaves). If the perception of the sequence were controlled entirely by binaural cues, the listener would hear just two tones on each cycle. One would be a lateralized tone, derived from the monaural signal; the other would occur at the midline, its location derived from the binaural signal.

There were five listeners experienced in auditory experiments, and they were asked to report on each cycle by marking what they heard on a two-by-five array of blanks on the answer sheet. The five horizontal blanks represented positions from left to right, and the upper and lower rows of blanks represented the first and second time slots in the cycle. The letters H and L, written in any of these blanks, indicated the pitch of the tone, high or low, heard in that position. Thus, listeners essentially drew a graphic representation of their percept of each pattern on time and space axes, indicating the pitch and the number of tones they heard.

The results were quite striking. For four out of the five subjects, there were conditions under which three, not two, tones were reported. These subjects reported three tones on 57 percent of all trials. When reporting three tones, the listeners almost always indicated that two of them were heard in succession at the same spatial position and that the third tone was at a different location. Three-quarters of these reports of three tones occurred when the frequency separation between the monaural and the binaural tone was small, suggesting that sequential integration was occurring by frequency proximity and that this was the factor that was competing with the binaural cues. Steiger looked to see whether it was always the binaural tone that had split to form two images. He was able to tell which one had supplied the extra tone because the monaural and the binaural tone were always at different pitches and the subjects gave a pitch label (H or L) for every tone. While it was the binaural tone that was often perceptually split (contributing two tones of the same pitch), the monaural tone could also be split to give two tones.

Although it is not clear why the monaural information should have been used in this way, the demonstration shows that in the case of contradictory information the listener may choose to resolve the contradiction by allocating the information to percepts in ways that we simply cannot predict on the basis of a simple theory of binaural perception.

An example of violation of the principle of exclusive allocation is sometimes observed when listening to the type of stimulus that was used by Pinker and myself, illustrated in figure 1.16 of chapter 1.[786] This stimulus is a cycle formed when a complex tone containing two pure tone partials, B and C, is alternated with a pure tone, A, that is close in frequency to B. Under some conditions, A captures B into a sequential stream A–B–A–B–. . . ; in other cases it does not. When it fails, the listener hears the cycle as containing a pure sound, A, alternating with a rich sound, BC. At the other extreme, when the conditions *strongly* favor capturing, the listener hears the sequence A–B–A–B–. . . as having a pure tone quality and also hears the stream C—C—C—. . . as being pure in sound. However, we have noticed that when the degree of segregation is not so strong, the listener still hears the A–B stream as pure in quality, but does not hear the C stream as being pure. It still retains much of the richness contributed by the fusion of B with C. Apparently, under these circumstances, which we might describe as an unresolved conflict between forces of sequential grouping of simultaneous grouping, we find a double use of evidence in which B's physical properties contribute to the experience of a pure tone in the A–B stream and also to the richness of the C stream.

Some of the cases of illusory continuity discussed in chapter 3 may qualify as violations of the principle of exclusive allocation. I am thinking of cases in which a sound of any sort appears to continue through a noise burst despite the fact that a segment of it has actually been deleted and replaced by the noise. The stimulation from the noise provides the frequency material for the restoration; at the same time it is heard as a noise burst. There is one uncertain point about this example, however. In some or all cases, the frequency components in the noise that are used to supply the restored material may be perceptually removed from the set that gives the noise its properties. If so, the exclusive allocation rule is not being violated.

The preceding few examples show possible cases of violations of exclusive allocation in sounds that are neither speech nor music. If any of them turns out, on further examination, to be real, we have to conclude that violations are not restricted to cases of conflict between two major biological systems of description, a general-purpose one and a specialized one.

DPS Is Not Immune from Low-Level Organizational Factors

I have been trying to pile up examples to show that the double use of evidence occurs in cases that do not involve speech. My purpose was to show that it was not true that speech and speech alone has the privilege of violating the principle of exclusive allocation. On the contrary, a conflict between two forms of primitive organization may lead to similar results. To conclude from these examples that the violation seen in DPS arises from the same causes would be to draw a stronger conclusion than is warranted. DPS could still derive from some special status of the speech mode that permits it to disregard the decisions of primitive organizations.

A much stronger argument against the idea that speech perception in insensitive to primitive scene analysis is derived from the large number of studies, presented earlier, that have shown that speech perception *is* affected by primitive grouping principles. The majority of these did not concern themselves with the transition-plus-base stimulus. Therefore, it might still be argued that this stimulus, because of some special property, allows us to see the essential fact that the speech system has a special exemption from the influence of primitive grouping. There have, however, been a few studies that have even demonstrated the effects of primitive grouping using the transition-plus-base stimulus itself.

First is the most basic factor of all, the dichotic presentation. The experiments by Cutting and by Repp and Bentin did show that the phonetic integration is made a little worse when the presentation is dichotic than when the signals are electronically mixed.

A much more direct assault was made on the integration of components in the transition-plus-base stimulus by Valter Ciocca at McGill.[787] To one ear he presented the base and to the other the formant transition signaling either "da" or "ga" (let us call the latter the *critical* transition). This gave the expected duplex effect. Then he used a sequence of formant transitions, all identical to the critical one (all sounding like chirps), and presented them to the same ear as the critical transition, both preceding and following it, so that the critical one fell into a regular rhythmic pattern with the others. This stimulus was made into a cyclic pattern in which the sequence of transitions occurred in a rhythmic pattern that was occasionally joined by the base (which occurred in the appropriate timing relation with one of them to form the syllable). The sequence of transitions succeeded in capturing the critical one into a separate stream of chirps, and markedly reduced its contribution to the phoneme identity. This worked only if the sequence of extra transitions was in the same frequency region as the critical transition. The influence of frequency proximity was a sign that the effect was due to primitive grouping. It is unlikely that the stream of added transitions had its effects simply by decreasing the sensitivity of the peripheral auditory system to the critical one, because we know from the research of Rand that as much as 30 db of intensity reduction of the transition relative to the base has no measurable effect on the phonetic integration.[788] It is improbable that the sequence could have reduced the ear's sensitivity to the critical transition by so much. This research, then, shows that phonetic integration, even with the transition-plus-base stimulus, is susceptible to the influence of primitive grouping. More generally, it shows that the speech system is not impervious to the effects of scene analysis.

Some unpublished research carried out in 1989 by Valter Ciocca at McGill also showed how scene analysis could affect DPS. Earlier observations had shown that the critical transition did not actually have to be a formant transition. A pure tone that glided along the path of the formant transition could be used as an alternative to the formant transition. It still would be integrated with the base to signal the difference between "da" and "ga". But Ciocca observed that the strength of this integration depended on the spatial location of the tonal transition relative to the base. When the two signals appeared to be coming from different locations, there was less phonetic integration than if they seemed to come from the same location. The scene-analysis explanation would say that whereas in the same-location presentation we are lacking only one of the cues that favor spectral integration (harmonicity), in the two-locations case two cues are missing (harmonicity and common spatial origin).

When we talk about a real formant changing in frequency, we are really referring to a change in the center frequency of a resonance peak in the spectrum, not the movement of any individual frequency component. The resonance peak can move in one direction while the individual harmonics are moving in another. In a natural speech sound or one that is synthesized in the usual way, even though the different formants move in different directions, their individual frequency components still continue to move in parallel (in frequency), continuing to bear a harmonic relation to a common fundamental. This harmonicity binds the spectrum together.

When the formant transition is mimicked by a tone gliding in frequency rather than by the movement of a spectral peak across a harmonic spectrum, this transition no longer maintains any harmonic relation to the rest of the spectrum. So we are missing one of the cues that favor the hearing of a single sound source. For this reason, the transition is probably on the verge of segregating from the base. When we present the base and transition at different locations, we add the additional cue of a spatial difference, causing the auditory system to definitively segregate the two sounds so that they no longer combine to specify a speech sound. This shows how the cumulation of evidence by the scene analysis system can determine whether or not a speech sound is heard.

Explanations of Violations of Exclusive Allocation

We have found that speech perception is not immune from the effects of primitive scene analysis. However, speech schemas are very powerful. They seem to have an impressive ability to put information together, even under circumstances in which primitive segregation is pulling it apart. The existence of duplex perception and other violations of the principle of exclusive allocation do not imply that speech is exempt from primitive organization. However, the apparent contradiction between the separation of the information to produce the sounds-in-space aspect of the perception and its combination to produce a phoneme tells us that something is wrong with our ideas about exclusive allocation. The next section works toward improving them.

Originally we justified the principle that properties should be exclusively allocated to one perceptual organization or another by the argument that if higher-order descriptions of environmental sources of sound were derived from mixtures of the evidence that arose from two different acoustic sources, the descriptions would be wrong. This seems like a valid argument, but perhaps it ignores an important point: the transparency of sound.

A clue to the puzzle of duplex perception may lie in the fact that sound is transparent. A sound in the foreground does not occlude a sound in the background in the same way as a visual object in the foreground occludes our view of objects behind it. This means that a region of the spectrum that is localized as being at a certain spatial position can actually bear the mixed effects of two different acoustic sources. Furthermore, the sounds at our two ears can come from the same acoustic sources.

In audition, the sensory effects of two co-occurring sounds can be described (approximately) via two transparent spectrograms that are laid on top of one another to give a picture like the one in figure 1.4 of chapter 1. Any local region of this summed spectrogram can represent the summation of properties of the two spectrograms. Even if the two ears were taken into account, so that we had a separate summed spectrogram for each ear, the local regions in each ear could represent energy from more than one source of sound. Therefore when we use the evidence from a particular region of the spectrogram in a particular ear, we cannot simply allocate it to only one of the two sounds. It should not be made totally unavailable for forming a second description. An example that seems to show that this guideline is actually followed by the auditory system is our ability to listen to a mixture of two synthesized vowels and to recognize both of them, even though they start and end together and have the same fundamental.[789]

If sounds are analogous to transparent visual objects, we should be able to find violations of the exclusive allocation of sensory evidence in cases of visual transparency. It is possible to use, as the analogy to the two ears of the DPS listener, two planes seen at different depths, the nearer plane looking transparent or having a hole in it. I have created, in collaboration with Valter Ciocca and Pierre Abdel Ahad, drawings in which different shapes are made to appear to lie on the two surfaces; however, there is an emergent figure that depends on information localized on both planes. To be similar to duplex perception, when this figure emerges it should appear to lie as a whole on one of the two planes. In our examples, it falls on the further surface.

A first example is a "ba-da" distinction in printed words. It is created by the alignment of one of the stripes of the pattern on the nearer surface with either the left side or the right side of a partial letter drawn on the further surface (see figure 7.2). The line that completes the "b" or the "d" serves that role and also appears as

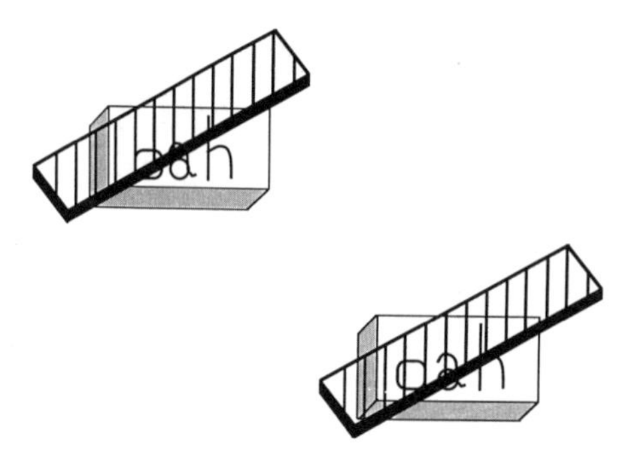

Figure 7.2
A visual "ba-da" distinction derived from information on two surfaces. The same line specifies both the vertical stroke of the "b" or "d" and a stripe on the nearer figure. (From Bregman 1987.)

Figure 7.3
Duplex perception of the subjective contours of a triangle drawn on the surface of an Easter egg. A wedge-shaped contour specifies a wedge cut out of a nearer form (disk) as well as the corner of the triangle. (From Bregman 1987.)

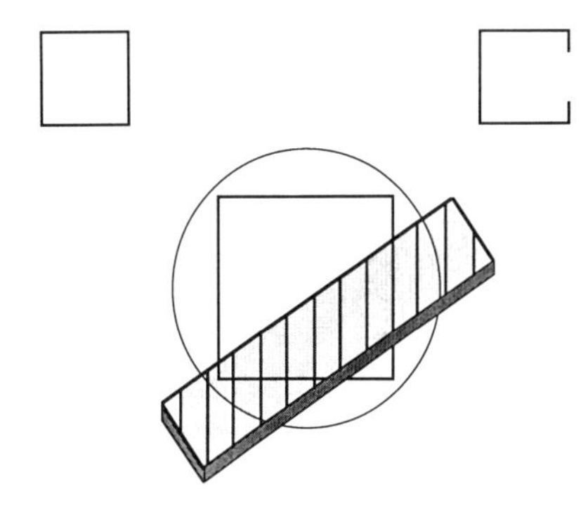

Figure 7.4
Duplex perception of a square. One of the lines specifies both a stripe on a nearer figure and part of the right side of the square (which is seen as the same as the one at the upper left). (From Bregman 1987.)

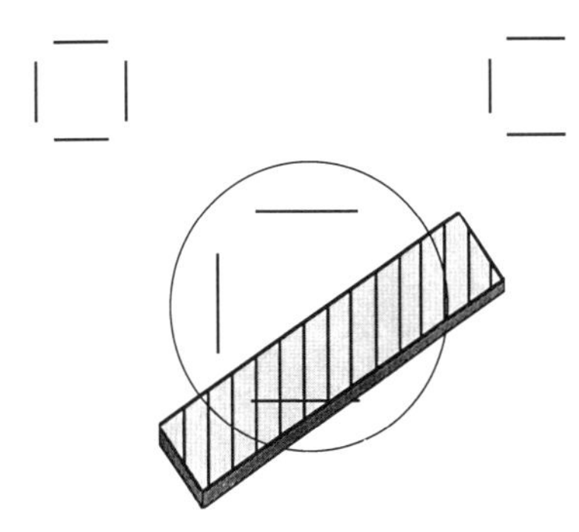

Figure 7.5
Non-duplex perception of a fragmented square. The fifth vertical stripe from the right on the nearer form could be used to complete the form shown on the upper left but is not so used. (From Bregman 1987.)

one of the stripes on the surface of the nearer form. The information is shared rather than being exclusively allocated.

A second case shows that the visual shapes that are involved need not be related to language. Figure 7.3 shows a subjective contour of the type described by Kanizsa.[790] We see a triangle lying on the surface of an Easter egg. The lines that define a wedge cut out of the circular form also serve to define one corner of the white triangle. Again there is a sharing of information.

To analyze the conditions under which the information is or is not shared, I have created two additional drawings, one showing sharing and the other showing exclusive allocation. In both figures, a striped bar seems to overlay a surface with a form drawn on it, with one of the stripes exactly replacing one of the lines of the underneath form. In figure 7.4 the line is shared and is seen as completing both the square shape and one of the stripes. The underneath form appears more like the comparison drawing seen at the upper left than the one seen at the upper right.

In figure 7.5, on the other hand, the underneath form is a square without corners, identical to the comparison drawing at the upper left. Despite the fact that the fourth line of the underneath form is actually present, we have removed it from our percept of that shape so that it now looks like the fragmented C shown at the upper right. The line is allocated fully to the striped bar. In this case exclusive allocation has occurred. The two examples are similar. Why, then, are the perceptual results so different? I think that the explanation lies in the fact that there is a strong integrative factor in figure 7.4—the continuity of the lines defining the right-hand side of the square. This binds the shared line into the square. The integrative factors are much weaker in figure 7.5.

This last example implies that before information will be shared, there must be cues that draw it into both organizations. This is the lesson of the visual illustrations.

How Unusual Is the Sharing of Evidence? In the violations of exclusive allocation that we have examined, both visual and auditory, different aspects of the same data are taken as evidence for two separate perceptual descriptions. How unusual is this? First let us look at vision. We can often find examples in normal viewing situations where a local bit of evidence (found in one region of space) can specify the features of more than one aspect of visual experience. Imagine a vase sitting on a shiny table top. Let us consider the small region below the vase where its reflection is visible. The color of that region tells the viewer about the color of the reflecting table top as well as about the color of the vase reflected in it. The boundary of the vase's reflection has a similar multiplicity of use. Its sharpness tells us how smooth the table top is and its shape contains information about how flat the table is as well as what the shape of the vase is. Jacob Beck has shown that the information for glossiness that is contained in brightness contrasts in local regions of an image of a surface will cause us to see the whole surface as glossy; this means that the information is used for specifying the properties of spatial positions other than the one containing the information.[791] The main reason that most of us have trouble drawing a realistic scene is that we are unaware of how much information is packed into local regions of the scene and of how much this evidence is used to specify different objects and properties of the scene.

We are not surprised when the same region of light is taken as evidence for both the gloss, color, and shape of a surface. We are, however, perplexed when the same bit of acoustic evidence contributes properties to our experiences of two sounds in different spatial positions. Perhaps this is because we are unaware of how often this happens in natural listening situations.

In audition, allowing one piece of evidence to contribute to two sounds can sometimes serve the useful purpose of preventing parts of different acoustical sources from merging inappropriately. To show how, let me describe an informal experiment that I did with the kind assistance of Pierre Divenyi. We used a program that he had implemented on a computer in his laboratory. This program allows a synthesized signal to be presented stereophonically over headphones in such a way that it sounds as if it were outside the head.[792] It also allows the perceived spatial origin of the sound to be controlled. We synthesized two sounds and presented one at 45° to our left and the other at 45° to our right. Each was constructed of four harmonics. The one at our left had a fundamental at 200 Hz and harmonics at 200, 400, 600, and 800 Hz. The one at our right had a fundamental of 300 Hz and harmonics at 300, 600, 900, and 1,200 Hz. All the harmonics in each sound were of equal intensity. We played each of the two notes at irregular intervals so that they never started or stopped at the same time; however, they overlapped for a substantial portion of the time.

Notice that both signals contained a partial at 600 Hz. Whenever the two sounds were on at the same time, our two ears were receiving the 600-Hz component at the same intensity and phase. According to the conventional scientific understanding of the cues to spatial location, this balance of energy should have caused the 600-Hz tone to pop out as a third sound, localized in the middle. There was no such experience. Only two tones were heard, one on each side of the midline. The absence of a centered tone was probably not due to masking, since the harmonics nearest in frequency to it were separated from it by more than a critical band.

In this demonstration, the 600-Hz tone was a good member of the harmonic series of both its parent tones, and it always went on and off in synchrony with one of them. Furthermore, at times when the opposite-side parent tone was silent, there was clear neural evidence that the 600-Hz component came from the same spatial position as the other harmonics in its parent spectrum. These factors could account for its assignment to the two different spectra at the same time.

Events that resemble this demonstration happen all the time in natural environments. Although steady-state tones are rare in nature, similar events would occur with tones that were moving slowly in frequency, such as two human voices. Different partials should briefly match and (if scene analysis were not preventing it) should pop out of the mixture. As phases changed, these disembodied sounds would go flying around the room. I have never heard this and neither has anybody whom I have asked. Instead the information from the offending partials is shared out. The matching spectral energy in the two ears that, taken alone, would specify a single sound is allocated to the two parent sounds instead. The cues that tell the auditory system that they belong to the parent spectra are the very same cues for spectral integration that we discussed in chapter 3.

A second demonstration shows how powerful the scene analysis is. Divenyi and I made a change in the signals that should have led us to hear a tone in the middle. We suppressed all the harmonics except the one at 600 Hz. As a result, the left-hand 600-Hz tone went through its own sequential pattern and the right-hand 600-Hz tone went though a different one, and they coincided at the same moments as in the previous demonstration, matched in phase and intensity. Again we heard no tone in the middle, just two pure tones, one at our right and another at our left, each pursuing its own temporal pattern. This was surprising because it violated the commonly held belief that identical energy sent to the two ears cannot contribute to more than one percept. How could the matched energy specify both a tone at our left and one at our right at the same time?

This demonstration requires a more complex explanation than the first one does to show why the balanced 600-Hz signal was assimilated to the streams at our left and right. Let us refer to figure 7.6 which illustrates the situation at a moment when the two tones overlap in time. For a certain period, there is an asymmetry of stimulation

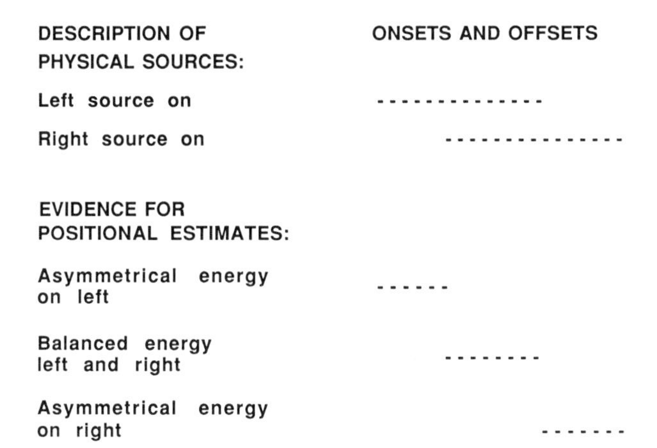

Figure 7.6
Diagram of the time relations between auditory events when two 600-Hz tones, one at the left and one at the right of the listener, overlap in time.

that is evidence for a tone on the left. Suddenly this changes to a situation in which there is a balanced stimulation at the left and right ears. Finally there is a third change to the asymmetrical stimulation that is characteristic of a sound coming from the right.

The timing of the changes at the two ears is important in telling the listener what is happening. When the left tone onset occurs, it reaches the left ear before the right. This says that the change came from the left. However, at the moment that the condition of balanced energy in the left and right ears begins (caused by the onset of the right-hand tone), there is a major cue that tells the listener that the balanced energy is a consequence of something happening on the right. As the right-hand signal is switched on, first there is an increment in energy at the right ear and then a smaller one at the left as the wave travels from right to left. This tells the auditory system that the new balanced state is the result of something that happened at the right, not in the middle. Although there is now steady-state evidence for a middle tone, the transition to that state did not arise from the middle. Eventually, when the left-hand source goes off, the ensuing decrease in energy reaches the left-hand ear first, telling the listener that the change came from the left. Despite the fact that a balanced state has ended, this ending did not originate in the center. Finally, when the right-hand tone goes off, the change reaches the right ear first. We can see how important the timing is in establishing the spatial origins of changes in the steady-state evidence. There were changes that arrived at the left ear first and some that did so on the right, but there were never any changes that arrived at both ears at the same time.

A second factor that might have contributed to the correct organization is the old-plus-new heuristic described in chapter 3. We must, however, expand this idea to include spatial information. Let me explain what an old-plus-new heuristic would mean as applied to spatial evidence. Because the auditory system is designed to deal with the mixtures that result when a second sound joins a first, whenever some change in the input evidence occurs, such as a new spatial estimate for a harmonic, it will try to interpret the new condition as resulting from some components that are continuing from the previous moment plus some new ones added to them. It will therefore try to subtract the binaural influences of the earlier sound out of the current evidence so as to leave binaural evidence that can be used to estimate the position and auditory qualities of the added sound.

In the example shown in figure 7.6, when the balanced 600-Hz energy appears, it occurs shortly after a left-of-center spatial estimate has been made for some 600-Hz energy. Therefore, when the balanced condition begins, since there is no evidence that the left-side energy has ceased, the auditory system subtracts, out of the balanced energy, sufficient evidence to account for this left-side location, leaving behind it an estimate for 600-Hz energy at a right-side location. Shortly afterward, this estimate, calculated by subtraction, is confirmed when the left-side tone goes off, leaving only the right-side tone. It is conceivable that a straight-ahead estimate is calculated as well but is discarded when it is found that the other two estimates can fully account for the balanced energy. Why would the left- and right-side estimates be treated as more reliable than the middle one? First, no other combination of two of these estimates can account for the third. Second, in our example, the left and right estimates either arise after silence (at that frequency) or disappear into silence. Being bracketed by silence indicates that a set of evidence arises from a single sound and not from a mixture. The center estimate is never bracketed by silence (at 600 Hz) either before or after it.

These last two explanations, although they were developed to explain the second demonstration, probably describe processes that are at work in the first example as well, since the factors used in the explanations would not be affected by the fact that the 600-Hz components were accompanied by other ones. We originally explained the first demonstration through the belongingness of the 600-Hz tone to the two harmonic series. To know how strong this factor is by itself, we would have to start the two complex tones at the same time.

Clearly there are a number of variations that could be tried, such as the use of nonharmonic spectra.

These experiments and others mentioned in chapter 3 show that the localization of sounds in space does not depend only on the simple binaural matches that are the subject of classical auditory theory. We have never really sat down and figured out, in a variety of real-life situations, whether the perceived localizations could really be predicted from classical theory. So we really do not know how often sensory evidence is allowed to be shared among multiple descriptions in real life. I expect that it is actually a routine occurrence. Incidentally, the experiments also suggest that the evidence on which Kubovy based his claim that location in space cannot be an "indispensable attribute" of hearing may have been too limited.[793]

A general trend can be seen to underlie all the examples in which sensory evidence is allocated to more than one description. They occur when the local evidence fits well into two different organizations. We saw this in vision, for example, in the case of the square with the transparent striped bar overlapping it. In audition, it occurred in the allocation of the frequency information when listening to two concurrent tones. However, we should not expect the factors that define "fitting in well" to be the same in vision as in audition.

Role of Schemas The fitting in of local evidence to larger descriptions can be defined by primitive grouping principles or by learned schemas. In the visual "ba-da" example, the ability of a line on the striped rectangle to complete a letter was probably affected by the familiarity of the letter. In DPS, our familiarity with the resulting syllable may have been one of the factors encouraging the integration.

Figure 7.7 shows a drawing that I used to show as an example of how the joining up of the circle's contour on both sides of the triangle allowed us to see the picture as a circle partly hidden by a triangle. Then my students became familiar with PAC-MAN, a character in a video game of the same name, who is represented by a simple disk with a wedge-shaped mouth and who eats the other characters in the game. As a result, I could no longer use the example. The partly covered circle looked too much like PAC-MAN: "It's PAC-MAN eating a triangle." Even if I drew the figure so that the triangle cast a shadow on the circle, the PAC-MAN concept was so strong that it overcame this cue. The learned schema was able to overcome fairly basic cues about objects in space.

The recognition of speech gives us another example of the use of highly overlearned schemas. We seem to be able to hear speech sounds in the most unlikely materials. For example, if you synthesize

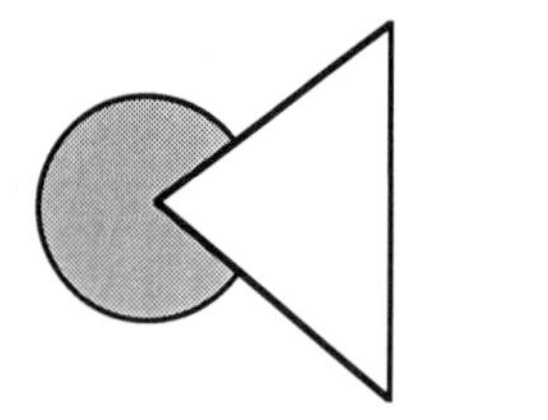
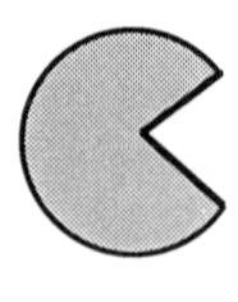

Figure 7.7
Left: PAC-MAN eating a triangle. Right: PAC-MAN alone.

speech by replacing each formant and its transitions with a pure tone that follows the frequency pattern of the formant, after a few moments listeners will begin to hear it as speech and can do reasonably well in recognizing the words.[794] It is even easier to hear it as speech if one is told in advance what the words are. This corresponds to our ability to see the pictures of familiar objects in clouds or in the scatter of tea leaves left over at the bottom of a cup, or to the tendency to interpret vague sounds as somebody calling out one's name. Years ago, B. F. Skinner reported experiments with a device called the verbal summator, which produced a burble of speech-like sound. He asked people what words they could hear in it and speculated that the strength of a listener's verbal responses could be tested by this method. (I would call them schemas, not responses.)

Two-Component Theory: Links and Schemas

We have seen, both in DPS and elsewhere, cases in which there was a sharing out of evidence. In some cases, primitive organizational processes seemed to be responsible; in others, schemas for familiar events seemed to be implicated. Generally speaking, the allocation is affected by how well parts of the sensory evidence fit into coherent patterns with other evidence. These cases imply that our earlier view of exclusive allocation was wrong. Yet we held this view for a reason. It allowed us to explain why we could capture a tone out of one stream by introducing some other tones with which it preferred to group. If no rule of exclusive allocation existed, the tone would have been able to be in both streams at the same time and no capturing would have been possible. We also saw a role for this principle in sorting out evidence for the more complex recognizers so that properties of different sources would not be used to construct a description of a single source. It is important to find a better view of the rule that explains how it makes capturing possible and helps to sort out sensory evidence while not imposing overly rigid partitions on that sensory evidence.

The principle of exclusive allocation was based on the Gestalt psychologists' demonstrations of belongingness in which a perceptual element was experienced as belonging to one perceptual organization and not to the alternative one. Yet it is possible that many of the demonstrations of this principle were in fact governed by the principle of *noncontradiction* rather than exclusive allocation. This idea can be illustrated with the help of the vase-faces ambiguous figure of the Gestalt psychologists (see figure 1.6 in chapter 1). When the boundary between one of the faces and the vase is seen as part of the face, we must actually be concluding that the face region is *nearer* to us than the other region. We are interpreting the edge as the occluding contour that one sees when a nearer object is seen against a background. If, on the other hand, we assign the edge to the vase, we are concluding that the vase region occludes the other one and is therefore nearer to the viewer. It would be a contradiction to reach both conclusions at the same time. It may be this contradiction that is being prevented and not merely the allocation of the shared edge to both regions at the same time. This may be why the shared edge cannot belong to both the vase and the faces.

What defines contradictions for our brains? Apparently certain relations (such as "A in front of B") cannot coexist with their opposites ("B in front of A") at the same time. If any of these relations is applied in the perceptual description of a situation, they will not tolerate their opposites also being applied. There are more complex connections between descriptions that have been referred to elsewhere as couplings.[795] Descriptions will be inhibited if they violate this coupling. For example, if, on the retina of a viewer, an apple projects an image that is half the size of the image of another apple, it may be that the first apple is half the size of the second or that it is twice as far away, but it cannot be both at the same time.

The requirement of not violating conditions of consistency would account for many of the visual illustrations in which the rule of exclusive allocation seems to be so strong. It is not obvious at this point what counts as a contradiction for the auditory system or what sorts of facts about the world would motivate having it treat certain descriptions as contradictory.

Perhaps we can reconcile the cases that do and do not show exclusive allocation of properties to descriptions. We need a theory that incorporates two different processes. The first, primitive scene analysis, assigns links between parts of the sensory evidence, basing the strength of a link on a competition among the cues that tell it whether the linked features derived from the same environmental event. These links describe the belongingness of a particular element in the sensory evidence to a particular stream. Because the system has evolved in a world in which no cue is utterly reliable in identifying parts of the evidence that *must* be combined, no cue is allowed to totally determine the strengths of the links. Furthermore, the links are not constrained to fall into closed patterns. That is, the data are not partitioned absolutely into disjunctive sets (although there may be a preference for such sets).

A second process builds descriptions. It decides, in an all-or-nothing manner, whether to include a particular perceptual property or subdescription in the current description. (An example of a property might be a certain level of loudness, and an example of a subdescription might be a "tone" included as part of a stream of tones.)

In sequential integration we observe often that a tone cannot be part of two streams at the same time. It is this all-or-nothing property that makes it possible to change the perception of a sequential pattern by capturing a tone out of it. The two-part theory would argue that this property is not enforced by the primitive heuristics for segregation. These only set up competing grouping tendencies that have different strengths, much in the manner described by Gestalt psychology. The description-building process is what enforces the definiteness of the resulting interpretation. The primitive process may nonetheless be a major determinant of *which* stream a given tone will be incorporated into.

Let us see whether this two-part analysis could help us to explain the decomposition of spectral mixtures. The primitive analysis process, using a large number of heuristics, such as the ones described in earlier chapters, would assign links of different strengths between spectral components. The links would have the function of suggesting possible groupings to the description-building processes. Then the latter processes would build pictures of event sequences. In the description itself, any distinct sonic event that was portrayed there would be required to have a single value on each of its essential descriptive dimensions. It could not have two different loudnesses, for example. So while the assignment of links by the primitive process might not be all-or-nothing, the creation of the final conscious description would embody rules of consistency.

Let us examine the case of the Bregman-Pinker experiment illustrated in figure 1.16 in chapter 1. In some conditions we experience two streams of sound, one consisting of repetitions of a pure tone and the other of slower repetitions of a rich tone. This involves the multiple use of sensory evidence. The same harmonic is used for the creation of a description of one of the pure tones and to contribute to the richness of the rich tone. However, the resulting description is not contradictory. Two tones with different properties are simply heard as co-occurring in time. If the same tone had two incompatible sets of properties at the same moment, that would be a contradiction; but that is not is what we hear.

The two-part account applied to vision can make sense of the Gestalt demonstrations of belongingness. The theory of primitive links would probably be able to explain some aspects of what happens with ambiguous figures of the vase-faces type. For instance, it could explain how properties of the drawing could favor one interpretation over the other. For example, one could probably bias the bounding edge to group with the region on the right side of it (possibly by making the edge more convex with respect to the right-hand region), and in this way predispose the later description-building process to interpret it as the outer edge of that surface. This biasing of the allocation of the edge to one of the components of the description would not be all-or-none, but the subsequent building of the description would be. The idea of a description-building process, governed by schemas and embodying rules of non-contradiction, would explain why we see the edge as defining the outline of only one of the forms at any particular moment, a fact that the links themselves cannot explain.

A crucial distinction has to be made between sensory evidence and perceptual descriptions. Sensory evidence is the raw input which the perceptual interpretation must account for. Perceptual descriptions, on the other hand, are the accounts themselves, built out of the qualities and patterns that populate our awareness. Sensory evidence can be multiplexed, shared out, or linked in different ways with different strengths. However, perceptual descriptions are constrained to be as definite and unequivocal as possible. By incorporating evidence in a more-or-less fashion, according to the suggestions of the primitive stage, but building definite descriptions with all-or-nothing properties, the description process makes it look as if the primitive stage had assigned properties in an exclusive manner to different perceptual descriptions. The all-or-noneness is imposed by the receiver of the suggestions, not the giver. The particular schemas that govern the building of a description at the moment that it is built will control whether a particular aspect (or part) of the sensory data will be allowed to contribute to more than one part of the description.

This account fits the example that I gave earlier, in which local bits of visual stimulation derived from a shiny table top were used to build many properties of both the surface of the table and the relation of the table to a vase sitting on it. Local bits of brightness are used for multiple purposes, but the perceptual qualities, the glossiness and the reflection, are given definite places in the descriptions that are composed.

The distinction between evidence and descriptions also fits the facts about the all-or-none inclusion of tones in streams, since "tones" are subdescriptions, not sensory evidence. Hence they are dealt with according to the all-or-none propensities of the description system. What I am saying is that *streams and the individual sounds within them are not created directly by primitive scene analysis.* Streams are perceptual descriptions. Primitive grouping merely establishes the links that *bias* the stream-building process in favor of including or excluding certain components of the sensory evidence.

When we form a perceptual representation of an event, we often have a choice about how to represent the event. For example, a timbre results (at least in part) from the partials that are present in the spectrum. However, the partials, if heard individually, would have timbres that are different from the timbre of the complex tone. Why do we hear the timbre of the overall spectrum and not the timbres of the individual components?

This is not a problem that is unique to timbre. In complex tones that have harmonic spectra we hear the pitch of the overall periodicity of the tone and not the pitch of the individual frequency components. In listening to a spoken vowel we hear the vowel quality and not the quality of individual formants. Although we are capable of hearing the properties of individual components when played alone, they are not heard when they contribute to a more global pattern.

The phenomenon is not limited to hearing. For example, when we see a long line, we are not aware of the short lines embedded in it. Many explanations have been offered for these facts. John Stuart Mill argued in the latter half of the nineteenth century that "when many impressions or ideas are operating in the mind together, there sometimes takes place a process of a similar kind to chemical combination." The qualities of the individual are lost, and "it is proper to say that the simple ideas *generate* rather than that they *compose* the complex one."[796] This notion was known as "mental chemistry."

While other theories have chosen different metaphors for this process, the problem has been widely recognized. The Gestalt psychologists just assumed that a self-organizing field that was activated by local properties would develop global properties and that the local properties would be either lost or distorted by this process. The physiological psychologist Donald Hebb thought that the global properties would emerge because the neural circuits activated by the simpler units, would, in combination, activate neural circuits that they would not do individually, and that these new neural activities would feed back and alter the pattern of the circuits activated by the simpler features of the stimulus.[797]

Stephen Grossberg, who has constructed hypothetical self-organizing neural models for pattern recognition, has incorporated the fact that the global properties of higher-level units (such as the word "myself") can suppress our awareness of properties of smaller embedded components (such as the word "elf") by means of his concept of a *masking field*, in which neural nodes that respond to "bigger" patterns suppress nodes that are responding simultaneously to the smaller components of such patterns.[798]

It is not clear by any of these accounts why this suppression does not always occur. Sometimes our awareness of embedded components is masked by the fact that the components are parts of higher-order units (such as the short pieces of wood that are embedded within a long piece) whereas other units that appear within higher-order ones are retained in our awareness as separable parts of the higher-order unit (such as fingers as parts of hands). In the example of the letter sequence that I gave earlier, hearing it as "myself" suppresses awareness of the "elf" component but not of the "self" component. "Myself" can be heard as a compound formed of "my" and "self". A full account of the suppression of lower-order units by higher-order ones would have to deal with the perception of part-whole relations. Whatever the reason, the fact that the brain often loses lower-order features when it forms higher-order ones is beyond dispute.

The connection with the notion of residuals is straightforward. The creation of lower-order units may be suppressed when the evidence that supports them is claimed by a schema that is building a higher-order unit of description.

If it is true that the acceptance of local features by a global schema makes the local properties invisible, does it make them equally invisible to all other analyses, or only to analyses of the same type as the one that claimed the local properties? If the latter alternative is true, it might explain two things. The first is that when we hear a sequence of sounds as the word "ground", this makes it impossible to hear part of it as "round". This occurs because "ground" and "round" are both recognized by schemas of the same type, namely word recognizers; so the "ground" recognizer hides the raw data from the "round" recognizer. On the other hand, recognizing the word as "ground" does not prevent us from hearing its pitch or loudness. This happens because the analyzers for pitch and loudness are not within the same competing set of schemas as the "ground" recognizer.

Let us try to account for duplex perception of speech (DPS) in the light of this two-part theory. We start by proposing that the primitive process establishes a set of links among the parts of the sensory data (perhaps one set that link right-side location estimates with the frequency region of the transition and another set that link left-side estimates with the frequency region of the base). The existence of two sets of links would be due to the fact that the sensory input from the base and transition stopped at different times, were separated in frequency, and occurred with different between-ear relations. These links would tend to bias the interpretation in favor of a description of two distinct sources. At the same time their strengths would not be strong enough to totally rule out alternative groupings. Links would also be assigned to connect the sensory inputs from the transition and the base because of their temporal proximity and because neither input has more plausible auditory material to group with. We would be left with a situation where the links tended, on the whole, to favor the establishment of two percepts but where there was some cross-linkage favoring a single percept.

So far, this is all the work of the primitive grouping process. Next, the definite descriptions of sounds in space, voices, words, and so on are built up. Both types of schemas, those that are concerned with distinct auditory sources in space and those concerned with speech sounds, operate at this level. Neither is prior. Information can be excluded from the formation of any description at this level if it does not fit appropriately into it (according to the particular rules that govern the formation of descriptions of that type). However, excluded information does not, by the fact of exclusion itself, form a connected body of data that can now be used more easily to build a separate part of the description. In terms of my earlier terminology, it does not form residuals. Connections are formed only by the primitive grouping or by inclusion *in* a schema, not by exclusion *from* a schema. Only if the set of evidence that is left out by a schema is interconnected by primitive links will it be more likely to be treated as a unit by other recognition schemas.

The chirp and the base would be heard as two separate sounds because the sources-in-space description mechanism built separate descriptions along the lines suggested by the primitive links, having no reason to do otherwise.

For the speech recognition process, the subdivision suggested by the links would be overcome by the fact that the combination of evidence from the transition and the base was acceptable as a basis for a speech sound. The right- and left-ear evidence would be put together. However, this decision by the speech recognizer would not affect those of the process that builds descriptions of sources in space, because the former has no say about the locations of sound in space, being a specialist in the interpretation of sounds as phonemes and not as sources in space.

It would be at this point that the descriptions formed by the sounds-in-space and the phonetic processes would have to be composed with one another to form a more complete description. To which sound in space should the phonetic description be attached? The choice would be between attaching it either (a) to the sources-in-space description of "low sound at the left", or (b) to the "high sound at the right", or (c) as part of a hierarchical description in which it was described as a property of the two sources taken in combination.

I do not know why the hierarchical solution is rejected and DPS occurs instead. Possibly speech-sound schemas do not normally build such hierarchies, since a particular speech sound normally comes from a single source in space, and therefore a single source tends to be chosen. The choice between the two individual sounds may be based on which package of sensory data contains most of the acoustic properties normally associated with voices. It is possible, then, that the left source description becomes the carrier of the syllable description because of its resemblance to a whole speech sound. (I am assuming here that the rules for building descriptions of speakers requires the phonetic description to be assigned to some source or other.)

This account sees two aspects of the description being created at the same level of processing: those concerned with the auditory properties of a source of sound with a spatial location and those concerned with the sound as speech. The primitive level does not build descriptions at all; it does some preliminary linking of the data, which usually has a strong influence on recognition processes but can be overcome by the latter if they have strong reasons for doing so. With normal sounds, the primitive processes and the schema-based ones will usually converge on the same groupings of evidence. A voice that says something sensible will also have a coherence in time, in space, and in acoustic properties.

When the normal constraints of the natural environment are violated, as in the perception laboratory, where the parts and properties of sound can be dissociated from one another, the usual heuristics for description formation can work at cross-purposes and odd assignments of properties to sources may occur. These do not happen only with speech. A good nonspeech example is Deutsch's octave illusion in which a tone is played at one ear at the same time as another tone, an octave higher, is played at the other. If the two tones are interchanged with one another at a regular rhythm, so that first the higher is at the left, then at the right, then at the left, and so on, many listeners hear only a single tone, but it has odd properties. It seems to bounce back and forth between the ears, governed by the position of the higher tone. But although it has the position of the higher tone it does not always have its pitch. Its pitch seems to alternate between high and low as if the listener were deriving a pitch by monitoring the sequence arriving at one ear. This erroneous assignment of a pitch to a location to derive a description is analogous to the erroneous assignment of a phonetic identity to a location in DPS.

Piecewise Verification of the Theory The theory, as I have so far presented it, has problems. These have to do with the question of the interaction of processes that build a description of sources in space and those that interpret these sources as voices saying words. How are their descriptions coordinated? Do we really know whether one precedes the other or whether they interact at the same level? Does one package the acoustic evidence such that the other can only access it in these packages?

How, in this account, are usable residuals derived? We believe that the formation of residuals is a powerful heuristic. In a mixture of evidence, if you can identify one of the components and subtract it out, it may be easier to recognize the remainder. Yet we do not know which types of processes are capable of forming such residuals and which are able to look at the residuals after they are formed. Liberman's view is that speech recognition can form residuals that the sounds-in-space system is capable of using. Earlier I offered a nonspeech example in which a continuing sound, constructed of a band of noise, was briefly replaced by a noise that had a greater bandwidth, and then continued after the interruption. We saw that stream-forming processes could subtract out part of the wide-band spectrum, hear it as a continuation of the narrower band of noise, and hear the spectral remainder of the wider noise band as an added sound that lacked the subtracted-out components. This was clearly carried out by the sounds-in-space part of the description process. Therefore we have before us claims that both speech and sounds-in-space analyses can leave residuals. There is also evidence from DPS that sounds-in-space packaging does not derail the speech-sound recognition. On the other hand, DPS also implies that speech recognition does not necessarily create packages that are compelling for the sounds-in-space description. The web of evidence is tangled and confused.

The explanation that I have offered is complex, but it is not without motivation. The reasons for proposing primitive links have been given in the earlier parts of this volume. The motivation for viewing perception as a description-building process is too lengthy to give here. I would simply refer the reader to my essay "Perception and behavior as compositions of ideals."[799]

An important question is how we can verify such a complex account. I think it would be futile to treat it as a formal theory at this point. It is really just a cluster of ideas. Therefore, research should be addressed toward verifying the component ideas. When we see which of these are right and wrong, we will be better able to assess the account as a whole.

The account that I have presented so far has many aspects, any of which could be wrong. Perhaps it would be useful to state them one at a time:

- The lowest-level analyses of auditory input are specific to local regions of time and frequency. Within such regions, such basic features as spatial estimates, periodicity, and frequency modulation are assessed.
- Primitive scene analysis involves the establishment of links between the low-level analyses that suggest which ones have come from the same acoustic source.
- Primitive scene analysis is performed on sensory input prior to the activity of more complex pattern-recognition processes.
- The principle of exclusive allocation does not describe the activity of primitive scene analysis. The latter involves competitions between groupings, but such competitions do not have to be resolved in an all-or-nothing manner.
- The complex processes that build descriptions are packaged in separable aspects called schemas. Each schema embodies knowledge of some particular kind of regularity in the sensory evidence. When it detects the sort of regularity that it knows about, it adds a representation of that fact to the description that is being built. Schemas can, as a result, also detect regularities in the descriptions built by other lower-order schemas.
- The principle of exclusive allocation refers to the way in which schemas build perceptual attributes into descriptions, not to the way in which sensory evidence is used to support the derivation of these attributes. Rather than talking about exclusive allocation, it might be more profitable to say that descriptions are constrained by criteria of consistency or noncontradiction.
- Schemas for speech recognition interact with primitive scene analysis in the same way that other schemas do.

• Speech schemas are the same as other recognition schemas in the following way: when they make use of the information that they need from a mixture, they do not remove it from the array of information that other description-building processes can use.

As a way to begin testing the theory, we could mount an experimental attack on the proposal that schemas cannot leave residuals that are coherent. It is a useful assumption because it provides a way to distinguish between primitive and schema-governed processes. The idea is based on observations such as those of Dowling, who discovered that familiarizing listeners with one melody in a mixture of two does not help them to recognize the second one.[800] This claim about schemas may be wrong or may apply only to certain kinds of schemas.

Another claim is that the speech-recognition processes are schemas of this type. It implies that they, too, cannot influence the grouping of material that they leave behind. This claim flies in the face of the example, given by Liberman and Studdert-Kennedy, of a synthetic sentence to which extra sounds had been added.[801] The added sounds failed to make the sentence unintelligible, and at least some of them segregated from the sentence and were heard as chirps and whistles. The authors assumed that the separability of these sounds in the mixture depended on their having been left out of the subset that was interpreted as speech. However, because there has been no follow-up to this research, we do not really know whether this was the reason. Did all the added sounds segregate? Would they have done so if the signal had not been interpreted as speech? Obviously a great deal of research needs to be done on the topic. This is an example of the method by which the piecewise testing of assumptions can lay constraints on the more global theory.

My account of speech and other forms of recognition could be wrong in any of the following ways:

• The speech system may indeed be schema-driven, but schemas may be capable of erasing the evidence that they claim; this would create a situation where the leaving of an isolated residual could not be used as a test to distinguish primitive from schema-driven processes.
• Some process in speech recognition (such as the recognition of sound as possibly coming from a human speaker) may be primitive rather than schema-driven and capable of leaving residuals, but schemas in general may not be.
• Many types of schemas can create residuals, and the examples that suggested that they could not may have been atypical.

• The whole dichotomy between primitive organization and the schema-based formation of descriptions may be wrong.

The thorny theoretical problem of precedence and interaction of speech and nonspeech recognition will not be solvable without future research specifically directed to the problem of how evidence is packaged and used up in the perception of sound.

Chapter 8

Summary and Conclusions: What We Do and Do Not Know about Auditory Scene Analysis

Summary of Previous Chapters

This chapter presents my conclusions about what we do and do not know about auditory scene analysis at present. The sequence of topics exactly follows that of the previous chapters, so if a point is not clear here, or if fuller details are wanted, the reader should have no difficulty in finding the corresponding material in the earlier discussion. In this chapter I present no references to the experiments on which the conclusions are based. The interested reader can look for them in the earlier chapters. Sometimes I have not undertaken to define a technical word here. In such cases, a rough definition can be found in the glossary at the end of the book.

Primitive Auditory Scene Analysis

The problem of scene analysis is this: Although we need to build separate mental descriptions of the different sound-producing events in our environments, the pattern of acoustic energy that is received by our ears is a mixture of the effects of the different events. It appears that our auditory systems solve the problem in two ways, by the use of primitive processes of auditory grouping and by governing the listening process by schemas that incorporate our knowledge of familiar sounds. This book has been mainly about the primitive process, although it has tried to discover whether the effects of the two kinds of processes can be distinguished from each other. I shall begin this summary by talking about the primitive process.

The primitive process of scene analysis seems to employ a strategy of first breaking down the incoming array of energy into a large number of separate analyses. These are local to particular moments of time and particular frequency regions in the acoustic spectrum. Each region is described in terms of its intensity, its fluctuation pattern, the direction of frequency transitions in it, an estimate of where the sound is coming from in space, and perhaps other features. After these numerous separate analyses have been done, the auditory system has the problem of deciding how to group them so that each group has been derived from the same environmental event. The grouping has to be done in two dimensions (at least), across time and across the spectrum. I have called the temporal grouping "sequential integration" and have referred to the other one as "simultaneous integration." The chapters in this volume have been laid out according to this division. However, I have pointed out that the two forms of grouping often operate in conjunction to solve the problem.

Sequential Integration: Auditory Stream Segregation

Sequential integration is visible in a number of contexts, but a popular stimulus pattern for studying it has been the one that gives rise to auditory stream segregation. This occurs when a sequence of tones jumps rapidly up and down between different frequency regions. The simplest case is a rapid repeated alternation of a high and a low tone. If the alternation is fast enough and the frequency separation great enough, listeners will not experience a single stream of tones alternating in pitch, but will perceive two streams of tones, one consisting of repetitions of the lower tone and the other consisting of repetitions of the higher one. When two streams are heard, the listener has the impression of two different sources of sound, one high pitched and the other low, whose tones happen to occur at about the same time. In more complex patterns, where a number of higher tones of slightly different frequencies are interleaved with a number of lower tones, listeners will still hear two streams, but this time each stream will have a melodic pattern that is restricted to the tones of that stream.

One sort of stimulus that has been used is a short repeating loop of tones. The tones are chosen from two different frequency regions, one high and one low. The properties of the tones have been varied and the effects on stream segregation observed.

Another form of stimulus has been a tune or other short tonal pattern interleaved with distractor tones. The frequency relations between the distractor and the relevant tones have been varied. When the two sets of tones are in the same frequency region, the tune disappears into a pattern formed out of all the tones, but if they are in two nonoverlapping frequency regions, the tune is readily heard as a separate stream. This sort of stimulus has been used to study primitive segregation but is more suited for the study of schema-based segregation.

Auditory stream segregation has been known by musicians since the Baroque period, when it was used to produce the impression of two lines of melody even though the instrument playing the sequence could produce only one note at a time. This could be done by having the instrument rapidly alternate between a higher and a lower melodic line.

Factors Influencing Stream Segregation The most important influences on the segregation of the streams are the rate of the tonal sequence and the frequency separation between the two subsets of tones that are interleaved. As the subsets are moved further apart in frequency, the segregation increases and it becomes harder and harder for a listener to hear the entire sequence as a single stream of sound. (A logarithmic scale seems to be one that reflects the segregability of the frequencies.) Furthermore the segregation increases when the sequence goes faster. As a consequence of these facts, the effects of frequency separation and time can be traded off against one another. As the frequency separation increases, the sequence must be slowed down if the listener is to be able to experience all the tones as part of a single, coherent stream of sound.

However, the effects of frequency separation and speed depend on what the listeners are trying to do. If they are trying to hear all the tones as part of a single sequence, the effects are as I have just described them. But if they are trying to focus their attention on the tones of just one of the streams, the effects of frequency separation and speed are different. The frequency separation of the high from the low tones need only exceed some small amount (a few semitones in the case of two alternating tones) before the target sequence can be followed by attention. Further increases in separation do not increase the segregation and the capacity to follow the selected stream is virtually unaffected by the speed of the sequence. Because of the difference in the effects when listeners are trying to hear coherence or segregation, I have proposed that two different factors are at work. One, primitive segregation, is affected by the rate and the frequency separation. The other, schema-based segregation that involves attention, is used for focusing on one of the streams. The attention of the listener can always be directed toward a narrow frequency range when required by the task. Beyond the minimum frequency separation that it requires so as not to confuse the notes of the stream that it is following with the tones of other streams, the attentional process is unaffected by the separation between the frequencies.

We know that the result of different speeds comes from the fact that certain temporal intervals have been affected. But we do not know exactly which ones. If the effect is based on bringing the tones from the same frequency range closer together in time, we would expect that the time interval between the end of one tone and the beginning of another in the same range would be the important one. Yet some evidence suggests that it is the separation of the *onsets* of the two that is important. There is another question too. Which is important: the interval between successive tones in the same frequency range or that between successive ones in the up-and-down sequence? Since most studies use sequences in which all tones and intertone silences are the same length, it is impossible to tell which of these intervals is the critical one.

It appears that the stream-forming process behaves in a manner analogous to the Gestalt principle of grouping by proximity. The high tones tend to group with other high ones if brought close to them in time by the speeding up of the sequence.

When we talk about the proximity of *tones* or *sounds* in frequency or in time, we are implying that the stream of sound is composed of discrete units. But what about cases in which the sound is more continuous? Where are the units? It appears as though there is a unit-forming process that is sensitive to discontinuities in the sound, particularly to sudden rises in intensity, and that creates unit boundaries when such discontinuities occur. Units can occur at different time scales and smaller units can be embedded in larger ones. When the sequence is speeded up, the changes that signal the smaller units may be missed by the auditory system, and other changes, too gradual to form units at the slower speed, may now be sudden enough to control the formation of units.

The units, once formed by these processes, can form groups with other similar ones. Similarity is determined by analyses that are applied to the units once they are formed. For example, suppose there is a glide in frequency, bounded by a rise and a fall in intensity. Between these boundaries, the change in frequency may be measured by the auditory system and assigned to the unit as one of its properties. This frequency-gliding unit will prefer to group with other ones whose frequency change has the same slope and which are in the same frequency region.

One of the similarities that affects the grouping of tones is their location in space. Engineers working on the automatic segregation of concurrent sounds have used spatial separation as a uniquely powerful way of determining whether the sounds have come from the same physical event (usually a talker). Humans use spatial origin too, but do not assign such an overwhelming role to it. They can do quite well at segregating more than one stream of sound coming from a single point in space, for example, from a single loudspeaker.

Primitive scene analysis tends to group sounds that come from the same point in space and to segregate those that come from different places. As a consequence, if two sounds, different in frequency, are alternated between the ears, they will not form a single coherent stream. The frequency separation, the rate, and the spatial separation combine to influence the segregation. Spatial differences seem to have their strongest effects on segregation when they are combined with other differences between the sounds. Illusions can be created by setting up a competition between the tendency to group sounds by their frequency similarity and by their spatial similarity. An example is Diana Deutsch's scale illusion.

When speech is rapidly switched back and forth between the ears, it is hard to follow. One reason is that when the switch occurs, it produces a sudden rise in intensity in one ear and a sudden drop in the other. If the listener simply combined the two changes there would be no net change in the signal. But this is not what happens. The changes in the two ears are treated as separate events. As a result, false beginnings and ends of syllables are perceived and this hurts the recognition of the speech.

When clicks are alternated between the two ears, the click rate seems to be slower than when all the clicks come to the same ear. When listeners are asked to count the total sequence, they are worse at doing so when the clicks are alternated than when they are not. Both effects seem to be the results of spatially based stream segregation.

So far I have spoken about frequency differences between tones. Most readers translate this to "pitch differences." This is all right as long as we are dealing with pure tones whose pitches are in one-to-one correspondence with their frequencies. Yet we know that in complex tones, having many frequency components, this simple equivalence can break down.

In a complex tone, the perceived pitch depends on the auditory system's estimate of the fundamental frequency of the set of harmonics in the tone. Yet this fundamental itself need not actually be present. All that is required (to a first approximation) is that all the partials that are present should be multiples of this fundamental. We can therefore have a case in which a tone with a lower pitch can have partials whose average is higher in frequency that the average of those in a tone whose pitch is higher. (The tone with the higher harmonics will sound "brighter" even though it has a lower pitch.)

This allows us to ask a question that we could not ask about sequences of pure tones. Is it the difference in the fundamental frequency (pitch) of the tones or the difference in the average frequency of its partials (brightness) that affects perceptual grouping? The answer is that they both do and that the effects are additive. A pure tone has a different spectral content than a complex tone; so even though the pitches of the two may be the same, the tones will tend to segregate from one another in rapid sequences. Another kind of grouping also occurs: A pure tone, instead of grouping with the entire complex tone that follows it, may group with one of the frequency components of the latter.

Pitch and brightness are both one-dimensional properties of a spectrum of sound. However, when a spectrum has a number of peaks in it (as the spectrum of of a vowel does), there can be many ways in which one spectrum resembles another. Few studies of the stream segregation of sequences containing such complex sounds have been done and those that have been carried out have not looked analytically at the dimensions that the auditory system uses to summarize the various complex shapes of spectra.

There is another type of highness that can be heard in bands of filtered noise. When the noise burst contains higher-frequency components, it sounds higher. Differences in frequency content can cause sequences formed out of bursts of noise to segregate into high and low streams in the same way as sequences formed out of tones.

Timbre Timbre is another factor that affects the similarity of tones and hence their grouping into streams. The difficulty is that timbre is not a simple one-dimensional property of tones. It may not even be reducible to a small number of dimensions.

Probably one distinct dimension of timbre is brightness. We know that tones that are similar in their brightness will tend to be assigned to the same stream. Brightness is, roughly speaking, the mean frequency that is obtained when all frequency components of a sound are weighted according to their loudness. Bright tones have more of their energy concentrated in higher frequencies than dull tones do.

The difference in quality between noises and tones can also be thought of as a timbre difference. The frequency components of noises constantly change in amplitude and phase whereas those of tones are fairly constant. A rapid sequence can be created by alternating pure tones with noises whose center frequencies have been matched to those of the tones. The sequence will segregate into one formed out of the noises and another formed out of the tones. Much more research needs to be done on the effects of spectral noisiness in controlling the grouping of sounds.

I have suggested that the pattern of peaks and valleys in the spectra of sounds may affect their grouping. Another way of saying this is that grouping is affected by the pattern of the intensities of various harmonics in the spectra of successive tones. However, we do not know how to compare the patterns in two successive tones whose fundamentals differ. We could consider two tones as having the same pattern of intensities if their harmonics had their peaks at exactly the same frequencies. In nature, this would probably mean that they had passed through the same set of resonators (the vocal tract of the same talker for example). On the other hand, we could also consider them the same if the corresponding harmonics were of proportional intensity. This would mean that if the fundamental frequency of the second tone were double that of the first, all the peaks in the spectrum would also be at double the frequency. In nature this would mean that the properties of the two vibrating bodies were similar (rather than the properties of the resonators that they had been passed through). The available evidence (and it is scanty) suggests that both forms of spectral similarity are used in auditory scene analysis to group successive tones.

Most of the research on the sequential grouping of sounds has used either tones or noise bursts that are presented in regular rhythmic patterns. Yet most of the sounds in the natural world are not like this. For example, natural sounds change their properties over time. Think of a voice, which has all kinds of sounds in it, or a plucked guitar string, which has a abrupt, noisy, and intense onset and dies out gradually to almost a pure tone. There has been almost no research on the sequential grouping of changing tones other than a few studies in the field of speech and studies on the grouping of pure-tone glides. The study of how changing tones are perceptually organized affords a rich opportunity for research. Among the factors that deserve study are the abruptness of the onset, the changes over time in the strengths of harmonics, the fluctuations in the overall intensity and pitch of the sound, and the granularity of the sound.

If you take each moment of each frequency component into account, you realize that sounds can differ from one another acoustically in an astonishingly large number of ways. Does the auditory system deal with this complexity by collapsing the differences into a small number of dimensions? We know that loudness, pitch, and possibly brightness are separable dimensions, but is there a limited number of other dimensions of timbre? A demonstration that we understood some set of dimensions would be our ability to construct metameric timbres. In vision, metameric colors are ones that look identical despite the fact that their spectral content is different. By analogy, metameric timbres would sound the same (in some respect) despite obvious acoustic differences. For our purposes in the study of scene analysis, it would not be so important that they sounded exactly alike as that their grouping tendencies were identical. That is, the substitution of one for the other would leave the groupings the same in patterns in which they appeared.

It has been argued that amplitude differences between sounds will control their grouping. Loud sounds will tend to group with other loud ones and soft ones with soft. However, the results obtained with tones differing in loudness makes me question whether the grouping based on loudness is the result of primitive scene analysis or of some schema-governed process of selection. The resolution of this issue may be as follows. Tones that differ only in loudness may not have a tendency to segregate from one another, but when there are also other differences between the sounds, the loudness differences may strengthen the segregation. Again we really do not know and research is required to resolve the question.

When you listen to a repeating alternation of high and low tones that are sufficiently far apart in frequency, at first you can follow the alternation of tones as a single stream, but eventually the sequence seems to split into two separate streams, one high and the other low. This shows that there is a cumulative effect of the alternation between frequency ranges. The tendency for primitive stream segregation to subdivide the sequence builds up for at least 4 seconds and takes at least 4 seconds to go away after the sequence stops. I have interpreted this sluggishness of the changes as having a useful function. It prevents the system from oscillating wildly among different ways of organizing the auditory scene. Once some interpretation of a number of sonic sources has occurred it does not disappear instantly just because some source has not been heard from for a second or two. This type of "hysteresis" is seen in a great number of perceptual phenomena in different sense modalities.

It appears, however, that a sudden change in the acoustic properties of the signal can reset the streaming mechanism more quickly than mere silence can. For instance, a sudden change in the frequency range occupied by the signal or the spatial location from which the sound seems to be coming can cause a segregated sequence to revert to being heard as unsegregated. Obviously the scene-analysis system treats these sorts of changes as indicating that it is now encountering a new sonic event.

The cumulative effect of exposure to a sequence that is alternating between frequency ranges has been explained in different ways. The explanation that I favor says that the auditory system is gradually building up evidence that the sequence actually contains different subsets of sounds with distinct properties and that they should be sorted into separate streams. An alternative explanation of the cumulative effects that are seen in extended exposures to the sequence is that the integration into a single stream is accomplished by means of frequency-jump detectors. When the sequence continues to jump back and forth in frequency the detectors get tired out. At this point only shorter jumps can be followed and the sequence breaks into sub-streams. Although the two explanations look different they are not necessarily incompatible. Notice that the first is a functional one while the latter is stated in terms of physiology. It may be that the physiological events described by the second are serving the function described by the first.

Continuous sounds hold together better as a single stream than discontinuous ones do. This can be shown by comparing two sorts of sequences. In a discontinuous sequence, there is an alternation of high and low tones and all the tones are steady in pitch and separate from their neighbors. In a continuous sequence, each high tone is joined to its two adjacent low neighbors by a frequency glide. The continuous sequence holds together better than the discontinuous one. The coherence of continuous sequences can be interpreted in functional terms as a heuristic of the auditory system. This heuristic is equivalent to a bet that any sequence that exhibits acoustic continuity has probably come from a single environmental event.

The use of continuity does not necessarily imply that the auditory system tracks changes and predicts the properties of the next moment of sound. I do not think that the primitive process does this. However, there is good reason to believe that schema-based processes of integration do employ this strategy.

Summary of Factors Promoting Sequential Grouping Many of the factors that favor the grouping of a sequence of auditory inputs are features that define the similarity and continuity of successive sounds. These include their fundamental frequency, their temporal proximity, the shape of their spectra, their intensity, and their apparent spatial origin. These characteristics affect the sequential aspect of scene analysis. My description has seemed to imply that the things that group sequentially can be thought of as sounds. This was because the examples that I have given were all stated in terms of rather simple sounds rather than in terms of mixtures of sound. We find that the same factors serve to promote the sequential grouping of sound in mixtures, but, in this case, it is not whole sounds but parts of the spectrum that are caused to group sequentially. The resulting grouping helps the brain to create separate descriptions of the component sounds in the mixture.

Effects of Stream Segregation Generally speaking, the perceptual effects of sequential integration and segregation follow from their role in scene analysis. Auditory material that is assigned to the same stream has a much stronger tendency to be used together in any perceptual computation. Emergent properties of the sound are likely to be computed from within-stream elements. Therefore sequential patterns that involve elements of the same stream will be more easily perceived. This general description takes many specific forms.

It can be shown that our perceptual representations of any pattern tend to include material that is within a stream and to exclude material that is not in that stream. For example, if listeners are asked to recognize a pattern that is interleaved with distractor sounds, any factor that causes the distractors to fall into a separate stream will make the pattern easier to recognize. This is true regardless of whether the pattern that they are trying to hear is a familiar melody or an unfamiliar sequence that they have just been played as a "standard" and are holding in their immediate memories.

In some sense we are talking about camouflage and are saying that only within-stream material can camouflage a target. Even such a simple task as counting a rapid sequence of tones can be carried out more accurately when all the tones fall into a single stream.

So far most of the recognition research has used pitch differences to segregate the streams, but there is no reason that the other factors that I have listed as affecting sequential integration could not be used.

Temporal relations can also be more easily perceived when they involve elements that have been grouped sequentially by auditory scene analysis. For example, it is difficult to detect the order of all the sounds in a rapid repeating cycle when they fall into more than one stream. (If we want to create a clear demonstration of this fact, we have to design the task in such a way that it is impossible for a listener to get the right answer by considering only one stream at a time.)

Stream segregation can also affect the rhythm of a perceived sequence. For example, if we were to create a sequence of equally spaced tones in which every third tone was an octave higher than the others, it would divide into two streams. The higher-pitched one would have this rhythm:

—H—H—H. . . .

The lower one would have this one:

LL–LL–LL–. . . .

A rhythm tends to be defined by sounds that fall into the same stream.

The perceived temporal overlap of sounds is also affected by segregation. If a rapid cycle of six tones consists of an alternation of three high and three low ones, all of equal duration, it splits perceptually into two streams. As you listen to the two streams you often get the impression that the high and the low cycles are running at different speeds. It is very difficult to judge whether the tones in the high stream are temporally overlapped with those in the lower one or not.

Our ability to detect a temporal gap between two tones seems to be affected by segregation even when the tones are not part of a longer sequence. It becomes harder and harder to judge the length of the gap as the frequency difference between the two adjacent tones increases. It is not absolutely certain whether this is really a result of stream segregation or is some other effect of frequency separation. To find out, we would have to see whether we could obtain the same effect if we replaced the frequency difference by some other factor that was known to affect stream segregation.

It appears that the factors that promote the grouping of auditory material act in a competitive way. For example, suppose we had a four-tone cycle, ABCD. If two of the tones, A and B, were separated in frequency from the other two, then A and B might form a separate stream of their own. Yet in a different four-tone cycle, ABXY, those same A and B tones might appear in two separate streams if one of these tones grouped more strongly with X and the other with Y. It appears that frequency proximities are competitive and that the system tries to form streams by grouping the elements that bear the strongest resemblance to one another. Because of this competition, we are able to create experiments in which we can capture an element out of a sequential grouping by giving it a better sound to group with.

This competition also occurs between different factors that favor grouping. For example, in a four-tone sequence ABXY, if similarity in fundamental frequency favors the groupings AB and XY, while similarity in spectral peaks favors the grouping AX and BY, then the actual grouping will depend on the relative sizes of the differences. If the differences in fundamental frequency are large while the differences in spectral peak positions are small, the fundamental frequency differences will control the grouping.

There is collaboration as well as competition. If a number of factors all favor the grouping of sounds in the same way, the grouping will be very strong and the sounds will always be heard as parts of the same stream. The process of competition and collaboration is simple to conceptualize. It is as if each acoustic dimension could vote for a grouping, with the number of votes it cast being determined by the degree of similarity on that dimension and on the importance of the dimension. Then the streams whose elements were grouped by the most votes would be formed. Such a voting system would be valuable in a natural environment in which it is not guaranteed that sounds that resemble one another in only one or two ways will always have arisen from the same acoustic source.

Competition and capturing would not be possible if a sound could be in two streams at the same time. Giving a sound something better to group with would not remove it from the original stream. The fact that we can capture sounds out of streams implies that the brain has a bias against having sounds in two different streams at the same time. However, this bias toward "exclusive allocation" is not absolute. When the auditory system encounters complex spectra, it sometimes decides that two sounds with shared spectral components are present at the same time. If this decision is made, some of the spectral components are used to derive the properties of more than one perceived sound.

Any of the effects that I have mentioned can be used to measure the strength of stream segregation. Some effects, however, are not as useful in experiments because they are strongly influenced by factors other than primitive grouping. The most reliable indication that a stream has been formed is the exclusion of certain sounds from a perceived pattern even though listeners are trying to include them. It is not as valid a measure if they are attempting to exclude them. Their success in doing so may not be due to primitive preattentive scene analysis but to schema-governed processes of attention. Therefore, failure of inclusion is a better measure than success in exclusion.

The sequential grouping that is observed in stream segregation has two analogies in vision. The first is the tendency for visual perception to group elements that are near to one another in space. We often see the same groupings in the visual diagrams of patterns of sounds as we hear in the sounds themselves. Apparently, proximity has similar effects on grouping in vision and audition. A more dynamic analogy to stream segregation in vision is apparent motion. Chapter 1 showed how the two phenomena display very similar effects.

Not only do vision and audition show certain similarities to each other but events in vision can affect how sounds are perceived and vice versa. We may already be disposed at birth to relate vision to audition. A newborn will spend more time looking at a face that appears visually to be speaking the same words that it is hearing than one that is not. An example of the interrelationship is that the grouping of sounds can influence the grouping of visual events with which they are synchronized and vice versa. For instance, suppose that two lights are too far apart to give good apparent motion when they are flashed in alternation (that is, they are not treated as parts of the same event). We can cause the perceived movement to be improved if the lights are synchronized with high and low tones, one light with each tone, provided that the two tones themselves are treated as parts of a single acoustic event. We can arrange this by placing them close enough together in frequency to fall into the same stream. It is not yet clear whether this particular form of coordination between vision and audition serves any useful purpose. Other forms of coordination between vision and audition have more obvious benefits. For example, the tendency to experience a sound as coming from a location at which visual events are occurring with the same temporal pattern (the so-called ventriloquism effect) can be interpreted as a way in which visual evidence about the location of an event can supplement unclear auditory evidence. The direction of influence is not just from vision to audition but in the reverse direction as well.

I have offered an explanation of stream segregation in terms of scene analysis. However, other forms of explanation have been offered by others. Some of them are physiological. One proposal is that overlapping hair cell populations in the inner ear must be stimulated by successive tones before a sequence can be integrated. When this condition is violated, separate streams are formed so as to group the tones that do conform to the requirement. A piece of evidence against this explanation is that under some circumstances tones from opposite ears can be grouped into the same stream. These tones are obviously not affecting the same hair cells. Another theory that I have already mentioned in this chapter is that a frequency-jump detector must register the transition between successive tones before the sequence can be integrated. With repeated frequency alternation, the detectors get tired out and can only follow shorter jumps. This theory has the advantage that it is the analogue of a motion-detector theory in vision that has been successful in explaining certain visual phenomena. Neither of these physiological theories can explain all the facts about the formation of auditory streams, but even if they could, they would not compete with the scene analysis explanation, which is functional rather than physiological in nature. They would merely describe the machinery by means of which scene analysis takes place.

However, functional theories have been offered that compete more directly with the theory of primitive preattentive grouping of acoustic evidence. These theories see the site of segregation and grouping as being within the attentional process itself. Attention is seen as trying to follow the changes in the stimulus. Rapid changes may exceed the capacity of attention to follow them. Sometimes the process that integrates successive sounds has been described as a filter that must pass all the sounds if they are to be incorporated into the same act of attention. The filter is conceptualized as being able to change its own setting with respect to the range of properties that it is tuned to (such as the range of frequencies that it will pass) but to be unable to change it very rapidly. Therefore it misses sudden changes in the sound. This is the explanation that is offered to explain why a sound is sometimes perceptually excluded from a stream. According to this view, only one stream of sound exists at a time, the one you are paying attention to. There is no such thing as a second grouping of perceptual evidence that is structured even if you are not paying attention to it. This is one important way in which this class of theory differs from the theory of primitive scene analysis. The latter says that links are formed between parts of the auditory evidence even though these parts may not currently be within the field of attention.

Another theory is similar to the attention-as-filter theory except that it sees the attention as being able to integrate a sequence when the changes in it can be anticipated as a result of prior learning. This tendency is seen as partially overcoming the inability to track sudden changes.

The Gestalt theory of grouping is similar to the idea of preattentive grouping. It sees the effects of similarity, temporal proximity, and continuity as innate principles that determine grouping. The idea of competitive grouping forces is also part of the theory. However, the Gestalt psychologists did not emphasize the relevance of these principles to the practical task of scene analysis.

Spectral Integration

I have summarized the facts about the sequential grouping of auditory evidence, but this is only a part of the story. In mixtures of sound the auditory system must decide which components, among those that are received concurrently, should be treated as arising from the same sound. This process was studied in simple experiments in which two concurrently presented pure tones, B and C, were alternated with a pure tone, A (see figure 1.16 of chapter 1). It was found that if B and C started and ended at the same time, they tended to be treated as two components of a single complex tone, BC, that was perceived as rich in quality. On the other hand, there was a tendency to treat B as a repetition of A whenever A was close in frequency to B. B seemed to be the object of a rivalry. When it was captured into a sequential stream with A, it was less likely to be heard as part of the complex tone, BC. Conversely, when it was captured by C and fused with it, it was less likely to be heard as a repetition of A. It seemed that sequential grouping and spectral grouping were in a competition that served to resolve competing evidence concerning the appropriate grouping of sensory material.

Gliding tones can be captured out of mixtures too (see figure 2.17 of chapter 2). A gliding complex tone that is really a mixture of simultaneously gliding pure tones can have one of its components captured out of it by a preceding pure-tone glide.

Factors Influencing Spectral Integration If we look at a spectrogram of a mixture of sounds, as in figure 1.4 of chapter 1, we find that the spectral content arriving from one sound overlaps the components of the remainder of the sound both in frequency and in time. How can the auditory system know which frequency components to group together to build a description of one of the sounds? It seems that it does so by looking for correlations or correspondences among parts of the spectral content that would be unlikely to have occurred by chance.

One type of correspondence is between the auditory properties of different moments of time. A complex spectrum may have, embedded within it, a simpler spectrum that was encountered a moment earlier. That simpler spectrum might, for example, abut against the more complex one with no discontinuity. In such a case, it is reasonable to treat the part of the spectrum that matches the earlier one as merely a continuation of it and treat the rest of the later one as resulting from the addition of a new sound to the mixture. This could be referred to as the "old-plus-new" heuristic. It is this strategy that is observed in experiments in which a component is captured out of a complex tone by a preceding pure tone.

The grouping of a part of the current auditory input with earlier material depends on how similar they are. We know that at least two factors influence the similarity: frequency separation and (in the case of gliding components) the direction of frequency change. They also group more strongly if there are shorter silences separating them. Recall that these factors are identical to those that determine sequential grouping of simple tones. This leads us to believe that the old-plus-new heuristic is just another manifestation of the principles that control sequential grouping.

Another aspect of this heuristic is that the factoring out of the old spectrum from the current one creates a residual whose properties are heard more clearly. There is even some evidence that the auditory system uses the amplitudes of the various spectral components of the earlier spectrum to decide not only *which* spectral components to subtract out but also *how much intensity* to leave behind at each frequency. This is a good strategy because the old and new sounds might have some frequency components that are the same. The subtraction (or a process roughly equivalent to subtraction) provides an estimate of the probable intensity of the frequency components of the sound that has been added to the first to create the complex spectrum.

We also have other ways of deciding which components, received at the same time, should be grouped to form a description of a single auditory event. Certain types of relations between these components can be used as clues that they should be grouped. The effect of this grouping is to allow global analyses of factors such as pitch, timbre, loudness, and even spatial origin to be computed on a set of sensory evidence that probably all came from the same event in the environment.

Some of the clues are based on the frequency relations between components. The first is their frequency separation. The further they are away from one another the less likely they are to be treated as parts of the same sound. Another fact is that partials that are more intense are easier to segregate from the spectrum. This may be because stronger tones better resist masking from nearby frequencies. The contribution of these two effects to scene analysis is not entirely clear, and they may be side-effects of other design principles in the auditory system.

However, there is an effect whose value is easy to appreciate. The scene-analysis system favors the grouping of partials that are harmonics of the same fundamental. This can be called the harmonicity principle. Its utility follows from the fact that when many types of physical bodies vibrate they tend to generate a harmonic spectrum in which the partials are all multiples (approximately) of the same fundamental. Instances include many animal sounds, including the human voice. Therefore if the auditory system can find a certain number of fundamentals that will account for all the partials that are present, then it is very likely that we are hearing that number of environmental sounds.

There are several effects of this grouping. One is that a pitch can be derived separately for each group of partials. This allows us to hear more than one pitch in a single spectrum. This grouping by harmonicity also explains why inharmonic spectra seem to have many pitches. A separate timbre can also be derived for each harmonic series, making it possible for us to segregate speech sounds (with their different timbres) when they have different pitches. The grouping also tends to cause the partials that are within the same group to be fused perceptually. When this happens, it becomes impossible to hear the pitches of the individual partials. Sometimes an incomplete fusion of a set of partials may occur even though they form more than one harmonic series, provided that many of the partials occur in more than one of the series. This is why a tone will fuse so strongly with one that is an octave higher. All of the partials of the higher tone will be matched by the even-numbered partials of the lower one.

Two factors that affect spectral integration are described by the Gestalt principle of common fate. The Gestalt psychologists discovered that when different parts of the perceptual field were changing in the same way at the same time, they tended to be grouped together and seen to be changing as a group because of their common fate. A visual example can be made by drawing two clusters of dots, each on a separate transparent sheet. When the two are superimposed, we see only one denser set of dots. However, if the two sheets are moved in different patterns, we see two sets of dots, each set defined by its own trajectory of motion.

Common fate in audition can be defined in terms of correlated changes in the frequencies of different partials or in their amplitudes. It will be convenient to take the human voice as an example. Variations in the pitch of a voice are represented acoustically by similar changes in all frequency components (parallel changes on a log-frequency scale). When the pitch rises, not only does the fundamental frequency go up but all the harmonics go up by the same proportion too. It is plausible to believe that this correlated change, if it could be detected auditorily, could tell us that the changing partials all came from the same voice. The auditory system could group all such correlated changes and hear only one changing sound.

There is evidence to suggest that two types of frequency change (or modulation) are used for this purpose. One is micromodulation, the tiny fluctuations of the pitch of human voices that occur even when speakers think that they are holding a steady pitch. A slightly larger version of such modulation occurs in singing where it is called vibrato. The other type of frequency modulation is the slow kind that occurs when we voluntarily vary the pitch of our voice in a smooth way, as we do, for example, when we raise our pitch at the end of a question. This sort of change is called portamento in music. The synchronization of micromodulation or of slow modulation in different parts of the spectrum seems to cause those parts to be treated as parts of a single sound. However, it is not yet clear whether these effects can be fully accounted for by an alternative explanation. This account argues that parallel frequency changes allow partials to maintain their harmonic relations to one another over time and that it is these sustained relations, rather than the change itself, that promotes the integration of the partials.

Another version of common fate in audition occurs when the auditory system detects synchronized amplitude changes in different parts of the spectrum. Just as with frequency modulation, this can occur on finer or grosser scales. The finer-scale modulation is not really a property of the physical signal itself but occurs within the auditory system. It happens when we listen to complex harmonic sounds such as the human voice. Because of the way in which our peripheral auditory systems filter the incoming sound, rapid fluctuations in intensity occur within the different auditory neural channels that respond to bands of frequencies in the voice. The fluctuations are periodic and have the same period in every channel; this happens to be the period of the fundamental of the voice. Experimental evidence supports the idea that this common neural periodicity can promote the integration of sensory evidence derived from different spectral regions.

We can also observe a grosser sort of correlated amplitude change in different parts of the spectrum. It is a property of the signal itself and occurs when sounds begin and end. All the frequency components derived from a single sound tend to start and stop at the same moment; those derived from different sounds tend to do so at different moments. This can be used to partition the set of frequency components derived from a mixture of sounds.

It seems that we ought to be able to pick out the auditory components contributed by a certain environmental event by watching the event and correlating visual changes with auditory ones. While it appears very probable that we can do this, the experimental evidence on this point is very indirect and more research is needed. We know that we look more closely at a talker's mouth in a noisy room, but we do not know what type of process uses this information. There is reason to believe that the recognition of a speech sound uses a schema that coordinates both the sound itself and the specific movements of the speaker's face that occur when that sound is made. It is not clear whether there exists, in addition, a more primitive process that notices visual-auditory correlations and uses them simply to partition the auditory sense material.

One of the most powerful strategies for grouping spectral components is to group those that have come from the same spatial direction and to segregate those groups that have come from different directions. That is why the individual instruments in an ensemble performance sound so much clearer in a stereophonic recording than in one that is monophonic. However, there is a requirement that has to be met before the auditory system can group spectral components by their spatial origin. It first has to be able to assign an independent estimate of spatial origin to each separable band of frequencies in the spectrum. Results from physiological experiments on animals and perceptual experiments on humans suggest that these independent estimates are indeed derived by the auditory system. For example, spatial cues that suggest two locations of origin can cause a band of noise to split perceptually into two different frequency bands. A location can be specified for each band by delaying the components of that band in one ear relative to the other.

Although it seems logical to treat components that come from the same direction as having come from the same sonic event, this strategy is not infallible. Different events can occur close together in space, or along the same line radiating outward from the body of the listener. Even when the events themselves are at quite distinguishable locations, the sensory evidence for their positions can be distorted by reflection of the sound waves from nearby surfaces, by the presence of bodies interposed between the ear and the sound source, and by asymmetrical masking of the evidence at the two ears by louder sounds. This may be why spectral organization does not depend too strongly on spatial cues. A person can do a creditable job at segregating concurrent sounds from one another even when listening to a monaural recording. Spatial evidence is just added up with all the other sorts of evidence in auditory scene analysis.

So far I have described how spatial information affects perceptual organization. But the influence can flow in the opposite direction as well. Because spatial cues are often unreliable, the auditory system seems to average different spatial estimates to arrive at the perceived location of an event. However, this strategy would be useless if it did not know how many sounds there were. It would be harmful to average the spatial estimates that had been derived from energy coming from different unrelated events. Therefore the system must group the evidence before averaging the estimates of location. As an example of how this works, we can set up a situation in which two different signals appear to come from different directions. If we then use correlated micromodulation in the two signals to tell the auditory system that they are one and the same event, it will derive only one (diffuse) spatial estimate for the whole sound. Another example is the use of correlated visual information to correct the perceived location of a sound (the ventriloquism effect).

The scene-analysis process uses the history of a signal to correct momentary spatial estimates. For example, if a pure-tone signal is split and sent to both ears in phase and with equal intensity, we will hear a tone coming from the center. However, if the tone at one ear is turned up and down in intensity fairly rapidly and abruptly, we will hear a pulsing tone at that ear and a steady tone at the other. The alternative perceptual solution, hearing a single tone move repeatedly from a central position to the side of the head receiving the louder tone, is not favored by the auditory system. It appears that an across-ear version of the old-plus-new heuristic concludes, instead, that there are two sources of sound. It decides that the balanced signal results accidentally from a continuation of the steady signal into the moments when a pulsing signal reaches its maximum. It partitions the balanced energy into a continuing (old) and an added (new) signal. Instead of one perceived location there are two.

We see, then, that there are more cues to the location of a sound-producing event than are usually mentioned in textbooks. We do not use only those cues that are based on the fact that our ears are on different sides of our heads and have a certain shape. We also use the fact that sound-producing events tend to persist over time, to move only slowly in space, and to give rise to sounds that have a coherent inner structure.

There are undoubtedly other factors that help a listener to partition the auditory evidence that arrives at a particular moment. It is possible that textural features (for example, ones that describe the temporal irregularity in the sound) may play a role in partitioning irregular spectra such as those we get when we tear a piece of paper, drag objects, or walk on crunchy snow. No research has been done on the partitioning of spectra that derive from combinations of such sounds. Yet it is worth noting that in the natural world these sounds are more numerous than the regular tones and noises that we have studied in the laboratory.

We also are ignorant of the role that rhythm plays in partitioning mixtures. Is it easier to decompose a mixture in which a component is changing in a regular repetitive fashion than one in which the changes are irregular? If so, what is the mechanism by which it is done, a primitive partitioning process or one that depends on our ability to guide our attention by rhythmic schemas?

When the scene-analysis process assigns different sensory components to the same analysis, we say that they are fused and no longer separately audible. There is another research context in which acoustic components become less audible in the presence of other ones. This is the research on masking. What is the relation between masking and fusion?

Masking and fusion differ in the tasks used to measure them. A sound is deemed to be masked if there is no way to tell whether it is present or absent in a mixture of sounds. It need not be audible as a separate sound. On the other hand, it is considered to be fused if it is not audible as a separate sound even if you can tell whether it is on or off by some change that it induces in the perceived quality of the spectrum.

One similarity between masking and fusion is that, in both cases, some components of a complex auditory mixture lose their ability to be heard individually. Another similarity is that many of the same factors that influence the audibility of components in experiments on auditory scene analysis also affect masking. Variables that help to segregate one acoustic component from others also prevent that component from being masked by the others. For example, if a target sound is micromodulated, it is harder to mask it by a sound that is not. It is also harder to mask it by a sound that does not start in synchrony with it or by one that comes from a different direction in space.

The masking effects of a band of frequencies (let us call it band A) can also be reduced by causing band A to group with a different band of frequencies (band B) that is too far away from the target to mask it. The grouping is induced by synchronizing the amplitude fluctuations in the two bands, a manipulation that affects spectral integration. This effect is called "comodulation release from masking."

The similarities in the factors that influence masking and fusion suggest that physiological mechanisms that have been evolved to serve the purpose of scene analysis are involved in the phenomenon of masking.

Any perceived property of an incoming array of sound is computed from a subset that the brain has selected from that array. The purpose of computing a property is to describe a meaningful quality, that is, a quality of a sound that has been created by some distinct happening in the world such as a speaker's voice. If the subset of sense data selected for the computation is too small, the computation may yield separate qualities for the individual acoustic components generated by the event (say individual harmonics in the voice) rather than some quality for the whole sound created by the event. I refer to the former properties as "partial" properties. If, on the other hand, the array that is used for the computation is too large, the perceived quality will represent an array that is really an accidental mixture of the acoustic energy from more than one event—for example, the sum of two vowels from different voices. I call this kind of quality chimeric. Arranging it so that the computed qualities are meaningful, rather than partial or chimeric, is the job of scene analysis. There is some evidence that there is a bias toward integration in audition. Properties will be computed on the whole incoming array of sound unless there is specific evidence that the array should be subdivided into subsets.

Results of experiments and of informal observations show that separate pitches, timbres (e.g., perceived roughness), vowel identities, and even locations can be computed separately on the streams created by scene analysis. If this were not possible we would be able to hear only one sound at a time and the qualities of that sound would always represent the sum of all ongoing events.

The Continuity Illusion and Contralateral Induction Principles of auditory scene analysis, particularly the subdivision of the array of sense data received at a particular moment, can explain two phenomena encountered in auditory research. One is the continuity illusion and the other is contralateral induction.

The continuity illusion was described in chapters 1 and 3. If a short segment of an ongoing sound is deleted and replaced by a much louder sound that has the right spectral content, the softer sound is perceived as continuing right through the louder one. The scene-analysis explanation is that the auditory system has taken part of the sensory evidence contributed by the louder sound and assigned it to the percept that represents the softer sound. This has been interpreted as a compensation for masking, since the louder sound would have masked the softer one even if it had been there.

The examples range from the simplest, in which the soft sound is a steady pure tone and the louder one is a louder version of that same tone, to the most complex case, in which the softer sound is speech and the louder one is a noise burst. In the latter example, the speech is heard as being complete. This is called phonemic restoration.

The explanation for the continuity illusion can be broken into two parts. One explains how the brain of the listener decides whether or not the soft sound is continuing behind the louder (the "whether" question). The other explains how the brain chooses what the content of the missing portion is (the "what" question). Only the "whether" question is decided by general scene-analysis principles.

The process of deciding whether a sound A has continued through an interruption by another sound B seems to be governed by some fundamental rules. They can be stated in terms of the labeling of the parts of the stimulus that is given in figure 3.22 of chapter 3. A1 and A2 are the parts of the softer tone, A, that precede and follow the interruption. B is the louder tone that replaces the deleted segment of A.

The continuity illusion involves the partitioning of the sensory stimulation received at time B (the period when B is on) into two bundles. One is interpreted as a continuation of sound A. The other is interpreted as a second sound that comes on suddenly, and its acoustic properties are perceived as consisting of ones that, when added to those of A, would yield the total stimulation received at time B. The scene-analysis system has concluded that A1 and A2 are not separate sounds but parts of the same one. This interpretation aids in the recognition of A, since the recognition process will try to identify a single long sound with properties of both A1 and A2 and not two sounds with separate sets of properties. When A1 and A2 are really parts of one sound, this will be an effective strategy.

The rules that govern the decision as to whether to restore A by partitioning the evidence supplied by B are as follows:

The "no discontinuity in A" rule. There should be no evidence that B is actually covering up a silence between A1 and A2 rather than covering the continuation of A. This means that there should be no evidence that A actually shuts off when B starts or turns on again when B finishes. There must be no audible silent gaps between A1, B, and A2, and there should be no changes in the amplitude of A1 or A2 near the boundary of B.

The "sufficiency of evidence" rule. During B, some subset of the neural activity in the auditory system should be indistinguishable from activity that would have occurred if A had actually continued. This implies that B should be sufficiently louder than A to provide adequate stimulation in the neural frequency channels normally stimulated by A. If B is a different frequency from A, then B will have to be of an even greater loudness so that the neural spread of excitation can supply a sufficient amount of activity in the frequency channels that normally signal A's presence. When a familiar signal (such as a spoken word) is being recognized by the schema-based recognition system, the latter will supply a hypothesis for what the missing part of A is. In this case, the stimulation will be required to contain the neural evidence that is normally activated by the missing part of A.

The "A1-A2 grouping" rule. There should be evidence that A1 and A2 have actually come from the same source. This means that the heuristics for sequential grouping would have put them into the same stream even if they had been separated by a silence instead of by B. If A1 and A2 do not fit well into the same stream, the restoration will not be favored. The rule allows the missing parts of two or more soft sounds, interrupted by the same louder sound, to be restored without confusion. The parts of each sound will be grouped into their own stream and a restored part will be computed for each stream.

The "A is not B" rule. The transition from A to B and back again should not be interpretable as sound A transforming into a new form, B, and then back again. If it is interpretable in this way, the listener should not hear two sounds, one continuing behind the other, but simply one sound, changing from one form into another and then back again. The criterion for hearing interruption rather than transformation is probably whether or not the rate of change exceeds a critical value, thereby giving evidence for a discontinuity in the signal.

Contralateral induction occurs when a soft sound presented to one ear is accompanied by a loud "inducing" sound in the other ear. As a result, the perceived location of the softer sound is pulled toward the center of the body. The interesting part of this is that the inducing sound is not required to be the same as the softer sound. If it were, contralateral induction would just be an example of the well-known fact that the binaural intensity balance for a particular sound determines its perceived location.

An example of contralateral induction can be created by sending a pure tone to one ear and a noise burst to the other. It is found that in order to serve as an inducer the noise must stimulate neural frequency channels that correspond to those stimulated by the pure tone in the other ear. This can happen either because the inducer contains the needed frequency components or because it is loud enough to stimulate the corresponding frequency channels through spread of neural excitation. Contralateral induction is a case in which the scene-analysis system pulls out of the noise the frequency components that match those of the tone and interprets the matching components on the left and the right as evidence for a centrally located tone.

The effect resembles the continuity illusion in that a complex sound is decomposed into two parts: one that matches another sound and a residual. The matching part is treated as belonging to the sound that it matches. In both cases, the sound that has to be decomposed must be much louder than the other one so that enough stimulation is received in the corresponding neural channel to supply a reasonable match to the softer tone.

Contralateral induction is actually a particular way of hearing a complex binaural event. The louder sound is interpreted as masking one ear's share of the binaurally balanced energy that has arisen from a centrally located softer tone. We should be aware that this interpretation is not guaranteed to be correct. However, it is correct often enough that we notice it, and realize that it is an "interpretation," only when unusual conditions that we set up in the laboratory cause it to be incorrect.

The percept of contralateral induction is not the only way of interpreting binaurally matched stimulation. We can block it if we arrange conditions appropriately. Here is a simple demonstration. Suppose we present a soft tone continuously to the left ear and a white noise continuously to the right. If we make the noise loud enough it pulls the localization of the tone to the center. This is the normal case of contralateral induction. Now we can eliminate the induction by simply pulsing the noise while holding the tone steady. If we do this, the scene-analysis system detects the fact that there are large amplitude changes in one ear that are not matched by any changes in the other, and this causes it to favor the interpretation of two streams of sound: a steady one on one side of the body and a pulsing one at the other. It refrains from centering the tone during the moments at which the noise burst is on, despite the fact that some of the right-ear stimulation could be used as a match for the stimulation on the left.

The examples of continuity that we have discussed show how the auditory system can resist momentary cases of masking. Masking occurs when there is no way to tell whether a part of the currently received sensory stimulation should be treated as a separate sound. (By analogy, we do not see a totally red piece of paper as containing a red spot at its center, since there is no border between the "spot" and the rest of the red.) Audition uses a number of methods to detect the fact that an embedded part of a complex mixture of stimulation should be extracted and interpreted as a separate sound. One type of clue is finding the sound in isolation before and after the complex mixture. Another is detecting a clearer, more isolated version of the sound in the other ear. A third is detecting a difference between the fundamental frequency of the embedded spectrum and the rest of the spectrum. In short, it can use any of the heuristics of the scene-analysis system.

Schema-Based Stream Segregation

Nature of Primitive and Schema-Based Organization

So far we have been focusing on primitive processes in scene analysis. These are assumed to establish basic groupings among parts of the sensory evidence so that the number and the qualities of the sounds that are ultimately perceived will be based on these groupings. The groupings are assumed to be based on rules that take advantage of fairly constant properties of the acoustic world, such as the fact that most sounds tend to be continuous, to change location slowly, and to have components that start and end together. However, the story of auditory organization would not be complete if it ended here. The experiences of the listener are also structured by more refined knowledge of particular classes of signals, such as speech, music, machine noises, and other familiar sounds of our environment. Psychologists (and many computer scientists) argue that this knowledge is captured in units of mental control called schemas. Each schema incorporates information about one particular regularity in our environment. Regularity can occur at different levels of size and spans of time. So in our knowledge of language, for example, we would have a schema for the sound "a", one for the word "apple", one for the grammatical structure of a passive sentence, one for the pattern of give and take in a conversation, and so on.

We think that schemas become active when they detect, in the incoming sense data, the particular pattern that they deal with. Because many of the patterns that schemas look for (such as the structure of a sentence) extend over time, when part of the evidence is present and the schema is activated, it can prepare the perceptual process for the remainder of the pattern. I will refer to this preparation as schema-governed attention. A schema can be activated not only by the specific sense data that it has been constructed to recognize but by other schemas with which it is associated. So if you read the word "apple" you will be more prepared to read the word "fruit" as well.

Any natural situation in the world exhibits many regularities and therefore will activate many schemas. But they do not just fire off in parallel. Their job is to compose themselves together to create a consistent description of the world at that moment.

A schema claims certain portions of the sensory evidence and groups them to create the particular description that it is responsible for. In so doing, it acts like a scene-analysis process. The goal of this part of my discussion is to consider the relations between the primitive preattentive clustering of sensory input that I have described up to now and the schema-governed, attention-based construction of perceived objects. A particularly important question is how we might distinguish the contributions of these two hypothetical mechanisms to the grouping effects that have been studied in the laboratory.

There are cases in the research literature in which primitive grouping processes seem not to be responsible for the perceptual groupings. For example, when two simultaneous vowels are synthesized on the same fundamental frequency, start and stop at the same time, and emanate from the same spatial position, we know of no rules of primitive grouping that could partition the spectrum into two parts, one for each vowel. Nonetheless, we can often distinguish two vowels in such a mixture. We suspect that the schema for each vowel is picking out what it needs from the total spectrum rather than requiring that a partitioning be done by the primitive process.

Another example of the schema-based selection of sense data occurs in the phonemic restoration of a speech sound that has been masked by a sudden loud noise (we hear the speech continue through the noise). Apparently we select certain frequency components out of the noise and hear them as if they were the missing speech sounds. This selection must be accomplished by a process that expects particular sounds to be there. Presumably, that process is a schema that represents the sound pattern of a particular word.

The previous two examples show that schemas can select evidence out of a mixture that has not been subdivided by primitive scene analysis. There are also examples that show another capacity: the ability to regroup evidence that has already been segregated by the primitive process. For example, if we synthesize a two-formant speech sound in which each formant is constructed from harmonics related to a different fundamental frequency, listeners will have an unusual experience. They will hear two sounds, one corresponding to each related group of harmonics. Yet at the same time they will hear a single speech sound, the one conveyed by the full set of harmonics. It seems that the schemas that recognize speech sounds can, at least in some cases, put together evidence that has been partitioned by the primitive process.

Let me summarize the differences between the concepts of primitive and schema-based scene analysis. Primitive segregation employs neither past learning nor voluntary attention. It is present in infants and, therefore, probably innate. It partitions the sensory evidence by being sensitive to relations that indicate that parts of the input have come from different sound-generating events. These relations tend to be valid clues over wide classes of acoustic events. By way of contrast, the schemas that are involved in schema-based organization have been developed for particular classes of sounds. They supplement the general knowledge that is packaged in the innate heuristics by using specific learned knowledge.

Our voluntary attention employs schemas. For example, when we are listening carefully for our name being called out among many others in a list, we are employing the schema for our name. Anything that is being "listened for" is part of a schema. Therefore whenever attention is accomplishing a task, schemas are participating. This means that if we can find cases of attention, we can find instances of schema-based segregation. But how do we know when attention is being used? One mark of attention is that it involves a subjective experience of effort. Another is that the number of things that can be attended to at the same time is quite limited. When we see the factors of effort and limited capacity operating in an auditory scene analysis task, we can infer the presence of attention.

This does not mean that the tasks that are used in experiments that seem to involve attention (and schemas) cannot be employed to demonstrate the influence of primitive grouping. The subjects in an experiment always have a conception of what they are listening for, and this "conception" is what we mean by a schema. However, the variables in the experiment may produce their results through their effects on primitive grouping. If the primitive process creates organizations that do not correspond to the grouping of evidence that the schemas need, the task of the schemas is made harder. The challenge to the theorist is to decide whether it is only one or both of these classes of processes that have been affected by the variables. This decision is made difficult by the fact that the two systems are likely to use the same sorts of sensory information. For example, if a tune that we are listening for is separated in frequency from distractor tones, this fact may affect both forms of organization. Primitive grouping would use the separation to put the tune and the distractors into separate streams. The schema-based process that was looking for the tune's notes might be more easily able to distinguish them from others that were far away in frequency than from nearby tones. Therefore we must look for two different patterns of causality that seem to correspond to the distinction between the primitive and the schema-governed process.

For example, we believe that regularity and familiarity of signals are dealt with by schemas. If we can find some sort of auditory organization that is independent of these factors, we have evidence for a primitive process that does not employ schemas.

The critical reader may ask why we should bother, in the first place, to distinguish schema-based segregation from primitive scene analysis. The answer is that there seems to be some empirical evidence that there are two classes of processes that show different patterns of causality. Let me mention some examples.

First, preliminary evidence shows that infants employ some of the grouping principles that I have called "primitive." Presumably the patterns of tones that were used to test them could not yet have been built into schemas.

Second, when listeners are presented with a sequence of alternating high and low tones, the effects of frequency separation and rate depend on what the listeners are trying to hear. If they are trying to hold the sequence together as a single stream, there is a strong segregating effect of the frequency difference between the high and low tones, and the effect is magnified by speed. However, if they are trying to listen only to a substream (say the lower tones), there is almost no effect of frequency separation, and the small effect that exists is independent of speed. We can interpret the difference in the causal pattern as follows. When the attention-based process is opposing primitive streaming by trying to include tones that are being segregated by the primitive process, this becomes harder as the primitive segregation becomes stronger. However, when it is trying to select a subset of tones, it requires only a minimum frequency separation to do this and can succeed whether the targets are in their own stream or in a stream with other tones. In other words, it seems that attention-based segregation can easily subdivide a stream but has difficulty integrating material across streams.

It appears also that the two processes have different effects on perception. Primitive processes *partition* the sensory evidence whereas schema-based attentional ones *select* from the evidence without partitioning it. This means that the effects of primitive segregation are symmetrical. When it segregates high tones from low ones, we can listen more easily to either the high ones alone or the low ones alone. Similarly, when it separates two sets of sounds by spatial location, we can more easily listen to the ones on the right or the ones on the left. However, the effects of schema-based selection do not show this symmetry. When my own name is embedded in a mixture of sounds the fact that it is my name makes it easier for me to hear it in the mixture, but it does not make it easier for me to tell what the remainder of the mixture consists of. Schema-based selection often seems to use the evidence that it needs without removing it from the mixture. For these reasons, it may be possible to use the asymmetry of the partitioning to detect the presence of schema-based segregation.

The effects of speed may also distinguish the two types of processes. It appears that segregation based on variables such as differences in frequency, timbre, or location actually gets stronger as the sequence speeds up. But the ability to select by loudness or by familiarity gets worse. This suggests to me that the first group of variables is used by the primitive process but the latter group is not.

There is also some indication that there is a difference in the time span across which primitive grouping and schema-based integration operate. It appears that the schema-based process can look at relations over a longer time span than the primitive one can.

Tests of the Existence of a Primitive Process

If we are to distinguish the role of a primitive organizational mechanism in the total process of interpreting sound, we have to find a mechanism that operates according to the description that I have just given. It must work independently of learning. It must not care about the regularity of the sequence and it must operate independently of attention. Let us look at these three issues, in turn, to try to determine whether the contribution of a primitive process can be detected.

It has been shown experimentally that learning can affect our ability to recognize a familiar tune whose notes have been interleaved with the notes of another one. If you tell the listeners the name of the tune to listen for, this will help them to hear it. However, if you tell them this name and then ask them to recognize the other tune, with which it is mixed, this information does not help them. This asymmetry shows that familiarity affects the schema-based process, rather than the primitive one.

Does Sequential Grouping Take Advantage of Trajectories? The question of whether a regular sequence of sounds (that is, where the sequence is predictable) is easier to recognize than an irregular one has also received some study. Auditory attention theorists have proposed that as we listen repeatedly to an auditory pattern we learn the regularities in it. This knowledge, because it allows us to anticipate the parts of the pattern before they occur, makes it possible for us to ready our attention and to integrate the sequence more easily into a coherent mental representation. The streaming phenomenon (that is, the exclusion of some of the tones in a sequence from an auditory stream) is interpreted, in this framework, as the failure of attention to follow the sequence. Therefore the regularity of the pattern of tones in a sequence, since it makes the readying of attention easier, ought to have very strong effects on the formation of streams.

This theory has received some confirmation from experiments on the listener's memory for regular and irregular sequences of tones. However, since the task of remembering is strongly affected by the schema-based process, it is not suitable for demonstrating the properties of primitive grouping.

Other experiments in which the listeners simply judged the number of streams without having to recognize or remember the patterns in them show quite different results. The regularity of the sequence does not affect the formation of streams. This suggests that streams are formed by a primitive process that is not affected by the predictability of the sequence.

One simple sort of predictable sequence is a regularly rising or falling sequence of pitches. We can call these simple trajectories. Can primitive scene analysis follow and segregate such trajectories from their acoustic contexts? Evidence both for and against such an ability exists. Let us start with the evidence against it. When a sequence is made up by interleaving a descending trajectory of tones with an ascending one, as in figure 4.2 of chapter 4, it is hard for a listener to follow one of these right through the crossover point. If we try to listen to the descending one, we find that we can follow its first half down to the crossover point. Then we find ourselves listening to the latter half of the rising sequence instead. Our intentions seem to be defeated by some process that opposes them. I think this process is a primitive one that prefers to group tones that fall in the same frequency range rather than to link tones that fall along a simple trajectory. You can make it possible for the ear to follow one of the trajectories by giving its tones a different timbre from the remaining ones, but this manipulation is simply introducing timbre as a new basis for segregation. It is not strengthening any primitive trajectory-based segregation.

There are also some data that derive from the continuity illusion. They are found when we present listeners with a connected sequence of alternately rising and falling pure-tone glides as shown in figure 1.15 of chapter 1. Noise bursts are inserted in the place of the peaks of the pattern (where the frequency reaches a maximum and then begins to fall). When the auditory system restores the missing peak, we do not hear it as having the frequency of the missing one but as being at the highest frequency that is actually present (the highest one that has been spared by the deletion). This occurs despite the fact that the missing peak's frequency is predictable from the slopes of the non-deleted parts. Apparently there exists a primitive restoration mechanism that does not use the trajectory to predict the missing parts.

Another failure of trajectories to control scene analysis is found when you try to capture a tone out of a mixture or out of a sequence of tones by preceding this mixture or sequence by a series of captor tones. The capturing is often successful when the captors are at the same frequency as the target tone but typically is unsuccessful when the captors merely fall on a common trajectory with the target tone.

Now for the positive evidence for the use of trajectories in scene analysis. Some examples come from research on the illusion of continuity. When segments of pure-tone glides precede and follow a loud noise burst, the listener more easily hears this as a single glide continuing behind the noise when the segments before and after the noise line up on a common trajectory. This stimulus is different from the one in the previous example. In that one, the glides that preceded and followed the peak did not line up on a common trajectory; rather, they pointed to the same frequency peak. Apparently this pointing is not used by the system.

Other evidence that seems to suggest a role for trajectories in scene analysis is that when listeners are asked to report the order of tones in a sequence, the task is easier when the tones follow a rising or falling trajectory. I would like to interpret these results, however, not in terms of perceptual grouping but in terms of the ease of encoding a regular trajectory into memory. In general, the effects of regularity tend to be seen most clearly in tasks that involve memory.

However, even if sequences of tones that form a trajectory are found to form more integrated streams, and we find the integration to be perceptual in origin, there is still an explanation that does not require the auditory system to make specific use of the regularity in the trajectory. Think of what happens when the tones are *not* on a trajectory. The reason that stream segregation breaks up this sort of sequence is that tones often prefer to group with tones that are nearest to them in frequency rather than with those that are nearest in time. Yet notice that in a trajectory no such conflict can arise; the nearest neighbors are nearest on both dimensions. It may be this continuity, rather than the fact that the sequence follows a rule, that is responsible for the perceptual integrity of a trajectory.

I have noticed that trajectory-based organization increases with more exposures to the stimulus. This points to an involvement of learned schemas in the integration of trajectories. My personal conclusion is that the primitive Gestalt-like grouping process does not make use of the fact that a sequence may be rule-governed or may point to some future position of a sound in frequency or in time. When it appears that it does, either it is just making use of the frequency proximity of tones that are present in trajectories or we are looking at a process of schema-governed integration.

We may be misled by visual analogies. It may well be a primitive process that is responsible for the enhanced grouping of the parts of a line that fall on two sides of an occluding surface when the parts fall on a common trajectory. Primitive organization may also be responsible for the fact that when a moving form disappears behind a barrier, the perceived continuity of motion depends on whether the entering and exiting paths fall on a common trajectory. We must not be seduced by these cases. The regularities, in the world of objects, that justify these kinds of grouping in vision are not the same ones that affect trajectories of sound. For example, visible objects have physical inertia that keeps them moving on straight lines. Sounds have no inertia to keep their pitch changes moving along a simple trajectory. Therefore the auditory system may not have evolved analogous rules for the primitive integration of trajectories.

A common form of regularity in sound is rhythm. This observation prompts us to ask whether this form of regularity affects primitive grouping. Theorists who argue that streams are formed by the attentional process have proposed that since predictability is what allows sequences to be integrated, then rhythmic regularity is responsible for the formation of streams. However, experiments on temporally irregular sequences that contain high- and low-frequency tones have found that streams are formed in the same way as in rhythmic sequences. The task in these experiments has merely been to decide on the number of streams, not to recognize patterns embedded in them. The recognition of patterns may have a heavy schema component and may therefore be affected by temporal regularity or by any other form of regularity.

It is important to evaluate the view that primitive organization operates independently of attention. Not every researcher believes it. Testing the idea is difficult because attention operates in most tasks. One approach to circumventing this problem is to manipulate the primitive grouping of sounds that we are trying to *exclude* from attention. If we could obtain evidence that they were actually organized, then we might conclude that organization does not require attention. Some results suggest that such organization exists, but they are not conclusive. Perhaps the most suggestive evidence comes from experiments in which the attention of the listener is controlled in different ways in the same experiment. It is found that the primitive factors of frequency separation have different effects in the two cases. Assuming that the primitive process has divided a sequence of sounds into two streams, it is easier for attention to further subdivide one of these streams than to reintegrate the divided streams. It is the conflict between attention and the primitive grouping process that reveals the existence of the latter.

Another approach to testing for the existence of a primitive preattentive process it to look for the formation of coherent residuals. I have assumed that when a schema extracts what it needs from a mixture of sense evidence, it does not create partitions that serve to bracket the excluded evidence as well as the included evidence. In other words, it selects rather than partitions. One could test this assertion by designing experiments that presented particular auditory patterns to listeners repeatedly so that they formed schemas for these patterns. Then extra sounds could be added to these patterns as distractors and the subjects asked to recognize the familiar patterns despite the distractors. Then one could test to see whether the sounds that were not used by the schema would be, as a consequence of exclusion, more likely to group with one another than if they had not been excluded by a schema.

Primitive Auditory Organization in Music

Role of Primitive Organization in Music

Both primitive scene analysis and complicated schemas play a role in our perception of music. Since the primitive process is the subject of this volume, let us consider its role.

Traditionally music is described as having a horizontal and a vertical dimension. These relate to the horizontal and vertical dimensions of a sheet of music. The horizontal one is concerned with the sequence of sounds that defines melody and the vertical one is concerned with the relations between simultaneous sounds that define harmony. Both these dimensions require primitive organization. The horizontal one is affected by sequential organization and the vertical one depends on simultaneous organization.

Perceptual organization plays a different role in music than in natural environments. In everyday life, its purpose is to segregate the streams of sound that are created by specific sound sources and to treat mixtures as accidental. If this always succeeded in music, instruments would never be able to blend to create new timbres or to define melodies that were carried in a succession of notes from different instruments. Music must defeat the stream-segregation tendencies (or at least work with them) to achieve its goals. Musical perceivers must perceive those organizations that are part of the architecture of the music itself rather than perceiving the individual pieces of hardware that are employed to produce the sound. They must hear fictional sources of sounds that have qualities that emerge from the set of sounds being grouped.

Fusion and segregation must therefore be carefully controlled in music. Their control has traditionally been carried out by rules of thumb, evolved over the course of musical history, rather than by an explicit understanding of principles of perceptual organization. However, a clear scientific understanding could contribute to a more exact theory of orchestration, particularly in relation to the newer musical forms for which pragmatic rules have not yet been evolved. For example, when composers generate musical sounds with a computer, they do not have to use distinct acoustic sound sources analogous to the instruments of the orchestra. The choice of whether to structure the sound as a collection of "instruments" is a decision that has to be made explicitly.

Sequential and simultaneous organization help to create many aspects of musical experience. Sequential grouping is the foundation of rhythm and of many aspects of melodic form, whereas simultaneous grouping is involved with such experiences as chord perception, timbre, consonance, and dissonance.

One form of segregation occurs between the musical piece that we are hearing and any accompanying nonmusical events, such as coughs or static. There is a second type of segregation between the different parts of the piece of music itself. This sort of organization has to be strong in some ways and weak in others. The segregation has to be strong enough for the listener to perceive each line of melody with its own distinct timbre. At the same time it must not be so strong as to keep us from perceiving the musical relations between the parts. The best solution would be to organize the music into a hierarchical form (parts within larger parts). Think of the way in which the fingers on a hand are perceived: distinct and yet united to create a larger form. We believe that perception is structured in this way, but we do not know whether these hierarchical structures are formed by primitive or by schema-based processes. I rather suspect that it is the latter. Since this book is primarily about the primitive process that is employed in all auditory perception, we will not be saying much more about either this hierarchical organization or the many forms of organization (scales, chord relations, and so on) that are specific to music.

Melody

Melody is the horizontal dimension of music. It is governed by principles of sequential organization. We saw earlier that when a sequence of tones contains large frequency transitions that occur in short periods of time, the sequence does not remain perceptually coherent. Music has adjusted itself to this fact. Small transitions in the fundamental frequencies (or pitches) of notes are much more common than large ones in traditional Western music, and when the speed has to be made very fast (as in trills, grace notes, and other ornamentation) the pitch jumps are made very small.

Rapid alternations of high and low tones are sometimes found in music, but composers are aware that such alternations segregate the low notes from the high. Transitions between high and low registers were used by the composers of the Baroque period to create compound melodic lines—the impression that a single instrument, such as a violin or flute, was playing more than one line of melody at the same time. These alternations were not fast enough to cause compulsory segregation of the pitch ranges, so the experience was ambiguous between one and two streams. Perhaps this was why it was interesting.

The segregation of high and low notes does not seem to be sensitive to musically significant relations such as the octave. A rapid succession of alternating high and low notes spaced an octave apart will segregate just as strongly from one another as notes that are not separated by this exact interval. The octave relation does not hold them together. This suggests that the formation of musical streams is strongly affected by a very primitive form of grouping that knows nothing about octaves.

Experiments have been done on the listener's ability to recognize melodies whose notes are interleaved with distractor tones. If the distractors fall into the same pitch range as the melody, the recognition is very hard. The further the distractors are in pitch from the melody, the easier the recognition becomes. In general, many of the findings with musical material have paralleled the results found in the laboratory with cycles of tones.

The transformations in pitch that occur over time define melodic form. For example, a rising sequence of tones is perceived as a rising "gesture." Unless the tones that define the beginning and end of the upward transition are perceived as part of the same stream, no sense of upward transition will be experienced. So transformations must be packaged within streams. Such a requirement makes sense in nature. Transformations signal important changes in the behavior of a sound source. The rise in intensity of a set of footsteps may tell us that the walker is drawing nearer. On the other hand, if each of a series of sounds derives from an event unrelated to the others, the intensity relation between them may be meaningless. Only if a single source (represented in our mind as a single stream) is creating the acoustic changes are they likely to really define a meaningful transformation in the world. We have presumably developed a perceptual system that looks for meaningful transitions within streams. Musical transformations have to be content to live within such a system.

My comments have so far been restricted to changes in pitch. But changes in timbre can also affect the integrity of a musical sequence. Sudden repeated changes in timbre can fragment our perception of a sequence of notes. This fact has been put to musical use in the technique of "klangfarbenmelodie," a rapid sequence of shifting timbres. More commonly, shifts in timbre are used to delineate musical units of larger sizes and to have their effects on phrasing. They are neither sudden enough nor frequent enough to affect the primitive coherence of the musical line.

Some notes in a line of music seem to define the overall form of the phrase whereas others, usually shorter (for example, grace notes), seem to serve as ornamentations that are appended to the form-bearing notes and seem to be subordinate to them. They seem to group with the note to which they are subordinate (let us call it the "anchor note") so as to create a larger event that has more complexity than a single note. The Gestalt psychologists called this relation "phenomenal dependency." Often the dependency is between successive notes played by a single instrument, but in ensembles it can be created between notes arising from different instruments. In this case the resulting complex auditory event can have qualities that a note from neither of the component instruments would have.

The tight perceptual binding between the sounds that generate these emergent events is accomplished by the Gestalt-like principles of primitive scene analysis. For example, the dependent note must be very close to the anchor note in frequency and time. Otherwise the two will not group to form a larger event. Ideally, both the time intervals and the pitch intervals between the sounds that are to form the event should be less than those between the notes that precede and follow them. The choice of which note is the dependent one and which the anchor depends on factors such as duration, intensity, and rhythm, the anchor typically being longer, louder, and on a major beat. The dependency can also be affected by the pattern of adjacent tones in ways that are predictable from Gestalt principles.

When component sounds are grouped sequentially to form a larger sonic event their own individual properties are to some extent lost. The loss is not as severe as with simultaneous sounds that are fused, but it is still noticeable. The perceived pitches of dependent tones tend to be altered or to become less distinct. This tends to happen less to the beginning and end tones than to the interior tones of rapid phrases. It also has less effect on tones that are the highest or lowest in their phrase.

I have emphasized the primitive processes that affect dependency, but schema-based ones that pertain to the musical style can also be involved. Dependent notes tend to be ones that are defined as unstable in the musical system, and they tend to resolve to stable anchor tones.

Timbre

Timbre can also play a role in the sequential organization of music. Timbre changes are rarely large enough and rapid enough to cause the line of melody to split into parallel streams, as in a "compound melodic line." Yet they could be used in that way. If the variations in pitch were small and those of timbre were large, we know from laboratory studies that timbre could control stream segregation. Often, as I have pointed out in the previous section, timbre is used as a sequential glue for musical phrases. Playing a phrase in a timbre different from the ones preceding and following it can help it to be perceived as a unit in the music. A textbook example of this technique can be seen in Webern's orchestration of the Ricercar from Bach's *Musical Offering*, in which the phrases are carved out almost surgically by timbre. On the other hand, if timbre is made to change repeatedly and rapidly within a phrase, the sequence becomes fragmented. This technique is used in hockets in which notes from different instruments follow in rapid succession. It also occurs in Webern's use of klangfarbenmelodie.

In using timbre to outline segments of the music, the composer is exploiting the scene-analysis principles that audition has evolved for arriving at accurate descriptions of natural sound-producing events. When there is a sudden change in timbre, it is usually valid to infer that some new event has begun. When the timbres change continuously, it is more likely that a single event is changing in some way. We perceive the change as a transformation that defines a "happening." If we knew what the dimensions of timbre were, we could use movements along them to define transformations that could serve as structural elements in a piece of music. This would be a stronger use of timbre than simply using it to color in the forms that have already been defined by pitch changes.

But what are the dimensions of timbre? There have been a number of different approaches to this question. One has been to ask people to rate the similarity between different pairs of sounds and then to try to infer how many dimensions could account for these judgments. Three dimensions have been found: the brightness of the spectrum, the bite of the attack, and the simplicity of the behavior of the harmonics over time. These are very general qualities of sound.

Another approach has been to look for general dimensions of timbre in the acoustic dimensions that define the differences between spoken vowels. The dimensions that have been chosen correspond to the frequencies of the lowest two prominent peaks (formants) in the spectrum of the sound. Music has been created in which timbral shapes were formed by the changes of the sounds along these dimensions.

A third approach is to try to synthesize imitations of natural sounds in which spectral details are eliminated. If these details do not matter, an imitation will be judged as an acceptable example of the timbre of the original sound. This method of "analysis by synthesis" is expected to identify the important dimensions of timbre by a process of elimination.

Other researchers have argued that our brains are not built to hear sounds in the abstract, but to form descriptions of environmental events. Therefore the important dimensions of timbre will correspond to possible changes in the actual physical objects that produce the sound. For example, a simple change in the force with which a person strikes a gong could have many different effects on the way in which the amplitudes of different spectral components evolve over time. Yet a change in the striking force might be a simple perceptual dimension for a listener. If this were true, it would imply that the brain has implicit models of the physical systems that can produce sound and can use them to "read off" the changes in the physical system from changes in the sound.

An understanding of the primitive organization of timbre by the brain would open the way for its use as a carrier of form in music.

So far the discussion has treated timbre as some property of the evolving spectrum of a sound. Yet auditory information does not come to us in the form of separate sounds. We receive an array of auditory properties simultaneously from an unknown number of sources. Therefore scene analysis is responsible for timbre. The identity of the component sounds is known as a result of the partitioning that is done by scene analysis and the partitioning allows us to hear different timbres at the same time. This means that the use of timbre in music depends on a practical understanding of the principles of auditory fusion and segregation. When composers understand these principles, they can use instruments as generators of auditory features and use the rules of spectral grouping to form new "orchestral timbres" as clusters of these properties. The instrument becomes analogous to a color on the palette of a painter, and the perceived instruments that result from this blending are entirely fictitious.

The control of spectral integration plays an important role in music. Musicians may present musical sounds together for many reasons. At one extreme they may want the sounds to fuse and generate a global timbre. At the other, they may wish to create a polyphonic texture in which two or more distinct lines of sound can be heard. It seems likely that all of the factors that have been found in the laboratory to affect spectral integration have already been used in music for this purpose. If the scientists succeed in making these factors explicit, it will probably not change musical practice very much. However, it may provide a rational basis for a theory of orchestration. If based on basic principles of auditory organization, such a theory could be independent of particular musical styles.

Let us look at some of the ways that music uses scene-analysis principles. As an example we could examine how soloists can be kept distinct from their accompaniments. Take the use of harmonic relations, for example. Since the auditory system looks for different sets of harmonic series and segregates them, one method available to a soloist to maintain perceptual distinctness is to be producing pitches that are not the same as those produced at the same time by the accompaniment. Another is to produce nominally identical pitches that are slightly mistuned relative to the accompaniment. This occurs automatically when the soloist's notes carry some vibrato. Since the soloist's vibrato is not likely to be phase-locked with the vibrato of the accompaniment, the note will frequently be at a slightly different pitch from any in the background. The wide vibrato of an opera singer is an example.

Another technique is to play or sing a pitch that is higher or lower than any in the accompaniment. The actual frequency band occupied by the energy produced by the soloist can also be somewhat different from that of the accompaniment. For example, singers learn to produce the *singing formant*, a peak in the singer's spectrum that occurs in a spectral region that tends not to contain much power from accompanying instruments.

Onsets and offsets are very important too. Soloists can employ a "rubato" style to minimize the synchronization of their note onsets with those of the rest of the ensemble. A tight synchronization of the other players will assist in segregating the soloist who is using this technique. In general, if the soloist tries to be different from the ensemble on any acoustic variable, it helps to have the other instruments of ensemble be as close together on that variable as possible.

Even spatial location can be used to segregate the soloist. The major advantage of stereophonic recording over monaural is not that it gives a sense of space (although it does that too) but that it allows the individual instruments and voices to be more distinctly heard. As a consequence, features of the music that would be blurred in a monaural recording can be distinguished. Some attempts have been made, even in live performances, to overcome the loss of definition of musical lines in dense textures (lines that are close together in pitch) by placing the players at quite different locations with respect to the audience. This seems to be quite effective.

It is interesting to look at the role of primitive scene analysis in counterpoint. Polyphonic music is a style in which there are two or more melodic lines running in parallel. Counterpoint is the technique for composing the lines. In polyphonic music, the parts must not be either totally segregated or totally integrated. If they were totally segregated there would be no overall coherence to the composition; if they were totally integrated there would be only one line of melody. Principles of auditory organization are employed to help achieve the level of vertical organization that is wanted at each point in the piece. Although schema-based principles, particular to the musical style, are also used, I will restrict my discussion to the primitive ones.

The segregation of one line from another can be improved by making sure that each one has a strong sequential organization within itself. This is controlled, in part, by the size of the pitch changes between one note and the next. Small steps favor sequential integration. Another requirement, if the lines are to remain distinct, is that they should be well separated in pitch and should not cross. Otherwise, as we have seen in corresponding laboratory examples, the perceived streams will not maintain a correspondence with the musical parts.

Segregation can also be improved by the weakening of fusion between corresponding notes of the different parts. Common fate between the parts (a factor that increases fusion) can be avoided by prohibiting synchronous onsets and offsets of the notes in different parts. This can be accomplished if the parts are given different rhythms. (These differences in rhythm will be appreciated, however, only when the parts end up being well segregated overall.) Also, when changes in pitch occur in two parts at the same time, they should not be parallel changes. We should avoid synchronous combinations of notes that have good harmonic relations, such as the octave (frequency ratio of 2:1) or the fifth (ratio of 3:2).

Traditional polyphonic music did not use spatial separation to keep the lines distinct, perhaps because this would have broken down the perceptual unity too much. However, present-day composers have employed this device.

To obtain vertical integration just violate these rules. Make large leaps from one pitch to the next within a part so as to weaken the sequential integration. Use harmonious combinations, such as the octave, and move the parts in parallel. Start and stop notes at the same time in the different parts.

Composers who worked in the polyphonic style were even able to control dissonance by the use of methods that exploited auditory scene analysis. I would like to distinguish two types of dissonance—psychoacoustic dissonance and musical dissonance. Psychoacoustic dissonance is the sense of roughness or unevenness that occurs when certain combinations of simultaneous tones are played. This sort of dissonance is not defined by the musical style. If two tones are spaced by a perfect fifth (seven semitones, or a ratio of 3:2) they sound smooth or consonant when played together, whereas if they are spaced by a tritone (six semitones, or a ratio of 45:32) they sound rough. The roughness is caused when the partials of the two tones beat at a large number of unrelated rates. This does not happen with consonant combinations of tones. Another feature of psychoacoustically consonant combinations is that they seem to blend better than dissonant ones.

Musical dissonance, on the other hand, is a more cognitive experience. In many musical styles, certain combinations of simultaneous sounds are treated as stable and others as unstable. The resting points in the music will fall on the stable combinations. Listeners will tend to experience unstable combinations as points of tension or dissonance in the music and stable ones as points of rest. Unstable combinations in a piece will tend to resolve to stable ones. By the terms musical consonance and dissonance, I am referring to this stability and instability. In the Western musical tradition, the tones treated as unstable tend to be the very ones that are heard as psychoacoustically dissonant. This is probably not an accident. The combinations used as resting points were probably chosen because they were perceived as having a smoother quality. Although such a choice is not compulsory, it is easy to see why it was made.

Many composers of polyphonic music wanted to be freer to use the combinations of tones that were viewed as dissonant. This led them to try to control the dissonance of the experience. They did so by certain techniques of composition that exploited the principles governing primitive stream segregation. The experience of psychoacoustic dissonance is reduced when the notes whose combination is dissonant are made to fall into different perceptual streams. This is an example of the fact that, as the Gestalt psychologists pointed out, perceived qualities belong to organized perceptual units rather than existing for their own sake. It appears that the mere registration of incoherent beating by the auditory system is not sufficient to cause the listener to experience dissonance. If the tone combination that generates the beating is interpreted as an accidental co-occurrence of unrelated events, the dissonance is not assigned to the mental description of any of these events. Somehow it gets lost.

The techniques that these composers employed to control the fusion of the potentially dissonant tones were varied. The tones were not allowed to start and stop at the same time. They were captured into separate sequential streams by preceding them by tones close to them in pitch or by capturing them into smooth trajectories or into repetitive sequences.

Another approach to segregation that can be used when there are many tones playing at the same time is to cause different groups to form separate simultaneous chords in which the internal relations are consonant and to try, at the same time, to dissociate these chords from one another perceptually. The technique of "polytriads" takes this approach. The triads, taken as units, are prevented from grouping with one another by separating them well in pitch range and keeping their onsets and offsets asynchronous. Furthermore, good harmonic relations within each triad can set up separate harmonic frameworks that help to keep the streams distinct in perception. It is also useful to change the pitches of the notes inside the triad in parallel so that the continued harmonic relations can assist the integration.

Not every method that could minimize the experience of dissonance has been tried. We might decorrelate the vibrato in the potentially dissonant tones, or might separate them in space. All this presupposes that we want to suppress the experience of psychophysical dissonance. If we wanted to enhance it, and if we could use the kind of precise control over the sound that computer-generated music offers, we could exactly synchronize onsets and offsets, vibrato, and so on.

Any sort of perceptual feature that depends on isolating some of the patterns in music can be influenced by primitive grouping. We can take the example of rhythm. Rhythms are relationships between auditory events in the same stream. We can show this by the example of the polyrhythm. A polyrhythm is generated by superimposing the pulses from two different rhythms going on at the same time—say three pulses per second and four per second. If the two sets of pulses are not segregated by primitive factors (for example, if they are carried by tones of the same pitch) the listener will hear only the complex pattern generated by the sum of the two rhythms. However, if they are segregated, say by moving them apart in pitch, the two component rhythms will be easily heard.

The purpose of setting out these examples in the field of music has been to show that many of the principles of voice leading and orchestration can be understood as taking advantage of the natural tendencies of the auditory system to group sounds. A knowledge of such principles cannot prescribe musical goals, but it is possible that it could provide a principled foundation for the most basic level of musical organization. It may be interesting for musicians to find out that these principles are the same as those that allow a person to cross a busy street without getting killed or to carry on a conversation in a noisy room.

Auditory Organization in Speech

The next topic is the role that primitive auditory scene analysis plays in the perception of speech. Discovering its contribution is made more difficult by the fact that special-purpose schemas are heavily involved. So sorting out the relations between primitive organization and the organization imposed by speech-sound schemas is not easy. Some theorists argue that special schemas for recognizing the basic sounds of speech are innate in the human species. For the purposes of the present discussion it is not necessary to take a position on this issue. The existence of speech-sound schemas, innate or learned, makes it harder to uncover the contribution of primitive organization.

The "cocktail party" problem, as it is called, refers to the difficulty that a listener has in following one voice in a mixture of conversations. Research on this problem has shown that the difficulty is reduced if the target voice has some qualities that distinguish it from the others. These include pitch and spatial location and possibly voice quality and rate. (The predictability of later from earlier parts is also important, but since we are focusing on primitive organization, we will not discuss this factor.)

The statement that distinctive qualities allow us to attend to one voice obscures an important point. If we can perceive two or more separate locations, pitches, or timbres in the incoming signal, we must have already done some scene analysis. These qualities are the product of a partitioning of the auditory evidence. Therefore, if they assist in the sequential organization (the tracking of a single voice over time), they must have been made available as the result of an organization of the simultaneously present auditory components.

I want to briefly review first the sequential organization of speech and then its simultaneous organization.

Sequential Organization of Speech Sounds

The sequential integration of speech must operate on both shorter and longer time scales. On the shorter scale, the successive parts of a single word must be integrated. The success of word recognition depends on such sequential integration. Here is an example. We can create a laboratory version of the phrase "say chop" in which a short silence before the "ch" tells the listener that it is a "ch" and not a "sh". Yet if the voice changes from male to female between the two words, the male's voice will be heard as pronouncing "say" and the female's as pronouncing "shop". The critical silence is not given a phonetic significance because it is no longer a within-voice event.

Here is another example. It is said that the rhythm of a sentence is very important for its recognition. Yet rhythm is computed across the events that lie within a single perceptual stream. Without the stream-forming process, the rhythm could not be used.

Some aspects of this short-term integration are easy to account for by using the principles that I introduced earlier, but some aspects are not so easily explained. It is easy to account for the integration of the successive parts of a single vowel. Its properties tend to change very continuously. But it is harder to account for the integration of sounds that have very different qualities, such as "s" and "a". Phonemes (such as "s" or "a") occur at the rate of 10 or more per second in fluent speech. Yet we know that at 10 tones per second, an alternation of a noise burst and a tone will segregate into two streams. In what way is speech different? Are speech sounds integrated by schemas that make them immune to primitive organization? Probably not. When speech is speeded up by a factor of 2.5 or more it has been observed to segregate into substreams. Perhaps the coherence of normal speech happens because of, rather than in spite of, its acoustic structure.

To compare the sequential integration of speech sounds with other sounds, researchers have made up short repeating loops of vowel sounds or syllables. The listener's ability to integrate these cycles is much worse than for sequences that occur in natural speech. In the cycles, qualitatively different subsets of speech sounds tend to be heard in separate streams. In one experiment, syllables (such as "bee") that started with a stop consonant tended to segregate from isolated vowels (such as "oo") that were in the same loop. This suggests that the sudden onset of a stop-consonant syllable was treated as an important feature of that sound. The role of suddenness of onset as a feature defining the similarity of events has not yet been studied in the sequential integration of nonspeech sounds.

The stream segregation of cycles of vowels depends on similarities of pitch and on the speed of the sequence. The effects are the same as those that occur with nonspeech cycles. Segregation is greater with larger pitch differences and higher speeds.

The effects of pitch-based segregation have been studied with ordinary speech as well. Listeners were required to shadow a running speech sample (that is, to repeat it as it was being said). They received two different prose passages, one to each ear, and were asked to shadow whatever came into one ear (say the left). Occasionally the two passages would be swapped between the ears. Frequently, listeners made errors by continuing to track the same message rather than the desired ear. It was shown that this had happened for two reasons. The first was a tendency to follow the message that continued the same conceptual content. This was clearly schema-based. But the second was a tendency to follow the same pitch contour over time. When the message suddenly switched ears, it would continue the contour that was begun before the switch, and this caused the listeners to follow the voice to the opposite side of the head. From this it appears that pitch continuity can hold a voice together even in the presence of a sudden change in location.

The converse of this fact is also true. Pitch discontinuities can break up a voice even when other factors favor continuity. A sudden pitch change occurring halfway through a synthesized word will make it sound as though a second voice has suddenly interrupted it. Here is another example. A formant pattern may sound like the syllable "wa" when the pitch is held constant, but if the pitch is suddenly changed in the middle of the "w", it sounds as if a first voice ends in the sound "oo" and a second begins with the sound "ba". The last part of the "w", presented with the second pitch, is interpreted as the brief transition of formants that defines a "b" rather than simply as part of the longer one that defines a "w". We can conclude that pitch continuities in the voice are important in holding it together as a perceptual unit.

The previous facts apply to voiced sounds, which, like tones, have pitch. Yet there are many sorts of consonants, such as "s" and "t", that have no pitch. How are they integrated with vowels? We know that when tones and noise bursts are spliced together into a repeating cycle, the tones and noises will segregate from one another and form separate streams. Yet this does not happen with natural connected speech.

Let us take an example of unrelated sounds in speech. Some African languages contain clicks whose position in a word can determine the word's meaning. This means that the perceptual stream must incorporate the clicks. Yet when a mechanical click is superimposed on a sentence, our perceptual systems segregate it from the speech sounds and we cannot decide on its exact position relative to them. What is the difference between a speech click and a superimposed mechanical click? When the click is produced in speech, it results from a movement that not only produces the click but affects the other adjacent sounds in the word. For example, the voicing will be briefly interrupted and the formants will undergo frequency transitions as the vocal tract moves into position to articulate the consonant. This synchronization of the click with changes in voicing may tie it to a definite location in the pattern of voicing. The situation is different with a mechanical click. If it is superimposed arbitrarily on a sentence, its occurrence will probably not be synchronized with other changes and there will be no cues for integration. Quite to the contrary, there will probably be clues for continuity that travel right through the click. The same considerations apply to the integration of other sorts of consonants, such as "s", "t", or "ch", with vowels.

We do not know whether the synchrony of the changes is used by a primitive integrating mechanism or by speech-specific schemas. It is natural to conclude, when our perception deals differently with speech and nonspeech signals, that the difference must be due to speech schemas, but we should not draw such a conclusion before exploring the possibility that the effect may be due to primitive auditory grouping.

The idea that formant continuities can have an important effect on sequential integration has been supported by research findings. If a repeating cycle of vowels contains transitions connecting the corresponding formants of successive vowels, the sequence will be heard as much more coherent than it would be without these transitions. This is similar to what happens with a cycle of alternating high and low pure tones. When the tones are connected by frequency transitions, the sequence is less likely to split perceptually into high and low streams. Continuity of formants can help to overcome discontinuities in other properties of the speech. When there is a sudden shift in the fundamental frequency from that of a male voice to that of a female in the middle of a word, the word is more likely to be heard as a unit when the pattern of formant trajectories travels smoothly through the point of change.

We have mentioned two speech features—pitch and formants—whose acoustic continuity is important for the integration of speech. Another is spatial continuity. We rarely think of this sort of stability, but our auditory systems use it just the same. Its effects can be observed most easily when it is violated. For example, if we switch speech repeatedly back and forth between the ears, intelligibility suffers.

There is another factor that prevents natural speech from suffering from the same sorts of segregation as occur in repeating cycles of nonspeech sounds. There is a difference between a sentence and a repeating cycle of unrelated sounds. In the cycle, the same class of sound will repeat at regular intervals, close together in time. The tendency to group with its own class will compete with the tendency to integrate with its true sequential neighbors. Furthermore, the tendency that favors the segregation of different classes will grow stronger with more repetitions. Speech is different. There is no regular repetition of classes of sounds. Occurrences of similar noise bursts, such as "t" and "ch", may be spaced by seconds, and when closer together may not be repetitive. However, if you repeatedly recycle a word formed of two classes of sound, such as "sissy", it will eventually segregate into two streams, one for the vowels and the other for the "s" sounds. This will happen more readily if the formant transitions from the "s" sounds to the vowels are spliced out. We must recall that the purpose of research with cycles is to force particular grouping tendencies to larger-than-life proportions. This means that the research on speech cycles has been successful in identifying factors involved in sequential integration and segregation, but it cannot accurately predict the actual amount of segregation in nonrepetitive material.

Simultaneous Organization of Speech Sounds

When we encounter speech, its sounds rarely occur alone. Therefore we face the problem of collecting those parts of the simultaneous jumble of auditory properties that define a single voice. This is the problem of simultaneous organization. The problem of extracting the sounds of a particular voice from a mixture is not independent of the problem of integrating them over time. If the auditory system can get a clear exposure to a single voice at one moment, it can select matching components from a mixture that occurs an instant later. This is an instance of the old-plus-new heuristic that we encountered in our study of the perceptual organization of nonspeech sounds. The auditory system can also use cues that depend directly on the relationships among simultaneously present components.

Much of the research on simultaneous organization has been concerned with how we decide how to allocate the components of the incoming spectrum to different voices. One important factor is fundamental frequency (experienced as pitch). Although it is only voiced sounds, such as vowels, that have a fundamental, they form a large enough part of the speech signal to make fundamental frequency very significant. The auditory system appears to look for one or more fundamentals that can account for as many of the frequency components in the spectrum as possible, and then to allocate all the components related to the same fundamental to the same stream. One experiment on this topic used speech spoken in a monotone. Two messages spoken on different pitches were much easier to distinguish than two spoken on the same pitch. The same effects of pitch differences have been obtained using pairs of synthesized vowels mixed together.

In normal speech the pitch is always changing. These changes are very important in the segregation of voices. Two voices are not likely to be following exactly the same pitch contour at the same time.

Therefore the accidental fit of the harmonics of two voices to a common fundamental is unlikely to persist for more than an instant.

Another important factor is location in space. Different spatial origins make voices easier to distinguish.

Differences in time of onset and in pulsations of intensity are important as well. When a voice rises suddenly in intensity, this increase is likely to be true of a number of its components. This shared property can tie them together.

Research on voice perception has tried to discover which properties of acoustic components occurring at the same time will tie those components together to define a voice. In this research there is usually only a single voice present and the perceptual choice is between integrating all of its components or missing some of them. Generally the need for manipulation of the features requires that the voice be synthesized. Different formants of the same voice are often given different properties and then the research tries to determine whether they resist integration. This kind of research has often produced paradoxical results. When the formants are given different properties, multiple sounds are heard, but these seem to be heard as a single speech phoneme or syllable.

The similarities in the formants that have been looked at are common spatial origin, common fundamental frequency, grouping with antecedent sounds, and asynchrony of onsets and offsets.

To look at the role of common spatial origin, different formants from the same synthetic voice have been sent to the opposite ears of listeners. If the other features of the formants match, the listeners will hear only a single sound and will integrate the formants to hear the phoneme that results from the combination. However, if the other features differ in some way, the listeners may hear two distinct *sounds* but only one phoneme or syllable. Whereas the left- and right-ear formants seem to be segregated to yield the experience of two sounds in space, the phonetic interpretation includes the information from both.

A similar effect is obtained when the formants differ in the fundamental frequency of their partials. Two sounds are heard, but the formants are integrated to derive a phonetic interpretation. There is one exception to this general pattern. When a number of formants are present and the listeners can draw different phonetic interpretations by grouping them in different ways, those with the same fundamental tend to be grouped together for phonetic purposes.

We have to explain why differences in raw acoustic properties will not affect phonetic integration unless there are alternative phonetic interpretations based on different groupings of formants. I think that the success in achieving a phonetic integration of the formants when there is no competition is based not on raw acoustic factors but on schemas for speech sounds that can select the auditory evidence that they need. However, when several of these schemas are activated equally strongly, the choice of which one gets which piece of evidence may be determined by primitive scene analysis. This conclusion agrees with two facts: (a) the segregation of a mixture into two whole voices by their acoustic properties usually makes it easier to recognize the words; but (b) the segregation of the formants in a single voice often does no harm. In the case of two voices, many formants and harmonics will be present; presumably, different schemas will generally be competing for the same evidence and the partitioning of the data will resolve the competition.

So far we have thought of formants as being properties of a spectrum that are immediately available to perception. This is not the case. When we encounter a spectrum, it surely has peaks, but the position of the center of each peak may not be the product of only a single environmental sound. It may be determined by the superimposition of the partials from two or more environmental sounds. Yet auditory perception is not thwarted by this superimposition. It has ways of finding the peaks in the speech portion of the mixture. Experiments have shown that if primitive scene analysis decides that one of the partials in a spectral peak actually comes from a different source than the others, the estimated frequency center of the formant will change and this will alter the perceived speech sound. The decision to exclude the partial can depend on the fact that it is heard as a continuation of an earlier sound, or that it does not fall into the same harmonic series as the other partials in the spectral peak, or that it is too intense relative to the other partials. Why do schemas not resist the segregation of parts of a formant in the same way that they resist the segregation of whole formants from one another? Perhaps because it is not the role of schemas to decide what is or is not a formant. The defining of the formants in the spectrum may be the job of lower-level processes of auditory organization.

Duplex Perception and the Problem of Exclusive Allocation

The next topic is the principle of exclusive allocation. I am referring to the tendency to allocate the perceived features of a stimulus to one or the other of the perceived objects or events in the perceptual field but not to more than one. A visual example can be seen in figure 1.6 of chapter 1. In this drawing, a given contour is seen either as the edge of the vase or as the edge of one of the faces, but never as both at once.

We have encountered similar examples in audition. A tone can be prevented from grouping with another one if it is captured by a better partner. This capturing would be impossible if a tone could be part of two unrelated organizations at the same time. It seems as if information is allocated exclusively to one organization or another. This might be a way of guaranteeing the most parsimonious perceptual description of the sensory input.

Despite the positive examples, we encounter cases in speech perception in which spectral information is used twice, once to define a speech sound and a second time to define a nonspeech sound. It has been claimed that this means that speech perception does not depend on primitive scene analysis. I would like to examine this issue by focusing on one example of the double use of evidence—duplex perception of speech.

The phenomenon can be produced in the following way. The first step is to synthesize a pair of syllables, say "da" and "ga", in such a way that only the initial transition of the third formant distinguishes them. Let us call this the *F3 transition*. Let us call the part common to the "da" and "ga" the *base*. Now let us present the base to one ear, say the left, and only the distinguishing F3 transition to the other ear. The two parts are temporally aligned as they would be in the full syllable. If we listen to this stimulus, we have an unexpected experience. At the ear that has the isolated transition sent to it we hear a chirp, and at the ear of the base a full "da" or "ga" syllable (depending on which F3 transition was sent to the other ear). We need the F3 transition to distinguish "da" from "ga", so we must have phonetically integrated the information from the two ears. Yet we heard two sounds, one at each ear. This means that we must have segregated the information from the two ears.

The experience is called duplex perception because the sensory evidence from the F3 transition is used twice. It contributes to the perception of the correct syllable at the left of the head and is also heard as a chirp at the right. Some theorists have used this duplexity of perception to argue that two independent systems have been activated: a speech-perception system and an "auditory" system. These systems have been conceptualized as being distinct in both a functional and a biological sense. The speech-perception system is seen as carrying out its own analysis without any dependence on the auditory system. The need for two systems to explain the effect seems to be justified by the belief that information cannot be used twice within each system. In other words, the rule of exclusive allocation must hold within each one. Furthermore, it is argued, phonetic interpretation is not built on the results of scene analysis; otherwise the primitive segregation into two sounds would have prevented the phonetic integration.

My reason for thinking that this interpretation is wrong and that speech perception actually takes advantage of primitive scene analysis is as follows. We know that when voices are mixed, the recognition of speech *is* affected by factors such as spatial separation and pitch difference. If this fact does not imply that speech perception takes advantage of primitive organization, it must mean, instead, that the speech system itself contains methods for the segregation of voices by these factors, and the methods must respond in exactly the same way to these stimulus factors as primitive analysis does. It is simpler to suppose that it uses the existing multipurpose machinery that has been evolved to do primitive grouping.

Nonetheless, phonetic integration is remarkably unaffected by the acoustic relations between the base and the F3 transition. The loss in phonetic recognition from splitting the signal to the two ears instead of sending it all to one is significant, but not large. Research has found that the parts presented to different ears can also have different fundamentals or be started asynchronously. Although each of these differences reduces phonetic integration a little, it remains fairly strong. Even the frequency alignment of the tail end of the F3 transition with the continuation of the same formant in the base is not critical. The recognition schema for the syllable seems to be able to pull together the information it needs despite strong tendencies for primitive processes to separate it.

Since the theoretical implications that have been drawn from duplex perception of speech depend on the belief that the rule of exclusive allocation must inevitably hold true within a single perceptual system, I want to examine whether this belief is valid. If it is not, then duplex perception may not have to be seen as the conflict between two systems. Let us examine, then, the conditions for obtaining violations of the rule of exclusive allocation.

Separating the formants and sending them to different ears does not always produce duplex perception. In a two-formant synthesis, if each formant remains whole and the two are sent to opposite ears, as long as the two formants match well acoustically, not only is there phonetic integration but only one sound is heard. It seems that other acoustic differences must be added to the difference in spatial location before the listener will hear two sounds. When there are very strong cues that only a single sound is present it affects both the phonetic integration and the sounds-in-space organization.

Furthermore, presentation to separate ears is not necessary for producing the duplex effect. You can play both formants to a single ear; but if the formants have different fundamentals, the listener will hear two distinct sounds, yet at the same time will integrate the formants phonetically. It does not appear that any one acoustic difference between parts of the signal is essential for hearing two sounds, as long as there is a sufficiently large difference. Whether two sounds are heard or not, the formants will be integrated into a single speech percept as long as there is no competition among speech schemas for the use of particular formants.

Violations of exclusive allocation are not restricted to speech. We can play the highest and lowest notes of a musical chord to one ear and the middle note to the other. Let us set it up so that the middle note tells the listener whether the chord is major or minor. Many listeners will report hearing a full chord at the ear that gets the two notes and an additional note at the other ear. The full chord will be experienced as either major or minor, depending on the identity of the isolated note.

Another case of violation of exclusive allocation can be obtained with environmental sound. A recording of a metal door closing can be filtered to obtain a low-frequency and a high-frequency part. The low part, played alone, sounds like a wooden door closing and the high part in isolation sounds like a rattle. These parts are sent to opposite ears. The listeners will hear a metal door at the ear that receives the low part and an extra rattle at the other ear. The high-frequency sound is used twice, once in combination with the low to produce a metal door and separately, as well, to produce a rattle.

Other cases of duplex perception occur. When there are conflicting cues to the spatial location of a sound, sometimes two sounds will be heard. Also, when a partial is captured from a complex spectrum by a preceding copy of that partial played in isolation, the partial will be heard out from the spectrum, but the spectrum will still have some of the quality contributed by that partial.

We see from these examples that the violation of the rule of exclusive allocation need not involve the simultaneous use of the speech system and the nonspeech auditory system. Nor need it result from the use of two biologically and functionally distinct systems.

While the previous examples show that the violation *need not* involve the independent actions of two biological systems, they do not rule out the possibility that in the particular case of duplex perception of speech this sort of independent action is actually the cause. Therefore we have to look more closely at the assumption that the analyses done by the speech-recognition system are not at all constrained by primitive auditory organization.

The first thing to remember is that the recognition of a speech sound when parts of it are sent to opposite ears is less accurate than when all parts are sent to the same ear. This, in itself, implies some constraint from auditory grouping. However, a stronger argument against the idea that the speech system can ignore primitive groupings comes from an experiment on duplex perception in which a perceptual grouping was shown to affect the recognition of the speech sound. In this experiment, the base was sent to the left ear and a formant transition (let us call it the "critical" transition) to the right as before. Together they made either the syllable "ga" or "da". But a series of additional formant transitions, short ones identical to the critical one, were played to the right ear before and after the syllable. These extra transitions grouped with the critical one and captured it into a stream of chirps at the right ear. This had the effect of reducing its contribution to the identification of the syllable. However, when the extra transitions were in a frequency range that was different from that of the critical one, they did not capture it into their stream and did not reduce its contribution to the phonetic identification of the syllable.

The violations of exclusive allocation seem to occur only in cases where two different sounds could be occurring at the same time. I do not know of cases that occur in the sequential grouping of pure tones. In cases of strictly sequential grouping, a tone seems to be required to be in only one stream at a time. It is only in cases of complex spectra that two percepts can be based on the same evidence. Perhaps the prohibition of the double allocation of evidence is weaker in complex spectra, where sounds might be overlapping in time. After all, sounds are transparent, so that a given spectral component at one ear could actually have resulted from the superimposition of components arising from more than one environmental event. Allocating the component to only one of these sonic events would be a mistake.

Here is an example. Suppose two sources of sound are active at the same time, one at my left and the other at my right. Suppose, in addition, that they both have a harmonic at 1,000 Hz and that the 1,000-Hz energy is balanced at my two ears. If the localization of sounds were determined by the balance of energy at the left and right ears, then I should hear a separate 1,000-Hz sound straight ahead of me. Such disembodied sounds should occur very frequently just by chance. But we never hear them. Instead, we allocate the energy to the larger sounds with which they have good acoustic relations. Such relations could include starting at the same time or fitting into the same harmonic series. In the present example it is probable that the 1,000-Hz harmonic is allocated to both the left-side and the right-side sonic events.

How is the auditory system to know whether a piece of sensory evidence should or should not be allocated to two percepts? A reasonable guess is that it uses basic acoustic relations (such as spatial relations, harmonic relations, and frequency continuity) to assess how well the properties of the local piece of sensory evidence fit together with other pieces of evidence. If these relations strongly favor the allocation of the piece of evidence to one stream rather to another, it is assigned in an exclusive manner; however, if there is ambiguity, the evidence is allocated to both.

Ideally, the scene-analysis system should *share out* the evidence rather than assigning it twice. For example, if the isolated transition in the duplex perception of speech is used in completing the base, its perception as a chirp should be weaker, the energy having been divided between the two percepts. Actually, we do not know for sure that the energy from the transition *is* doubly allocated rather than being divided up. If it turns out that it is not shared out in some proportional way, this may be because it is too hard to estimate how much energy to allocate to each percept.

The multiple use of local bits of sensory data is not unusual in human perception. Many examples are found in vision. If we are looking at a shiny table top, the color of a small bit of the visual field will contribute (together with other bits, of course) to our perception of the color of the surface, to its glossiness, to the color of an object reflected in it, and to the color and compactness of the source of illumination. As the Gestalt psychologists were fond of pointing out, it is not true that the perceiver's knowledge about a local property of an object in the world is derived exclusively from the sensory properties of the corresponding local part of the visual field.

I have presented some examples to show that sensory evidence need not always be allocated in an all-or-nothing fashion. But if such examples can be found, why were we so convinced earlier that the rule of exclusive allocation was valid? It appears that this conviction was based on many confirming examples in audition and vision. Two examples that we can focus on are the ambiguous vase-faces example illustrated in figure 1.6 of chapter 1 and the capturing of tones from a sequential pattern that was shown in figure 1.7 of that chapter.

The argument that I have given up to this point seems to show that exclusive allocation occurs when the local sensory evidence fits in strongly with one organization and not with another. When the fit is more ambiguous, the evidence can be used twice. However, this argument does not work well for the vase-faces drawing. The shared contour between the vase and a face must have about equally strong visual relations connecting it with both organizations. Otherwise the figure would not be ambiguous. Yet despite this ambiguity, the information is allocated in an exclusive fashion. It is either the edge of a face or the edge of the vase—never both at the same time.

The mutual exclusion of interpretations in the vase-faces drawing probably does not originate with a primitive analysis of the strengths of the connections among the components of the evidence. It may be a result of rules that govern the building of certain specific kinds of perceptual interpretations. There are two mutually contradictory interpretations of the spatial relations in the vase-faces picture. When an edge is seen as the outer contour of a face, we are interpreting the face region as being in front of the other region (the vase region). On the other hand, when we see the edge as defining an outer contour of the vase we are seeing the vase as in front of the other region (the faces region). It may be the contradictory interpretations of two regions that are being prevented (A in front of B and B in front of A), not merely the allocation of the edge to both regions. In general, exclusive allocation may be enforced by rules that prevent contradictions in the building of perceptual "descriptions."

We are left with a two-part account of perceptual organization. A first process, primitive auditory scene analysis, lays down links of different strengths between parts of the sensory evidence. This process uses the sequential and simultaneous relations that I have described earlier. Then a second process builds descriptions, using schemas (definitions of regularity) that may be either innate or learned. This process is strongly governed by requirements for consistency of interpretation. For example, a given simple sound cannot have two pitches at the same time. (It could have distinct *parts* with different pitches, but then it would no longer be the whole sound but its parts that were simple and were obliged to obey the rule.)

This line of reasoning can be applied to cases in which a tone is captured out of a sequence by other tones in an all-or-nothing fashion. I would argue that the all-or-noneness does not result from the fact that it now fits in better with the capturing tones. That fact just alters the strength of the links. It results from a rule that says that a tone cannot be part of two streams at the same time. This rule is part of a description-building system.

The two-part theory draws an important distinction between sensory evidence and perceptual descriptions. Sensory evidence is the raw input for which the descriptions must account. Its components may be shared out and used in multiple ways to build different aspects of the descriptions as long as the descriptions account appropriately for the evidence. Descriptions, on the other hand, are required to be definite. A thing is this and not that, here and not there. If it is both here and there, it must be two things, and so on. The *things* of descriptions and the *components* of sensory evidence are two different sorts of entities and subject to different kinds of rules.

This theory can be applied to duplex perception of speech. At the first stage of the perceptual analysis of the dichotic stimulus, the acoustic relations set up fairly weak links between the sensory evidence arising from the two ears. Then schemas begin to build definite descriptions. I would propose that it is at this stage that both the schemas concerned with voices and those that describe sounds in space come into play. Neither is prior. The sounds-in-space system builds two descriptions, one for a low sound on the left and another for a high one at the right. It does so because the primitive links favor this interpretation. For the speech schemas, the subdivision favored by the primitive links is overcome by the fact that the combination of evidence from the two ears is favored by the fact that the combination is acceptable as a syllable of speech. The sharing of the right-ear evidence is permitted because of the transparency of sound, a fact about the world that often requires such sharing of evidence to take place if descriptions are to be arrived at correctly.

Next the sounds-in-space description must be composed with the speech interpretation to determine a location and other properties for the speech. Disembodied speech is apparently not a preferred percept. Why the system chooses to identify the speech with the left-side sound rather than treating it as a property of a compound left-and-right-side sound is not clear. Perhaps it is because the left-side sound has more of the qualities of a voice.

Directions for the Future

There is no chance that the reader will have arrived at this point in the discussion with the sense that anything is settled. Even if one accepts the general framework of auditory scene analysis, there still remains the problem of filling it out. I have assumed that the auditory system has a set of methods by which it untangles the mass of input and interprets it into a description of distinct sources of sound with their own separate properties. However, only certain experimental approaches and choices of sounds have been explored. Other broad avenues are untouched. Even within those areas in which there has been some research, many issues are unresolved and the detailed knowledge that could resolve them is not yet available. Let me suggest, following the outline of the previous chapters, what some of these unknowns are.

On the topic of *sequential grouping*, a fairly general question is what sorts of similarities will affect the sequential grouping of frequency components. In order to answer this question we will have to decide whether the same process is responsible for two kinds of sequential grouping. The first is the grouping of already fused spectra to create a stream of tones or sounds. This first kind of grouping is seen in the streaming phenomenon. The second type is the sequential grouping that serves to decompose a complex spectrum into simpler ones by capturing components out of it. It would be simpler to believe that the principles are the same, but not enough studies have been done comparing them. For example, does the time interval between a capturing tone and its target harmonic in a larger spectrum affect their grouping in the same way that the time interval between pure tones does in the streaming experiment?

Other questions on this issue are also puzzling. For example, we know that a sequence of *already formed* tones can be grouped by their timbre. However, when it was a question of capturing a subset of components out of a complex spectrum, this could not be done by the use of timbre. We could not argue that the subset's timbre resembled that of an earlier component, because the computation of its timbre would depend on its having already been segregated from the rest of the spectrum. Spectral components do not have timbres; only "sounds" do. It is more reasonable to suppose that after the properties of spectral components have caused them to be grouped into distinct sounds, and global properties (such as timbre) have been computed for them, these computed properties are able to serve as the basis for another level of grouping (such as by timbre).

Even when puzzles about the level of grouping are not involved, we do not know which properties of sounds will cause primitive scene analysis to group them with others. Will spectrally shaped noises have a tendency to group with tones whose spectra have peaks in the same places? The answer to this question is important if we are to understand the perceptual integration of speech. What about the common environmental sounds, with their myriad of qualities: rasping, tinkling, grating, clanking, thumping, and so on? Can every nameable quality affect how sounds will group? We must hope that it is not so and that a limited number of measurable properties will affect their grouping. Otherwise the prediction of grouping from physical measurements may be impossible.

There are also questions about the *formation of units* in the sound stream. Do sudden rises in amplitude tell the auditory system that a new event is beginning and that the computation of new global properties such as pitch and timbre should be started?

Many issues concerned with the segregation and integration of *simultaneous auditory components* also remain unresolved. For instance, does the parallel frequency modulation of partials actually improve their spectral integration? Is this an example of the Gestalt principle of common fate or is it just that the parallel movement (on a log frequency scale) preserves the "good" frequency relations between the harmonics over time? This question could be studied with inharmonic partials. In these sounds the maintaining of "bad" frequency relations over time by frequency modulation would not be expected to assist the integration.

We also do not know what evidence is used by the auditory system to decide that a particular harmonic is too loud to be incorporated into a larger spectrum, but we know that the system does so. Given the fact that a natural spectrum, such as found in the human voice, has many peaks and valleys, what mechanism decides that a harmonic is too loud to simply be a spectral peak?

There are still many unanswered questions about how the perceived qualities of a spectrum can be affected when scene analysis partitions it. For example, we know that more than one pitch can be derived at the same time when more than one harmonic series is detected. But we do not know whether the computation of pitch can be altered if we induce the partitioning of the spectrum by factors *other than* harmonic relations. For example, consider a spectrum, A, consisting only of every third harmonic of a certain fundamental. It sounds an octave and a fifth higher than spectrum B, which has all the harmonics of the specified fundamental. Suppose we rapidly alternate the two spectra. Would A capture its corresponding harmonics out of B so that the pitch of A was also heard as part of the B tone? If so, it would mean that the local pitch computation during B had been affected by stream segregation. What other global properties can be affected by auditory organization?

We also need further research on how the spatial separation of sources allows the spectra from those sources to be segregated. Even if the auditory system is capable of getting an independent estimate of the spatial origin of a large number of spectral bands, are these bands narrow enough to permit the separation of sources whose harmonics are interlaced in the spectrum? What are the limits of location-based segregation?

We also need to find out to what extent perceptual fusion and *masking* can be accounted for by the same mechanisms. Despite the differences in their definitions, is the difference between the factors that influence them merely a matter of degree?

Is it really possible to decide whether fusion is or is not the default condition of the spectrum? Does the auditory system always need specific evidence to override this default?

The *perceived continuity* of soft sounds through louder masking ones deserves more study. In particular, we must test the assumption that before continuity can be heard the auditory system must decide that the soft sound that enters the masking noise and the one that exits from it are the same sound. How much of this decision is determined by primitive links set up by similarity relations between the entering and exiting sounds and how much is based on a model of what the sound is and how it might have changed during the time that it was not clearly heard? It is possible that we can use the phenomenon of perceived continuity through a masking sound as a way of discovering how our brain expects a nonspeech environmental sound to change over time. For example, many sources of sound generate a richer spectrum when more energy is forcing the vibration. The voice, the trumpet, and the violin exhibit this kind of correlation between intensity and richness. Is knowledge of this correlation built into our auditory system as a general rule for integration? If it is, then a sound that violated the correlation (entering a masking noise burst at low intensity, but rich in harmonics, and exiting louder but purer) should be less likely to be heard as continuous than one that obeyed the correlation.

The questions that have been raised by considering the *role of schemas* in perception are many, but there is one central one. We do not know for sure whether there actually are two separate phases of scene analysis, one based on primitive grouping and using regularities in the auditory input that are shared by broad classes of sounds, and a second that builds detailed and coherent descriptions of the sound, employing schemas that incorporate knowledge about specific domains such as speech, music, or specific environmental sounds. If the two exist, they are sure to be present in every experiment. What research could separate their effects? What properties distinguish them: the effects of learning, the involvement of attention, the use they make of complex rhythmic patterns, the ability to remove the effects of certain sensory evidence from a mixture so that the residual can be more easily recognized?

How do schemas and primitive organization interact? When can schemas ignore the boundaries created by primitive organization?

The consideration of *music* presents us with issues that go unnoticed in other forms of sound. The basic one is that it is not sufficient to think of the auditory system as organizing its input into separate simple sounds, each arising from a separate source. A piece of music is heard as separate from the coughs of the audience, yet it often has a part-whole structure with several lines going on within it. Is the primitive process that segregates the lines from one another exactly like the process that segregates the music from other sounds? What maintains the perceptual integrity of the music as a whole? Is the hierarchical structure maintained purely by musical schemas or by primitive grouping principles as well? (We should recall that a non-musical sound, such as the one produced by a machine, can also have a part-whole structure.)

It is important for musicians to be able to predict whether a sequence of sounds will be experienced as a progression or a transformation. Is this determined entirely by our learning to expect the later parts when we hear the earlier ones or does the progression have to satisfy certain acoustic requirements so that the primitive organizing system will integrate it?

When will we hear two timbres at the same time in musical sound? Can segregation prevent us from hearing qualities of the unpartitioned spectrum, such as psychoacoustic dissonance? The research to really answer these questions has not yet been done. If it were carried out, it might make possible a science of orchestration.

There are several issues in *speech perception* that need to be resolved. What holds sequences of speech sounds of different categories together (such as fricatives and vowels)? For example, do the formants present in unvoiced sounds play a role in keeping them integrated with their voiced neighbors? Also, do changes in the voiced spectrum reveal the exact position at which a consonant is inserted? If so, is the integration of the vowels and consonants accomplished by primitive scene analysis or by speech-specific schemas?

We know that the depth of the spectral valleys between formants is not very important when only a single synthesized voice is played, but does the energy in the valleys play a role in holding the voice together as a coherent sound when other sounds are present?

How do the listener's mental model of speech, general models of sounds, and low-level grouping rules based on acoustic properties function in speech perception? How could these different types of constraints interact smoothly in a cooperative fashion? When the mental model accepts only some of the acoustic components that are present as being part of a speech sound, does the nonacceptance of some of them cause them to be formed into a separate stream that can be heard as an extraneous sound? What does it take to camouflage speech sounds (as opposed to masking them)? Does it require other speech sounds, or can nonspeech sounds do it? In general, how do low-level properties and mental models (both for speech and for other types of sounds) cooperate in effecting the perceptual result?

This volume has looked at the part played by the Gestalt-like processes of primitive grouping in perception. However, the need to account for certain grouping processes in speech, such as duplex perception, has made it clear that an understanding of primitive grouping will take us only so far in understanding auditory perception. We have to go on to study the processes that use the sensory evidence to build descriptions.

There are several important questions about description building that have attracted some research but deserve to be pursued with greater effort. One is the question of whether some features of signals can be excluded from awareness when they cannot be given a solid home in a description. We have encountered some apparent examples in this volume. We found that in listening to music, the listener's awareness of the psychophysical dissonance between co-occurring notes could be suppressed if primitive grouping led to the notes being perceived in separate streams. The evidence came from examining musical practice and scholarship, not from direct experimentation. The latter need to be done.

There are issues in the formation of even simple tone sequences that may require an understanding of the roles of consistency and contradiction in the building of descriptions. For example, when a sound consisting of several spectral components is followed by a lower-frequency version of itself we will typically hear a single tone moving downward in pitch. Yet if one of the components of the first spectrum was at the same frequency as one of those in the second, you might expect the pair of matching components to be heard as a repeating pure tone. When will this happen? In general, when does a sound act as a whole in grouping with later sounds and when do its spectral components try to find matches, either individually or in groups? Does the decision among these percepts use principles that are outside the scope of primitive scene analysis? What is the role of the consistency of the derived interpretation in determining the choice of percept?

Other illusions—such as Deutsch's octave illusion, in which properties derived from different environmental events are assigned to the same perceived sound—also seem to require an explanation in terms of a description-building process.

Practical Applications

In the preceding chapters, I have not considered in any detail the practical applications of our understanding of auditory scene analysis. However there are many.

An important area of application is the automatic recognition of sounds by computers. Many of the methods that are currently in use, for example, in speech recognition, deteriorate badly when extraneous sounds are present. Incorporating a primitive scene-analysis stage into the recognition process might allow the systems to resist being derailed by these sounds. Some beginnings have been made by using a few features of a voice, such as its fundamental or its spatial location, to track it through a mixture, but no computational system has so far attempted to implement the full range of heuristics described in the earlier chapters.

Similar issues arise in automatic music transcription by computers. Before an incoming acoustic signal can be accurately transcribed into musical notation, the computer must decide how many instruments are playing at the same time and which instrument is playing which note. These decisions require the incoming spectrum to have been decomposed to derive a number of separate pitches and timbres. Only when such a capability is present can more "musical" properties of the sound, such as rhythm, tonality, and so forth, be derived. Current attempts have segregated the parts by using only the harmonic relations in the spectrum and the tendency of individual parts to take small steps. As a result they have been able to separate only simple mixtures of sounds. The difficulty in using a multiplicity of acoustic relations all at the same time seems to be due to the large computational load that is involved in handling a lot of information about alternative groupings of spectral components.

Another area of application is in designing signals for the workplace. It should be evident that the perceptual segregation of signals in work environments (for example, the segregation of instructions or of warning signals) is critical for the safe and effective execution of the activity. If a warning signal is perceptually grouped with an environmental sound or with another warning to create a global sound with new qualities, it will not be responded to appropriately. As advances in artificial intelligence give us machines that both talk and listen to us, the importance of knowledge about auditory scene analysis will increase for psychologists and engineers concerned with ergonomics.

A more detailed understanding of auditory perception should also make it easier for us to understand how people differ in their auditory perceptual capacities. In our laboratory we have noticed consistent differences between people. In one experiment, different cues for the grouping of sounds—sequential, spectral, and spatial relations—were pitted against one another. Different people with normal hearing tended to resolve the conflict in different ways. That is, they heard different kinds of illusions. But the same person would resolve the contradiction in the same way on different occasions. This led me to suspect that different people give different weights to the various clues that point to the correct organization of the auditory evidence. In good listening environments, all the clues point in the same direction and people, despite their differences, generally come up with the same answers. But when conditions deteriorate, this no longer happens. Perhaps an individual can be characterized by a profile that describes the weights that he or she assigns to different clues. This might enable us to predict the kinds of failures that might be expected in different listening situations or with different types of hearing loss or different sorts of hearing aids for that person.

It is possible, finally, that certain types of neurological conditions that lead to a deficit in being able to deal with the order of sounds, or with mixtures of sounds, may be understandable as damage to the system that performs primitive organization.

Another point concerns computer models of human auditory perception. I have come to the conclusion after writing these chapters that we are now in a substantially different position than we were some years ago. At that time I decided that it was too early to attempt to construct explicit computational models of primitive scene analysis. But we have now reached the point where we have a good appreciation of many of the kinds of evidence that the human brain uses for partitioning sound, and it seems appropriate to begin to explore the formal patterns of computation by which the process could be accomplished. Unfortunately, as a psychologist, I do not personally have the skills and knowledge that are needed in this endeavor. I hope that some researchers who do have them will, after reading these chapters, accept the challenge of constructing an explicit model.

The level at which the research reported in this volume attacks the problem of the perception of sound is somewhere between the levels of auditory psychophysics and auditory pattern recognition. I find this level attractive because it deals with the issue of pattern but is, in some sense, content-free and therefore quite general. It is relevant to questions of everyday life, and yet the questions are often answerable in acoustic terms; we are never very far away from the sound.

A few final observations: What seems remarkable to me in rereading this volume is that many things we take as self-evident, such as the coherence of a single note or of a single voice, are perceived through a process of grouping. Another nonintuitive idea is that many qualities that seem to be the automatic products of simple acoustic properties also depend on grouping. These include pitch, loudness, timbre, location, and dissonance. Finally, I am struck by the realization that the processes of audition that can accomplish the grouping and use it to derive these experiences must be doing so in time periods that we have to measure in milliseconds.

Notes

1. For example, those described by Deutsch (1975a).
2. From Guzman (1969).
3. Bregman and Rudnicky (1975).
4. Treisman and Schmidt (1982).
5. Julesz and Hirsh (1972).
6. Forms of this effect have been described by Vicario (1965, 1982) and Bregman and Achim (1973).
7. See discussion in van Noorden (1975). A more elaborate form of Körte's law in audition has been offered by Jones (1976).
8. Ogasawara (1936), Corbin (1942), and Attneave and Block (1973).
9. Bregman and Mills (1982).
10. See review in Warren (1982).
11. Bregman and Pinker (1978).
12. Cutting (1976).
13. Anstis and Saida (1985).
14. Shepard (1981).
15. Demany (1982).
16. This computer was kindly supplied by Martin Levine of the McGill University Department of Electrical Engineering.
17. Warren, Obusek, Farmer, and Warren (1969).
18. Bregman and Campbell (1971).
19. Miller (1947).
20. Miller and Heise (1950).
21. Researchers who seem to have independently rediscovered the extreme dissociation of streams in rapid sequences of alternating high and low pitched tones include Bozzi and Vicario (1960), Warren (1968), Bregman and Campbell (1971), van Noorden (1975).
22. Bozzi and Vicario (1960). The phenomenon of the splitting of streams the Gestalt approach to explaining it can also be found in Vicario (1965, 1982).
23. Jones, Kidd, and Wetzel (1981).
24. van Noorden (1975, 1977).
25. Bregman (1971).
26. Anstis and Saida (1985).
27. van Noorden (1975).
28. Jones (1976).
29. van Noorden (1975) p. 53.
30. Dannenbring and Bregman (1976a).
31. The importance of onset-to-onset time in controlling the amount of stream segregation was also apparent in a different experiment by the same authors

(Dannenbring and Bregman, 1976b). There was no effect of the silent gap between tones when onset-to-onset time was held constant.
32. van Noorden (1975) p. 56.
33. Vos and Rasch (1981).
34. Tuller and Fowler (1980).
35. Hirsh (1959) and Hirsh and Sherrick (1961).
36. Hirsh (1959).
37. Broadbent and Ladefoged (1959).
38. Warren (1982), Ch. 5.
39. For example, Hirsh (1974).
40. Royer and Robin (1986).
41. van Noorden (1975).
42. Royer and Robin (1986).
43. Ideas related to this notion of hierarchy have been discussed by Jones (1976), but her view of temporal units is tied to the notion of perceptual rhythms that result from oscillators in the auditory system becoming entrained to periodicities of different length in the signal. In the view that I am presenting here, the notion of a unit does not rely on the existence of periodicities.
44. Steiger and Bregman (1981).
45. Shepard (1981).
46. The evidence involves the time taken to imagine visual transformations of different sizes, (Cooper and Shepard, 1973a, 1973b; Shepard and Metzler, 1971) or the time required to shift one's attention across different distances in two-dimensional space (Tsal, 1983; Shulman, Remington and McLean, 1979) and in three-dimensional space (Downing and Pinker, 1985). Evidence for analog tactile representation comes from experiments by Carpenter and Eisenberg (1978) and Marmor and Zaback (1976).
47. Rhodes (1985).
48. This has been found in birds (Knudsen 1982, 1984) and mammals (Drager and Hubel, 1975, Palmer and King, 1982)
49. I am indebted to Michael Cohen for finding this interpretation of the experiment.
50. Examples of signal-processing approaches to the separation of signals by their spatial location include Mitchell, Ross, and Yates (1971) and Strube (1981). There have been two attempts that I know of to use other sorts of cues, by Parsons (1976) and Weintraub (1984). A number of approaches to the separation of speech from interfering noise are described in Lim (1983).
51. Norman (1966).
52. van Noorden (1975) p. 22.
53. Deutsch (1975).
54. Judd (1977).
55. Deutsch (1979).
56. Butler (1979a, 1979b).
57. Cherry and Taylor (1954).
58. Broadbent (1954).
59. Schubert and Taylor (1956).
60. Axelrod and Guzy, (1968), Axelrod, Guzy, and Diamond (1968), Axelrod and Powazek (1972), Guzy and Axelrod (1971, 1972).
61. Huggins (1974).
62. ten Hoopen (1982), ten Hoopen and Akerboom (1982), ten Hoopen, Vos and Dispa (1982), and ten Hoopen, van Meurs and Akerboom (1982).

63. ten Hoopen, Akerboom and Boelaarts (1985).
64. Deutsch (1979), Judd (1977), and Schubert and Parker (1956).
65. See Moore (1982), Ch. 4, for a review of pitch phenomena.
66. van Noorden (1975).
67. Bregman, Pinker (1978).
68. A result of spectral position on segregation of tones in the absence of a difference between them in (missing) fundamental frequency was also found by Kinney (1961). The segregation affected the listener's ability to judge the duration of a gap between the tones.
69. Bregman and Levitan (1983). See also Singh (1987).
70. Bregman and Liao (1984).
71. Bregman and Levitan (1983).
72. van Noorden (1975).
73. Darwin and Bethell-Fox (1977).
74. Dannenbring and Bregman (1976).
75. American Standards Association (1960).
76. Smith, Hausfeld, Power, and Gorta (1982).
77. Warren, Obusek, Farmer and Warren (1969).
78. See also the review of the research relating to this phenomenon in Warren (1982), Ch. 5.
79. McNally and Handel (1977).
80. The matching in frequency was studied by Bregman and Pinker (1978) and the density of the simultaneous components by Vicario (1982).
81. Steiger (1980).
82. Wessel (1979).
83. The role of the higher harmonics in increasing the brightness of a tone was described by Helmholtz (1859), p. 62.
84. Risset and Wessel (1982) caution that the estimate of brightness would also have to take into account the masking of one partial by another, and the fact that the loudness of any group of harmonics depends upon whether its components are in the same critical band or in different ones.
85. Kinney (1961), Bregman and Levitan (1983), Bregman and Liao (1984), and van Noorden (1975).
86. Green and Kidd (1983), Green, Kidd, and Mason (1983), Green, Kidd, and Picardi (1983), Green and Mason (1983), Green and Mason (1985), and Green, Mason, and Kidd (1984).
87. van Noorden (1975).
88. McAdams and Bregman (1979).
89. Halpern (1977).
90. Tougas and Bregman (1985a).
91. Plomp and Steenecken (1971).
92. Described by Plomp (1976), pp. 107–109.
93. Dannenbring and Bregman (1976).
94. Plomp (1976), p. 97.
95. Warren and Verbrugge (1984).
96. For example, Grey (1977).
97. Steiger and Bregman (1981).
98. The notion of pitch movement detectors has been supported by evidence from psychophysical observations (Regan and Tansley, 1979). Kay and Matthews (1972), Green and Kay (1973), and Gardner and Wilson (1979) have found that the auditory system can be habituated to particular kinds of frequency

sweeps without at the same time being habituated to different orientations or rates of frequency modulation. Pollack (1968) has also found psychophysical evidence for channels in the auditory system sensitive to particular directions of frequency change. Physiological measurement on bats (Suga 1965a, 1965b) shows FM-sensitive auditory neurons. Other physiological observations have been reported by Evans and Whitfield (1964) and Vartanian (1974).
99. Steiger and Bregman (1981).
100. Steiger (1980).
101. Grey (1977), Grey and Gordon (1978), and Grey and Moorer, (1977).
102. Cutting and Rosner (1976).
103. Butler (1979b), Wessel (1979).
104. van Noorden (1975).
105. Erickson (1974).
106. E.g., Zucker (1977, 1985a, 1985b).
107. Julesz (1981a, 1981b) and Pomerantz (1981).
108. Warren and Verbrugge (1984).
109. Gabor (1947), p. 591.
110. Bastiaans (1980).
111. Julesz (1981a, 1981b) and Julesz and Bergen (1983).
112. I would like to express my thanks to Bela Julesz for discussing the topic of auditory texture with me and helping me to clarify my thinking on the topic.
113. Roads (1985), p. 156.
114. See chapter 3.
115. Ciocca and Bregman (1987).
116. Goldstein (1980), pp. 116–119.
117. Shepard (1962).
118. Reviewed in Plomp (1976), ch.6.
119. von Bismarck (1974).
120. Grey (1977). See also Grey (1975), Grey and Gordon (1978), Gordon and Grey (1978), Grey and Moorer (1977), Wessel (1978, 1979).
121. The actual analyses in experiments by Grey and his colleagues used an algorithm called INDSCAL that takes individual differences between listeners into account (Carroll and Chang, 1970).
122. van Noorden (1975).
123. van Noorden (1975).
124. Bregman (1978a).
125. Anstis and Saida (1985).
126. Bregman (1978a), pp. 386–387.
127. For example, Ladefoged (1959), Ladefoged and Broadbent (1960), and Fodor and Bever (1965).
128. For example, Kinney (1961), Perrott and Williams (1970), Divenyi (1971), Williams and Perrott (1971), Divenyi and Hirsh (1972), Collyer (1974), Williams and Elfner (1976), Williams, Elfner and Howse (1979), Fitzgibbons, Pollatsek, and Thomas (1974), Divenyi and Danner (1977), and Divenyi and Sachs (1978).
129. Anstis and Saida (1985).
130. van Noorden (1975).
131. Bregman and Rudnicky (1975).
132. Bregman (1978a), p. 386.
133. Jones, Kidd, and Wetzel (1981).
134. Also see the preliminary observations made by Bregman and Rudnicky on simultaneous cycles of tones with different tone repetition rates (reported in

chapter 3). It took a little while for the sense of two distinct streams to build up despite the fact that the listener was not trying to follow a sequence that was alternating between frequency ranges.
135. Bregman and Dannenbring (1973).
136. A related experiment was performed for a "ramped" condition by Anstis and Saida (1985). Despite using a different methodology and a different type of ramp (sinusoidal), they obtained similar results.
137. Heise and Miller (1951).
138. Jones (1976).
139. Bregman and Campbell (1971).
140. Bregman and Campbell (1971).
141. Dowling (1973).
142. See also Warren (1968).
143. Bregman and Rudnicky (1975).
144. Ortmann (1926), Divenyi and Hirsh (1975), Watson, Kelly, and Wroton (1976), Watson, Wroton, Kelly, and Benbasset (1975), Idson and Massaro (1976), and Divenyi and Hirsh (1978).
145. Divenyi and Hirsh (1975).
146. Divenyi and Hirsh (1978).
147. Massaro (1970, 1975).
148. Idson and Massaro (1976).
149. Sparks (1976).
150. Holding, Loeb, and Yoder (1972) and Sparks (1976).
151. Dannenbring and Bregman (1976b).
152. Woods (1979).
153. Massaro (1977).
154. Warren, Obusek, Farmer, and Warren (1969).
155. Hirsh (1959).
156. See also Thomas and Fitzgibbons (1971) who reported that successive tones within recycled sequences of four items all have to be within half an octave for accurate identification of order at the limiting value of 125 msec per item.
157. Similar cases of grouping similar items together in the report were found by McNally and Handel (1977) and by Bregman (1972).
158. Bregman and Campbell (1971).
159. Broadbent and Ladefoged (1959).
160. Norman (1966), p. 4. See also Norman (1967).
161. Vicario (1973), pp. 64–72.
162. McNally and Handel (1977).
163. Nickerson and Freeman (1974) and Warren and Byrnes (1975).
164. Warren and Obusek (1972) and Warren and Ackroff (1976).
165. Wilcox, Neisser, and Roberts (1972), Watson (1976), Watson, Wroton, Kelly, and Benbasset (1975), Watson, Kelly, and Wroton (1976), and Warren (1974).
166. Warren and Obusek (1972).
167. Warren (1982), p. 125.
168. Nickerson and Freeman (1974).
169. Neisser (1971, 1972) and Neisser and Hirst (1974).
170. For example, Warren (1974).
171. Broadbent and Ladefoged (1959).
172. Warren (1982), p. 132.
173. Hirsh (1959), Hirsh and Sherrick (1961), Kinney (1961), and Fay (1966).

174. Patterson and Green (1970), Yund and Efron (1974), and Wier and Green (1975).
175. Neisser (1972).
176. Neisser and Hirst (1974).
177. Warren and Byrnes (1975).
178. For example, Warren (1982), p. 129.
179. Warren (1982), p. 123–125, reviews many of these studies, including those of Warren, Obusek, Farmer and Warren (1969), Thomas, Hill, Carroll, and Garcia (1970), Thomas, Cetti, and Chase (1971), and Dorman, Cutting, and Raphael (1975).
180. Neisser (1971).
181. Cole and Scott (1973).
182. Neisser and Hirst (1974).
183. Ortmann (1926), Warren (1972, 1974), Watson, Kelly, and Wroton (1975), Watson, Wroton, Kelly, and Benbasset (1975), and Divenyi and Hirsh (1978).
184. Bregman (1978a) and Anstis and Saida (1985).
185. This term was used by Neisser (1967). It has also been called "precategorical acoustic store" by Crowder and Morton (1969). See also Darwin, Turvey, and Crowder (1972).
186. Divenyi and Hirsh (1978).
187. For example, Bregman (1978b) and Handel, Weaver, and Lawson (1983).
188. For example, Neisser and Hirst (1974) and Barsz (1988).
189. Warren and Ackroff (1976) employed this method.
190. Warren (1982).
191. van Noorden (1975).
192. Norman and Bobrow (1977).
193. Hirsh (1959).
194. See Warren (1982), pp. 120–139.
195. van Noorden (1975).
196. Bregman (1978b).
197. van Noorden (1975), p. 56.
198. See experiments reviewed by Handel (1984) and studies by Klapp, Hill, Tyler, Martin, Jagacinski, and Jones (1985) and Beauvillain (1983).
199. Dannenbring and Bregman (1976b). This was a more carefully controlled study based on an earlier pilot study by Bregman (1972b).
200. Kinney (1961).
201. Fitzgibbons, Pollatsek, and Thomas (1974).
202. van Noorden (1975), p. 47.
203. For example, Perrott and Williams (1970), Divenyi (1971), Williams and Perrott (1971), Divenyi and Hirsh (1972), Collyer (1974), Williams and Elfner (1976), Williams, Elfner and Howse (1979), Divenyi and Danner (1977), and Divenyi and Sachs (1978).
204. Neff, Jesteadt and Brown (1982).
205. Bregman and Liao (1984).
206. Dowling (1973).
207. Warren and Ackroff (1976).
208. ten Hoopen, van Meurs, and Akerboom (1982) and ten Hoopen, Akerboom and Boelaarts (1985).
209. Bregman and Rudnicky (1975).
210. van Noorden (1975), pp. 46–48; see also Norman (1967).
211. Bregman (1978b).

212. McNally and Handel (1977) p. 455.
213. Idson and Massaro (1976).
214. For a discussion of recognition masking see Massaro (1975); other related articles are Massaro (1970, 1970, 1972).
215. Bregman and Rudnicky (1975).
216. Bregman and Levitan (1983) and Bregman and Liao (1984).
217. Smith, Hausfeld, Power and Gorta (1982); the scale illusion is described in the earlier section of the present volume on the effect of spatial factors on stream segregation and in Deutsch (1975b, 1982).
218. Bregman and Pinker (1978).
219. Among them, in chronological order: Ortmann (1926), Koffka (1935), Fox (1948), Miller and Heise (1950), Heise and Miller (1951), Bozzi and Vicario (1960), Vicario (1965), Bregman and Campbell (1971), Julesz and Hirsh (1972), Bregman and Achim (1973), Vicario (1973), van Noorden (1975), Deutsch (1975a), Divenyi and Hirsh (1978), Bregman (1978b), Kubovy (1981), Vicario (1982), Deutsch (1982), Handel, Weaver, and Lawson (1983), and Anstis and Saida (1985),
220. For example, Helmholtz (1862) and Koffka (1935), p. 435.
221. Divenyi and Hirsh (1971) and Bregman and Achim (1973).
222. This account is given by van Noorden (1975, p. 50).
223. Kolers (1964) and Anstis, Giaschi and Cogan (1985).
224. Bregman and Achim (1973).
225. Vicario (1965).
226. Tougas and Bregman (1985a).
227. Ramachandran and Anstis (1984).
228. Ramachandran and Anstis (1983).
229. Körte (1915).
230. The notion of pitch movement detectors has been supported by evidence from psychophysical observations (Regan and Tansley, 1979). Kay and Matthews (1972), Green and Kay (1973), and Gardner and Wilson (1979) have found that the auditory system can be habituated to particular kinds of frequency sweeps without at the same time being habituated to different orientations or rates of frequency modulation. Pollack (1968) has also found psychophysical evidence for direction-specific channels in the auditory system. Physiological measurement on bats (Suga 1965a, 1965b) shows FM-sensitive auditory neurons. Other physiological observations have been reported by Evans and Whitfield (1964) and Vartanian (1974).
231. van Noorden (1975), Anstis and Saida (1985).
232. Bregman and Dannenbring (1973).
233. Anstis, Giaschi, and Cogan (1985).
234. van Noorden (1975).
235. Bregman and Dannenbring (1973).
236. Burke (1952); see also Wertheimer (1912) and Knops (1947).
237. But see Sigman and Rock (1974), who showed that if the screen is shown, its own properties (for example, whether it is seen as being in motion itself) can change the perceived motion of the events going on behind it.
238. Spelke and Cortelyou (1981); see also Spelke (1979).
239. Dodd (1979).
240. O'Leary (1981), p. 7.
241. O'Leary and Rhodes (1984).
242. Gilbert (1939).

243. Staal and Donderi (1983).
244. Radeau and Bertelson (1976) and Bertelson and Radeau (1981). See also Hay, Pick, and Ikeda (1965), Jackson (1953), Thomas (1941), Witkin, Wapner, and Leventhal (1952), and Jack and Thurlow (1973).
245. This is supported by experiments done by Dodd (1977, 1980).
246. McGurk and MacDonald (1976).
247. van Noorden (1975).
248. Judd (1977), Deutsch (1979).
249. Bregman and Liao (1984).
250. van Noorden (1975) and Anstis and Saida (1985).
251. For a list of some of the research on cortical detectors see my earlier discussion on the sequential grouping of frequency glides, and my discussion of the research of Anstis and Saida (1985).
252. van Noorden (1975), p. 41.
253. Bregman and Rudnicky (1975).
254. Bregman and Pinker (1978); a similar sort of capturing was demonstrated by van Noorden (1975).
255. Pattison, Gardner and Darwin (1986).
256. Bregman and Rudnicky (1975).
257. van Noorden (1975).
258. Norman (1967).
259. Anstis and Saida (1985).
260. Idson and Massaro (1976), p. 173.
261. Bregman and Rudnicky (1975).
262. Bregman (1978a).
263. Bregman (1981b).
264. Jones (1976).
265. Jones, Maser and Kidd (1978).
266. van Noorden (1975).
267. Bregman (1978a).
268. Bregman and Rudnicky (1975).
269. See Bregman (1981a).
270. Tougas and Bregman (1985a).
271. Gottschaldt (1926).
272. Demany (1982).
273. Bregman (1984), Deutsch (1982), Fox (1948), Handel (1985), Julesz and Hirsh (1972), Vicario (1965, 1973, 1980, 1982).
274. I thank Meg Withgott for pointing this out.
275. Witkin and Tenenbaum (1983).
276. Rock (1985), Bregman (1977).
277. Steiger (1980).
278. Discussions of hierarchies in the representation of temporal patterns are presented by Handel and Todd (1981), Jones (1976, 1978), Jones, Boltz, and Kidd (1982), Jones, Kidd, and Wetzel (1981), and Jones, Maser, and Kidd (1978); it is discussed specifically in relation to music by Jackendoff and Lehrdahl (1981).
279. Norman (1966), Jones (1976).
280. Jones, Maser and Kidd (1978).
281. Bregman and Rudnicky (1975). This experiment is discussed in detail elsewhere in this volume.
282. Summarized in Warren (1982), pp. 185–186.
283. Carried out by von Wright, Anderson, and Stenman (1975).

284. Bregman and Pinker (1978).
285. van Noorden (1975).
286. Helmholtz (1859), p. 50.
287. van Noorden (1975), p. 88.
288. Steiger and Bregman (1981).
289. Helmholtz (1859), pp. 59–60.
290. Helmholtz (1859), p. 50.
291. van Noorden (1975), pp. 23, 87–89.
292. The experiment was carried out by Warren, Obusek, and Ackroff (1972) and is described in Warren (1982), p. 141.
293. Bregman (1977).
294. For example, in Shepard (1981).
295. van Noorden (1975).
296. For example, Helmholtz (1859) and Plomp (1964).
297. Moore (1982), Ch. 1.
298. This explanation for the unequal ability of different harmonics to resist being captured out of the complex tone was offered by van Noorden (1975).
299. Vicario (1982).
300. This assumption was required to explain certain results in the experiments of Bregman, Abramson, Doehring, and Darwin (1985). An unpublished result by Margo Taylor at McGill also produced confirming evidence.
301. Bregman and Pinker (1978).
302. Plomp's studies of the hearing out of partials are reported in Plomp (1964, 1976), and Plomp and Mimpen (1968).
303. Dannenbring and Bregman (1978).
304. Moore (1982), Ch.3.
305. van Noorden (1975), p. 87.
306. Dannenbring and Bregman (1978).
307. Denes and Pinson (1963).
308. Martens (1984) and Moore, Peters, and Glasberg (1985).
309. See McAdams (1984), pp. 41–43.
310. One of the best of these is by Moore (1982).
311. McAdams (1984), p. 41.
312. See Moore (1982), Ch. 4, for a review of the phenomena associated with shifting a harmonic series.
313. Goldstein (1973).
314. Theories of this type are reviewed in Moore (1982), pp. 123–127.
315. The perceptual qualities of sounds with "stretched partials" were reported by Slaymaker (1970), Cohen (1979, 1980a, 1980b), and Mathews and Pierce (1980).
316. Personal communication, 1982.
317. Houtsma (1985) and Weintraub (1985).
318. Martens (1984) showed that a 7 percent mistuning of the third harmonic increased its audibility as much as adding 23 dB to its intensity did.
319. Moore, Glasberg, and Peters (1985a), p. 13. See also Moore, Glasberg, and Peters (1985b) and Moore, Peters, and Glasberg (1985).
320. This notion has been proposed as an extension of the pitch model of Goldstein (1973) by Duifhius, Willems, and Sluyter (1982), Scheffers (1983), and Grandori (1984). "According to this idea, a partial will only be accepted by the pitch mechanism as part of a given harmonic series if its estimated frequency falls within a pre-set range around each harmonic frequency . . . about 2–3 for com-

plex tones 410 ms in duration" (Moore, Glasberg, and Peters, 1985a).
321. This argument can be read in more detail in Moore (1982), p. 154.
322. Plomp (1964).
323. Bregman and Doehring (1984).
324. Summerfield, Haggard, Foster, and Gray (1984).
325. It was discovered by Summerfield and his co-workers before 1985 but had not been published as of the writing of this chapter.
326. A case that we will not consider here is one where one of the tones is harmonic and the other inharmonic. There can be more than a fifty percent overlap in such a case. However, we will probably find that there is only one dominant global pitch and a number of partial pitches, as in the case of mixed inharmonic partials.
327. Stumpf (1890).
328. Vicario (1982).
329. This idea has, in effect, been proposed by Rasch (1978).
330. Houtsma (1983).
331. While there are certain nonlinearities in acoustic systems that cause violations of this principle, it remains, on the whole, a valid one.
332. Chowning (1980).
333. McAdams (1984).
334. McAdams (1984). He actually used a mixture of two different kinds of modulation functions to generate the FM. The first (called vibrato) was a 6.5-Hz sinusoid, the second (called jitter) was an irregular function containing frequency components from 0 to 150 Hz with the amplitude falling off greatly for the higher frequency components.
335. McAdams (1984), p. 106.
336. McAdams (1984), p. 193.
337. Thurlow and Small (1955) and Plomp (1976).
338. McAdams (1984), p. 200.
339. The sound was used in the 1983 composition "Archipelago" by Roger Reynolds and was made with the assistance of Thierry Lancino.
340. This was reported in Bregman, McAdams, and Halpern (1978) and in McAdams and Bregman (1979), and was an undergraduate project at McGill University. Replications and extensions were done subsequently with the assistance of Magda Halikia (also spelled Chalikia).
341. Bregman and Doehring (1984).
342. Bregman and Pinker (1978).
343. Vicario (1973).
344. Dannenbring and Bregman (1978).
345. Rasch (1978).
346. See Kubovy (1981), pp. 66–69.
347. Kubovy and Jordan (1979).
348. They pointed out that if the waveform is subject to a compressive nonlinearity, such as a cubic root transformation, at some peripheral stage of processing, it can be shown that there is a peak in the power spectrum at precisely the frequency of the shifted component.
349. Cohen (1979, 1980).
350. Risset and Mathews (1969).
351. Some of these are given by McAdams (1984), p. 50.
352. Bacon and Viemeister (1985a, 1985b).
353. Malsburg and Schneider (1986).

354. Schubert and Nixon (1970), cited in McAdams (1984), p. 57.
355. Broadbent and Ladefoged (1957).
356. Hall, Haggard, and Fernandes (1984), p. 56.
357. The computations underlying the cochleagram are described by Lyon (1982, 1983).
358. Broadbent and Ladefoged (1957) have argued that "the key to the fusion of sounds which stimulate different parts of the basilar membrane is the envelope of the waveform of these sounds" (p. 709).
359. Moore (1982), pp. 140–144.
360. Moore (1982), p. 133.
361. Warren (1982), p. 101.
362. Halikia (1985). See also Chalikia and Bregman (1989).
363. Moore (1982).
364. Moore (1982), p. 193.
365. Bregman, Abramson, Doehring, and Darwin (1985).
366. Bregman, Levitan, and Liao (1990). Experiments 1A and 1B.
367. Bregman, Levitan, and Liao (1990). Experiments 2A and 2B.
368. See experiment 2 of Bregman, Abramson, Doehring, and Darwin (1985).
369. Warren (1982), p. 79–80 and Warren and Bashford (1981).
370. Békésy (1963).
371. Reviewed in Deutsch (1982a).
372. Bregman and Abdel Ahad (1985).
373. See Moore (1982), p. 104.
374. Bertelson and Radeau (1981), Hay, Pick, and Ikeda (1965), Jack and Thurlow (1973), Jackson (1953), Radeau and Bertelson (1976), Thomas (1941), and Witkin, Wapner, and Leventhal (1952).
375. Dodd (1979), Spelke (1979), and Spelke and Cortelyou (1981).
376. O'Leary and Rhodes (1984).
377. See, for example, Dodd (1977, 1980).
378. For example, McGurk and MacDonald (1976).
379. Cherry (1953).
380. Kubovy (1981).
381. See chapter 7, the section entitled *How Unusual is the Sharing of Evidence?*
382. Jenkins and Merzenich (1984).
383. Perrott and Barry (1969).
384. Kubovy and Howard (1976).
385. This pattern was created by Roger Reynolds and Thierry Lancino at the Institut de Recherche et Coordination Acoustique/Musique (Institute for Research and Coordination in Acoustics and Music, abbreviated IRCAM) in Paris, for Reynolds' composition, *Archipelago*. It was reported by McAdams (1984), p. 55.
386. This description is based on an experiment by Cramer and Huggins (1958).
387. Meyer (1978).
388. Green and Kidd (1983).
389. For reviews, see Broadbent (1958, 1971), Kahneman (1973), Norman (1976), Underwood (1976), and Moray (1970).
390. Efron, Crandall, Koss, Divenyi, and Yund (1983).
391. Strube (1981).
392. Mitchell, Ross, and Yates (1971).
393. Strube (1981).
394. Lyon (1983).

395. The model is described in Lyon (1983).
396. Steiger and Bregman (1982).
397. van den Brink, Sintnicolaas, and van Stam (1976).
398. Cutting (1976).
399. Deutsch (1974, 1975a, 1982).
400. Bertelson and Radeau (1981), Hay, Pick, and Ikeda (1965), Jack and Thurlow (1973), Jackson (1953), Radeau and Bertelson (1976), Thomas (1941), and Witkin, Wapner, and Leventhal (1952). A recent general review of the effects of discrepancies between the senses is given by Welch and Warren (1980).
401. It has been noted in experiments on discrepancy between information derived from different senses that the subject's awareness that a discrepancy has been experimentally induced can affect the interaction (Welch and Warren, 1980). For example, Miller (1972), experiment 3, found in studying how sight and touch interact in the perception of the shape of an object that only when the observer believes that the visual and touch cues are from the same object does vision correct the shape perception derived from touching.
402. Jack and Thurlow (1973).
403. Bregman and Steiger (1980).
404. Pratt (1930).
405. Butler (1969), Roffler (1968), and Searle, Braida, Cuddy, and Davis (1975).
406. Broadbent and Ladefoged (1957).
407. For example, Julesz (1981a).
408. Helmholtz (1859), p. 62.
409. The effect of harmonicity on masking was shown by Moore, Peters, and Glasberg (1985) and the effect on perceptual isolation by Moore, Glasberg, and Peters (1986).
410. Rasch (1978).
411. Kubovy (1976) described in Kubovy (1981), pp. 66–69.
412. Scheffers (1983a).
413. Dannenbring and Bregman (1978).
414. Rasch (1979).
415. Bacon and Viemeister (1985b).
416. Hall, Haggard, and Fernandes (1984) and Hall (1986). Closely related research has been done by Buus (1985), Haggard, Harvey, and Carlyon (1985), and Hall, Haggard, and Harvey (1984).
417. The noise was amplitude modulated by a 0–50 Hz noise band.
418. Hall, Haggard, and Fernandes (1984), p. 56.
419. See Buus (1985).
420. Schooneveldt and Moore (1988). However, other research by Hall and Grose (1988) shows that multiple cues may be involved in the release from masking.
421. This argument has been made by Moore (1982).
422. Bronkhorst and Plomp (1987) and Plomp and Mimpen (1981).
423. Kock (1950), Schubert (1956), Carhart, Tillman, and Johnson (1967), and Levitt and Rabiner (1967).
424. A more complete discussion of the binaural masking level difference and related effects is given by Moore (1982), Ch. 5.
425. de Laat and Plomp (1985).
426. McAdams (1984), p. 176.
427. Thurlow and Small (1955) and Plomp (1976).
428. Houtsma and Goldstein (1972).

429. Green and Kidd (1983).
430. Stern (1972).
431. Treisman and Schmidt (1982), p. 119.
432. Helmholtz (1859), pp. 60–61.
433. Attneave (1974).
434. van Noorden (1975).
435. Bregman (1977).
436. Bregman and Tougas (1989).
437. This will be discussed under the topic of duplex perception of speech in the section on speech.
438. Winston (1975), Ch.3.
439. Waltz (1975).
440. Zucker (1977).
441. For example, van Noorden (1975). The sequence-integrating theory of Mari Riess Jones, which sees the integrative process as the action of a single sequence building process, would have the same problems; see Jones (1976), Jones, Boltz, and Kidd (1982), and Jones, Kidd, and Wetzel (1981).
442. Warren (1982).
443. Dannenbring (1976).
444. See Warren and Bashford (1976).
445. Warren (1982).
446. For example, Vicario (1960).
447. Warren, Obusek, and Ackroff (1972).
448. Elfner and Caskey (1965) and Houtgast (1972).
449. Bregman and Dannenbring (1977).
450. Plomp (1982).
451. Houtgast (1972), cited by Warren (1982).
452. Elfner and Caskey (1965) and Elfner and Homick (1966, 1967).
453. Warren, Obusek, and Ackroff (1972).
454. Warren, Obusek, and Ackroff (1972).
455. Verschuure, personal communication in 1974, cited by van Noorden (1975).
456. Moore (1982), pp. 97–105.
457. Ciocca (1985) and Dannenbring (1976).
458. This perceptual result is predictable from unpublished experiments done by Yves Tougas in my laboratory.
459. Layton (1975) and Samuel (1981).
460. Warren (1982), p. 151.
461. Zwicker, Flottorp, and Stevens, (1957).
462. Houtgast (1972).
463. Houtgast (1974).
464. Steiger (1980).
465. Tougas and Bregman (1985b).
466. Ciocca (1985) and Ciocca and Bregman (1987).
467. A mild deception in the name of science.
468. Steiger and Bregman (1981), for example, found that it did not.
469. Vicario (1973).
470. Warren, Sherman (1974).
471. Warren, Warren (1970).
472. Warren, Obusek, and Ackroff (1972).
473. Thurlow (1957), Thurlow and Elfner (1959), and Warren, Obusek, Ackroff (1972).

474. Bregman and Dannenbring (1973).
475. Vicario (1960, 1982) and Sasaki (1980), cited in Warren (1982). Musical scale restoration has also been observed in unpublished research by Gary Dannenbring.
476. Warren (1982), Ch.6.
477. Warren, Obusek, and Ackroff (1972) and Warren (1982), p. 141.
478. Warren, Obusek, and Ackroff (1972) and van Noorden (1975).
479. Miller and Licklider (1950).
480. Vicario (1960). The visual tunnel effect was studied by Wertheimer (1912), Knops (1947), and Burke (1952).
481. Bashford and Warren (1986).
482. Thurlow (1957); see also subsequent research by Elfner (1969, 1971), Elfner and Caskey (1965), Elfner and Homick (1966, 1967), Thurlow and Elfner (1959), Thurlow and Marten (1962), and Thurlow and Erschul (1978).
483. Dannenbring (1976).
484. Ciocca (1985) and Ciocca and Bregman (1987).
485. Vicario (1982).
486. Miller and Licklider (1950); this result was also found by Dirks and Bower (1970).
487. Cherry and Wiley (1967), Holloway (1970), Powers and Wilcox (1977), and Verschuure and Brocaar (1983).
488. This was first proposed by Huggins (1964) and later by Powers and Wilcox (1977).
489. This suggestion was first made by Cherry and Wiley (1967).
490. The research on the different types of spoken material was done by Bashford and Warren (1979) and on the different rates of speaking by Bashford, Meyers, Brubaker, and Warren (1988).
491. Warren (1970), Warren and Obusek (1971), Obusek and Warren (1973), and Warren and Sherman (1974).
492. Warren and Obusek (1971).
493. Warren and Sherman (1974).
494. Layton (1975), Samuel (1981), and Samuel and Ressler (1986). This finding has been confirmed using the method of periodic interruption of running speech by Bashford and Warren (1986).
495. Wrightson and Warren (1981), described in Warren (1982); the tone was 70 dB at 1,000 Hz; the narrow band was 80 dB, centered at 1,000 Hz.
496. I am indebted to John Pierce for this story.
497. Warren, Obusek, and Ackroff (1972).
498. van Noorden (1975).
499. van Noorden (1975), pp. 31–36.
500. The speech-noise case was reported by Egan (1948), and the tone-tone case by Thurlow and Elfner (1959).
501. Butler and Naunton (1962, 1964).
502. Warren and Bashford (1976).
503. Steiger and Bregman (1982a).
504. Steiger (1983).
505. Deutsch (1979).
506. For example, Warren (1982), Ch.6.
507. Bregman and Pinker (1978).
508. Rasch (1978).

509. Helmholtz (1859).
510. Nordmark (1970).
511. Scheffers (1979, 1982, 1983a).
512. Cutting (1976).
513. Cutting (1975), Darwin (1979, 1981), Isenberg and Liberman (1979), Liberman, Isenberg, and Rakerd (1981), Mann (1980), Mann, Madden, Russell, and Liberman (1981), Mattingly, Liberman, Syrdal, and Halwes (1971), Mattingly and Liberman (1989), Liberman and Mattingly (1985), Rand (1974), and Repp (1984).
514. Cherry (1953), Broadbent (1958).
515. Bregman (1971).
516. Dowling (1973).
517. DeWitt and Samuels (1986).
518. "Schema," or actually "scheme," was the term employed by Jean Piaget. A good general outline of his work on the analysis of certain mental capacities is found in Flavell (1963). "Frame" is a term introduced in the field of artificial intelligence by Minsky (1975). The term "ideal" was used by Bregman (1977).
519. Watson, Wroton, Kelly, and Benbasset (1975).
520. Watson, Kelly, and Wroton (1976).
521. Spiegel and Watson (1981).
522. McBride (1986).
523. Leek and Colleran (1984).
524. Demany (1982).
525. van Noorden (1975).
526. For a discussion of the concept of the critical band, see Zwislocki (1978) and Moore (1982), Ch. 3.
527. Dowling (1973).
528. Deutsch (1972).
529. Warren and Warren (1970).
530. Anstis and Saida (1985).
531. Dowling (1973).
532. Jones (1976).
533. van Noorden (1975).
534. Jones, Maser, and Kidd (1978).
535. Jones, Maser, and Kidd (1978) required listeners to write down a description of the sequence while Jones, Boltz, and Kidd (1982) and Kidd, Boltz, and Jones (1984) used a sequence-comparison task.
536. van Noorden (1975), p. 41.
537. This phenomenon was first described by van Noorden (1975), p. 76.
538. Deutsch (1975a).
539. Tougas and Bregman (1985a).
540. Smith, Hausfeld, Power, and Gorta (1982) also promoted the crossing of streams in a more complex situation in which tones were also being alternated between ears in the manner of the Deutsch (1975) scale illusion. They isolated the streams on the basis of timbre by having a synthesized piano play one stream and a synthesized saxophone the other. Again the effect cannot be interpreted as showing the existence of a trajectory principle.
541. Steiger and Bregman (1981).
542. Ciocca and Bregman (1987).
543. Dannenbring (1976).
544. Bregman and Rudnicky (1975).

545. Pattison, Gardner, and Darwin (1986) and Darwin and Gardner (1986), p. 16.
546. Bregman and Dannenbring (1973).
547. Ciocca and Bregman (1987).
548. Dannenbring (1976).
549. Heise and Miller (1951).
550. Nickerson and Freeman (1974).
551. Warren and Byrnes (1975).
552. van Noorden (1975), p. 15.
553. McNally and Handel (1977).
554. Handel, Weaver, and Lawson (1983).
555. Divenyi and Hirsh (1974, 1975).
556. Idson and Massaro (1976).
557. Bregman (1978c).
558. van Noorden (1975), pp. 77–78.
559. Guilford and Hilton (1933) and Guilford and Nelson (1936); cited by Heise and Miller (1951), p. 69.
560. Scott (1971) and Scott and Cole (1972).
561. Cole and Scott (1973).
562. Warren and Warren (1970) and Warren and Sherman (1974).
563. Ciocca and Bregman (1987).
564. Bregman and Achim (1973).
565. Ramachandran and Anstis (1983); see also Ramachandran and Anstis (1981).
566. Shepard (1981).
567. Martin (1972).
568. Jones (1976).
569. Jones, Kidd, and Wetzel (1981), quotations from pp. 1060 and 1071.
570. Jones, Kidd, and Wetzel (1981).
571. Jones, Kidd, and Wetzel (1981), p. 1071.
572. Jones, Boltz, and Kidd (1982).
573. Dowling (1973).
574. Handel, Weaver, and Lawson (1983).
575. This is observable, for example, in the results of Bregman and Campbell (1971) and in those of Handel, Weaver, and Lawson (1983).
576. Tougas and Bregman (1985a).
577. French-St. George and Bregman (1989).
578. Bregman (1978a) and Anstis and Saida (1985).
579. Jones, Kidd, and Wetzel (1981).
580. Bregman and Rudnicky (1975).
581. Erickson (1982), p. 520.
582. I am not a musician. Fortunately, I have been privileged to associate with musicians and this chapter is the fruit of that contact. I particularly had the pleasure of a year-long dialogue with James Wright when I helped to supervise a Master's thesis that he submitted to the McGill University Faculty of Music. Many of the ideas that appear in this chapter are the result. Since the thesis and a subsequent paper by Wright and myself are not widely available, I have taken this opportunity to present many of our ideas. I have also had the benefit of discussions with composers at the Center for Computer Research in Music and Acoustics at Stanford who kept me honest in my statements about music. The citation for the thesis is Wright (1986) and for the article is Wright and Bregman (1987).
583. Boulez (1985).

584. The ideas of this chapter were evolved with little contact with the literature on music theory. They come from the ideas about scene analysis that have been the basis for the earlier parts of this book. They draw strongly upon the ideas of the Gestalt psychologists. In preparing this chapter it became obvious that music theorists have also been influenced by Gestalt theory. In particular, C. W. Fox in his 1948 article on modern counterpoint put forward a view of music based on Gestalt theory (Fox, 1948). He argued that a musical pattern was to be considered as a Gestalt (an integrated pattern) that had other smaller patterns such as melodic patterns, chords, and rhythmic patterns embedded within it. He pointed out the importance of frequency proximity and smooth continuity over time and pitch as factors that strengthened the melodic dimension of music. Similarity between the timbres of successive notes also strengthened the horizontal integration. He was aware of two factors in the integration of patterns, similarity and familiarity. These correspond roughly to what I have referred to, in chapter 4, as primitive and schema-based integration.
585. McAdams (1984).
586. Bregman and Levitan (1983), Bregman and Liao (1984), Noteboom, Brokx, and de Rooij (1978), Ortmann (1926), Singh (1987), Wessel (1979).
587. van Noorden (1975), p. 69.
588. Babbitt (1964).
589. Fraisse (1963), p. 89.
590. Winckel (1967), Warren (1982), p. 120.
591. Dowling (1973).
592. Ortmann (1926).
593. Fucks (1962).
594. Merriam (1964), cited by Dowling (1973).
595. Some of these terms can be found in the following sources: "compound melodic line" in Piston (1947), p. 23, "implied polyphony" in Bukofzer (1958), and "melodic segregation" in Fox (1948).
596. Erickson (1982), pp. 524–525.
597. Ortmann (1926), p. 7.
598. van Noorden (1975), p. 13.
599. Dowling (1973).
600. The research using cycles of unrelated sounds is extensively reviewed in chapter 2.
601. Dowling (1973, 1978) and Dowling and Fujitani (1971).
602. van Noorden (1975), p. 72.
603. Erickson (1975), p. 12.
604. Boulez (1985).
605. Webern (1935).
606. Bompiani (1987).
607. For example, Vicario (1982).
608. van Noorden (1975, 1977).
609. For example, Royer and Garner (1970) and Royer and Robin (1986).
610. Guilford and Nelson (1936); see also Guilford and Hilton (1933).
611. Bregman and Rudnicky (1975).
612. Bharucha (1984).
613. Sloboda (1985).
614. Vicario (1982), p. 272.
615. Vicario (1982), p. 270.
616. van Noorden (1975).

617. See Erickson (1975).
618. Boulez (1985).
619. Slawson (1968, 1981, 1985).
620. McAdams and Saariaho (1985) and Balzano (1986).
621. Cadoz (1985).
622. Balzano (1986) and Gibson (1966).
623. Huggins (1952).
624. Risset and Wessel (1982).
625. McAdams (1984), p. 18.
626. Boulez (1985).
627. Cited by Erickson (1982), p. 518.
628. Schoenberg (1911), p. 470f, introduced the term "klangfarbenmelodie". Robert Erickson (1974) has created an experimental composition called LOOPS to investigate the role of timbre contrasts, pitch sequence, and pitch range in the experience of klangfarbenmelodie.
629. Moore, Glasberg, and Peters (1985a). See also Moore, Peters, and Glasberg (1985) and Moore, Glasberg, and Peters (1985b).
630. Cutting (1976).
631. Sundberg (1977, 1978).
632. Rasch (1979) described the performance asynchronies and Rasch (1978) described their perceptual effects and the effects of vibrato.
633. Stern (1972).
634. Erickson (1982), p. 531.
635. These were codified by Fux (1725).
636. Fox (1948).
637. van Noorden (1975).
638. van Noorden (1975), p. 76, McAdams and Bregman (1979), and Tougas and Bregman (1985a); see also Deutsch's "scale illusion" (Deutsch, 1975a).
639. Wright (1986), pp. 106–108. The experiment was done in the Speech and Hearing Laboratory of the McGill University Psychology Department.
640. Erickson (1975).
641. Jeppesen (1939).
642. Brant (1967).
643. A psychological approach to musical dissonance is offered by Bharucha (1984).
644. Wright and Bregman (1987).
645. Roberts (1983).
646. Helmholtz (1859); See also Helmholtz' essay "On the physiological causes of harmony in music" in Warren and Warren (1976).
647. Stumpf (1890); see the description in Sadie (1980).
648. DeWitt and Crowder (1987).
649. Schenker (1925).
650. Zuckerkandl (1956).
651. Wright and Bregman (1987).
652. Fox (1948), p. 52.
653. The term "reckless counterpoint" is defined by the *Harvard Dictionary of Music* as "the modern type of counterpoint that takes little account of harmonic combination and euphony (Apel, 1972).
654. Bregman (1978a) and Anstis and Saida (1985).
655. This is another version of the illusion described by Galli and Zama (1931), illustrated in Vicario (1982).

656. Wright (1986).
657. Wright (1986).
658. See experiments reviewed by Handel (1984) and studies by Klapp, Hill, Tyler, Martin, Jagacinski, and Jones (1985), and Beauvillain (1983). Also Sachs (1953).
659. Piston (1978), p. 501.
660. Krumhansl and Schmuckler (1984).
661. Krumhansl and Shepard (1979) and Krumhansl and Kessler (1982).
662. Chowning (1970).
663. Chafe, Jaffe, Kashima, Mont-Reynaud, and Smith (1985) and Chafe and Jaffe (1985).
664. Moorer (1977).
665. Cherry (1953).
666. Speith, Curtis, and Webster (1954).
667. Darwin (1984), p. 1646.
668. Dorman, Raphael, and Liberman (1979); see also Price and Levitt (1983).
669. Warren (1982) Ch.5.
670. Orr, Friedman, and Williams (1965).
671. Foulke and Sticht (1969).
672. van Noorden (1975), p. 80.
673. See the research reviewed in chapter 2 of this volume and in chapter 5 of Warren (1982).
674. Hirsh (1959).
675. Warren (1968); see also Warren and Warren (1970), Warren, Obusek, Farmer and Warren (1969), and Warren (1982), Ch.5.
676. Thomas, Hill, Carroll, and Garcia (1970), Thomas, Cetti, and Chase (1971).
677. Cullinan, Erdos, Schaeffer, and Tekieli (1977).
678. Lackner and Goldstein (1974).
679. Noteboom, Brokx, and de Rooij (1978).
680. Treisman (1960).
681. Darwin (1975), the reported experiment was carried out in collaboration with Davina Simmonds.
682. Noteboom, Brokx, and de Rooij (1978).
683. Darwin and Bethell-Fox (1977).
684. Darwin and Bethell-Fox (1977).
685. Dorman, Raphael, and Liberman (1979); see also Price and Levitt (1983).
686. Ladefoged (1959); also reported by Ladefoged and Broadbent (1960) and Fodor and Bever (1965).
687. See reviews by Warren (1982) and by Bashford and Warren (1986).
688. Bregman and Dannenbring (1977).
689. Dorman, Cutting, and Raphael (1975).
690. Bregman and Dannenbring (1973).
691. Rakerd, Dechovitz, and Verbrugge (1982) and Verbrugge and Rakerd (1986).
692. Cole and Scott (1973).
693. Bregman and Dannenbring (1973).
694. Bregman and Dannenbring (1977).
695. Personal communication from Jared Bernstein.
696. Cherry and Taylor (1954).

697. Huggins (1964).
698. Cole and Scott (1973).
699. Liberman, Cooper, Shankweiler, and Studdert-Kennedy (1967); see also Liberman (1982), Liberman and Mattingly (1985), and Mattingly and Liberman (in press).
700. For example, Searle (1982), Yilmaz (1967, 1968), Stevens (1980), Blumstein and Stevens (1979), Stevens and Blumstein (1981), and Bladon (1982).
701. For example, Treisman (1964). For reviews, see Broadbent (1958, 1971), Kahneman (1973), Norman (1976), Underwood (1976), and Moray (1970).
702. Egan, Carterette, and Thwing (1954).
703. Brokx and Noteboom (1982).
704. The speech was subjected to LPC analysis and a subsequent formant analysis and then resynthesized with a digital speech synthesizer.
705. Scheffers (1979, 1982, 1983a). See also Zwicker (1984).
706. Scheffers (1983), p. 97. The formants were synthesized using a software serial five-formant synthesizer.
707. Duifhuis, Willems, and Sluyter (1982).
708. Darwin and Gardner (1986) and Moore, Glasberg and Peters (1985a).
709. Halikia (1985). See also Chalikia and Bregman (1989).
710. Broadbent (1955).
711. The filters attenuated at about 18 dB per octave above (or below) the cutoff frequency.
712. Broadbent and Ladefoged (1957).
713. Darwin, Howell, and Brady (1978).
714. Cutting (1976).
715. Darwin (1981); see also Darwin and Sutherland (1984), as well as unpublished research by Sally Gaskill described by Darwin and Gardner (1986).
716. Darwin and Gardner (1986). See also Roberts (1988).
717. Moore, Glasberg, and Peters (1985a).
718. Parsons (1976), Weintraub (1984, 1985, 1986).
719. Lyon (1982, 1983).
720. Darwin (1984), experiment 2.
721. Rodet (1983), cited by McAdams (1984), pp. 38–39. Also McAdams and Rodet (1988).
722. Chowning (1980).
723. McAdams (1984).
724. Marin (1987).
725. Halikia (1985) and Chalikia and Bregman (1989). (Halikia and Chalikia are alternate spellings).
726. Gardner and Darwin (1986).
727. McAdams (1984), experiment 6.
728. Dorman, Cutting, and Raphael (1975).
729. McAdams (1984), p. 200.
730. Warren, Obusek, and Ackroff (1972), van Noorden (1975), Bregman and Pinker (1978), and Dannenbring and Bregman (1978).
731. Scheffers (1983), p. 97.
732. Rasch (1978, 1979).
733. Kubovy (1976), described in Kubovy (1981).
734. Darwin (1981, 1983, 1984) and Darwin and Sutherland (1984).
735. Pattison, Gardner, and Darwin (1986) and Darwin and Gardner (1986), p. 16.

736. Dannenbring and Bregman (1978).
737. Darwin and Sutherland (1984).
738. Cutting (1976).
739. Darwin (1981), experiment 1.
740. Experiment 4 in Darwin (1981).
741. Weintraub (1984, 1985, 1986).
742. The early research was done by Cherry (1953) and Speith, Curtis and Webster (1954); reviews of the field are given by Broadbent (1958, 1971), Kahneman (1973), Norman (1976), Underwood (1976), and Moray (1970).
743. Schubert and Schultz (1962).
744. Broadbent (1955).
745. One signal was low-pass filtered at 450 Hz and the other was high-pass filtered at 2,000 Hz. The filters both attenuated at about 18 dB per octave and so that at the middle frequency (on a log-frequency scale) of about 950 Hz, there would have been some energy, attenuated by about 19 dB, that was common to the two ears.
746. Cutting (1976).
747. Darwin (1979).
748. Darwin (1981).
749. Scheffers (1983).
750. See, for example, Bregman (1978b), Bregman and Pinker (1978), Darwin (1983), Pattison, Gardner, and Darwin (1986), Steiger (1983), van Noorden (1975), and Vicario (1980).
751. For example, Liberman (1982); it has also been referred to as "spectral/temporal fusion" by Cutting (1976) and by Repp and Bentin (1984).
752. Rand (1974).
753. The example is taken from Liberman (1982).
754. Reviewed by Liberman (1982). See also Repp, Milburn, and Ashkenas (1983).
755. This research is reviewed by Liberman (1982). See also Mann, Madden, Russell, and Liberman (1981).
756. Liberman (1982) and Liberman and Mattingly (1985).
757. Rand (1974).
758. Cutting (1976).
759. Similar effects of asynchrony were found by Bentin and Mann (1983).
760. Broadbent and Ladefoged (1957) and Darwin (1981).
761. Darwin (1981).
762. Repp and Bentin (1984).
763. Repp and Bentin (1984), p. 528.
764. Liberman and Mattingly (1985), p. 16.
765. McAdams (1984), p. 27, has given a similar argument about the conflicts in duplex perception.
766. Liberman (1982).
767. Bregman (1981b, 1977) and Bregman and Mills (1982).
768. Mattingly and Liberman (in press).
769. Liberman and Studdert-Kennedy (1978).
770. Mattingly and Liberman (in press).
771. Broadbent and Ladefoged (1957).
772. Darwin (1981).
773. The experiment was carried out by Sally Gaskill and reported in Darwin and Gardner (1986).

774. Liberman and Mattingly (1985), p. 16.
775. Repp and Bentin (1984), p. 528.
776. Whalen and Liberman (1987).
777. McAdams (1984), p. 197.
778. This method, known as linear predictive coefficient (LPC) analysis and resynthesis, is described in the textbook by Rabiner and Schaffer (1978).
779. Pastore, Schmuckler, Rosenblum, and Szczesiul (1983).
780. Collins (1985).
781. See, for example, Liberman and Mattingly (1985), p. 16, and McAdams (1984), p. 27.
782. Pastore, Schmuckler, Rosenblum, and Szczesiul (1983), p. 470.
783. Fowler and Rosenblum (1988).
784. Hafter and Jeffress (1968) and Hafter and Carrier (1972).
785. Steiger (1983).
786. Bregman and Pinker (1978).
787. Ciocca and Bregman (1989).
788. Rand (1974), figure 5.
789. Scheffers (1983a).
790. Kanizsa (1955).
791. Beck (1975).
792. The method involves filtering the signal to the left and right ear so as to impose the same transfer function as measured on an artificial head for a signal arriving from the desired position in space. The filtering also takes the characteristics of the headphone into account. The method is described by Blauert (1983). Divenyi's laboratory is located at the Speech and Hearing Research Facility, Veterans Administration Hospital, Martinez, California.
793. Kubovy (1981).
794. Bailey, Dorman, and Summerfield (1977) and Remez, Rubin, Pisoni, and Carrell (1981).
795. See Bregman (1977).
796. Mill (1874), p. 592.
797. Hebb (1949).
798. A brief review is given in Cohen and Grossberg (1986); see also Grossberg (1986).
799. Bregman (1977).
800. Dowling (1973).
801. Liberman and Studdert-Kennedy (1978).

Glossary

AM. Abbreviation of *amplitude modulation.*

AMPLITUDE MODULATION. A process of changing the amplitude of a tone (called a *carrier tone*). If the modulation is done periodically, its effects on the carrier tone can be described in two equivalent ways. The first is by simply describing the result as a repeating change in the amplitude of the carrier. The second is to describe it as a mixture of a fixed intensity carrier with a number of additional fixed intensity tones. The latter are described as *side bands*. If the pattern of amplitude variation is supplied by the wave shape of a second tone, the latter is called the modulating tone or modulator.

APERIODIC SOUND. A sound is said to be aperiodic if the *period* of all the waves is not the same. The extreme of aperiodic sound is *white noise*, in which there is no regularity at all to the wave pattern. See *periodic sound.*

APPARENT MOTION. When two lamps at different locations in space are flashed in succession, the viewer obtains an impression of motion between the first light and the second. This is called "apparent motion."

ASPIRATION. A type of very soft noise appearing in speech sounds. It occurs in the *phoneme* "h" in English, or with less duration after the release of an unvoiced consonant, for example, after the "p" in "pie".

ATTACK. A musical term that means the same as *rise time.*

BAND-PASS. See *filter.*

BANDWIDTH. See *filter* and *spectrum.*

BASILAR MEMBRANE. The organ of hearing. It is a long, coiled, ribbon-like membrane suspended in a liquid-filled chamber in the inner ear. As sound reaches it, it goes into vibration. Because of differences in width and stiffness from one end to the other, each site along the membrane vibrates maximally to a particular frequency in the incoming acoustic signal. These vibrations are translated to neural firing and the pattern of activity at each site is carried away by a separate group of neurons. The pattern of activity along the basilar membrane encodes the frequency content of the signal. This is called "place information." In addition, the actual pattern of motion of the membrane at each frequency-selective site reflects the *period* and *phase* of the frequency component to which it is maximally sensitive.

BEATS. Because of the mathematical properties of waves, the mixing (addition) of two pure tones can be described in either as a sum of the two frequencies of the tones or as a single frequency with *sinusoidal* variations in amplitude called "beats." In practice, listeners hear the pattern as consisting of beats when their auditory system does not have a fine enough frequency resolution to distinguish the component frequencies. This description applies also to the mixture of complex tones, since they have pure-tone components whose mixture can be described as above.

BINAURAL. Pertaining to two ears. A presentation of sound is binaural when both ears are presented with the sound. Sometimes this term is also used as a synonym for *diotic*, with the meaning of the latter.

CARRIER TONE. See *amplitude modulation* and *frequency modulation*.

CENT. In musical research, a unit of pitch change equal to 0.01 semitones.

CHORD. Three or more notes played at the same time. (If there are only two, it is called an *interval*.)

COMPLEX TONE. A tone containing many frequency components or *partials*. See *pure tone*.

CONSONANT. 1. (noun) A speech sound in which an articulatory gesture stops or modifies the flow of the voiced sounds (vowels). Examples are "b", "k", and "n". 2. (adjective) Smooth and harmonious. The opposite of *dissonant*.

COUNTERPOINT. In music, the art of creating a *polyphonic* composition in which two or more lines of melody occur at the same time.

CRITICAL BAND. A range of frequencies surrounding the frequency of a designated pure tone. When other pure tones whose frequencies are within this range are played at the same time as the designated one, the auditory system does not hear the two completely independently. The designated tone may be masked, beats may be heard, or other forms of interaction may occur. The size of the critical band increases for higher frequency tones, ranging from about 100 Hz for low-frequency tones to above 2,000 Hz for very high ones.

DB. Abbreviation of *decibel*.

DECIBEL. A unit of *intensity* of sound. The abbreviation is dB. The decibel is a relational measure, expressing the relative intensity of the described sound to a reference sound. If no specific other reference sound is mentioned, or if the suffix SPL is attached to the unit of measurement, as in the expression 70 dB SPL, the standard is taken to be a sound with a power of 10^{-16} watts per square centimeter, which is a bit below the threshold of human hearing. The decibel is a logarithmic measure. A difference of 20 dB between two sounds means that the more intense one has 10 times the amplitude (100 times the power) of the softer.

DENSITY OF A SPECTRUM. A spectrum is dense when the frequency components are closely packed on the frequency dimension.

DIATONIC SCALE. The scale on which most Western European music is built. The names given to its notes are do, re, mi, fa, sol, la, ti (si), do. The diatonic scale of C major can be produced using only the white keys of a piano keyboard.

DICHOTIC PRESENTATION. Simultaneous presentation of different signals to the two ears. See *diotic*, *binaural*.

DIOTIC PRESENTATION. Presentation of the same signal to the two ears.

DISSONANCE. See *psychoacoustic dissonance*, *musical dissonance*.

F1, F2, F3, ... The successive *formants* in the *spectrum* of a speech signal, numbering them from low to high.

FILTER. A device that can change the relative amplitudes and phases of the frequency components in the *spectrum* of a signal. A *high-pass* filter attentuates low frequencies and lets the high ones pass through. A *low-pass* filter does the opposite. A *band-pass* filter allows a range of frequencies through, attenuating those that are lower and higher than the desired band of frequencies.

Other types of filters can change the *spectral shape* in other ways, such as allowing amplitude to vary inversely with frequency.

FM. Abbreviation of *frequency modulation*.

FORMANT. A peak in the *spectrum* of a speech signal. It is caused by resonant cavities in the *vocal tract* of the speaker. The *vowels* differ from one another in the frequencies at which these peaks occur in their *spectra*. A formant, when it occurs in natural speech, is just a peak in a spectrum. But in some synthesized speech used in research, it may be an isolated band of frequencies. It appears that these isolated bands are sufficient to induce the perception of vowels or other *voiced* sounds. A formant is described by its order, counting from low to high, in the set of formants in a speech spectrum. F1 is the lowest, F2 the next, and so on.

FORMANT FREQUENCY. The frequency of the peak of some *formant* in a speech signal. Because the formant is formed of a number of *harmonics* it is related to a particular *fundamental frequency*. Therefore two independent frequency values can be given for a formant (center and fundamental).

FOURIER ANALYSIS. A mathematical analysis of waves, discovered by the French mathematician Fourier. He proved that any periodic sound, or any nonperiodic sound of limited duration, could be represented (Fourier analysis) or created out of (Fourier synthesis) the sum of a set of *pure tones* with different frequencies, amplitudes, and phases.

FREQUENCY. The number of repetitions of the wave in a *periodic* vibration in a fixed *time*.

FREQUENCY MODULATION. A process of changing the frequency of a tone (called a *carrier tone*). If the modulation is done periodically, its effects on the carrier tone can be described in two equivalent ways. The first is by simply describing the result as a *periodic* change in the frequency of the carrier. The second is to describe it as a mixture of a fixed intensity carrier with a number of additional fixed intensity tones. The latter are described as *side bands*. If the pattern of frequency variation is supplied by the wave shape of a second tone, the latter is called the *modulating tone* or *modulator*.

FRICATION. See *fricative*.

FRICATIVE. A speech sound produced by *frication*, that is by forcing air through a constriction in the vocal tract. Examples are "s" and "f".

FUNDAMENTAL. A shortening of the expression *fundamental frequency*.

FUNDAMENTAL FREQUENCY. Its abbreviation is F0. For its definition, see *harmonic*.

F0. Abbreviation of *fundamental frequency*.

GLISSANDO (PL. GLISSANDI) A rapid succession of notes that forms an ascending or descending trajectory.

HARMONIC. A harmonic is the name given to a frequency component that occurs as one of a number of such components in a spectrum in which the frequency of every component is a multiple of a low frequency called the *fundamental frequency*. Therefore a harmonic is always a "harmonic of" some particular fundamental frequency. See *partial*.

HARMONIC INTERVAL. In music, the number of pitch steps (in the musical scale) separating two simultaneously played notes. See *melodic interval*.

HARMONIC NUMBER. The *harmonics* related to a given *fundamental frequency* in a *spectrum* are numbered as follows: The factor that the *fundamental* has to be multiplied by to derive the frequency of the harmonic is used as the number of that harmonic. Therefore the fundamental itself is called the first harmonic.

HARMONIC SERIES. The set of harmonics whose frequencies are multiples of a certain *fundamental frequency*. For example, the harmonic series based on the fundamental 100 Hz are 100, 200, 300, 400. . . . The members of the series are separated by a frequency equal to the fundamental.

HARMONIC TONE. A tone whose *partials* are all harmonics of a given *fundamental frequency*, although not all the harmonics need be present. See *inharmonic tone*.

HIGH-PASS. See *filter*.

HZ. Abbreviation of hertz, the unit of *frequency* in wave motion. One hertz is one complete occurrence of the wave per second.

INHARMONIC TONE. A tone composed of *partials* that are not all multiples of a common *fundamental*.

INNER EAR. The deepest part of the ear. It includes the cochlea, a snail-shaped cavity in the bone that contains the *basilar membrane* which is the organ of hearing.

INTENSITY. The name given to the physical energy with which a sound is present. It contrasts with *loudness*, which is the perceptual experience correlated (but not perfectly) with that physical intensity.

INTERVAL (IN MUSIC). A shorter form that means the same as *harmonic interval* or *melodic interval*, depending on context.

ISOCHRONOUS. An isochronous series of sounds is one whose components are spaced at equal *time* intervals.

LATERALIZATION. The identification of a sound that is presented over headphones is described as "lateralization" rather than *localization*. Lateralization is the identification of the position of the sound on the left-right dimension. With conventional recording and playback, the sound usually is experienced as inside the head.

LOCALIZATION. The judgment of the place of spatial origin of a sound. See *lateralization*.

LOG SCALE (LOGARITHMIC SCALE). A scale in which the logarithm of the physical variable is used instead of the raw value. This has the effect that equal steps along the scale represent equal ratios between the raw values. Examples in audition are the *decibel* scale and the scale of musical *pitch*.

LOUDNESS. See *intensity*.

LOW-PASS. See *filter*.

MAJOR TRIAD. A *chord* of three notes that is the foundation of the major *diatonic scale* in Western music. They are the first, third, and fifth notes of that scale.

MASKING. A phenomenon in which the presence of a loud sound, called the *masker*, makes it impossible to decide whether a weaker sound, called the "target," is also present. The masker is more effective in masking the target the louder it is and the closer it is in frequency to the target. Low-frequency tones mask higher ones better than vice versa.

MELODIC INTERVAL. The number of pitch steps (in a musical scale) separating two successively played notes. See *harmonic interval*.

MICROMODULATION. Tiny fluctuations in the frequency of a tone (on the order of 1 percent) that occur naturally in speech and music even when the pitch is thought of as steady.

MILLISECOND. One one-thousandth of a second. Abbreviated as msec.

MISSING FUNDAMENTAL. The phenomenon of the "missing fundamental" is one in which a listener, presented with a *harmonic tone* in which the *fundamental* is absent, hears the same pitch as would be heard if the fundamental had been present. Therefore only some of the *harmonics* are needed to hear the pitch. This used to be thought of as "hearing the fundamental" because the fundamental, played alone, would also have that *pitch*. The pitch that is heard when the fundamental is absent is called *periodicity pitch* because the period of the wave is the same whether the fundamental is present or not.

MODULATING TONE. See *frequency modulation* and *amplitude modulation*.

MODULATION. Variation (usually, but not necessarily, *periodic*) in some property of a tone. See *frequency modulation* and *amplitude modulation*.

MODULATOR. See *frequency modulation* and *amplitude modulation*.

MONAURAL PRESENTATION. Presentation of a signal to only one ear. See *dichotic*, *diotic*, *binaural*.

MSEC. The abbreviation of *millisecond*.

MUSICAL DISSONANCE. A role assigned to certain simultaneous combinations of notes in music. The combination is considered to induce tension, which is later to be resolved by the presentation of a musically *consonant* combination.

NEURAL SPECTROGRAM. The idea that the auditory system takes apart the acoustic information in the same way that a *spectrogram* does. The separation of different frequencies is done by the *basilar membrane*. Information about the intensity and phase of different frequency components is kept separate in different neural pathways originating at different sites on the membrane. This separation of frequency information is maintained all the way up to the brain. Intensity activity in each neural pathway corresponds to the darkness of the streak on the spectrogram for the corresponding frequency.

NOISE. Sound that is irregular. That is, it is not formed of regular repeating waves. Noise can, however, be described by its frequency content. Since the frequencies and phases change from one instant to the next, this description represents an average taken over *time*. In *white noise* all audible frequencies are present with equal (average) amplitude. The moment-by-moment sequence of amplitudes in white noise is essentially random. If white noise is passed through a *filter*, its *spectral shape* can be altered and it is no longer considered white noise.

OCTAVE. One of the pitch *intervals* in music. Tones separated by an octave have an equivalent quality and are assigned the same note name (for example, "C") in western music and the same role in harmony. The equivalent perceptual quality of tones separated by an octave has been given the name "chroma," and the quality that distinguishes them has been named "pitch height." Physically, a note that is an octave higher than another has a frequency that is twice that of the lower one.

PARTIAL. A frequency component of a tone. This component need not be harmonically related to a fundamental. See *harmonic*.

PERIOD. In a *periodic sound*, the period is the *time* required for one repetition of the wave.

PERIODIC SOUND. A periodic sound is one in which each wave is identical to the one before it. As a consequence, it can be represented as the sum of a set of *harmonics*. If this is not true, the sound is said to be *aperiodic*, or nonperiodic. See *Fourier analysis* and *harmonic tone*.

PERIODICITY PITCH. See *missing fundamental*.

PHASE. The phase is the particular point in a wave that is passing a position in space at a certain instant of *time*. Phase is measured in units of degrees, with 360 degrees representing one complete cycle of the wave. If two tones have the same *period* and are occurring at the same time, the *temporal* lag of one with respect to the other can be described in terms of phase. If two waves are out of phase by 180 degrees, the later one is lagging by one-half a period.

PHONEME. The basic classes of sounds used to form the words in a language. Examples in English are "k", "oo", and "th". They often are represented by single written letters.

PHONETIC. Pertaining to the sounds of a language.

PHONETIC IDENTIFICATION. Phonetic identification means identifying a sound as a sequence of one or more speech sounds.

PITCH. The quality that distinguishes the sound of two different notes on the same instrument when they are played with equal force. In periodic sounds, it is correlated with the physical property of frequency. Periodic sounds with higher frequencies are heard as having higher pitches. See *periodicity pitch*.

POLYPHONY. See *counterpoint*.

PSYCHOACOUSTIC DISSONANCE. The sense of roughness or lack of blending that is heard when certain combinations of musical tones are played together outside a musical context.

PURE TONE. A tone with only a single frequency component. Its wave form will be that of a sine wave.

RESONATOR. A physical system that acts to enhance the intensity of some frequency components of a sound and to attenuate others. It is a type of *filter*. The air chambers in the *vocal tract* of a talker act as resonators that produce the *formants* of the voice.

RISE TIME. The time taken for a signal to rise from silence to full intensity. The tones of different instruments can be distinguished by their rise time, the tones of percussive instruments like the piano rising very rapidly and of others like the tuba, more slowly. In music, "rise time" is called *attack*.

SCHEMA. In cognitive theory, an organization (in a person's brain) of information pertaining to some regularity in his or her environment. Sometimes it is conceptualized as an active structure analogous to a computer program, and sometimes as similar to a complex organization of "memory" records in a computer. In all cases it is abstract enough to be able to fit a range of environmental situations. Schemas are conceived of as being at different levels of generality. Examples are the schemas for "causality", "space", and "bread".

SEC. Abbreviation of "second" when it means a unit of time.

SEMITONE. The smallest pitch *interval* in the Western musical scale. It corresponds to the pitch difference between a white note on a piano and the black note immediately adjacent to it. If two tones are a semitone apart, the frequency of the higher one is 1.06 times the frequency of the lower.

SHADOWING. A task used in psychological experiments on auditory attention. A stream of speech is played and a listener is required to repeat it in a continuous fashion while it is still being said. That is, the listener's response is made while listening to the next part of the signal.

SIDE BAND. See *amplitude modulation* and *frequency modulation*.

SIMPLE TONE. Same as *pure tone*

SINE WAVE. The simplest form of periodic wave motion. All other forms can be created by adding (mixing) a number of sine waves. The wave form of a *pure tone* is a sine wave.

SINUSOIDAL. Having the shape of a *sine wave*.

SOURCE VIBRATION. The original wave form produced by a vibrating body before it passes through any structures that act as *resonators* altering the shape of the *spectrum* of the sound. The source vibration in speech is produced by the *vocal folds*.

SPECTRA. Plural of *spectrum*.

SPECTRAL BAND. A part of a spectrum containing a range of adjacent frequencies. See *filter*.

SPECTRAL ENVELOPE. An imaginary *spectral shape* represented by a line drawn on a graph of a spectrum. In the graph, the horizontal axis represents frequency and the vertical axis represents the intensity. Points drawn on the graph represent the intensity of each spectral component. The shortest smooth line that touches all these points is the spectral envelope, and defines the spectral shape.

SPECTRAL REGION. A particular range of frequencies in the *spectrum*.

SPECTRAL SHAPE. See *spectral envelope*

SPECTROGRAM. A graphic representation of a time-varying spectrum, such as occurs in speech. An example is figure 1.3 of chapter 1. The horizontal axis represents time and the vertical axis represents frequency. The darkness of any point on the graph represents the amplitude of the frequency that is designated on the vertical axis at the time designated on the horizontal axis.

SPECTRUM. The spectrum of a particular sound is a description giving the amplitude (and/or phase) of each frequency component in it. The description of an amplitude spectrum is given under *spectral envelope*.

SQUARE WAVE. A square wave is one in which there are only two values of the displacement of the wave from the neutral position, a positive displacement and an equally large negative displacement. The wave moves instantaneously from one state to the other and remains equally long in each state. Its *spectrum* contains odd *harmonics* only, whose *intensities* are inversely proportional to their *harmonic number*.

STOP CLOSURE. The closing off of the *vocal tract* to produce the *stops*.

STOPS. In phonetics, the class of consonants produced by a complete closure of the flow of air in the *vocal tract*. Examples are "p", "d", and "k".

TEMPORAL. An adjective meaning "pertaining to *time*."

TIME. That property of the universe that lets you say, "I'll see you later."

TRIAD. In music, a chord of three notes. See *major triad*.

UNVOICED SOUND. See *voiced sound*.

VOCAL CORDS. Same as *vocal folds*.

VOCAL FOLDS. Fold of tissue in the larynx whose vibration creates the *periodic sound* present in the *voiced sounds* of speech.

VOCAL TRACT. A series of cavities, above the vocal folds, forming a long, connected tube, in which voiced sounds are shaped and many unvoiced sounds are created. They include the structures of the pharynx, the mouth, and the nose.

VOICED SOUND. A speech sound in which the vocal folds are creating a regular wave form in the sound. Examples are the vowels, or consonants such as "m" or "l". This type of sound is contrasted with an unvoiced sound in which the vocal folds are silent and the sound is produced by a sustained noise, as in "s", an explosion, as in "p", or an implosion as in the clicks of some African languages.

VOWELS. The *voiced sounds* of speech that are combined with *consonants* to form syllables. Examples are "ah", "oo", and "ee".

WHITE NOISE. See *noise*.

WHOLE TONE. In music, the pitch interval equal to two semitones. The ratio of the frequency of a tone to one that is a whole tone below it is 9:8 (relative frequency approximately 1.12). The notes C and D are separated by a whole tone.

Bibliography

American Standards Association (1960). *Acoustical Terminology SI. 1-1960.* New York: American Standards Association.

Anstis, S., and Saida, S. (1985). Adaptation to auditory streaming of frequency-modulated tones. *Journal of Experimental Psychology: Human Perception and Performance, 11,* 257–271.

Anstis, S., Giaschi, D., and Cogan, A. I. (1985). Adaptation to apparent motion. *Vision Research, 25,* 1051–1062.

Apel, W. (ed.) (1972). *Harvard Dictionary of Music.* (Second edition) Cambridge, Mass.: Belnap Press of Harvard University Press.

Attneave, F. (1974). Apparent movement and the what-where connection. *Psychologia, 17,* 108–120.

Attneave, F., and Block, G. (1973). Apparent movement in tridimensional space. *Perception & Psychophysics, 13,* 301–307.

Axelrod, S., and Guzy, L. T. (1968). Underestimation of dichotic click rates: Results using methods of absolute estimation and constant stimuli. *Psychonomic Science, 12,* 133–134.

Axelrod, S., and Powazek, M. (1972). Dependence of apparent rate of alternating clicks on azimuthal separation between sources. *Psychonomic Science, 26,* 217–218.

Axelrod, S., Guzy, L. T., and Diamond, I. T. (1968). Perceived rate of monotic and dichotically alternating clicks. *Journal of the Acoustical Society of America, 43,* 51–55.

Babbitt, M. (1964). The synthesis, perception and specification of musical time. *Journal of the International Folk Music Council, 16,* 92–95.

Bacon, S. P., and Viemeister, N. F. (1985a). Simultaneous masking by gated and continuous sinusoidal maskers. *Journal of the Acoustical Society of America, 78,* 1220–1230.

Bacon, S. P., and Viemeister, N. F. (1985b). The temporal course of simultaneous tone-on-tone masking. *Journal of the Acoustical Society of America, 78,* 1231–1235.

Bailey, P. J., Dorman, M. F., Summerfield, A. Q. (1977). Identification of sine-wave analogs of CV syllables in speech and non-speech modes. *Journal of the Acoustical Society of America, 61,* S(A).

Balzano, G. J. (1986). What are musical pitch and timbre? *Music Perception, 3,* 297–314.

Barsz, K. (1988). Auditory pattern perception: The effect of tonal frequency range on the perception of temporal order. *Perception & Psychophysics, 43,* 293–303.

Bashford, J. A., Meyers, M. D., Brubaker, B. S., and Warren, R. M. (1988). Illusory continuity of interrupted speech: Speech rate determines durational limits. *Journal of the Acoustical Society of America, 84,* 1635–1638.

Bashford, J. A., and Warren, R. M. (1987). Multiple phonemic restorations follow the rules for auditory induction. *Perception & Psychophysics, 42,* 114–121.

Bashford, J. A., Jr., and Warren, R. M. (1979). Perceptual synthesis of deleted phonemes. In J. J. Wolf and D. H. Klatt (eds.), *Speech Communication Papers,* New York: Acoustical Society of America.

Bastiaans, M. (1980). Gabor's expansion of a signal into Gaussian elementary signals. *Proceedings of the IEEE, 68,* 538–539.

Beauvillain, C. (1983). Auditory perception of dissonant polyrhythms. *Perception & Psychophysics, 34,* 585–592.

Beck, J. (1975). The perception of surface color. *Scientific American, 232(2),* 62–75.

Békésy, G. von. (1963). Three experiments concerned with speech perception. *Journal of the Acoustical Society of America, 35,* 602–606.

Bentin, S., and Mann, V. A. (1983). Selective effects of masking on speech and non-speech in the duplex perception paradigm. *Haskins Laboratories Status Report on Speech Research, SR-6,* 65–85.

Beauvillain, C. (1983). Auditory perception of dissonant polyrhythms. *Perception & Psychophysics, 34,* 585–592.

Bertelson, P., and Radeau, M. (1981). Cross-modal bias and perceptual fusion with auditory-visual spatial discordance. *Perception & Psychophysics, 29,* 578–584.

Bharucha, J. J. (1984). Anchoring effects in music: The resolution of dissonance. *Cognitive Psychology, 16,* 485–518.

Bladon, A. (1982). Arguments against formants in the auditory representation of speech. In R. Carlson and B. Granstöm (eds.) *The Representation of Speech in the Peripheral Auditory System.* Amsterdam: Elsevier Biomedical Press.

Blauert, J. (1983). *Spatial Hearing: The Psychophysics of Human Sound Localization.* Cambridge, Mass.: MIT Press.

Blumstein, S. E., and Stevens, K. N. (1979). Acoustic invariance in speech production: Evidence from measurements of the spectral characteristics of stop consonants. *Journal of the Acoustical Society of America, 66,* 1001–1017.

Bompiani (Publisher). (1987). *Effeto Archimboldo.* Milan: Bompiani.

Boulez, P. (1985). Le timbre dans la littérature instrumentale de la XXième siecle. Presented at the Seminar on Timbre, Institut de Recherche et Coordination Acoustique/Musique, Paris, April 13–17, 1985.

Bozzi, P., and Vicario, G. (1960). Due fattori di unificazione fra note musicali: La vicinanza temporale e la vicinanza tonale. *Rivista di Psycologia, 54,* 235–258.

Brant, Henry (1967). Space as an essential aspect of music composition. In E. Schwartz and B. Childs (eds.), *Contemporary Composers on Contemporary Music.* New York: Holt, Rinehart & Winston.

Bregman, A. S. (1971). *Primary Auditory Stream Segregation and the Perception of Tunes.* Unpublished manuscript, Department of Psychology, McGill University.

Bregman, A. S. (1972). *Stream Segregation in Sequences of Tones and Hisses.* Unpublished Manuscript, Department of Psychology, McGill University.

Bregman, A. S. (1977). Perception and behavior as compositions of ideals. *Cognitive Psychology, 9,* 250–292.

Bregman, A. S. (1978a). Auditory streaming is cumulative. *Journal of Experimental Psychology: Human Perception and Performance, 4*, 380–387.
Bregman, A. S. (1978b). Auditory streaming: Competition among alternative organizations. *Perception & Psychophysics, 23*, 391–398.
Bregman, A. S. (1978c). The formation of auditory streams. In J. Requin (ed.), *Attention and Performance VII*. Hillsdale, N.J.: Erlbaum.
Bregman, A. S. (1981a). Chomsky without language. *Cognition, 10*, 33–38.
Bregman, A. S. (1981b). Asking the "what for" question in auditory perception. In M. Kubovy and J. R. Pomerantz, (eds.) *Perceptual Organization*. Hillsdale, N.J.: Erlbaum.
Bregman, A. S. (1984). Auditory scene analysis. *Proceedings of the Seventh International Conference on Pattern Recognition*. Silver Spring, Md.: IEEE Computer Society Press. (Library of Congress No. 84-80909.)
Bregman, A. S. (1987). The meaning of duplex perception: Sounds as transparent objects. In M. E. H. Schouten (ed.), *The Psychophysics of Speech Perception*. Dordrecht: Martinus Nijhoff NATO-ASI Series.
Bregman, A. S., and Abdel Ahad, P. (1985). Fusion of Simultaneous Sounds: Effects of Three Types of Modulation. Unpublished research, Psychology Department, McGill University.
Bregman, A. S., Abramson, J., Doehring, P., and Darwin, C. J. (1985). Spectral integration based on common amplitude modulation. *Perception & Psychophysics, 37*, 483–493.
Bregman, A. S., and Achim, A. (1973). Visual stream segregation. *Perception & Psychophysics, 13*, 451–454.
Bregman, A. S., and Campbell, J. (1971). Primary auditory stream segregation and perception of order in rapid sequences of tones. *Journal of Experimental Psychology, 89*, 244–249.
Bregman, A. S., and Dannenbring, G. (1973). The effect of continuity on auditory stream segregation. *Perception & Psychophysics, 13*, 308–312.
Bregman, A. S., and Dannenbring, G. L. (1977). Auditory continuity and amplitude edges. *Canadian Journal of Psychology, 31*, 151–159.
Bregman, A. S., and Doehring, P. (1984). Fusion of simultaneous tonal glides: The role of parallelness and simple frequency relations. *Perception & Psychophysics, 36*, 251–256.
Bregman, A. S., and Levitan, R. (1983). Stream Segregation Based on Fundamental Frequency and Spectral Peak. I: Effects of Shaping by filters. Unpublished manuscript, Psychology Department, McGill University.
Bregman, A. S., Levitan, R., and Liao, C. (1990). Fusion of Auditory Components: Effects of the Frequency of Amplitude Modulation. *Perception & Psychophysics, 47*, 68–73.
Bregman, A. S., and Liao, C. (1984). Stream Segregation Based on Fundamental Frequency and Spectral Peak. II: Effects of fixed Spectral Window and Local Peak Shaping through Additive Synthesis. Unpublished manuscript, Psychology Department, McGill University.
Bregman, A. S., McAdams, S., and Halpern, L. (1978). *Auditory Segregation and Timbre*. Presented at meeting of the Psychonomic Society, November 1978, San Antonio, Texas.
Bregman, A. S., and Mills, M. I. (1982). Perceived movement: The Flintstone constraint. *Perception, 11*, 201–206.
Bregman, A. S., and Pinker, S. (1978). Auditory streaming and the building of timbre. *Canadian Journal of Psychology, 32*, 19–31.

Bregman, A. S., and Rudnicky, A. (1975). Auditory segregation: Stream or streams? *Journal of Experimental Psychology: Human Perception and Performance, 1*, 263–267.

Bregman, A. S., and Steiger, H. (1980). Auditory streaming and vertical localization: Interdependence of "what" and "where" decisions in audition. *Perception & Psychophysics, 28*, 539–546.

Bregman, A. S., and Tougas, Y. (1989). Propagation of constraints in auditory organization. *Perception & Psychophysics, 46*, 395–396.

Broadbent, D. E. (1955). A note on binaural fusion. *Quarterly Journal of Experimental Psychology*, 7, 46–47.

Broadbent, D. E. (1958). *Perception and Communication*. London: Pergamon.

Broadbent, D. E. (1971). *Decision and Stress*. London: Academic Press.

Broadbent, D. E., and Ladefoged, P. (1957). On the fusion of sounds reaching different sense organs. *Journal of the Acoustical Society of America, 29*, 708–710.

Broadbent, D. E., and Ladefoged, P. (1959). Auditory perception of temporal order. *Journal of the Acoustical Society of America, 31*, 1539.

Brokx, J. P. L., and Noteboom, S. G. (1982). Intonation and the perceptual separation of simultaneous voices. *Journal of Phonetics, 10*, 23–36.

Bronkhorst, A. W., and Plomp, R. (1987). The effect of head-induced interaural time and level differences on speech intelligibility in noise. *Journal of the Acoustical Society of America, 83*, 1508–1516.

Bukofzer, M. (1958). *Music in the Baroque Era*. New York: Pergamon.

Burke, L. (1952). On the tunnel effect. *Quarterly Journal of Experimental Psychology, 4*, 121–138.

Butler, D. (1979a). *Melodic Channeling in a Musical Environment*. Research Symposium on the Psychology and Acoustics of Music, February 22–23, 1979, University of Kansas.

Butler, D. (1979b). A further study of melodic channeling. *Perception & Psychophysics, 25*, 264–268.

Butler, R. (1969). Monaural and binaural localization of noise bursts in the median sagittal plane. *Journal of Auditory Research, 3*, 320–235.

Butler, R. A., and Naunton, R. F. (1962). Some effects of unilateral auditory masking upon the localization of sounds in space. *Journal of the Acoustical Society of America, 34*, 1100–1107.

Butler, R. A., and Naunton, R. F. (1964). Role of stimulus frequency and duration in the phenomenon of localization shifts. *Journal of the Acoustical Society of America, 36*, 917–922.

Buus, S. (1985). Release from masking caused by amplitude fluctuations. *Journal of the Acoustical Society of America, 78*, 1958–1965.

Cadoz, C. (1985). Timbre et Causalité. Unpublished paper. Seminar on Timbre, Institut de Recherche et Coordination Acoustique/Musique, Paris, France, April 13–17.

Carhart, R., Tillman, T. W., and Johnson, K. R. (1967). Release of masking for speech through interaural time delay. *Journal of the Acoustical Society of America, 42*, 124–138.

Carpenter, P. A., and Eisenberg, P. (1978). Mental rotation and frame of reference in blind and sighted individuals. *Perception & Psychophysics, 23*, 117–124.

Carroll, J. D., and Chang; J. J. (1970). Analysis of individual differences in multidimensional scaling via an n-way generalization of "Eckart-Young" decomposition. *Psychometrika, 35*, 283–319.

Chafe, C., and Jaffe, D. (1986). Source separation and note identification in polyphonic music. *Proceedings of the International Conference on Acoustics, Speech, and Signal Processing (ICASSP)*, Vol. 2, 25.6.1–25.6.2, Tokyo.

Chafe, C., Jaffe, D., Kashima, K., Mont-Reynaud, B., and Smith, J. (1985). Techniques for note identification in polyphonic music. *Proceedings of the International Conference on Computer Music (ICMC)*, Vancouver, Computer Music Association.

Chalikia, M. H., and Bregman, A. S. (1989). The perceptual segregation of simultaneous auditory signals: Pulse train segregation and vowel segregation. *Perception & Psychophysics, 46*, 487–497.

Cherry, C., and Wiley, R. (1967). Speech communication in very noisy environments. *Nature (London), 214*, 1164.

Cherry, E. C. (1953). Some experiments on the recognition of speech with one and with two ears. *Journal of the Acoustical Society of America, 25*, 975–979.

Cherry, E. C., and Taylor, W. K. (1954). Some further experiments upon the recognition of speech, with one and with two ears. *Journal of the Acoustical Society of America, 26*, 554–559.

Chowning, J. M. (1970). The simulation of moving sound sources. Presented at the 38th convention, The Audio Engineering Society, May 4–7. (Available from Center for Computer Research in Music and Acoustics, Department of Music, Stanford University, Stanford, Calif.)

Chowning, J. M. (1980). Computer synthesis of the singing voice. In *Sound Generation in Winds, Strings, Computers*. Stockholm: Royal Swedish Academy of Music, Publ. No. 29. Kungl. Musikaliska Akademien.

Ciocca, V., and Bregman, A. S. (1989). The effects of auditory streaming on duplex perception. *Perception & Psychophysics, 46*, 39–48.

Ciocca, V. (1985). Perceived Continuity of Steady-State and Glided Tones through a Louder Noise: Evidence Concerning a Trajectory Effect. Master's thesis, McGill University.

Ciocca, V., and Bregman, A. S. (1987). Perceived continuity of gliding and steady-state tones through interrupting noise. *Perception & Psychophysics, 42*, 476–484.

Cohen, E. A. (1979). Fusion and consonance relations for tones with inharmonic partials. *Journal of the Acoustical Society of America, 65*, Suppl. 1, S123.

Cohen, E. A. (1980a). The Influence of Non-Harmonic Partials on Tone Perception. Ph.D. dissertation, Program in Acoustics, Stanford University.

Cohen, E. A. (1980b). Pitch processing of non-harmonic tones: A search for an auditory mechanism that recognizes spectral patterns. *Journal of the Acoustical Society of America, 68*, Suppl. 1, S110.

Cohen, M., and Grossberg, S. (1986). Neural dynamics of speech and language coding: Developmental programs, perceptual grouping, and competition for short-term memory. *Human Neurobiology, 5*, 1–22.

Cole, R. A., and Scott, B. (1973). Perception of temporal order in speech: The role of vowel transitions. *Canadian Journal of Psychology, 27*, 441–449.

Collins, S. (1985). Duplex perception with musical stimuli: A further investigation. *Perception & Psychophysics, 38*, 172–177.

Collyer, C. E. (1974). The detection of a temporal gap between two disparate stimuli. *Perception & Psychophysics, 16*, 96–100.

Cooper, L. A., and Shepard, R. N. (1973a). The time required to prepare for a rotated stimulus. *Memory and Cognition, 1*, 246–250.

Cooper, L. A., and Shepard, R. N. (1973b). Chronometric studies of the rotation of mental images. In W. Chase (ed.), *Visual Information Processing*. New York: Academic Press.

Corbin, H. H. (1942). The perception of grouping and apparent movement in visual depth. *Archives of Psychology*, No. 273.

Cramer, E. M., and Huggins, W. H. (1958). Creation of pitch through binaural interaction. *Journal of the Acoustical Society of America*, *30*, 413–417.

Crowder, R. G., and Morton, J. (1969). Precategorical acoustic storage. *Perception & Psychophysics*, *5*, 365–373.

Cullinan, W. L., Erdos, E., Schaefer, R., and Tekieli, M. E. (1977). Perception of temporal order of vowels and consonant-vowel syllables. *Journal of Speech and Hearing Research*, *20*, 742–751.

Cutting J. E. (1975). Aspects of phonological fusion. *Journal of Experimental Psychology: Human Perception and Performance*, *104*, 105–120.

Cutting, J. E. (1976). Auditory and linguistic processes in speech perception: Inferences from six fusions in dichotic listening. *Psychological Review*, *83*, 114–140.

Cutting, J. E., and Rosner, B. S. (1976). Discrimination functions predicted from categories in speech and music. *Perception & Psychophysics*, *20*, 87–88.

Dannenbring, G. L. (1976). Perceived auditory continuity with alternately rising and falling frequency transitions. *Canadian Journal of Psychology*, *30*, 99–114.

Dannenbring, G. L., and Bregman, A. S. (1976a). The effect of silence on auditory stream segregation. *Journal of the Acoustical Society of America*, *59*, 987–989.

Dannenbring, G. L., and Bregman, A. S. (1976b). Stream segregation and the illusion of overlap. *Journal of Experimental Psychology: Human Perception and Performance*, *2*, 544–555.

Dannenbring, G. L., and Bregman, A. S. (1978). Streaming vs. fusion of sinusoidal components of complex waves. *Perception & Psychophysics*, *24*, 369–376.

Darwin, C. J. (1975). On the dynamic use of prosody in speech perception. In A. Cohen and S. G. Noteboom (eds.) Structure and Process in Speech Perception: Proceedings of the Symposium on Dynamic Aspects of Speech Perception. Held at I. P. O., Eindhoven, The Netherlands, August 4–6, 1975.

Darwin, C. J. (1981). Perceptual grouping of speech components differing in fundamental frequency and onset-time. *Quarterly Journal of Experimental Psychology*, *33A*, 185–207.

Darwin, C. J. (1983). Auditory processing and speech perception. In H. Bouma and D. G. Bouwhuis (eds.), *Attention and Performance X*. Hillsdale, N.J.: Erlbaum.

Darwin, C. J. (1984). Perceiving vowels in the presence of another sound: Constraints on formant perception. *Journal of the Acoustical Society of America*, *76*, 1636–1647.

Darwin, C. J., and Bethell-Fox, C. E. (1977). Pitch continuity and speech source attribution. *Journal of Experimental Psychology: Human Perception and Performance*, *3*, 665–672.

Darwin, C. J., and Gardner, R. B. (1986). Mistuning a harmonic of a vowel: Grouping and phase effects on vowel quality. *Journal of the Acoustical Society of America*, *79*, 838–845.

Darwin, C. J., Howell, P., and Brady, S. A. (1978). Laterality and localization: A right ear advantage for speech heard on the left. In J. Requin (ed.), *Attention and Performance VII*. Hillsdale, N.J.: Erlbaum.

Darwin, C. J., and Sutherland, N. S. (1984). Grouping frequency components of vowels: When is a harmonic not a harmonic? *Quarterly Journal of Experimental Psychology, 36A*, 193–208.

Darwin, C. J., Turvey, M. T., and Crowder, R. G. (1972). An auditory analog of the Sperling partial report procedure: Evidence for brief auditory storage. *Cognitive Psychology, 3*, 255–267.

de Laat, J. A. P. M., and Plomp, R. (1985). The effect of competing melodies on melody recognition by hearing-impaired and normal-hearing listeners. *Journal of the Acoustical Society of America, 78*, 1574–1577.

Demany, L. (1982). Auditory stream segregation in infancy. *Infant Behavior and Development, 5*, 261–276.

Denes, P. B., and Pinson, E. N. (1963). *The Speech Chain*. Bell Telephone Laboratories, Inc.

Deutsch, D. (1972). Octave generalization and tune recognition. *Perception & Psychophysics, 11*, 411–412.

Deutsch, D. (1974). An auditory illusion. *Nature (London), 251*, 307–309.

Deutsch, D. (1975a). Musical illusions. *Scientific American, 233*, 92–104.

Deutsch, D. (1975b). Two-channel listening to musical scales. *Journal of the Acoustical Society of America, 57*, 1156–1160.

Deutsch, D. (1979). Binaural integration of melodic patterns. *Perception & Psychophysics, 25*, 399–405.

Deutsch, D. (1982). Grouping mechanisms in music. In D. Deutsch (ed.) *The Psychology of Music*. New York: Academic Press.

DeWitt, L. A., and Crowder, R. G. (1987). Tonal fusion of consonant musical intervals. *Perception & Psychophysics, 41*, 73–84.

DeWitt, L. A., and Samuel, A. G. (1986). Perceptual restoration of music. *Journal of the Acoustical Society of America, 80*, Suppl.1, S110.

Dirks, D. D., and Bower, D. (1970). Effects of forward and backward masking on speech intelligibility. *Journal of the Acoustical Society of America, 47*, 1003–1007.

Divenyi, P. L. (1971). The rhythmic perception of micromelodies: Detectability by human observers of a time increment between sinusoidal pulses of two different, successive frequencies. *University of Iowa Studies in the Psychology of Music*, 7, 41–130.

Divenyi, P. L., and Danner, W. F. (1977). Discrimination of time intervals marked by brief acoustic pulses of various intensities and spectra. *Perception & Psychophysics, 21*, 125–142.

Divenyi, P. L., and Hirsh, I. J. (1972). Discrimination of the silent gap in two-tone sequences of different frequencies. *Journal of the Acoustical Society of America, 52*, 166(A).

Divenyi, P. L., and Hirsh, I. J. (1974). Identification of temporal order in three-tone sequences. *Journal of the Acoustical Society of America, 56*, 144–151.

Divenyi, P. L., and Hirsh, I. J. (1975). The effect of blanking on the identification of temporal order in three-tone sequences. *Perception & Psychophysics, 17*, 246–252.

Divenyi, P. L., and Hirsh, I. J. (1978). Some figural properties of auditory patterns. *Journal of the Acoustical Society of America, 64*, 1369–1386.

Divenyi, P. L., and Sachs, R. M. (1978). Discrimination of time intervals bounded by tone bursts. *Perception & Psychophysics, 24*, 429–436.

Dodd, B. (1977). The role of vision in the perception of speech. *Perception, 6*, 31–40.

Dodd, B. (1979). Lip reading in infants: Attention to speech presented in- and out-of-synchrony *Cognitive Psychology, 11*, 478–484.

Dodd, B. (1980). Interaction of auditory and visual information in speech perception. *British Journal of Psychology, 71*, 541–549.

Dorman, M. F., Cutting, J. E., and Raphael, L. J. (1975). Perception of temporal order in vowel sequences with and without formant transitions. *Journal of Experimental Psychology: Human Perception and Performance, 1*, 121–129.

Dorman, M. F., Raphael, L. J., and Liberman, A. M. (1979). Some experiments on the sound of silence in phonetic perception. *Journal of the Acoustical Society of America, 65*, 1518–1532.

Dowling, W. J. (1973). Rhythmic groups and subjective chunks in memory for melodies. *Perception & Psychophysics, 14*, 37–40.

Dowling, W. J. (1978). Scale and contour: Two components of a scale of memory for melodies. *Psychological Review, 85*, 341–354.

Dowling, W. J., and Fujitani, D. S. (1971). Contour, interval and pitch recognition in memory for melodies. *Journal of the Acoustical Society of America, 49*, 524–531.

Downing, C. J., and Pinker, S. (1985). The spatial structure of visual attention. In M. I. Posner and O. S. M. Marin (eds.), *Attention and Performance XI*. Hillsdale, N.J.: Erlbaum.

Drager, U. C., and Hubel, D. H. (1975). Responses to visual stimulation and relationship between visual, auditory and somatosensory inputs in mouse superior colliculum. *Journal of Neurophysiology, 38*, 690–713.

Duifhuis, H., Willems, L. F., and Sluyter, R. J. (1982). Measurement of pitch in speech: An implementation of Goldstein's theory of pitch perception. *Journal of the Acoustical Society of America, 71*, 1568–1580.

Efron, R., Crandall, P. H., Koss, B., Divenyi, P. L., and Yund, E. W. (1983). Central auditory processing: III. The cocktail party effect and anterior temporal lobectomy. *Brain and Language, 19*, 254–263.

Egan, J. P. (1948). The effect of noise in one ear upon the loudness of speech in the other ear. *Journal of the Acoustical Society of America, 20*, 58–62.

Egan, J. P., Carterette, E. C., and Thwing, E. J. (1954). Some factors affecting multi-channel listening. *Journal of the Acoustical Society of America, 26*, 774–782.

Elfner, L. F. (1969). Continuity in alternately sounded tone and noise signals in a free field. *Journal of the Acoustical Society of America, 46*, 914–917.

Elfner, L. F. (1971). Continuity in alternately sounded tonal signals in a free field. *Journal of the Acoustical Society of America, 49*, 447–449.

Elfner, L. F., and Caskey, W. E. (1965). Continuity effects with alternately sounded tones under dichotic stimulation. *Journal of the Acoustical Society of America, 49*, 447–449.

Elfner, L. F., and Homick, J. L. (1966). Some factors affecting the perception of continuity in alternately sounded tone and noise signals. *Journal of the Acoustical Society of America, 40*, 27–31.

Elfner, L. F., and Homick, J. L. (1967). Continuity effects with alternately sounding tones under dichotic presentation. *Perception & Psychophysics, 2*, 34–36.

Erickson, R. (1974). *LOOPS, an Informal Timbre Experiment*. Center for Music Experiment, University of California, San Diego.

Erickson, R. (1975). *Sound Structure in Music.* Berkeley, Calif.: University of California Press.
Erickson, R. (1982). New music and psychology. In. D. Deutsch (ed.), *The Psychology of Music.* New York: Academic Press.
Evans, E. F., and Whitfield, J. C. (1964). Responses of cortical neurones to acoustic stimuli varying periodically in frequency. *Journal of Physiology* (London), *172*, 52P–53P.
Fay, W. H. (1966). *Temporal Sequence in the Perception of Speech.* The Hague: Mouton.
Fitzgibbons, P. J., Pollatsek, A, and Thomas, I. B. (1974). Detection of temporal gaps within and between perceptual tonal groups. *Perception & Psychophysics, 16*, 522–528.
Flavell, J. H. (1963). *The Developmental Psychology of Jean Piaget.* New York: Van Nostrand.
Fodor, J. A., and Bever, T. G. (1965). The psychological reality of linguistic segments. *Journal of Verbal Learning and Verbal Behavior, 4*, 414–420.
Foulke, E., and Sticht, T. G. (1969). Review of research on the intelligibility and comprehension of accelerated speech. *Psychological Bulletin, 72*, 50–62.
Fowler, C. A., and Rosenblum, L. D. (1988). The perception of phonetic gestures. Presentation in the conference, Modularity and the Motor Theory of Speech Perception. Haskins Laboratories, New Haven, Conn., June 5–8, 1988.
Fox, C. W. (1948). Modern counterpoint: A phenomenological approach. *Notes, 6*, 46–57.
Fraisse, P. (1963). *The psychology of time.* (J. Leith, Translator). New York: Harper and Row.
French-St. George, M., and Bregman, A. S. (1989). Stream segregation as a function of predictability of frequency and timing. *Perception & Psychophysics, 46*, 384–386.
Fucks, W. (1962). Mathematical analysis of formal structure of music. *IRE Transactions on Information Theory, IT 8*, 225–228.
Fux, J. J. (1725). *Gradus ad Parnassum* Annotated and translated by A. Mann and J. Edmunds, New York: Norton, 1965
Gabor, D. (1947). Acoustical quanta and the theory of hearing. *Nature (London), 159*, 591–594.
Galli, A., and Zama, A. (1931). Untersuchungen über die Wahrnehmung ebener geometrischen figuren die ganz oder teilweise von anderen geometrischen figuren verdekt sind. *Zeitschrift für Psychologie, 123*, 308–348.
Gardner, R. B., and Darwin, C. J. (1986). *Grouping of vowel harmonics by frequency modulation: Absence of effects on phonemic categorization. Perception & Psychophysics, 40*, 183–187.
Gardner, R. B., and Wilson, J. P. (1979). Evidence for direction-specific channels in the processing of frequency modulation. *Journal of the Acoustical Society of America, 66*, 704–709.
Gibson, J. J. (1966). *The Senses Considered as Perceptual Systems.* Boston: Houghton Mifflin.
Gilbert, G. M. (1939). Dynamic psychophysics and the phi phenomenon. *Archives of Psychology, No. 237.*
Goldstein, E. B. (1980). *Sensation and Perception.* Belmont, Calif.: Wadsworth.
Goldstein, J. L. (1973). An optimum processor theory for the central formation

of the pitch of complex tones. *Journal of the Acoustical Society of America, 54*, 1496–1516.

Gordon, J. W., and Grey, J. M. (1978). Perception of spectral modifications on orchestral instrument tones. *Computer Music Journal, 2*, 24–31.

Gottschaldt, K. (1926). Uber den Einfluss der Ehrfahrung auf die Wehrnehmung von Figuren. *Psychologische Forschung, 8*, 261–317. Excerpts translated in M. D. Vernon (ed.) *Experiments in Visual Perception*. Baltimore: Penguin, 1966, pp. 29–44.

Green, D. M., and Kidd, G. (1983). Further studies of auditory profile analysis. *Journal of the Acoustical Society of America, 73*, 1260–1265.

Green, D. M., Kidd, G., and Mason, C. R. (1983). Profile analysis and the critical band. *Journal of the Acoustical Society of America, 73*, 1261–1265.

Green, D. M., Kidd, G., and Picardi, M. C. (1983). Successive versus simultaneous comparison in auditory intensity discrimination. *Journal of the Acoustical Society of America, 73*, 639–643.

Green, D. M., and Mason, C. R. (1983). Phase effects and profile analysis. *Journal of the Acoustical Society of America*, 74:S71(A).

Green, D. M., and Mason, C. R. (1985). Auditory profile analysis: Frequency, phase, and Weber's law. *Journal of the Acoustical Society of America, 77*, 1155–1161.

Green, D. M., Mason, C. R., and Kidd, G. Jr. (1984). Profile analysis: Critical bands and duration. *Journal of the Acoustical Society of America, 74*, 1163–1167.

Green, G. G. R., and Kay, R. H. (1973). The adequate stimulus for channels in the human auditory pathway concerned with the modulation present in frequency-modulated tones. *Journal of Physiology, 234*, 50–52P.

Grey, J. M. (1975). *An Exploration of Musical Timbre*. Center for Computer Research in Music and Acoustics, Department of Music Report No. STAN-M- 2, Stanford University, February, 1975

Grey, J. M. (1977). Multidimensional perceptual scaling of musical timbres. *Journal of the Acoustical Society of America, 61*, 1270–1277.

Grey, J. M., and Gordon, J. W. (1978). Perceptual effects of spectral modifications on musical timbres. *Journal of the Acoustical Society of America, 63*, 1493–1500.

Grey, J. M., and Moorer, J. A. (1977). Perceptual evaluation of synthesized musical instrument tones. *Journal of the Acoustical Society of America, 62*, 454–462.

Grossberg, S. (1986). The adaptive self-organization of serial-order in behavior: Speech, language, and motor control. In E. C. Schwab, and H. C. Nusbaum (eds.), *Pattern Recognition by Humans and Machines*. Orlando, Fla.: Academic Press.

Guilford, J. P., and Hilton, R. A. (1933). Configurational properties of melodies. *Journal of Experimental Psychology, 16*, 32–54.

Guilford, J. P., and Nelson, H. M. (1936). Changes in the pitch of tones when melodies are repeated. *Journal of Experimental Psychology, 19*, 193–202.

Guzman, A. (1969). Decomposition of a visual scene into three-dimensional bodies. In A. Grasselli (ed.), *Automatic Interpretation and Classification of Images*. New York: Academic Press.

Guzy, L. T., and Axelrod, S. (1971). Synchronization of unimanual and bimanual responses with monotic and dichotic clicks. *Perception & Psychophysics, 9*, 161–164.

Guzy, L. T., and Axelrod, S. (1972). Interaural attention shifting *Journal of Experimental Psychology, 95*, 290–294.
Hafter, E. R., and Carrier, S. C. (1972). Binaural interaction in low-frequency stimuli: The inability to trade time and intensity completely. *Journal of the Acoustical Society of America, 51*, 1852–1862.
Hafter, E. R., and Jeffress, L. A. (1968). Two-image lateralization of tones and clicks. *Journal of the Acoustical Society of America, 44*, 563–569.
Haggard, M. P., Harvey, A. D. G., and Carlyon, R. P. (1985). Peripheral and central components of comodulation masking release. *Journal of the Acoustical Society of America*, Suppl. 1 *78*, S63.
Halikia, M. H. (1985). *The Perceptual Segregation of Simultaneous Sounds.* Unpublished Ph.D. dissertation, McGill University.
Hall, J. W. (1986). The effect of across frequency differences in masking level on spectro-temporal pattern analysis. *Journal of the Acoustical Society of America, 79*, 781–787.
Hall, J. W., and Grose, J. H. (1988). Comodulation masking release: Evidence for multiple cues. *Journal of the Acoustical Society of America, 84*, 1669–1675.
Hall, J. W., Haggard, M. P., and Fernandes, M. A. (1984). Detection in noise by spectro-temporal pattern analysis. *Journal of the Acoustical Society of America, 76*, 50–56.
Hall, J. W., Haggard, M. P. and Harvey, A. D. G. (1984). Release from masking through ipsilateral and contralateral comodulation of a flanking band. *Journal of the Acoustical Society of America, 76*, S76.
Halpern, L. (1977). The Effect of Harmonic Ratio Relationships on Auditory Stream Segregation. Unpublished research report, Psychology Department, McGill University.
Handel, S. (1984). Using polyrhythms to study rhythm. *Music Perception, 1*, 465–484.
Handel, S., and Todd, P. (1981). Segmentation of sequential patterns. *Journal of Experimental Psychology: Human Perception and Performance*, 7, 41–55.
Handel, S., Weaver, M. S., and Lawson, G. (1983). Effect of rhythmic grouping on stream segregation. *Journal of Experimental Psychology: Human Perception and Performance, 9*, 637–651.
Hay, J. C., Pick, H. L., and Ikeda, K. (1965). Visual capture produced by prism spectacles. *Psychonomic Science, 2*, 215–216.
Hebb, D. O. (1949). *The Organization of Behavior.* New York: Wiley.
Heise, G. A., and Miller, G. A. (1951). An experimental study of auditory patterns. *American Journal of Psychology, 64*, 68–77.
Helmholtz, H. von (1859). *On the Sensations of Tone as a Physiological Basis for the Theory of Music.* (Second English edition; Translated by A. J. Ellis, 1885). Reprinted by Dover Publications, 1954.
Helmholtz, H. von (1862). *Die lehre von den Tonempfindungen als physiologische Grundlage fur die Theorie der Musik. (6th edition, 1913).* Braunschweig: Vieweg & Son.
Hirsh, I. J. (1959). Auditory perception of temporal order. *Journal of the Acoustical Society of America, 31*, 759–767.
Hirsh, I. J. (1974). Temporal order and auditory perception. In H. R. Moskowitz et al. (eds.), *Sensation and Measurement.* Dordrecht, Holland: Reidel.
Hirsh, I. J., and Sherrick, C. E. (1961). Perceived order in different sense modalities. *Journal of Experimental Psychology, 62*, 423–432.

Holding, D., Loeb, M., and Yoder, D. (1972). Masking vs. interference in pitch perception. *Journal of Auditory Research, 12*, 247–254.

Holloway, C. M. (1970). Passing the strongly voiced components of noisy speech. *Nature (London), 226*, 178–179.

Houtgast, T. (1972). Psychophysical evidence for lateral inhibition in hearing. *Journal of the Acoustical Society of America, 51*, 1885–1894.

Houtgast, T. (1974). *Lateral Suppression in Hearing*. Doctoral dissertation, Free University, Amsterdam.

Houtsma, A. J. M. (1983). Perception of harmonic intervals made by simultaneous complex tones. *Journal of the Acoustical Society of America, 73*, S77(A).

Houtsma, A. J. M. (1985). *Perception of Simultaneous Harmonic and Inharmonic Complex Tones*. Paper presented at The Fifth Workshop on Physical and Neuropsychological Foundations of Music, Ossiach, Austria. August 6–10, 1985.

Houtsma, A. J. M., and Goldstein, J. L. (1972). The central origin of the pitch of complex tones: Evidence from musical interval recognition. *Journal of the Acoustical Society of America, 51*, 520–529.

Huggins, A. W. F. (1964). Distortion of temporal patterns of speech: Interruption and alternation. *Journal of the Acoustical Society of America, 36*, 1055–1065.

Huggins, A. W. F. (1974). On perceptual integration of dichotically alternated pulse trains. *Journal of the Acoustical Society of America, 56*, 939–943.

Huggins, W. H. (1952). A phase principle for complex frequency analysis and its implication in auditory theory. *Journal of the Acoustical Society of America, 24*, 582–589.

Idson, W. L., and Massaro, D. W. (1976). Cross-octave masking of single tones and musical sequences: The effects of structure on auditory recognition. *Perception & Psychophysics, 19*, 155–175.

Isenberg, D., and Liberman, A. M. (1979). The use of duplex perception to study silence as a cue for the stop consonants. *Journal of the Acoustical Society of America, 65*, S79(A).

Jack, C. E., and Thurlow, W. R. (1973). Effects of degree of visual association and angle of displacement on the "ventriloquism" effect. *Perceptual and Motor Skills, 37*, 967–979.

Jackendoff, R. and Lehrdahl, F. (1981). Generative music theory and its relation to psychology. *Journal of Music theory, 25*, 45–90.

Jackson, C. V. (1953). Visual factors in auditory localization. *Quarterly Journal of Experimental Psychology, 5*, 52–66.

Jenkins, W. M., and Merzenich, M. M. (1984). Role of cat primary auditory cortex for sound-localization behavior. *Journal of Neurophysiology, 52*, 819–847.

Jeppesen, K. (1939). *Counterpoint: The Polyphonic Vocal Style of the Sixteenth Century*. (translated by G. Haydon) Englewood Cliffs, N.J.: Prentice-Hall.

Jones, M. R. (1976). Time, our lost dimension: Toward a new theory of perception, attention, and memory. *Psychological Review, 83*, 323–355.

Jones, M. R. (1978). Auditory patterns. In E. C. Carterette and M. P. Friedman (eds.), *Handbook of Perception: Space and Object Perception*. Vol 8. New York: Academic Press.

Jones, M. R., Boltz, M., and Kidd, G. (1982). Controlled attending as a function of melodic and temporal context. *Perception & Psychophysics, 32*, 211–218.

Jones, M. R., Kidd, G., and Wetzel, R. (1981). Evidence for rhythmic attention.

Journal of Experimental Psychology: Human Perception and Performance, 7, 1059–1073.

Jones, M. R., Maser, D. J., and Kidd, G. R. (1978). Rate and structure in memory for auditory patterns. *Memory and Cognition*, *6*, 246–258.

Judd, T. (1977). *An Explanation of Deutsch's Scale Illusion.* Unpublished manuscript, Department of Psychology, Cornell University.

Julesz, B. (1981a). Textons, the elements of texture perception, and their interactions. *Nature (London)*, *290*, 91–97.

Julesz, B. (1981b). Figure and ground perception in briefly presented isodipole patterns. In J. R. Pomerantz, and M. Kubovy (eds.), *Perceptual Organization.* Hillsdale, N.J.: Erlbaum.

Julesz, B. and Bergen, J. R. (1983). Textons, the fundamental elements in in preattentive vision and perception of texture. *The Bell System Technical Journal*, *62(6)*, 1619–1645.

Julesz, B., and Hirsh, I. J. (1972). Visual and auditory perception—An essay of comparison. In E. E. David, Jr., and P. B. Denes (eds.), *Human Communication: A Unified View*. New York: McGraw-Hill

Kahneman, D. (1973). *Attention and Effort.* Englewood Cliffs, N.J.: Prentice-Hall.

Kanizsa, G. (1955). Margini quasi-percettivi in campi con stimulazione omogenea. *Rivista di Psicologia*, *49*, 7–30.

Kay, R. H., and Matthews, D. R. (1972). On the existence in human auditory pathways of channels selectively tuned to the modulation present in frequency-modulated tones. *Journal of Physiology*, *225*, 657–677.

Kidd, G., Boltz, M., and Jones, M. R. (1984). Some effects of rhythmic context on melody recognition. *American Journal of Psychology*, *97*, 153–173.

Kinney, J. A. S. (1961). Discrimination in auditory and visual patterns. *American Journal of Psychology*, *74*, 529–541.

Klapp, S. T., Hill, M. D., Tyler, J. G., Martin, Z. E., Jagacinski, R. J., and Jones, M. R. (1985). On marching to two different drummers: Perceptual aspects of the difficulties. *Journal of Experimental Psychology: Human Perception and Performance*, *11*, 814–827.

Knops, L. (1947). Contribution à l'étude de la "naissance" et de la "permanence" phenomenales dans le champ visuel. In *Miscellanea Psychologica Albert Michotte*. Paris: Vrin.

Knudsen, E. I. (1982). Auditory and visual maps of space in the optic tectum of the owl. *Journal of Neuroscience*, *2(9)*, 1177–1194.

Knudsen, E. I. (1984). Synthesis of a neural map of auditory space in the owl. In G. M. Edelman, W. M. Cowan, and W. E. Gall (eds.), *Dynamic Aspects of Neocortical Function*. New York: Wiley.

Kock, W. E. (1958). Binaural localization and masking. *Journal of the Acoustical Society of America*, *22*, 801–804.

Koffka, K. (1935). *Principles of Gestalt Psychology*. New York: Harcourt, Brace and World.

Kolers, P. A. (1964). Some illusions of movement. *Scientific American*, *211*, 98–106.

Körte, A. (1915). Kinomatoscopishe Untersuchungen. *Zeitschrift für Psychologie der Sinnesorgane*, *72*, 193–296.

Krumhansl, C. L. (1984). *Bitonality: A Naturalistic Test of Divided Attention in Music*. Paper presented at the Psychonomic Society, November 9, 1984.

Krumhansl, C. L., and Kessler, E. J. (1982). Tracing the dynamic changes in perceived tonal organization in a spatial representation of musical keys. *Psychological Review, 89*, 334–368.

Krumhansl, C. L., and Shepard, R. N. (1979). Quantification of the hierarchy of tonal functions within a diatonic context. *Journal of Experimental Psychology, 5*, 579–594.

Kubovy, M. (1981). Concurrent-pitch segregation and the theory of indispensable attributes. In M. Kubovy and J. R. Pomerantz (eds.), *Perceptual Organization*. Hillsdale, N.J.: Erlbaum.

Kubovy, M., and Howard, F. P. (1976). Persistence of a pitch-segregating echoic memory. *Journal of Experimental Psychology: Human Perception and Performance, 2*, 531–537.

Kubovy, M., and Jordan, R. (1979). Tone segregation by phase: On the phase sensitivity of the single ear. *Journal of the Acoustical Society of America, 66*, 100–106.

Lackner, J. R., and Goldstein, L. M. (1974). Primary auditory stream segregation of repeated consonant-vowel sequences. *Journal of the Acoustical Society of America, 56*, 1651–1652.

Ladefoged, P. (1959). The perception of speech. *National Physical Laboratory Symposium No. 10, Mechanism of Thought Processes. 1*, 309–417. London: Her Majesty's Stationery Office.

Ladefoged P., and Broadbent, D. E. (1960). Perception of sequence in auditory events. *Quarterly Journal of Experimental Psychology, 12*, 162–170.

Layton, B. (1975). Differential effects of two non-speech sounds on phonemic restoration. *Bulletin of the Psychonomic Society, 6*, 487–490.

Leek, M. R., and Colleran, E. (1984). Individual differences in pattern discrimination by trained listeners. *Journal of the Acoustical Society of America, 76*, S14.

Levitt, H., and Rabiner, L. R. (1967). Binaural release from masking for speech and gain in intelligibility. *Journal of the Acoustical Society of America, 42*, 601–608.

Liberman, A. M. (1982). On finding that speech is special. *American Psychologist, 37*, 148–167

Liberman, A. M., Cooper, F. S., Shankweiler, D. P., and Studdert-Kennedy, M. (1967). Perception of the speech code. *Psychological Review, 74*, 431–461.

Liberman, A. M., Isenberg, D., and Rakerd, B. (1981). Duplex perception of cues for stop consonants: Evidence for a phonetic mode. *Perception & Psychophysics, 30*, 133–143.

Liberman, A. M., and Mattingly, I. G. (1985). The motor theory of speech perception revised. *Cognition, 21*, 1–36.

Liberman, A. M., and Studdert-Kennedy, M. (1978). Phonetic perception. In *Handbook of Sensory Physiology. Vol VIII: Perception.* Berlin: Springer-Verlag.

Lim, J. S. (1983). *Speech Enhancement.* Englewood Cliffs, New Jersey: Prentice Hall.

Lyon, R. F. (1982). *A Computational Model of filtering, Detection, and Compression in the Cochlea.* Paper presented at the International Conference on Acoustics Speech and Signal Processing, Paris. 1982

Lyon, R. F. (1983). *A Computational Model of Binaural Localization and Separation.* Presented at the International Conference on Acoustics Speech and Signal Processing, Boston, Mass., April 1983.

Malsberg, C. von der, and Schneider, W. (1986). A neural cocktail-party processor. Unpublished manuscript, Abteilung Neurobiologie, Max-Planck Institut für Biophysikalische Chemie, Göttingen.

Mann, V. A. (1980). Influence of preceding liquid on stop-consonant perception *Perception & Psychophysics*, *28*, 407–412.

Mann, V. A., Madden, J., Russell, J. M., and Liberman, A. M. (1981). Further investigations into the influence of preceding liquids on stop consonant perception. *Journal of the Acoustical Society of America*, *69*, S91. (Abstract).

Marin, C. (1987). Rôle de l'enveloppe spectrale dans la perception des sources sonores. Memoire de la DEA de Phonétique, Université de la Sorbonne Nouvelle, Paris III.

Marmor, G. S., and Zaback, L. A. (1976). Mental rotation by the blind: Does mental rotation depend on visual imagery? *Journal of Experimental Psychology: Human Perception and Performance*, *2*, 515–521.

Martens, J. P. (1984). Comment on "Algorithm for the extraction of pitch and pitch salience from complex tonal signals." [*Journal of the Acoustical Society of America*, *71*, 679–688 (1982)] *Journal of the Acoustical Society of America*, *75*, 626–628.

Martin, J. G. (1972). Rhythmic (hierarchical) versus serial structure in speech and other behavior. *Psychological Review*, *79*, 487–509.

Massaro, D. W. (1970). Preperceptual auditory images. *Journal of Experimental Psychology*, *85*, 411–417.

Massaro, D. W. (1972). Stimulus information versus processing time in auditory recognition. *Perception & Psychophysics*, *12*, 50–56.

Massaro, D. W. (1975). Backward recognition masking. *Journal of the Acoustical Society of America*, *58*, 1059–1065.

Massaro, D. W. (1977). Perceptual grouping in audition. *Perception*, *6*, 541–553.

Mathews, M. V., and Pierce, J. R. (1980). Harmony and non-harmonic partials. *Journal of the Acoustical Society of America*, *68*, 1252–1257

Mattingly, I. G., and Liberman, A. M. (in press). Speech and other auditory modules. In G. M. Edelman et al. (eds.), *Signal and Sense*. New York: Wiley.

Mattingly, I. G., Liberman, A. M., Syrdal, A., and Halwes, T. (1971). Discrimination in speech and non-speech modes. *Cognitive Psychology*, *2*, 131–157.

McAdams, S. (1984). *Spectral Fusion, Spectral Parsing, and the Formation of Auditory Images*. Unpublished doctoral dissertation, Stanford University.

McAdams, S., and Bregman A. S. (1979). Hearing musical streams. *Computer Music Journal*, *3*, 26–43.

McAdams, S., and Rodet, X. (1988). The role of FM-induced AM in dynamic spectral profile analysis. In H. Duifhuis, J. Horst, and H. Wit (eds.), *Basic Issues in Hearing*. London: Academic Press.

McAdams, S., and Saariaho, K. (1985). Qualities and functions of musical timbre. *Proceedings of the International Computer Music Conference*, 367–374.

McBride, D. L. (1986). Rhythm and Frequency Factors in the Perception of Tone Sequences. M.Sc. Thesis, Arizona State University, Tempe.

McGurk, H., and MacDonald, J. (1976). Hearing lips and seeing voices. *Nature (London)*, *264*, 746–748.

McNally, K. A., and Handel, S. (1977). Effect of element composition on streaming and the ordering of repeating sequences. *Journal of Experimental Psychology: Human Perception and Performance*, *3*, 451–460.

Merriam, A. P. (1964). *The Anthropology of Music*. Evanston, Ill.: Northwestern University Press.

, J. (1978). *Acoustics and the performance of music*. Frankfurt/ Main: Verlag as Musikinstrumenten.
J. S. (1874). *A System of Logic*. New York: Harper (first edition, 1843)
, E. A. (1972). Interaction of vision and touch in conflict and non-conflict orm perception. *Journal of Experimental Psychology, 96*, 114–123.
r, G. A. (1947). The masking of speech. *Psychological Bulletin, 44*, 105–129.
r, G. A., and Heise, G. A. (1950). The trill threshold. *Journal of the Acoustical Society of America, 22*, 637–638.
r, G. A., and Licklider, J. C. R. (1950). Intelligibility of interrupted speech. *Journal of the Acoustical Society of America, 22*, 167–173.
ky, M. (1975). A framework for presenting knowledge. In P. H. Winston (ed.) *The Psychology of Computer Vision*. New York: McGraw-Hill.
hell, O. M. M., Ross, C. A., and Yates, G. H. (1971). Signal processing for a cocktail party effect. *Journal of the Acoustical Society of America, 50*, 656–660.
re, B. C. J. (1982). *An Introduction to the Psychology of Hearing*. (Second edition) London: Academic Press.
re, B. C. J., Glasberg, B. R., and Peters, R. W. (1985a). Thresholds for Hearing Mistuned Partials as Separate Tones in Harmonic Complexes. Unpublished manuscript, Department of Experimental Psychology, University of Cambridge.
ore, B. C. J., Glasberg, B. R., and Peters, R. W. (1985b). Relative dominance of individual partials in determining the pitch of complex tones. *Journal of the Acoustical Society of America, 77*, 1853–1860.
ore, B. C. J., Glasberg, B. R., and Peters, R. W. (1986). Thresholds for hearing mistuned partials as separate tones in harmonic complexes. *Journal of the Acoustical Society of America, 80*, 479–483.
ore, B. C. J., Peters, R. W., and Glasberg, B. R. (1985). Thresholds for the detection of inharmonicity in complex tones. *Journal of the Acoustical Society of America, 77*, 1861–1867.
oorer, J. A. (1977). On the transcription of musical sound by computer. *Computer Music Journal, 1(4)*, 32–38.
Moray, N. (1970). *Attention*. New York: Academic Press.
Neff, D. L., Jesteadt, W., and Brown, E. L. (1982). The relation between ga discrimination and auditory stream segregation. *Perception & Psychophysic 31*, 493–501.
Neisser, U. (1967). *Cognitive Psychology*. New York: Appleton-Century-Croft
Neisser, U. (1971). *Perceiving and Judging Temporal Order: Preliminary Definitio and Concepts*. Unpublished "purple peril." Department of Psychology, Co nell University. Ithaca, New York.
Neisser, U. (1972). *On the Perception of Auditory Sequences* Presented at the sy posium Perception of Temporal Order in Hearing: Old Pattern Recogniti Problems in a New Guise. American Psychological Association meeti Honolulu, September, 1972.
Neisser, U., and Hirst, W. (1974). Effect of practice on the identification of au tory sequences. *Perception & Psychophysics, 15*, 391–398.
Nickerson, R. S., and Freeman, B. (1974). Discrimination of the order of co ponents of repeating tone sequences: Effects of frequency separation and tensive practice. *Perception & Psychophysics, 16*, 471–477.
Nordmark, J. O. (1970). Time and frequency analysis. In J. V. Tobias (*Foundations of Modern Auditory Theory, Vol 1*. New York: Academic Pr
Norman, D. A. (1966). *Rhythmic fission: Observations on Attention, Temporal*

ments and the Critical Band. Unpublished manuscript, Center t
Studies, Harvard University.
Norman, D. A. (1967). Temporal confusions and limited capacity p
Acta Psychologica, 27, 293–297.
Norman, D. A. (1976). *Memory and Attention: An Introduction to Human In*
tion Processing. Second edition. New York: Wiley.
Norman, D. A., and Bobrow, D. G. (1977). On data-limited and resour
limited processes. *Cognitive Psychology,* 7, 44–64.
Noteboom, S. G., Brokx, J. P. L., and De Rooij, J. J. (1976). Contributions of prosody to speech perception. In W. J. M. Levelt and G. B. Flores d'Arcais (eds.) *Studies in the Perception of Language.* Chichester: Wiley.
O'Leary, A. (1981). Effects of Cross-Modal Stimulation on Perceptual Organization. Unpublished manuscript, Department of Psychology, Stanford University.
O'Leary, A., and Rhodes, G. (1984). Cross-modal effects on visual and auditory object perception. *Perception & Psychophysics, 35,* 565–569.
Obusek, C., and Warren, R. M. (1973). Relation of the verbal transformation and the phonemic restoration effects. *Cognitive Psychology, 5,* 97–107.
Ogasawara, J. (1936). Effect of apparent separation on apparent movement. *Japanese Journal of Psychology, 11,* 109–122.
Orr, D. B., Friedman, H. L., and Williams, J. C. (1965). Trainability of listening comprehension of speeded discourse. *Journal of Educational Psychology, 56,* 148–156.
Ortmann, O. (1926). On the melodic relativity of tones. *Psychological Monographs, 35,* Whole No. 162.
Palmer, A. R., and King, A. J. (1982). The representation of auditory space in the mammalian superior colliculus. *Nature (London), 299,* 248–249.
Parsons, T. W. (1976). Separation of speech from interfering speech by means of harmonic selection. *Journal of the Acoustical Society of America, 60,* 911–918.
Pastore, R. E., Schmuckler, M. A., Rosenblum, L., and Szczesiul, R. (1983). Duplex perception with musical stimuli. *Perception & Psychophysics, 33,* 469–474.
Patterson, J. H., and Green, D. M. (1970). Discrimination of transient signals having identical energy spectra. *Journal of the Acoustical Society of America, 48,* 894–905.
Pattison, H., Gardner, R. B., and Darwin, C. J. (1986). Effects of acoustical context on perceived vowel quality. *Journal of the Acoustical Society of America, 80 Suppl. 1,* Fall.
Perrott, D. R., and Barry, S. H. (1969). Binaural fusion. *The Journal of Auditory Research, 3,* 263–269.
Perrott, D. R., and Williams, K. H. (1970). Auditory temporal resolution as a function of interpulse frequency disparity. *Psychonomic Science, 25,* 73–74.
Piston, W. (1947). *Counterpoint* New York: W. W. Norton and Co.
Piston, W. (1978). *Harmony* (4th edition). New York: Norton.
Plomp, R. (1964). The ear as a frequency analyzer. *Journal of the Acoustical Society of America, 36,* 1628–1636.
Plomp, R. (1976). *Aspects of Tone Sensation.* London: Academic Press.
Plomp, R. (1982). Continuity effects in the perception of sounds. Paper presented at summer workshop on the Psychoacoustics of Music, Jablonna, Poland, July 5–11, 1982.

Plomp, R., and Mimpen, A. M. (1968). The ear as a frequency analyzer II. *Journal of the Acoustical Society of America, 43*, 764–767.
Plomp, R., and Mimpen, A. M. (1981). Effect of the orientation of the speaker's head and the azimuth of a noise source on the speech reception threshold for sentences. *Acustica, 48*, 325–328.
Plomp, R., and Steenecken, H. J. M. (1971). Pitch versus timbre. *Proceedings of the 7th International Congress on Acoustics, Budapest, 3*, 377–380.
Pollack, J. (1968). Detection of rate of change of auditory frequency. *Journal of Experimental Psychology, 77*, 535–541.
Pomerantz, J. R. (1981). Perceptual organization in information processing. In J. R. Pomerantz, and M. Kubovy (eds.), *Perceptual Organization*. Hillsdale, N.J.: Erlbaum.
Powers, G. L., and Wilcox, J. C. (1977). Intelligibility of temporally interrupted speech with and without intervening noise. *Journal of the Acoustical Society of America, 61*, 195–199.
Pratt, C. C. (1930). The spatial character of high and low notes. *Journal of Experimental Psychology, 13*, 278–285.
Price, P. J., and Levitt, A. G. (1983). The relative roles of syntax and prosody in the perception of the /š/-/č/ distinction. *Language and Speech, 26*, 291–304.
Rabiner, L. R., and Schaffer, R. W. (1978). *Digital Processing of Speech Signals*. Englewood Cliffs, N.J.: Prentice-Hall.
Radeau, M., and Bertelson, P. (1976). The effect of a textured field on modality dominance in a ventriloquism situation. *Perception & Psychophysics, 20*, 227–235.
Rakerd, B., Dechovitz, D. R., and Verbrugge, R. R. (1982). An effect of sentence finality on the phonetic significance of silence. *Language and Speech, 25*, 267–282.
Ramachandran, V. S., and Anstis, S. M. (1981). *Studies in the Cognitive Sciences*. Vol. 10 (September). School of Social Sciences, University of California.
Ramachandran, V. S., and Anstis, S. M. (1983). Perceptual organization in moving patterns. *Nature (London), 304*, 529–531.
Ramachandran, V. S., and Anstis, S. M. (1984). *Crossing trajectories in Long-Range Apparent Motion*. "7th ECVP," Cambridge, 1984
Rand, T. C. (1974). Dichotic release from masking for speech. *Journal of the Acoustical Society of America, 55*, 678–680(L).
Rasch, R. A. (1978). The perception of simultaneous notes such as in polyphonic music. *Acustica, 40*, 21–33.
Rasch, R. A. (1979). Synchronization in performed ensemble music. *Acustica, 43*, 121–131.
Regan, D., and Tansley, B. W. (1979). Selective adaptation to frequency- modulated tones: Evidence for an information-processing channel selectively sensitive to frequency changes. *Journal of the Acoustical Society of America, 65*, 1249–1257.
Remez, R. E., Rubin, P. E., Pisoni D. B., and Carrell, T. D. (1981). Speech perception without traditional speech cues. *Science, 212*, 947–950.
Repp, B. H. (1984). Categorical perception: Issues, methods, findings. In N. J. Lass (ed.) *Speech and Language: Advances in Basic Research and Practice. Vol. 10*. New York: Academic Press.
Repp, B. H., and Bentin, S. (1984). Parameters of spectral/temporal fusion in speech perception. *Perception & Psychophysics, 36*, 523–530.

Repp, B. H., Milburn, C., and Ashkenas, J. (1983). Duplex perception: Confirmation of fusion. *Perception & Psychophysics, 33,* 333–337.

Rhodes, G. (1985). *Auditory Attention and the Representation of Spatial Information.* Unpublished manuscript, Stanford University.

Risset, J. C., and Mathews, M. V. (1969). Analysis of musical instrument tones. *Physics Today, 22* No. 2, 23–30.

Risset, J. C., and Wessel, D. L. (1982). Exploration of timbre by analysis and synthesis. In D. Deutsch (ed.), *The Psychology of Music.* New York: Academic Press.

Roads, C. (1985). Granular synthesis of sound. In C. Roads and J. Strawn (eds.) *Foundations of Computer Music.* Cambridge, Mass.: The MIT Press.

Roberts, B. (1988). Vowel Identification in the Presence of Extraneous Sounds. Unpublished doctoral dissertation. University of Cambridge.

Roberts, L. A. (1983). *Consonance and Dissonance: A Review of the Literature.* Unpublished manuscript. Bell Laboratories and Rutgers University.

Rock, I. (1985). *The Logic of Perception.* Cambridge, Mass.: The MIT Press.

Rodet, X. (1983). Unpublished research. Institut de Recherche et Coordination Acoustique/Musique, Paris.

Roffler, S. (1968). Factors that influence the localization of sound in the vertical plane. *Journal of the Acoustical Society of America, 43,* 1255–1259.

Royer, F. L., and Garner, W. R. (1970). Perceptual organization of nine- element auditory temporal patterns. *Perception & Psychophysics,* 7, 115–120.

Royer, F. L., and Robin, D. (1986). On the perceived unitization of repetitive auditory patterns. *Perception & Psychophysics, 39,* 9–18.

Sachs, C. (1953). *Rhythm and Tempo.* New York: Norton.

Sadie, S. (ed.) (1980). *The New Grove Dictionary of Music and Musicians.* London: Macmillan.

Samuel, A. G. (1981). The role of bottom-up confirmation in the phonemic restoration illusion. *Journal of Experimental Psychology: Human Perception and Performance,* 7, 1124–1131.

Samuel, A. G., and Ressler, W. H. (1986). Attention within auditory word perception: Insights from the phonemic restoration illusion. *Journal of Experimental Psychology: Human Perception and Performance, 12,* 70–79.

Sasaki, T. (1980). Sound restoration and temporal localization of noise in speech and music sounds. *Tohuku Psychologica Folia, 39,* 79–88.

Scheffers, M. T. M. (1982). The role of pitch in the perceptual separation of simultaneous vowels II. *IPO Annual Progress Report, 17,* 41–45. Institute for Perception Research, Eindhoven.

Scheffers, M. T. M. (1983). *Sifting Vowels: Auditory Pitch Analysis and Sound Segregation.* Unpublished doctoral dissertation, Groningen University.

Schenker, H. (1925–30/1973). Das Meisterwerk in der Musik, 3 vols. Munich: Drei Masken Verlag, 1925, 1926, 1930. Translated by Sylvan Kalib, In Thirteen Essays from the Three Yearbooks 'Das Meisterwerk in der Musik' (1925); An Annotated Translation. Ph.D. dissertation, Northwestern University, Evanston, Ill., 1973.

Schoenberg, A. (1911). *Harmonielehre.* [English: *Theory of Harmony.* Translated by R. E. Carter, 1978]. Berkeley: University of California Press.

Schooneveldt, G. P., and Moore, B. C. J. (1988). Failure to obtain comodulation masking release with frequency-modulated maskers. *Journal of the Acoustical Society of America, 83,* 2290–2292.

Schubert, E. D. (1956). Some preliminary experiments on binaural time delay and intelligibility. *Journal of the Acoustical Society of America, 28*, 895–901.

Schubert, E. D., and Nixon, J. C. (1970). *On the Relation Between Temporal Envelope Patterns at Two Different Points in the Cochlea*. Technical Report, Hearing Science Laboratories, Stanford University.

Schubert, E. D., and Parker, C. D. (1956). Addition to Cherry's findings on switching speech between the two ears. *Journal of the Acoustical Society of America, 27*, 792–793.

Schubert, E. D., and Schultz, M. C. (1962). Some aspects of binaural signal selection. *Journal of the Acoustical Society of America, 34*, 844–849.

Scott, B. (1971). The Verbal Transformation Effect as a Function of Imbedded Sounds. Unpublished Master's thesis, University of Waterloo.

Scott, B., and Cole, R. (1972). Auditory Illusions as a function of imbedded sounds. *Journal of the Acoustical Society of America, 51*, 112 (abstract).

Searle, C. L., Braida, L. D., Cuddy, D. R., and Davis, M. F. (1975). Binaural pinna disparity: another auditory localization cue. *Journal of the Acoustical Society of America, 57*, 448–455.

Searle, C. L. (1982). Speech perception from an auditory and visual viewpoint. *Canadian Journal of Psychology, 36*, 402–419.

Shepard, R. N. (1962). The analysis of proximities: Multidimensional scaling with an unknown distance function, I and II. *Psychometrika, 27*, 219–246.

Shepard, R. N. (1981). Psychophysical complementarity. In M. Kubovy and J. R. Pomerantz (eds.) *Perceptual Organization*, Hillsdale, N.J.: Erlbaum.

Shepard, R. N., and Metzler, J. (1971). Mental rotation of three-dimensional objects. *Science, 171*, 701–703.

Shulman, G. L., Remington, R. W., and McLean, J. P. (1979). Moving attention through visual space. *Journal of Experimental Psychology: Human Perception and Performance, 5*, 522–526.

Sigman, E., and Rock, I. (1974). Stroboscopic movement based on perceptual intelligence. *Perception, 3*, 9–28.

Singh, P. (1987). Perceptual organization of complex-tone sequences: A tradeoff between pitch and timbre? *Journal of the Acoustical Society of America, 82*, 886–899.

Slawson, A. W. (1968). Vowel quality and musical timbre as functions of spectrum envelope and fundamental frequency. *Journal of the Acoustical Society of America, 43*, 87–101.

Slawson, A. W. (1981). The musical control of sound color. *Canadian University Music Review, No. 3*, 67–79.

Slawson, A. W. (1985). Sound Color. Berkeley: University of California Press. (With two sound discs.)

Slaymaker, F. H. (1970). Chords from tones having stretched partials. *Journal of the Acoustical Society of America, 47*, 1569–1571.

Sloboda, J. A. (1985). *The Musical Mind*. New York: Clarendon (Oxford University Press).

Smith, J., Hausfeld, S., Power, R. P., and Gorta, A. (1982). Ambiguous musical figures and auditory streaming. *Perception & Psychophysics, 32*, 454–464.

Sparks, D. W. (1976). Temporal recognition masking—or interference. *Journal of the Acoustical Society of America, 60*, 347–353.

Speith, W., Curtis, J. F., and Webster, J. C. (1954). Responding to one of two simultaneous messages. *Journal of the Acoustical Society of America, 26*, 391–396.

Spelke, E. S. (1979). Perceiving bimodally specified events in infancy. *Developmental Psychology, 15*, 626–636.

Spelke, E. S., and Cortelyou, A. (1981). Perceptual aspects of social knowing: Looking and listening in infancy. In M. E. Lamb and L. R. Sherrod (eds.), *Infant Social Cognition*. Hillsdale, N.J.: Erlbaum.

Spiegel, M. F., and Watson, C. I. (1981). Frequency discrimination with components of well-learned patterns. *Journal of the Acoustical Society of America, 89*, 223–230.

Staal, H. E., and Donderi, D. C. (1983). The effect of sound on visual apparent motion. *American Journal of Psychology, 96*, 95–105.

Steiger, H. (1980). *Some Informal Observations Concerning the Perceptual Organization of Patterns Containing Frequency Glides*. Unpublished report. McGill University.

Steiger, H. (1983). *Influences of Sequential Organization Processes on the Use of Binaural Cues*. Unpublished Ph.D. dissertation, McGill University.

Steiger, H., and Bregman A. S. (1981). Capturing frequency components of glided tones: Frequency separation, orientation and alignment. *Perception & Psychophysics, 30*, 425–435.

Steiger, H., and Bregman A. S. (1982a). Negating the effects of binaural cues: Competition between auditory streaming and contralateral induction. *Journal of Experimental Psychology: Human Perception and Performance, 8*, 602–613.

Steiger, H., and Bregman A. S. (1982b). Competition among auditory streaming, dichotic fusion, and diotic fusion. *Perception & Psychophysics, 32*, 153–162.

Stern, R. M. (1972). Perception of simultaneously presented musical timbres. Quarterly Progress Report, Research Laboratory of Electronics, Massachusetts Institute of Technology, Cambridge, Mass. July 15, 1972. pp.202–210.

Stevens, K. N. (1980). Acoustic correlates of some phonetic categories. *Journal of the Acoustical Society of America, 68*, 836–842.

Stevens, K. N., and Blumstein, S. E. (1981). The search for invariant acoustic correlates of phonetic features. In P. D. Eimas and J. L. Miller (eds.). *Perspectives in the Study of Speech*. Hillsdale, N.J.: Erlbaum.

Strube, H. W. (1981). Separation of several speakers recorded by two microphones (cocktail party processing). *Signal Processing, 3*, 355–364.

Stumpf, C. (1890). *Tonpsychologie*. Leipzig: S. Hinzel-Verlag.

Suga, N. (1965a). Analysis of frequency-modulated sounds by auditory neurones of echo-locating bats. *Journal of Physiology, 179*, 26–53.

Suga, N. (1965b). Responses of auditory cortical neurones to frequency modulated sounds in echo-locating bats. *Nature (London), 206*, 890–891.

Summerfield, Q., Haggard, M., Foster, J., and Gray, S. (1984). Perceiving vowels from uniform spectra: Phonetic exploration of an auditory aftereffect. *Perception & Psychophysics, 35*, 203–213.

Sundberg, J. (1977). The acoustics of the singing voice. *Scientific American, 236 (3)*, 82–91.

Sundberg, J. (1978). Synthesis of singing. *Swedish Journal of Musicology, 60 (1)*, 107–112.

ten Hoopen, G. (1982). *The Perceptual Organization of Alternating Tone Sequences*. Doctoral dissertation, University of Leiden.

ten Hoopen, G., and Akerboom, S. (1982). The perceived tempi of coherent and streaming tone sequences: II. *Perception & Psychophysics, 32*, 481–485.

ten Hoopen, G. Akerboom, S., and Boelaarts, L. (1985). *Streaming by Locus or Interaural Time Dilatation?* Unpublished manuscript. Unit of Experimental Psychology, University of Leiden.

ten Hoopen, G., van Meurs, G., and Akerboom, S. P. (1982). The perceived tempi of coherent and streaming tone sequences. *Perception & Psychophysics, 31*, 256–260.

ten Hoopen, G. T., Vos J., and Dispa, J. (1982). Interaural and monaural clicks and clocks: Tempo difference versus attention switching. *Journal of Experimental Psychology: Human Perception and Performance, 8*, 422–434.

Thomas, G. J. (1941). Experimental study of the influence of vision on sound localization. *Journal of Experimental Psychology, 28*, 167–177.

Thomas, I. B., Cetti, R. P., and Chase, P. W. (1971). Effect of silent intervals on the perception of temporal order. *Journal of the Acoustical Society of America, 49*, 85(A).

Thomas, I. B., and Fitzgibbons, P. J. (1971). Temporal order and perceptual classes. *Journal of the Acoustical Society of America, 50*, 86–87 (Abstract).

Thomas, I. B., Hill, P. B., Carroll, F. S., and Garcia, B. (1970). Temporal order in the perception of vowels. *Journal of the Acoustical Society of America, 48*, 1010–1013.

Thurlow, W. R. (1957). An auditory figure-ground effect. *American Journal of Psychology, 70*, 653–654.

Thurlow, W. R., and Elfner, L. F. (1959). Continuity effects with alternately sounding tones. *Journal of the Acoustical Society of America, 31*, 1337–1339.

Thurlow, W. R., and Erschul, W. P. (1978). Understanding continuity effects with complex stimuli. *Journal of the American Auditory Society, 4*, 113–116.

Thurlow, W. R., and Marten, A. E. (1962). Perception of steady and intermittent sound with alternating noise-burst stimuli. *Journal of the Acoustical Society of America, 34*, 1853–1858.

Thurlow, W. R., and Small, A. M. (1955). Pitch perception for certain periodic auditory stimuli. *Journal of the Acoustical Society of America, 27*, 132–137.

Tougas, Y. and Bregman, A. S. (1985a). The crossing of auditory streams. *Journal of Experimental Psychology: Human Perception and Performance, 11*, 788–798.

Tougas, Y. and Bregman, A. S. (in press). Auditory streaming and the continuity illusion. *Perception & Psychophysics.*

Treisman, A. M., and Schmidt, H. (1982). Illusory conjunctions in the perception of objects. *Cognitive Psychology, 14*, 107–141.

Treisman, A. M. (1960). Contextual cues in selective listening. *Quarterly Journal of Experimental Psychology, 12*, 242–248.

Treisman, A. M. (1964). Verbal cues, language, and meaning in selective attention. *American Journal of Psychology, 77*, 206–219.

Tsal, Y. (1983). Movements of attention across the visual field. *Journal of Experimental Psychology: Human Perception and Performance, 9*, 523–530.

Tuller, B., and Fowler, C. A. (1980). Some articulatory correlates of perceptual isochrony. *Perception & Psychophysics, 27*, 277–283.

Underwood, G. (1976). *Attention and Memory*. Oxford: Pergamon.

Van den Brink, G., Sintnicolaas, K., and van Stam, W. S. (1976). Dichotic pitch fusion. *Journal of the Acoustical Society of America, 59*, 1471–1476.

Van Noorden, L. P. A. S. (1975). *Temporal Coherence in the Perception of Tone Sequences.* Unpublished doctoral dissertation, Eindhoven University of Technology.

Van Noorden, L. P. A. S. (1977). Minimum differences of level and frequency for perceptual fission of tone sequences ABAB. *Journal of the Acoustical Society of America, 61,* 1041–1045.

Vartanian, T. A. (1974). On mechanisms of specialized reactions of central auditory neurons to frequency-modulated sounds. *Acustica, 31,* 305–310.

Verbrugge, R. R., and Rakerd, B. (1986). Evidence for talker-independent information for vowels. *Language and Speech, 25,* 267–282.

Verschuure, J., and Brocaar, M. P. (1983). Intelligibility of interrupted meaningful and nonsense speech with and without intervening noise. *Perception & Psychophysics, 33,* 232–240.

Vicario, G. (1960). L'effetto tunnel acustico. *Rivista di Psicologia, 54* , 41–52.

Vicario, G. (1965). Vicinanza spaziale e vicinanza temporale nella segregazione degli eventi. *Rivista di Psicologia, 59,* 843–863.

Vicario, G. (1973). *Tempo Psicologico ed Eventi.* Florence: C/E Giunti—G. Barbera.

Vicario, G. (1980). Gottschaldt figures in hearing. *Italian Journal of Psychology, 7,* 197–202.

Vicario, G. (1982). Some observations in the auditory field. In J. Beck (ed.). *Organization and Representation in Perception.* Hillsdale, N.J.: Erlbaum.

von Bismarck, G. (1974). Timbre of steady sounds: a factorial investigation of its verbal attributes. *Acustica, 30,* 146–159.

von Wright, J. M., Anderson, K., and Stenman, U. (1975). Generalization of conditioned GSR's in dichotic listening. In P. M. A. Rabbitt and S. Dornic (eds.), *Attention and Performance V.* New York: Academic Press.

Vos, J., and Rasch, R. (1981). The perceptual onset of musical tones. *Perception & Psychophysics, 29,* 323–335.

Waltz, D. (1975). Understanding line drawings of scenes with shadows. In P. H. Winston (ed.) *The Psychology of Computer Vision,* New York: McGraw-Hill.

Warren, R. M. (1968). *Relation of Verbal Transformations to Other Perceptual Phenomena.* In Conference Publication No. 42, IEEE/NPL Conference on Pattern Recognition. Teddington, England: Institute of Electrical Engineers (Suppl., 8 pp.).

Warren, R. M. (1970). Perceptual restoration of missing speech sounds. *Science, 167,* 392–393.

Warren, R. M. (1972). Perception of temporal order: Special rules for initial and terminal sounds of sequences. *Journal of the Acoustical Society of America, 52,* 167 (Abstract).

Warren, R. M. (1974). Auditory temporal discrimination by trained listeners. *Cognitive Psychology, 6,* 237–256.

Warren, R. M. (1982). *Auditory Perception: A New Synthesis.* New York: Pergamon.

Warren, R. M., and Ackroff, J. M. (1976). Two types of auditory sequence perception. *Perception & Psychophysics, 20,* 387–394.

Warren, R. M., and Bashford, J. A. (1976). Auditory contralateral induction: An early stage in binaural processing. *Perception & Psychophysics, 20,* 380–386.

Warren, R. M., and Bashford, J. A., Jr. (1981). Perception of acoustic iterance: Pitch and infrapitch. *Perception & Psychophysics, 29,* 323–335.

Warren, R. M., and Byrnes, D. L. (1975). Temporal discrimination of recycled tonal sequences: Pattern matching and naming of order by untrained listeners. *Perception & Psychophysics, 18,* 273–280.

Warren, R. M., and Obusek, C. J. (1971). Speech perception and phonemic restorations. *Perception & Psychophysics, 9*, 358–362.

Warren, R. M., and Obusek, C. J. (1972). Identification of temporal order within auditory sequences. *Perception & Psychophysics, 12*, 86–90.

Warren, R. M., and Sherman, G. L. (1974). Phonemic restorations based on subsequent context. *Perception & Psychophysics, 16*, 150–156.

Warren, R. M., and Warren, R. P. (1970). Auditory illusions and confusions. *Scientific American, 233*, 30–36.

Warren, R. M., and Warren, R. P. (1976). *Helmholtz on Perception: Its Physiology and Development*. New York: Wiley.

Warren, R. M., Obusek, C. J., and Ackroff, J. M. (1972). Auditory induction: Perceptual synthesis of absent sounds. *Science, 176*, 1149–1151.

Warren, R. M., Obusek, C. J., Farmer, R. M., and Warren, R. P. (1969). Auditory sequence: Confusion of patterns other than speech or music. *Science, 164*, 586–587.

Warren, W. H., and Verbrugge, R. R. (1984). Auditory perception of breaking and bouncing events: A case study of ecological acoustics. *Journal of Experimental Psychology: Human Perception and Performance, 10*, 704–712.

Watson, C. S. (1976). Factors in the discrimination of word-length auditory patterns. In S. K. Hirsh, D. H. Eldredge, I. J. Hirsh, and S. R. Silverman (eds.), *Hearing and Davis: Essays Honoring Hallowell Davis*. Saint Louis: Washington University Press.

Watson, C. S., Kelly, W. J., Wroton, H. W. (1976). Factors in the discrimination of tonal patterns. II. Selective attention and learning under various levels of uncertainty. *Journal of the Acoustical Society of America, 60*, 1176–1186.

Watson, C. S., Wroton, H. W., Kelly, W. J., and Benbasset, C. A. (1975). Factors in the discrimination of tonal patterns. I. Component frequency, temporal position, and silent intervals. *Journal of the Acoustical Society of America, 57*, 1175–1185.

Webern, A. (1935). Orchestration of the fugue from the Musical Offering of Bach. (without opus) The complete works of Anton Webern. Vol. 1. (Conducted by Pierre Boulez). Columbia Masterworks MA 35193, 1978.

Weintraub, M. (1984). The GRASP sound separation system. *ICASSP 84*, San Diego, CA, 19–21 March 1984, *2*, 18A.6/1–4 (IEEE, New York, 1984). Phys. Abstr. 103134 (15 November 1984)

Weintraub, M. (1985). A Theory and Compositional Model of Auditory Monaural Speech Separation. Doctoral dissertation, Department of Electrical Engineering, Stanford University.

Weintraub, M. (1986). A computational model for separating two simultaneous talkers. *IEEE-IECEJ-ASJ International Conference on Acoustics, Speech, and Signal Processing (ICASSP 86)*, pp. 3.1–3.4, Tokyo, 7–11 April, 1986. (IEEE, New York, 1986).

Welch, R. B., and Warren, D. H. (1980). Immediate perceptual response to intersensory discrepancy. *Psychological Bulletin, 88*, 638–667.

Wertheimer, M. (1912). Experimentelle Studien über das Sehen von Bewegung. *Zeitschrift für Psychologie, 61*, 161–265.

Wessel, D. L. (1978). Low dimensional control of musical timbre. *Rapports IRCAM*, Centre Georges Pompidou, Paris, France, December.

Wessel, D. L. (1979). Timbre space as a musical control structure. *Computer Music Journal, 3*, No. 2, 45–52.

Whalen, D. H., and Liberman, A. M. (1987). Speech perception takes precedence over non-speech perception. *Science, 237,* 169–171.

Wier, C. C., and Green, D. M. (1975). Temporal acuity as a function of frequency difference. *Journal of the Acoustical Society of America, 57,* 1512–1515.

Wilcox, G. W., Neisser, U., and Roberts, J. (1972). *Recognition of Auditory Temporal Order.* Presented at the Spring meeting of the Eastern Psychological Association, Boston.

Williams, K. N., and Perrott, D. R. (1971). Temporal resolution of tonal pulses. *Journal of the Acoustical Society of America, 51,* 644–647.

Williams, K. N., and Elfner, L. F. (1976). Gap detection with three auditory events: A single-channel process. *Journal of the Acoustical Society of America, 60,* 423–428.

Williams, K. N., Elfner, L. F., and Howse, W. R. (1979). Auditory temporal resolution: Effects of sensation level. *Journal of Auditory Research, 19,* 265–270.

Winston, P. H. (ed.) (1975). *The Psychology of Computer Vision.* New York: McGraw-Hill.

Witkin, A. P., and Tenenbaum, J. M. (1986). On the role of structure in vision. In J. Beck, B. Hope, and A. Rosenfeld, (eds.) *Human and Machine Vision.* New York: Academic Press.

Witkin, H. A., Wapner, S., and Leventhal, T. (1952). Sound localization with conflicting cues. *Journal of Experimental Psychology, 43,* 58–67.

Woods, D. D. (1979). *Role of Context in Auditory Perception: Organizational Processes in Detection.* Ph.D. dissertation, Purdue University, December, 1979.

Wright, J. K. (1986). Auditory Object Perception: Counterpoint in a New Context. Unpublished Master's thesis. Faculty of Music, McGill University.

Wright, J. K., and Bregman, A. S. (1987). Auditory stream segregation and the control of dissonance in polyphonic music. *Contemporary Music Review, 2,* 63–93.

Wrightson, J. M., and Warren, R. M. (1981). Incomplete auditory induction of tones alternated with noise: Effects occurring below the pulsation threshold. *Journal of the Acoustical Society of America, 69,* S105–S106 (Abstract).

Yilmaz, H. A. (1968). A theory of speech perception, II. *Bulletin of Mathematical Biophysics, 30,* 455–479.

Yund, E. W., and Efron, R. (1974). Dichoptic and dichotic micropattern discrimination. *Perception & Psychophysics, 15,* 383–390.

Zucker, S. W. (1977). Relaxation labeling and the reduction of local ambiguity. In C. H. Chen (ed.), *Pattern Recognition and Artificial Intelligence.* New York: Academic Press.

Zucker, S. W. (1985a). The diversity of perceptual grouping. In M. Arbib and A. Hanson (eds.), *Vision, Brain, and Cooperative Computation.* Cambridge, Mass.: MIT Press.

Zucker, S. W. (1985b). Early orientation selection: Tangent fields and the dimensionality of their support. *Computer Vision, Graphics, and Image Processing, 32,* 74–103.

Zuckerkandl, V. (1956). *Sound and Symbol: Music and the External World.* New York: Pantheon Books.

Zwicker, E., Flottorp, G., and Stevens, S. S. (1957). Critical bandwidth in loudness summation. *Journal of the Acoustical Society of America, 29,* 548–557.

Zwicker, U. T. (1984). Auditory recognition of diotic and dichotic vowel pairs. *Speech Communication, 3,* 265–277.

Index